D0849586

XENOPHON

IN SEVEN VOLUMES

IV

MEMORABILIA AND OECONOMICUS

WITH AN ENGLISH TRANSLATION BY

E. C. MARCHANT

SUB-RECTOR OF LINCOLN COLLEGE, OXFORD

SYMPOSIUM AND APOLOGY

WITH AN ENGLISH TRANSLATION BY

O. J. TODD

UNIVERSITY OF BRITISH COLUMBIA

CAMBRIDGE, MASSACHUSETTS
HARVARD UNIVERSITY PRESS

LONDON
WILLIAM HEINEMANN LTD

MCMLXXIX

American ISBN 0–674–99186–9
British ISBN 0 434 99168 6

First printed 1923
Reprinted 1938, 1953, 1959, 1965, 1968, 1979

Printed in Great Britain by
Fletcher & Son Ltd, Norwich

CONTENTS

INTRODUCTION

Note on the Titles : (*a*) The *Memorabilia.*

THE title by which this work is familiarly known
to us, dates only from 1569, when Johann Lenklau
prefixed it to the Latin version that accompanied his
great edition of Xenophon's works. Before that
time scholars had commonly used the Greek title
Apomnemoneumata, *i.e.* Memoirs, or the awkward
description *De factis et dictis Socratis memoratu dignis.*
The correct Latin equivalent of the Greek name is
Commentarii, which, in fact, occurs in the description
of the book given by Aulus Gellius (XIV. iii.), viz.
*libri quos dictorum et factorum Socratis commentarios
composuit* (*Xenophon*).

The Greek title itself is not altogether satisfactory ;
for in reality the *Memorabilia* consists of four separate
parts, which were certainly not all composed at the
same time, and to the first of these parts the title
does not apply.

(*b*) The *Oeconomicus.*

" In many respects," writes Cicero in a well-known
passage of the *de Senectute,* "Xenophon's works are
very useful. How eloquently he praises agriculture
in his book entitled *Oeconomicus,* which deals with
the care of one's property." Philodemus and Galen
refer to the book as the *Oeconomica.* The ancients
certainly did not suppose that the title meant the
Economist or *Householder,* but understood it to denote

exactly what Cicero's words suggest—*a Discourse on Estate Management.* The same holds good *mutatis mutandis* of the titles *Hipparchicus* and *Cynegeticus.*

I

The first part of the *Memorabilia,* which is confined to the first two chapters of the First Book,[1] is a Defence of Socrates, who had been tried and condemned to death on a charge of "impiety," in the spring of 399 B.C. At the time of the trial Xenophon was absent in Asia. No speech delivered by any one of the three prosecutors—Anytus, Meletus and Lycon—had been published, and Xenophon in consequence is only able to give the gist, not the exact form, of the indictment (I. i. 1), which had been drawn by Meletus. His reply to this indictment extends to the eighth section of the second chapter.

At this point a surprise is in store for the reader. For in the next sentence (I. ii. 9) Xenophon suddenly refers to "the prosecutor" in the singular, and proceeds to combat a series of accusations that he had brought. This " prosecutor " had charged against Socrates: (1) that he encouraged his companions to despise the laws (ii. 9); (2) that Critias and Alcibiades, who had done great evil to the state, were his associates (ii. 12); (3) that he taught young men to despise their fathers and their other relations, and to be false to their friends (ii. 49); (4) that he encouraged unscrupulous conduct and an anti-democratic spirit by the use he made of the poets (ii. 56).

Xenophon at first sight appears to be replying here

[1] The absurd division into books and chapters is, of course, not due to Xenophon himself.

to a speech actually delivered for the prosecution. But, as we have just seen, this cannot be the case. To whom, then, and to what is he replying? The correct solution of this problem was first given by Cobet, and it has been supported by a series of indisputable proofs by several subsequent scholars. The man Socrates had died in 399 B.C., and had left nothing written. But his ardent and gifted disciples —especially Antisthenes, a fanatical admirer, and a little later Plato—very soon began to publish works about Socrates, especially dialogues in which Socrates appeared as the chief interlocutor. One of these earlier Socratic works is, of course, the *Apology* of Plato. And so it came about that a literary Socrates grew into being—a figure that retained much, doubtless, of the historical man, but was not identical with him, and might be variously represented by the different authors, and even by the same author in different works.

This cult of Socrates actually provoked opposition. For shortly after the year 393 B.C. a well-known " sophist " named Polycrates published an attack on his memory, throwing his attack into the form of an imaginary speech delivered by one of the three prosecutors, Anytus, at the trial. In after ages a belief not unnaturally grew up that Anytus had actually employed this man, Polycrates, to write his speech for the prosecution. In reality the "Accusation of Socrates" written by Polycrates was nothing more than a literary exercise, based no doubt on reminiscences of the trial, but strongly coloured by the writer's own views. Xenophon was now living in exile at Scillus near Olympia; and there he must have read the work of Polycrates. He resolved to compose a reply, traversing the accusation step by step.[1] The "prosecutor" then, is Polycrates, or rather Polycrates masquerading as Anytus.

Xenophon's *Defence* of Socrates, therefore (occupying Book I. i. and ii.), has a double purpose. It is intended, first, to be an answer to the actual indictment, so far as Xenophon was aware of its terms; and, secondly, to refute the attack of Polycrates on the memory of the martyred Socrates. As for the substance of the *Defence*, we note that although Plato's *Apology* was certainly written already, Xenophon has not drawn upon it. In fact, throughout these two chapters there are no trustworthy indications that he has laid any of Plato's published work under contribution. At I. ii. 20, indeed, Xenophon quotes in support of his arguments two passages from the poets that are in the *Meno* and the *Protagoras* of Plato, but it would be absurd to suppose that he went to Plato for two commonplace passages that would be familiar to every educated Athenian. In one passage (I. ii. 10) Xenophon expresses an opinion that is known to have been maintained by Antisthenes; in another (I. ii. 19) he combats that Cynic's doctrine of the permanence of Virtue. In neither place is he professing to report the views of Socrates; and even if it is safe to conclude from these two instances that he had consulted the works of Antisthenes, there is, so far as can be ascertained, no trace in the *Defence* that he borrowed such knowledge as he shows of Socrates from Antisthenes. The most likely inference from these negative facts is that

---

[1] In after ages another rejoinder was written to Polycrates by Libanius (fourth century A.D.), from whose *Defence* a good deal more can be learned about the lost *Accusation* of Polycrates.

he incorporated only such knowledge of Socrates as he had gained himself by intercourse with the Master. This knowledge, to be sure, is superficial, and does not point to a close intimacy. On the other hand, since Xenophon is concerned only to rebut the specific charges brought by the prosecutors and by Polycrates, we are scarcely entitled to assume that he has told us *all* that he really knew about Socrates in these two chapters.

II

The Socratic literature rapidly grew in bulk. Antisthenes, who developed the Cynic system out of the teaching of Socrates, was probably the first to write " Socratic " dialogues. Plato, a much younger man, soon entered the field in sharp opposition to the Cynic. And others tried their hand. It seems that somewhere about the year 385 B.C., Xenophon, who had perhaps now read what Plato had so far published, and had certainly pondered on the works of Antisthenes and assimilated much of his doctrine, decided to compose a series of memoirs and dialogues as illustrations of his " Defence of Socrates." These illustrations cover the remainder of the First (I. iii. onwards) and the whole of the Second Book of the *Memorabilia*. " I propose to show," he says (I. iii. 1), " how Socrates helped his companions both by his deeds and his words : and, in order to do so, I shall relate all that I remember about them."

Though he makes no reference here to his earlier work, he follows its arrangement closely. He first gives details to prove that Socrates accepted the gods of the state (I. iii. 1–4). Then he insists on the moral tendency of the conduct and teachings of Socrates

INTRODUCTION

(5–15); and here he recalls an outspoken conversation between the Master and himself about love. It is the only conversation in the collection in which Xenophon himself takes part. Having proceeded thus far, he suddenly modifies his plan; and writes a new and controversial introduction to a complete series of dialogues, dealing again with the two topics already handled—the piety and the morality of Socrates—before proceeding to illustrate his third topic. He says no more about the *actions* of Socrates; and the reason presumably is, that he was conscious that he could not add anything new to what he had already said in the *Defence*, little as that was. At any rate, it is noteworthy that, having undertaken to tell all that he remembers about the helpful deeds of Socrates, he has after all told us so very little, but has in the main confined himself to the conversations.

It will be convenient to have a list of the ensuing topics side by side with the corresponding passages of the *Defence*:

INTRODUCTION

Xenophon's statement that he himself "heard" these conversations is a mere literary device. Some of them may quite possibly be based on actual recollection. But others are almost certainly pure invention. Who could suppose, for instance, that Socrates lectured his son on his duty to his mother (II. ii.), or urged Chaerecrates to make up a quarrel with his brother (II. iii.), while a third person, Xenophon, stood by silent, storing up all that good advice in a capacious memory? The supposition of Mr. Dakyns that such conversations were repeated to Xenophon by Lamprocles, Chaerecrates and others is very unlikely, unless we could imagine that Xenophon went about Athens gathering reports of Socrates' conversations before he left for Asia, and when as yet he had no notion that he would ever come to write Socratic memoirs. The opening conversation of the collection, that on Piety (I. iv.), probably owes much to the study of Antisthenes. The chapters on the education of the Ruler (II. i.) and on the proper relations between parents and children, brothers, relatives and friends, contain much that we associate with Xenophon himself rather than with Socrates; and it is difficult to imagine Socrates declaiming to Aristippus a long passage from a work of Prodicus which was often part of its author's own programmes (II. i. 21).

Does Xenophon owe anything to Plato in this part of the *Memorabilia*? The question hardly admits of a confident answer. The passage about the "Kingly Art" and "Happiness" in II. i. 17 bears a close resemblance to a sentence in the *Euthydemus* of Plato (p. 291 b). But we know that the "Kingly Art" was a commonplace with Antisthenes, as may be seen from some words put

into his mouth in Xenophon's *Banquet* (iv. 6).
Again, the opening words of I. vi. 14 strongly
suggest a passage in Plato's *Lysis* (p. 211 d).
But a similar sentiment is attributed to Socrates by
Epictetus (III. v. 14) and reappears in Dio Chrysostom
(III. 128), and as both these authors borrow largely
from Cynic sources, the common source of all four
passages may possibly be Antisthenes again, though
it certainly looks as if Xenophon here had borrowed
from Plato, so close is the correspondence.

However that may be, we have here a series of
imaginary conversations to which Xenophon's study
of the Socratic literature has contributed not a little.
But no doubt many of his reflections are really based
on his recollection of Socrates himself. There is no
proof in them, however, that Xenophon had really
been one of his intimate companions, and indeed he
nowhere makes any such claim. These remarks
apply equally to the Collections which make up the
Third and the Fourth Books.

III

The Third Book of the *Memorabilia*, which
consists of miscellaneous dialogues loosely strung
together, and an appendix of aphorisms, clearly
forms yet another separate work. The first seven
chapters are linked together by a common subject—
the civil and military service of the state. But
at the eighth chapter the writer passes abruptly
to the relation of a dialectical encounter between
Socrates and Aristippus the Cyrenaic, on the
identity of the Beautiful and the Useful, and
appends to it a discourse of Socrates on the same
theme. Next we come on a series of definitions.

Then follow other conversations on detached topics. The aphorisms that fill the last two chapters are concerned with very small things: and they are quite in the Cynic manner. The talk between Socrates and the younger Pericles (c. v.) may really have occurred in the year 411 B.C.; but the ambitions of Thebes are alluded to in a manner that suggests the period of the Theban Supremacy, the years following the battle of Leuctra (fought in 371 B.C.), as the time of composition, and there is a suspiciously Xenophontine ring in the allusions of Pericles to the excellence of the Spartan institutions (v. 15–16).

The fact is, the whole of the subjects dealt with in the first seven chapters of this Third Book are just those in which Xenophon, the old campaigner and worshipper of efficiency, took a special interest. Ten passages in the conversations on the duties and qualifications of commanders are repeated from the *Cyropaedia*; and here and there the author of the *Anabasis* and the *Hipparchicus* reveals himself pretty clearly.

Nevertheless, the spirit of these dialogues, with their insistence on Knowledge as the only sure basis of efficiency, is genuinely Socratic. Nor does the rest of the Third Book, from c. viii. onwards, contain anything inconsistent with the Socrates of Plato's early dialogues. Thus the cross-examination of the artists in the tenth chapter is entirely in keeping with the Platonic Socrates, whose habit it is to appose all sorts and conditions of men respecting their special work. The amusing interview with Theodoté, the courtesan, is surprising in its context. The intention of it, apparently, is to show Socrates in a lighter vein, in the mood that we associate with the persiflage of a *Banquet*. The definitions in the ninth chapter are not alien to Socrates; but it may be that Xenophon drew them from the works of Antisthenes, whose opinions are known to have coincided with those expressed in them.

We may fairly accept as historical the explicit declaration in the *Defence* (I. ii. 4) that Socrates attached importance to physical culture. In the Dialogues of Plato, so far as I recollect, he does not display much real interest in the physical exercises of the wrestling-ground and the gymnasium; at any rate his chief interest is clearly in other matters when he enters those places. But in the *Republic* Plato on his part fully recognizes the value of "gymnastic" in education, and indeed builds up in his own way a complete theory of the subject. The germs of this theory may very well have come from Socrates himself. If that is true, then just as Plato develops the opinions of Socrates in his way, so Xenophon in the twelfth chapter of this book colours the same opinions with notions of his own, drawn from his experience in Asia, his admiration of Spartan institutions, and very likely, from his study of Antisthenes.

Lastly, what are we to say of the dispute with Aristippus about the Good and the Beautiful (c. viii.)? The truth of the account that Xenophon gives of Socrates' views on this matter must clearly be rejected if we suppose that Plato derived from Socrates himself the theory of eternal, unchanging Ideas or Forms of Goodness and Beauty; for, according to the Socrates of Xenophon nothing is good, beautiful or useful in *itself*, but only in relation to *something*. But it is, to say the least, exceedingly doubtful whether Socrates is responsible for the "Theory of Forms or Ideas," which makes no appearance in the early Dialogues of Plato. The doctrine of the Xenophontine Socrates is that all things Good and Beautiful must contribute to the advantage or enjoyment of man : nothing is Good but what is Useful for the particular purpose for which it is intended. The very same doctrine is propounded by Socrates in the *Greater Hippias* (rightly or wrongly attributed to Plato), but on examination is rejected by him as untenable. But Plato in the *Gorgias* makes Socrates declare that a thing is Beautiful because it is pleasant or useful or both ; and the doctrine is unchallenged. Lastly, there is a passage of similar import in the *First Alcibiades.* If the *Greater Hippias* was really written by Plato, it must be later in date than the *Gorgias*, but earlier than the Third Book of the *Memorabilia ;* and Xenophon, assuming that he had read it, has tacitly implied that the views of Socrates are not correctly represented there. Whence did he derive his knowledge ? If not from the *Gorgias*, it is very significant that his exposition agrees with what Plato puts into the mouth of Socrates in that Dialogue.

IV

We pass now to the Fourth Book. In the noble and impassioned peroration with which this book concludes, the virtues of Socrates are summed up. Socrates was pious, just, self-controlled and wise : he was masterly in exposition and definition, in refuting error and exhorting to goodness. This concluding sentence is clearly a summary of the contents of this Fourth Book in the form in which it has come down to us ; and it is

INTRODUCTION

in itself a sufficient refutation of the widely held opinion that large portions of the Fourth Book are spurious. The peroration applies only to this last book; at any rate it contains no reference to many of the topics that have been dealt with in the preceding portions of the collection, whereas it entirely covers the topics of the last. The natural inference is that the Fourth Book is yet another independent work.

This inference gains strong support from the actual contents of the book. The subject throughout is Education. Many topics already treated recur without any indication given that they have already been discussed. The style too differs to some extent from that of the preceding parts, in that it is somewhat fuller and more elaborate. The matter is arranged in an orderly fashion, in striking contrast with the desultory miscellany that makes up the latter part of the preceding book. Most of the conversations (c. ii., iii., v., vi.) are carried on with Euthydemus, a handsome, bookish and self-confident young man, eager to distinguish himself "in speech and action." The first of these conversations with the youth shows how Socrates convinced young men like Euthydemus that their essential need was to get real education. Next we are introduced to something like a complete system of Socratic education. The first object of Socrates was to make his followers "prudent," *i. e.* to train the character. Training in power to "speak and act" came after training of character, and it turns out presently that Socrates put speech and action in the inverse order of importance; and, moreover, held that sound action could come only from one who was master of himself. Competence in "speech" depended on power to reason and to define correctly.

INTRODUCTION

We have seen that Euthydemus hoped to excel in "speech and action." Socrates brings him to see that the right way to attain the goal of his ambition is first to learn Prudence, then to realize what is the only sure foundation of right action, and lastly to study the laws of sound reasoning.

We should certainly have expected that throughout the book Socrates would have been represented as addressing himself to Euthydemus, and to none other. But this is, in fact, not the case. The fourth chapter contains an argument on Justice. If we regard the subject with which it deals, it is quite in place where it stands; but it is strange to find the series of hortatory discourses interrupted by an argument addressed to Hippias, the "sophist," on the identity of Law and Justice. Moreover, in the opening sentence of the seventh chapter Xenophon apparently disregards this argument with Hippias; and yet it is clear from the wording of the peroration, which is in exact correspondence with the topics of the discourses, that he had, when he wrote it, dealt with the topic of Justice.

All the conditions will be satisfied if we suppose that when he had written the fourth chapter down to the point where he was to relate what Socrates *said* about Justice by means of a dialogue (iv. 5), he incorporated this argument between Socrates and Hippias, which he had composed at some previous time, instead of writing a new dialogue in conformity with the others.

The talk with Hippias is in itself remarkable. For it represents Socrates as identifying Law and Justice. We have read in the *Defence* of Socrates (I. ii. 9) that Polycrates charged him with "despising the established laws," and we find that Xenophon there really makes no reply to that charge. Socrates, of course, insisted on obedience to the laws and held that " it was just to do what the laws ordain " ;[1] but that is a very different thing from saying that he thought the laws to be the embodiment of Justice. This latter opinion runs counter to the whole trend of the *Gorgias* of Plato, and is indeed not wholly consistent with what Socrates says in other parts of the *Memorabilia.* Plato's work may well have seemed to Xenophon to lend countenance to the very charge that he had failed to rebut in his own earlier work ; and because Plato had written so, he may have felt it incumbent on him to come forward with an answer. He found a convenient place for its insertion here. It is really unconvincing as an exposition of Socrates' views on Justice, and the concluding sentence of the chapter does not square with it.

The fifth chapter brings us to that "efficiency in speech and action" coveted by such men as Euthydemus, and it turns out that Socrates put "action" before "speech." The secret and essential condition of efficiency in action was Prudence or Self-control.[2] The curious passage appended to this conversation, in which "sound reasoning," by a fanciful derivation, is declared to mean "sorting things out, and choosing what is right and rejecting what is wrong in speech and action," looks like a genuine, but rather crude, reminiscence of something actually said by Socrates, who was fond of such word-play.

As for "efficiency in speech," that is arrived at by

[1] Compare IV. vi. 5-6, where the question, "Is what the laws order necessarily just?" is entirely shirked.

[2] As a matter of convenience I have consistently rendered σωφροσύνη "prudence" in the translation.

INTRODUCTION

mastering the art of Reasoning; and the art of Reasoning depends on correct definition of terms. Accordingly, in the sixth chapter we have a series of definitions. Some of these overlap the definitions contained in the ninth chapter of the Third Book; but, as the Fourth Book is independent of the Third, the omission of all reference to the earlier passage need not cause surprise. There is much in this sixth chapter that certainly reflects the opinions of the historical Socrates; but, as usual, the manner in which they are reflected is unmistakably Xenophontine. It is strange that there is nothing about Pleasure and its relation to the Good and Beautiful, seeing that this problem is handled by Plato already in the *Protagoras* and *Gorgias*, which dialogues belong to his earlier or "Socratic" stage, and of which Xenophon certainly takes account in his Fourth Book. One cannot but suspect that, in thus ignoring the problem of Pleasure, Xenophon was influenced by the works of Antisthenes. The speculations on Pleasure attributed to Socrates by Plato were, no doubt, much too subtle for Xenophon, and they were, outwardly at least, inconsistent. It was wiser for a plain man to pass them by.

The superficial account of Socratic induction and assumption, or "hypothesis," with which the sixth chapter concludes (§§ 13–15) has raised a sharp dispute as to the sources of Xenophon's information. Is all this derived from Socrates himself, or is it gleaned from the *Phaedo* and, possibly, other dialogues of Plato? The question admits of no certain answer. But if we assume that the information really comes from certain dialogues of Plato, then it is surely strange that Xenophon selected just this one point,

INTRODUCTION

"hypothesis," from them, and ignored other theories —for instance, Knowledge as Recollection and the doctrine of Forms—that Plato in those same dialogues attributes, truly or falsely, to Socrates.

In the seventh chapter we come to mathematics and astronomy, and the views of Socrates thereon. We are told that he recommended the study of them for practical purposes only—just so far as they were "useful." What Xenophon says is not inconsistent with the earlier Socrates of Plato, and can be brought into harmony with the *Clouds* of Aristophanes and, even with Plato's *Phaedo*. It is, on the other hand, wholly inconsistent with the system of education that Socrates is made to recommend for the "Guardians" in the *Republic* of Plato. The very uncomplimentary reference to Anaxagoras (IV. vii. 6) is thought by some to be based on a famous passage of the *Phaedo*, in which Socrates expresses disappointment with the Anaxagorean theory of the classification of Matter by Mind. But it is difficult to think that Xenophon could have justified to himself the taunt he attributes to Socrates by the regretful complaint of the Platonic Socrates, or even that he was capable of building this insult on so slender a substructure.

In the sentence that immediately follows this passage about the sciences, Xenophon refers to the importance that Socrates attached to divination (§ 10). Then he argues that the belief in "the divine voice"—the belief that gave rise to the charge of introducing strange gods—was no delusion, and finally launches out into a noble description of the attitude of Socrates towards his trial and condemnation. The total effect of this epilogue is not greatly marred by one serious blemish it exhibits—the series of futile questions,[1] so characteristic of our author at his worst, in the third section of the last chapter.

Although this Fourth Book was written a generation after the death of Socrates, the tone of the peroration is still controversial. The object of Xenophon throughout the book is to prove that the system of education inculcated by Socrates was the best possible; that Socrates was himself the embodiment of that system, and was therefore the pattern of a good and happy man. Clearly there were many still who maintained that the infamous Critias [2] had been trained by Socrates, and that this fact was enough to condemn the system. Nor can it escape notice that the depreciation of the higher mathematics and other sciences in the seventh chapter, and the sharp limitation of scientific studies by Socrates in the training of himself that is implied in the peroration,[3] are argumentative. Evidently, even after so long a time, controversy about Socrates had not been silenced, and there was still something to be done for his memory by an ardent believer.

V

The chronological relationship of the *Oeconomicus* to Xenophon's other Socratic writings cannot be

[1] Similar questions, in which the obvious is put in the form of a conundrum, are often attributed to Socrates by Xenophon. They are, of course, invariably the product of Xenophon's own mind.

[2] Aeschines, *against Timarchus*, § 173.

[3] The passage in the peroration referring to chapter seven is, "So wise that he was unerring in his judgment of the better and the worse and needed no counsellor, but relied on himself for his knowledge of them."

established with confidence. Certain linguistic indications point to a date earlier than the *Memorabilia*;
but the tone of the work, calm and detached from
controversy, strongly suggests that it was at least
put into its final shape after the so-called Fourth
Book of that work was written. The thoughts and
reflections, whether put into the mouth of Socrates
or Ischomachus, are so entirely Xenophon's own
that we may wonder why he did not frankly produce
a treatise on the management of an estate instead of
a Socratic dialogue. And it is evident that he found
the dialogue form which he selected inconvenient.
Socrates by this time was clearly a literary figure, and
almost any amount of freedom might be taken with his
name. But at least some measure of verisimilitude
must be kept up; and to represent Socrates, the
wandering philosopher, as a landowner, an authority
on household craft, land development and agriculture, devoted to his home, would carry the author
too far away from the truth. An ingenious com-
promise suggested itself. What was impossible in
the mouth of Socrates might be put into the mouth
of another, and reported by Socrates. But this
other person must be a man of standing and of
mature years, and therefore could not be Xenophon
himself, who had no established position during the
life of Socrates. Hence Ischomachus. According
to Plutarch this worthy but self-complacent gentleman is a historic personage; but little credence
attaches to the kind of story that he tells. Anyhow, Ischomachus, as he appears in this book, is
quite clearly Xenophon—Xenophon home from the
wars, living happily and prosperously on his own
estate at Scillus.

The beginning and end of the *Oeconomicus* are as

abrupt as the end of Borrow's *Lavengro* and the beginning of *The Romany Rye*. Even the name of Socrates is not given in the first few sentences : he is referred to as if he had been already mentioned ; and there is no epilogue. But of course this does not show, as Galen supposed, that we have here a continuation of the *Memorabilia*, intended to follow on the Fourth Book. The second portion of the *Memorabilia* ends (II. x.) and the third portion opens (III. i.) and ends (III. xiv.) with similar abruptness. We may group the *Oeconomicus* with these miscellaneous dialogues, doubtless not all composed at the same time, that make up the Third Book of the *Memorabilia*. The plan of the work is curious, for the first six chapters form a lengthy preamble to the reported conversation with Ischomachus. The work must of course not be judged as though it were a complete treatise on Estate Management, indoor and outdoor. That is precisely what Xenophon has not chosen to write. The practical value, therefore, of the teaching is not anything like so great as that of the treatise *On Horsemanship*. But so far as it goes, the teaching is sound—for it is not certain that Xenophon believed that straw added to the manurial value, as well as to the bulk, of our old friends from farmyard and stable.[1]

The abiding interest of the book, however, lies less in the edification it offers and in its literary merit (which is not great), than in the light that it sheds on Xenophon's intimate life, his tastes and pursuits. Readers will differ in their opinion of that paragon " Ischomachus." None will object to his having his boots and his pots and

[1] See xviii. 2, where εἰς κόπρον ἐμβληθὲν means "thrown on the manure heap," not "applied (to the land) as manure."

pans neatly set out in rows; but some will mock with the wits at his notion that there was any particular beauty in the spectacle afforded by these homely articles so carefully bestowed. However that may be, one cannot but sympathize with that long-suffering little saint, his wife, the most arresting figure in Xenophon's gallery of women. We glance at Theodoté in the *Memorabilia* and Syennesis in the *Anabasis*, and we linger for a time over Panthea in the *Cyropaedia;* but we return again and again to this unnamed heroine of the household.

This unnamed heroine! But Ischomachus is Xenophon, and the little lady is wife of Ischomachus—that is she is Xenophon's wife, Philesia. "My dear, where is it?" asked her methodical husband; and Philesia, not knowing the answer, could only hang her head and blush. So she had to listen to a long homily on the beauty of *order* in the house, with illustrations drawn from the army and the navy. It is pleasant to know, that henceforward, at least in one home at Scillus, regimental order reigned among the household paraphernalia, from the boots to the works of art.

And this regimental order in his house is the mirror of Xenophon's mind; for his mind is a series of labelled pigeon-holes, each hole filled with a commonplace thought remorselessly analysed. These elementary thoughts he produces again and again, for his reader's edification.

The *Oeconomicus* was reviewed and criticized by the Epicurean philosopher Philodemus, an elder contemporary of Cicero, in his treatise *On Vices and their Opposite Virtues,* but only a small part of what he had to say has survived, recovered from the ashes of Herculaneum. Further it was translated into

INTRODUCTION

Latin by Cicero[1] in the days of his youth: it was
familiar to the Roman writers on agriculture, including Virgil, was admired and imitated by the
Italians of the Renaissance, and in our own times
has found a doughty champion in Ruskin. Xenophon
writes with an infectious enthusiasm, and with that
easy charm of manner and diction of which he
is a great master. But as with his thoughts,
so with his words: he too often irritates the
reader by incessant repetition of the same pattern
of sentence, of the same formula, and even of the
same word. How prone Xenophon is to repetition
may be judged from the many references added in
the translation of both *Memorabilia* and *Oeconomicus*
to other works; and of course these references are
not exhaustive. His mind moves in a narrow circle
of ideas. But he is master of an extensive and
multifarious vocabulary; so that it is strange that
he constantly uses the same word over and over
again in the compass of a few lines. A translator
is often compelled to have recourse to synonyms.

[1] There is some ground for the conjecture that in the time
of Philodemus and Cicero an edition of the *Oeconomicus* divided
into four books existed.

MANUSCRIPTS AND EDITIONS

I. Of the Greek text the following papyrus fragments have been discovered:—

1. *Mem.* I. iii. 15, IV. i. 3, third or fourth century A.D. (Grenfell and Hunt, II., the original in the British Museum).
2. *Mem.* II. i. 5–16, first or second century A.D. (Vitelli, *Papiri greci e latini*, II.).
3. *Oec.* ii. 8–17; ix. 2, first century A.D. (G. and H., II.).

The best manuscripts are the following:—

1. *Memorabilia:*
   A. (*Parisinus*, 1302), thirteenth century, containing only Books I. and II.
   B. (*Parisinus*, 1740), fourteenth century.

These represent two different classes. Between them, but nearer to B, stand:

   C. (*Parisinus*, 1642).
   D. (*Parisinus*, 1643), fifteenth century.
   M. (*Marcianus*, 511), thirteenth century.

2. *Oeconomicus:*
   E. (*Laurentianus*, lxxx. 13), thirteenth century.
   M. (*Lipsiensis*, 9), fourteenth century, wanting c. xii. 9 to xix. 16.
   F. (*Laurentianus*, lxxxv. 9), thirteenth century.
   V. (*Marcianus*, 511), thirteenth century.
   H. (*Reginensis*, 96), twelfth or thirteenth century.

II. Principal Editions:—

(a) Complete Works of Xenophon.

JUNTA : Florence, 1516. *Editio Princeps.*
ALDUS : Venice, 1525.
STEPHANUS, H. : Geneva, 1561 and 1581.
LENKLAU, J. : Frankfurt, 1594; 2nd ed. with notes of Aemilius Portius, 1596.

xxviii

MANUSCRIPTS AND EDITIONS

ZEUNE, J. C. : Leipzig, 1778–
SCHNEIDER, J. G. : Leipzig, 1790–
WEISKE, B. : Leipzig, 1798–
SCHAEFER, G. H. : Leipzig, 1811–
DINDORF, L. : Leipzig, 1824–
SCHNEIDER and DINDORF : Oxford, 1810–
SAUPPE, G. : Leipzig, 1865–
MARCHANT, E. C. : Oxford, 1900–

(b) *Separate Editions with Commentaries.*

(i) *Of the Memorabilia:*
BREITENBACH, L. : Berlin, 1854.
KÜHNER, R. : Gotha, 1858.

(ii) *Of the Oeconomicus:*
BREITENBACH, L. : Berlin, 1841.
HOLDEN, H. A. : London, 1884.

(c) The best German critical edition of the *Memorabilia* next is Gilbert's (Berlin, 1888–); of the *Oeconomicus*, Thalheim's (Berlin, 1910).

Very important work on the MSS. was done by Karl Schenkl, and has been continued by his son. A recent work of great value is A. W. Persson's *Zur Textgeschichte Xenophons.*

The above list is, of course, very far from being complete, and does not even include reference to some scholars of the first rank, such as Cobet and J. J. Hartman, who have dealt with the text.

The present edition follows the text of G. Sauppe, except where stated in the footnotes.

Recent work includes the following:

Memorabilia.
  Ed. Maior. C. Hude. Leipzig, Teubner, 1934.

Oeconomicus.
  Text and French translation (Budé), P. Chantraine. Paris, 1949.

Banquet and Socrates' Defence.
  Text and French Translation (Budé), F. Ollier. Paris, 1961.

XENOPHON'S MEMORABILIA

BOOK I

ΞΕΝΟΦΩΝΤΟΣ
ΑΠΟΜΝΗΜΟΝΕΥΜΑΤΑ

Α

I. Πολλάκις ἐθαύμασα, τίσι ποτὲ λόγοις Ἀθηναίους ἔπεισαν οἱ γραψάμενοι Σωκράτην, ὡς ἄξιος
εἴη θανάτου τῇ πόλει. ἡ μὲν γὰρ γραφὴ κατ᾽
αὐτοῦ τοιάδε τις ἦν· Ἀδικεῖ Σωκράτης οὓς μὲν ἡ
πόλις νομίζει θεοὺς οὐ νομίζων, ἕτερα δὲ καινὰ
δαιμόνια εἰσφέρων· ἀδικεῖ δὲ καὶ τοὺς νέους
διαφθείρων.

2 Πρῶτον μὲν οὖν, ὡς οὐκ ἐνόμιζεν οὓς ἡ πόλις
νομίζει θεούς, ποίῳ ποτ᾽ ἐχρήσαντο τεκμηρίῳ ;
θύων τε γὰρ φανερὸς ἦν πολλάκις μὲν οἴκοι,
πολλάκις δὲ καὶ[1] ἐπὶ τῶν κοινῶν τῆς πόλεως
βωμῶν καὶ μαντικῇ χρώμενος οὐκ ἀφανὴς ἦν·
διετεθρύλητο γάρ, ὡς φαίη Σωκράτης τὸ δαιμόνιον
ἑαυτῷ σημαίνειν· ὅθεν δὴ καὶ μάλιστά μοι
δοκοῦσιν αὐτὸν αἰτιάσασθαι καινὰ δαιμόνια
3 εἰσφέρειν. ὁ δ᾽ οὐδὲν καινότερον εἰσέφερε τῶν
ἄλλων, ὅσοι μαντικὴν νομίζοντες οἰωνοῖς τε
χρῶνται καὶ φήμαις καὶ συμβόλοις καὶ θυσίαις.
οὗτοί τε γὰρ ὑπολαμβάνουσιν οὐ τοὺς ὄρνιθας
οὐδὲ τοὺς ἀπαντῶντας εἰδέναι τὰ συμφέροντα τοῖς
μαντευομένοις, ἀλλὰ τοὺς θεοὺς διὰ τούτων αὐτὰ

---

[1] καὶ A : Sauppe omits.

4 σημαίνειν, κἀκεῖνος δὲ οὕτως ἐνόμιζεν. ἀλλ' οἱ
μὲν πλεῖστοί φασιν ὑπό τε τῶν ὀρνίθων καὶ τῶν
ἀπαντώντων ἀποτρέπεσθαί τε καὶ προτρέπεσθαι·
Σωκράτης δ' ὥσπερ ἐγίγνωσκεν, οὕτως ἔλεγε· τὸ
δαιμόνιον γὰρ ἔφη σημαίνειν. καὶ πολλοῖς τῶν
συνόντων προηγόρευε τὰ μὲν ποιεῖν, τὰ δὲ μὴ
ποιεῖν, ὡς τοῦ δαιμονίου προσημαίνοντος. καὶ
τοῖς μὲν πειθομένοις αὐτῷ συνέφερε, τοῖς δὲ μὴ
5 πειθομένοις μετέμελε. καίτοι τίς οὐκ ἂν ὁμο-
λογήσειεν αὐτὸν βούλεσθαι μήτ' ἠλίθιον μήτ'
ἀλαζόνα φαίνεσθαι τοῖς συνοῦσιν; ἐδόκει δ' ἂν
ἀμφότερα ταῦτα, εἰ προαγορεύων ὡς ὑπὸ θεοῦ
φαινόμενα ψευδόμενος ἐφαίνετο. δῆλον οὖν ὅτι
οὐκ ἂν προέλεγεν, εἰ μὴ ἐπίστευεν ἀληθεύσειν.
ταῦτα δὲ τίς ἂν ἄλλῳ πιστεύσειεν ἢ θεῷ;
πιστεύων δὲ θεοῖς πῶς οὐκ εἶναι θεοὺς ἐνόμιζεν;
6 ἀλλὰ μὴν ἐποίει καὶ τάδε πρὸς τοὺς ἐπιτηδείους.
τὰ μὲν γὰρ ἀναγκαῖα συνεβούλευε καὶ πράττειν,
ὡς νομίζοιεν ἄριστ' ἂν πραχθῆναι· περὶ δὲ
τῶν ἀδήλων ὅπως ἀποβήσοιτο μαντευσομένους
7 ἔπεμπεν, εἰ ποιητέα· καὶ τοὺς μέλλοντας οἴκους
τε καὶ πόλεις καλῶς οἰκήσειν μαντικῆς ἔφη
προσδεῖσθαι· τεκτονικὸν μὲν γὰρ ἢ χαλκευτικὸν
ἢ γεωργικὸν ἢ ἀνθρώπων ἀρχικὸν ἢ τῶν τοιούτων
ἔργων ἐξεταστικὸν ἢ λογιστικὸν ἢ οἰκονομικὸν ἢ
στρατηγικὸν γενέσθαι, πάντα τὰ τοιαῦτα μαθή-
ματα καὶ ἀνθρώπου γνώμη αἱρετὰ ἐνόμιζεν εἶναι·
8 τὰ δὲ μέγιστα τῶν ἐν τούτοις ἔφη τοὺς θεοὺς
ἑαυτοῖς καταλείπεσθαι, ὧν οὐδὲν δῆλον εἶναι τοῖς
ἀνθρώποις. οὔτε γάρ τοι τῷ καλῶς ἀγρὸν
φυτευσαμένῳ δῆλον, ὅστις καρπώσεται, οὔτε

4

XENOPHON'S MEMORABILIA

BOOK I

I. I HAVE often wondered by what arguments those who drew up the indictment against Socrates could persuade the Athenians that his life was forfeit to the state. The indictment against him was to this effect: *Socrates is guilty of rejecting the gods acknowledged by the state and of bringing in strange deities: he is also guilty of corrupting the youth.*

First then, that he rejected the gods acknowledged by the state—what evidence did they produce of that? He offered sacrifices constantly, and made no secret of it, now in his home, now at the altars of the state temples, and he made use of divination with as little secrecy. Indeed it had become notorious that Socrates claimed to be guided by 'the deity'[1]: it was out of this claim, I think, that the charge of bringing in strange deities arose. He was no more bringing in anything strange than are other believers in divination, who rely on augury, oracles, coincidences and sacrifices. For these men's belief is not that the birds or the folk met by accident know what profits the inquirer, but that they are the instruments by which the gods mak

---

[1] That immanent 'divine something,' as Cicero terms which Socrates claimed as his peculiar possession.

this known; and that was Socrates' belief too. Only, whereas most men say that the birds or the 4 folk they meet dissuade or encourage them, Socrates said what he meant: for he said that the deity gave him a sign. Many of his companions were counselled by him to do this or not to do that in accordance with the warnings of the deity: and those who followed his advice prospered, and those who rejected it had cause for regret. And yet who would 5 not admit that he wished to appear neither a knave nor a fool to his companions? but he would have been thought both, had he proved to be mistaken when he alleged that his counsel was in accordance with divine revelation. Obviously, then, he would not have given the counsel if he had not been confident that what he said would come true. And who could have inspired him with that confidence but a god? And since he had confidence in the gods, how can he have disbelieved in the existence of the gods? Another way he had of dealing with 6 intimate friends was this: if there was no room for doubt, he advised them to act as they thought best; but if the consequences could not be foreseen, he sent them to the oracle to inquire whether the thing ought to be done. Those who intended to 7 control a house or a city, he said, needed the help of divination. For the craft of carpenter, smith, farmer or ruler, and the theory of such crafts, and arithmetic and economics and generalship might be learned and mastered by the application of human powers; but the deepest secrets of these matters 8 the gods reserved to themselves; they were dark to men. You may plant a field well; but you know not who shall gather the fruits: you may build a

τῷ καλῶς οἰκίαν οἰκοδομησαμένῳ δῆλον, ὅστις
ἐνοικήσει, οὔτε τῷ στρατηγικῷ δῆλον, εἰ συμφέρει
στρατηγεῖν, οὔτε τῷ πολιτικῷ δῆλον, εἰ συμφέρει
τῆς πόλεως προστατεῖν, οὔτε τῷ καλὴν γήμαντι,
ἵν᾽ εὐφραίνηται, δῆλον, εἰ διὰ ταύτην ἀνιάσεται,
οὔτε τῷ δυνατοὺς ἐν τῇ πόλει κηδεστὰς λαβόντι
δῆλον, εἰ διὰ τούτους στερήσεται τῆς πόλεως.

9 τοὺς δὲ μηδὲν τῶν τοιούτων οἰομένους εἶναι
δαιμόνιον, ἀλλὰ πάντα τῆς ἀνθρωπίνης γνώμης
δαιμονᾶν ἔφη· δαιμονᾶν δὲ καὶ τοὺς μαντευο-
μένους ἃ τοῖς ἀνθρώποις ἔδωκαν οἱ θεοὶ μαθοῦσι
διακρίνειν, οἷον εἴ τις ἐπερωτῴη, πότερον ἐπιστάμενον ἡνιοχεῖν ἐπὶ ζεῦγος λαβεῖν κρεῖττον ἢ μὴ
ἐπιστάμενον ἢ πότερον ἐπιστάμενον κυβερνᾶν ἐπὶ
τὴν ναῦν κρεῖττον λαβεῖν ἢ μὴ ἐπιστάμενον ἢ ἃ
ἔξεστιν ἀριθμήσαντας ἢ μετρήσαντας ἢ στήσαντας
εἰδέναι, τοὺς τὰ τοιαῦτα παρὰ τῶν θεῶν πυνθανο-
μένους ἀθέμιτα ποιεῖν ἡγεῖτο. ἔφη δὲ δεῖν ἃ μὲν
μαθόντας ποιεῖν ἔδωκαν οἱ θεοὶ μανθάνειν, ἃ δὲ
μὴ δῆλα τοῖς ἀνθρώποις ἐστὶ πειρᾶσθαι διὰ
μαντικῆς παρὰ τῶν θεῶν πυνθάνεσθαι· τοὺς
θεοὺς γὰρ οἷς ἂν ὦσιν ἵλεῳ σημαίνειν.

10 Ἀλλὰ μὴν ἐκεῖνός γε ἀεὶ μὲν ἦν ἐν τῷ φανερῷ·
πρωί τε γὰρ εἰς τοὺς περιπάτους καὶ τὰ γυμνάσια
ᾔει καὶ πληθούσης ἀγορᾶς ἐκεῖ φανερὸς ἦν καὶ τὸ
λοιπὸν ἀεὶ τῆς ἡμέρας ἦν ὅπου πλείστοις μέλλοι
συνέσεσθαι· καὶ ἔλεγε μὲν ὡς τὸ πολύ, τοῖς δὲ βου-

---

[1] *Cyropaedia*, I. vi. 6.

house well; but you know not who shall dwell in it: able to command, you cannot know whether it is profitable to command: versed in statecraft, you know not whether it is profitable to guide the state: though, for your delight, you marry a pretty woman, you cannot tell whether she will bring you sorrow: though you form a party among men mighty in the state, you know not whether they will cause you to be driven from the state. If any 9 man thinks that these matters are wholly within the grasp of the human mind and nothing in them is beyond our reason, that man, he said, is irrational. But it is no less irrational to seek the guidance of heaven in matters which men are permitted by the gods to decide for themselves by study: to ask, for instance, Is it better to get an experienced coach-man to drive my carriage or a man without experience?[1] Is it better to get an experienced seaman to steer my ship or a man without experience? So too with what we may know by reckoning, measurement or weighing. To put such questions to the gods seemed to his mind profane. In short, what the gods have granted us to do by help of learning, we must learn; what is hidden from mortals we should try to find out from the gods by divination: for to him that is in their grace the gods grant a sign.

Moreover, Socrates lived ever in the open; for 10 early in the morning he went to the public promenades and training-grounds; in the forenoon he was seen in the market; and the rest of the day he passed just where most people were to be met: he was generally talking, and anyone might listen. Yet none ever knew him to offend against piety

7

11 λομένοις ἐξῆν ἀκούειν. οὐδεὶς δὲ πώποτε Σωκράτους οὐδὲν ἀσεβὲς οὐδὲ ἀνόσιον οὔτε πράττοντος
εἶδεν οὔτε λέγοντος ἤκουσεν. οὐδὲ γὰρ περὶ τῆς
τῶν πάντων φύσεως ᾗπερ τῶν ἄλλων οἱ πλεῖστοι
διελέγετο σκοπῶν, ὅπως ὁ καλούμενος ὑπὸ τῶν
σοφιστῶν κόσμος ἔφυ καὶ τίσιν ἀνάγκαις ἕκαστα
γίγνεται τῶν οὐρανίων, ἀλλὰ καὶ τοὺς φροντίζοντας
12 τὰ τοιαῦτα μωραίνοντας ἀπεδείκνυε. καὶ πρῶτον
μὲν αὐτῶν ἐσκόπει πότερά ποτε νομίσαντες ἱκανῶς
ἤδη τἀνθρώπινα εἰδέναι ἔρχονται ἐπὶ τὸ περὶ τῶν
τοιούτων φροντίζειν ἢ τὰ μὲν ἀνθρώπεια παρέντες,
τὰ δαιμόνια δὲ σκοποῦντες ἡγοῦνται τὰ προσή-
13 κοντα πράττειν. ἐθαύμαζε δ᾽ εἰ μὴ φανερὸν
αὐτοῖς ἐστιν, ὅτι ταῦτα οὐ δυνατόν ἐστιν ἀνθρώποις
εὑρεῖν· ἐπεὶ καὶ τοὺς μέγιστον φρονοῦντας ἐπὶ τῷ
περὶ τούτων λέγειν οὐ ταὐτὰ δοξάζειν ἀλλήλοις,
ἀλλὰ τοῖς μαινομένοις ὁμοίως διακεῖσθαι πρὸς
14 ἀλλήλους. τῶν τε γὰρ μαινομένων τοὺς μὲν οὐδὲ
τὰ δεινὰ δεδιέναι, τοὺς δὲ καὶ τὰ μὴ φοβερὰ
φοβεῖσθαι· καὶ τοῖς μὲν οὐδ᾽ ἐν ὄχλῳ δοκεῖν
αἰσχρὸν εἶναι λέγειν ἢ ποιεῖν ὁτιοῦν, τοῖς δὲ οὐδ᾽
ἐξιτητέον εἰς ἀνθρώπους εἶναι δοκεῖν· καὶ τοὺς
μὲν οὔθ᾽ ἱερὸν οὔτε βωμὸν οὔτ᾽ ἄλλο τῶν θείων
οὐδὲν τιμᾶν, τοὺς δὲ καὶ λίθους καὶ ξύλα τὰ
τυχόντα καὶ θηρία σέβεσθαι· τῶν τε περὶ τῆς
τῶν πάντων φύσεως μεριμνώντων τοῖς μὲν δοκεῖν
ἓν μόνον τὸ ὂν εἶναι, τοῖς δ᾽ ἄπειρα τὸ πλῆθος·
καὶ τοῖς μὲν ἀεὶ πάντα κινεῖσθαι, τοῖς δ᾽ οὐδὲν ἂν
ποτε κινηθῆναι· καὶ τοῖς μὲν πάντα γίγνεσθαί τε
καὶ ἀπόλλυσθαι, τοῖς δὲ οὔτ᾽ ἂν γενέσθαι ποτὲ
15 οὐδὲν οὔτε ἀπολέσθαι.[1] ἐσκόπει δὲ περὶ αὐτῶν
καὶ τάδε, ἆρ᾽ ὥσπερ οἱ τἀνθρώπεια μανθάνοντες

8

and religion in deed or word. He did not even 11
discuss that topic so favoured by other talkers,
"the Nature of the Universe": and avoided speculation on the so-called "Cosmos" of the Professors,
how it works, and on the laws that govern the
phenomena of the heavens: indeed he would argue
that to trouble one's mind with such problems is
sheer folly. In the first place, he would inquire, 12
did these thinkers suppose that their knowledge of
human affairs was so complete that they must seek
these new fields for the exercise of their brains ; or
that it was their duty to neglect human affairs and
consider only things divine? Moreover, he mar- 13
velled at their blindness in not seeing that man
cannot solve these riddles ; since even the most
conceited talkers on these problems did not agree
in their theories, but behaved to one another like
madmen. As some madmen have no fear of danger 14
and others are afraid where there is nothing to be
afraid of, as some will do or say anything in a crowd
with no sense of shame, while others shrink even
from going abroad among men, some respect neither
temple nor altar nor any other sacred thing, others
worship stocks and stones and beasts, so is it, he
held, with those who worry with " Universal Nature."
Some hold that *What is* is one, others that it is
infinite in number: some that all things are in
perpetual motion, others that nothing can ever be
moved at any time : some that all life is birth and
decay, others that nothing can ever be born or ever
die. Nor were those the only questions he asked 15
about such theorists. Students of human nature, he

---

¹ ἀπολέσθαι Stobaeus : ἀπολεῖσθαι Sauppe.

ἡγοῦνται τοῦθ' ὅ τι ἂν μάθωσιν ἑαυτοῖς τε καὶ
τῶν ἄλλων ὅτῳ ἂν βούλωνται ποιήσειν, οὕτω καὶ
οἱ τὰ θεῖα ζητοῦντες νομίζουσιν, ἐπειδὰν γνῶσιν,
αἷς ἀνάγκαις ἕκαστα γίγνεται, ποιήσειν, ὅταν
βούλωνται, καὶ ἀνέμους καὶ ὕδατα καὶ ὥρας καὶ
ὅτου ἂν ἄλλου δέωνται τῶν τοιούτων, ἢ τοιοῦτο
μὲν οὐδὲν οὐδ' ἐλπίζουσιν, ἀρκεῖ δ' αὐτοῖς γνῶναι
μόνον, ᾗ τῶν τοιούτων ἕκαστα γίγνεται.

16 Περὶ μὲν οὖν τῶν ταῦτα πραγματευομένων
τοιαῦτα ἔλεγεν· αὐτὸς δὲ περὶ τῶν ἀνθρωπίνων ἀεὶ διελέγετο σκοπῶν, τί εὐσεβές, τί ἀσεβές,
τί καλόν, τί αἰσχρόν, τί δίκαιον, τί ἄδικον, τί
σωφροσύνη, τί μανία, τί ἀνδρεία, τί δειλία, τί
πόλις, τί πολιτικός, τί ἀρχὴ ἀνθρώπων, τί
ἀρχικὸς ἀνθρώπων, καὶ περὶ τῶν ἄλλων, ἃ τοὺς
μὲν εἰδότας ἡγεῖτο καλοὺς κἀγαθοὺς εἶναι, τοὺς δ'
ἀγνοοῦντας ἀνδραποδώδεις ἂν δικαίως κεκλῆσθαι.

17 Ὅσα μὲν οὖν μὴ φανερὸς ἦν ὅπως ἐγίγνωσκεν,
οὐδὲν θαυμαστὸν ὑπὲρ τούτων περὶ αὐτοῦ παρα-
γνῶναι τοὺς δικαστάς· ὅσα δὲ πάντες ᾔδεσαν, οὐ

18 θαυμαστὸν εἰ μὴ τούτων ἐνεθυμήθησαν; βουλεύσας
γάρ ποτε καὶ τὸν βουλευτικὸν ὅρκον ὀμόσας, ἐν ᾧ
ἦν κατὰ τοὺς νόμους βουλεύσειν, ἐπιστάτης ἐν τῷ
δήμῳ γενόμενος, ἐπιθυμήσαντος τοῦ δήμου παρὰ
τοὺς νόμους ἐννέα στρατηγοὺς μιᾷ ψήφῳ τοὺς
ἀμφὶ Θράσυλλον καὶ Ἐρασινίδην ἀποκτεῖναι
πάντας, οὐκ ἠθέλησεν ἐπιψηφίσαι, ὀργιζομένου
μὲν αὐτῷ τοῦ δήμου, πολλῶν δὲ καὶ δυνατῶν
ἀπειλούντων· ἀλλὰ περὶ πλείονος ἐποιήσατο

said, think that they will apply their knowledge in due course for the good of themselves and any others they choose. Do those who pry into heavenly phenomena imagine that, once they have discovered the laws by which these are produced, they will create at their will winds, waters, seasons and such things to their need? Or have they no such expectation, and are they satisfied with knowing the causes of these various phenomena?

Such, then, was his criticism of those who meddle 16 with these matters. His own conversation was ever of human things. The problems he discussed were, What is godly, what is ungodly; what is beautiful, what is ugly; what is just, what is unjust; what is prudence, what is madness; what is courage, what is cowardice; what is a state, what is a statesman; what is government, and what is a governor;—these and others like them, of which the knowledge made a "gentleman," in his estimation, while ignorance should involve the reproach of "slavishness."

So, in pronouncing on opinions of his that were 17 unknown to them it is not surprising that the jury erred: but is it not astonishing that they should have ignored matters of common knowledge? For 18 instance, when he was on the Council and had taken the counsellor's oath by which he bound himself to give counsel in accordance with the laws, it fell to his lot to preside in the Assembly when the people wanted to condemn Thrasyllus and Erasinides and their colleagues to death by a single vote. That was illegal, and he refused the motion in spite of popular rancour and the threats of many powerful persons. It was more to him that he should keep his oath than that he should humour

εὐορκεῖν ἢ χαρίσασθαι τῷ δήμῳ παρὰ τὸ δίκαιον
19 καὶ φυλάξασθαι τοὺς ἀπειλοῦντας. καὶ γὰρ
ἐπιμελεῖσθαι θεοὺς ἐνόμιζεν ἀνθρώπων οὐχ ὃν
τρόπον οἱ πολλοὶ νομίζουσιν· οὗτοι μὲν γὰρ
οἴονται τοὺς θεοὺς τὰ μὲν εἰδέναι, τὰ δ' οὐκ
εἰδέναι· Σωκράτης δὲ πάντα μὲν ἡγεῖτο θεοὺς
εἰδέναι, τά τε λεγόμενα καὶ πραττόμενα καὶ τὰ
σιγῇ βουλευόμενα, πανταχοῦ δὲ παρεῖναι καὶ
σημαίνειν τοῖς ἀνθρώποις περὶ τῶν ἀνθρωπείων
πάντων.

20   Θαυμάζω οὖν, ὅπως ποτὲ ἐπείσθησαν Ἀθηναῖοι
Σωκράτην περὶ τοὺς θεοὺς μὴ σωφρονεῖν, τὸν
ἀσεβὲς μὲν οὐδέν ποτε περὶ θεοὺς οὔτ' εἰπόντα
οὔτε πράξαντα, τοιαῦτα δὲ καὶ λέγοντα καὶ
πράττοντα [περὶ θεῶν], οἷά τις ἂν καὶ λέγων καὶ
πράττων εἴη τε καὶ νομίζοιτο εὐσεβέστατος.

II. Θαυμαστὸν δὲ φαίνεταί μοι καὶ τὸ πεισθῆ-
ναί τινας, ὡς Σωκράτης τοὺς νέους διέφθειρεν, ὃς
πρὸς τοῖς εἰρημένοις πρῶτον μὲν ἀφροδισίων καὶ
γαστρὸς πάντων ἀνθρώπων ἐγκρατέστατος ἦν,
εἶτα πρὸς χειμῶνα καὶ θέρος καὶ πάντας πόνους
καρτερικώτατος, ἔτι δὲ πρὸς τὸ μετρίων δεῖσθαι
πεπαιδευμένος οὕτως, ὥστε πάνυ μικρὰ κεκτημένος
2 πάνυ ῥᾳδίως ἔχειν ἀρκοῦντα. πῶς οὖν αὐτὸς ὢν
τοιοῦτος ἄλλους ἂν ἢ ἀσεβεῖς ἢ παρανόμους ἢ
λίχνους ἢ ἀφροδισίων ἀκρατεῖς ἢ πρὸς τὸ πονεῖν
μαλακοὺς ἐποίησεν; ἀλλ' ἔπαυσε μὲν τούτων
πολλούς, ἀρετῆς ποιήσας ἐπιθυμεῖν καὶ ἐλπίδας
παρασχών, ἂν ἑαυτῶν ἐπιμελῶνται, καλοὺς
3 κἀγαθοὺς ἔσεσθαι. καίτοι γε οὐδεπώποτε
ὑπέσχετο διδάσκαλος εἶναι τούτου, ἀλλὰ τῷ
φανερὸς εἶναι τοιοῦτος ὢν ἐλπίζειν ἐποίει τοὺς

the people in an unjust demand and shield himself from threats. For, like most men, indeed, he be- 19 lieved that the gods are heedful of mankind, but with an important difference; for whereas they do not believe in the omniscience of the gods, Socrates thought that they know all things, our words and deeds and secret purposes; that they are present everywhere, and grant signs to men of all that concerns man.[1]

I wonder, then, how the Athenians can have been 20 persuaded that Socrates was a freethinker, when he never said or did anything contrary to sound religion, and his utterances about the gods and his behaviour towards them were the words and actions of a man who is truly religious and deserves to be thought so.

II. No less wonderful is it to me that some believed the charge brought against Socrates of corrupting the youth. In the first place, apart from what I have said, in control of his own passions and appetites he was the strictest of men; further, in endurance of cold and heat and every kind of toil he was most resolute; and besides, his needs were so schooled to moderation that having very little he was yet very content. Such was his own character: how then 2 can he have led others into impiety, crime, gluttony, lust, or sloth? On the contrary, he cured these vices in many, by putting into them a desire for goodness, and by giving them confidence that self-discipline would make them gentlemen. To be sure 3 he never professed to teach this; but, by letting his own light shine, he led his disciples to hope that

---

[1] IV. iii, 2; *Cyropaedia*, I. vi. 46.

συνδιατρίβοντας ἑαυτῷ μιμουμένους ἐκεῖνον τοιού-
4 τους γενήσεσθαι. ἀλλὰ μὴν καὶ τοῦ σώματος
αὐτός τε οὐκ ἠμέλει τούς τ' ἀμελοῦντας οὐκ
ἐπήνει. τὸ μὲν οὖν ὑπερεσθίοντα ὑπερπονεῖν
ἀπεδοκίμαζε, τὸ δὲ ὅσα γ' ἡδέως ἡ ψυχὴ δέχεται,
ταῦτα ἱκανῶς ἐκπονεῖν ἐδοκίμαζε. ταύτην γὰρ
τὴν ἕξιν ὑγιεινήν τε ἱκανῶς εἶναι καὶ τὴν τῆς
5 ψυχῆς ἐπιμέλειαν οὐκ ἐμποδίζειν ἔφη. ἀλλ' οὐ
μὴν θρυπτικός γε οὐδὲ ἀλαζονικὸς ἦν οὔτ'
ἀμπεχόνῃ οὔθ' ὑποδέσει οὔτε τῇ ἄλλῃ διαίτῃ.
οὐ μὴν οὐδ' ἐρασιχρημάτους γε τοὺς συνόντας
ἐποίει. τῶν μὲν γὰρ ἄλλων ἐπιθυμιῶν ἔπαυε,
τοὺς δὲ ἑαυτοῦ ἐπιθυμοῦντας οὐκ ἐπράττετο
6 χρήματα. τούτου δ' ἀπεχόμενος ἐνόμιζεν ἐλευθερίας ἐπιμελεῖσθαι· τοὺς δὲ λαμβάνοντας τῆς
ὁμιλίας μισθὸν ἀνδραποδιστὰς ἑαυτῶν ἀπεκάλει
διὰ τὸ ἀναγκαῖον αὐτοῖς εἶναι διαλέγεσθαι παρ'
7 ὧν λάβοιεν τὸν μισθόν. ἐθαύμαζε δ', εἴ τις
ἀρετὴν ἐπαγγελλόμενος ἀργύριον πράττοιτο καὶ
μὴ νομίζοι τὸ μέγιστον κέρδος ἕξειν φίλον ἀγαθὸν
κτησάμενος, ἀλλὰ φοβοῖτο, μὴ ὁ γενόμενος καλὸς
κἀγαθὸς τῷ τὰ μέγιστα εὐεργετήσαντι μὴ τὴν
8 μεγίστην χάριν ἕξοι. Σωκράτης δὲ ἐπηγγείλατο
μὲν οὐδενὶ πώποτε τοιοῦτον οὐδέν, ἐπίστευε δὲ
τῶν συνόντων ἑαυτῷ τοὺς ἀποδεξαμένους ἅπερ
αὐτὸς ἐδοκίμαζεν εἰς τὸν πάντα βίον ἑαυτῷ τε καὶ
ἀλλήλοις φίλους ἀγαθοὺς ἔσεσθαι. πῶς ἂν οὖν
ὁ τοιοῦτος ἀνὴρ διαφθείροι τοὺς νέους; εἰ μὴ ἄρα
ἡ τῆς ἀρετῆς ἐπιμέλεια διαφθορά ἐστιν.

9 Ἀλλὰ νὴ Δία, ὁ κατήγορος ἔφη, ὑπερορᾶν ἐποίει
τῶν καθεστώτων νόμων τοὺς συνόντας λέγων, ὡς
μῶρον εἴη τοὺς μὲν τῆς πόλεως ἄρχοντας ἀπὸ

14

they through imitation of him would attain to such
excellence. Furthermore, he himself never neg- 4
lected the body, and reproved such neglect in others.
Thus over-eating followed by over-exertion he dis-
approved. But he approved of taking as much
hard exercise as is agreeable to the soul[1]; for the
habit not only insured good health, but did not
hamper the care of the soul. On the other hand, 5
he disliked foppery and pretentiousness in the
fashion of clothes or shoes or in behaviour. Nor,
again, did he encourage love of money in his companions. For while he checked their other desires,
he would not make money himself out of their
desire for his companionship. He held that this 6
self-denying ordinance insured his liberty. Those
who charged a fee for their society he denounced
for selling themselves into bondage ; since they were
bound to converse with all from whom they took the
fee. He marvelled that anyone should make money 7
by the profession of virtue, and should not reflect
that his highest reward would be the gain of a good
friend ; as though he who became a true gentleman
could fail to feel deep gratitude for a benefit so
great. Socrates indeed never promised any such 8
boon to anyone ; but he was confident that those of
his companions who adopted his principles of conduct would throughout life be good friends to him
and to one another. How, then, should such a man
" corrupt the youth " ? Unless, perchance, it be
corruption to foster virtue.

But, said his accuser, he taught his companions to 9
despise the established laws by insisting on the
folly of appointing public officials by lot, when none

----

[1] *Cyropaedia*, I. vi. 17.

κυάμου καθιστάναι, κυβερνήτῃ δὲ μηδένα ἐθέλειν
χρῆσθαι κυαμευτῷ μηδὲ τέκτονι μηδ' αὐλητῇ μηδ'
ἐπ' ἄλλα τοιαῦτα, ἃ πολλῷ ἐλάττονας βλάβας
ἁμαρτανόμενα ποιεῖ τῶν περὶ τὴν πόλιν ἁμαρτα-
νομένων· τοὺς δὲ τοιούτους λόγους ἐπαίρειν ἔφη
τοὺς νέους καταφρονεῖν τῆς καθεστώσης πολιτείας
10 καὶ ποιεῖν βιαίους. ἐγὼ δ' οἶμαι τοὺς φρόνησιν
ἀσκοῦντας καὶ νομίζοντας ἱκανοὺς ἔσεσθαι[1] τὰ
συμφέροντα διδάσκειν τοὺς πολίτας ἥκιστα
γίγνεσθαι βιαίους, εἰδότας, ὅτι τῇ μὲν βίᾳ
πρόσεισιν ἔχθραι καὶ κίνδυνοι, διὰ δὲ τοῦ πείθειν
ἀκινδύνως τε καὶ μετὰ φιλίας ταὐτὰ γίγνεται.
οἱ μὲν γὰρ βιασθέντες ὡς ἀφαιρεθέντες μισοῦσιν,
οἱ δὲ πεισθέντες ὡς κεχαρισμένοι φιλοῦσιν.
οὔκουν τῶν φρόνησιν ἀσκούντων τὸ βιάζεσθαι,
ἀλλὰ τῶν ἰσχὺν ἄνευ γνώμης ἐχόντων [τὰ τοιαῦτα
11 πράττειν] ἐστίν. ἀλλὰ μὴν καὶ συμμάχων ὁ μὲν
βιάζεσθαι τολμῶν δέοιτ' ἂν οὐκ ὀλίγων, ὁ δὲ
πείθειν δυνάμενος οὐδενός· καὶ γὰρ μόνος ἡγοῖτ'
ἂν δύνασθαι πείθειν. καὶ φονεύειν δὲ τοῖς τοιούτοις ἥκιστα συμβαίνει· τίς γὰρ ἀποκτεῖναί τινα
βούλοιτ' ἂν μᾶλλον ἢ ζῶντι πειθομένῳ χρῆσθαι;
12 Ἀλλ' ἔφη γε ὁ κατήγορος, Σωκράτει ὁμιλητὰ
γενομένω Κριτίας τε καὶ Ἀλκιβιάδης πλεῖστα
κακὰ τὴν πόλιν ἐποιησάτην. Κριτίας μὲν γὰρ
τῶν ἐν τῇ ὀλιγαρχίᾳ πάντων κλεπτίστατός τε
καὶ βιαιότατος καὶ φονικώτατος ἐγένετο, Ἀλκιβιάδης δὲ αὖ τῶν ἐν τῇ δημοκρατίᾳ πάντων ἀκρα-
τέστατός τε καὶ ὑβριστότατος καὶ βιαιότατος.
13 ἐγὼ δ', εἰ μέν τι κακὸν ἐκείνω τὴν πόλιν
ἐποιησάτην, οὐκ ἀπολογήσομαι· τὴν δὲ πρὸς

would choose a pilot or builder or flautist by lot, nor any other craftsman for work in which mistakes are far less disastrous than mistakes in statecraft. Such sayings, he argued, led the young to despise the established constitution and made them violent. But I hold[1] that they who cultivate wisdom and 10 think they will be able to guide the people in prudent policy never lapse into violence: they know that enmities and dangers are inseparable from violence, but persuasion produces the same results safely and amicably. For violence, by making its victims sensible of loss, rouses their hatred: but persuasion, by seeming to confer a favour, wins goodwill. It is not, then, cultivation of wisdom that leads to violent methods, but the possession of power without prudence. Besides, many sup- 11 porters are necessary to him who ventures to use force: but he who can persuade needs no confederate, having confidence in his own unaided power of persuasion. And such a man has no occasion to shed blood; for who would rather take a man's life than have a live and willing follower?

But his accuser argued thus. Among the 12 associates of Socrates were Critias and Alcibiades; and none wrought so many evils to the state. For Critias in the days of the oligarchy bore the palm for greed and violence: Alcibiades, for his part, exceeded all in licentiousness and insolence under the democracy. Now I have no intention of excusing 13 the wrong these two men wrought the state; but I

[1] *Cyropaedia*, I. iv. 21.

---

[1] ἔσεσθαι MSS. : εἶναι Sauppe.

Σωκράτην συνουσίαν αὐτοῖν ὡς ἐγένετο διηγή-
14 σομαι. ἐγενέσθην μὲν γὰρ δὴ τὼ ἄνδρε τούτω
φύσει φιλοτιμοτάτω πάντων Ἀθηναίων βουλομένω
τε πάντα δι᾽ ἑαυτῶν πράττεσθαι καὶ πάντων
ὀνομαστοτάτω γενέσθαι. ᾔδεσαν δὲ Σωκράτην
ἀπ᾽ ἐλαχίστων μὲν χρημάτων αὐταρκέστατα
ζῶντα, τῶν ἡδονῶν δὲ πασῶν ἐγκρατέστατον ὄντα,
τοῖς δὲ διαλεγομένοις αὐτῷ πᾶσι χρώμενον ἐν τοῖς
15 λόγοις ὅπως βούλοιτο. ταῦτα δὲ ὁρῶντε καὶ ὄντε
οἵω προείρησθον, πότερόν τις αὐτὼ φῇ τοῦ βίου
τοῦ Σωκράτους ἐπιθυμήσαντε καὶ τῆς σωφροσύνης,
ἣν ἐκεῖνος εἶχεν, ὀρέξασθαι τῆς ὁμιλίας αὐτοῦ ἢ
νομίσαντε, εἰ ὁμιλησαίτην ἐκείνῳ, γενέσθαι ἂν
16 ἱκανωτάτω λέγειν τε καὶ πράττειν; ἐγὼ μὲν γὰρ
ἡγοῦμαι, θεοῦ διδόντος αὐτοῖς ἢ ζῆν ὅλον τὸν βίον
ὥσπερ ζῶντα Σωκράτην ἑώρων ἢ τεθνάναι, ἑλέσθαι
ἂν αὐτὼ μᾶλλον τεθνάναι. δῆλω δ᾽ ἐγενέσθην ἐξ
ὧν ἐπραξάτην· ὡς γὰρ τάχιστα κρείττονε τῶν
συγγιγνομένων ἡγησάσθην εἶναι, εὐθὺς ἀποπηδή-
σαντε Σωκράτους ἐπραττέτην τὰ πολιτικά, ὧνπερ
ἕνεκα Σωκράτους ὠρεχθήτην.
17 Ἴσως οὖν εἴποι τις ἂν πρὸς ταῦτα, ὅτι ἐχρῆν
τὸν Σωκράτην μὴ πρότερον τὰ πολιτικὰ διδάσκειν
τοὺς συνόντας ἢ σωφρονεῖν. ἐγὼ δὲ πρὸς τοῦτο
μὲν οὐκ ἀντιλέγω· πάντας δὲ τοὺς διδάσκοντας
ὁρῶ αὐτοὺς δεικνύντας τε τοῖς μανθάνουσιν, ᾗπερ
αὐτοὶ ποιοῦσιν ἃ διδάσκουσι, καὶ τῷ λόγῳ προσ-
18 βιβάζοντας. οἶδα δὲ καὶ Σωκράτην δεικνύντα τοῖς
συνοῦσιν ἑαυτὸν καλὸν κἀγαθὸν ὄντα καὶ διαλεγόμενον κάλλιστα περὶ ἀρετῆς καὶ τῶν ἄλλων
ἀνθρωπίνων. οἶδα δὲ κἀκείνω σωφρονοῦντε, ἔστε
Σωκράτει συνήστην, οὐ φοβουμένω, μὴ ζημιοῖντο

will explain how they came to be with Socrates. Ambition was the very life-blood of both: no 14 Athenian was ever like them. They were eager to get control of everything and to outstrip every rival in notoriety. They knew that Socrates was living on very little, and yet was wholly independent; that he was strictly moderate in all his pleasures; and that in argument he could do what he liked with any disputant. Sharing this knowledge and the principles 15 I have indicated, is it to be supposed that these two men wanted to adopt the simple life of Socrates, and with this object in view sought his society? Did they not rather think that by associating with him they would attain the utmost proficiency in speech and action? For my part 16 I believe that, had heaven granted them the choice between the life they saw Socrates leading and death, they would have chosen rather to die. Their conduct betrayed their purpose; for as soon as they thought themselves superior to their fellow-disciples they sprang away from Socrates and took to politics; it was for political ends that they had wanted Socrates.

But it may be answered: Socrates should have 17 taught his companions prudence before politics. I do not deny it; but I find that all teachers show their disciples how they themselves practise what they teach, and lead them on by argument. And I know that it was so with Socrates: he showed his companions that he was a gentleman himself, and talked most excellently of goodness and of all things that concern man. I know further that even those 18 two were prudent so long as they were with Socrates,

19

ἢ παίοιντο ὑπὸ Σωκράτους, ἀλλ' οἰομένω τότε
κράτιστον εἶναι τοῦτο πράττειν.

19 Ἴσως οὖν εἴποιεν ἂν πολλοὶ τῶν φασκόντων
φιλοσοφεῖν, ὅτι οὐκ ἄν ποτε ὁ δίκαιος ἄδικος
γένοιτο οὐδὲ ὁ σώφρων ὑβριστὴς οὐδὲ ἄλλο οὐδὲν
ὧν μάθησίς ἐστιν ὁ μαθὼν ἀνεπιστήμων ἄν ποτε
γένοιτο. ἐγὼ δὲ περὶ τούτων οὐχ οὕτω γιγνώσκω·
ὁρῶ γὰρ ὥσπερ τὰ τοῦ σώματος ἔργα τοὺς μὴ τὰ
σώματα ἀσκοῦντας οὐ δυναμένους ποιεῖν, οὕτω
καὶ τὰ τῆς ψυχῆς ἔργα τοὺς μὴ τὴν ψυχὴν
ἀσκοῦντας οὐ δυναμένους· οὔτε γὰρ ἃ δεῖ πράττειν
20 οὔτε ὧν δεῖ ἀπέχεσθαι δύνανται. διὸ καὶ τοὺς
υἱεῖς οἱ πατέρες, κἂν ὦσι σώφρονες, ὅμως ἀπὸ
τῶν πονηρῶν ἀνθρώπων εἴργουσιν, ὡς τὴν μὲν
τῶν χρηστῶν ὁμιλίαν ἄσκησιν οὖσαν τῆς ἀρετῆς,
τὴν δὲ τῶν πονηρῶν κατάλυσιν. μαρτυρεῖ δὲ καὶ
τῶν ποιητῶν ὅ τε λέγων,

Ἐσθλῶν μὲν γὰρ ἀπ' ἐσθλὰ διδάξεαι· ἢν δὲ
κακοῖσι
συμμίσγῃς, ἀπολεῖς καὶ τὸν ἐόντα νόον·

καὶ ὁ λέγων,

Αὐτὰρ ἀνὴρ ἀγαθὸς τοτὲ μὲν κακός, ἄλλοτε δ'
ἐσθλός.

21 Κἀγὼ δὲ μαρτυρῶ τούτοις· ὁρῶ γὰρ ὥσπερ τῶν
ἐν μέτρῳ πεποιημένων ἐπῶν τοὺς μὴ μελετῶντας
ἐπιλανθανομένους, οὕτω καὶ τῶν διδασκαλικῶν
λόγων τοῖς ἀμελοῦσι λήθην ἐγγιγνομένην. ὅταν
δὲ τῶν νουθετικῶν λόγων ἐπιλάθηταί τις, ἐπιλέ-
λησται καὶ ὧν ἡ ψυχὴ πάσχουσα τῆς σωφροσύνης ἐπεθύμει· τούτων δ' ἐπιλαθόμενον οὐδὲν

not from fear of fine or blow, but because at that time they really believed in prudent conduct.

But many self-styled lovers of wisdom may reply : 19 A just man can never become unjust ; a prudent man can never become wanton ; in fact no one having learned any kind of knowledge can become ignorant of it. I do not hold with this view.[1] I notice that as those who do not train the body cannot perform the functions proper to the body, so those who do not train the soul cannot perform the functions of the soul : for they cannot do what they ought to do nor avoid what they ought not to do. For this cause fathers try to keep their sons, even if 20 they are prudent lads, out of bad company : for the society of honest men is a training in virtue, but the society of the bad is virtue's undoing. As one of the poets says :

" From the good shalt thou learn good things ; but if thou minglest with the bad thou shalt lose even what thou hast of wisdom." [2]

And another says :

"Ah, but a good man is at one time noble, at another base." [3]

My testimony agrees with theirs ; for I see that, 21 just as poetry is forgotten unless it is often repeated, so instruction, when no longer heeded, fades from the mind. To forget good counsel is to forget the experiences that prompted the soul to desire prudence : and when those are forgotten, it is not

[1] *Cyropaedia*, VII. v. 75. Against Antisthenes.
[2] Theognis.
[3] Author unknown.

θαυμαστὸν καὶ τῆς σωφροσύνης ἐπιλαθέσθαι.
22 ὁρῶ δὲ καὶ τοὺς εἰς φιλοποσίαν προαχθέντας καὶ
τοὺς εἰς ἔρωτας ἐκκυλισθέντας ἧττον δυναμένους
τῶν τε δεόντων ἐπιμελεῖσθαι καὶ τῶν μὴ δεόντων
ἀπέχεσθαι. πολλοὶ γὰρ καὶ χρημάτων δυνάμενοι
φείδεσθαι, πρὶν ἐρᾶν, ἐρασθέντες οὐκέτι δύνανται·
καὶ τὰ χρήματα καταναλώσαντες ὧν πρόσθεν
ἀπείχοντο κερδῶν, αἰσχρὰ νομίζοντες εἶναι, τού-
23 των οὐκ ἀπέχονται. πῶς οὖν οὐκ ἐνδέχεται
σωφρονήσαντα πρόσθεν αὖθις μὴ σωφρονεῖν καὶ
δίκαια δυνηθέντα πράττειν αὖθις ἀδυνατεῖν;
πάντα μὲν οὖν ἔμοιγε δοκεῖ τὰ καλὰ καὶ τἀγαθὰ
ἀσκητὰ εἶναι, οὐχ ἥκιστα δὲ σωφροσύνη. ἐν γὰρ
τῷ αὐτῷ σώματι συμπεφυτευμέναι τῇ ψυχῇ αἱ
ἡδοναὶ πείθουσιν αὐτὴν μὴ σωφρονεῖν, ἀλλὰ τὴν
ταχίστην ἑαυταῖς τε καὶ τῷ σώματι χαρίζεσθαι.
24 Καὶ Κριτίας δὴ καὶ Ἀλκιβιάδης ἕως μὲν
Σωκράτει συνήστην, ἐδυνάσθην ἐκείνῳ χρωμένῳ
συμμάχῳ τῶν μὴ καλῶν ἐπιθυμιῶν κρατεῖν·
ἐκείνου δ᾽ ἀπαλλαγέντε Κριτίας μὲν φυγὼν εἰς
Θετταλίαν ἐκεῖ συνῆν ἀνθρώποις ἀνομίᾳ μᾶλλον
ἢ δικαιοσύνῃ χρωμένοις, Ἀλκιβιάδης δ᾽ αὖ διὰ
μὲν κάλλος ὑπὸ πολλῶν καὶ σεμνῶν γυναικῶν
θηρώμενος, διὰ δὲ δύναμιν τὴν ἐν τῇ πόλει καὶ
τοῖς συμμάχοις ὑπὸ πολλῶν καὶ δυνατῶν
[κολακεύειν] ἀνθρώπων διαθρυπτόμενος, ὑπὸ δὲ
τοῦ δήμου τιμώμενος καὶ ῥᾳδίως πρωτεύων, ὥσπερ
οἱ τῶν γυμνικῶν ἀγώνων ἀθληταὶ ῥᾳδίως πρω-
τεύοντες ἀμελοῦσι τῆς ἀσκήσεως, οὕτω κἀκεῖνος
25 ἠμέλησεν αὐτοῦ. τοιούτων δὲ συμβάντων αὐτοῖν
καὶ ὠγκωμένω μὲν ἐπὶ γένει, ἐπηρμένω δ᾽ ἐπὶ
πλούτῳ, πεφυσημένω δ᾽ ἐπὶ δυνάμει, διατεθρυμ-

surprising that prudence itself is forgotten. I see 22
also that men who take to drink or get involved in
love intrigues lose the power of caring about right
conduct and avoiding evil. For many who are
careful with their money no sooner fall in love than
they begin to waste it : and when they have spent
it all, they no longer shrink from making more by
methods which they formerly avoided because they
thought them disgraceful. How then can it be 23
impossible for one who was prudent to lose his
prudence, for one who was capable of just action to
become incapable ? To me indeed it seems that
whatever is honourable, whatever is good in conduct is the result of training, and that this is
especially true of prudence. For in the same body
along with the soul are planted the pleasures which
call to her : " Abandon prudence, and make haste
to gratify us and the body."

And indeed it was thus with Critias and Alcibiades. 24
So long as they were with Socrates, they found in
him an ally who gave them strength to conquer
their evil passions. But when they parted from
him, Critias fled to Thessaly, and got among men
who put lawlessness before justice; while Alcibiades,
on account of his beauty, was hunted by many great
ladies, and because of his influence at Athens and
among her allies he was spoilt by many powerful
men : and as athletes who gain an easy victory in
the games are apt to neglect their training, so the
honour in which he was held, the cheap triumph
he won with the people, led him to neglect himself.
Such was their fortune : and when to pride of 25
birth, confidence in wealth, vainglory and much

μένω δὲ ὑπὸ πολλῶν ἀνθρώπων, ἐπὶ δὲ πᾶσι
τούτοις [διεφθαρμένω] καὶ πολὺν χρόνον ἀπὸ
Σωκράτους γεγονότε τί θαυμαστὸν εἰ ὑπερηφάνω
26 ἐγενέσθην; εἶτα εἰ μέν τι ἐπλημμελησάτην, τούτου Σωκράτην ὁ κατήγορος αἰτιᾶται; ὅτι δὲ νέω
ὄντε αὐτώ, ἡνίκα καὶ ἀγνωμονεστάτω καὶ ἀκρατε-
στάτω εἰκὸς εἶναι, Σωκράτης παρέσχε σώφρονε,
οὐδενὸς ἐπαίνου δοκεῖ τῷ κατηγόρῳ ἄξιος εἶναι;
27 οὐ μὴν τά γε ἄλλα οὕτω κρίνεται. τίς μὲν γὰρ
αὐλητής, τίς δὲ κιθαριστής, τίς δὲ ἄλλος
διδάσκαλος ἱκανοὺς ποιήσας τοὺς μαθητάς, ἐὰν
πρὸς ἄλλους ἐλθόντες χείρους φανῶσιν, αἰτίαν
ἔχει τούτου; τίς δὲ πατήρ, ἐὰν ὁ παῖς αὐτοῦ
συνδιατρίβων τῳ σωφρονῇ, ὕστερον δὲ ἄλλῳ τῳ
συγγενόμενος πονηρὸς γένηται, τὸν πρόσθεν
αἰτιᾶται, ἀλλ' οὐχ ὅσῳ ἂν παρὰ τῷ ὑστέρῳ
χείρων φαίνηται, τοσούτῳ μᾶλλον ἐπαινεῖ τὸν
πρότερον; ἀλλ' οἵ γε πατέρες αὐτοὶ συνόντες
τοῖς υἱέσι, τῶν παίδων πλημμελούντων, οὐκ αἰτίαν
28 ἔχουσιν, ἐὰν αὐτοὶ σωφρονῶσιν. οὕτω δὲ καὶ
Σωκράτην δίκαιον ἦν κρίνειν· εἰ μὲν αὐτὸς ἐποίει
τι φαῦλον, εἰκότως ἂν ἐδόκει πονηρὸς εἶναι· εἰ δ'
αὐτὸς σωφρονῶν διετέλει, πῶς ἂν δικαίως τῆς οὐκ
ἐνούσης αὐτῷ κακίας αἰτίαν ἔχοι; /
29 Ἀλλ' εἰ καὶ μηδὲν αὐτὸς πονηρὸν ποιῶν
ἐκείνους φαῦλα πράττοντας ὁρῶν ἐπῄνει, δικαίως
ἂν ἐπιτιμῷτο. Κριτίαν μὲν τοίνυν αἰσθανόμενος
ἐρῶντα Εὐθυδήμου καὶ πειρῶντα χρῆσθαι καθάπερ
οἱ πρὸς τἀφροδίσια τῶν σωμάτων ἀπολαύοντες,
ἀπέτρεπε φάσκων ἀνελεύθερόν τε εἶναι καὶ οὐ
πρέπον ἀνδρὶ καλῷ κἀγαθῷ τὸν ἐρώμενον, ᾧ
βούλεται πολλοῦ ἄξιος φαίνεσθαι, προσαιτεῖν
24

yielding to temptation were added corruption and long separation from Socrates, what wonder if they grew overbearing? For their wrongdoing, then, is Socrates to be called to account by his accuser? And does he deserve no word of praise for having controlled them in the days of their youth, when they would naturally be most reckless and licentious? Other cases, at least, are not so judged. For what teacher of flute, lyre, or anything else, after making his pupils proficient, is held to blame if they leave him for another master, and then turn out incompetent? What father, whose son bears a good character so long as he is with one master, but goes wrong after he has attached himself to another, throws the blame on the earlier teacher? Is it not true that the worse the boy turns out with the second, the higher is his father's praise of the first? Nay, fathers themselves, living with their sons, are not held responsible for their boys' wrongdoing if they are themselves prudent men. This is the test which should have been applied to Socrates too. If there was anything base in his own life, he might fairly have been thought vicious. But, if his own conduct was always prudent, how can he be fairly held to blame for the evil that was not in him?

Nevertheless, although he was himself free from vice, if he saw and approved of base conduct in them, he would be open to censure. Well, when he found that Critias loved Euthydemus [1] and wanted to lead him astray, he tried to restrain him by saying that it was mean and unbecoming in a gentleman to sue like a beggar to the object of his affection, whose

[1] iv. ii. 1.

XENOPHON

ὥσπερ τοὺς πτωχοὺς ἱκετεύοντα καὶ δεόμενον
30 προσδοῦναι, καὶ ταῦτα μηδενὸς ἀγαθοῦ. τοῦ δὲ
Κριτίου τοῖς τοιούτοις οὐχ ὑπακούοντος οὐδὲ
ἀποτρεπομένου, λέγεται τὸν Σωκράτην ἄλλων τε
πολλῶν παρόντων καὶ τοῦ Εὐθυδήμου εἰπεῖν, ὅτι
ὑικὸν αὑτῷ δοκοίη πάσχειν ὁ Κριτίας ἐπιθυμῶν
Εὐθυδήμῳ προσκνῆσθαι ὥσπερ τὰ ὕδια τοῖς
31 λίθοις. ἐξ ὧν δὴ καὶ ἐμίσει τὸν Σωκράτην ὁ
Κριτίας, ὥστε καὶ ὅτε τῶν τριάκοντα ὢν νομοθέτης
μετὰ Χαρικλέους ἐγένετο, ἀπεμνημόνευσεν αὐτῷ
καὶ ἐν τοῖς νόμοις ἔγραψε λόγων τέχνην μὴ
διδάσκειν, ἐπηρεάζων ἐκείνῳ καὶ οὐκ ἔχων ὅπη
ἐπιλάβοιτο, ἀλλὰ τὸ κοινῇ τοῖς φιλοσόφοις ὑπὸ
τῶν πολλῶν ἐπιτιμώμενον ἐπιφέρων αὐτῷ καὶ
διαβάλλων πρὸς τοὺς πολλούς. οὐδὲ γὰρ ἔγωγε
οὔτ᾽ αὐτὸς τοῦτο πώποτε Σωκράτους ἤκουσα
οὔτ᾽ ἄλλου του φάσκοντος ἀκηκοέναι ᾐσθόμην.
32 ἐδήλωσε δέ· ἐπεὶ γὰρ οἱ τριάκοντα πολλοὺς μὲν
τῶν πολιτῶν καὶ οὐ τοὺς χειρίστους ἀπέκτεινον,
πολλοὺς δὲ προετρέποντο ἀδικεῖν, εἶπέ που ὁ
Σωκράτης, ὅτι θαυμαστόν οἱ δοκοίη εἶναι, εἴ τις
γενόμενος βοῶν ἀγέλης νομεὺς καὶ τὰς βοῦς
ἐλάττους τε καὶ χείρους ποιῶν μὴ ὁμολογοίη
κακὸς βουκόλος εἶναι, ἔτι δὲ θαυμαστότερον, εἴ
τις προστάτης γενόμενος πόλεως καὶ ποιῶν τοὺς
πολίτας ἐλάττους τε καὶ χείρους μὴ αἰσχύνεται
μηδ᾽ οἴεται κακὸς εἶναι προστάτης τῆς πόλεως.
33 ἀπαγγελθέντος δὲ αὐτοῖς τούτου, καλέσαντε ὅ τε
Κριτίας καὶ ὁ Χαρικλῆς τὸν Σωκράτην τόν τε
26

good opinion he coveted, stooping to ask a favour that it was wrong to grant. As Critias paid no heed 30 whatever to this protest, Socrates, it is said, exclaimed in the presence of Euthydemus and many others, " Critias seems to have the feelings of a pig : he can no more keep away from Euthydemus than pigs can help rubbing themselves against stones." Now Critias bore a grudge against Socrates for this ; 31 and when he was one of the Thirty and was drafting laws with Charicles, he bore it in mind. He inserted a clause which made it illegal " to teach the art of words." It was a calculated insult to Socrates, whom he saw no means of attacking, except by imputing to him the practice constantly attributed to philosophers,[1] and so making him unpopular. For I myself never heard Socrates indulge in the practice, nor knew of anyone who professed to have heard him do so. The truth came out. When the Thirty were 32 putting to death many citizens of the highest respectability and were encouraging many in crime, Socrates had remarked : " It seems strange enough to me that a herdsman [2] who lets his cattle decrease and go to the bad should not admit that he is a poor cowherd ; but stranger still that a statesman when he causes the citizens to decrease and go to the bad, should feel no shame nor think himself a poor statesman." This remark was reported to 33 Critias and Charicles, who sent for Socrates, showed

---

[1] *i.e.* the practice of "making the worse appear the better argument." In Plato, *Apol.* 19b, Socrates makes Aristophanes (*Clouds*) author of this charge against him. Aristotle in the *Rhetoric* (B 24, 11) associates the practice with the name of Protagoras : *cp. Diog. Laert.* ix. 51.

[2] *Cyropaedia*, VIII. ii. 14.

νόμον ἐδεικνύτην αὐτῷ καὶ τοῖς νέοις ἀπειπέτην
μὴ διαλέγεσθαι.

Ὁ δὲ Σωκράτης ἐπήρετο αὐτώ, εἰ ἐξείη πυνθά-
νεσθαι, εἴ τι ἀγνοοῖτο τῶν προαγορευομένων.

Τὼ δ' ἐφάτην.

34 Ἐγὼ τοίνυν, ἔφη, παρεσκεύασμαι μὲν πείθεσθαι
τοῖς νόμοις· ὅπως δὲ μὴ δι' ἄγνοιαν λάθω τι
παρανομήσας, τοῦτο βούλομαι σαφῶς μαθεῖν παρ'
ὑμῶν, πότερον τὴν τῶν λόγων τέχνην σὺν τοῖς
ὀρθῶς λεγομένοις εἶναι νομίζοντες ἢ σὺν τοῖς μὴ
ὀρθῶς ἀπέχεσθαι κελεύετε αὐτῆς. εἰ μὲν γὰρ σὺν
τοῖς ὀρθῶς, δῆλον ὅτι ἀφεκτέον ἂν εἴη τοῦ ὀρθῶς
λέγειν· εἰ δὲ σὺν τοῖς μὴ ὀρθῶς, δῆλον ὅτι
πειρατέον ὀρθῶς λέγειν.

35 Καὶ ὁ Χαρικλῆς ὀργισθεὶς αὐτῷ, Ἐπειδή, ἔφη,
ὦ Σώκρατες, ἀγνοεῖς, τάδε σοι εὐμαθέστερα ὄντα
προαγορεύομεν, τοῖς νέοις ὅλως μὴ διαλέγεσθαι.

Καὶ ὁ Σωκράτης, Ἵνα τοίνυν, ἔφη, μὴ ἀμφίβολον
ᾖ, ὡς ἄλλο τι ποιῶ ἢ τὰ προηγορευμένα, ὁρίσατέ
μοι, μέχρι πόσων ἐτῶν δεῖ νομίζειν νέους εἶναι
τοὺς ἀνθρώπους.

Καὶ ὁ Χαρικλῆς, Ὅσουπερ, εἶπε, χρόνου βου-
λεύειν οὐκ ἔξεστιν, ὡς οὔπω φρονίμοις οὖσι· μηδὲ
σὺ διαλέγου νεωτέροις τριάκοντα ἐτῶν.

36 Μηδ' ἐάν τι ὠνῶμαι, ἔφη, ἢν πωλῇ νεώτερος
τριάκοντα ἐτῶν, ἔρωμαι, ὁπόσου πωλεῖ;

Ναὶ τά γε τοιαῦτα, ἔφη ὁ Χαρικλῆς· ἀλλά τοι
σύγε, ὦ Σώκρατες, εἴωθας εἰδὼς πῶς ἔχει τὰ
πλεῖστα ἐρωτᾶν. ταῦτα οὖν μὴ ἐρώτα.

Μηδ' ἀποκρίνωμαι οὖν, ἔφη, ἄν τίς με ἐρωτᾷ
νέος, ἐὰν εἰδῶ, οἷον ποῦ οἰκεῖ Χαρικλῆς ἢ ποῦ ἐστι
Κριτίας;

him the law and forbade him to hold conversation
with the young.

"May I question you," asked Socrates, "in case I do
not understand any point in your orders?"

"You may," said they.

"Well now," said he, " I am ready to obey the laws. 34
But lest I unwittingly transgress through ignorance,
I want clear directions from you. Do you think that
the art of words from which you bid me abstain is
associated with sound or unsound reasoning? For
if with sound, then clearly I must abstain from
sound reasoning: but if with unsound, clearly I must
try to reason soundly."

"Since you are ignorant, Socrates," said Charicles 35
in an angry tone, "we put our order into language
easier to understand. You may not hold any converse whatever with the young."

"Well then," said Socrates, "that there may be no
question raised about my obedience, please fix the
age limit below which a man is to be accounted
young."

"So long," replied Charicles, "as he is not permitted to sit in the Council, because as yet he lacks
wisdom. You shall not converse with anyone who
is under thirty."

"Suppose I want to buy something, am I not even 36
then to ask the price if the seller is under thirty?"

"Oh yes," answered Charicles, "you may in such
cases. But the fact is, Socrates, you are in the habit
of asking questions to which you know the answer:
so that is what you are not to do."

"Am I to give no answer, then, if a young man asks
me something that I know?—for instance, 'Where
does Charicles live?' or 'Where is Critias?'"

Ναὶ τά γε τοιαῦτα, ἔφη ὁ Χαρικλῆς.

37 Ὁ δὲ Κριτίας, Ἀλλὰ τῶνδέ τοί σε ἀπέχεσθαι ἔφη, δεήσει, ὦ Σώκρατες, τῶν σκυτέων καὶ τῶν τεκτόνων καὶ τῶν χαλκέων· καὶ γὰρ οἶμαι αὐτοὺς ἤδη κατατετρῖφθαι διαθρυλουμένους ὑπὸ σοῦ.

Οὐκοῦν, ἔφη ὁ Σωκράτης, καὶ τῶν ἑπομένων τούτοις τοῦ τε δικαίου καὶ τοῦ ὁσίου καὶ τῶν ἄλλων τῶν τοιούτων;

Ναὶ μὰ Δί, ἔφη ὁ Χαρικλῆς, καὶ τῶν βουκόλων γε· εἰ δὲ μή, φυλάττου, ὅπως μὴ καὶ σὺ
38 ἐλάττους τὰς βοῦς ποιήσῃς.

Ἔνθα καὶ δῆλον ἐγένετο, ὅτι ἀπαγγελθέντος αὐτοῖς τοῦ περὶ τῶν βοῶν λόγου ὠργίζοντο τῷ Σωκράτει.

Οἷα μὲν οὖν ἡ συνουσία ἐγεγόνει Κριτίᾳ πρὸς Σωκράτην καὶ ὡς εἶχον πρὸς ἀλλήλους, εἴρηται.
39 φαίην δ᾽ ἂν ἔγωγε μηδενὶ μηδεμίαν εἶναι παίδευσιν παρὰ τοῦ μὴ ἀρέσκοντος. Κριτίας δὲ καὶ Ἀλκιβιάδης οὐκ ἀρέσκοντος αὐτοῖς Σωκράτους ὡμιλησάτην ὃν χρόνον ὡμιλείτην αὐτῷ, ἀλλ᾽ εὐθὺς ἐξ ἀρχῆς ὡρμηκότε προεστάναι τῆς πόλεως. ἔτι γὰρ Σωκράτει συνόντες οὐκ ἄλλοις τισὶ μᾶλλον ἐπεχείρουν διαλέγεσθαι ἢ τοῖς μάλιστα πράττουσι
40 τὰ πολιτικά. λέγεται γὰρ Ἀλκιβιάδην, πρὶν εἴκοσιν ἐτῶν εἶναι, Περικλεῖ, ἐπιτρόπῳ μὲν ὄντι ἑαυτοῦ, προστάτῃ δὲ τῆς πόλεως, τοιάδε διαλεχθῆναι περὶ νόμων.

41 Εἰπέ μοι, φάναι, ὦ Περίκλεις, ἔχοις ἄν με διδάξαι, τί ἐστι νόμος ;

Πάντως δήπου, φάναι τὸν Περικλέα.

Δίδαξον δὴ πρὸς τῶν θεῶν, φάναι τὸν Ἀλκιβιάδην· ὡς ἐγὼ ἀκούων τινῶν ἐπαινουμένων, ὅτι

30

"Oh yes," answered Charicles, "you may, in such cases."

"But you see, Socrates," explained Critias, "you 37 will have to avoid your favourite topic,—the cobblers, builders and metal workers [1]; for it is already worn to rags by you in my opinion."

"Then must I keep off the subjects of which these supply illustrations, Justice, Holiness, and so forth ? "

"Indeed yes," said Charicles, "and cowherds too : else *you* may find the cattle decrease."

Thus the truth was out : the remark about the 38 cattle had been repeated to them : and it was this that made them angry with him.

So much, then, for the connexion of Critias with Socrates and their relation to each other. I venture 39 to lay it down that learners get nothing from a teacher with whom they are out of sympathy. Now, all the time that Critias and Alcibiades associated with Socrates they were out of sympathy with him, but from the very first their ambition was political advancement. For while they were still with him, they tried to converse, whenever possible, with prominent politicians. Indeed, there is a story 40 told of Alcibiades, that, when he was less than twenty years old, he had a talk about laws with Pericles, his guardian, the first citizen in the State.

"Tell me, Pericles," he said, "can you teach me 41 what a law is ? "

"Certainly," he replied.

"Then pray teach me. For whenever I hear men praised for keeping the laws, it occurs to me

[1] *Cyropaedia*, VI. ii. 37.

XENOPHON

νόμιμοι ἄνδρες εἰσίν, οἶμαι μὴ ἂν δικαίως τούτου
τυχεῖν τοῦ ἐπαίνου τὸν μὴ εἰδότα, τί ἐστι
νόμος.

42 Ἀλλ᾽ οὐδέν τι χαλεποῦ πράγματος ἐπιθυμεῖς,
ὦ Ἀλκιβιάδη, φάναι τὸν Περικλέα, βουλόμενος
γνῶναι, τί ἐστι νόμος· πάντες γὰρ οὗτοι νόμοι
εἰσίν, οὓς τὸ πλῆθος συνελθὸν καὶ δοκιμάσαν
ἔγραψε, φράζον ἅ τε δεῖ ποιεῖν καὶ ἃ μή.

Πότερον δὲ τἀγαθὰ νομίσαν δεῖν ποιεῖν ἢ τὰ
κακά ;

Τἀγαθὰ νὴ Δία, φάναι, ὦ μειράκιον, τὰ δὲ
κακὰ οὔ.

43 Ἐὰν δὲ μὴ τὸ πλῆθος, ἀλλ᾽ ὥσπερ ὅπου
ὀλιγαρχία ἐστίν, ὀλίγοι συνελθόντες γράψωσιν
ὅ τι χρὴ ποιεῖν, ταῦτα τί ἐστι ;

Πάντα, φάναι, ὅσα ἂν τὸ κρατοῦν τῆς πόλεως
βουλευσάμενον ἃ χρὴ ποιεῖν γράψῃ, νόμος
καλεῖται.

Καὶ ἂν τύραννος οὖν κρατῶν τῆς πόλεως
γράψῃ τοῖς πολίταις ἃ χρὴ ποιεῖν, καὶ ταῦτα
νόμος ἐστί ;

Καὶ ὅσα τύραννος ἄρχων, φάναι, γράφει, καὶ
ταῦτα νόμος καλεῖται.

44 Βία δέ, φάναι, καὶ ἀνομία τί ἐστιν, ὦ Περίκλεις ; ἆρ᾽ οὐχ ὅταν ὁ κρείττων τὸν ἥττω μὴ
πείσας, ἀλλὰ βιασάμενος ἀναγκάσῃ ποιεῖν ὅ τι
ἂν αὐτῷ δοκῇ ;

Ἔμοιγε δοκεῖ, φάναι τὸν Περικλέα.

Καὶ ὅσα ἄρα τύραννος μὴ πείσας τοὺς πολίτας
ἀναγκάζει ποιεῖν γράφων, ἀνομία ἐστί ;

Δοκεῖ μοι, φάναι τὸν Περικλέα· ἀνατίθεμαι
γὰρ τὸ ὅσα τύραννος μὴ πείσας γράφει νόμον εἶναι.

32

that no one can really deserve that praise who does not know what a law is."

"Well, Alcibiades, there is no great difficulty 42 about what you desire. You wish to know what a law is. Laws are all the rules approved and enacted by the majority in assembly, whereby they declare what ought and what ought not to be done."

"Do they suppose it is right to do good or evil?"

"Good, of course, young man,—not evil."

"But if, as happens under an oligarchy, not the 43 majority, but a minority meet and enact rules of conduct, what are these?"

"Whatsoever the sovereign power in the State, after deliberation, enacts and directs to be done is known as a law."

"If, then, a despot, being the sovereign power, enacts what the citizens are to do, are his orders also a law?"

"Yes, whatever a despot as ruler enacts is also known as a law."

"But force, the negation of law, what is that, 44 Pericles? Is it not the action of the stronger when he constrains the weaker to do whatever he chooses, not by persuasion, but by force?"

"That is my opinion."

"Then whatever a despot by enactment constrains the citizens to do without persuasion, is the negation of law?"

"I think so: and I withdraw my answer that whatever a despot enacts without persuasion is a law."

45 Ὅσα δὲ οἱ ὀλίγοι τοὺς πολλοὺς μὴ πείσαντες, ἀλλὰ κρατοῦντες γράφουσι, πότερον βίαν φῶμεν ἢ μὴ φῶμεν εἶναι ;

Πάντα μοι δοκεῖ, φάναι τὸν Περικλέα, ὅσα τις μὴ πείσας ἀναγκάζει τινὰ ποιεῖν, εἴτε γράφων εἴτε μή, βία μᾶλλον ἢ νόμος εἶναι.

Καὶ ὅσα ἄρα τὸ πᾶν πλῆθος κρατοῦν τῶν τὰ χρήματα ἐχόντων γράφει μὴ πεῖσαν, βία μᾶλλον ἢ νόμος ἂν εἴη ;

46 Μάλα τοι, φάναι τὸν Περικλέα, ὦ Ἀλκιβιάδη, καὶ ἡμεῖς τηλικοῦτοι ὄντες δεινοὶ τὰ τοιαῦτα ἦμεν· τοιαῦτα γὰρ καὶ ἐμελετῶμεν καὶ ἐσοφιζόμεθα, οἷάπερ καὶ σὺ νῦν ἐμοὶ δοκεῖς μελετᾶν.

Τὸν δὲ Ἀλκιβιάδην φάναι· Εἴθε σοι, ὦ Περίκλεις, τότε συνεγενόμην, ὅτε δεινότατος 47 σαυτοῦ ταῦτα ἦσθα. ἐπεὶ τοίνυν τάχιστα τῶν πολιτευομένων ὑπέλαβον κρείττονες εἶναι, Σωκράτει μὲν οὐκέτι προσῄεσαν· οὔτε γὰρ αὐτοῖς ἄλλως ἤρεσκεν εἴ τε προσέλθοιεν, ὑπὲρ ὧν ἡμάρτανον ἐλεγχόμενοι ἤχθοντο· τὰ δὲ τῆς πόλεως ἔπραττον, ὧνπερ ἕνεκεν καὶ Σωκράτει προσῆλθον.

48 Ἀλλὰ Κρίτων τε Σωκράτους ἦν ὁμιλητὴς καὶ Χαιρεφῶν καὶ Χαιρεκράτης καὶ Ἑρμογένης καὶ Σιμμίας καὶ Κέβης καὶ Φαιδώνδας καὶ ἄλλοι, οἳ ἐκείνῳ συνῆσαν οὐχ ἵνα δημηγορικοὶ ἢ δικανικοὶ γένοιντο, ἀλλ᾿ ἵνα καλοί τε κἀγαθοὶ γενόμενοι καὶ οἴκῳ καὶ οἰκέταις καὶ οἰκείοις καὶ φίλοις καὶ πόλει καὶ πολίταις δύναιντο καλῶς χρῆσθαι. καὶ τούτων οὐδεὶς οὔτε νεώτερος οὔτε πρεσβύτερος ὢν οὔτ᾿ ἐποίησε κακὸν οὐδὲν οὔτ᾿ αἰτίαν ἔσχεν.

"And when the minority passes enactments, not 45 by persuading the majority, but through using its power, are we to call that force or not?"

"Everything, I think, that men constrain others to do 'without persuasion,' whether by enactment or not, is not law, but force."

"It follows then, that whatever the assembled majority, through using its power over the owners of property, enacts without persuasion is not law, but force?"

"Alcibiades," said Pericles, "at your age, I may 46 tell you, we, too, were very clever at this sort of thing. For the puzzles we thought about and exercised our wits on were just such as you seem to think about now."

"Ah, Pericles," cried Alcibiades, "if only I had known you intimately when you were at your cleverest in these things!"

So soon, then, as they presumed themselves to be 47 the superiors of the politicians, they no longer came near Socrates. For apart from their general want of sympathy with him, they resented being cross-examined about their errors when they came. Politics had brought them to Socrates, and for politics they left him. But Criton was a true asso- 48 ciate of Socrates, as were Chaerophon, Chaerecrates, Hermogenes, Simmias, Cebes, Phaedondas, and others who consorted with him not that they might shine in the courts or the assembly, but that they might become gentlemen, and be able to do their duty by house and household, and relatives and friends, and city and citizens. Of these not one, in his youth or old age, did evil or incurred censure.

49 Ἀλλὰ Σωκράτης γ᾽, ἔφη ὁ κατήγορος, τοὺς
πατέρας προπηλακίζειν ἐδίδασκε, πείθων μὲν
τοὺς συνόντας ἑαυτῷ σοφωτέρους ποιεῖν τῶν
πατέρων, φάσκων δὲ κατὰ νόμον ἐξεῖναι παρα-
νοίας ἑλόντι καὶ τὸν πατέρα δῆσαι, τεκμηρίῳ
τούτῳ χρώμενος, ὡς τὸν ἀμαθέστερον ὑπὸ τοῦ
50 σοφωτέρου νόμιμον εἴη δεδέσθαι. Σωκράτης δὲ
τὸν μὲν ἀμαθίας ἕνεκα δεσμεύοντα δικαίως ἂν
καὶ αὐτὸν ᾤετο δεδέσθαι ὑπὸ τῶν ἐπισταμένων
ἃ μὴ αὐτὸς ἐπίσταται· καὶ τῶν τοιούτων ἕνεκα
πολλάκις ἐσκόπει, τί διαφέρει μανίας ἀμαθία·
καὶ τοὺς μὲν μαινομένους ᾤετο συμφερόντως ἂν
δεδέσθαι καὶ αὐτοῖς καὶ τοῖς φίλοις, τοὺς δὲ μὴ
ἐπισταμένους τὰ δέοντα δικαίως ἂν μανθάνειν
παρὰ τῶν ἐπισταμένων.

51 Ἀλλὰ Σωκράτης γε, ἔφη ὁ κατήγορος, οὐ μόνον
τοὺς πατέρας, ἀλλὰ καὶ τοὺς ἄλλους συγγενεῖς
ἐποίει ἐν ἀτιμίᾳ εἶναι παρὰ τοῖς ἑαυτῷ συνοῦσι,
λέγων, ὡς οὔτε τοὺς κάμνοντας οὔτε τοὺς δικαζο-
μένους οἱ συγγενεῖς ὠφελοῦσιν, ἀλλὰ τοὺς μὲν οἱ
52 ἰατροί, τοὺς δὲ οἱ συνδικεῖν ἐπιστάμενοι. ἔφη δὲ
καὶ περὶ τῶν φίλων αὐτὸν λέγειν, ὡς οὐδὲν ὄφελος
εὔνους εἶναι, εἰ μὴ καὶ ὠφελεῖν δυνήσονται·
μόνους δὲ φάσκειν αὐτὸν ἀξίους εἶναι τιμῆς τοὺς
εἰδότας τὰ δέοντα καὶ ἑρμηνεῦσαι δυναμένους·
ἀναπείθοντα οὖν τοὺς νέους αὐτόν, ὡς αὐτὸς εἴη
σοφώτατός τε καὶ ἄλλους ἱκανώτατος ποιῆσαι
σοφούς, οὕτω διατιθέναι τοὺς ἑαυτῷ συνόντας,
ὥστε μηδαμοῦ παρ᾽ αὐτοῖς τοὺς ἄλλους εἶναι πρὸς
53 αὐτόν. ἐγὼ δ᾽ αὐτὸν οἶδα μὲν καὶ περὶ πατέρων
τε καὶ τῶν ἄλλων συγγενῶν καὶ περὶ φίλων ταῦτα
λέγοντα· καὶ πρὸς τούτοις γε δή, ὅτι τῆς ψυχῆς

"But," said his accuser, "Socrates taught sons to 49
treat their fathers with contempt: he persuaded
them that he made his companions wiser than their
fathers: he said that the law allowed a son to put
his father in prison if he convinced a jury that he
was insane; and this was a proof that it was lawful
for the wiser to keep the more ignorant in gaol."
In reality Socrates held that, if you clap fetters on 50
a man for his ignorance, you deserve to be kept in
gaol yourself by those whose knowledge is greater
than your own: and such reasoning led him
frequently to consider the difference between Madness and Ignorance. That madmen should be kept
in prison was expedient, he thought, both for themselves and for their friends: but those who are
ignorant of what they ought to know deserve to
learn from those who know it.

"But," said his accuser, "Socrates caused his 51
companions to dishonour not only their fathers, but
their other relations as well, by saying that invalids
and litigants get benefit not from their relations,
but from their doctor or their counsel. Of friends 52
too he said that their goodwill was worthless,
unless they could combine with it some power to
help one: only those deserved honour who knew
what was the right thing to do, and could explain it.
Thus by leading the young to think that he excelled
in wisdom and in ability to make others wise, he
had such an effect on his companions that no one
counted for anything in their estimation in comparison with him." Now I know that he did use 53
this language about fathers, relations and friends.
And, what is more, he would say that so soon as

XENOPHON

ἐξελθούσης, ἐν ᾗ μόνῃ γίγνεται φρόνησις, τὸ σῶμα
τοῦ οἰκειοτάτου ἀνθρώπου τὴν ταχίστην ἐξενέγ-
54 καντες ἀφανίζουσιν. ἔλεγε δέ, ὅτι καὶ ζῶν ἕκαστος
ἑαυτοῦ, ὃ πάντων μάλιστα φιλεῖ, τοῦ σώματος
ὅ,τι ἂν ἀχρεῖον ᾖ καὶ ἀνωφελές, αὐτός τε ἀφαιρεῖ
καὶ ἄλλῳ παρέχει. αὐτοί τέ γε αὑτῶν ὄνυχάς τε
καὶ τρίχας καὶ τύλους ἀφαιροῦσι καὶ τοῖς ἰατροῖς
παρέχουσι μετὰ πόνων τε καὶ ἀλγηδόνων καὶ
ἀποτέμνειν καὶ ἀποκάειν καὶ τούτου χάριν οἴονται
δεῖν αὐτοῖς καὶ μισθὸν τίνειν· καὶ τὸ σίαλον ἐκ
τοῦ στόματος ἀποπτύουσιν ὡς δύνανται πορρω-
τάτω, διότι ὠφελεῖ μὲν οὐδὲν αὐτοὺς ἐνόν, βλάπτει
55 δὲ πολὺ μᾶλλον. ταῦτ᾽ οὖν ἔλεγεν οὐ τὸν μὲν
πατέρα ζῶντα κατορύττειν διδάσκων, ἑαυτὸν δὲ
κατατέμνειν, ἀλλ᾽ ἐπιδεικνύων, ὅτι τὸ ἄφρον
ἄτιμόν ἐστι, παρεκάλει ἐπιμελεῖσθαι τοῦ ὡς
φρονιμώτατον εἶναι καὶ ὠφελιμώτατον, ὅπως, ἐάν
τε ὑπὸ πατρὸς ἐάν τε ὑπὸ ἀδελφοῦ ἐάν τε ὑπ᾽
ἄλλου τινὸς βούληται τιμᾶσθαι, μὴ τῷ οἰκεῖος
εἶναι πιστεύων ἀμελῇ, ἀλλὰ πειρᾶται ὑφ᾽ ὧν ἂν
βούληται τιμᾶσθαι, τούτοις ὠφέλιμος εἶναι.

56 Ἔφη δ᾽ αὐτὸν ὁ κατήγορος καὶ τῶν ἐνδοξοτάτων
ποιητῶν ἐκλεγόμενον τὰ πονηρότατα καὶ τούτοις
μαρτυρίοις χρώμενον διδάσκειν τοὺς συνόντας
κακούργους τε εἶναι καὶ τυραννικούς, Ἡσιόδου
μὲν τὸ

Ἔργον δ᾽ οὐδὲν ὄνειδος, ἀεργίη δέ τ᾽ ὄνειδος·

τοῦτο δὴ λέγειν αὐτὸν ὡς ὁ ποιητὴς κελεύει μηδενὸς ἔργου μήτ᾽ ἀδίκου μήτ᾽ αἰσχροῦ ἀπέχεσθαι,
57 ἀλλὰ καὶ ταῦτα ποιεῖν ἐπὶ τῷ κέρδει. Σωκράτης
δ᾽ ἐπεὶ διομολογήσαιτο τὸ μὲν ἐργάτην εἶναι

the soul, the only seat of intelligence, is gone out of a man, even though he be our nearest and dearest, we carry out his body and hide it in the tomb. Moreover, a man's dearest friend is himself: yet, 54 even in his lifetime he removes or lets another remove from his body whatever is useless and unprofitable. He removes his own nails, hair, corns: he lets the surgeon cut and cauterize him, and, aches and pains notwithstanding, feels bound to thank and fee him for it. He spits out the saliva from his mouth as far away as he can, because to retain it doesn't help him, but harms him rather.

Now in saying all this, he was not giving a lesson 55 on "the duty of burying one's father alive, or making mincemeat of one's body": he meant to show that unreason is unworth, and was urging the necessity of cultivating sound sense and usefulness, in order that he who would fain be valued by father or by brother or by anyone else may not rely on the bond of familiarity and neglect him, but may try to be useful to all those by whom he would be valued.

Again, his accuser alleged that he selected 56 from the most famous poets the most immoral passages, and used them as evidence in teaching his companions to be tyrants and malefactors: for example, Hesiod's line:

"No work is a disgrace, but idleness is a disgrace."[1]

He was charged with explaining this line as an injunction to refrain from no work, dishonest or disgraceful, but to do anything for gain. Now, 57 though Socrates would fully agree that it is a

[1] *Works and Days*, 309.

ὠφέλιμόν τε ἀνθρώπῳ καὶ ἀγαθὸν εἶναι, τὸ δὲ
ἀργὸν βλαβερόν τε καὶ κακόν, καὶ τὸ μὲν
ἐργάζεσθαι ἀγαθόν, τὸ δ' ἀργεῖν κακόν, τοὺς μὲν
ἀγαθόν τι ποιοῦντας ἐργάζεσθαί τε ἔφη καὶ
ἐργάτας εἶναι, τοὺς δὲ κυβεύοντας ἤ τι ἄλλο
πονηρὸν καὶ ἐπιζήμιον ποιοῦντας ἀργοὺς ἀπεκάλει. ἐκ δὲ τούτων ὀρθῶς ἂν ἔχοι τὸ

Ἔργον δ' οὐδὲν ὄνειδος, ἀεργίη δέ τ' ὄνειδος.

58 τὸ δὲ Ὁμήρου ἔφη ὁ κατήγορος πολλάκις αὐτὸν
λέγειν, ὅτι Ὀδυσσεὺς

Ὅντινα μὲν βασιλῆα καὶ ἔξοχον ἄνδρα κιχείη,
τὸν δ' ἀγανοῖς ἐπέεσσιν ἐρητύσασκε παραστάς·
δαιμόνι', οὔ σε ἔοικε κακὸν ὣς δειδίσσεσθαι,
ἀλλ' αὐτός τε κάθησο καὶ ἄλλους ἵδρυε λαούς.
ὃν δ' αὖ δήμου τ' ἄνδρα ἴδοι βοόωντά τ' ἐφεύροι,
τὸν σκήπτρῳ ἐλάσασκεν ὁμοκλήσασκέ τε μύθῳ·
δαιμόνι', ἀτρέμας ἧσο καὶ ἄλλων μῦθον ἄκουε,
οἳ σέο φέρτεροί εἰσι· σὺ δ' ἀπτόλεμος καὶ
  ἄναλκις,
οὔτε ποτ' ἐν πολέμῳ ἐναρίθμιος οὔτ' ἐνὶ βουλῇ.

ταῦτα δὴ αὐτὸν ἐξηγεῖσθαι, ὡς ὁ ποιητὴς ἐπαινοίη
59 παίεσθαι τοὺς δημότας καὶ πένητας. Σωκράτης
δ' οὐ ταῦτ' ἔλεγε, καὶ γὰρ ἑαυτὸν οὕτω γ' ἂν ᾤετο
δεῖν παίεσθαι, ἀλλ' ἔφη δεῖν τοὺς μήτε λόγῳ μήτ'
ἔργῳ ὠφελίμους ὄντας καὶ μήτε στρατεύματι μήτε
πόλει μήτε αὐτῷ τῷ δήμῳ, εἴ τι δέοι, βοηθεῖν
ἱκανούς, ἄλλως τ' ἐὰν πρὸς τούτῳ καὶ θρασεῖς
ὦσι, πάντα τρόπον κωλύεσθαι, κἂν πάνυ πλού-
60 σιοι τυγχάνωσιν ὄντες. ἀλλὰ Σωκράτης γε

benefit and a blessing to a man to be a worker, and a disadvantage and an evil to be an idler—that work, in fact, is a blessing, idleness an evil—"working," "being a worker," meant to him doing good work; but gambling and any occupation that is immoral and leads to loss he called idling. When thus interpreted there is nothing amiss with the line:

"No work is a disgrace, but idleness is a disgrace."

Again, his accuser said that he often quoted the 58 passage from Homer, showing how Odysseus:

"Whenever he found one that was a captain and a man of mark, stood by his side, and restrained him with gentle words: 'Good sir, it is not seemly to affright thee like a coward, but do thou sit thyself and make all thy folk sit down. . . .' But whatever man of the people he saw and found him shouting, him he drove with his sceptre and chid him with loud words: 'Good sir, sit still and hearken to the words of others that are thy betters: but thou art no warrior and a weakling, never reckoned whether in battle or in council.'" [1]

This passage, it was said, he explained to mean that the poet approved of chastising common and poor folk. But Socrates never said that: indeed, 59 on that view he would have thought himself worthy of chastisement. But what he did say was that those who render no service either by word or deed, who cannot help army or city or the people itself in time of need, ought to be stopped, even if they have riches in abundance, above all if they are insolent as well as inefficient. But Socrates, at least, was just 60

---

[1] *Iliad*, ii. 188 ; Leaf's translation.

XENOPHON

τἀναντία τούτων φανερὸς ἦν καὶ δημοτικὸς καὶ
φιλάνθρωπος ὤν. ἐκεῖνος γὰρ πολλοὺς ἐπιθυ-
μητὰς καὶ ἀστοὺς καὶ ξένους λαβὼν οὐδένα
πώποτε μισθὸν τῆς συνουσίας ἐπράξατο, ἀλλὰ
πᾶσιν ἀφθόνως ἐπήρκει τῶν ἑαυτοῦ· ὧν τινες
μικρὰ μέρη παρ' ἐκείνου προῖκα λαβόντες πολλοῦ
τοῖς ἄλλοις ἐπώλουν καὶ οὐκ ἦσαν ὥσπερ ἐκεῖνος
δημοτικοί. τοῖς γὰρ μὴ ἔχουσι χρήματα διδόναι
61 οὐκ ἤθελον διαλέγεσθαι. ἀλλὰ Σωκράτης γε καὶ
πρὸς τοὺς ἄλλους ἀνθρώπους κόσμον τῇ πόλει
παρεῖχε, πολλῷ μᾶλλον ἢ Λίχας τῇ Λακε-
δαιμονίων, ὃς ὀνομαστὸς ἐπὶ τούτῳ γέγονε.
Λίχας μὲν γὰρ ταῖς γυμνοπαιδίαις τοὺς ἐπιδη-
μοῦντας ἐν Λακεδαίμονι ξένους ἐδείπνιζε, Σωκράτης δὲ διὰ παντὸς τοῦ βίου τὰ ἑαυτοῦ
δαπανῶν τὰ μέγιστα πάντας τοὺς βουλομένους
ὠφέλει· βελτίους γὰρ ποιῶν τοὺς συγγιγνομένους
ἀπέπεμπεν.

62 Ἐμοὶ μὲν δὴ Σωκράτης τοιοῦτος ὢν ἐδόκει
τιμῆς ἄξιος εἶναι τῇ πόλει μᾶλλον ἢ θανάτου.
καὶ κατὰ τοὺς νόμους δὲ σκοπῶν ἄν τις τοῦθ'
εὕροι. κατὰ γὰρ τοὺς νόμους, ἐάν τις φανερὸς
γένηται κλέπτων ἢ λωποδυτῶν ἢ βαλαντιοτομῶν
ἢ τοιχωρυχῶν ἢ ἀνδραποδιζόμενος ἢ ἱεροσυλῶν,
τούτοις θάνατός ἐστιν ἡ ζημία· ὧν ἐκεῖνος πάντων
63 ἀνθρώπων πλεῖστον ἀπεῖχεν. ἀλλὰ μὴν τῇ
πόλει γε οὔτε πολέμου κακῶς συμβάντος οὔτε
στάσεως οὔτε προδοσίας οὔτε ἄλλου κακοῦ
οὐδενὸς πώποτε αἴτιος ἐγένετο· οὐδὲ μὴν ἰδίᾳ γε
οὐδένα πώποτε ἀνθρώπων οὔτε ἀγαθῶν ἀπε-
στέρησεν οὔτε κακοῖς περιέβαλεν, ἀλλ' οὐδ'

the opposite of all that: he showed himself to be one of the people and a friend of mankind. For although he had many eager disciples among citizens and strangers, yet he never exacted a fee for his society from one of them, but of his abundance he gave without stint to all. Some indeed, after getting from him a few trifles for nothing, became vendors of them at a great price to others, and showed none of his sympathy with the people, refusing to talk with those who had no money to give them.[1] But Socrates did far more to win 61 respect for the State in the world at large than Lichas, whose services to Sparta have made his name immortal. For Lichas used to entertain the strangers staying at Sparta during the Feast of the Dancing Boys;[2] but Socrates spent his life in lavishing his gifts and rendering the greatest services to all who cared to receive them. For he always made his associates better men before he parted with them.

Such was the character of Socrates. To me he 62 seemed to deserve honour rather than death at the hands of the State. And a consideration of his case in its legal aspect will confirm my opinion. Under the laws, death is the penalty inflicted on persons proved to be thieves, highwaymen, cutpurses, kidnappers, robbers of temples; and from such criminals no man was so widely separated as he. Moreover, 63 to the State he was never the cause of disaster in war, or strife or treason or any evil whatever. Again, in private life no man by him was ever

---

[1] Aristippus especially is meant.
[2] According to Eusebius this festival, which was held in the summer, was instituted in honour of the Spartans who fell fighting against the Argives for the possession of Thyrea.

64 αἰτίαν τῶν εἰρημένων οὐδενὸς πώποτ᾽ ἔσχε. πῶς
οὖν ἂν ἔνοχος εἴη τῇ γραφῇ; ὃς ἀντὶ μὲν τοῦ
μὴ νομίζειν θεούς, ὡς ἐν τῇ γραφῇ ἐγέγραπτο,
φανερὸς ἦν θεραπεύων τοὺς θεοὺς μάλιστα πάντων
ἀνθρώπων, ἀντὶ δὲ τοῦ διαφθείρειν τοὺς νέους, ὃ
δὴ ὁ γραψάμενος αὐτὸν ᾐτιᾶτο, φανερὸς ἦν τῶν
συνόντων τοὺς πονηρὰς ἐπιθυμίας ἔχοντας τούτων μὲν παύων, τῆς δὲ καλλίστης καὶ μεγαλο-
πρεπεστάτης ἀρετῆς, ᾗ πόλεις τε καὶ οἶκοι εὖ
οἰκοῦσι, προτρέπων ἐπιθυμεῖν· ταῦτα δὲ πράττων
πῶς οὐ μεγάλης ἄξιος ἦν τιμῆς τῇ πόλει;

III. Ὡς δὲ δὴ καὶ ὠφελεῖν ἐδόκει μοι τοὺς συνόντας τὰ μὲν ἔργῳ δεικνύων ἑαυτὸν οἷος ἦν, τὰ δὲ καὶ
διαλεγόμενος, τούτων δὴ γράψω ὁπόσα ἂν διαμνη-
μονεύσω.

Τὰ μὲν τοίνυν πρὸς τοὺς θεοὺς φανερὸς ἦν καὶ
ποιῶν καὶ λέγων ᾗπερ ἡ Πυθία ἀποκρίνεται
τοῖς ἐρωτῶσι, πῶς δεῖ ποιεῖν ἢ περὶ θυσίας ἢ
περὶ προγόνων θεραπείας ἢ περὶ ἄλλου τινὸς τῶν
τοιούτων· ἥ τε γὰρ Πυθία νόμῳ πόλεως ἀναιρεῖ
ποιοῦντας εὐσεβῶς ἂν ποιεῖν Σωκράτης τε οὕτω
καὶ αὐτὸς ἐποίει καὶ τοῖς ἄλλοις παρῄνει, τοὺς δὲ
ἄλλως πως ποιοῦντας περιέργους καὶ ματαίους
2 ἐνόμιζεν εἶναι. καὶ εὔχετο δὲ πρὸς τοὺς θεοὺς
ἁπλῶς τἀγαθὰ διδόναι, ὡς τοὺς θεοὺς κάλλιστα
εἰδότας, ὁποῖα ἀγαθά ἐστι· τοὺς δ᾽ εὐχομένους
χρυσίον ἢ ἀργύριον ἢ τυραννίδα ἢ ἄλλο τι τῶν
τοιούτων οὐδὲν διάφορον ἐνόμιζεν εὔχεσθαι ἢ εἰ
κυβείαν ἢ μάχην ἢ ἄλλο τι εὔχοιντο τῶν φανερῶς
3 ἀδήλων ὅπως ἀποβήσοιτο. θυσίας δὲ θύων

deprived of good or involved in ill. None of these 64
crimes was ever so much as imputed to him. How
then could he be guilty of the charges? For so far
was he from "rejecting the gods," as charged in the
indictment, that no man was more conspicuous for
his devotion to the service of the gods: so far from
"corrupting the youth," as his accuser actually
charged against him, that if any among his companions had evil desires, he openly tried to reform
them and exhorted them to desire the fairest and
noblest virtue, by which men prosper in public life
and in their homes. By this conduct did he not
deserve high honour from the State?

III. In order to support my opinion that he
benefited his companions, alike by actions that
revealed his own character and by his conversation,
I will set down what I recollect of these.

First, then, for his attitude towards religion; his
deeds and words were clearly in harmony with the
answer given by the Priestess at Delphi to such
questions as "What is my duty about sacrifice?" or
about "cult of ancestors." For the answer of the
Priestess is, "Follow the custom of the State: that
is the way to act piously." And so Socrates acted
himself and counselled others to act. To take any
other course he considered presumption and folly.

And again, when he prayed he asked simply for 2
good gifts,[1] "for the gods know best what things are
good." To pray for gold or silver or sovereignty or
any other such thing, was just like praying for a
gamble or a fight or anything of which the result
is obviously uncertain.

Though his sacrifices were humble, according to 3

[1] *Cyropaedia*, I. vi. 5.

μικρὰς ἀπὸ μικρῶν οὐδὲν ἡγεῖτο μειοῦσθαι τῶν
ἀπὸ πολλῶν καὶ μεγάλων πολλὰ καὶ μεγάλα
θυόντων. οὔτε γὰρ τοῖς θεοῖς ἔφη καλῶς ἔχειν,
εἰ ταῖς μεγάλαις θυσίαις μᾶλλον ἢ ταῖς μικραῖς
ἔχαιρον· πολλάκις γὰρ ἂν αὐτοῖς τὰ παρὰ τῶν
πονηρῶν μᾶλλον ἢ τὰ παρὰ τῶν χρηστῶν εἶναι
κεχαρισμένα· οὔτ' ἂν τοῖς ἀνθρώποις ἄξιον εἶναι
ζῆν, εἰ τὰ παρὰ τῶν πονηρῶν μᾶλλον ἦν
κεχαρισμένα τοῖς θεοῖς ἢ τὰ παρὰ τῶν χρηστῶν·
ἀλλ' ἐνόμιζε τοὺς θεοὺς ταῖς παρὰ τῶν εὐσε-
βεστάτων τιμαῖς μάλιστα χαίρειν. ἐπαινέτης δ'
ἦν καὶ τοῦ ἔπους τούτου,

 Καδδύναμιν δ' ἔρδειν ἱερ' ἀθανάτοισι θεοῖσι.

καὶ πρὸς φίλους δὲ καὶ ξένους καὶ πρὸς τὴν ἄλλην
δίαιταν καλὴν ἔφη παραίνεσιν εἶναι τὴν Καδδύ-
4 ναμιν ἔρδειν. εἰ δέ τι δόξειεν αὐτῷ σημαίνεσθαι
παρὰ τῶν θεῶν, ἧττον ἂν ἐπείσθη παρὰ τὰ
σημαινόμενα ποιῆσαι ἢ εἴ τις αὐτὸν ἔπειθεν
ὁδοῦ λαβεῖν ἡγεμόνα τυφλὸν καὶ μὴ εἰδότα τὴν
ὁδὸν ἀντὶ βλέποντος καὶ εἰδότος· καὶ τῶν ἄλλων
δὲ μωρίαν κατηγόρει, οἵτινες παρὰ τὰ ὑπὸ τῶν
θεῶν σημαινόμενα ποιοῦσί τι φυλαττόμενοι τὴν
παρὰ τοῖς ἀνθρώποις ἀδοξίαν. αὐτὸς δὲ πάντα
τἀνθρώπινα ὑπερεώρα πρὸς τὴν παρὰ τῶν θεῶν
συμβουλίαν.

5 Διαίτῃ δὲ τήν τε ψυχὴν ἐπαίδευσε καὶ τὸ
σῶμα, ᾗ χρώμενος ἄν τις, εἰ μή τι δαιμόνιον εἴη,
θαρραλέως καὶ ἀσφαλῶς διάγοι καὶ οὐκ ἂν
ἀπορήσειε τοσαύτης δαπάνης. οὕτω γὰρ εὐτελὴς

---

[1] Hesiod, *Works and Days*, 336.

his means, he thought himself not a whit inferior to those who made frequent and magnificent sacrifices out of great possessions. The gods (he said) could not well delight more in great offerings than in small—for in that case must the gifts of the wicked often have found more favour in their sight than the gifts of the upright—and man would not find life worth having, if the gifts of the wicked were received with more favour by the gods than the gifts of the upright. No, the greater the piety of the giver, the greater (he thought) was the delight of the gods in the gift. He would quote with approval the line:

"According to thy power render sacrifice to the immortal gods,"[1]

and he would add that in our treatment of friends and strangers, and in all our behaviour, it is a noble principle to *render according to our power*. If ever 4 any warning seemed to be given him from heaven, he would more easily have been persuaded to choose a blind guide who did not know the road in preference to one who could see and knew the way, than to disregard the admonition. All men, in fact, who flouted the warnings of the gods in their anxiety to avoid the censure of men, he denounced for their foolishness. He himself despised all human opinions in comparison with counsel given by the gods.

He schooled his body and soul by following a 5 system which, in all human calculation, would give him a life of confidence and security, and would make it easy to meet his expenses. For he was so

47

ἦν, ὥστ᾽ οὐκ οἶδ᾽ εἴ τις οὕτως ἂν ὀλίγα ἐργάζοιτο,
ὥστε μὴ λαμβάνειν τὰ Σωκράτει ἀρκοῦντα. σίτῳ
μὲν γὰρ τοσούτῳ ἐχρῆτο, ὅσον ἡδέως ἤσθιε· καὶ
ἐπὶ τοῦτο οὕτω παρεσκευασμένος ᾖει, ὥστε τὴν
ἐπιθυμίαν τοῦ σίτου ὄψον αὐτῷ εἶναι· ποτὸν δὲ
πᾶν ἡδὺ ἦν αὐτῷ διὰ τὸ μὴ πίνειν, εἰ μὴ διψῴη.
6 εἰ δέ ποτε κληθεὶς ἐθελήσειεν ἐπὶ δεῖπνον ἐλθεῖν,
ὃ τοῖς πλείστοις ἐργωδέστατόν ἐστιν, ὥστε
φυλάξασθαι τὸ ὑπὲρ τὸν κόρον ἐμπίπλασθαι,
τοῦτο ῥᾳδίως πάνυ ἐφυλάττετο. τοῖς δὲ μὴ δυναμένοις τοῦτο ποιεῖν συνεβούλευε φυλάττεσθαι
τὰ πείθοντα μὴ πεινῶντας ἐσθίειν μηδὲ διψῶντας
πίνειν· καὶ γὰρ τὰ λυμαινόμενα γαστέρας καὶ
7 κεφαλὰς καὶ ψυχὰς ταῦτ᾽ ἔφη εἶναι. οἴεσθαι δ᾽
ἔφη ἐπισκώπτων καὶ τὴν Κίρκην ὗς ποιεῖν τοιούτοις πολλοῖς δειπνίζουσαν· τὸν δὲ Ὀδυσσέα
Ἑρμοῦ τε ὑποθημοσύνῃ καὶ αὐτὸν ἐγκρατῆ ὄντα
καὶ ἀποσχόμενον τὸ ὑπὲρ τὸν κόρον τῶν τοιούτων
8 ἅπτεσθαι διὰ ταῦτα οὐ γενέσθαι ὗν. τοιαῦτα μὲν
περὶ τούτων ἔπαιζεν ἅμα σπουδάζων.

Ἀφροδισίων δὲ παρῄνει τῶν καλῶν ἰσχυρῶς
ἀπέχεσθαι· οὐ γὰρ ἔφη ῥᾴδιον εἶναι τῶν τοιούτων ἁπτόμενον σωφρονεῖν. ἀλλὰ καὶ Κριτό-
βουλόν ποτε τὸν Κρίτωνος πυθόμενος ὅτι ἐφίλησε
τὸν Ἀλκιβιάδου υἱὸν καλὸν ὄντα, παρόντος τοῦ
9 Κριτοβούλου ἤρετο Ξενοφῶντα, Εἰπέ μοι, ἔφη,
ὦ Ξενοφῶν, οὐ σὺ Κριτόβουλον ἐνόμιζες εἶναι τῶν
σωφρονικῶν ἀνθρώπων μᾶλλον ἢ τῶν θρασέων
καὶ τῶν προνοητικῶν μᾶλλον ἢ τῶν ἀνοήτων τε
καὶ ῥιψοκινδύνων;

Πάνυ μὲν οὖν, ἔφη ὁ Ξενοφῶν.

Νῦν τοίνυν νόμιζε αὐτὸν θερμουργότατον εἶναι

frugal that it is hardly possible to imagine a man doing so little work as not to earn enough to satisfy the needs of Socrates. He ate just sufficient food to make eating a pleasure, and he was so ready for his food that he found appetite the best sauce [1]: and any kind of drink he found pleasant, because he drank only when he was thirsty. Whenever 6 he accepted an invitation to dinner, he resisted without difficulty the common temptation to exceed the limit of satiety; and he advised those who could not do likewise to avoid appetizers that encouraged them to eat and drink what they did not want: for such trash was the ruin of stomach and brain and soul. "I believe," he said in jest, 7 "it was by providing a feast of such things that Circe made swine; and it was partly by the prompting of Hermes,[2] partly through his own self-restraint and avoidance of excessive indulgence in such things, that Odysseus was not turned into a pig." This was 8 how he would talk on the subject, half joking, half in earnest.

Of sensual passion he would say: "Avoid it resolutely: it is not easy to control yourself once you meddle with that sort of thing." Thus, on hearing that Critobulus had kissed Alcibiades' pretty boy, he put this question to Xenophon before Critobulus: "Tell me, Xenophon, did you not 9 suppose Critobulus to be a sober person, and by no means rash; prudent, and not thoughtless or adventurous?"

"Certainly," said Xenophon.

"Then you are to look on him henceforth as

---

[1] *Cyropaedia*, I. v. 12.
[2] In *Odyssey*, x. 281 f.

καὶ λεωργότατον· οὗτος κἂν εἰς μαχαίρας κυβι-
στήσειε κἂν εἰς πῦρ ἅλοιτο.

10 Καὶ τί δή, ἔφη ὁ Ξενοφῶν, ἰδὼν ποιοῦντα
τοιαῦτα κατέγνωκας αὐτοῦ ;

Οὐ γὰρ οὗτος, ἔφη, ἐτόλμησε τὸν Ἀλκιβιάδου
υἱὸν φιλῆσαι, ὄντα εὐπροσωπότατον καὶ ὡραιό-
τατον ;

Ἀλλ' εἰ μέντοι, ἔφη ὁ Ξενοφῶν, τοιοῦτόν ἐστι
τὸ ῥιψοκίνδυνον ἔργον, κἂν ἐγὼ δοκῶ μοι τὸν
κίνδυνον τοῦτον ὑπομεῖναι.

11 Ὦ τλῆμον, ἔφη ὁ Σωκράτης, καὶ τί ἂν οἴει
παθεῖν καλὸν φιλήσας ; ἆρ' οὐκ ἂν αὐτίκα μάλα
δοῦλος μὲν εἶναι ἀντ' ἐλευθέρου, πολλὰ δὲ
δαπανᾶν εἰς βλαβερὰς ἡδονάς, πολλὴν δὲ
ἀσχολίαν ἔχειν τοῦ ἐπιμεληθῆναί τινος καλοῦ
κἀγαθοῦ, σπουδάζειν δ' ἀναγκασθῆναι ἐφ' οἷς
οὐδ' ἂν μαινόμενος σπουδάσειεν ;

12 Ὦ Ἡράκλεις, ἔφη ὁ Ξενοφῶν, ὡς δεινήν τινα
λέγεις δύναμιν τοῦ φιλήματος εἶναι.

Καὶ τοῦτο, ἔφη ὁ Σωκράτης, θαυμάζεις ; οὐκ
οἶσθα, ἔφη, τὰ φαλάγγια οὐδ' ἡμιωβολιαῖα τὸ
μέγεθος ὄντα προσαψάμενα μόνον τῷ στόματι
ταῖς τε ὀδύναις ἐπιτρίβει τοὺς ἀνθρώπους καὶ τοῦ
φρονεῖν ἐξίστησι ;

Ναὶ μὰ Δί', ἔφη ὁ Ξενοφῶν· ἐνίησι γάρ τι τὰ
φαλάγγια κατὰ τὸ δῆγμα.

13 Ὦ μῶρε, ἔφη ὁ Σωκράτης, τοὺς δὲ καλοὺς οὐκ
οἴει φιλοῦντας ἐνιέναι τι, ὅτι σὺ οὐχ ὁρᾷς ; οὐκ
οἶσθ', ὅτι τοῦτο τὸ θηρίον, ὃ καλοῦσι καλὸν καὶ
ὡραῖον, τοσούτῳ δεινότερόν ἐστι τῶν φαλαγγίων,
ὅσῳ ἐκεῖνα μὲν ἁψάμενα, τοῦτο δὲ οὐδ' ἁπτόμενον,
ἐὰν δέ τις αὐτὸ θεᾶται, ἐνίησί τι καὶ πάνυ

utterly hot-headed and reckless : the man would do a somersault into a ring of knives ; he would jump into fire."

"What on earth has he done to make you think 10 so badly of him ? " asked Xenophon.

"What has the man done ? He dared to kiss Alcibiades' son, and the boy is very good-looking and attractive."

"Oh, if that is the sort of adventure you mean, I think I might make that venture myself."

"Poor fellow ! What do you think will happen 11 to you through kissing a pretty face ? Won't you lose your liberty in a trice and become a slave, begin spending large sums on harmful pleasures, have no time to give to anything fit for a gentleman, be forced to concern yourself with things that no madman even would care about ? "

"Heracles ! what alarming power in a kiss ! " 12 cried Xenophon.

"What ? Does that surprise you ? " continued Socrates. "Don't you know that the scorpion, though smaller than a farthing, if it but fasten on the tongue, inflicts excruciating and maddening pain ? "

"Yes, to be sure ; for the scorpion injects something by its bite."

"And do you think, you foolish fellow, that the 13 fair inject nothing when they kiss, just because you don't see it ? Don't you know that this creature called 'fair and young' is more dangerous than the scorpion, seeing that it need not even come in contact, like the insect, but at any distance can

πρόσωθεν τοιοῦτον, ὥστε μαίνεσθαι ποιεῖν ; [ἴσως
δὲ καὶ οἱ Ἔρωτες τοξόται διὰ τοῦτο καλοῦνται,
ὅτι καὶ πρόσωθεν οἱ καλοὶ τιτρώσκουσιν.] ἀλλὰ
συμβουλεύω σοι, ὦ Ξενοφῶν, ὁπόταν ἴδῃς τινὰ
καλόν, φεύγειν προτροπάδην, σοὶ δ', ὦ Κριτόβουλε, συμβουλεύω ἀπενιαυτίσαι· μόλις γὰρ ἂν
ἴσως ἐν τοσούτῳ χρόνῳ [τὸ δῆγμα] ὑγιὴς γένοιο.

14 Οὕτω δὴ καὶ ἀφροδισιάζειν τοὺς μὴ ἀσφαλῶς
ἔχοντας πρὸς ἀφροδίσια ᾤετο χρῆναι πρὸς
τοιαῦτα, οἷα μὴ πάνυ μὲν δεομένου τοῦ σώματος
οὐκ ἂν προσδέξαιτο ἡ ψυχή, δεομένου δὲ οὐκ ἂν
πράγματα παρέχοι. αὐτὸς δὲ πρὸς ταῦτα φανερὸς
ἦν οὕτω παρεσκευασμένος, ὥστε ῥᾷον ἀπέχεσθαι
τῶν καλλίστων καὶ ὡραιοτάτων ἢ οἱ ἄλλοι τῶν
15 αἰσχίστων καὶ ἀωροτάτων. περὶ μὲν δὴ βρώσεως
καὶ πόσεως καὶ ἀφροδισίων οὕτω κατεσκευασμένος
ἦν, καὶ ᾤετο οὐδὲν ἂν ἧττον ἀρκούντως ἥδεσθαι
τῶν πολλὰ ἐπὶ τούτοις πραγματευομένων, λυπεῖσθαι δὲ πολὺ ἔλαττον.[1]

IV. Εἰ δέ τινες Σωκράτην νομίζουσιν, ὡς ἔνιοι
γράφουσί τε καὶ λέγουσι περὶ αὐτοῦ τεκμαιρόμενοι,
προτρέψασθαι μὲν ἀνθρώπους ἐπ' ἀρετὴν κράτιστον γεγονέναι, προαγαγεῖν δ' ἐπ' αὐτὴν οὐχ
ἱκανόν, σκεψάμενοι μὴ μόνον ἃ ἐκεῖνος κολα-
στηρίου ἕνεκα τοὺς πάντ' οἰομένους εἰδέναι ἐρωτῶν
ἤλεγχεν, ἀλλὰ καὶ ἃ λέγων συνημέρευε τοῖς συνδιατρίβουσι, δοκιμαζόντων, εἰ ἱκανὸς ἦν βελτίους

---

[1] § 15 Sauppe and others bracket as a spurious addition.

---

[1] Sophists.

inject a maddening poison into anyone who only looks at it?

"Maybe, too, the loves are called archers for this reason, that the fair can wound even at a distance.

"Nay, I advise you, Xenophon, as soon as you see a pretty face to take to your heels and fly: and you, Critobulus, I advise to spend a year abroad. It will certainly take you at least as long as that to recover from the bite."

Thus in the matter of carnal appetite, he held 14 that those whose passions were not under complete control should limit themselves to such indulgence as the soul would reject unless the need of the body were pressing, and such as would do no harm when the need was there. As for his own conduct in this matter, it was evident that he had trained himself to avoid the fairest and most attractive more easily than others avoid the ugliest and most repulsive. Concerning eating and drinking then and carnal in- 15 dulgence such were his views, and he thought that a due portion of pleasure would be no more lacking to him than to those who give themselves much to these, and that much less trouble would fall to his lot.

IV. If any hold the opinion expressed in some written and spoken criticisms of Socrates that are based on inference, and think, that though he was consummate in exhorting men to virtue, he was an incompetent guide to it, let them consider not only the searching cross-examination with which he chastised those who thought themselves omniscient,[1] but his daily talks with his familiar friends, and then judge whether he was capable of improving his companions.

2 ποιεῖν τοὺς συνόντας. λεξω δὲ πρῶτον ἅ ποτε
αὐτοῦ ἤκουσα περὶ τοῦ δαιμονίου διαλεγομένου
πρὸς Ἀριστόδημον τὸν μικρὸν ἐπικαλούμενον.
καταμαθὼν γὰρ αὐτὸν οὔτε θύοντα τοῖς θεοῖς
οὔτε <εὐχόμενον δῆλον ὄντα οὔτε>[1] μαντικῇ
χρώμενον, ἀλλὰ καὶ τῶν ποιούντων ταῦτα κατα-
γελῶντα, Εἰπέ μοι, ἔφη, ὦ Ἀριστόδημε, ἔστιν
οὕστινας ἀνθρώπους τεθαύμακας ἐπὶ σοφίᾳ ;
Ἔγωγε, ἔφη.

3 Καὶ ὅς, Λέξον ἡμῖν, ἔφη, τὰ ὀνόματα αὐτῶν.
Ἐπὶ μὲν τοίνυν ἐπῶν ποιήσει Ὅμηρον ἔγωγε
μάλιστα τεθαύμακα, ἐπὶ δὲ διθυράμβῳ Μελα-
νιππίδην, ἐπὶ δὲ τραγῳδίᾳ Σοφοκλέα, ἐπὶ δὲ
ἀνδριαντοποιίᾳ Πολύκλειτον, ἐπὶ δὲ ζωγραφίᾳ
Ζεῦξιν.

4 Πότερά σοι δοκοῦσιν οἱ ἀπεργαζόμενοι εἴδωλα
ἄφρονά τε καὶ ἀκίνητα ἀξιοθαυμαστότεροι εἶναι
ἢ οἱ ζῷα ἔμφρονά τε καὶ ἐνεργά ;
Πολὺ νὴ Δία οἱ ζῷα, εἴπερ γε μὴ τύχῃ τινί,
ἀλλ' ἀπὸ γνώμης ταῦτα γίγνεται.
Τῶν δὲ ἀτεκμάρτως ἐχόντων ὅτου ἕνεκά ἐστι
καὶ τῶν φανερῶς ἐπ' ὠφελείᾳ ὄντων πότερα τύχης
καὶ πότερα γνώμης ἔργα κρίνεις ;
Πρέπει μὲν τὰ ἐπ' ὠφελείᾳ γιγνόμενα γνώμης
εἶναι ἔργα.

5 Οὔκουν δοκεῖ σοι ὁ ἐξ ἀρχῆς ποιῶν ἀνθρώπους
ἐπ' ὠφελείᾳ προσθεῖναι αὐτοῖς δι' ὧν αἰσθάνονται
ἕκαστα, ὀφθαλμοὺς μὲν ὥσθ' ὁρᾶν τὰ ὁρατά, ὦτα
δὲ ὥστ' ἀκούειν τὰ ἀκουστά ; ὀσμῶν γε μήν, εἰ μὴ
ῥῖνες προσετέθησαν, τί ἂν ἡμῖν ὄφελος ἦν ; τίς δ'
ἂν αἴσθησις ἦν γλυκέων καὶ δριμέων καὶ πάντων
τῶν διὰ στόματος ἡδέων, εἰ μὴ γλῶττα τούτων

I will first state what I once heard him say about 2
the godhead in conversation with Aristodemus the
dwarf, as he was called. On learning that he was
not known to sacrifice or pray or use divination, and
actually made a mock of those who did so, he said:
"Tell me, Aristodemus, do you admire any human
beings for wisdom?"

"I do," he answered.

"Tell us their names." 3

"In epic poetry Homer comes first, in my opinion;
in dithyramb, Melanippides; in tragedy, Sophocles;
in sculpture, Polycleitus; in painting, Zeuxis."

"Which, think you, deserve the greater admira- 4
tion, the creators of phantoms without sense and
motion, or the creators of living, intelligent, and
active beings?"

"Oh, of living beings, by far, provided only they
are created by design and not mere chance."

"Suppose that it is impossible to guess the
purpose of one creature's existence, and obvious that
another's serves a useful end, which, in your judgment, is the work of chance, and which of design?"

"Presumably the creature that serves some useful
end is the work of design."

"Do you not think then that he who created man 5
from the beginning had some useful end in view
when he endowed him with his several senses, giving
eyes to see visible objects, ears to hear sounds?
Would odours again be of any use to us had we not
been endowed with nostrils? What perception should
we have of sweet and bitter and all things pleasant
to the palate had we no tongue in our mouth

---

[1] These words are wanting in the MSS. but are supplied
from the papyrus fragment.

6 γνώμων ἐνειργάσθη; πρὸς δὲ τούτοις οὐ δοκεῖ
σοι καὶ τόδε προνοίας ἔργοις ἐοικέναι, τὸ ἐπεὶ
ἀσθενὴς μέν ἐστιν ἡ ὄψις, βλεφάροις αὐτὴν
θυρῶσαι, ἃ ὅταν μὲν αὐτῇ χρῆσθαί τι δέῃ, ἀναπε-
τάννυται, ἐν δὲ τῷ ὕπνῳ συγκλείεται; ὡς δ' ἂν
μηδὲ ἄνεμοι βλάπτωσιν, ἠθμὸν βλεφαρίδας
ἐμφῦσαι· ὀφρύσι τε ἀπογεισῶσαι τὰ ὑπὲρ τῶν
ὀμμάτων, ὡς μηδ' ὁ ἐκ τῆς κεφαλῆς ἱδρὼς
κακουργῇ· τὸ δὲ τὴν ἀκοὴν δέχεσθαι μὲν πάσας
φωνάς, ἐμπίπλασθαι δὲ μήποτε· καὶ τοὺς μὲν
πρόσθεν ὀδόντας πᾶσι ζῴοις οἵους τέμνειν εἶναι,
τοὺς δὲ γομφίους οἵους παρὰ τούτων δεξαμένους
λεαίνειν· καὶ στόμα μέν, δι' οὗ ὧν ἐπιθυμεῖ τὰ
ζῷα εἰσπέμπεται, πλησίον ὀφθαλμῶν καὶ ῥινῶν
καταθεῖναι· ἐπεὶ δὲ τὰ ἀποχωροῦντα δυσχερῆ,
ἀποστρέψαι τοὺς τούτων ὀχετοὺς καὶ ἀπενεγκεῖν
ᾗ δυνατὸν προσωτάτω ἀπὸ τῶν αἰσθήσεων· ταῦτα
οὕτω προνοητικῶς πεπραγμένα ἀπορεῖς πότερα
τύχης ἢ γνώμης ἔργα ἐστίν;

7 Οὐ μὰ τὸν Δί', ἔφη, ἀλλ' οὕτω γε σκοπουμένῳ
πάνυ ἔοικε ταῦτα σοφοῦ τινος δημιουργοῦ καὶ
φιλοζῴου τεχνήματι.

Τὸ δὲ ἐμφῦσαι μὲν ἔρωτα τῆς τεκνοποιίας,
ἐμφῦσαι δὲ ταῖς γειναμέναις ἔρωτα τοῦ ἐκτρέφειν,
τοῖς δὲ τραφεῖσι μέγιστον μὲν πόθον τοῦ ζῆν,
μέγιστον δὲ φόβον τοῦ θανάτου;

Ἀμέλει καὶ ταῦτα ἔοικε μηχανήμασί τινος ζῷα
εἶναι βουλευσαμένου.

8 Σὺ δὲ σαυτὸν φρόνιμόν τι δοκεῖς ἔχειν;

Ἐρώτα γ' οὖν καὶ ἀποκρινοῦμαι.

Ἄλλοθι δὲ οὐδαμοῦ οὐδὲν οἴει φρόνιμον εἶναι;
καὶ ταῦτ' εἰδώς, ὅτι γῆς τε μικρὸν μέρος ἐν τῷ

56

to discriminate between them? Besides these, are 6
there not other contrivances that look like the results
of forethought? Thus the eyeballs, being weak, are
set behind eyelids, that open like doors when we
want to see, and close when we sleep: on the lids
grow lashes through which the very winds filter
harmlessly: above the eyes is a coping of brows that
lets no drop of sweat from the head hurt them. The
ears catch all sounds, but are never choked with
them. Again, the incisors of all creatures are
adapted for cutting, the molars for receiving food
from them and grinding it. And again, the mouth,
through which the food they want goes in, is set
near the eyes and nostrils; but since what goes out
is unpleasant, the ducts through which it passes are
turned away and removed as far as possible from the
organs of sense. With such signs of forethought in
these arrangements, can you doubt whether they are
the works of chance or design?"

"No, of course not. When I regard them in this 7
light they do look very like the handiwork of a wise
and loving creator."

"What of the natural desire to beget children,
the mother's desire to rear her babe, the child's
strong will to live and strong fear of death?"

"Undoubtedly these, too, look like the contrivances of one who deliberately willed the
existence of living creatures."

"Do you think you have any wisdom yourself?" 8

"Oh! Ask me a question and judge from my
answer."

"And do you suppose that wisdom is nowhere else
to be found, although you know that you have a mere
speck of all the earth in your body and a mere

σώματι πολλῆς οὔσης ἔχεις καὶ ὑγροῦ βραχὺ
πολλοῦ ὄντος καὶ τῶν ἄλλων δήπου μεγάλων
ὄντων ἑκάστου μικρὸν μέρος λαβόντι τὸ σῶμα
συνήρμοσταί σοι· νοῦν δὲ μόνον ἄρα οὐδαμοῦ ὄντα
σε εὐτυχῶς πως δοκεῖς συναρπάσαι καὶ τάδε τὰ
ὑπερμεγέθη καὶ πλῆθος ἄπειρα δι' ἀφροσύνην
τινὰ οὕτως οἴει εὐτάκτως ἔχειν ;

9 Μὰ Δί', οὐ γὰρ ὁρῶ τοὺς κυρίους, ὥσπερ τῶν
ἐνθάδε γιγνομένων τοὺς δημιουργούς.

Οὐδὲ γὰρ τὴν σαυτοῦ σύγε ψυχὴν ὁρᾷς, ἢ τοῦ
σώματος κυρία ἐστίν· ὥστε κατά γε τοῦτο ἔξεστί
σοι λέγειν, ὅτι οὐδὲν γνώμῃ, ἀλλὰ τύχῃ πάντα
πράττεις.

10 Καὶ ὁ Ἀριστόδημος, Οὗτοι, ἔφη, ἐγώ, ὦ
Σώκρατες, ὑπερορῶ τὸ δαιμόνιον, ἀλλ' ἐκεῖνο
μεγαλοπρεπέστερον ἡγοῦμαι ἢ ὡς τῆς ἐμῆς
θεραπείας προσδεῖσθαι.

Οὐκοῦν, ἔφη, ὅσῳ μεγαλοπρεπέστερον ἀξιοῖ σε
θεραπεύειν, τοσούτῳ μᾶλλον τιμητέον αὐτό.

11 Εὖ ἴσθι, ἔφη, ὅτι εἰ νομίζοιμι θεοὺς ἀνθρώπων
τι φροντίζειν, οὐκ ἂν ἀμελοίην αὐτῶν.

Ἔπειτ' οὐκ οἴει φροντίζειν ; οἳ πρῶτον μὲν
μόνον τῶν ζῴων ἄνθρωπον ὀρθὸν ἀνέστησαν· ἡ
δὲ ὀρθότης καὶ προορᾶν πλέον ποιεῖ δύνασθαι καὶ
τὰ ὕπερθεν μᾶλλον θεᾶσθαι καὶ ἧττον κακοπαθεῖν·
ἔπειτα τοῖς μὲν ἄλλοις ἑρπετοῖς πόδας ἔδωκαν, οἳ
τὸ πορεύεσθαι μόνον παρέχουσιν, ἀνθρώπῳ δὲ
καὶ χεῖρας προσέθεσαν, αἳ τὰ πλεῖστα, οἷς
εὐδαιμονέστεροι ἐκείνων ἐσμέν, ἐξεργάζονται.

12 καὶ μὴν γλῶτταν γε πάντων τῶν ζῴων ἐχόντων
μόνην τὴν τῶν ἀνθρώπων ἐποίησαν οἵαν ἄλλοτε

drop of all the water, and that of all the other mighty elements you received, I suppose, just a scrap towards the fashioning of your body? But as for mind, which alone, it seems, is without mass, do you think that you snapped it up by a lucky accident, and that the orderly ranks of all these huge masses, infinite in number, are due, forsooth, to a sort of absurdity?"

"Yes; for I don't see the master hand, whereas I 9 see the makers of things in this world."

"Neither do you see your own soul,[1] which has the mastery of the body; so that, as far as that goes, you may say that you do nothing by design, but everything by chance."

Here Aristodemus exclaimed: "Really, Socrates, 10 I don't despise the godhead. But I think it is too great to need my service."

"Then the greater the power that deigns to serve you, the more honour it demands of you."

"I assure you, that if I believed that the gods pay 11 any heed to man, I would not neglect them."

"Then do you think them unheeding? In the first place, man is the only living creature that they have caused to stand upright; and the upright position gives him a wider range of vision in front and a better view of things above, and exposes him less to injury. Secondly, to grovelling creatures they have given feet that afford only the power of moving, whereas they have endowed man with hands, which are the instruments to which we chiefly owe our greater happiness. Again, though all creatures have 12 a tongue, the tongue of man alone has been formed by them to be capable of contact with different parts

[1] *Cyropaedia*, VIII. vii. 17.

ἀλλαχῇ ψαύουσαν τοῦ στόματος ἀρθροῦν τε τὴν
φωνὴν καὶ σημαίνειν πάντα ἀλλήλοις, ἃ βουλόμεθα. τὸ δὲ καὶ τὰς τῶν ἀφροδισίων ἡδονὰς τοῖς
μὲν ἄλλοις ζῴοις δοῦναι περιγράψαντας τοῦ
ἔτους χρόνον, ἡμῖν δὲ συνεχῶς μέχρι γήρως ταῦτα
παρέχειν ; [1]

13 Οὐ τοίνυν μόνον ἤρκεσε τῷ θεῷ τοῦ σώματος
ἐπιμεληθῆναι, ἀλλ' ὅπερ μέγιστόν ἐστι, καὶ τὴν
ψυχὴν κρατίστην τῷ ἀνθρώπῳ ἐνέφυσε. τίνος
γὰρ ἄλλου ζῴου ψυχὴ πρῶτα μὲν θεῶν τῶν τὰ
μέγιστα καὶ κάλλιστα συνταξάντων ᾔσθηται ὅτι
εἰσί ; τί δὲ φῦλον ἄλλο ἢ ἄνθρωποι θεοὺς θερα-
πεύουσι ; ποία δὲ ψυχὴ τῆς ἀνθρωπίνης ἱκανωτέρα προφυλάττεσθαι ἢ λιμὸν ἢ δίψος ἢ ψύχη ἢ
θάλπη ἢ νόσοις ἐπικουρῆσαι ἢ ῥώμην ἀσκῆσαι
ἢ πρὸς μάθησιν ἐκπονῆσαι, ἢ ὅσα ἂν ἀκούσῃ ἢ
14 ἴδῃ ἢ μάθῃ ἱκανωτέρα ἐστὶ διαμεμνῆσθαι ; οὐ
γὰρ πάνυ σοι κατάδηλον, ὅτι παρὰ τἆλλα ζῷα
ὥσπερ θεοὶ ἄνθρωποι βιοτεύουσι, φύσει καὶ τῷ
σώματι καὶ τῇ ψυχῇ κρατιστεύοντες ; οὔτε γὰρ
βοὸς ἂν ἔχων σῶμα, ἀνθρώπου δὲ γνώμην ἐδύνατ'
ἂν πράττειν ἃ ἐβούλετο, οὔθ' ὅσα χεῖρας ἔχει,
ἄφρονα δ' ἐστί, πλέον οὐδὲν ἔχει. σὺ δ' ἀμφοτέρων τῶν πλείστου ἀξίων τετυχηκὼς οὐκ οἴει
σου θεοὺς ἐπιμελεῖσθαι ; ἀλλ' ὅταν τί ποιήσωσι,
νομιεῖς αὐτούς σου φροντίζειν ;

15 Ὅταν πέμπωσιν, ὥσπερ σὺ φῂς πέμπειν
αὐτούς, συμβούλους ὅτι χρὴ ποιεῖν καὶ μὴ ποιεῖν.
Ὅταν δὲ Ἀθηναίοις, ἔφη, πυνθανομένοις τι διὰ
μαντικῆς φράζωσιν, οὐ καὶ σοὶ δοκεῖς φράζειν

_____
[1] § 12 τὸ δὲ . . . παρέχειν is bracketed as spurious by
Sauppe.

of the mouth, so as to enable us to articulate the voice and express all our wants to one another. Once more, for all other creatures they have prescribed a fixed season of sexual indulgence; in our case the only time limit they have set is old age.

"Nor was the deity content to care for man's body. 13 What is of yet higher moment, he has implanted in him the noblest type of soul. For in the first place what other creature's soul has apprehended the existence of gods who set in order the universe, greatest and fairest of things? And what race of living things other than man worships gods? And what soul is more apt than man's to make provision against hunger and thirst, cold and heat, to relieve sickness and promote health, to acquire knowledge by toil, and to remember accurately all that is heard, seen, or learned? For is it not obvious to you that, in com- 14 parison with the other animals, men live like gods, by nature peerless both in body and in soul? For with a man's reason and the body of an ox we could not carry out our wishes, and the possession of hands without reason is of little worth. Do you, then, having received the two most precious gifts, yet think that the gods take no care of you? What are they to do, to make you believe that they are heedful of you?"

"I will believe when they send counsellors, as you 15 declare they do, saying, 'Do this, avoid that.'"

"But when the Athenians inquire of them by divination and they reply, do you not suppose that

61

αὐτούς ; οὐδ' ὅταν τοῖς "Ελλησι τέρατα πέμποντες προσημαίνωσιν, οὐδ' ὅταν πᾶσιν ἀνθρώποις, ἀλλὰ μόνον σὲ ἐξαιροῦντες ἐν ἀμελείᾳ κατατίθενται ;

16 οἴει δ' ἂν τοὺς θεοὺς τοῖς ἀνθρώποις δόξαν ἐμφῦσαι, ὡς ἱκανοί εἰσιν εὖ καὶ κακῶς ποιεῖν, εἰ μὴ δυνατοὶ ἦσαν, καὶ τοὺς ἀνθρώπους ἐξαπατωμένους τὸν πάντα χρόνον οὐδέποτ' ἂν αἰσθέσθαι ; οὐχ ὁρᾷς, ὅτι τὰ πολυχρονιώτατα καὶ σοφώτατα τῶν ἀνθρωπίνων, πόλεις καὶ ἔθνη, θεοσεβέστατά ἐστι καὶ αἱ φρονιμώταται ἡλικίαι

17 θεῶν ἐπιμελέσταται ; ὠγαθέ, ἔφη, κατάμαθε, ὅτι καὶ ὁ σὸς νοῦς ἐνὼν τὸ σὸν σῶμα ὅπως βούλεται μεταχειρίζεται. οἴεσθαι οὖν χρὴ καὶ τὴν ἐν τῷ παντὶ φρόνησιν τὰ πάντα ὅπως ἂν αὐτῇ ἡδὺ ᾖ, οὕτω τίθεσθαι, καὶ μὴ τὸ σὸν μὲν ὄμμα δύνασθαι ἐπὶ πολλὰ στάδια ἐξικνεῖσθαι, τὸν δὲ τοῦ θεοῦ ὀφθαλμὸν ἀδύνατον εἶναι ἅμα πάντα ὁρᾶν, μηδὲ τὴν σὴν μὲν ψυχὴν καὶ περὶ τῶν ἐνθάδε καὶ περὶ τῶν ἐν Αἰγύπτῳ καὶ ἐν Σικελίᾳ δύνασθαι φροντίζειν, τὴν δὲ τοῦ θεοῦ φρόνησιν μὴ ἱκανὴν

18 εἶναι ἅμα πάντων ἐπιμελεῖσθαι. ἢν μέντοι ὥσπερ ἀνθρώπους θεραπεύων γιγνώσκεις τοὺς ἀντιθεραπεύειν ἐθέλοντας καὶ χαριζόμενος τοὺς ἀντιχαριζομένους καὶ συμβουλευόμενος καταμανθάνεις τοὺς φρονίμους, οὕτω καὶ τῶν θεῶν πεῖραν λαμβάνῃς θεραπεύων, εἴ τί σοι θελήσουσι περὶ τῶν ἀδήλων ἀνθρώποις συμβουλεύειν, γνώσῃ τὸ θεῖον ὅτι τοσοῦτον καὶ τοιοῦτόν ἐστιν, ὥσθ' ἅμα πάντα ὁρᾶν καὶ πάντα ἀκούειν καὶ πανταχοῦ παρεῖναι καὶ ἅμα πάντων ἐπιμελεῖσθαι.

19 Ἐμοὶ μὲν οὖν ταῦτα λέγων οὐ μόνον τοὺς συνόντας ἐδόκει ποιεῖν, ὁπότε ὑπὸ τῶν ἀνθρώπων

to you, too, the answer is given? Or when they send portents for warning to the Greeks, or to all the world? Are you their one exception, the only one consigned to neglect? Or do you suppose that 16 the gods would have put into man a belief in their ability to help and harm, if they had not that power; and that man throughout the ages would never have detected the fraud? Do you not see that the wisest and most enduring of human institutions, cities and nations, are most god-fearing, and that the most thoughtful period of life is the most religious? Be 17 well assured, my good friend, that the mind within you directs your body according to its will; and equally you must think that Thought indwelling in the Universal disposes all things according to its pleasure. For think not that your eye can travel over many furlongs and yet god's eye cannot see the the whole world at once; that your soul can ponder on things in Egypt and in Sicily, and god's thought is not sufficient to pay heed to the whole world at once. Nay, but just as by serving men you find out 18 who is willing to serve you in return, by being kind who will be kind to you in return, and by taking counsel, discover the masters of thought, so try the gods by serving them, and see whether they will vouchsafe to counsel you in matters hidden from man. Then you will know that such is the greatness and such the nature of the deity that he sees all things [1] and hears all things alike, and is present in all places and heedful of all things."

To me at least it seemed that by these sayings he 19 kept his companions from impiety, injustice, and

---

[1] *Cyropaedia*, VIII. vii. 22.

ὁρῷντο, ἀπέχεσθαι τῶν ἀνοσίων τε καὶ ἀδίκων
καὶ αἰσχρῶν, ἀλλὰ καὶ ὁπότε ἐν ἐρημίᾳ εἶεν,
ἐπείπερ ἡγήσαιντο μηδὲν ἄν ποτε ὧν πράττοιεν
θεοὺς διαλαθεῖν.

V. Εἰ δὲ δὴ καὶ ἐγκράτεια καλόν τε κἀγαθὸν
ἀνδρὶ κτῆμά ἐστιν, ἐπισκεψώμεθα, εἴ τι προὐβί-
βαζε λέγων εἰς ταύτην τοιάδε·

Ὦ ἄνδρες, εἰ πολέμου ἡμῖν γενομένου βουλοί-
μεθα ἑλέσθαι ἄνδρα, ὑφ' οὗ μάλιστ' ἂν αὐτοὶ μὲν
σωζοίμεθα, τοὺς δὲ πολεμίους χειροίμεθα, ἆρ'
ὅντιν' αἰσθανοίμεθα ἥττω γαστρὸς ἢ οἴνου ἢ
ἀφροδισίων¹ ἢ ὕπνου, τοῦτον ἂν αἱροίμεθα; καὶ
πῶς ἂν οἰηθείημεν τὸν τοιοῦτον ἢ ἡμᾶς σώσειν ἢ
2 τοὺς πολεμίους κρατήσειν; εἰ δ' ἐπὶ τελευτῇ τοῦ
βίου γενόμενοι βουλοίμεθά τῳ ἐπιτρέψαι ἢ παῖδας
ἄρρενας παιδεῦσαι ἢ θυγατέρας παρθένους δια-
φυλάξαι ἢ χρήματα διασῶσαι, ἆρ' ἀξιόπιστον
εἰς ταῦτα ἡγησόμεθα τὸν ἀκρατῆ; δούλῳ δ'
ἀκρατεῖ ἐπιτρέψαιμεν ἂν ἢ βοσκήματα ἢ ταμιεῖα
ἢ ἔργων ἐπιστασίαν; διάκονον δὲ καὶ ἀγοραστὴν
3 τοιοῦτον ἐθελήσαιμεν ἂν προῖκα λαβεῖν; ἀλλὰ
μὴν εἴ γε μηδὲ δοῦλον ἀκρατῆ δεξαίμεθ' ἄν, πῶς
οὐκ ἄξιον αὐτόν γε φυλάξασθαι τοιοῦτον γενέσθαι;
καὶ γὰρ οὐχ ὥσπερ οἱ πλεονέκται τῶν ἄλλων
ἀφαιρούμενοι χρήματα ἑαυτοὺς δοκοῦσι πλουτίζειν, οὕτως ὁ ἀκρατὴς τοῖς μὲν ἄλλοις βλαβερός,
ἑαυτῷ δ' ὠφέλιμος, ἀλλὰ κακοῦργος μὲν τῶν
ἄλλων, ἑαυτοῦ δὲ πολὺ κακουργότερος, εἴ γε
κακουργότατόν ἐστι μὴ μόνον τὸν οἶκον τὸν
ἑαυτοῦ φθείρειν, ἀλλὰ καὶ τὸ σῶμα καὶ τὴν
4 ψυχήν. ἐν συνουσίᾳ δὲ τίς ἂν ἡσθείη τῷ
τοιούτῳ, ὃν εἰδείη τῷ ὄψῳ τε καὶ τῷ οἴνῳ

baseness, and that not only when they were seen by men, but even in solitude; since they ever felt that no deed of theirs could at any time escape the gods.

V. But if Self-control too is a fair and noble possession, let us now consider whether he led men up to that virtue by discourse like the following:

"My friends, if we were at war and wanted to choose a leader most capable of helping us to save ourselves and conquer the enemy, should we choose one whom we knew to be the slave of the belly, or of wine, or lust, or sleep? How could we expect that such an one would either save us or defeat the enemy? Or if at the end of our life we should wish 2 to appoint a guardian to educate our boys or protect our girls or to take care of our goods, should we think a loose liver a trustworthy man to choose? Should we entrust live stock or storehouses or the management of works to a vicious slave? Should we be willing to take as a gift a page or an errand-boy with such a character? Surely then, if we should 3 refuse a vicious slave, the master must look to it that he does not grow vicious himself? For whereas the covetous, by robbing other men of their goods, seem to enrich themselves, a vicious man reaps no advantage from the harm he does to others. If he is a worker of mischief to others, he brings much greater mischief on himself, if indeed the greatest mischief of all is to ruin not one's home merely, but the body and the soul. In social intercourse what 4 pleasure could you find in such a man, knowing that

---

¹ Sauppe adds ἢ πόνου with the MSS. and Stobaeus, but it can hardly be right.

χαίροντα μᾶλλον ἢ τοῖς φίλοις καὶ τὰς πόρνας
ἀγαπῶντα μᾶλλον ἢ τοὺς ἑταίρους; ἆρά γε οὐ
χρὴ πάντα ἄνδρα ἡγησάμενον τὴν ἐγκράτειαν
ἀρετῆς εἶναι κρηπῖδα ταύτην πρῶτον ἐν τῇ ψυχῇ
5 κατασκευάσασθαι; τίς γὰρ ἄνευ ταύτης ἢ μάθοι
τι ἂν ἀγαθὸν ἢ μελετήσειεν ἀξιολόγως; ἢ τίς οὐκ
ἂν ταῖς ἡδοναῖς δουλεύων αἰσχρῶς διατεθείη καὶ
τὸ σῶμα καὶ τὴν ψυχήν; ἐμοὶ μὲν δοκεῖ νὴ τὴν
Ἥραν ἐλευθέρῳ μὲν ἀνδρὶ εὐκτὸν εἶναι μὴ τυχεῖν
δούλου τοιούτου, δουλεύοντα δὲ ταῖς τοιαύταις
ἡδοναῖς ἱκετεύειν τοὺς θεοὺς δεσποτῶν ἀγαθῶν
τυχεῖν· οὕτως γὰρ ἂν μόνως ὁ τοιοῦτος σωθείη.

6 Τοιαῦτα δὲ λέγων ἔτι ἐγκρατέστερον τοῖς ἔργοις
ἢ τοῖς λόγοις ἑαυτὸν ἐπεδείκνυεν· οὐ γὰρ μόνον
τῶν διὰ τοῦ σώματος ἡδονῶν ἐκράτει, ἀλλὰ καὶ
τῆς διὰ τῶν χρημάτων, νομίζων τὸν παρὰ τοῦ
τυχόντος χρήματα λαμβάνοντα δεσπότην ἑαυτοῦ
καθιστάναι καὶ δουλεύειν δουλείαν οὐδεμιᾶς ἧττον
αἰσχράν.

VI. Ἄξιον δ᾽ αὐτοῦ καὶ ἃ πρὸς Ἀντιφῶντα
τὸν σοφιστὴν διελέχθη μὴ παραλιπεῖν. ὁ γὰρ
Ἀντιφῶν ποτε βουλόμενος τοὺς συνουσιαστὰς
αὐτοῦ παρελέσθαι προσελθὼν τῷ Σωκράτει
παρόντων αὐτῶν ἔλεξε τάδε·

2 Ὦ Σώκρατες, ἐγὼ μὲν ᾤμην τοὺς φιλοσοφοῦντας
εὐδαιμονεστέρους χρῆναι γίγνεσθαι· σὺ δέ μοι
δοκεῖς τἀναντία τῆς φιλοσοφίας ἀπολελαυκέναι.
ζῇς γοῦν οὕτως, ὡς οὐδ᾽ ἂν εἷς δοῦλος ὑπὸ δεσπότῃ
διαιτώμενος μείνειε· σῖτά τε σιτῇ καὶ ποτὰ πίνεις
τὰ φαυλότατα καὶ ἱμάτιον ἠμφίεσαι οὐ μόνον
φαῦλον, ἀλλὰ τὸ αὐτὸ θέρους τε καὶ χειμῶνος,
3 ἀνυπόδητός τε καὶ ἀχίτων διατελεῖς. καὶ μὴν

he prefers your sauces and your wines to your friends, and likes the women [1] better than the company? Should not every man hold self-control to be the foundation of all virtue, and first lay this foundation firmly in his soul? For who without 5 this can learn any good or practise it worthily? Or what man that is the slave of his pleasures is not in an evil plight body and soul alike? From my heart I declare that every free man should pray not to have such a man among his slaves; and every man who is a slave to such pleasures should entreat the gods to give him good masters: thus, and only thus, may he find salvation."

Such were his words; but his own self-control 6 was shown yet more clearly by his deeds than by his words. For he kept in subjection not only the pleasures of the body, but those too that money brings, in the belief that he who takes money from any casual giver puts himself under a master and endures the basest form of slavery.

VI. It is due to him that a conversation he had with Antiphon the Sophist should not go unrecorded. Antiphon came to Socrates with the intention of drawing his companions away from him, and spoke thus in their presence.

"Socrates, I supposed that philosophy must add 2 to one's store of happiness. But the fruits you have reaped from philosophy are apparently very different. For example, you are living a life that would drive even a slave to desert his master. Your meat and drink are of the poorest: the cloak you wear is not only a poor thing, but is never changed summer or winter; and you never wear shoes or tunic. Besides 3

[1] Employed to entertain the guests at the banquet.

χρήματά γε οὐ λαμβάνεις, ἃ καὶ κτωμένους
εὐφραίνει καὶ κεκτημένους ἐλευθεριώτερόν τε καὶ
ἥδιον ποιεῖ ζῆν. εἰ οὖν ὥσπερ καὶ τῶν ἄλλων
ἔργων οἱ διδάσκαλοι τοὺς μαθητὰς μιμητὰς
ἑαυτῶν ἀποδεικνύουσιν, οὕτω καὶ σὺ τοὺς συνόντας διαθήσεις, νόμιζε κακοδαιμονίας διδάσκαλος
εἶναι.

4   Καὶ ὁ Σωκράτης πρὸς ταῦτα εἶπε· Δοκεῖς μοι,
ὦ Ἀντιφῶν, ὑπειληφέναι με οὕτως ἀνιαρῶς ζῆν,
ὥστε πέπεισμαι σὲ μᾶλλον ἀποθανεῖν ἂν ἑλέσθαι
ἢ ζῆν ὥσπερ ἐγώ. ἴθι οὖν ἐπισκεψώμεθα, τί
5 χαλεπὸν ᾔσθησαι τοὐμοῦ βίου. πότερον ὅτι
τοῖς μὲν λαμβάνουσιν ἀργύριον ἀναγκαῖόν ἐστιν
ἀπεργάζεσθαι τοῦτο, ἐφ' ᾧ ἂν μισθὸν λαμβά-
νωσιν, ἐμοὶ δὲ μὴ λαμβάνοντι οὐκ ἀνάγκη
διαλέγεσθαι ᾧ ἂν μὴ βούλωμαι; ἢ τὴν δίαιτάν
μου φαυλίζεις ὡς ἧττον μὲν ὑγιεινὰ ἐσθίοντος
ἐμοῦ ἢ σοῦ, ἧττον δὲ ἰσχὺν παρέχοντα; ἢ ὡς
χαλεπώτερα πορίσασθαι τὰ ἐμὰ διαιτήματα τῶν
σῶν διὰ τὸ σπανιώτερά τε καὶ πολυτελέστερα
εἶναι; ἢ ὡς ἡδίω σοι ἃ σὺ παρασκευάζῃ ὄντα ἢ
ἐμοὶ ἃ ἐγώ; οὐκ οἶσθ', ὅτι ὁ μὲν ἥδιστα ἐσθίων
ἥκιστα ὄψου δεῖται, ὁ δὲ ἥδιστα πίνων ἥκιστα
6 τοῦ μὴ παρόντος ἐπιθυμεῖ ποτοῦ; τά γε μὴν
ἱμάτια οἶσθ' ὅτι οἱ μεταβαλλόμενοι ψύχους καὶ
θάλπους ἕνεκα μεταβάλλονται καὶ ὑποδήματα
ὑποδοῦνται, ὅπως μὴ διὰ τὰ λυποῦντα τοὺς
πόδας κωλύωνται πορεύεσθαι· ἤδη οὖν ποτε
ᾔσθου ἐμὲ ἢ διὰ ψῦχος μᾶλλόν του ἔνδον μένοντα
ἢ διὰ θάλπος μαχόμενόν τῳ περὶ σκιᾶς ἢ διὰ τὸ
ἀλγεῖν τοὺς πόδας οὐ βαδίζοντα ὅποι ἂν βούλω-
7 μαι; οὐκ οἶσθ', ὅτι οἱ φύσει ἀσθενέστατοι τῷ

you refuse to take money, the mere getting of which is a joy, while its possession makes one more independent and happier. Now the professors of other subjects try to make their pupils copy their teachers : if you too intend to make your companions do that, you must consider yourself a professor of unhappiness."

To this Socrates replied : 4

" Antiphon, you seem to have a notion that my life is so miserable, that I feel sure you would choose death in preference to a life like mine. Come then, let us consider together what hardship you have noticed in my life. Is it that those who take money 5 are bound to carry out the work for which they get a fee, while I, because I refuse to take it, am not obliged to talk with anyone against my will? Or do you think my food poor because it is less whole-some than yours or less nourishing? or because my viands are harder to get than yours, being scarcer and more expensive? or because your diet is more enjoyable than mine? Do you not know that the greater the enjoyment of eating the less the need of sauce ; the greater the enjoyment of drinking, the less the desire for drinks that are not available? As for cloaks, they are changed, as you know, on 6 account of cold or heat. And shoes are worn as a protection to the feet against pain and inconvenience in walking. Now did you ever know me to stay indoors more than others on account of the cold, or to fight with any man for the shade because of the heat, or to be prevented from walking anywhere by sore feet? Do you not know that by training, a puny 7

σώματι μελετήσαντες τῶν ἰσχυροτάτων ἀμελη-
σάντων κρείττους τε γίγνονται πρὸς ἂν μελετῶσι
καὶ ῥᾷον αὐτὰ φέρουσιν ; ἐμὲ δὲ ἄρα οὐκ οἴει τῷ
σώματι ἀεὶ τὰ συντυγχάνοντα μελετῶντα καρτε-
8 ρεῖν πάντα ῥᾷον φέρειν σοῦ μὴ μελετῶντος ; τοῦ
δὲ μὴ δουλεύειν γαστρὶ μηδ᾽ ὕπνῳ καὶ λαγνείᾳ
οἴει τι ἄλλο αἰτιώτερον εἶναι ἢ τὸ ἕτερα ἔχειν
τούτων ἡδίω, ἃ οὐ μόνον ἐν χρείᾳ ὄντα εὐφραίνει,
ἀλλὰ καὶ ἐλπίδας παρέχοντα ὠφελήσειν ἀεί ; καὶ
μὴν τοῦτό γε οἶσθα, ὅτι οἱ μὲν οἰόμενοι μηδὲν εὖ
πράττειν οὐκ εὐφραίνονται, οἱ δὲ ἡγούμενοι καλῶς
προχωρεῖν ἑαυτοῖς ἢ γεωργίαν ἢ ναυκληρίαν ἢ
ἄλλ᾽ ὅτι ἂν τυγχάνωσιν ἐργαζόμενοι ὡς εὖ
9 πράττοντες εὐφραίνονται. οἴει οὖν ἀπὸ πάντων
τούτων τοσαύτην ἡδονὴν εἶναι ὅσην ἀπὸ τοῦ
ἑαυτόν τε ἡγεῖσθαι βελτίω γίγνεσθαι καὶ φίλους
ἀμείνους κτᾶσθαι ; ἐγὼ τοίνυν διατελῶ ταῦτα
νομίζων.[1]

Ἐὰν δὲ δὴ φίλους ἢ πόλιν ὠφελεῖν δέῃ, ποτέρῳ
ἡ πλείων σχολὴ τούτων ἐπιμελεῖσθαι, τῷ ὡς ἐγὼ
νῦν ἢ τῷ ὡς σὺ μακαρίζεις διαιτωμένῳ ; στρα-
τεύοιτο δὲ πότερος ἂν ῥᾷον, ὁ μὴ δυνάμενος ἄνευ
πολυτελοῦς διαίτης ζῆν ἢ ᾧ τὸ παρὸν ἀρκοίη ;
ἐκπολιορκηθείη δὲ πότερος ἂν θᾶττον, ὁ τῶν
χαλεπωτάτων εὑρεῖν δεόμενος ἢ ὁ τοῖς ῥᾴστοις
ἐντυγχάνειν ἀρκούντως χρώμενος ;

10 Ἔοικας, ὦ Ἀντιφῶν, τὴν εὐδαιμονίαν οἰομένῳ
τρυφὴν καὶ πολυτέλειαν εἶναι· ἐγὼ δὲ νομίζω τὸ
μὲν μηδενὸς δεῖσθαι θεῖον εἶναι, τὸ δ᾽ ὡς ἐλαχίστων

---

[1] § 9 ἐγὼ . . . νομίζων is bracketed by Sauppe as spurious.

weakling comes to be better at any form of exercise he practises, and gets more staying power, than the muscular prodigy who neglects to train? Seeing then that I am always training my body to answer any and every call on its powers, do you not think that I can stand every strain better than you can without training? For avoiding slavery to the belly 8 or to sleep and incontinence, is there, think you, any more effective specific than the possession of other and greater pleasures, which are delightful not only to enjoy, but also because they arouse hopes of lasting benefit? And again, you surely know that while he who supposes that nothing goes well with him is unhappy, he who believes that he is successful in farming or a shipping concern or any other business he is engaged in is happy in the thought of his prosperity. Do you think then that out of all 9 this thinking there comes anything so pleasant as the thought: 'I am growing in goodness and I am making better friends?' And that, I may say, is my constant thought.

"Further, if help is wanted by friends or city, which of the two has more leisure to supply their needs, he who lives as I am living or he whose life you call happy? Which will find soldiering the easier task, he who cannot exist without expensive food or he who is content with what he can get? Which when besieged will surrender first, he who wants what is very hard to come by or he who can make shift with whatever is at hand?

"You seem, Antiphon, to imagine that happiness 10 consists in luxury and extravagance. But my belief is that to have no wants is divine;[1] to have as few as

---

[1] *Cyropaedia*, viii. iii. 40.

ἐγγυτάτω τοῦ θείου, καὶ τὸ μὲν θεῖον κράτιστον,
τὸ δ' ἐγγυτάτω τοῦ θείου ἐγγυτάτω τοῦ κρατίστου.

11 Πάλιν δέ ποτε ὁ Ἀντιφῶν διαλεγόμενος τῷ
Σωκράτει εἶπεν·

Ὦ Σώκρατες, ἐγώ τοί σε δίκαιον μὲν νομίζω,
σοφὸν δὲ οὐδ' ὁπωστιοῦν· δοκεῖς δέ μοι καὶ αὐτὸς
τοῦτο γιγνώσκειν· οὐδένα γὰρ τῆς συνουσίας
ἀργύριον πράττῃ. καίτοι τό γε ἱμάτιον ἢ τὴν
οἰκίαν ἢ ἄλλο τι ὧν κέκτησαι νομίζων ἀργυρίου
ἄξιον εἶναι οὐδενὶ ἂν μὴ ὅτι προῖκα δοίης, ἀλλ'
12 οὐδ' ἔλαττον τῆς ἀξίας λαβών. δῆλον δή, ὅτι εἰ
καὶ τὴν συνουσίαν ᾤου τινὸς ἀξίαν εἶναι, καὶ
ταύτης ἂν οὐκ ἔλαττον τῆς ἀξίας ἀργύριον
ἐπράττου. δίκαιος μὲν οὖν ἂν εἴης, ὅτι οὐκ
ἐξαπατᾷς ἐπὶ πλεονεξίᾳ, σοφὸς δὲ οὐκ ἄν, μηδενός
γε ἄξια ἐπιστάμενος.

13 Ὁ δὲ Σωκράτης πρὸς ταῦτα εἶπεν· Ὦ Ἀντιφῶν,
παρ' ἡμῖν νομίζεται τὴν ὥραν καὶ τὴν σοφίαν
ὁμοίως μὲν καλόν, ὁμοίως δὲ αἰσχρὸν διατίθεσθαι
εἶναι. τήν τε γὰρ ὥραν ἐὰν μέν τις ἀργυρίου
πωλῇ τῷ βουλομένῳ, πόρνον αὐτὸν ἀποκαλοῦσιν,
ἐὰν δέ τις ὃν ἂν γνῷ καλόν τε κἀγαθὸν ἐραστὴν
ὄντα, τοῦτον φίλον ἑαυτῷ ποιῆται, σώφρονα
νομίζομεν· καὶ τὴν σοφίαν ὡσαύτως τοὺς μὲν
ἀργυρίου τῷ βουλομένῳ πωλοῦντας σοφιστὰς
ὥσπερ πόρνους [1] ἀποκαλοῦσιν, ὅστις δὲ ὃν ἂν γνῷ
εὐφυᾶ ὄντα διδάσκων ὅτι ἂν ἔχῃ ἀγαθὸν φίλον
ποιεῖται, τοῦτον νομίζομεν ἃ τῷ καλῷ κἀγαθῷ
14 πολίτῃ προσήκει, ταῦτα ποιεῖν. ἐγὼ δ' οὖν καὶ
αὐτός, ὦ Ἀντιφῶν, ὥσπερ ἄλλος τις ἢ ἵππῳ
ἀγαθῷ ἢ κυνὶ ἢ ὄρνιθι ἥδεται, οὕτω καὶ ἔτι

possible comes next to the divine; and as that which is divine is supreme, so that which approaches nearest to its nature is nearest to the supreme."

In another conversation with Socrates Antiphon 11 said :

"Socrates, I for my part believe you to be a just, but by no means a wise man. And I think you realise it yourself. Anyhow, you decline to take money for your society. Yet if you believed your cloak or house or anything you possess to be worth money, you would not part with it for nothing or even for less than its value. Clearly, then, if you 12 set any value on your society, you would insist on getting the proper price for that too. It may well be that you are a just man because you do not cheat people through avarice; but wise you cannot be, since your knowledge is not worth anything."

To this Socrates replied : 13

"Antiphon, it is common opinion among us in regard to beauty and wisdom that there is an honourable and a shameful way of bestowing them. For to offer one's beauty for money to all comers is called prostitution; but we think it virtuous to become friendly with a lover who is known to be a man of honour. So is it with wisdom. Those who offer it to all comers for money are known as sophists, prostitutors of wisdom, but we think that he who makes a friend of one whom he knows to be gifted by nature, and teaches him all the good he can, fulfils the duty of a citizen and a gentleman. That is my 14 own view, Antiphon. Others have a fancy for a good horse or dog or bird : my fancy, stronger even

---

[1] ὥσπερ πόρνους is bracketed by Sauppe after Ruhnken.

μᾶλλον ἥδομαι φίλοις ἀγαθοῖς καὶ ἐάν τι ἔχω
ἀγαθόν, διδάσκω καὶ ἄλλοις συνίστημι, παρ' ὧν
ἂν ἡγῶμαι ὠφελήσεσθαί τι αὐτοὺς εἰς ἀρετήν.
καὶ τοὺς θησαυροὺς τῶν πάλαι σοφῶν ἀνδρῶν,
οὓς ἐκεῖνοι κατέλιπον ἐν βιβλίοις γράψαντες,
ἀνελίττων κοινῇ σὺν τοῖς φίλοις διέρχομαι, καὶ
ἄν τι ὁρῶμεν ἀγαθόν, ἐκλεγόμεθα καὶ μέγα νομίζομεν κέρδος, ἐὰν ἀλλήλοις ὠφέλιμοι γιγνώμεθα.
ἐμοὶ μὲν δὴ ταῦτα ἀκούοντι ἐδόκει αὐτός τε
μακάριος εἶναι καὶ τοὺς ἀκούοντας ἐπὶ καλοκά-
γαθίαν ἄγειν.

15 Καὶ πάλιν ποτὲ τοῦ Ἀντιφῶντος ἐρομένου
αὐτόν, πῶς ἄλλους μὲν ἡγοῖτο πολιτικοὺς ποιεῖν,
αὐτὸς δὲ οὐ πράττοι τὰ πολιτικά, εἴπερ ἐπίσταιτο·
Ποτέρως δ' ἄν, ἔφη, ὦ Ἀντιφῶν, μᾶλλον τὰ
πολιτικὰ πράττοιμι, εἰ μόνος αὐτὰ πράττοιμι ἢ
εἰ ἐπιμελοίμην τοῦ ὡς πλείστους ἱκανοὺς εἶναι
πράττειν αὐτά;

VII. Ἐπισκεψώμεθα δέ, εἰ καὶ ἀλαζονείας
ἀποτρέπων τοὺς συνόντας ἀρετῆς ἐπιμελεῖσθαι
προέτρεπεν· ἀεὶ γὰρ ἔλεγεν, ὡς οὐκ εἴη καλλίων
ὁδὸς ἐπ' εὐδοξίαν ἢ δι' ἧς ἄν τις ἀγαθὸς τοῦτο
γένοιτο, ὃ καὶ δοκεῖν βούλοιτο.

2 Ὅτι δ' ἀληθῆ ἔλεγεν, ὧδ' ἐδίδασκεν· Ἐνθυ-
μώμεθα γάρ, ἔφη, εἴ τις μὴ ὢν ἀγαθὸς αὐλητὴς
δοκεῖν βούλοιτο, τί ἂν αὐτῷ ποιητέον εἴη. ἆρ'
οὐ τὰ ἔξω τῆς τέχνης μιμητέον τοὺς ἀγαθοὺς
αὐλητάς; καὶ πρῶτον μὲν ὅτι ἐκεῖνοι σκευήν τε
καλὴν κέκτηνται καὶ ἀκολούθους πολλοὺς περι-
άγονται, καὶ τούτῳ ταῦτα ποιητέον· ἔπειτα ὅτι
ἐκείνους πολλοὶ ἐπαινοῦσι, καὶ τούτῳ πολλοὺς
ἐπαινέτας παρασκευαστέον. ἀλλὰ μὴν ἔργον γε

than theirs, is for good friends. And I teach them all the good I can, and recommend them to others from whom I think they will get some moral benefit. And the treasures that the wise men of old have left us in their writings I open and explore with my friends. If we come on any good thing, we extract it, and we set much store on being useful to one another."

For my part, when I heard these words fall from his lips, I judged him to be a happy man himself and to be putting his hearers in the way of being gentlemen.

On yet another occasion Antiphon asked him: 15 "How can you suppose that you make politicians of others, when you yourself avoid politics even if you understand them?"

"How now, Antiphon?" he retorted, "should I play a more important part in politics by engaging in them alone or by taking pains to turn out as many competent politicians as possible?"

VII. Let us next consider whether by discouraging imposture he encouraged his companions to cultivate virtue.[1] For he always said that the best road to glory is the way that makes a man as good as he wishes to be thought. And this was how he demonstrated the truth of this saying:

"Suppose a bad flute-player wants to be thought 2 a good one, let us note what he must do. Must he not imitate good players in the accessories of the art? First, as they wear fine clothes and travel with many attendants, he must do the same. Further, seeing that they win the applause of crowds, he must provide himself with a large *claque*. But, of

---

[1] *Cyropaedia*, I. vi. 22.

οὐδαμοῦ ληπτέον ἡ εὐθὺς ἐλεγχθήσεται γελοῖος
ὢν καὶ οὐ μόνον αὐλητὴς κακός, ἀλλὰ καὶ
ἄνθρωπος ἀλαζών. καίτοι πολλὰ μὲν δαπανῶν,
μηδὲν δ' ὠφελούμενος, πρὸς δὲ τούτοις κακοδοξῶν
πῶς οὐκ ἐπιπόνως τε καὶ ἀλυσιτελῶς καὶ κατα-
3 γελάστως βιώσεται; ὡς δ' αὕτως εἴ τις βούλοιτο
στρατηγὸς ἀγαθὸς μὴ ὢν φαίνεσθαι ἢ κυβερνήτης,
ἐννοῶμεν, τί ἂν αὐτῷ συμβαίνοι. ἆρ' οὐκ ἄν, εἰ
μὲν ἐπιθυμῶν τοῦ δοκεῖν ἱκανὸς εἶναι ταῦτα
πράττειν μὴ δύναιτο πείθειν, τοῦτ' εἴη λυπηρόν,
εἰ δὲ πείσειεν, ἔτι ἀθλιώτερον; δῆλον γὰρ ὅτι
κυβερνᾶν καταστάθεὶς ὁ μὴ ἐπιστάμενος ἢ
στρατηγεῖν ἀπολέσειεν ἂν οὓς ἥκιστα βούλοιτο
καὶ αὐτὸς αἰσχρῶς ἂν καὶ κακῶς ἀπαλλάξειεν.
4 Ὡσαύτως δὲ καὶ τὸ πλούσιον καὶ τὸ ἀνδρεῖον καὶ
τὸ ἰσχυρὸν μὴ ὄντα δοκεῖν ἀλυσιτελὲς ἀπέφαινε·
προστάττεσθαι γὰρ αὐτοῖς ἔφη μείζω ἢ κατὰ
δύναμιν καὶ μὴ δυναμένους ταῦτα ποιεῖν δοκοῦντας
ἱκανοὺς εἶναι συγγνώμης οὐκ ἂν τυγχάνειν.
5 ἀπατεῶνα δ' ἐκάλει οὐ μικρὸν μέν, εἴ τις ἀργύριον
ἢ σκεῦος παρά του πειθοῖ λαβὼν ἀποστεροίη,
πολὺ δὲ μέγιστον ὅστις μηδενὸς ἄξιος ὢν ἐξηπατή-
κοι πείθων, ὡς ἱκανὸς εἴη τῆς πόλεως ἡγεῖσθαι.

Ἐμοὶ μὲν οὖν ἐδόκει καὶ τοῦ ἀλαζονεύεσθαι
ἀποτρέπειν τοὺς συνόντας τοιάδε διαλεγόμενος.

course, he must never accept an engagement, or he will promptly expose himself to ridicule as an incompetent player and an impostor to boot. And so, what with incurring heavy expense and gaining nothing, and bringing disgrace on himself as well, he will make his life burdensome, unprofitable and ridiculous. So too if a man who is not a general or 3 a pilot wanted to be thought a good one, let us imagine what would happen to him. If his efforts to seem proficient in these duties failed to carry conviction, would not his failure be galling to him? if they succeeded, would not his success be still more disastrous? for it is certain that if a man who knew nothing about piloting a ship or commanding an army were appointed to such work, he would lose those whom he least wanted to lose and would bring ruin and disgrace on himself."

By similar reasoning he would show how un- 4 profitable is a reputation for wealth or courage or strength when it is undeserved. "Tasks beyond their powers," he would say, "are laid on the incompetent, and no mercy is shown to them when they disappoint the expectation formed of their capability. The man who persuades you to lend 5 him money or goods and then keeps them is without doubt a rogue; but much the greatest rogue of all is the man who has gulled his city into the belief that he is fit to direct it."

For my part I thought that such talks did discourage imposture among his companions.

BOOK II

B

Ι. Ἐδόκει δέ μοι καὶ τοιαῦτα λέγων προτρέπειν τοὺς συνόντας ἀσκεῖν ἐγκράτειαν [πρὸς ἐπιθυμίαν] βρωτοῦ καὶ ποτοῦ καὶ λαγνείας καὶ ὕπνου καὶ ῥίγους καὶ θάλπους καὶ πόνου. γνοὺς δέ τινα τῶν συνόντων ἀκολαστοτέρως ἔχοντα πρὸς τὰ τοιαῦτα, Εἰπέ μοι, ἔφη, ὦ Ἀρίστιππε, εἰ δέοι σε παιδεύειν παραλαβόντα δύο τῶν νέων, τὸν μὲν ὅπως ἱκανὸς ἔσται ἄρχειν, τὸν δ' ὅπως μηδ' ἀντιποιήσεται ἀρχῆς, πῶς ἂν ἑκάτερον παιδεύοις; βούλει σκοπῶμεν ἀρξάμενοι ἀπὸ τῆς τροφῆς ὥσπερ ἀπὸ τῶν στοιχείων;

Καὶ ὁ Ἀρίστιππος ἔφη· Δοκεῖ γοῦν μοι ἡ τροφὴ ἀρχὴ εἶναι· οὐδὲ γὰρ ζώη γ' ἄν τις, εἰ μὴ τρέφοιτο.

2   Οὐκοῦν τὸ μὲν βούλεσθαι σίτου ἅπτεσθαι, ὅταν ὥρα ἥκῃ, ἀμφοτέροις εἰκὸς παραγίγνεσθαι;

Εἰκὸς γάρ, ἔφη.

Τὸ οὖν προαιρεῖσθαι τὸ κατεπεῖγον μᾶλλον πράττειν ἢ τῇ γαστρὶ χαρίζεσθαι πότερον ἂν αὐτῶν ἐθίζοιμεν;

Τὸν εἰς τὸ ἄρχειν, ἔφη, νὴ Δία παιδευόμενον, ὅπως μὴ τὰ τῆς πόλεως ἄπρακτα γίγνηται παρὰ τὴν ἐκείνου ἀρχήν.

Οὐκοῦν, ἔφη, καὶ ὅταν πιεῖν βούλωνται, τὸ δύνασθαι διψῶντα ἀνέχεσθαι τῷ αὐτῷ προσθετέον;

Πάνυ μὲν οὖν, ἔφη.

BOOK II

I. In other conversations I thought that he exhorted his companions to practise self-control in the matter of eating and drinking, and sexual indulgence, and sleeping, and endurance of cold and heat and toil. Aware that one of his companions was rather intemperate in such matters, he said: "Tell me, Aristippus, if you were required to take charge of two youths and educate them so that the one would be fit to rule and the other would never think of putting himself forward, how would you educate them? Shall we consider it, beginning with the elementary question of food?"

"Oh yes," replied Aristippus, "food does seem to come first; for one can't live without food."

"Well, now, will not a desire for food naturally 2 arise in both at certain times?"

"Yes, naturally."

"Now which of the two should we train in the habit of transacting urgent business before he satisfies his hunger?"

"The one who is being trained to rule, undoubtedly; else State business might be neglected during his tenure."

"And must not the same one be given power to resist thirst when both want to drink?"

"Certainly."

3   Τὸ δὲ ὕπνου ἐγκρατῆ εἶναι, ὥστε δύνασθαι καὶ
ὀψὲ κοιμηθῆναι καὶ πρωὶ ἀναστῆναι καὶ ἀγρυ-
πνῆσαί, εἴ τι δέοι, ποτέρῳ ἂν προσθείημεν ;
    Καὶ τοῦτο, ἔφη, τῷ αὐτῷ.
    Τί δέ, ἔφη, τὸ ἀφροδισίων ἐγκρατῆ εἶναι, ὥστε
μὴ διὰ ταῦτα κωλύεσθαι πράττειν, εἴ τι δέοι ;
    Καὶ τοῦτο, ἔφη, τῷ αὐτῷ.
    Τί δέ, τὸ μὴ φεύγειν τοὺς πόνους, ἀλλ᾽ ἐθελοντὴν
ὑπομένειν, ποτέρῳ ἂν προσθείημεν ;
    Καὶ τοῦτο, ἔφη, τῷ ἄρχειν παιδευομένῳ.
    Τί δέ, τὸ μαθεῖν εἴ τι ἐπιτήδειόν ἐστι μάθημα
πρὸς τὸ κρατεῖν τῶν ἀντιπάλων ποτέρῳ ἂν
προσθεῖναι μᾶλλον πρέποι ;
    Πολὺ νὴ Δί᾽, ἔφη, τῷ ἄρχειν παιδευομένῳ· καὶ
γὰρ τῶν ἄλλων οὐδὲν ὄφελος ἄνευ τῶν τοιούτων
μαθημάτων.

4   Οὐκοῦν ὁ οὕτω πεπαιδευμένος ἧττον ἂν δοκεῖ
σοι ὑπὸ τῶν ἀντιπάλων ἢ τὰ λοιπὰ ζῷα ἁλίσκεσθαι ; τούτων γὰρ δήπου τὰ μὲν γαστρὶ δελεαζό-
μενα, καὶ μάλα ἔνια δυσωπούμενα, ὅμως τῇ
ἐπιθυμίᾳ τοῦ φαγεῖν ἀγόμενα πρὸς τὸ δέλεαρ
ἁλίσκεται, τὰ δὲ ποτῷ ἐνεδρεύεται.
    Πάνυ μὲν οὖν, ἔφη.
    Οὐκοῦν καὶ ἄλλα ὑπὸ λαγνείας, οἷον οἵ τε
ὄρτυγες καὶ οἱ πέρδικες, πρὸς τὴν τῆς θηλείας
φωνὴν τῇ ἐπιθυμίᾳ καὶ τῇ ἐλπίδι τῶν ἀφροδισίων
φερόμενοι καὶ ἐξιστάμενοι τοῦ τὰ δεινὰ ἀναλογί-
ζεσθαι τοῖς θηράτροις ἐμπίπτουσι ;

5   Συνέφη καὶ ταῦτα.
    Οὐκοῦν δοκεῖ σοι αἰσχρὸν εἶναι ἀνθρώπῳ ταὐτὰ
πάσχειν τοῖς ἀφρονεστάτοις τῶν θηρίων ; ὥσπερ
οἱ μοιχοὶ εἰσέρχονται εἰς τὰς εἱρκτὰς εἰδότες, ὅτι

"And to which shall we give the power of limiting 3
his sleep so that he can go late to bed and get up
early, and do without sleep if need be?"

"To the same again."

"And the power to control his passions, so that he
may not be hindered in doing necessary work?"

"To the same again."

"And to which shall we give the habit of not
shirking a task, but undertaking it willingly?"

"That too will go to the one who is being trained
to rule."

"And to which would the knowledge needful
for overcoming enemies be more appropriately
given?"

"Without doubt to the one who is being trained to
rule; for the other lessons would be useless without such knowledge."

"Don't you think that with this education he will 4
be less likely to be caught by his enemy than other
creatures? Some of them, you know, are so greedy,
that in spite of extreme timidity in some cases, they
are drawn irresistibly to the bait to get food, and are
caught; and others are snared by drink."

"Yes, certainly."

"Others again—quails and partridges, for instance
—are so amorous, that when they hear the cry of
the female, they are carried away by desire and
anticipation, throw caution to the winds and blunder
into the nets. Is it not so?"

He agreed again.   5

"Now, don't you think it disgraceful that a man
should be in the same plight as the silliest of wild
creatures? Thus an adulterer enters the women's

κίνδυνος τῷ μοιχεύοντι ἅ τε ὁ νόμος ἀπειλεῖ
παθεῖν καὶ ἐνεδρευθῆναι καὶ ληφθέντα ὑβρισθῆναι·
καὶ τηλικούτων μὲν ἐπικειμένων τῷ μοιχεύοντι
κακῶν τε καὶ αἰσχρῶν, ὄντων δὲ πολλῶν τῶν
ἀπολυσόντων τῆς τῶν ἀφροδισίων ἐπιθυμίας ἐν
ἀδείᾳ, ὅμως εἰς τὰ ἐπικίνδυνα φέρεσθαι, ἆρ' οὐκ
ἤδη τοῦτο παντάπασι κακοδαιμονῶντός ἐστιν ;

Ἔμοιγε δοκεῖ, ἔφη.

6 Τὸ δὲ εἶναι μὲν τὰς ἀναγκαιοτάτας πλείστας
πράξεις τοῖς ἀνθρώποις ἐν ὑπαίθρῳ, οἷον τάς τε
πολεμικὰς καὶ τὰς γεωργικὰς καὶ τῶν ἄλλων οὐ
τὰς ἐλαχίστας, τοὺς δὲ πολλοὺς ἀγυμνάστως ἔχειν
πρός τε ψύχη καὶ θάλπη οὐ δοκεῖ σοι πολλὴ
ἀμέλεια εἶναι ;

Συνέφη καὶ τοῦτο.

Οὐκοῦν δοκεῖ σοι τὸν μέλλοντα ἄρχειν ἀσκεῖν
δεῖν καὶ ταῦτα εὐπετῶς φέρειν ;

Πάνυ μὲν οὖν, ἔφη.

7 Οὐκοῦν εἰ τοὺς ἐγκρατεῖς τούτων ἁπάντων εἰς
τοὺς ἀρχικοὺς τάττομεν, τοὺς ἀδυνάτους ταῦτα
ποιεῖν εἰς τοὺς μηδ' ἀντιποιησομένους τοῦ ἄρχειν
τάξομεν ;

Συνέφη καὶ τοῦτο.

Τί οὖν ; ἐπειδὴ καὶ τούτων ἑκατέρου τοῦ φύλου
τὴν τάξιν οἶσθα, ἤδη ποτ' ἐπεσκέψω, εἰς ποτέραν
τῶν τάξεων τούτων σαυτὸν δικαίως ἂν τάττοις ;

8 Ἔγωγ', ἔφη ὁ Ἀρίστιππος, καὶ οὐδαμῶς γε
τάττω ἐμαυτὸν εἰς τὴν τῶν ἄρχειν βουλομένων
τάξιν. καὶ γὰρ πάνυ μοι δοκεῖ ἄφρονος ἀνθρώπου
εἶναι τὸ μεγάλου ἔργου ὄντος τοῦ ἑαυτῷ τὰ δέοντα
παρασκευάζειν μὴ ἀρκεῖν τοῦτο, ἀλλὰ προσανα-
θέσθαι τὸ καὶ τοῖς ἄλλοις πολίταις ὧν δέονται

quarters, knowing that by committing adultery he is in danger of incurring the penalties threatened by the law, and that he may be trapped, caught and ill-treated. When such misery and disgrace hang over the adulterer's head, and there are many remedies to relieve him of his carnal desire without risk, is it not sheer lunacy to plunge headlong into danger?"

"Yes, I think it is."

"And considering that the great majority of essential occupations, warfare, agriculture and very many others, are carried on in the open air, don't you think it gross negligence that so many men are untrained to withstand cold and heat?"

He agreed again.

"Don't you think then, that one who is going to rule must adapt himself to bear them lightly?"

"Certainly."

"If then we classify those who control themselves in all these matters as 'fit to rule,' shall we not classify those who cannot behave so as men with no claim to be rulers?"

He agreed again.

"Well now, as you know the category to which each of these species belongs, have you ever considered in which category you ought to put yourself?"

"I have; and I do not for a moment put myself in the category of those who want to be rulers.[1] For considering how hard a matter it is to provide for one's own needs, I think it absurd not to be content to do that, but to shoulder the burden of supplying the wants of the community as well. That

---

[1] *Cyropaedia*, i. vi. 7 ; vii. ii. 26 f.

πορίζειν· καὶ ἑαυτῷ μὲν πολλὰ ὧν βούλεται
ἐλλείπειν, τῆς δὲ πόλεως προεστῶτα, ἐὰν μὴ
πάντα, ὅσα ἡ πόλις βούλεται, καταπράττῃ,
τούτου δίκην ὑπέχειν, τοῦτο πῶς οὐ πολλὴ
9 ἀφροσύνη ἐστί; καὶ γὰρ ἀξιοῦσιν αἱ πόλεις τοῖς
ἄρχουσιν ὥσπερ ἐγὼ τοῖς οἰκέταις χρῆσθαι. ἐγώ
τε γὰρ ἀξιῶ τοὺς θεράποντας ἐμοὶ μὲν ἄφθονα
τὰ ἐπιτήδεια παρασκευάζειν, αὐτοὺς δὲ μηδενὸς
τούτων ἅπτεσθαι, αἵ τε πόλεις οἴονται χρῆναι
τοὺς ἄρχοντας ἑαυταῖς μὲν ὡς πλεῖστα ἀγαθὰ
πορίζειν, αὐτοὺς δὲ πάντων τούτων ἀπέχεσθαι.
ἐγὼ οὖν τοὺς μὲν βουλομένους πολλὰ πράγματα
ἔχειν αὐτοῖς τε καὶ ἄλλοις παρέχειν οὕτως ἂν
παιδεύσας εἰς τοὺς ἀρχικοὺς καταστήσαιμι·
ἐμαυτόν γε μέντοι τάττω εἰς τοὺς βουλομένους ᾗ
ῥᾷστά τε καὶ ἥδιστα βιοτεύειν.

10 Καὶ ὁ Σωκράτης ἔφη· Βούλει οὖν καὶ τοῦτο
σκεψώμεθα, πότεροι ἥδιον ζῶσιν, οἱ ἄρχοντες ἢ
οἱ ἀρχόμενοι; Πάνυ μὲν οὖν, ἔφη.

Πρῶτον μὲν τοίνυν τῶν ἐθνῶν ὧν ἡμεῖς ἴσμεν
ἐν μὲν τῇ Ἀσίᾳ Πέρσαι μὲν ἄρχουσιν, ἄρχονται
δὲ Σύροι καὶ Φρύγες καὶ Λυδοί· ἐν δὲ τῇ Εὐρώπῃ
Σκύθαι μὲν ἄρχουσι, Μαιῶται δὲ ἄρχονται· ἐν δὲ
τῇ Λιβύῃ Καρχηδόνιοι μὲν ἄρχουσι, Λίβυες δὲ
ἄρχονται. τούτων οὖν ποτέρους ἥδιον οἴει ζῆν;
ἢ τῶν Ἑλλήνων, ἐν οἷς καὶ αὐτὸς εἶ, πότεροί σοι
δοκοῦσιν ἥδιον, οἱ κρατοῦντες ἢ οἱ κρατούμενοι,
ζῆν;

11 Ἀλλ᾽ ἐγώ τοι, ἔφη ὁ Ἀρίστιππος, οὐδὲ εἰς τὴν
δουλείαν αὖ ἐμαυτὸν τάττω, ἀλλ᾽ εἶναί τίς μοι
δοκεῖ μέση τούτων ὁδός, ἣν πειρῶμαι βαδίζειν,
οὔτε δι᾽ ἀρχῆς οὔτε διὰ δουλείας, ἀλλὰ δι᾽

anyone should sacrifice a large part of his own wishes and make himself accountable as head of the state for the least failure to carry out all the wishes of the community is surely the height of folly. For states claim to treat their rulers just as I claim to treat my servants. I expect my men to provide me with necessaries in abundance, but not to touch any of them ; and states hold it to be the business of the ruler to supply them with all manner of good things, and to abstain from all of them himself. And so, should anyone want to bring plenty of trouble on himself and others, I would educate him as you propose and number him with ' those fitted to be rulers ' : but myself I classify with those who wish for a life of the greatest ease and pleasure that can be had."

Here Socrates asked : " Shall we then consider whether the rulers or the ruled live the pleasanter life ? "

" Certainly," replied Aristippus.

" To take first the nations known to us. In Asia the rulers are the Persians; the Syrians, Lydians and Phrygians are the ruled. In Europe the Scythians rule, and the Maeotians are ruled. In Africa the Carthaginians rule, and the Libyans are ruled. Which of the two classes, think you, enjoys the pleasanter life ? Or take the Greeks, of whom you yourself are one ; do you think that the controlling or the controlled communities enjoy the pleasanter life ? "

" Nay," replied Aristippus, " for my part I am no candidate for slavery ; but there is, as I hold, a middle path in which I am fain to walk. That way leads neither through rule nor slavery, but

ἐλευθερίας, ἥπερ μάλιστα πρὸς εὐδαιμονίαν
ἄγει.

12 Ἀλλ' εἰ μέν, ἔφη ὁ Σωκράτης, ὥσπερ οὔτε δι'
ἀρχῆς οὔτε διὰ δουλείας ἡ ὁδὸς αὕτη φέρει, οὕτως
μηδὲ δι' ἀνθρώπων, ἴσως ἄν τι λέγοις· εἰ μέντοι
ἐν ἀνθρώποις ὢν μήτε ἄρχειν ἀξιώσεις μήτε
ἄρχεσθαι μηδὲ τοὺς ἄρχοντας ἑκὼν θεραπεύσεις,
οἶμαί σε ὁρᾶν, ὡς ἐπίστανται οἱ κρείττονες τοὺς
ἥττονας καὶ κοινῇ καὶ ἰδίᾳ κλαίοντας καθίσαντες
13 δούλοις χρῆσθαι. ἢ λανθάνουσί σε οἱ ἄλλωι
σπειράντων καὶ φυτευσάντων τόν τε σῖτον
τέμνοντες καὶ δενδροκοποῦντες καὶ πάντα τρόπον
πολιορκοῦντες τοὺς ἥττονας καὶ μὴ θέλοντας
θεραπεύειν, ἕως ἂν πείσωσιν ἑλέσθαι δουλεύειν
ἀντὶ τοῦ πολεμεῖν τοῖς κρείττοσι; καὶ ἰδίᾳ αὖ
οἱ ἀνδρεῖοι καὶ δυνατοὶ τοὺς ἀνάνδρους καὶ
ἀδυνάτους οὐκ οἶσθα ὅτι καταδουλωσάμενοι
καρποῦνται;

Ἀλλ' ἐγώ τοι, ἔφη, ἵνα μὴ πάσχω ταῦτα, οὐδ'
εἰς πολιτείαν ἐμαυτὸν κατακλείω, ἀλλὰ ξένος
πανταχοῦ εἰμι.

14 Καὶ ὁ Σωκράτης ἔφη· Τοῦτο μέντοι ἤδη λέγεις
δεινὸν πάλαισμα. τοὺς γὰρ ξένους, ἐξ οὗ ὅ τε
Σίνις καὶ ὁ Σκείρων καὶ ὁ Προκρούστης ἀπέθανον,
οὐδεὶς ἔτι ἀδικεῖ· ἀλλὰ νῦν οἱ μὲν πολιτευόμενοι
ἐν ταῖς πατρίσι καὶ νόμους τίθενται, ἵνα μὴ
ἀδικῶνται, καὶ φίλους πρὸς τοῖς ἀναγκαίοις
καλουμένοις ἄλλους κτῶνται βοηθοὺς καὶ ταῖς
πόλεσιν ἐρύματα περιβάλλονται καὶ ὅπλα
κτῶνται, οἷς ἀμυνοῦνται τοὺς ἀδικοῦντας, καὶ
πρὸς τούτοις ἄλλους ἔξωθεν συμμάχους κατα-
σκευάζονται· καὶ οἱ μὲν πάντα ταῦτα κεκτημένοι

through liberty, which is the royal road to happiness."

"Ah," said Socrates, "if only that path can avoid 12 the world as well as rule and slavery, there may be something in what you say. But, since you are in the world, if you intend neither to rule nor to be ruled, and do not choose to truckle to the rulers—I think you must see that the stronger have a way of making the weaker rue their lot both in public and 13 in private life, and treating them like slaves. You cannot be unaware that where some have sown and planted, others cut their corn and fell their trees, and in all manner of ways harass the weaker if they refuse to bow down, until they are persuaded to accept slavery as an escape from war with the stronger. So, too, in private life do not brave and mighty men enslave and plunder the cowardly and feeble folk ? "

"Yes, but my plan for avoiding such treatment is this. I do not shut myself up in the four corners of a community, but am a stranger in every land."

"A very cunning trick, that ! " cried Socrates, 14 "for ever since the death of Sinis and Sceiron and Procrustes [1] no one injures strangers! And yet nowadays those who take a hand in the affairs of their homeland pass laws to protect themselves from injury, get friends to help them over and above those whom nature has given them, encompass their cities with fortresses, get themselves weapons to ward off the workers of mischief ; and besides all this seek to make allies in other lands ; and in spite of all these precautions, they are still wronged.

---

[1] Highwaymen slain by Theseus, Plutarch, *Thes.* c. 8 f.

XENOPHON

15 ὅμως ἀδικοῦνται· σὺ δὲ οὐδὲν μὲν τούτων ἔχων,
ἐν δὲ ταῖς ὁδοῖς, ἔνθα πλεῖστοι ἀδικοῦνται, πολὺν
χρόνον διατρίβων, εἰς ὁποίαν δ' ἂν πόλιν ἀφίκῃ,
τῶν πολιτῶν πάντων ἥττων ὢν καὶ τοιοῦτος οἵοις
μάλιστα ἐπιτίθενται οἱ βουλόμενοι ἀδικεῖν, ὅμως
διὰ τὸ ξένος εἶναι οὐκ ἂν οἴει ἀδικηθῆναι; ἢ
διότι αἱ πόλεις σοι κηρύττουσιν ἀσφάλειαν καὶ
προσιόντι καὶ ἀπιόντι, θαρρεῖς; ἢ διότι καὶ
δοῦλος ἂν οἴει τοιοῦτος εἶναι οἷος μηδενὶ δεσπότῃ
λυσιτελεῖν; τίς γὰρ ἂν ἐθέλοι ἄνθρωπον ἐν οἰκίᾳ
ἔχειν πονεῖν μὲν μηδὲν ἐθέλοντα, τῇ δὲ πολυτελε-
στάτῃ διαίτῃ χαίροντα;

16 Σκεψώμεθα δὲ καὶ τοῦτο, πῶς οἱ δεσπόται τοῖς
τοιούτοις οἰκέταις χρῶνται. ἆρα οὐ τὴν μὲν
λαγνείαν αὐτῶν τῷ λιμῷ σωφρονίζουσι; κλέπτειν
δὲ κωλύουσιν ἀποκλείοντες ὅθεν ἄν τι λαβεῖν ἦ;
τοῦ δὲ δραπετεύειν δεσμοῖς ἀπείργουσι; τὴν
ἀργίαν δὲ πληγαῖς ἐξαναγκάζουσιν; ἢ σὺ πῶς
ποιεῖς, ὅταν τῶν οἰκετῶν τινα τοιοῦτον ὄντα
καταμανθάνῃς;

17 Κολάζω, ἔφη, πᾶσι κακοῖς, ἕως ἂν δουλεύειν
ἀναγκάσω. ἀλλὰ γάρ, ὦ Σώκρατες, οἱ εἰς τὴν
βασιλικὴν τέχνην παιδευόμενοι, ἣν δοκεῖς μοι σὺ
νομίζειν εὐδαιμονίαν εἶναι, τί διαφέρουσι τῶν
ἐξ ἀνάγκης κακοπαθούντων, εἴ γε πεινήσουσι καὶ
διψήσουσι καὶ ῥιγώσουσι καὶ ἀγρυπνήσουσι καὶ
τἆλλα πάντα μοχθήσουσιν ἑκόντες; ἐγὼ μὲν γὰρ
οὐκ οἶδ' ὅτι διαφέρει τὸ αὐτὸ δέρμα ἑκόντα ἢ
ἄκοντα μαστιγοῦσθαι ἢ ὅλως τὸ αὐτὸ σῶμα πᾶσι
τοῖς τοιούτοις ἑκόντα ἢ ἄκοντα πολιορκεῖσθαι·
ἄλλο γε ἢ ἀφροσύνη πρόσεστι τῷ θέλοντι τὰ
λυπηρὰ ὑπομένειν;

But you, with none of these advantages, spend 15
much time on the open road, where so many come
to harm; and into whatever city you enter, you rank
below all its citizens, and are one of those specially
marked down for attack by intending wrongdoers;
and yet, because you are a stranger, do you expect
to escape injury? What gives you confidence? Is
it that the cities by proclamation guarantee your
safety in your coming and going? Or is it the
thought that no master would find you worth having
among his slaves? For who would care to have a
man in his house who wants to do no work and has
a weakness for high living?

"But now let us see how masters treat such 16
servants. Do they not starve them to keep them
from immorality, lock up the stores to stop their
stealing, clap fetters on them so that they can't run
away, and beat the laziness out of them with whips?
What do you do yourself to cure such faults among
your servants?"

"I make their lives a burden to them until I 17
reduce them to submission. But how about those
who are trained in the art of kingship, Socrates,
which you appear to identify with happiness? How
are they better off than those whose sufferings are
compulsory, if they must bear hunger, thirst, cold,
sleeplessness, and endure all these tortures willingly?
For if the same back gets the flogging whether its
owner kicks or consents, or, in short, if the same
body, consenting or objecting, is besieged by all
these torments, I see no difference, apart from the
folly of voluntary suffering."

18 Τί δέ, ὦ 'Αρίστιππε, ὁ Σωκράτης ἔφη, οὐ δοκεῖ
σοι τῶν τοιούτων διαφέρειν τὰ ἑκούσια τῶν
ἀκουσίων, ᾗ ὁ μὲν ἑκὼν πεινῶν φάγοι ἂν ὁπότε
βούλοιτο καὶ ὁ ἑκὼν διψῶν πίοι καὶ τἆλλα
ὡσαύτως, τῷ δ' ἐξ ἀνάγκης ταῦτα πάσχοντι οὐκ
ἔξεστιν ὁπόταν βούληται παύεσθαι; ἔπειτα ὁ
μὲν ἑκουσίως ταλαιπωρῶν ἐπ' ἀγαθῇ ἐλπίδι
πονῶν εὐφραίνεται, οἷον οἱ τὰ θηρία θηρῶντες
19 ἐλπίδι τοῦ λήψεσθαι ἡδέως μοχθοῦσι. καὶ τὰ μὲν
τοιαῦτα ἆθλα τῶν πόνων μικροῦ τινος ἄξιά ἐστι·
τοὺς δὲ πονοῦντας, ἵνα φίλους ἀγαθοὺς κτήσωνται
ἢ ὅπως ἐχθροὺς χειρώσονται ἢ ἵνα δυνατοὶ γενόμενοι καὶ τοῖς σώμασι καὶ ταῖς ψυχαῖς καὶ τὸν
ἑαυτῶν οἶκον καλῶς οἰκῶσι καὶ τοὺς φίλους εὖ
ποιῶσι καὶ τὴν πατρίδα εὐεργετῶσι, πῶς οὐκ
οἴεσθαι χρὴ τούτους καὶ πονεῖν ἡδέως εἰς τὰ
τοιαῦτα καὶ ζῆν εὐφραινομένους, ἀγαμένους μὲν
ἑαυτούς, ἐπαινουμένους δὲ καὶ ζηλουμένους ὑπὸ
20 τῶν ἄλλων; ἔτι δὲ αἱ μὲν ῥᾳδιουργίαι καὶ ἐκ τοῦ
παραχρῆμα ἡδοναὶ οὔτε σώματι εὐεξίαν ἱκαναί
εἰσιν ἐνεργάζεσθαι, ὥς φασιν οἱ γυμνασταί, οὔτε
ψυχῇ ἐπιστήμην ἀξιόλογον οὐδεμίαν ἐμποιοῦσιν,
αἱ δὲ διὰ καρτερίας ἐπιμέλειαι τῶν καλῶν τε
κἀγαθῶν ἔργων ἐξικνεῖσθαι ποιοῦσιν, ὥς φασιν
οἱ ἀγαθοὶ ἄνδρες. λέγει δέ που καὶ Ἡσίοδος·

Τὴν μὲν γὰρ κακότητα καὶ ἰλαδὸν ἔστιν
ἑλέσθαι
ῥηιδίως· λείη μὲν ὁδός, μάλα δ' ἐγγύθι ναίει.
τῆς δ' ἀρετῆς ἱδρῶτα θεοὶ προπάροιθεν ἔθηκαν
ἀθάνατοι· μακρὸς δὲ καὶ ὄρθιος οἶμος ἐς αὐτὴν
καὶ τρηχὺς τὸ πρῶτον· ἐπὴν δ' εἰς ἄκρον ἵκηαι,
ῥηιδίη δὴ ἔπειτα πέλει, χαλεπή περ ἐοῦσα.

"What, Aristippus," exclaimed Socrates, "don't 18 you think that there is just this difference between these voluntary and involuntary sufferings, that if you bear hunger or thirst willingly, you can eat, drink, or what not, when you choose, whereas compulsory suffering is not to be ended at will? Besides, he who endures willingly enjoys his work because he is comforted by hope; hunters, for instance, toil gladly in hope of game. Rewards like these are 19 indeed of little worth after all the toil; but what of those who toil to win good friends, or to subdue enemies, or to make themselves capable in body and soul of managing their own homes well, of helping their friends and serving their country? Surely these toil gladly for such prizes and live a joyous life, well content with themselves, praised and envied by everyone else? Moreover, indolence and present 20 enjoyment can never bring the body into good condition, as trainers say, neither do they put into the soul knowledge of any value, but strenuous effort leads up to good and noble deeds, as good men say. And so says Hesiod somewhere: [1]

'Wickedness can be had in abundance easily: smooth is the road and very nigh she dwells. But in front of virtue the gods immortal have put sweat: long and steep is the path to her and rough at first; but when you reach the top, then at length the road is easy, hard though it was.'

[1] *Works and Days*, 285.

μαρτυρεῖ δὲ καὶ Ἐπίχαρμος ἐν τῷδε·

Τῶν πόνων πωλοῦσιν ἡμῖν πάντα τἀγάθ᾽ οἱ θεοί.

καὶ ἐν ἄλλῳ δὲ τόπῳ φησίν·

Ὦ πονηρέ, μὴ τὰ μαλακὰ μῶσο, μὴ τὰ σκλήρ᾽ ἔχῃς.[1]

21 Καὶ Πρόδικος δὲ ὁ σοφὸς ἐν τῷ συγγράμματι τῷ περὶ Ἡρακλέους, ὅπερ δὴ καὶ πλείστοις ἐπιδείκνυται, ὡσαύτως περὶ τῆς ἀρετῆς ἀποφαίνεται, ὧδέ πως λέγων, ὅσα ἐγὼ μέμνημαι.

Φησὶ γὰρ Ἡρακλέα, ἐπεὶ ἐκ παίδων εἰς ἥβην ὡρμᾶτο, ἐν ᾗ οἱ νέοι ἤδη αὐτοκράτορες γιγνόμενοι δηλοῦσιν, εἴτε τὴν δι᾽ ἀρετῆς ὁδὸν τρέψονται ἐπὶ τὸν βίον εἴτε τὴν διὰ κακίας, ἐξελθόντα εἰς ἡσυχίαν καθῆσθαι ἀποροῦντα, ποτέραν τῶν ὁδῶν τράπηται·
22 καὶ φανῆναι αὐτῷ δύο γυναῖκας προσιέναι μεγάλας, τὴν μὲν ἑτέραν εὐπρεπῆ τε ἰδεῖν καὶ ἐλευθέριον φύσει, κεκοσμημένην τὸ μὲν σῶμα καθαρότητι, τὰ δὲ ὄμματα αἰδοῖ, τὸ δὲ σχῆμα σωφροσύνῃ, ἐσθῆτι δὲ λευκῇ, τὴν δ᾽ ἑτέραν τεθραμμένην μὲν εἰς πολυσαρκίαν τε καὶ ἁπαλότητα, κεκαλλωπισμένην δὲ τὸ μὲν χρῶμα, ὥστε λευκοτέραν τε καὶ ἐρυθροτέραν τοῦ ὄντος δοκεῖν φαίνεσθαι, τὸ δὲ σχῆμα, ὥστε δοκεῖν ὀρθοτέραν τῆς φύσεως εἶναι, τὰ δὲ ὄμματα ἔχειν ἀναπεπταμένα, ἐσθῆτα δέ, ἐξ ἧς ἂν μάλιστα ὥρα διαλάμποι, κατασκοπεῖσθαι δὲ θαμὰ ἑαυτήν, ἐπισκοπεῖν δὲ καὶ εἴ τις ἄλλος αὐτὴν θεᾶται, πολλάκις δὲ καὶ εἰς τὴν ἑαυτῆς
23 σκιὰν ἀποβλέπειν. Ὡς δ᾽ ἐγένοντο πλησιαίτερον τοῦ Ἡρακλέους, τὴν μὲν πρόσθεν ῥηθεῖσαν

"And we have the testimony of Epicharmus too in the line:

'The gods demand of us toil as the price of all good things.'

"And elsewhere he says:

'Knave, yearn not for the soft things, lest thou earn the hard.'

"Aye, and Prodicus the wise expresses himself 21 to the like effect concerning Virtue in the essay 'On Heracles' that he recites to throngs of listeners. This, so far as I remember, is how he puts it:

"When Heracles was passing from boyhood to youth's estate, wherein the young, now becoming their own masters, show whether they will approach life by the path of virtue or the path of vice, he went out into a quiet place, and sat pondering 22 which road to take. And there appeared two women of great stature making towards him. The one was fair to see and of high bearing; and her limbs were adorned with purity, her eyes with modesty; sober was her figure, and her robe was white. The other was plump and soft, with high feeding. Her face was made up to heighten its natural white and pink, her figure to exaggerate her height. Open-eyed was she; and dressed so as to disclose all her charms. Now she eyed herself; anon looked whether any noticed her; and often stole a glance at her own shadow.

"When they drew nigh to Heracles, the first 23

---

[1] καὶ ἐν ἄλλῳ . . . ἔχῃς is bracketed by Sauppe as spurious.

ἰέναι τὸν αὐτὸν τρόπον, τὴν δ' ἑτέραν φθάσαι
βουλομένην προσδραμεῖν τῷ Ἡρακλεῖ καὶ εἰπεῖν·
Ὁρῶ σε, ὦ Ἡράκλεις, ἀποροῦντα, ποίαν ὁδὸν
ἐπὶ τὸν βίον τράπῃ. ἐὰν οὖν ἐμὲ φίλην ποιησά-
μενος, ἐπὶ[1] τὴν ἡδίστην τε καὶ ῥᾴστην ὁδὸν ἄξω
σε καὶ τῶν μὲν τερπνῶν οὐδενὸς ἄγευστος ἔσῃ,
24 τῶν δὲ χαλεπῶν ἄπειρος διαβιώσῃ. πρῶτον μὲν
γὰρ οὐ πολέμων οὐδὲ πραγμάτων φροντιεῖς, ἀλλὰ
σκοπούμενος διέσῃ,[2] τί ἂν κεχαρισμένον ἢ σιτίον
ἢ ποτὸν εὕροις ἢ τί ἂν ἰδὼν ἢ τί ἀκούσας τερ-
φθείης ἢ τίνων ἂν ὀσφραινόμενος ἢ ἁπτόμενος
ἡσθείης, τίσι δὲ παιδικοῖς ὁμιλῶν μάλιστ' ἂν
εὐφρανθείης, καὶ πῶς ἂν μαλακώτατα καθεύδοις
καὶ πῶς ἂν ἀπονώτατα τούτων πάντων τυγχά-
25 νοις. ἐὰν δέ ποτε γένηταί τις ὑποψία σπάνεως
ἀφ' ὧν ἔσται ταῦτα, οὐ φόβος, μή σε ἀγάγω ἐπὶ
τὸ πονοῦντα καὶ ταλαιπωροῦντα τῷ σώματι καὶ
τῇ ψυχῇ ταῦτα πορίζεσθαι, ἀλλ' οἷς ἂν οἱ ἄλλοι
ἐργάζωνται, τούτοις σὺ χρήσῃ, οὐδενὸς ἀπεχόμενος ὅθεν ἂν δυνατὸν ᾖ τι κερδᾶναι. πανταχόθεν γὰρ ὠφελεῖσθαι τοῖς ἐμοὶ συνοῦσιν ἐξουσίαν
ἐγὼ παρέχω.
26 Καὶ ὁ Ἡρακλῆς ἀκούσας ταῦτα, Ὦ γύναι, ἔφη,
ὄνομα δέ σοι τί ἐστιν; ἡ δέ, Οἱ μὲν ἐμοὶ φίλοι,
ἔφη, καλοῦσί με Εὐδαιμονίαν, οἱ δὲ μισοῦντές με
ὑποκοριζόμενοι ὀνομάζουσι Κακίαν.
27 Καὶ ἐν τούτῳ ἡ ἑτέρα γυνὴ προσελθοῦσα εἶπε·
Καὶ ἐγὼ ἥκω πρὸς σέ, ὦ Ἡράκλεις, εἰδυῖα τοὺς
γεννήσαντάς σε καὶ τὴν φύσιν τὴν σὴν ἐν τῇ
παιδείᾳ καταμαθοῦσα· ἐξ ὧν ἐλπίζω, εἰ τὴν πρὸς
ἐμὲ ὁδὸν τράποιο, σφόδρ' ἄν σε τῶν καλῶν καὶ
σεμνῶν ἐργάτην ἀγαθὸν γενέσθαι καὶ ἐμὲ ἔτι

pursued the even tenor of her way: but the other, all eager to outdo her, ran to meet him, crying: ' Heracles, I see that you are in doubt which path to take towards life. Make me your friend; follow me, and I will lead you along the pleasantest and easiest road. You shall taste all the sweets of life; and hardship you shall never know. First, of wars 24 and worries you shall not think, but shall ever be considering what choice food or drink you can find, what sight or sound will delight you, what touch or perfume; what tender love can give you most joy, what bed the softest slumbers; and how to come by all these pleasures with least trouble. And should 25 there arise misgiving that lack of means may stint your enjoyments, never fear that I may lead you into winning them by toil and anguish of body and soul. Nay; you shall have the fruits of others' toil, and refrain from nothing that can bring you gain. For to my companions I give authority to pluck advantage where they will.'

" Now when Heracles heard this, he asked, ' Lady, 26 pray what is your name?'

" ' My friends call me Happiness,' she said, ' but among those that hate me I am nicknamed Vice.'

" Meantime the other had drawn near, and she 27 said: ' I, too, am come to you, Heracles: I know your parents and I have taken note of your character during the time of your education. Therefore I hope that, if you take the road that leads to me, you will turn out a right good doer of high and noble

---

[1] Sauppe reads ἐπὶ τὴν ἡδίστην with the MSS.; ἐπὶ was removed by Hirschig.

[2] διέσῃ is wrong, but cannot be corrected with certainty.

πολὺ ἐντιμοτέραν καὶ ἐπ᾽ ἀγαθοῖς διαπρεπεστέ-
ραν φανῆναι. οὐκ ἐξαπατήσω δέ σε προοιμίοις
ἡδονῆς, ἀλλ᾽ ᾗπερ οἱ θεοὶ διέθεσαν τὰ ὄντα διηγή-
28 σομαι μετ᾽ ἀληθείας. τῶν γὰρ ὄντων ἀγαθῶν
καὶ καλῶν οὐδὲν ἄνευ πόνου καὶ ἐπιμελείας θεοὶ
διδόασιν ἀνθρώποις, ἀλλ᾽ εἴτε τοὺς θεοὺς ἵλεως
εἶναί σοι βούλει, θεραπευτέον τοὺς θεούς, εἴτε
ὑπὸ φίλων ἐθέλεις ἀγαπᾶσθαι, τοὺς φίλους εὐερ-
γετητέον, εἴτε ὑπό τινος πόλεως ἐπιθυμεῖς τιμᾶσθαι, τὴν πόλιν ὠφελητέον, εἴτε ὑπὸ τῆς Ἑλλά-
δος πάσης ἀξιοῖς ἐπ᾽ ἀρετῇ θαυμάζεσθαι, τὴν
Ἑλλάδα πειρατέον εὖ ποιεῖν, εἴτε γῆν βούλει σοι
καρποὺς ἀφθόνους φέρειν, τὴν γῆν θεραπευτέον,
εἴτε ἀπὸ βοσκημάτων οἴει δεῖν πλουτίζεσθαι, τῶν
βοσκημάτων ἐπιμελητέον, εἴτε διὰ πολέμου ὁρμᾷς
αὔξεσθαι καὶ βούλει δύνασθαι τούς τε φίλους
ἐλευθεροῦν καὶ τοὺς ἐχθροὺς χειροῦσθαι, τὰς
πολεμικὰς τέχνας αὐτάς τε παρὰ τῶν ἐπισταμένων μαθητέον καὶ ὅπως αὐταῖς δεῖ χρῆσθαι
ἀσκητέον· εἰ δὲ καὶ τῷ σώματι βούλει δυνατὸς
εἶναι, τῇ γνώμῃ ὑπηρετεῖν ἐθιστέον τὸ σῶμα καὶ
γυμναστέον σὺν πόνοις καὶ ἱδρῶτι.

29 Καὶ ἡ Κακία ὑπολαβοῦσι εἶπεν, ὥς φησι Πρό-
δικος· Ἐννοεῖς, ὦ Ἡράκλεις, ὡς χαλεπὴν καὶ
μακρὰν ὁδὸν ἐπὶ τὰς εὐφροσύνας ἡ γυνή σοι αὕτη
διηγεῖται ; ἐγὼ δὲ ῥᾳδίαν καὶ βραχεῖαν ὁδὸν ἐπὶ
30 τὴν εὐδαιμονίαν ἄξω σε. καὶ ἡ Ἀρετὴ εἶπεν· Ὦ
τλῆμον, τί δὲ σὺ ἀγαθὸν ἔχεις ; ἢ τί ἡδὺ οἶσθα
μηδὲν τούτων ἕνεκα πράττειν ἐθέλουσα ; ἥτις
οὐδὲ τὴν τῶν ἡδέων ἐπιθυμίαν ἀναμένεις, ἀλλὰ
πρὶν ἐπιθυμῆσαι πάντων ἐμπίπλασαι, πρὶν μὲν
πεινῆν ἐσθίουσα, πρὶν δὲ διψῆν πίνουσα, καὶ ἵνα

deeds, and I shall be yet more highly honoured and more illustrious for the blessings I bestow. But I will not deceive you by a pleasant prelude: I will rather tell you truly the things that are, as the gods have ordained them. For of all things good and fair, 28 the gods give nothing to man without toil and effort. If you want the favour of the gods, you must worship the gods: if you desire the love of friends, you must do good to your friends: if you covet honour from a city, you must aid that city: if you are fain to win the admiration of all Hellas for virtue, you must strive to do good to Hellas: if you want land to yield you fruits in abundance, you must cultivate that land: if you are resolved to get wealth from flocks, you must care for those flocks: if you essay to grow great through war and want power to liberate your friends and subdue your foes, you must learn the arts of war from those who know them and must practise their right use: and if you want your body to be strong, you must accustom your body to be the servant of your mind, and train it with toil and sweat.'

"And Vice, as Prodicus tells, answered and said: 29 'Heracles, mark you how hard and long is that road to joy, of which this woman tells? but I will lead you by a short and easy road to happiness.'

"And Virtue said: 'What good thing is thine, 30 poor wretch, or what pleasant thing dost thou know, if thou wilt do nought to win them? Thou dost not even tarry for the desire of pleasant things, but fillest thyself with all things before thou desirest them, eating before thou art hungry, drinking before

XENOPHON

μὲν ἡδέως φάγῃς, ὀψοποιοὺς μηχανωμένη, ἵνα δὲ
ἡδέως πίῃς, οἴνους τε πολυτελεῖς παρασκευάζῃ
καὶ τοῦ θέρους χιόνα περιθέουσα ζητεῖς, ἵνα δὲ
καθυπνώσῃς ἡδέως, οὐ μόνον τὰς στρωμνὰς μαλακάς, ἀλλὰ¹ καὶ τὰ ὑπόβαθρα ταῖς κλίναις
παρασκευάζῃ· οὐ γὰρ διὰ τὸ πονεῖν, ἀλλὰ διὰ τὸ
μηδὲν ἔχειν ὅ,τι ποιῇς ὕπνου ἐπιθυμεῖς. τὰ δ᾽
ἀφροδίσια πρὸ τοῦ δεῖσθαι ἀναγκάζεις, πάντα
μηχανωμένη καὶ γυναιξὶ τοῖς ἀνδράσι χρωμένη·
οὕτω γὰρ παιδεύεις τοὺς σεαυτῆς φίλους, τῆς μὲν
νυκτὸς ὑβρίζουσα, τῆς δ᾽ ἡμέρας τὸ χρησιμώτα-
31 τον κατακοιμίζουσα. ἀθάνατος δὲ οὖσα ἐκ θεῶν
μὲν ἀπέρριψαι, ὑπὸ δὲ ἀνθρώπων ἀγαθῶν ἀτι-
μάζῃ· τοῦ δὲ πάντων ἡδίστου ἀκούσματος, ἐπαίνου ἑαυτῆς, ἀνήκοος εἶ καὶ τοῦ πάντων ἡδίστου
θεάματος ἀθέατος· οὐδὲν γὰρ πώποτε σεαυτῆς
ἔργον καλὸν τεθέασαι. τίς δ᾽ ἄν σοι λεγούσῃ τι
πιστεύσειε; τίς δ᾽ ἂν δεομένῃ τινὸς ἐπαρκέσειεν;
ἢ τίς ἂν εὖ φρονῶν τοῦ σοῦ θιάσου τολμήσειεν
εἶναι; οἳ νέοι μὲν ὄντες τοῖς σώμασιν ἀδύνατοί
εἰσι, πρεσβύτεροι τὲ γενόμενοι ταῖς ψυχαῖς ἀνό-
ητοι, ἀπόνως μὲν λιπαροὶ διὰ νεότητος τρεφόμενοι, ἐπιπόνως δὲ αὐχμηροὶ διὰ γήρως περῶντες,
τοῖς μὲν πεπραγμένοις αἰσχυνόμενοι, τοῖς δὲ πρατ-
τομένοις βαρυνόμενοι, τὰ μὲν ἡδέα ἐν τῇ νεότητι
διαδραμόντες, τὰ δὲ χαλεπὰ εἰς τὸ γῆρας ἀποθέ-
32 μενοι. ἐγὼ δὲ σύνειμι μὲν θεοῖς, σύνειμι δὲ
ἀνθρώποις τοῖς ἀγαθοῖς· ἔργον δὲ καλὸν οὔτε
θεῖον οὔτ᾽ ἀνθρώπινον χωρὶς ἐμοῦ γίγνεται. τιμῶμαι δὲ μάλιστα πάντων καὶ παρὰ θεοῖς καὶ
παρ᾽ ἀνθρώποις οἷς προσήκει, ἀγαπητὴ μὲν συνερ-
γὸς τεχνίταις, πιστὴ δὲ φύλαξ οἴκων δεσπόταις,

100

thou art thirsty, getting thee cooks, to give zest to eating, buying thee costly wines and running to and fro in search of snow in summer, to give zest to drinking; to soothe thy slumbers it is not enough for thee to buy soft coverlets, but thou must have frames for thy beds.¹ For not toil, but the tedium of having nothing to do, makes thee long for sleep. Thou dost rouse lust by many a trick, when there is no need, using men as women: thus thou trainest thy friends, waxing wanton by night, consuming in sleep the best hours of day. Immortal art thou, 31 yet the outcast of the gods, the scorn of good men. Praise, sweetest of all things to hear, thou hearest not: the sweetest of all sights thou beholdest not, for never yet hast thou beheld a good work wrought by thyself. Who will believe what thou dost say? who will grant what thou dost ask? Or what sane man will dare join thy throng? While thy votaries are young their bodies are weak, when they wax old, their souls are without sense; idle and sleek they thrive in youth, withered and weary they journey through old age, and their past deeds bring them shame, their present deeds distress. Pleasure they ran through in their youth: hardship they laid up for their old age. But I company with gods and 32 good men, and no fair deed of god or man is done without my aid. I am first in honour among the gods and among men that are akin to me: to craftsmen a beloved fellow-worker, to masters a faithful

---

¹ Sauppe read καὶ τὰς κλίνας καὶ with the MSS.

XENOPHON

εὐμενὴς δὲ παραστάτις οἰκέταις, ἀγαθὴ δὲ συλ-
λήπτρια τῶν ἐν εἰρήνῃ πόνων, βεβαία δὲ τῶν ἐν
πολέμῳ σύμμαχος ἔργων, ἀρίστη δὲ φιλίας κοι-
33 νωνός. ἔστι δὲ τοῖς μὲν ἐμοῖς φίλοις ἡδεῖα μὲν
καὶ ἀπράγμων σίτων καὶ ποτῶν ἀπόλαυσις· ἀνέ-
χονται γάρ, ἕως ἂν ἐπιθυμήσωσιν αὐτῶν. ὕπνος
δ᾽ αὐτοῖς πάρεστιν ἡδίων ἢ τοῖς ἀμόχθοις καὶ
οὔτε ἀπολείποντες αὐτὸν ἄχθονται οὔτε διὰ τοῦτον μεθιᾶσι τὰ δέοντα πράττειν. καὶ οἱ μὲν νέοι
τοῖς τῶν πρεσβυτέρων ἐπαίνοις χαίρουσιν, οἱ δὲ
γεραίτεροι ταῖς τῶν νέων τιμαῖς ἀγάλλονται καὶ
ἡδέως μὲν τῶν παλαιῶν πράξεων μέμνηνται, εὖ
δὲ τὰς παρούσας ἥδονται πράττοντες, δι᾽ ἐμὲ
φίλοι μὲν θεοῖς ὄντες, ἀγαπητοὶ δὲ φίλοις, τίμιοι
δὲ πατρίσιν. ὅταν δ᾽ ἔλθῃ τὸ πεπρωμένον τέλος,
οὐ μετὰ λήθης ἄτιμοι κεῖνται, ἀλλὰ μετὰ μνήμης
τὸν ἀεὶ χρόνον ὑμνούμενοι θάλλουσι. τοιαῦτά
σοι, ὦ παῖ τοκέων ἀγαθῶν Ἡράκλεις, ἔξεστι δια-
πονησαμένῳ τὴν μακαριστοτάτην εὐδαιμονίαν
34 κεκτῆσθαι.

Οὕτω πως διώκει Πρόδικος τὴν ὑπ᾽ Ἀρετῆς
Ἡρακλέους παίδευσιν, ἐκόσμησε μέντοι τὰς
γνώμας ἔτι μεγαλειοτέροις ῥήμασιν ἢ ἐγὼ νῦν.
σοὶ δ᾽ οὖν ἄξιον, ὦ Ἀρίστιππε, τούτων ἐνθυμου-
μένῳ πειρᾶσθαί τι καὶ τῶν εἰς τὸν μέλλοντα
χρόνον τοῦ βίου φροντίζειν.

II. Αἰσθόμενος δέ ποτε Λαμπροκλέα, τὸν πρεσ-
βύτατον υἱὸν αὐτοῦ, πρὸς τὴν μητέρα χαλεπαί-
νοντα, Εἰπέ μοι, ἔφη, ὦ παῖ, οἶσθά τινας ἀνθρώπους ἀχαρίστους καλουμένους;

Καὶ μάλα, ἔφη ὁ νεανίσκος.

guardian of the house, to servants a kindly protector : good helpmate in the toils of peace, staunch ally in the deeds of war, best partner in friendship. To my friends meat and drink bring sweet and simple enjoyment : for they wait till they crave them. And a sweeter sleep falls on them than on idle folk : they are not vexed at awaking from it, nor for its sake do they neglect to do their duties. The young rejoice to win the praise of the old ; the elders are glad to be honoured by the young ; with joy they recall their deeds past, and their present well-doing is joy to them, for through me they are dear to the gods, lovely to friends, precious to their native land. And when comes the appointed end, they lie not forgotten and dishonoured, but live on, sung and remembered for all time. O Heracles, thou son of goodly parents, if thou wilt labour earnestly on this wise, thou mayest have for thine own the most blessed happiness.'

"Such, in outline, is Prodicus' story of the training of Heracles by Virtue ; only he has clothed the thoughts in even finer phrases than I have done now. But anyhow, Aristippus, it were well that you should think on these things and try to show some regard for the life that lies before you."

II. On noticing that his eldest son, Lamprocles, was out of humour with his mother, he said : "Tell me, my boy, do you know that some men are called ungrateful ? "

"Indeed I do," replied the young man.

XENOPHON

Καταμεμάθηκας οὖν, τοὺς τί ποιοῦντας τὸ ὄνομα τοῦτο ἀποκαλοῦσιν ;

Ἔγωγ᾽, ἔφη· τοὺς γὰρ εὖ παθόντας, ὅταν δυνάμενοι χάριν ἀποδοῦναι μὴ ἀποδῶσιν, ἀχαρίστους καλοῦσιν.

Οὐκοῦν δοκοῦσί σοι ἐν τοῖς ἀδίκοις καταλογίζεσθαι τοὺς ἀχαρίστους ;

Ἔμοιγε, ἔφη.

2 Ἤδη δέ ποτ᾽ ἐσκέψω, εἰ ἄρα ὥσπερ τὸ ἀνδραποδίζεσθαι τοὺς μὲν φίλους ἄδικον εἶναι δοκεῖ, τοὺς δὲ πολεμίους δίκαιον, καὶ τὸ ἀχαριστεῖν πρὸς μὲν τοὺς φίλους ἄδικόν ἐστι, πρὸς δὲ τοὺς πολεμίους δίκαιον ;

Καὶ μάλα, ἔφη· καὶ δοκεῖ μοι, ὑφ᾽ οὗ ἄν τις εὖ παθὼν εἴτε φίλου εἴτε πολεμίου μὴ πειρᾶται χάριν ἀποδιδόναι, ἄδικος εἶναι.

3 Οὐκοῦν εἴ γ᾽ οὕτως ἔχει τοῦτο, εἰλικρινής τις ἂν εἴη ἀδικία ἡ ἀχαριστία ; συνωμολόγει.

Οὐκοῦν ὅσῳ ἄν τις μείζω ἀγαθὰ παθὼν μὴ ἀποδιδῷ χάριν, τοσούτῳ ἀδικώτερος ἂν εἴη ; συνέφη καὶ τοῦτο.

Τίνας οὖν, ἔφη, ὑπὸ τίνων εὕροιμεν ἂν μείζω εὐεργετημένους ἢ παῖδας ὑπὸ γονέων ; οὓς οἱ γονεῖς ἐκ μὲν οὐκ ὄντων ἐποίησαν εἶναι, τοσαῦτα δὲ καλὰ ἰδεῖν καὶ τοσούτων ἀγαθῶν μετασχεῖν, ὅσα οἱ θεοὶ παρέχουσι τοῖς ἀνθρώποις· ἃ δὴ καὶ οὕτως ἡμῖν δοκεῖ παντὸς ἄξια εἶναι, ὥστε πάντες τὸ καταλιπεῖν αὐτὰ πάντων μάλιστα φεύγομεν· καὶ αἱ πόλεις ἐπὶ τοῖς μεγίστοις ἀδικήμασι ζημίαν θάνατον πεποιήκασιν, ὡς οὐκ ἂν μείζονος κακοῦ 4 φόβῳ τὴν ἀδικίαν παύσαντες. καὶ μὴν οὐ τῶν γε ᾽φροδισίων ἕνεκα παιδοποιεῖσθαι τοὺς ἀνθρώ-

" Do you realise how they come to have this bad name ? "

" I do ; the word is used of those who do not show the gratitude that it is in their power to show for benefits received."

" You take it, then, that the ungrateful are reckoned among the unjust ? "

" Yes."

" Now, seeing that enslavement is considered a 2 just or an unjust act according as the victims are friends or enemies, have you ever considered whether the case of ingratitude is analogous, ingratitude being unjust towards friends, but just towards enemies ? "

" Indeed I have ; and I think that it is always unjust not to show gratitude for a favour from whomsoever it is received, be he friend or enemy."

" If that is so, must not ingratitude be injustice 3 pure and simple ? "

He assented.

" Therefore the greater the benefits received the greater the injustice of not showing gratitude ? "

He agreed again.

" Now what deeper obligation can we find than that of children to their parents ? To their parents children owe their being and their portion of all fair sights and all blessings that the gods bestow on men —gifts so highly prized by us that all will sacrifice anything rather than lose them ; and the reason why governments have made death the penalty for the greatest crimes is that the fear of it is the strongest deterrent against crime. Of course you 4 don't suppose that lust provokes men to beget

πους ὑπολαμβάνεις, ἐπεὶ τούτου γε τῶν ἀπολυσόντων μεσταὶ μὲν αἱ ὁδοί, μεστὰ δὲ τὰ οἰκήματα.
φανεροὶ δ' ἐσμὲν καὶ σκοπούμενοι, ἐξ ὁποίων ἂν
γυναικῶν βέλτιστα ἡμῖν τέκνα γένοιτο, αἷς συνελ-
5 θόντες τεκνοποιούμεθα. καὶ ὁ μέν γε ἀνὴρ τήν
τε συντεκνοποιήσουσαν ἑαυτῷ τρέφει καὶ τοῖς
μέλλουσιν ἔσεσθαι παισὶ προπαρασκευάζει πάντα,
ὅσα ἂν οἴηται συνοίσειν αὐτοῖς πρὸς τὸν βίον, καὶ
ταῦτα ὡς ἂν δύνηται πλεῖστα· ἡ δὲ γυνὴ ὑποδε-
ξαμένη τε φέρει τὸ φορτίον τοῦτο βαρυνομένη τε
καὶ κινδυνεύουσα περὶ τοῦ βίου καὶ μεταδιδοῦσα
τῆς τροφῆς, ᾗ καὶ αὐτὴ τρέφεται, καὶ σὺν πολλῷ
πόνῳ διενεγκοῦσα καὶ τεκοῦσα τρέφει τε καὶ ἐπιμελεῖται, οὔτε προπεπονθυῖα οὐδὲν ἀγαθὸν οὔτε
γιγνῶσκον τὸ βρέφος, ὑφ' ὅτου εὖ πάσχει οὐδὲ
σημαίνειν δυνάμενον, ὅτου δεῖται, ἀλλ' αὐτὴ
στοχαζομένη τά τε συμφέροντα καὶ τὰ κεχαρισμένα πειρᾶται ἐκπληροῦν καὶ τρέφει πολὺν
χρόνον καὶ ἡμέρας καὶ νυκτὸς ὑπομένουσα πονεῖν, οὐκ εἰδυῖα, τίνα τούτων χάριν ἀπολήψεται.
6 καὶ οὐκ ἀρκεῖ θρέψαι μόνον, ἀλλὰ καὶ ἐπειδὰν
δόξωσιν ἱκανοὶ εἶναι οἱ παῖδες μανθάνειν τι, ἃ
μὲν ἂν αὐτοὶ ἔχωσιν οἱ γονεῖς ἀγαθὰ πρὸς
τὸν βίον διδάσκουσιν, ἃ δ' ἂν οἴωνται ἄλλον
ἱκανώτερον εἶναι διδάξαι, πέμπουσι πρὸς τοῦτον
δαπανῶντες καὶ ἐπιμελοῦνται πάντα ποιοῦντες,
ὅπως οἱ παῖδες αὐτοῖς γένωνται ὡς δυνατὸν
βέλτιστοι.
7   Πρὸς ταῦτα ὁ νεανίσκος εἶπεν· Ἀλλά τοι εἰ καὶ
πάντα ταῦτα πεποίηκε καὶ ἄλλα τούτων πολλα-
πλάσια, οὐδεὶς ἂν δύναιτο αὐτῆς ἀνασχέσθαι τὴν
χαλεπότητα.

children, when the streets and the stews are full of means to satisfy that? We obviously select for wives the women who will bear us the best children, and then marry them to raise a family. The man 5 supports the woman who is to share with him the duty of parentage and provides for the expected children whatever he thinks will contribute to their benefit in life, and accumulates as much of it as he can. The woman conceives and bears her burden in travail, risking her life, and giving of her own food; and, with much labour, having endured to the end and brought forth her child, she rears and cares for it, although she has not received any good thing, and the babe neither recognises its benefactress nor can make its wants known to her: still she guesses what is good for it and what it likes, and seeks to supply these things, and rears it for a long season, enduring toil day and night, nothing knowing what return she will get.

" Nor are the parents content just to supply food, 6 but so soon as their children seem capable of learning they teach them what they can for their good, and if they think that another is more competent to teach them anything, they send them to him at a cost, and strive their utmost that the children may turn out as well as possible."

To this the young man replied: " Nay, but even 7 if she has done all this and far more than this, no one could put up with her vile temper."

XENOPHON

Καὶ ὁ Σωκράτης, Πότερα δέ, ἔφη, οἴει θηρίου ἀγριότητα δυσφορωτέραν εἶναι ἢ μητρός ;

Ἐγὼ μὲν οἶμαι, ἔφη, μητρὸς τῆς γε τοιαύτης.

Ἤδη πώποτε οὖν ἢ δακοῦσα κακόν τί σοι ἔδωκεν ἢ λακτίσασα, οἶα ὑπὸ θηρίων ἤδη πολλοὶ ἔπαθον ;

8 Ἀλλὰ νὴ Δί’, ἔφη, λέγει ἃ οὐκ ἄν τις ἐπὶ τῷ βίῳ παντὶ βούλοιτο ἀκοῦσαι.

Σὺ δὲ πόσα, ἔφη ὁ Σωκράτης, οἴει ταύτῃ [δυσάνεκτα] καὶ τῇ φωνῇ καὶ τοῖς ἔργοις ἐκ παιδίου δυσκολαίνων καὶ ἡμέρας καὶ νυκτὸς πράγματα παρασχεῖν, πόσα δὲ λυπῆσαι κάμνων;

Ἀλλ’ οὐδεπώποτε αὐτήν, ἔφη, οὔτ’ εἶπα οὔτ’ ἐποίησα οὐδέν, ἐφ’ ᾧ ᾐσχύνθη.

9 Τί δέ ; οἴει, ἔφη, χαλεπώτερον εἶναί σοι ἀκούειν ὧν αὕτη λέγει ἢ τοῖς ὑποκριταῖς, ὅταν ἐν ταῖς τραγῳδίαις ἀλλήλους τὰ ἔσχατα λέγωσιν ;

Ἀλλ’, οἶμαι, ἐπειδὴ οὐκ οἴονται τῶν λεγόντων οὔτε τὸν ἐλέγχοντα ἐλέγχειν, ἵνα ζημιώσῃ, οὔτε τὸν ἀπειλοῦντα ἀπειλεῖν, ἵνα κακόν τι ποιήσῃ, ῥᾳδίως φέρουσι.

Σὺ δ’ εὖ εἰδώς, ὅτι ἃ λέγει σοι ἡ μήτηρ, οὐ μόνον οὐδὲν κακὸν νοοῦσα λέγει, ἀλλὰ καὶ βουλομένη σοι ἀγαθὰ εἶναι ὅσα οὐδενὶ ἄλλῳ, χαλεπαίνεις ; ἢ νομίζεις κακόνουν τὴν μητέρα σοι εἶναι ;

Οὐ δῆτα, ἔφη, τοῦτό γε οὐκ οἶμαι.

10 Καὶ ὁ Σωκράτης, Οὐκοῦν, ἔφη, σὺ ταύτην, εὔνουν τέ σοι οὖσαν καὶ ἐπιμελομένην ὡς μάλιστα δύναται κάμνοντος, ὅπως ὑγιανεῖς τε καὶ ὅπως τῶν ἐπιτηδείων μηδενὸς ἐνδεὴς ἔσῃ, καὶ πρὸς τούτοις πολλὰ τοῖς θεοῖς εὐχομένην ἀγαθὰ ὑπὲρ σοῦ

"Which, think you," asked Socrates, "is the harder to bear, a wild beast's brutality or a mother's?"

"I should say a mother's, when she is like mine."

"Well now, many people get bitten or kicked by wild beasts; has she ever done you an injury of that sort?"

"Oh no, but she says things one wouldn't listen 8 to for anything in the world."

"Well, how much trouble do you think you have given her by your peevish words and froward acts day and night since you were a little child; and how much pain when you were ill?"

"But I have never yet said or done anything to cause her shame."

"Now do you really think it harder for you to 9 listen to what she says than for actors when they abuse one another in a tragedy?"

"But an actor, I suppose, doesn't think that a question put to him will lead to punishment, or that a threat means any harm: and so he makes light of it."

"And why should you be annoyed? You know well that there is no malice in what your mother says to you; on the contrary, she wishes you to be blessed above all other beings—unless, indeed, you suppose that your mother is maliciously set against you?"

"Oh no, I don't think that."

Then Socrates exclaimed: "So this mother of 10 yours is kindly disposed towards you; she nurses you devotedly in sickness and sees that you want for nothing; more than that, she prays the gods to

καὶ εὐχὰς ἀποδιδοῦσαν, χαλεπὴν εἶναι φῄς ; ἐγὼ
μὲν οἶμαι, εἰ τοιαύτην μὴ δύνασαι φέρειν μητέρα,
11 τἀγαθά σε οὐ δύνασθαι φέρειν. εἰπὲ δέ μοι, ἔφη,
πότερον ἄλλον τινὰ οἴει δεῖν θεραπεύειν ; ἢ παρεσκεύασαι μηδενὶ ἀνθρώπων πειρᾶσθαι ἀρέσκειν
μηδὲ πείθεσθαι μήτε στρατηγῷ μήτε ἄλλῳ
ἄρχοντι ;

Ναὶ μὰ Δί᾽ ἔγωγε, ἔφη.

12 Οὐκοῦν, ἔφη ὁ Σωκράτης, καὶ τῷ γείτονι βούλει
σὺ ἀρέσκειν, ἵνα σοι καὶ πῦρ ἐναύῃ, ὅταν τούτου
δέῃ, καὶ ἀγαθοῦ τέ σοι γίγνηται συλλήπτωρ καί,
ἄν τι σφαλλόμενος τύχῃς, εὐνοϊκῶς ἐγγύθεν
βοηθῇ σοι ;

Ἔγωγε, ἔφη.

Τί δέ ; συνοδοιπόρον ἢ σύμπλουν ἢ εἴ τῳ ἄλλῳ
ἐντυγχάνοις, οὐδὲν ἄν σοι διαφέροι φίλον ἢ
ἐχθρὸν γενέσθαι ἢ καὶ τῆς παρὰ τούτων εὐνοίας
οἴει δεῖν ἐπιμελεῖσθαι ;

Ἔγωγε, ἔφη.

13 Εἶτα τούτων μὲν ἐπιμελεῖσθαι παρεσκεύασαι,
τὴν δὲ μητέρα τὴν πάντων μάλιστά σε φιλοῦσαν
οὐκ οἴει δεῖν θεραπεύειν ; οὐκ οἶσθ᾽, ὅτι καὶ ἡ
πόλις ἄλλης μὲν ἀχαριστίας οὐδεμιᾶς ἐπιμελεῖται οὐδὲ δικάζει, ἀλλὰ περιορᾷ τοὺς εὖ πεπον-
θότας χάριν οὐκ ἀποδιδόντας, ἐὰν δέ τις γονέας
μὴ θεραπεύῃ, τούτῳ δίκην τε ἐπιτίθησι καὶ
ἀποδοκιμάζουσα οὐκ ἐᾷ ἄρχειν τοῦτον, ὡς οὔτε
ἂν τὰ ἱερὰ εὐσεβῶς θυόμενα ὑπὲρ τῆς πόλεως
τούτου θύοντος αὖτε ἄλλο καλῶς καὶ δικαίως
οὐδὲν ἂν τούτου πράξαντος ; καὶ νὴ Δία ἐάν τις
τῶν γονέων τελευτησάντων τοὺς τάφους μὴ κοσμῇ,
καὶ τοῦτο ἐξετάζει ἡ πόλις ἐν ταῖς τῶν ἀρχόντων

bless you abundantly and pays vows on your behalf; and yet you say she is a trial! It seems to me that, if you can't endure a mother like her, you can't endure a good thing. Now tell me, is there any 11 other being whom you feel bound to regard? Or are you set on trying to please nobody, and obeying neither general nor other ruler?"

"Of course not!"

"Do you want to please your neighbour, for 12 instance, so that he may kindle a fire for you at your need, may support you in prosperity, and in case of accident or failure may be ready to hold out a helping hand?"

"Yes, I do."

"When you find yourself with a travelling companion on land or at sea, or happen to meet anyone, is it a matter of indifference to you whether he prove a friend or an enemy? Or do you think his goodwill worth cultivating?"

"Yes, I do."

"And yet, when you are resolved to cultivate 13 these, you don't think courtesy is due to your mother, who loves you more than all? Don't you know that even the state ignores all other forms of ingratitude and pronounces no judgment on them,[1] caring nothing if the recipient of a favour neglects to thank his benefactor, but inflicts penalties on the man who is discourteous to his parents and rejects him as unworthy of office, holding that it would be a sin for him to offer sacrifices on behalf of the state and that he is unlikely to do anything else honourably and rightly? Aye, and if one fail to honour his parents' graves, the state inquires into that too, when

---

[1] *Cyropaedia*, i. ii. 7.

14 δοκιμασίαις. σὺ οὖν, ὦ παῖ, ἐὰν σωφρονῇς, τοὺς μὲν θεοὺς παραιτήσῃ συγγνώμονάς σοι εἶναι, εἴ τι παρημέληκας τῆς μητρός, μή σε καὶ οὗτοι νομίσαντες ἀχάριστον εἶναι οὐκ ἐθελήσωσιν εὖ ποιεῖν, τοὺς δὲ ἀνθρώπους φυλάξῃ, μή σε αἰσθόμενοι τῶν γονέων ἀμελοῦντα πάντες ἀτιμάσωσιν, εἶτα ἐν ἐρημίᾳ φίλων ἀναφανῇς. εἰ γάρ σε ὑπολάβοιεν πρὸς τοὺς γονεῖς ἀχάριστον εἶναι, οὐδεὶς ἂν νομίσειεν εὖ σε ποιήσας χάριν ἀπολήψεσθαι.

III. Χαιρεφῶντα δέ ποτε καὶ Χαιρεκράτην, ἀδελφὼ μὲν ὄντε ἀλλήλοιν, ἑαυτῷ δὲ γνωρίμω, αἰσθόμενος διαφερομένω, ἰδὼν τὸν Χαιρεκράτην, Εἰπέ μοι, ἔφη, ὦ Χαιρέκρατες, οὐ δήπου καὶ σὺ εἶ τῶν τοιούτων ἀνθρώπων, οἳ χρησιμώτερον νομίζουσι χρήματα ἢ ἀδελφούς; καὶ ταῦτα τῶν μὲν ἀφρόνων ὄντων, τοῦ δὲ φρονίμου, καὶ τῶν μὲν βοηθείας δεομένων, τοῦ δὲ βοηθεῖν δυναμένου, καὶ πρὸς τούτοις τῶν μὲν πλειόνων ὑπαρχόντων, τοῦ

2 δὲ ἑνός. θαυμαστὸν δὲ καὶ τοῦτο, εἴ τις τοὺς μὲν ἀδελφοὺς ζημίαν ἡγεῖται, ὅτι οὐ καὶ τὰ τῶν ἀδελφῶν κέκτηται, τοὺς δὲ πολίτας οὐχ ἡγεῖται ζημίαν, ὅτι οὐ καὶ τὰ τῶν πολιτῶν ἔχει, ἀλλ' ἐνταῦθα μὲν δύνανται λογίζεσθαι, ὅτι κρεῖττον σὺν πολλοῖς οἰκοῦντα ἀσφαλῶς τἀρκοῦντα ἔχειν ἢ μόνον διαιτώμενον τὰ τῶν πολιτῶν ἐπικινδύνως πάντα κεκτῆσθαι, ἐπὶ δὲ τῶν ἀδελφῶν τὸ αὐτὸ

3 τοῦτο ἀγνοοῦσι. καὶ οἰκέτας μὲν οἱ δυνάμενοι ὠνοῦνται, ἵνα συνεργοὺς ἔχωσι, καὶ φίλους κτῶνται ὡς βοηθῶν δεόμενοι, τῶν δ' ἀδελφῶν ἀμελοῦσιν, ὥσπερ ἐκ πολιτῶν μὲν γιγνομένους φίλους,

it examines the candidates for office. Therefore, my 14
boy, if you are prudent, you will pray the gods to
pardon your neglect of your mother, lest they in
turn refuse to be kind to you, thinking you an
ingrate; and you will beware of men, lest all cast
you out, perceiving that you care nothing for your
parents, and in the end you are found to be without a friend. For, should men suppose you to be
ungrateful to your parents, none would think you
would be grateful for any kindness he might show
you."

III. On another occasion he found that two
brothers, Chaerophon and Chaerecrates, whom he
knew well, were quarrelling. On seeing the latter,
he cried, "Surely, Chaerecrates, you are not one of
those who hold that there is more value in goods
and chattels than in a brother, when they are senseless but he is sensible; they are helpless but he is
helpful; when, moreover, you have many goods, but
only one brother. It is strange too that a man 2
should think he loses by his brothers because he
cannot have their possessions as well as his own,
and yet should not think that he loses by his fellow-
citizens because their possessions are not his; and
whereas in this case men can reflect that it is better
to belong to a community, secure in the possession
of a sufficiency, than to dwell in solitude with a
precarious hold on all the property of their fellow-
citizens, they fail to see that the same principle
applies to brothers. Again, those who have the 3
means buy servants to relieve them of work, and
make friends because they feel the need of help;
but they care nothing for their brothers, as though
friendship can exist between fellow-citizens, but not

4 ἐξ ἀδελφῶν δὲ οὐ γιγνομένους. καὶ μὴν πρὸς
φιλίαν μέγα μὲν ὑπάρχει τὸ ἐκ τῶν αὐτῶν φῦναι,
μέγα δὲ τὸ ὁμοῦ τραφῆναι, ἐπεὶ καὶ τοῖς θηρίοις
πόθος τις ἐγγίγνεται τῶν συντρόφων· πρὸς δὲ
τούτοις καὶ οἱ ἄλλοι ἄνθρωποι τιμῶσί τε μᾶλλον
τοὺς συναδέλφους ὄντας τῶν ἀναδέλφων καὶ
ἧττον τούτοις ἐπιτίθενται.

5 Καὶ ὁ Χαιρεκράτης εἶπεν· Ἀλλ' εἰ μέν, ὦ
Σώκρατες, μὴ μέγα εἴη τὸ διάφορον, ἴσως ἂν δέοι
φέρειν τὸν ἀδελφὸν καὶ μὴ μικρῶν ἕνεκα φεύγειν·
ἀγαθὸν γάρ, ὥσπερ καὶ σὺ λέγεις, ἀδελφὸς ὢν
οἷον δεῖ· ὁπότε μέντοι παντὸς ἐνδέοι καὶ πᾶν τὸ
ἐναντιώτατον εἴη, τί ἄν τις ἐπιχειροίη τοῖς
ἀδυνάτοις;

6 Καὶ ὁ Σωκράτης ἔφη· Πότερα δέ, ὦ Χαιρέκρατες, οὐδενὶ ἀρέσαι δύναται Χαιρεφῶν, ὥσπερ
οὐδὲ σοί, ἢ ἔστιν οἷς καὶ πάνυ ἀρέσκει;
Διὰ τοῦτο γάρ τοι, ἔφη, ὦ Σώκρατες, ἄξιόν
ἐστιν ἐμοὶ μισεῖν αὐτόν, ὅτι ἄλλοις μὲν ἀρέσκειν
δύναται, ἐμοὶ δὲ ὅπου ἂν παρῇ πανταχοῦ καὶ
ἔργῳ καὶ λόγῳ ζημία μᾶλλον ἢ ὠφέλειά ἐστιν.

7 Ἆρ' οὖν, ἔφη ὁ Σωκράτης, ὥσπερ ἵππος τῷ
ἀνεπιστήμονι μέν, ἐγχειροῦντι δὲ χρῆσθαι ζημία
ἐστίν, οὕτω καὶ ἀδελφός, ὅταν τις αὐτῷ μὴ ἐπιστάμενος ἐγχειρῇ χρῆσθαι, ζημία ἐστί;

8 Πῶς δ' ἂν ἐγώ, ἔφη ὁ Χαιρεκράτης, ἀνεπιστήμων
εἴην ἀδελφῷ χρῆσθαι, ἐπιστάμενός γε καὶ εὖ
λέγειν τὸν εὖ λέγοντα καὶ εὖ ποιεῖν τὸν εὖ
ποιοῦντα; τὸν μέντοι καὶ λόγῳ καὶ ἔργῳ πειρώμενον ἐμὲ ἀνιᾶν οὐκ ἂν δυναίμην οὔτ' εὖ λέγειν
οὔτ' εὖ ποιεῖν, ἀλλ' οὐδὲ πειράσομαι.

between brothers! Yet common parentage and 4
common upbringing are strong ties of affection,[1] for
even brute beasts reared together feel a natural
yearning for one another. Besides, our fellow-men
respect those of us who have brothers more than
those who have none, and are less ready to quarrel
with them."

"If only the difference between us were a slight 5
one, Socrates," replied Chaerecrates, "it might perhaps be my duty to put up with my brother and not
allow trifles to separate us. For a brother who
behaves like a brother is, as you say, a blessing ;
but if his conduct is nothing like that, and is, in fact,
just the opposite of what it should be, what is the
use of attempting impossibilities?"

"Does everyone find Chaerophon as disagreeable 6
as you do, Chaerecrates, or do some people think
him very pleasant?"

"Ah, Socrates," replied he, "this is precisely my
reason for hating him : he is pleasant enough to other
people, but whenever he is near me, he invariably
says and does more to hurt than to help me."

"Well now," said Socrates, "if you try to manage 7
a horse without knowing the right way, he hurts
you. Is it so with a brother? Does he hurt if you
try to deal with him when you don't know the
way?"

"What," exclaimed Chaerecrates, "don't I know 8
how to deal with a brother, when I know how to
requite a kind word and a generous deed? But I
can't speak or act kindly to one who tries to annoy
me by his words and actions—and what's more, I
won't try."

---

[1] *Cyropaedia*, II. i. 28.

9 Καὶ ὁ Σωκράτης ἔφη· Θαυμαστά γε λέγεις, ὦ
Χαιρέκρατες, εἰ κύνα μέν, εἴ σοι ἦν ἐπὶ προβάτοις
ἐπιτήδειος ὢν καὶ τοὺς μὲν ποιμένας ἠσπάζετο,
σοὶ δὲ προσιόντι ἐχαλέπαινεν, ἀμελήσας ἂν τοῦ
ὀργίζεσθαι ἐπειρῶ εὖ ποιήσας πραΰνειν αὐτόν,
τὸν δὲ ἀδελφὸν φὴς μὲν μέγα ἂν ἀγαθὸν εἶναι
ὄντα πρὸς σὲ οἷον δεῖ, ἐπίστασθαι δὲ ὁμολογῶν
καὶ εὖ ποιεῖν καὶ εὖ λέγειν οὐκ ἐπιχειρεῖς
μηχανᾶσθαι, ὅπως σοι ὡς βέλτιστος ᾖ.

10 Καὶ ὁ Χαιρεκράτης, Δέδοικα, ἔφη, ὦ Σώκρατες,
μὴ οὐκ ἔχω ἐγὼ τοσαύτην σοφίαν, ὥστε Χαιρεφῶντα ποιῆσαι πρὸς ἐμὲ οἷον δεῖ.

Καὶ μὴν οὐδέν γε ποικίλον, ἔφη ὁ Σωκράτης,
οὐδὲ καινὸν δεῖ ἐπ' αὐτόν, ὡς ἐμοὶ δοκεῖ, μηχανᾶσθαι, οἷς δὲ καὶ σὺ ἐπίστασαι αὐτὸς οἴομαι
ἂν αὐτὸν ἁλόντα περὶ πολλοῦ ποιεῖσθαί σε.

11 Οὐκ ἂν φθάνοις, ἔφη, λέγων, εἴ τι ᾔσθησαί
με φίλτρον ἐπιστάμενον, ὃ ἐγὼ εἰδὼς λέληθα
ἐμαυτόν.

Λέγε δή μοι, ἔφη, εἴ τινα τῶν γνωρίμων
βούλοιο κατεργάσασθαι, ὁπότε θύοι, καλεῖν σε
ἐπὶ δεῖπνον, τί ἂν ποιοίης;

Δῆλον ὅτι κατάρχοιμι ἂν τοῦ αὐτός, ὅτε θύοιμι,
καλεῖν ἐκεῖνον.

12 Εἰ δὲ βούλοιο τῶν φίλων τινὰ προτρέψασθαι,
ὁπότε ἀποδημοίης, ἐπιμελεῖσθαι τῶν σῶν, τί ἂν
ποιοίης;

Δῆλον ὅτι πρότερος ἂν ἐγχειροίην ἐπιμελεῖσθαι
τῶν ἐκείνου, ὁπότε ἀποδημοίη.

13 Εἰ δὲ βούλοιο ξένον ποιῆσαι ὑποδέχεσθαι
σεαυτόν, ὁπότε ἔλθοις εἰς τὴν ἐκείνου, τί ἂν
ποιοίης;

"Chaerecrates, you astonish me! Had you a 9
sheep dog that was friendly to the shepherds, but
growled when you came near him, it would never
occur to you to get angry, but you would try to
tame him by kindness. You say that, if your
brother treated you like a brother, he would be a
great blessing, and you confess that you know how
to speak and act kindly: yet you don't set yourself
to contriving that he shall be the greatest possible
blessing to you."

"I fear, Socrates, that I lack the wisdom to make 10
Chaerophon treat me as he should."

"And yet," said Socrates, "there is no need, so
far as I see, of any subtle or strange contriving on
your part: I think you know the way to win him
and to get his good opinion."

"If you have observed that I know some spell 11
without being conscious of my knowledge, pray tell
me at once."

"Then tell me, now; if you wanted to get an
invitation to dine with an acquaintance when he
offers sacrifice, what would you do?"

"Of course I should begin by inviting him myself
when I offered sacrifice."

"And suppose you wanted to encourage one of 12
your friends to look after your affairs during your
absence from home, what would you do?"

"Of course I should first undertake to look after
his affairs in his absence."

"And suppose you wanted a stranger to entertain 13
you when you visited his city, what would you do?"

Δῆλον ὅτι καὶ τοῦτον πρότερος ὑποδεχοίμην
ἄν, ὁπότε ἔλθοι Ἀθήναζε· καὶ εἴ γε βουλοίμην
αὐτὸν προθυμεῖσθαι διαπράττειν μοι ἐφ' ἃ ἥκοιμι,
δῆλον ὅτι καὶ τοῦτο δέοι ἂν πρότερον αὐτὸν
ἐκείνῳ ποιεῖν.

14 Πάντ' ἄρα σύγε τὰ ἐν ἀνθρώποις φίλτρα
ἐπιστάμενος πάλαι ἀπεκρύπτου· ἢ ὀκνεῖς, ἔφη,
ἄρξαι, μὴ αἰσχρὸς φανῇς, ἐὰν πρότερος τὸν
ἀδελφὸν εὖ ποιῇς; καὶ μὴν πλείστου γε δοκεῖ
ἀνὴρ ἐπαίνου ἄξιος εἶναι, ὃς ἂν φθάνῃ τοὺς μὲν
πολεμίους κακῶς ποιῶν, τοὺς δὲ φίλους εὐεργετῶν. εἰ μὲν οὖν ἐδόκει μοι Χαιρεφῶν ἡγεμον-
ικώτερος εἶναι σοῦ πρὸς τὴν φιλίαν ταύτην,
ἐκεῖνον ἂν ἐπειρώμην πείθειν πρότερον ἐγχειρεῖν
τῷ σὲ φίλον ποιεῖσθαι· νῦν δέ μοι σὺ δοκεῖς
ἡγούμενος μᾶλλον ἂν ἐξεργάζεσθαι τοῦτο.

15 Καὶ ὁ Χαιρεκράτης εἶπεν· Ἄτοπα λέγεις, ὦ
Σώκρατες, καὶ οὐδαμῶς πρὸς σοῦ, ὅς γε κελεύεις
ἐμὲ νεώτερον ὄντα καθηγεῖσθαι· καίτοι τούτου
γε παρὰ πᾶσιν ἀνθρώποις τἀναντία νομίζεται, τὸν
πρεσβύτερον ἡγεῖσθαι παντὸς καὶ ἔργου καὶ λόγου.

16 Πῶς; ἔφη ὁ Σωκράτης· οὐ γὰρ καὶ ὁδοῦ
παραχωρῆσαι τὸν νεώτερον πρεσβυτέρῳ συν-
τυγχάνοντι πανταχοῦ νομίζεται καὶ καθήμενον
ὑπαναστῆναι καὶ κοίτῃ μαλακῇ τιμῆσαι καὶ
λόγων ὑπεῖξαι; ὠγαθέ, μὴ ὄκνει, ἔφη, ἀλλ'
ἐγχείρει τὸν ἄνδρα καταπραΰνειν· καὶ πάνυ ταχύ
σοι ὑπακούσεται. οὐχ ὁρᾷς, ὡς φιλότιμός ἐστι
καὶ ἐλευθέριος; τὰ μὲν γὰρ πονηρὰ ἀνθρώπια
οὐκ ἂν ἄλλως μᾶλλον ἕλοις ἢ εἰ δοίης τι, τοὺς
δὲ καλοὺς κἀγαθοὺς ἀνθρώπους προσφιλῶς χρώμενος μάλιστ' ἂν κατεργάσαιο.

"Obviously I should first entertain him when he came to Athens. Yes, and if I wanted him to show himself eager in forwarding the business on which I had come, it is obvious that I should first have to do the same by him."

"It seems that you have long concealed a know- 14 ledge of all spells that were ever discovered. Or is it that you hesitate to make a beginning, for fear of disgracing yourself by first showing kindness to your brother? Yet it is generally thought worthy of the highest praise to anticipate the malevolence of an enemy and the benevolence of a friend. So if I thought Chaerophon more capable than you of showing the way to this friendship, I would try to persuade him to take the first step towards an understanding with you. But as things are, I think the enterprise more likely to succeed under your direction."

"Strange sentiments, these, Socrates! It's quite 15 unlike you to urge me, the junior, to lead the way! And surely all hold the contrary opinion, that the senior, I mean, should always act and speak first?"

"How so?" said Socrates. "Is it not the general 16 opinion that a young man should make way for an older when they meet,[1] offer his seat to him, give him a comfortable bed, let him have the first word? My good friend, don't hesitate, but take up the task of pacifying your man, and in no time he will respond to your overtures. Don't you see how keen and frank he is? Low fellows, it is true, yield most readily to gifts, but kindness is the weapon most likely to prevail with a gentleman."

---

[1] *Cyropaedia*, VIII. vii. 10.

17 Καὶ ὁ Χαιρεκράτης εἶπεν· Ἐὰν οὖν ἐμοῦ ταῦτα
ποιοῦντος ἐκεῖνος μηδὲν βελτίων γίγνηται;

Τί γὰρ ἄλλο, ἔφη ὁ Σωκράτης, ἢ κινδυνεύσεις
ἐπιδεῖξαι σὺ μὲν χρηστός τε καὶ φιλάδελφος εἶναι,
ἐκεῖνος δὲ φαῦλός τε καὶ οὐκ ἄξιος εὐεργεσίας;
ἀλλ' οὐδὲν οἶμαι τούτων ἔσεσθαι· νομίζω γὰρ
αὐτόν, ἐπειδὰν αἴσθηταί σε προκαλούμενον ἑαυτὸν
εἰς τὸν ἀγῶνα τοῦτον, πάνυ φιλονεικήσειν, ὅπως
περιγένηταί σου καὶ λόγῳ καὶ ἔργῳ εὖ ποιῶν.

18 νῦν μὲν γὰρ οὕτως, ἔφη, διάκεισθον, ὥσπερ εἰ
τὼ χεῖρε, ἃς ὁ θεὸς ἐπὶ τῷ συλλαμβάνειν ἀλ-
λήλαις ἐποίησεν, ἀφεμένω τούτου τράποιντο
πρὸς τὸ διακωλύειν ἀλλήλω ἢ εἰ τὼ πόδε θείᾳ
μοίρᾳ πεποιημένω πρὸς τὸ συνεργεῖν ἀλλήλοιν

19 ἀμελήσαντε τούτου ἐμποδίζοιεν ἀλλήλω. οὐκ ἂν
πολλὴ ἀμαθία εἴη καὶ κακοδαιμονία τοῖς ἐπ'
ὠφελείᾳ πεποιημένοις ἐπὶ βλάβῃ χρῆσθαι; καὶ
μὴν ἀδελφώ γε, ὡς ἐμοὶ δοκεῖ, ὁ θεὸς ἐποίησεν
ἐπὶ μείζονι ὠφελείᾳ ἀλλήλοιν ἢ χεῖρέ τε καὶ
πόδε καὶ ὀφθαλμὼ καὶ τἆλλα, ὅσα ἀδελφὰ
ἔφυσεν ἀνθρώποις. χεῖρες μὲν γάρ, εἰ δέοι αὐτὰς
τὰ πλέον ὀργυιᾶς διέχοντα ἅμα ποιῆσαι, οὐκ ἂν
δύναιντο· πόδες δὲ οὐδ' ἂν ἐπὶ τὰ ὀργυιὰν διέχοντα ἔλθοιεν ἅμα· ὀφθαλμοὶ δὲ οἱ καὶ δοκοῦντες
ἐπὶ πλεῖστον ἐξικνεῖσθαι οὐδ' ἂν τῶν ἔτι ἐγγυτέρω ὄντων τὰ ἔμπροσθεν ἅμα καὶ τὰ ὄπισθεν
ἰδεῖν δύναιντο· ἀδελφὼ δὲ φίλω ὄντε καὶ πολὺ
διεστῶτε πράττετον ἅμα καὶ ἐπ' ὠφελείᾳ
ἀλλήλοιν.

IV. Ἤκουσα δέ ποτε αὐτοῦ καὶ περὶ φίλων
διαλεγομένου, ἐξ ὧν ἔμοιγε ἐδόκει μάλιστ' ἄν τις
ὠφελεῖσθαι πρὸς φίλων κτῆσίν τε καὶ χρείαν.

"And what," asked Chaerecrates, "if all my 17
efforts lead to no improvement?"

"Well, in that case, I presume you will have shown
that you are honest and brotherly, he that he is base
and unworthy of kindness. But I am confident that
no such result will follow; for I think that, as soon
as he is aware of your challenge to this contest, he
will be all eagerness to outdo your kind words and
actions. What if a pair of hands refused the office 18
of mutual help for which God made them, and tried
to thwart each other; or if a pair of feet neglected
the duty of working together, for which they were
fashioned, and took to hampering each other? That
is how you two are behaving at present. Would it 19
not be utterly senseless and disastrous to use for
hindrance instruments that were made for help?
And, moreover, a pair of brothers, in my judgment,
were made by God to render better service one to
the other than a pair of hands and feet and eyes
and all the instruments that he meant to be used as
fellows. For the hands cannot deal simultaneously
with things that are more than six feet or so apart:
the feet cannot reach in a single stride things that
are even six feet apart: and the eyes, though they
seem to have a longer range, cannot at the same
moment see things still nearer than that, if some
are in front and some behind. But two brothers,
when they are friends, act simultaneously for mutual
benefit, however far parted one from the other."

IV. Again, I once heard him give a discourse on
friendship[1] that was likely, as I thought, to help
greatly in the acquisition and use of friends.

---

[1] *Cyropaedia*, VIII. vii. 13.

Τοῦτο μὲν γὰρ δὴ πολλῶν ἔφη ἀκούειν, ὡς
πάντων κτημάτων κράτιστον εἴη φίλος σαφὴς
καὶ ἀγαθός· ἐπιμελομένους δὲ παντὸς μᾶλλον
2 ὁρᾶν ἔφη τοὺς πολλοὺς ἢ φίλων κτήσεως. καὶ
γὰρ οἰκίας καὶ ἀγροὺς καὶ ἀνδράποδα καὶ βοσκήματα καὶ σκεύη κτωμένους τε ἐπιμελῶς ὁρᾶν ἔφη
καὶ τὰ ὄντα σώζειν πειρωμένους, φίλον δέ, ὃ
μέγιστον ἀγαθὸν εἶναί φασιν, ὁρᾶν ἔφη τοὺς πολλοὺς οὔτε ὅπως κτήσονται φροντίζοντας οὔτε
3 ὅπως οἱ ὄντες ἑαυτοῖς σῴζωνται. ἀλλὰ καὶ κα-
μνόντων φίλων τε καὶ οἰκετῶν ὁρᾶν τινας ἔφη
τοῖς μὲν οἰκέταις καὶ ἰατροὺς εἰσάγοντας καὶ
τἆλλα τὰ πρὸς ὑγίειαν ἐπιμελῶς παρασκευά-
ζοντας, τῶν δὲ φίλων ὀλιγωροῦντας, ἀποθανόντων
τε ἀμφοτέρων ἐπὶ μὲν τοῖς οἰκέταις ἀχθομένους
τε καὶ ζημίαν ἡγουμένους, ἐπὶ δὲ τοῖς φίλοις
οὐδὲν οἰομένους ἐλαττοῦσθαι, καὶ τῶν μὲν ἄλλων
κτημάτων οὐδὲν ἐῶντας ἀθεράπευτον οὐδ' ἀνεπί-
σκεπτον, τῶν δὲ φίλων ἐπιμελείας δεομένων
4 ἀμελοῦντας. ἔτι δὲ πρὸς τούτοις ὁρᾶν ἔφη τοὺς
πολλοὺς τῶν μὲν ἄλλων κτημάτων καὶ πάνυ
πολλῶν αὐτοῖς ὄντων τὸ πλῆθος εἰδότας, τῶν δὲ
φίλων ὀλίγων ὄντων οὐ μόνον τὸ πλῆθος ἀγνοοῦντας, ἀλλὰ καὶ τοῖς πυνθανομένοις τοῦτο
καταλέγειν ἐγχειρήσαντας οὓς ἐν τοῖς φίλοις
ἔθεσαν, πάλιν τούτους ἀνατίθεσθαι· τοσοῦ-
5 τον αὐτοὺς τῶν φίλων φροντίζειν. καίτοι πρὸς
ποῖον κτῆμα τῶν ἄλλων παραβαλλόμενος
φίλος ἀγαθὸς οὐκ ἂν πολλῷ κρείττων φανείη;
ποῖος γὰρ ἵππος ἢ ποῖον ζεῦγος οὕτω χρήσιμον
ὥσπερ ὁ χρηστὸς φίλος; ποῖον δὲ ἀνδράποδον
οὕτως εὔνουν καὶ παραμόνιμον; ἢ ποῖον ἄλλο

For he said that he often heard it stated that of all possessions the most precious is a good and sincere friend. "And yet," he said, "there is no transaction most men are so careless about as the acquisition of friends. For I find that they are 2 careful about getting houses and lands and slaves and cattle and furniture, and anxious to keep what they have; but though they tell one that a friend is the greatest blessing, I find that most men take no thought how to get new friends or how to keep their old ones. Indeed, if one of their friends and 3 one of their servants fall ill at the same time, I find that some call in the doctor to attend the servant and are careful to provide everything that may contribute to his recovery, whereas they take no heed of the friend. In the event of both dying, they are vexed at losing the servant, but don't feel that the death of the friend matters in the least. And though none of their other possessions is uncared for and unconsidered, they are deaf to their friends' need of attention. And besides all this, I find that 4 most men know the number of their other possessions, however great it may be, yet cannot tell the number of their friends, few as they are; and, if they are asked and try to make a list, they will insert names and presently remove them. So much for the thought they give to their friends! Yet 5 surely there is no other possession that can compare with a good friend. For what horse, what yoke of oxen is so good a servant as the good friend? What slave so loyal and constant? or what possession so

6 κτῆμα οὕτω πάγχρηστον; ὁ γὰρ ἀγαθὸς φίλος
ἑαυτὸν τάττει πρὸς πᾶν τὸ ἐλλεῖπον τῷ φίλῳ
καὶ τῆς τῶν ἰδίων κατασκευῆς καὶ τῶν κοινῶν
πράξεων, καὶ ἄν τέ τινα εὖ ποιῆσαι δέῃ, συν-
επισχύει, ἄν τέ τις φόβος ταράττῃ, συμβοηθεῖ
τὰ μὲν συναναλίσκων, τὰ δὲ συμπράττων καὶ
τὰ μὲν συμπείθων, τὰ δὲ βιαζόμενος καὶ εὖ μὲν
πράττοντας πλεῖστα εὐφραίνων, σφαλλομένους
7 δὲ πλεῖστα ἐπανορθῶν. ἃ δὲ αἵ τε χεῖρες ἑκάστῳ
ὑπηρετοῦσι καὶ οἱ ὀφθαλμοὶ προορῶσι καὶ τὰ
ὦτα προακούουσι καὶ οἱ πόδες διανύτουσι, τούτων φίλος εὐεργετῶν οὐδενὸς λείπεται· πολλάκις
δὲ ἃ πρὸ αὑτοῦ τις ἢ οὐκ ἐξειργάσατο ἢ οὐκ
εἶδεν ἢ οὐκ ἤκουσεν ἢ οὐ διήνυσε, ταῦθ' ὁ φίλος
πρὸ τοῦ φίλου ἐξήρκεσεν. ἀλλ' ὅμως ἔνιοι δένδρα
μὲν πειρῶνται θεραπεύειν τοῦ καρποῦ ἕνεκεν, τοῦ
δὲ παμφορωτάτου κτήματος, ὃ καλεῖται φίλος,
ἀργῶς καὶ ἀνειμένως οἱ πλεῖστοι ἐπιμέλονται.

V. Ἤκουσα δέ ποτε καὶ ἄλλον αὐτοῦ λόγον,
ὃς ἐδόκει μοι προτρέπειν τὸν ἀκούοντα ἐξετάζειν
ἑαυτόν, ὁπόσου τοῖς φίλοις ἄξιος εἴη. ἰδὼν γάρ
τινα τῶν συνόντων ἀμελοῦντα φίλου πενίᾳ πιε-
ζομένου ἤρετο Ἀντισθένη ἐναντίον τοῦ ἀμε-
2 λοῦντος αὐτοῦ καὶ ἄλλων πολλῶν, Ἆρ', ἔφη,
ὦ Ἀντίσθενες, εἰσί τινες ἀξίαι φίλων, ὥσπερ
οἰκετῶν; τῶν γὰρ οἰκετῶν ὁ μέν που δυοῖν μναῖν
ἄξιός ἐστιν, ὁ δὲ οὐδ' ἡμιμναίου, ὁ δὲ πέντε μνῶν,
ὁ δὲ καὶ δέκα· Νικίας δὲ ὁ Νικηράτου λέγεται
ἐπιστάτην εἰς τἀργύρεια πρίασθαι ταλάντου.
σκοποῦμαι δὴ τοῦτο, ἔφη, εἰ ἄρα ὥσπερ τῶν
οἰκετῶν, οὕτω καὶ τῶν φίλων εἰσὶν ἀξίαι.

3 Ναὶ μὰ Δί', ἔφη ὁ Ἀντισθένης· ἐγὼ γοῦν

serviceable? The good friend is on the watch to 6
supply whatever his friend wants for building up his
private fortune and forwarding his public career.
If generosity is called for, he does his part: if fear
harasses, he comes to the rescue, shares expenses,
helps to persuade, bears down opposition: he is
foremost in delighting him when he is prosperous
and raising him up when he falls. Of all that a man 7
can do with his hands, see for himself with his eyes,
hear for himself with his ears or accomplish with his
feet, in nothing is a friend backward in helping.
Nevertheless, while some strive to cultivate a tree
for its fruit, most bestow but an idle and listless care
on their most fruitful possession, the name of which
is 'friend.'"

V. Again, I once heard him exhort a listener—for
so I interpreted his words—to examine himself and
to ask how much he was worth to his friends. For
he had noticed that one of his companions was neglecting a poverty-stricken friend; so he put a question
to Antisthenes in the presence of several others,
including the careless friend. "Antisthenes," he 2
said, "have friends like servants their own values?
For one servant, I suppose, may be worth two minas,[1]
another less than half a mina, another five minas,
another no less than ten. Nicias, son of Niceratus,
is said to have given a whole talent[2] for a manager
of his silver-mine. So I am led to inquire whether
friends too may not differ in value."

"Oh yes," replied Antisthenes, "there are men 3

[1] Some £8.   [2] Some £240.

βουλοίμην ἂν τὸν μέν τινα φίλον μοι εἶναι μᾶλλον ἢ δύο μνᾶς, τὸν δ' οὐδ' ἂν ἡμιμναίου προτιμησαίμην, τὸν δὲ καὶ πρὸ δέκα μνῶν ἑλοίμην ἄν, τὸν δὲ πρὸ πάντων χρημάτων καὶ πόνων πριαίμην ἂν φίλον μοι εἶναι.

4 Οὐκοῦν, ἔφη ὁ Σωκράτης, εἴ γε ταῦτα τοιαῦτά ἐστι, καλῶς ἂν ἔχοι ἐξετάζειν τινὰ ἑαυτόν, πόσου ἄρα τυγχάνει τοῖς φίλοις ἄξιος ὤν, καὶ πειρᾶθαι ὡς πλείστου ἄξιος εἶναι, ἵνα ἧττον αὐτὸν οἱ φίλοι προδιδῶσιν. ἐγὼ γάρ τοι, ἔφη, πολλάκις ἀκούω τοῦ μέν, ὅτι προὔδωκεν αὐτὸν φίλος ἀνήρ, τοῦ δ', ὅτι μνᾶν ἀνθ' ἑαυτοῦ μᾶλλον εἵλετο 5 ἀνήρ, ὃν ᾤετο φίλον εἶναι. τὰ τοιαῦτα πάντα σκοπῶ, μὴ ὥσπερ ὅταν τις οἰκέτην πονηρὸν πωλῇ καὶ ἀποδίδοται[1] τοῦ εὑρόντος, οὕτω καὶ τὸν πονηρὸν φίλον, ὅταν ἐξῇ τὸ πλέον τῆς ἀξίας λαβεῖν, ἐπαγωγὸν ᾖ ἀποδίδοσθαι. τοὺς δὲ χρηστοὺς οὔτε οἰκέτας πάνυ τι πωλουμένους ὁρῶ οὔτε φίλους προδιδομένους.

VI. Ἐδόκει δέ μοι καὶ εἰς τὸ δοκιμάζειν φίλους ὁποίους ἄξιον κτᾶσθαι φρενοῦν τοιάδε λέγων·

Εἰπέ μοι, ἔφη, ὦ Κριτόβουλε, εἰ δεοίμεθα φίλου ἀγαθοῦ, πῶς ἂν ἐπιχειροίημεν σκοπεῖν; ἆρα πρῶτον μὲν ζητητέον, ὅστις ἄρχει γαστρός τε καὶ φιλοποσίας καὶ λαγνείας καὶ ὕπνου καὶ ἀργίας; ὁ γὰρ ὑπὸ τούτων κρατούμενος οὔτ' αὐτὸς ἑαυτῷ δύναιτ' ἂν οὔτε φίλῳ τὰ δέοντα πράττειν.

Μὰ Δί' οὐ δῆτα, ἔφη.

Οὐκοῦν τοῦ μὲν ὑπὸ τούτων ἀρχομένου ἀφεκτέον δοκεῖ σοι εἶναι;

Πάνυ μὲν οὖν, ἔφη.

whose friendship I, at any rate, would rather have
than two minas: others I should value at less than
half a mina: others I would prefer to ten minas:
others I would sacrifice any sum and take any trouble
to have among my friends."

"Then if that is so," said Socrates, "were it not 4
well that one should ask himself how much he is
really worth to his friends, and try to make himself
as precious as possible, in order that his friends may
not be tempted to betray him? For my part, I
often hear complaints of this sort: 'A friend betrayed me,' 'one whom I regarded as my friend gave
me up for the sake of a mina.' I think over such 5
matters and reflect that, when a man sells a bad
slave he takes anything he can get for him; and
perhaps it is tempting to sell a bad friend when there
is a chance of getting more than he is worth. Good
servants, I find, are not offered for sale, nor are
good friends betrayed."

VI. In the following conversation I thought he
gave instruction for testing the qualities that make a
man's friendship worth winning.

"Tell me, Critobulus," he said, "if we wanted a
good friend, how should we start on the quest?
Should we seek first for one who is no slave to eating
and drinking, lust, sleep, idleness? For the thrall
of these masters cannot do his duty by himself or his
friend."

"No, of course not."

"Then you think we should avoid one who is
subject to them?"

"I do, certainly."

---

[1] ἀποδίδοται wtih *M* : ἀποδιδῶται Sauppe.

2 Τί γάρ; ἔφη, ὅστις δαπανηρὸς ὢν μὴ αὐτάρχης
ἐστίν, ἀλλ' ἀεὶ τῶν πλησίον δεῖται καὶ λαμβάνων
μὲν μὴ δύναται ἀποδιδόναι, μὴ λαμβάνων δὲ τὸν
μὴ διδόντα μισεῖ, οὐ δοκεῖ σοι καὶ οὗτος χαλεπὸς
φίλος εἶναι;
    Πάνυ γ', ἔφη.
    Οὐκοῦν ἀφεκτέον καὶ τούτου;
    Ἀφεκτέον μέντοι, ἔφη.

3 Τί γάρ; ὅστις χρηματίζεσθαι μὲν δύναται,
πολλῶν δὲ χρημάτων ἐπιθυμεῖ καὶ διὰ τοῦτο
δυσσύμβολός ἐστι καὶ λαμβάνων μὲν ἥδεται,
ἀποδιδόναι δὲ μὴ βούλεται;
    Ἐμοὶ μὲν δοκεῖ, ἔφη, οὗτος ἔτι πονηρότερος
ἐκείνου εἶναι.

4 Τί δ'; ὅστις διὰ τὸν ἔρωτα τοῦ χρηματίζεσθαι
μηδὲ πρὸς ἓν ἄλλο σχολὴν ποιεῖται ἢ ὁπόθεν
αὐτὸς κερδανεῖ;
    Ἀφεκτέον καὶ τούτου, ὡς ἐμοὶ δοκεῖ· ἀνωφελὴς
γὰρ ἂν εἴη τῷ χρωμένῳ.
    Τί δέ; ὅστις στασιώδης τέ ἐστι καὶ θέλων
πολλοὺς τοῖς φίλοις ἐχθροὺς παρέχειν;
    Φευκτέον νὴ Δία καὶ τοῦτον.
    Εἰ δέ τις τούτων μὲν τῶν κακῶν μηδὲν ἔχοι,
εὖ δὲ πάσχων ἀνέχεται, μηδὲν φροντίζων τοῦ
ἀντευεργετεῖν;
    Ἀνωφελὴς ἂν εἴη καὶ οὗτος. ἀλλὰ ποῖον, ὦ
Σώκρατες, ἐπιχειρήσομεν φίλον ποιεῖσθαι;

5 Οἶμαι μέν, ὅστις τἀναντία τούτων ἐγκρατὴς
μέν ἐστι τῶν διὰ τοῦ σώματος ἡδονῶν, εὔοικος[1]
δὲ καὶ εὐσύμβολος ὢν τυγχάνει καὶ φιλόνικος πρὸς

---

[1] εὔοικος B (first hand): εὔνους Sauppe with A : εὔορκος C.

"Now what about the spendthrift who is never 2
satisfied, who is always appealing to his neighbours
for help, if he receives something, makes no return,
if he receives nothing, resents it? Don't you think
he too is a troublesome friend?"

"Certainly."

"Then we must avoid him too?"

"We must indeed."

"Again, what about the skilful man of business 3
who is eager to make money, and consequently
drives a hard bargain, who likes to receive but is
disinclined to repay?"

"So far as I see, he is even worse than the
last."

"And what of the man who is such a keen man 4
of business that he has no leisure for anything but
the selfish pursuit of gain?"

"We must avoid him too, I think. There is no
profit in knowing him."

"And what of the quarrelsome person who is willing to provide his friends with plenty of enemies?"

"We must shun him too, of course."

"Suppose that a man is free from all these faults,
but stoops to receive kindness with no thought of
returning it?"

"There is no profit in him either. But what are
the qualities for which we shall try to win a man's
friendship, Socrates?"

"The opposite of these, I suppose. We shall look 5
for one who controls his indulgence in the pleasures
of the body, who is truly hospitable[1] and fair in his

---

[1] Or εὔνους, "loyal," or εὔορκος, "scrupulous," "a man of
his word."

τὸ μὴ ἐλλείπεσθαι εὖ ποιῶν τοὺς εὐεργετοῦντας
αὐτόν, ὥστε λυσιτελεῖν τοῖς χρωμένοις.

6 Πῶς οὖν ἂν ταῦτα δοκιμάσαιμεν, ὦ Σώκρατες,
πρὸ τοῦ χρῆσθαι ;

Τοὺς μὲν ἀνδριαντοποιούς, ἔφη, δοκιμάζομεν
οὐ τοῖς λόγοις αὐτῶν τεκμαιρόμενοι, ἀλλ' ὃν ἂν
ὁρῶμεν τοὺς πρόσθεν ἀνδριάντας καλῶς εἰργασμένον, τούτῳ πιστεύομεν καὶ τοὺς λοιποὺς εὖ
ποιήσειν.

7 Καὶ ἄνδρα δὴ λέγεις, ἔφη, ὃς ἂν τοὺς φίλους
τοὺς πρόσθεν εὖ ποιῶν φαίνηται, δῆλον εἶναι καὶ
τοὺς ὕστερον εὐεργετήσοντα ;

Καὶ γὰρ ἵπποις, ἔφη, ὃν ἂν ὁρῶ τοῖς πρόσθεν
καλῶς χρώμενον, τοῦτον κἂν ἄλλοις οἶμαι καλῶς
χρῆσθαι.

8 Εἶεν, ἔφη· ὃς δ' ἂν ἡμῖν ἄξιος φιλίας δοκῇ
εἶναι, πῶς χρὴ φίλον τοῦτον ποιεῖσθαι ;

Πρῶτον μέν, ἔφη, τὰ παρὰ τῶν θεῶν ἐπισκε-
πτέον, εἰ συμβουλεύουσιν αὐτὸν φίλον ποιεῖσθαι.

Τί οὖν ; ἔφη, ὃν ἂν ἡμῖν τε δοκῇ καὶ οἱ θεοὶ μὴ
ἐναντιῶνται, ἔχεις εἰπεῖν ὅπως οὗτος θηρατέος ;

9 Μὰ Δί', ἔφη, οὐ κατὰ πόδας ὥσπερ ὁ λαγῶς
οὐδ' ἀπάτῃ ὥσπερ αἱ ὄρνιθες οὐδὲ βίᾳ ὥσπερ
οἱ ἐχθροί.[1] ἄκοντα γὰρ φίλον ἑλεῖν ἐργῶδες·
χαλεπὸν δὲ καὶ δήσαντα κατέχειν ὥσπερ δοῦλον·
ἐχθροὶ γὰρ μᾶλλον ἢ φίλοι γίγνονται οἱ τοιαῦτα
πάσχοντες.

10 Φίλοι δὲ πῶς ; ἔφη.

Εἶναι μέν τινάς φασιν ἐπῳδάς, ἃς οἱ ἐπιστάμενοι ἐπᾴδοντες οἷς ἂν βούλωνται φίλους αὐτοὺς

---

[1] ἐχθροί MSS. : κάπροι Ernesti, Sauppe.

dealings and eager to do as much for his benefactors as he receives from them, so that he is worth knowing."

"Then how can we test these qualities, Socrates, 6 before intimacy begins?"

"What test do we apply to a sculptor? We don't judge by what he says, but we look at his statues, and if we see that the works he has already produced are beautiful, we feel confident that his future works will be as good."

"You mean that anyone whose good works wrought 7 upon his old friends are manifest will clearly prove a benefactor to new friends also?"

"Yes; for when I find that an owner of horses has been in the habit of treating his beasts well I think that he will treat others equally well."

"Granted! but when we have found a man who 8 seems worthy of our friendshp, how are we to set about making him our friend?"

"First we should seek guidance from the gods, whether they counsel us to make a friend of him."

"And next? Supposing that we have chosen and the gods approve him, can you say how is he to be hunted?"

"Surely not like a hare by swift pursuit, nor like 9 birds by cunning, nor like enemies[1] by force. It is no light task to capture a friend against his will, and hard to keep him a prisoner like a slave. Hatred, rather than friendship, comes of that treatment."

"But how does friendship come?" 10

"There are spells, they say, wherewith those who know charm whom they will and make friends of

---

[1] Or κάπροι, "boars."

ποιοῦνται, εἶναι δὲ καὶ φίλτρα, οἷς οἱ ἐπιστάμενοι πρὸς οὓς ἂν βούλωνται χρώμενοι φιλοῦνται
ὑπ' αὐτῶν.

11   Πόθεν οὖν, ἔφη, ταῦτα μάθοιμεν ἄν ;
῝Α μὲν αἱ Σειρῆνες ἐπῇδον τῷ Ὀδυσσεῖ,
ἤκουσας Ὁμήρου, ὧν ἐστιν ἀρχὴ τοιάδε τις·

Δεῦρ' ἄγε δή, πολύαιν' Ὀδυσεῦ, μέγα κῦδος
Ἀχαιῶν.

Ταύτην οὖν, ἔφη, τὴν ἐπῳδήν, ὦ Σώκρατες,
καὶ τοῖς ἄλλοις ἀνθρώποις αἱ Σειρῆνες ἐπᾴδου-
σαι κατεῖχον, ὥστε μὴ ἀπιέναι ἀπ' αὐτῶν τοὺς
ἐπασθέντας ;

12   Οὐκ ἀλλὰ τοῖς ἐπ' ἀρετῇ φιλοτιμουμένοις
οὕτως ἐπῇδον.

Σχεδόν τι λέγεις τοιαῦτα χρῆναι ἑκάστῳ ἐπᾴ-
δειν, οἷα μὴ νομιεῖ ἀκούων τὸν ἐπαινοῦντα κατα-
γελῶντα λέγειν.

Οὕτω μὲν γὰρ ἐχθίων τ' ἂν εἴη καὶ ἀπελαύνοι
τοὺς ἀνθρώπους ἀφ' ἑαυτοῦ, εἰ τὸν εἰδότα, ὅτι
μικρός τε καὶ αἰσχρὸς καὶ ἀσθενής ἐστιν, ἐπαινοίη
λέγων, ὅτι καλός τε καὶ μέγας καὶ ἰσχυρός ἐστιν.

Ἄλλας δέ τινας οἶσθα ἐπῳδάς ;

13   Οὐκ ἀλλ' ἤκουσα μέν, ὅτι Περικλῆς πολλὰς
ἐπίσταιτο, ἃς ἐπᾴδων τῇ πόλει ἐποίει αὐτὴν
φιλεῖν αὐτόν.

Θεμιστοκλῆς δὲ πῶς ἐποίησε τὴν πόλιν φιλεῖν
αὐτόν ;

Μὰ Δι' οὐκ ἐπᾴδων, ἀλλὰ περιάψας τι ἀγαθὸν
αὐτῇ.

14   Δοκεῖς μοι λέγειν, ὦ Σώκρατες, ὡς εἰ μέλλομεν

them, and drugs which those who know give to whom they choose and win their love."

"How then can we learn them?" **11**

"You have heard from Homer the spell that the Sirens put on Odysseus. It begins like this:

' Hither, come hither, renowned Odysseus, great
    glory of the Achaeans.' [1]

"Then did the Sirens chant in this strain for other folk too, Socrates, so as to keep those who were under the spell from leaving them?"

"No, only for those that yearned for the fame **12** that virtue gives."

"You mean, I take it, that the spell must be fitted to the listener, so that he may not take the praise for mockery."

"Yes; for to praise one for his beauty, his stature and his strength who is conscious that he is short, ugly and puny, is the way to repel him and make him dislike you more."

"Do you know any other spells?"

"No, but I have heard that Pericles knew many **13** and put them on the city, and so made her love him."

"And how did Themistocles make the city love him?"

"Not by spells: no, no; but by hanging some good amulet about her." [2]

"I think you mean, Socrates, that if we are to **14**

---

[1] *Odyssey*, xii. 184.
[2] *i. e.* not by his words, but by protecting Athens with ships and fortifications.

ἀγαθόν τινα κτήσεσθαι φίλον, αὐτοὺς ἡμᾶς ἀγαθοὺς δεῖ γενέσθαι λέγειν τε καὶ πράττειν.[1]

Σὺ δ' ᾤου, ἔφη ὁ Σωκράτης, οἷόν τ' εἶναι καὶ
πονηρὸν ὄντα χρηστοὺς φίλους κτήσασθαι ;

15 Ἑώρων γάρ, ἔφη ὁ Κριτόβουλος, ῥήτοράς τε
φαύλους ἀγαθοῖς δημηγόροις φίλους ὄντας καὶ
στρατηγεῖν οὐχ ἱκανοὺς πάνυ στρατηγικοῖς ἀνδράσιν ἑταίρους.

16 Ἆρ' οὖν, ἔφη, καί, περὶ οὗ διαλεγόμεθα, οἶσθά
τινας, οἳ ἀνωφελεῖς ὄντες ὠφελίμους δύνανται
φίλους ποιεῖσθαι ;

Μὰ Δί' οὐ δῆτ', ἔφη· ἀλλ' εἰ ἀδύνατόν ἐστι
πονηρὸν ὄντα καλοὺς κἀγαθοὺς φίλους κτήσασθαι,
ἐκεῖνο ἤδη μέλει μοι, εἰ ἔστιν αὐτὸν καλὸν κἀγαθὸν γενόμενον ἐξ ἑτοίμου τοῖς καλοῖς κἀγαθοῖς
φίλον εἶναι.

17 Ὃ ταράττει σε, ὦ Κριτόβουλε, ὅτι πολλάκις
ἄνδρας καὶ τὰ καλὰ πράττοντας καὶ τῶν αἰσχρῶν
ἀπεχομένους ὁρᾷς ἀντὶ τοῦ φίλους εἶναι στασιά-
ζοντας ἀλλήλοις καὶ χαλεπώτερον χρωμένους τῶν
μηδενὸς ἀξίων ἀνθρώπων.

18 Καὶ οὐ μόνον γ', ἔφη ὁ Κριτόβουλος, οἱ ἰδιῶται
τοῦτο ποιοῦσιν, ἀλλὰ καὶ πόλεις αἱ τῶν τε καλῶν
μάλιστα ἐπιμελόμεναι καὶ τὰ αἰσχρὰ ἥκιστα
προσιέμεναι πολλάκις πολεμικῶς ἔχουσι πρὸς
19 ἀλλήλας. ἃ λογιζόμενος πάνυ ἀθύμως ἔχω πρὸς
τὴν τῶν φίλων κτῆσιν· οὔτε γὰρ τοὺς πονηροὺς
ἀλλήλοις δυναμένους εἶναι· πῶς γὰρ ἂν ἢ ἀχά-
ριστοι ἢ ἀμελεῖς ἢ πλεονέκται ἢ ἄπιστοι ἢ ἀκρατεῖς ἄνθρωποι δύναιντο φίλοι γενέσθαι ; οἱ μὲν
οὖν πονηροὶ πάντως ἔμοιγε δοκοῦσιν ἀλλήλοις
20 ἐχθροὶ μᾶλλον ἢ φίλοι πεφυκέναι. ἀλλὰ μήν,

win a good man's friendship, we ourselves must be good in word and deed alike?"

"But you imagined that a bad man could win the friendship of honest men?"

"I did," answered Critobulus, "for I saw that 15 poor orators have good speakers among their friends, and some who are incapable of commanding an army are intimate with great generals."

"Coming then to the point under discussion, do 16 you know cases of useless persons making useful friends?"

"Assuredly not; but if it is impossible that the bad should gain the friendship of gentlemen, then I am anxious to know whether it is quite easy for a gentleman as a matter of course to be the friend of gentlemen?"

"Your trouble is, Critobulus, that you often find 17 men who do good and shun evil not on friendly terms, but apt to quarrel and treat one another more harshly than worthless fellows."

"Yes," said Critobulus, "and such conduct is not 18 confined to individuals, but even the cities that care most for the right and have least liking for the wrong are often at enmity. These thoughts make 19 me despair about the acquisition of friends. For I see on the one hand that rogues cannot be friends with one another—for how could the ungrateful, the careless, the selfish, the faithless, the incontinent, form friendships? I feel sure, then, that rogues are by their nature enemies rather than friends. But 20

---

[1] λέγειν τε καὶ πράττειν is bracketed by Sauppe as spurious.

ὥσπερ σὺ λέγεις, οὐδ ἂν τοῖς χρηστοῖς οἱ πονηροί
ποτε συναρμόσειαν εἰς φιλίαν. πῶς γὰρ οἱ τὰ
πονηρὰ ποιοῦντες τοῖς τὰ τοιαῦτα μισοῦσι φίλοι
γένοιντ' ἄν; εἰ δὲ δὴ καὶ οἱ ἀρετὴν ἀσκοῦντες
στασιάζουσί τε περὶ τοῦ πρωτεύειν ἐν ταῖς πόλεσι
καὶ φθονοῦντες ἑαυτοῖς μισοῦσιν ἀλλήλους, τίνες
ἔτι φίλοι ἔσονται καὶ ἐν τίσιν ἀνθρώποις εὔνοια
καὶ πίστις ἔσται;

21 Ἀλλ' ἔχει μέν, ἔφη ὁ Σωκράτης, ποικίλως πως
ταῦτα, ὦ Κριτόβουλε. φύσει γὰρ ἔχουσιν οἱ
ἄνθρωποι τὰ μὲν φιλικά· δέονταί τε γὰρ ἀλλήλων καὶ ἐλεοῦσι καὶ συνεργοῦντες ὠφελοῦσι
καὶ τοῦτο συνιέντες χάριν ἔχουσιν ἀλλήλοις· τὰ
δὲ πολεμικά· τά τε γὰρ αὐτὰ καλὰ καὶ ἡδέα
νομίζοντες ὑπὲρ τούτων μάχονται καὶ διχο-
γνωμονοῦντες ἐναντιοῦνται. πολεμικὸν δὲ καὶ
ἔρις καὶ ὀργή· καὶ δυσμενὲς μὲν ὁ τοῦ πλεονεκτεῖν
22 ἔρως, μισητὸν δὲ ὁ φθόνος. ἀλλ' ὅμως διὰ τούτων πάντων ἡ φιλία διαδυομένη συνάπτει τοὺς
καλούς τε κἀγαθούς. διὰ γὰρ τὴν ἀρετὴν αἱροῦνται μὲν ἄνευ πόνου τὰ μέτρια κεκτῆσθαι
μᾶλλον ἢ διὰ πολέμου πάντων κυριεύειν καὶ
δύνανται πεινῶντες καὶ διψῶντες ἀλύπως σίτου
καὶ ποτοῦ κοινωνεῖν καὶ τοῖς τῶν ὡραίων ἀφροδισίοις ἡδόμενοι καρτερεῖν, ὥστε μὴ λυπεῖν οὓς
23 μὴ προσήκει· δύνανται δὲ καὶ χρημάτων οὐ μόνον τοῦ πλεονεκτεῖν ἀπεχόμενοι νομίμως κοινωνεῖν, ἀλλὰ καὶ ἐπαρκεῖν ἀλλήλοις· δύνανται
δὲ καὶ τὴν ἔριν οὐ μόνον ἀλύπως, ἀλλὰ καὶ
συμφερόντως ἀλλήλοις διατίθεσθαι καὶ τὴν ὀργὴν
κωλύειν εἰς τὸ μεταμελησόμενον προϊέναι. τὸν
δὲ φθόνον παντάπασιν ἀφαιροῦσι τὰ μὲν ἑαυτῶν

then, as you point out, neither can rogues ever join in friendship with honest men, for how can wrong-doers become friendly with those who hate their conduct? And if we must add that the votaries of virtue strive with one another for headship in cities, and envy and hate one another, who then will be friends and where shall loyalty and faithfulness be found?"

"Ah, Critobulus, but there is a strange complica- 21 tion in these matters. Some elements in man's nature make for friendship: men need one another, feel pity, work together for their common good, and, conscious of the facts, are grateful to one another. But there are hostile elements in men. For, holding the same things to be honourable and pleasant, they fight for them, fall out and take sides. Strife and anger lead to hostility, covetousness to enmity, jealousy to hatred. Nevertheless through all these 22 barriers friendship slips, and unites the gentle natures. For thanks to their virtue these prize the untroubled security of moderate possessions above sovereignty won by war; despite hunger and thirst, they can share their food and drink without a pang; and although they delight in the charms of beauty they can resist the lure and avoid offending those whom they should respect; they can not only share 23 wealth lawfully and keep from covetousness, but also supply one another's wants; they can compose strife not only without pain, but with advantage to one another, and prevent anger from pursuing its way towards remorse: but jealousy they take away utterly, regarding their own good things as belong-

ἀγαθὰ τοῖς φίλοις οἰκεῖα παρέχοντες, τὰ δὲ τῶν
24 φίλων ἑαυτῶν νομίζοντες. πῶς οὖν οὐκ εἰκὸς
τοὺς καλοὺς κἀγαθοὺς καὶ τῶν πολιτικῶν τιμῶν
μὴ μόνον ἀβλαβεῖς, ἀλλὰ καὶ ὠφελίμους ἀλλήλοις κοινωνοὺς εἶναι; οἱ μὲν γὰρ ἐπιθυμοῦντες
ἐν ταῖς πόλεσι τιμᾶσθαί τε καὶ ἄρχειν, ἵνα
ἐξουσίαν ἔχωσι χρήματά τε κλέπτειν καὶ ἀνθρώπους βιάζεσθαι καὶ ἡδυπαθεῖν, ἄδικοί τε καὶ
πονηροὶ ἂν εἶεν καὶ ἀδύνατοι ἄλλῳ συναρμόσαι.
25 εἰ δέ τις ἐν πόλει τιμᾶσθαι βουλόμενος, ὅπως
αὐτός τε μὴ ἀδικῆται καὶ τοῖς φίλοις τὰ δίκαια
βοηθεῖν δύνηται, καὶ ἄρξας ἀγαθόν τι ποιεῖν τὴν
πατρίδα πειρᾶται, διὰ τί ὁ τοιοῦτος ἄλλῳ τοιούτῳ
οὐκ ἂν δύναιτο συναρμόσαι; πότερον τοὺς φίλους
ὠφελεῖν μετὰ τῶν καλῶν κἀγαθῶν ἧττον δυ-
νήσεται ἢ τὴν πόλιν εὐεργετεῖν ἀδυνατώτερος
26 ἔσται καλοὺς κἀγαθοὺς ἔχων συνεργούς; ἀλλὰ
καὶ ἐν τοῖς γυμνικοῖς ἀγῶσι δῆλόν ἐστιν, ὅτι εἰ
ἐξῆν τοῖς κρατίστοις συνθεμένους ἐπὶ τοὺς χείρους
ἰέναι, πάντας ἂν τοὺς ἀγῶνας οὗτοι ἐνίκων καὶ
πάντα τὰ ἆθλα οὗτοι ἐλάμβανον. ἐπεὶ οὖν ἐκεῖ
μὲν οὐκ ἐῶσι τοῦτο ποιεῖν, ἐν δὲ τοῖς πολιτικοῖς,
ἐν οἷς οἱ καλοὶ κἀγαθοὶ κρατιστεύουσιν, οὐδεὶς
κωλύει μεθ' οὗ ἄν τις βούληται τὴν πόλιν
εὐεργετεῖν, πῶς οὐ λυσιτελεῖ τοὺς βελτίστους
φίλους κτησάμενον πολιτεύεσθαι, τούτοις κοι-
νωνοῖς καὶ συνεργοῖς τῶν πράξεων μᾶλλον ἢ
27 ἀνταγωνισταῖς χρώμενον; ἀλλὰ μὴν κἀκεῖνο
δῆλον, ὅτι κἂν πολεμῇ τίς τινι, συμμάχων δε-
ήσεται καὶ τούτων πλειόνων, ἐὰν καλοῖς κἀγαθοῖς
ἀντιτάττηται. καὶ μὴν οἱ συμμαχεῖν ἐθέλοντες
εὖ ποιητέοι, ἵνα θέλωσι προθυμεῖσθαι. πολὺ δὲ
138

ing to their friends, and thinking their friend's good things to be their own. Surely, then, it is likely 24 that true gentlemen will share public honours too not only without harm to one another, but to their common benefit? For those who desire to win honour and to bear rule in their cities that they may have power to embezzle, to treat others with violence, to live in luxury, are bound to be unjust, unscrupulous, incapable of unity. But if a man 25 seeks to be honoured in a state that he may not be the victim of injustice himself and may help his friends in a just cause, and when he takes office may try to do some good to his country, why should he be incapable of union with one like himself? Will his connexion with other gentlemen render him less capable of serving his friends? Will he be less able to benefit his city with the help of other gentlemen? Even in the public games it is clear that, if the 26 strongest competitors were allowed to join forces against the weaker, they would win all the events, they would carry off all the prizes. True, that is not permitted in the games; but in politics, where the gentlemen are the strongest, nobody prevents anyone from forming any combination he may choose for the benefit of the state; surely, then, in public life it is a gain to make friends with the best, and to see in them partners and fellow-workers in a common cause, and not rivals. But, again, it is equally clear 27 that anyone who goes to war will need allies, and more of them if he is to fight an army of gentlemen. Moreover, those who are willing to fight at your side must be well treated that they may be willing to exert themselves; and it is a far sounder plan to

κρεῖττον τοὺς βελτίστους ἐλάττονας εὖ ποιεῖν ἢ
τοὺς χείρονας πλείονας ὄντας· οἱ γὰρ πονηροὶ
πολὺ πλειόνων εὐεργεσιῶν ἢ οἱ χρηστοὶ δέονται.

28 ἀλλὰ θαρρῶν, ἔφη, ὦ Κριτόβουλε, πειρῶ ἀγαθὸς
γίγνεσθαι καὶ τοιοῦτος γενόμενος θηρᾶν ἐπιχείρει
τοὺς καλούς τε κἀγαθούς. ἴσως δ' ἄν τί σοι
κἀγὼ συλλαβεῖν εἰς τὴν τῶν καλῶν τε κἀγαθῶν
θήραν ἔχοιμι διὰ τὸ ἐρωτικὸς εἶναι. δεινῶς γὰρ
ὧν ἂν ἐπιθυμήσω ἀνθρώπων ὅλος ὥρμημαι ἐπὶ τὸ
φιλῶν τε αὐτοὺς ἀντιφιλεῖσθαι ὑπ' αὐτῶν καὶ
ποθῶν ἀντιποθεῖσθαι καὶ ἐπιθυμῶν συνεῖναι καὶ
29 ἀντεπιθυμεῖσθαι τῆς συνουσίας. ὁρῶ δὲ καὶ σοὶ
τούτων δεήσον, ὅταν ἐπιθυμήσῃς φιλίαν πρός τινας
ποιεῖσθαι. μὴ οὖν ἀποκρύπτου με οἷς ἂν βούλοιο
φίλος γενέσθαι· διὰ γὰρ τὸ ἐπιμελεῖσθαι τοῦ
ἀρέσαι τῷ ἀρέσκοντί μοι οὐκ ἀπείρως οἶμαι ἔχειν
πρὸς θήραν ἀνθρώπων.

30 Καὶ ὁ Κριτόβουλος ἔφη· Καὶ μήν, ὦ Σώκρατες,
τούτων ἐγὼ τῶν μαθημάτων πάλαι ἐπιθυμῶ
ἄλλως τε καὶ εἰ ἐξαρκέσει μοι ἡ αὐτὴ ἐπιστήμη
ἐπὶ τοὺς ἀγαθοὺς τὰς ψυχὰς καὶ ἐπὶ τοὺς καλοὺς
τὰ σώματα.

31 Καὶ ὁ Σωκράτης ἔφη· Ἀλλ', ὦ Κριτόβουλε,
οὐκ ἔνεστιν ἐν τῇ ἐμῇ ἐπιστήμῃ τὸ τὰς χεῖρας
προσφέροντα ποιεῖν ὑπομένειν τοὺς καλούς. πέπεισμαι δὲ καὶ ἀπὸ τῆς Σκύλλης διὰ τοῦτο
φεύγειν τοὺς ἀνθρώπους, ὅτι τὰς χεῖρας αὐτοῖς
προσέφερε· τὰς δέ γε Σειρῆνας, ὅτι τὰς χεῖρας
οὐδενὶ προσέφερον, ἀλλὰ πᾶσι πόρρωθεν ἐπῇδον,
πάντας φασὶν ὑπομένειν καὶ ἀκούοντας αὐτῶν
κηλεῖσθαι.

32 Καὶ ὁ Κριτόβουλος ἔφη· Ὡς οὐ προσοίσοντος

show kindness to the best, who are fewer in number, than to the worst, who are the greater company; for the bad want many more kindnesses than the good. Courage, Critobulus; try to be good, and 28 when you have achieved that, set about catching your gentleman. Maybe, I myself, as an adept in love, can lend you a hand in the pursuit of gentlemen. For when I want to catch anyone it's surprising how I strain every nerve to have my love returned, my longing reciprocated by him, in my eagerness that he shall want me as much as I want him. I see that you too will feel this need when 29 you want to form a friendship. So do not hide from me the names of those whom you wish to make your friends; for I am careful to please him who pleases me, and so, I think, I am not without experience in the pursuit of men."

"Well, Socrates," said Critobulus in reply, "these 30 are the lessons I have long wished to learn, especially if the same skill will serve to win a good soul and a fair face."

"Ah no, Critobulus," said Socrates, "it belongs 31 not to my skill to lay hands on the fair and force them to submit. I am convinced that the reason why men fled from Scylla was that she laid hands on them; but the Sirens laid hands on no man; from far away they sang to all, and therefore, we are told, all submitted, and hearing were enchanted." [1]

"I am not going to put a hand on anyone," said 32

---

[1] *Odyssey* xii. 39 f., adapted.

τὰς χεῖρας, εἴ τι ἔχεις ἀγαθὸν εἰς φίλων κτῆσιν, δίδασκε. Οὐδὲ τὸ στόμα οὖν, ἔφη ὁ Σωκράτης, πρὸς τὸ στόμα προσοίσεις;

Θάρρει, ἔφη ὁ Κριτόβουλος· οὐδὲ γὰρ τὸ στόμα προσοίσω οὐδενί, ἐὰν μὴ καλὸς ᾖ.

Εὐθύς, ἔφη, σύγε, ὦ Κριτόβουλε, τοὐναντίον τοῦ συμφέροντος εἴρηκας. οἱ μὲν γὰρ καλοὶ τὰ τοιαῦτα οὐχ ὑπομένουσιν, οἱ δὲ αἰσχροὶ καὶ ἡδέως προσίενται, νομίζοντες διὰ τὴν ψυχὴν καλοὶ καλεῖσθαι.

33 Καὶ ὁ Κριτόβουλος ἔφη· Ὡς τοὺς μὲν καλοὺς φιλήσοντός μου, τοὺς δ᾽ ἀγαθοὺς καταφιλήσοντος, θαρρῶν δίδασκε τῶν φίλων τὰ θηρατικά.

Καὶ ὁ Σωκράτης ἔφη· Ὅταν οὖν, ὦ Κριτόβουλε, φίλος τινὶ βούλῃ γενέσθαι, ἐάσεις με κατειπεῖν σου πρὸς αὐτόν, ὅτι ἄγασαί τε αὐτοῦ καὶ ἐπιθυμεῖς φίλος αὐτοῦ εἶναι;

Κατηγόρει, ἔφη ὁ Κριτόβουλος· οὐδένα γὰρ οἶδα μισοῦντα τοὺς ἐπαινοῦντας.

34 Ἐὰν δέ σου προσκατηγορήσω, ἔφη, ὅτι διὰ τὸ ἄγασθαι αὐτοῦ καὶ εὐνοϊκῶς ἔχεις πρὸς αὐτόν, ἆρα μὴ διαβάλλεσθαι δόξεις ὑπ᾽ ἐμοῦ;

Ἀλλὰ καὶ αὐτῷ μοι, ἔφη, ἐγγίγνεται εὔνοια πρὸς οὓς ἂν ὑπολάβω εὐνοϊκῶς ἔχειν πρὸς ἐμέ.

35 Ταῦτα μὲν δή, ἔφη ὁ Σωκράτης, ἐξέσται μοι λέγειν περὶ σοῦ πρὸς οὓς ἂν βούλῃ φίλους ποιήσασθαι· ἐὰν δέ μοι ἔτι ἐξουσίαν δῷς λέγειν περὶ σοῦ, ὅτι ἐπιμελής τε τῶν φίλων εἶ καὶ οὐδενὶ οὕτω χαίρεις ὡς φίλοις ἀγαθοῖς καὶ ἐπί τε τοῖς καλοῖς ἔργοις τῶν φίλων ἀγάλλῃ οὐχ ἧττον ἢ ἐπὶ τοῖς σαυτοῦ καὶ ἐπὶ τοῖς ἀγαθοῖς τῶν φίλων χαίρεις οὐδὲν ἧττον ἢ ἐπὶ τοῖς σαυτοῦ,

Critobulus, "so teach me any good plan you know for making friends."

"Then won't you put lip to lip either?"

"Courage!" answered Critobulus, "I won't touch a lip with mine either—unless the owner is fair!"

"That's an unfortunate beginning for you, Critobulus! The fair [1] won't submit to such conduct; but the ugly like it, supposing that they are called fair for the beauty of their souls."

"A kiss for the fair," exclaimed Critobulus, "and 33 a thousand kisses for the good! That shall be my motto, so take courage, and teach me the art of catching friends."

"Well then, Critobulus," said Socrates, "when you want to make a new friend, will you let me warn him that you admire him and want his friendship?"

"Warn him by all means: no one hates those who praise him, so far as I know."

"Suppose I go on to warn him that your admira- 34 tion makes you well disposed towards him, you won't think I am slandering you, will you?"

"Nay; when I guess that anyone feels well disposed towards me, a like goodwill towards him is begotten in me."

"Then you will permit me to say this about you 35 to those whose friendship you desire. Now if you will give me permission to tell them besides that you are devoted to your friends and nothing gives you so much pleasure as good friends; that you take as much pride in your friends' fair achievements as in your own, and as much pleasure in your friends'

---

[1] *i.e.* beautiful in character (soul).

ὅπως τε ταῦτα γίγνηται τοῖς φίλοις οὐκ ἀπο-
κάμνεις μηχανώμενος, καὶ ὅτι ἔγνωκας ἀνδρὸς
ἀρετὴν εἶναι νικᾶν τοὺς μὲν φίλους εὖ ποιοῦντα,
τοὺς δ' ἐχθροὺς κακῶς, πάνυ ἂν οἶμαί σοι
ἐπιτήδειον εἶναί με σύνθηρον τῶν ἀγαθῶν φίλων.

36   Τί οὖν, ἔφη ὁ Κριτόβουλος, ἐμοὶ τοῦτο λέγεις,
ὥσπερ οὐκ ἐπὶ σοὶ ὂν ὅ,τι ἂν βούλῃ περὶ ἐμοῦ
λέγειν;

Μὰ Δί' οὔχ, ὥς ποτε ἐγὼ Ἀσπασίας ἤκουσα·
ἔφη γὰρ τὰς ἀγαθὰς προμνηστρίδας μετὰ μὲν
ἀληθείας τἀγαθὰ διαγγελλούσας δεινὰς εἶναι
συνάγειν ἀνθρώπους εἰς κηδείαν, ψευδομένας δ'
οὐκ ἐθέλειν ἐπαινεῖν· τοὺς γὰρ ἐξαπατηθέντας
ἅμα μισεῖν ἀλλήλους τε καὶ τὴν προμνησαμένην.
ἃ δὴ καὶ ἐγὼ πεισθεὶς ὀρθῶς ἔχειν ἡγοῦμαι οὐκ
ἐξεῖναί μοι περὶ σοῦ λέγειν ἐπαινοῦντι οὐδὲν ὅ,τι
ἂν μὴ ἀληθεύω.

37   Σὺ μὲν ἄρα, ἔφη ὁ Κριτόβουλος, τοιοῦτός μοι
φίλος εἶ, ὦ Σώκρατες, οἷος, ἂν μέν τι αὐτὸς ἔχω
ἐπιτήδειον εἰς τὸ φίλους κτήσασθαι, συλλαμβάνειν μοι· εἰ δὲ μή, οὐκ ἂν ἐθέλοις πλάσας τι
εἰπεῖν ἐπὶ τῇ ἐμῇ ὠφελείᾳ.

Πότερα δ' ἄν, ἔφη ὁ Σωκράτης, ὦ Κριτόβουλε,
δοκῶ σοι μᾶλλον ὠφελεῖν σε τὰ ψευδῆ ἐπαινῶν
ἢ πείθων πειρᾶσθαί σε ἀγαθὸν ἄνδρα γενέσθαι;

38 εἰ δὲ μὴ φανερὸν οὕτω σοι, ἐκ τῶνδε σκέψαι· εἰ
γάρ σε βουλόμενος φίλον ποιῆσαι ναυκλήρῳ
ψευδόμενος ἐπαινοίην, φάσκων ἀγαθὸν εἶναι
κυβερνήτην, ὁ δέ μοι πεισθεὶς ἐπιτρέψειέ σοι
τὴν ναῦν μὴ ἐπισταμένῳ κυβερνᾶν, ἔχεις τινὰ
ἐλπίδα μὴ ἂν σαυτόν τε καὶ τὴν ναῦν ἀπολέσαι;
ἢ εἴ σοι πείσαιμι κοινῇ τὴν πόλιν ψευδόμενος

good as in your own, and never weary of contriving
it for your friend's; and you have made up your
mind that a man's virtue consists in outdoing his
friends in kindness and his enemies in mischief;
then I think you will find me a useful companion in
the quest of good friends."

"Now why do you say this to me? as if you were 36
not free to say what you choose about me."

"Not so indeed: I can quote Aspasia against you.
She once told me that good matchmakers are successful in making marriages only when the good
reports they carry to and fro are true; false reports
she would not recommend, for the victims of deception hate one another and the matchmaker too. I
am convinced that this is sound, and so I think it is
not open to me to say anything in your praise that I
can't say truthfully."

"It appears, Socrates, that you are the sort of 37
friend to help me if I am in any way qualified to
make friends: but if not, you won't make up a story
to help me."

"How do you think I shall help you best,
Critobulus, by false praise, or by urging you to try
to be a good man? If you don't yet see clearly, 38
take the following cases as illustrations. Suppose
that I wanted to get a shipmaster to make you his
friend, and as a recommendation told him that you
are a good skipper, which is untrue; and suppose
that he believed me and put you in charge of his
ship in spite of your not knowing how to steer it:
have you any reason to hope that you would not
lose the ship and your life as well? Or suppose
that I falsely represented to the Assembly that you

ὡς ἂν στρατηγικῷ τε καὶ δικαστικῷ καὶ πολιτικῷ
ἑαυτὴν ἐπιτρέψαι, τί ἂν οἴει σεαυτὸν καὶ τὴν
πόλιν ὑπὸ σοῦ παθεῖν; ἢ εἴ τινας ἰδίᾳ τῶν
πολιτῶν πείσαιμι ψευδόμενος ὡς ὄντι οἰκονομικῷ
τε καὶ ἐπιμελεῖ τὰ ἑαυτῶν ἐπιτρέψαι, ἆρ' οὐκ
ἂν πεῖραν διδοὺς ἅμα τε βλαβερὸς εἴης καὶ κατα-
39 γέλαστος φαίνοιο; ἀλλὰ συντομωτάτη τε καὶ
ἀσφαλεστάτη καὶ καλλίστη ὁδός, ὦ Κριτόβουλε,
ὅ,τι ἂν βούλῃ δοκεῖν ἀγαθὸς εἶναι, τοῦτο καὶ
γενέσθαι ἀγαθὸν πειρᾶσθαι. ὅσαι δ' ἐν ἀνθρώποις ἀρεταὶ λέγονται, σκοπούμενος εὑρήσεις
πάσας μαθήσει τε καὶ μελέτῃ αὐξανομένας.
ἐγὼ μὲν οὖν, ὦ Κριτόβουλε, οὕτως οἶμαι δεῖν
ἡμᾶς θηρᾶν.[1] εἰ δὲ σύ πως ἄλλως γιγνώσκεις,
δίδασκε.

Καὶ ὁ Κριτόβουλος, Ἀλλ' αἰσχυνοίμην ἄν,
ἔφη, ὦ Σώκρατες, ἀντιλέγων τούτοις· οὔτε γὰρ
καλὰ οὔτε ἀληθῆ λέγοιμ' ἄν.

VII. Καὶ μὴν τὰς ἀπορίας γε τῶν φίλων τὰς
μὲν δι' ἄγνοιαν ἐπειρᾶτο γνώμῃ ἀκεῖσθαι, τὰς
δὲ δι' ἔνδειαν διδάσκων κατὰ δύναμιν ἀλλήλοις
ἐπαρκεῖν. ἐρῶ δὲ καὶ ἐν τούτοις ἃ σύνοιδα
αὐτῷ.

Ἀρίσταρχον γάρ ποτε ὁρῶν σκυθρωπῶς
ἔχοντα, Ἔοικας, ἔφη, ὦ Ἀρίσταρχε, βαρέως
φέρειν τι. χρὴ δὲ τοῦ βάρους τοῖς φίλοις
μεταδιδόναι· ἴσως γὰρ ἄν τί σε καὶ ἡμεῖς
κουφίσαιμεν.

2 Καὶ ὁ Ἀρίσταρχος, Ἀλλὰ μήν, ἔφη, ὦ

---

[1] θηρᾶν is a conjecture in one MS. to fill a gap, and is not
right.

are a born general, jurist and statesman in one, and
so persuaded the state to commit her fortunes to
you, what do you suppose would happen to the
state and to yourself under your guidance? Or
again, suppose that I falsely described you to certain
citizens in private as a thrifty, careful person, and
persuaded them to place their affairs in your hands,
wouldn't you do them harm and look ridiculous
when you came to the test? Nay, Critobulus, if 39
you want to be thought good at anything, you must
try to be so; that is the quickest, the surest, the
best way.[1] You will find on reflection that every
kind of virtue named among men is increased by
study and practice. Such is the view I take of our
duty, Critobulus. If you have anything to say
against it, tell me."

"Why, Socrates," said Critobulus, "I should be
ashamed to contradict you, for I should be saying
what is neither honourable nor true."

VII. To pass to another subject. The distresses
of his friends that arose from ignorance he tried to
cure by advice, those that were due to want by
telling them how to help one another according to
their power. On this subject too I will state what
I know about him.

One day, noticing that Aristarchus looked glum,
he said: "Aristarchus, you seem to have a burden
on your mind. You should let your friends share
it; possibly we may do something to ease you."

"Ah yes, Socrates," replied Aristarchus, "I am 2

[1] *Cyropaedia*, I. vi. 22.

Σώκρατες, ἐν πολλῇ γέ εἰμι ἀπορίᾳ. ἐπεὶ γὰρ
ἐστασίασεν ἡ πόλις, πολλῶν φυγόντων εἰς τὸν
Πειραιᾶ, συνεληλύθασιν ὡς ἐμὲ καταλελειμμέναι
ἀδελφαί τε καὶ ἀδελφιδαῖ καὶ ἀνεψιαὶ τοσαῦται,
ὥστ᾽ εἶναι ἐν τῇ οἰκίᾳ τέτταρας καὶ δέκα τοὺς
ἐλευθέρους. λαμβάνομεν δὲ οὔτε ἐκ τῆς γῆς
οὐδέν· οἱ γὰρ ἐναντίοι κρατοῦσιν αὐτῆς· οὔτ᾽
ἀπὸ τῶν οἰκιῶν· ὀλιγανθρωπία γὰρ ἐν τῷ ἄστει
γέγονε. τὰ ἔπιπλα δὲ οὐδεὶς ὠνεῖται οὐδὲ δανείσασθαι οὐδαμόθεν ἔστιν ἀργύριον, ἀλλὰ πρότερον
ἄν τίς μοι δοκεῖ ἐν τῇ ὁδῷ ζητῶν εὑρεῖν ἢ δανειζό-
μενος λαβεῖν. χαλεπὸν μὲν οὖν ἐστιν, ὦ Σώκρατες,
τοὺς οἰκείους περιορᾶν ἀπολλυμένους, ἀδύνατον
δὲ τοσούτους τρέφειν ἐν τοιούτοις πράγμασιν.

3 Ἀκούσας οὖν ταῦτα ὁ Σωκράτης, Τί ποτέ
ἐστιν, ἔφη, ὅτι Κεράμων μὲν πολλοὺς τρέφων
οὐ μόνον ἑαυτῷ τε καὶ τούτοις τἀπιτήδεια δύναται
παρέχειν, ἀλλὰ καὶ περιποιεῖται τοσαῦτα, ὥστε
καὶ πλουτεῖν, σὺ δὲ πολλοὺς τρέφων δέδοικας, μὴ
δι᾽ ἔνδειαν τῶν ἐπιτηδείων ἅπαντες ἀπόλησθε ;

Ὅτι νὴ Δί᾽, ἔφη, ὁ μὲν δούλους τρέφει, ἐγὼ δ᾽
ἐλευθέρους.

4 Καὶ πότερον, ἔφη, τοὺς παρὰ σοὶ ἐλευθέρους
οἴει βελτίους εἶναι ἢ τοὺς παρὰ Κεράμωνι
δούλους ;

Ἐγὼ μὲν οἶμαι, ἔφη, τοὺς παρ᾽ ἐμοὶ ἐλευθέρους.

Οὐκοῦν, ἔφη, αἰσχρὸν τὸν μὲν ἀπὸ τῶν πονηρο-
τέρων εὐπορεῖν, σὲ δὲ πολλῷ βελτίους ἔχοντα ἐν
ἀπορίᾳ εἶναι ;

Νὴ Δί᾽, ἔφη· ὁ μὲν γὰρ τεχνίτας τρέφει, ἐγὼ δ᾽
ἐλευθερίως πεπαιδευμένους.

in great distress. Since the revolution there has been an exodus to the Piraeus, and a crowd of my women-folk, being left behind, are come to me,—sisters, nieces and cousins,—so that we are fourteen in the house without counting the slaves. We get nothing from our land, because our enemies have seized it, and nothing from our house property, now there are so few residents in the city. Portable property finds no buyers, and it's quite impossible to borrow money anywhere: I really think a search in the street would have better result than an application for a loan. It's hard, Socrates, to let one's people die, but impossible to keep so many in times like these."

When Socrates heard this, he asked: " How is it that with so many mouths to feed Ceramon not only contrives to provide for the needs of himself and his family, but actually saves enough to make him a rich man, whereas you, with so many mouths to feed, fear you will all be starved to death?"

"The explanation, of course, is this: my dependants are gentlefolk, his are slaves."

"And which do you think are the better, his slaves or your gentlefolk?"

"My gentlefolk, I think."

"Then is it not disgraceful that you with your gentlefolk should be in distress, while he is kept in affluence by his meaner household?"

"Of course his dependants are artisans, while mine have had a liberal education."

5 Ἆρ᾽ οὖν, ἔφη, τεχνῖταί εἰσιν οἱ χρήσιμόν τι
ποιεῖν ἐπιστάμενοι ;
  Μάλιστά γ᾽, ἔφη.
  Οὐκοῦν χρήσιμά γ᾽ ἄλφιτα ;
  Σφόδρα γε.
  Τί δ᾽ ἄρτοι ;
  Οὐδὲν ἧττον.
  Τί γάρ ; ἔφη, ἱμάτιά τε ἀνδρεῖα καὶ γυναικεῖα
καὶ χιτωνίσκοι καὶ χλαμύδες καὶ ἐξωμίδες ;
  Σφόδρα γ᾽, ἔφη, καὶ πάντα ταῦτα χρήσιμα.
  Ἔπειτα, ἔφη, οἱ παρὰ σοὶ τούτων οὐδὲν
ἐπίστανται ποιεῖν ;
  Πάντα μὲν οὖν, ὡς ἐγῷμαι.

6 Εἶτ᾽ οὐκ οἶσθ᾽, ὅτι ἀφ᾽ ἑνὸς μὲν τούτων, ἀλφι-
τοποιίας, Ναυσικύδης οὐ μόνον ἑαυτόν τε καὶ
τοὺς οἰκέτας τρέφει, ἀλλὰ πρὸς τούτοις καὶ ὗς
πολλὰς καὶ βοῦς, καὶ περιποιεῖται τοσαῦτα,
ὥστε καὶ τῇ πόλει πολλάκις λειτουργεῖν, ἀπὸ
δὲ ἀρτοποιίας Κύρηβος τήν τε οἰκίαν πᾶσαν
διατρέφει καὶ ζῇ δαψιλῶς, Δημέας δ᾽ ὁ Κολλυτεὺς
ἀπὸ χλαμυδουργίας, Μένων δ᾽ ἀπὸ χλανιδοποιίας,
Μεγαρέων δ᾽ οἱ πλεῖστοι ἀπὸ ἐξωμιδοποιίας
διατρέφονται ;
  Νὴ Δί᾽, ἔφη· οὗτοι μὲν γὰρ ὠνούμενοι βαρβάρους ἀνθρώπους ἔχουσιν, ὥστ᾽ ἀναγκάζειν
ἐργάζεσθαι ἃ καλῶς ἔχει· ἐγὼ δ᾽ ἐλευθέρους τε
καὶ συγγενεῖς.

7 Ἔπειτ᾽, ἔφη, ὅτι ἐλεύθεροί τ᾽ εἰσὶ καὶ συγγενεῖς σοι, οἴει χρῆναι αὐτοὺς μηδὲν ἄλλο ποιεῖν ἢ ἐσθίειν καὶ καθεύδειν ; πότερον καὶ τῶν
ἄλλων ἐλευθέρων τοὺς οὕτω ζῶντας ἄμεινον
διάγοντας ὁρᾷς καὶ μᾶλλον εὐδαιμονίζεις ἢ τοὺς

150

" What is an artisan? one who knows how to 5
produce something useful? "

" Certainly."

" Are groats useful? "

" Yes, very."

" And bread? "

" No less so."

" What about men's and women's cloaks, shirts,
capes, smocks? "

" Yes, all these things too are very useful."

" Then don't the members of your household
know how to make any of these? "

" I believe they can make all of them."

" Don't you know, then, that by manufacturing 6
one of these commodities, namely groats, Nausicydes
keeps not only himself and his family, but large
herds of swine and cattle as well, and has so much
to spare that he often undertakes costly public
duties; that Cyrebus feeds his whole family well
and lives in luxury by baking bread, Demeas of
Collytus by making capes, Menon by making cloaks;
and most of the Megarians make a good living out
of smocks? "

" Yes, of course; for they buy foreign slaves
and can force them to make what is convenient,
but my household is made up of gentlefolk and
relations."

" And so, just because they are gentlefolk and 7
related to you, you think they should do nothing
but eat and sleep? Do you find that other gentlefolk who live this sort of life are better off and

ἃ ἐπίστανται χρήσιμα πρὸς τὸν βίον τούτων
ἐπιμελομένους ; ἢ τὴν μὲν ἀργίαν καὶ τὴν ἀμέλειαν αἰσθάνῃ τοῖς ἀνθρώποις πρός τε τὸ μαθεῖν
ἃ προσήκει ἐπίστασθαι καὶ πρὸς τὸ μνημονεύειν
ἃ ἂν μάθωσι καὶ πρὸς τὸ ὑγιαίνειν τε καὶ ἰσχύειν
τοῖς σώμασι καὶ πρὸς τὸ κτήσασθαί τε καὶ σώζειν
τὰ χρήσιμα πρὸς τὸν βίον ὠφέλιμα ὄντα, τὴν δ'
8 ἐργασίαν καὶ τὴν ἐπιμέλειαν οὐδὲν χρήσιμα ; ἔμαθον δὲ ἃ φῂς αὐτὰς ἐπίστασθαι πότερον ὡς οὔτε
χρήσιμα ὄντα πρὸς τὸν βίον οὔτε ποιήσουσαι
αὐτῶν οὐδὲν ἢ τοὐναντίον ὡς καὶ ἐπιμελησόμεναι
τούτων καὶ ὠφεληθησόμεναι ἀπ' αὐτῶν ; ποτέρως
γὰρ ἂν μᾶλλον ἄνθρωποι σωφρονοῖεν, ἀργοῦντες
ἢ τῶν χρησίμων ἐπιμελόμενοι ; ποτέρως δ' ἂν
δικαιότεροι εἶεν, εἰ ἐργάζοιντο ἢ εἰ ἀργοῦντες
9 βουλεύοιντο περὶ τῶν ἐπιτηδείων ; ἀλλὰ καὶ νῦν
μέν, ὡς ἐγῷμαι, οὔτε σὺ ἐκείνας φιλεῖς οὔτ'
ἐκεῖναι σέ, σὺ μὲν ἡγούμενος αὐτὰς ἐπιζημίους
εἶναι σεαυτῷ, ἐκεῖναι δὲ σὲ ὁρῶσαι ἀχθόμενον
ἐφ' ἑαυταῖς. ἐκ δὲ τούτων κίνδυνος μείζω τε
ἀπέχθειαν γίγνεσθαι καὶ τὴν προγεγονυῖαν χάριν
μειοῦσθαι. ἐὰν δὲ προστατήσῃς, ὅπως ἐνεργοὶ
ὦσι, σὺ μὲν ἐκείνας φιλήσεις ὁρῶν ὠφελίμους
σεαυτῷ οὔσας, ἐκεῖναι δὲ σὲ ἀγαπήσουσιν αἰσθό-
μεναι χαίροντα αὐταῖς, τῶν δὲ προγεγονυιῶν
εὐεργεσιῶν ἥδιον μεμνημένοι τὴν ἀπ' ἐκείνων
χάριν αὐξήσετε καὶ ἐκ τούτων φιλικώτερόν τε
10 καὶ οἰκειότερον ἀλλήλοις ἕξετε. εἰ μὲν τοίνυν
αἰσχρόν τι ἔμελλον ἐργάσεσθαι, θάνατον ἀντ'
αὐτοῦ προαιρετέον ἦν· νῦν δὲ ἃ μὲν δοκεῖ κάλλιστα
καὶ πρεπωδέστατα γυναιξὶν εἶναι ἐπίστανται, ὡς
ἔοικε. πάντες δὲ ἃ ἐπίστανται ῥᾷστά τε καὶ

happier than those who are usefully employed in
work that they understand? Or is it your experience that idleness and carelessness help men
to learn what they ought to know and remember
what they learn, to make themselves healthy and
strong, and to get and keep things that are of
practical use, but industry and carefulness are
useless things? When these women learned the 8
work that you say they understand, did they regard
it as of no practical use, and had they no intention
of taking it up, or did they mean to occupy themselves in it and obtain some benefit from it? Which
makes men more prudent, idleness or useful employ-
ment? Which makes men more just, work or idle
discussions about supplies? Besides, at present, I 9
fancy, you don't love these ladies and they don't
love you: you think they are a tax on you, and they
see that you feel them to be a burden. And the
danger in this state of things is that dislike may
grow and their former gratitude fade away; but if
you exert your authority and make them work, you
will love them, when you find that they are profitable
to you, and they will be fond of you, when they feel
that you are pleased with them. Both you and
they will like to recall past kindnesses and will
strengthen the feeling of gratitude that these en-
gender; thus you will be better friends and feel
more at home. To be sure, if they were going to do 10
something disgraceful, death would be a better fate.
But in point of fact the work they understand is, as
it appears, the work considered the most honourable
and the most suitable for a woman; and the work
that is understood is always done with the greatest

τάχιστα καὶ κάλλιστα καὶ ἥδιστα ἐργάζονται.
μὴ οὖν ὄκνει, ἔφη, ταῦτα εἰσηγεῖσθαι αὐταῖς, ἃ
σοί τε λυσιτελήσει κἀκείναις, καί, ὡς εἰκός,
ἡδέως ὑπακούσονται.

11   Ἀλλὰ νὴ τοὺς θεούς, ἔφη ὁ Ἀρίσταρχος,
οὕτως μοι δοκεῖς καλῶς λέγειν, ὦ Σώκρατες,
ὥστε πρόσθεν μὲν οὐ προσιέμην δανείσασθαι
εἰδώς, ὅτι ἀναλώσας ὃ ἂν λάβω οὐχ ἕξω ἀποδοῦναι, νῦν δέ μοι δοκῶ εἰς ἔργων ἀφορμὴν
ὑπομενεῖν αὐτὸ ποιῆσαι.

12   Ἐκ τούτων δὲ ἐπορίσθη μὲν ἀφορμή, ἐωνήθη
δὲ ἔρια, καὶ ἐργαζόμεναι μὲν ἠρίστων, ἐργασάμεναι δὲ ἐδείπνουν, ἱλαραὶ δὲ ἀντὶ σκυθρωπῶν
ἦσαν καὶ ἀντὶ ὑφορωμένων ἑαυτοὺς ἡδέως ἀλλήλους ἑώρων, καὶ αἱ μὲν ὡς κηδεμόνα ἐφίλουν, ὁ
δὲ ὡς ὠφελίμους ἠγάπα. τέλος δὲ ἐλθὼν πρὸς
τὸν Σωκράτην χαίρων διηγεῖτο ταῦτά τε καὶ ὅτι
αἰτιῶνται αὐτὸν μόνον τῶν ἐν τῇ οἰκίᾳ ἀργὸν
ἐσθίειν.

13   Καὶ ὁ Σωκράτης ἔφη· Εἶτ᾽ οὐ λέγεις αὐταῖς
τὸν τοῦ κυνὸς λόγον; φασὶ γάρ, ὅτε φωνήεντα
ἦν τὰ ζῷα, τὴν οἶν πρὸς τὸν δεσπότην εἰπεῖν·
Θαυμαστὸν ποιεῖς, ὃς ἡμῖν μὲν ταῖς καὶ ἔριά σοι
καὶ ἄρνας καὶ τυρὸν παρεχούσαις οὐδὲν δίδως
ὅ,τι ἂν μὴ ἐκ τῆς γῆς λάβωμεν, τῷ δὲ κυνί, ὃς
οὐδὲν τοιοῦτόν σοι παρέχει, μεταδίδως οὗπερ
14   αὐτὸς ἔχεις σίτου.   τὸν κύνα οὖν ἀκούσαντα
εἰπεῖν· Ναὶ μὰ Δί᾽· ἐγὼ γάρ εἰμι ὁ καὶ ὑμᾶς
αὐτὰς σώζων, ὥστε μήτε ὑπ᾽ ἀνθρώπων κλέπτεσθαι μήτε ὑπὸ λύκων ἁρπάζεσθαι, ἐπεὶ ὑμεῖς
γε, εἰ μὴ ἐγὼ προφυλάττοιμι ὑμᾶς, οὐδ᾽ ἂν
νέμεσθαι δύναισθε φοβούμεναι, μὴ ἀπόλησθε.

ease, speed, pride and pleasure. So do not hesitate to offer them work that will yield a return both to you and to them, and probably they will welcome your proposal."

"Well, well," said Aristarchus, "your advice 11 seems so good, Socrates, that I think I shall now bring myself to borrow capital to make a start. Hitherto I have had no inclination to do so, knowing that when I had spent the loan I should not have the wherewithal to repay it."

The consequence was that capital was provided 12 and wool purchased. The women worked during dinner and only stopped at the supper hour. There were happy instead of gloomy faces: suspicious glances were exchanged for pleasant smiles. They loved him as a guardian and he liked them because they were useful. Finally Aristarchus came to Socrates and told him this with delight. "One objection they have to me," he added: "I am the only member of the household who eats the bread of idleness."

"Then why not tell them the story of the dog?" 13 asked Socrates. "It is said that when beasts could talk, a sheep said to her master: 'It is strange that you give us sheep nothing but what we get from the land, though we supply you with wool and lambs and cheese, and yet you share your own food with your dog, who supplies you with none of these things.' The dog heard this, and said: 'Of course 14 he does. Do not I keep you from being stolen by thieves, and carried off by wolves? Why, but for my protection you couldn't even feed for fear of

οὕτω δὴ λέγεται καὶ τὰ πρόβατα συγχωρῆσαι τὸν κύνα προτιμᾶσθαι. καὶ σὺ οὖν ἐκείναις λέγε, ὅτι ἀντὶ κυνὸς εἶ φύλαξ καὶ ἐπιμελητὴς καὶ διὰ σὲ οὐδ᾽ ὑφ᾽ ἑνὸς ἀδικούμεναι ἀσφαλῶς τε καὶ ἡδέως ἐργαζόμεναι ζῶσιν.

VIII. Ἄλλον δέ ποτε ἀρχαῖον ἑταῖρον διὰ χρόνου ἰδών, Πόθεν, ἔφη, Εὔθηρε, φαίνῃ;

Ὑπὸ μὲν τὴν κατάλυσιν τοῦ πολέμου, ἔφη, ὦ Σώκρατες, ἐκ τῆς ἀποδημίας, νυνὶ μέντοι αὐτόθεν. ἐπειδὴ γὰρ ἀφῃρέθην μὲν τὰ ἐν τῇ ὑπερορίᾳ κτήματα, ἐν δὲ τῇ Ἀττικῇ ὁ πατήρ μοι οὐδὲν κατέλιπεν, ἀναγκάζομαι νῦν ἐπιδημήσας τῷ σώματι ἐργαζόμενος τὰ ἐπιτήδεια πορίζεσθαι. δοκεῖ δέ μοι τοῦτο κρεῖττον εἶναι ἢ δεῖσθαί τινος ἀνθρώπων, ἄλλως τε καὶ μηδὲν ἔχοντα, ἐφ᾽ ὅτῳ ἂν δανειζοίμην.

2 Καὶ πόσον ἂν χρόνον οἴει σοι, ἔφη, τὸ σῶμα ἱκανὸν εἶναι μισθοῦ τὰ ἐπιτήδεια ἐργάζεσθαι;

Μὰ τὸν Δί᾽, ἔφη, οὐ πολὺν χρόνον.

Καὶ μήν, ἔφη, ὅταν γε πρεσβύτερος γένῃ, δῆλον ὅτι δαπάνης μὲν δεήσῃ, μισθὸν δὲ οὐδείς σοι ἐθελήσει τῶν τοῦ σώματος ἔργων διδόναι.

3 Ἀληθῆ λέγεις, ἔφη.

Οὐκοῦν, ἔφη, κρεῖττόν ἐστιν αὐτόθεν τοῖς τοιούτοις τῶν ἔργων ἐπιτίθεσθαι, ἃ καὶ πρεσβυτέρῳ γενομένῳ ἐπαρκέσει, καὶ προσελθόντα τῷ τῶν πλείονα χρήματα κεκτημένων, τῷ δεομένῳ τοῦ συνεπιμελησομένου, ἔργων τε ἐπιστατοῦντα καὶ συγκομίζοντα τοὺς καρποὺς καὶ συμφυλάττοντα τὴν οὐσίαν ὠφελοῦντα ἀντωφελεῖσθαι.

4 Χαλεπῶς ἄν, ἔφη, ἐγώ, ὦ Σώκρατες, δουλείαν ὑπομείναιμι.

being killed.' And so, they say, the sheep admitted the dog's claim to preference. Do you then tell these women that you are their watch-dog and keeper, and it is due to you that they live and work in safety and comfort, with none to harm them."

VIII. Again, on meeting an old comrade after long absence he said: "Where do you come from, Eutherus?"

"I came home when the war ended, Socrates, and am now living here," he replied. "Since we have lost our foreign property, and my father left me nothing in Attica, I am forced to settle down here now and work for my living with my hands. I think it's better than begging, especially as I have no security to offer for a loan."

"And how long will you have the strength, do 2 you think, to earn your living by your work?"

"Oh, not long, of course."

"But remember, when you get old you will have to spend money, and nobody will be willing to pay you for your labour."

"True."

"Then it would be better to take up some kind 3 of work at once that will assure you a competence when you get old, and to go to somebody who is better off and wants an assistant, and get a return for your services by acting as his bailiff, helping to get in his crops and looking after his property."

"I shouldn't like to make myself a slave, 4 Socrates."

157

Καὶ μὴν οἵ γε ἐν ταῖς πόλεσι προστατεύοντες
καὶ τῶν δημοσίων ἐπιμελόμενοι οὐ δουλοπρεπέ-
στεροι ἕνεκα τούτου, ἀλλ᾽ ἐλευθεριώτεροι
νομίζονται.

5 Ὅλως, ἔφη, ὦ Σώκρατες, τὸ ὑπαίτιον εἶναί
τινι οὐ πάνυ προσίεμαι. Καὶ μήν, ἔφη, Εὔθηρε,
οὐ πάνυ γε ῥᾴδιόν ἐστιν εὑρεῖν ἔργον, ἐφ᾽ ᾧ οὐκ
ἄν τις αἰτίαν ἔχοι. χαλεπὸν γὰρ οὕτω τι ποιῆσαι, ὥστε μηδὲν ἁμαρτεῖν, χαλεπὸν δὲ καὶ ἀναμαρτήτως τι ποιήσαντα μὴ ἀγνώμονι κριτῇ περι-
τυχεῖν· ἐπεὶ καὶ οἷς νῦν ἐργάζεσθαι φὴς θαυμάζω
6 εἰ ῥᾴδιόν ἐστιν ἀνέγκλητον διαγίγνεσθαι. χρὴ
οὖν πειρᾶσθαι τοὺς φιλαιτίους φεύγειν καὶ τοὺς
εὐγνώμονας διώκειν καὶ τῶν πραγμάτων ὅσα μὲν
δύνασαι ποιεῖν ὑπομένειν, ὅσα δὲ μὴ δύνασαι
φυλάττεσθαι, ὅ,τι δ᾽ ἂν πράττῃς, τούτου ὡς
κάλλιστα καὶ προθυμότατα ἐπιμελεῖσθαι. οὕτω
γὰρ ἥκιστ᾽ ἂν μέν σε οἶμαι ἐν αἰτίᾳ εἶναι, μάλιστα
δὲ τῇ ἀπορίᾳ βοήθειαν εὑρεῖν, ῥᾷστα δὲ καὶ
ἀκινδυνότατα ζῆν καὶ εἰς τὸ γῆρας διαρκέστατα.

IX. Οἶδα δέ ποτε αὐτὸν καὶ Κρίτωνος ἀκούσαντα, ὡς χαλεπὸν ὁ βίος Ἀθήνησιν εἴη ἀνδρὶ
βουλομένῳ τὰ ἑαυτοῦ πράττειν. Νῦν γάρ, ἔφη,
ἐμέ τινες εἰς δίκας ἄγουσιν, οὐχ ὅτι ἀδικοῦνται
ὑπ᾽ ἐμοῦ, ἀλλ᾽ ὅτι νομίζουσιν ἥδιον ἄν με ἀργύριον
τελέσαι ἢ πράγματα ἔχειν.

2 Καὶ ὁ Σωκράτης, Εἰπέ μοι, ἔφη, ὦ Κρίτων,
κύνας δὲ τρέφεις, ἵνα σοι τοὺς λύκους ἀπὸ τῶν
προβάτων ἀπερύκωσι;

Καὶ μάλα, ἔφη· μᾶλλον γάρ μοι λυσιτελεῖ
τρέφειν ἢ μή.

Οὐκ ἂν οὖν θρέψαις καὶ ἄνδρα, ὅστις ἐθέλοι

"But surely those who control their cities and take charge of public affairs are thought more respectable, not more slavish on that account."

"Briefly, Socrates, I have no inclination to expose 5 myself to any man's censure."

"But, you see, Eutherus, it is by no means easy to find a post in which one is not liable to censure. Whatever one does, it is difficult to avoid mistakes, and it is difficult to escape unfair criticism even if one makes no mistakes. I wonder if you find it easy to avoid complaints entirely even from your present employers. You should try, therefore, to 6 have no truck with grumblers and to attach yourself to considerate masters; to undertake such duties as you can perform and beware of any that are too much for you, and, whatever you do, to give of your best and put your heart into the business. In this way, I think, you are most likely to escape censure, find relief from your difficulties, live in ease and security, and obtain an ample competence for old age."

IX. I remember that he once heard Criton say that life at Athens was difficult for a man who wanted to mind his own business. "At this moment," Criton added, "actions are pending against me not because I have done the plaintiffs an injury, but because they think that I would sooner pay than have trouble."

"Tell me, Criton," said Socrates, "do you keep 2 dogs to fend the wolves from your sheep?"

"Certainly," replied Criton, "because it pays me better to keep them."

"Then why not keep a man who may be able

τε καὶ δύναιτό σου ἀπερύκειν τοὺς ἐπιχειροῦντας
ἀδικεῖν σε ;

Ἡδέως γ᾿ ἄν, ἔφη, εἰ μὴ φοβοίμην, ὅπως μὴ
ἐπ᾿ αὐτόν με τράποιτο.

3   Τί δ᾿ ; ἔφη, οὐχ ὁρᾶς, ὅτι πολλῷ ἥδιόν ἐστι
χαριζόμενον οἵῳ σοὶ ἀνδρὶ ἢ ἀπεχθόμενον ὠφελεῖσθαι ; εὖ ἴσθι, ὅτι εἰσὶν ἐνθάδε τῶν τοιούτων
ἀνδρῶν οἳ πάνυ ἂν φιλοτιμηθεῖεν φίλῳ σοι
χρῆσθαι.

4   Καὶ ἐκ τούτων ἀνευρίσκουσιν Ἀρχέδημον,
πάνυ μὲν ἱκανὸν εἰπεῖν τε καὶ πρᾶξαι, πένητα
δέ· οὐ γὰρ ἦν οἷος ἀπὸ παντὸς κερδαίνειν, ἀλλὰ
φιλόχρηστός τε καὶ ἔφη ῥᾷστον εἶναι ἀπὸ τῶν
συκοφαντῶν λαμβάνειν. τούτῳ οὖν ὁ Κρίτων,
ὁπότε συγκομίζοι ἢ σῖτον ἢ ἔλαιον ἢ οἶνον ἢ
ἔρια ἤ τι ἄλλο τῶν ἐν ἀγρῷ γιγνομένων χρησίμων
πρὸς τὸν βίον, ἀφελὼν ἐδίδου καὶ ὁπότε θύοι,
5   ἐκάλει καὶ τὰ τοιαῦτα πάντα ἐπεμελεῖτο. νομίσας
δὲ ὁ Ἀρχέδημος ἀποστροφήν οἱ τὸν Κρίτωνος
οἶκον μάλα περιεῖπεν αὐτόν. καὶ εὐθὺς τῶν
συκοφαντούντων τὸν Κρίτωνα ἀνευρίσκει πολλὰ
μὲν ἀδικήματα, πολλοὺς δ᾿ ἐχθρούς, καὶ αὐτῶν
τινα προσεκαλεσαῖτο[1] εἰς δίκην δημοσίαν, ἐν
ᾗ αὐτὸν ἔδει κριθῆναι, ὅ,τι δεῖ παθεῖν ἢ ἀπο-
6   τῖσαι. ὁ δὲ συνειδὼς αὑτῷ πολλὰ καὶ πονηρὰ
πάντ᾿ ἐποίει, ὥστε ἀπαλλαγῆναι τοῦ Ἀρχεδήμου.
ὁ δὲ Ἀρχέδημος οὐκ ἀπηλλάττετο, ἕως τόν τε
7   Κρίτωνα ἀφῆκε καὶ αὐτῷ χρήματα ἔδωκεν. ἐπεὶ
δὲ τοῦτό τε καὶ ἄλλα τοιαῦτα ὁ Ἀρχέδημος διε-
πράξατο, ἤδη τότε, ὥσπερ ὅταν νομεὺς ἀγαθὸν
κύνα ἔχῃ, καὶ οἱ ἄλλοι νομεῖς βούλονται πλησίον
αὐτοῦ τὰς ἀγέλας ἱστάναι, ἵνα τοῦ κυνὸς ἀπο-

and willing to fend off the attempts to injure you?"

"I would gladly do so were I not afraid that he might turn on me."

"What? don't you see that it is much pleasanter 3 to profit by humouring a man like you than by quarrelling with him? I assure you there are men in this city who would take pride in your friendship."

Thereupon they sought out Archedemus, an 4 excellent speaker and man of affairs, but poor. For he was not one of those who make money unscrupu- lously, but an honest man, and he would say that it was easy to take forfeit from false accusers. So whenever Criton was storing corn, oil, wine, wool or other farm produce, he would make a present of a portion to Archedemus, and when he sacrificed, he invited him, and in fact lost no similar opportu- nity of showing courtesy. Archedemus came to 5 regard Criton's house as a haven of refuge and con- stantly paid his respects to him. He soon found out that Criton's false accusers had much to answer for and many enemies. He brought one of them to trial on a charge involving damages or imprison- ment. The defendant, conscious that he was guilty 6 on many counts, did all he could to get quit of Archedemus. But Archedemus refused to let him off until he withdrew the action against Criton and compensated him. Archedemus carried through 7 several other enterprises of a similar kind; and now many of Criton's friends begged him to make Archedemus their protector, just as when a shepherd

---

[1] προσεκαλεῖτο, Sauppe with A.

λαύωσιν, οὕτω δὴ καὶ Κρίτωνος πολλοὶ τῶν
φίλων ἐδέοντο καὶ σφίσι παρέχειν φύλακα τὸν
8 Ἀρχέδημον. ὁ δὲ Ἀρχέδημος τῷ Κρίτωνι ἡδέως
ἐχαρίζετο, καὶ οὐχ ὅτι μόνος ὁ Κρίτων ἐν ἡσυχίᾳ
ἦν, ἀλλὰ καὶ οἱ φίλοι αὐτοῦ. εἰ δέ τις αὐτῷ
τούτων, οἷς ἀπήχθετο, ὀνειδίζοι, ὡς ὑπὸ Κρίτωνος
ὠφελούμενος κολακεύοι αὐτόν, Πότερον οὖν, ἔφη
ὁ Ἀρχέδημος, αἰσχρόν ἐστιν εὐεργετούμενον ὑπὸ
χρηστῶν ἀνθρώπων καὶ ἀντευεργετοῦντα τοὺς
μὲν τοιούτους φίλους ποιεῖσθαι, τοῖς δὲ πονηροῖς
διαφέρεσθαι, ἢ τοὺς μὲν καλοὺς κἀγαθοὺς ἀδικεῖν
πειρώμενον ἐχθροὺς ποιεῖσθαι, τοῖς δὲ πονηροῖς
συνεργοῦντα πειρᾶσθαι φίλους ποιεῖσθαι καὶ
χρῆσθαι τούτοις ἀντ᾽ ἐκείνων;

Ἐκ δὲ τούτου εἷς τε τῶν Κρίτωνος φίλων
Ἀρχέδημος ἦν καὶ ὑπὸ τῶν ἄλλων Κρίτωνος
φίλων ἐτιμᾶτο.

X. Οἶδα δὲ καὶ Διοδώρῳ αὐτὸν ἑταίρῳ ὄντι
τοιάδε διαλεχθέντα·

Εἰπέ μοι, ἔφη, ὦ Διόδωρε, ἄν τίς σοι τῶν οἰκετῶν ἀποδρᾷ, ἐπιμελῇ, ὅπως ἀνασώσῃ;

2 Καὶ ἄλλους γε νὴ Δί᾽, ἔφη, παρακαλῶ σῶστρα
τούτου ἀνακηρύττων.

Τί γάρ; ἔφη, ἐάν τίς σοι κάμνῃ τῶν οἰκετῶν,
τούτου ἐπιμελῇ καὶ παρακαλεῖς ἰατρούς, ὅπως
μὴ ἀποθάνῃ;

Σφόδρα γ᾽, ἔφη.

Εἰ δέ τίς σοι τῶν γνωρίμων, ἔφη, πολὺ τῶν
οἰκετῶν χρησιμώτερος ὢν κινδυνεύοι δι᾽ ἔνδειαν
ἀπολέσθαι, οὐκ οἴει σοι ἄξιον εἶναι ἐπιμεληθῆναι,

has a good dog the other shepherds want to pen their flocks near his, in order to get the use of his dog. Archedemus was glad to humour Criton, and 8 so there was peace not only for Criton but for his friends as well. If anyone whom he had offended reproached Archedemus with flattering Criton because he found him useful, he would answer: "Which, then, is disgraceful: to have honest men for your friends, by accepting and returning their favours, and to fall out with rogues; or to treat gentlemen as enemies by trying to injure them, and to make friends of rogues by siding with them, and to prefer their intimacy?"[1]

Henceforward Archedemus was respected by Criton's friends and was himself numbered among them.

X. Again I recall the following conversation between him and his companion Diodorus.

"Tell me, Diodorus," he said, "if one of your servants runs away, do you take steps to bring him back safe?"

"Yes, of course," he replied, "and I invite others 2 to help, by offering a reward for the recovery of the man."

"And further, if one of your servants is ill, do you take care of him and call in doctors to prevent him dying?"

"Indeed I do."

"Well, suppose that one of your acquaintance, who is much more useful than your servants, is near being ruined by want, don't you think it worth your

---

[1] The Archedemus surpasses even the Socrates of Xenophon in the art of dressing up the obvious in the guise of a conundrum.

3 ὅπως διασωθῇ; καὶ μὴν οἶσθά γε, ὅτι οὐκ
ἀγνώμων ἐστὶν Ἑρμογένης· αἰσχύνοιτο δ᾽ ἄν,
εἰ ὠφελούμενος ὑπὸ σοῦ μὴ ἀντωφελοίη σε.
καίτοι τὸ ὑπηρέτην ἑκόντα τε καὶ εὔνουν καὶ
παραμόνιμον καὶ τὸ κελευόμενον ἱκανὸν ὄντα
ποιεῖν ἔχειν καὶ μὴ μόνον τὸ κελευόμενον ἱκανὸν
ὄντα ποιεῖν, ἀλλὰ δυνάμενον καὶ ἀφ᾽ ἑαυτοῦ
χρήσιμον εἶναι καὶ προνοεῖν καὶ προβουλεύεσθαι
4 πολλῶν οἰκετῶν οἶμαι ἀντάξιον εἶναι. οἱ μέντοι
ἀγαθοὶ οἰκονόμοι, ὅταν τὸ πολλοῦ ἄξιον μικροῦ
ἐξῇ πρίασθαι, τότε φασὶ δεῖν ὠνεῖσθαι. νῦν
δὲ διὰ τὰ πράγματα εὐωνοτάτους ἔστι φίλους
ἀγαθοὺς κτήσασθαι.

5   Καὶ ὁ Διόδωρος, Ἀλλὰ καλῶς γε, ἔφη, λέγεις,
ὦ Σώκρατες, καὶ κέλευσον ἐλθεῖν ὡς ἐμὲ τὸν
Ἑρμογένην.

Μὰ Δί᾽, ἔφη, οὐκ ἔγωγε· νομίζω γὰρ οὔτε σοὶ
κάλλιον εἶναι τὸ. καλέσαι ἐκεῖνον τοῦ αὐτὸν
ἐλθεῖν πρὸς ἐκεῖνον οὔτ᾽ ἐκείνῳ μεῖζον ἀγαθὸν τὸ
πραχθῆναι ταῦτα ἢ σοί.

6   Οὕτω δὴ ὁ Διόδωρος ᾤχετο πρὸς τὸν
Ἑρμογένην, καὶ οὐ πολὺ τελέσας ἐκτήσατο
φίλον, ὃς ἔργον εἶχε σκοπεῖν ὅ τι ἂν ἢ λέγων
ἢ πράττων ὠφελοίη τε καὶ εὐφραίνοι Διόδωρον.

while to take steps to save him? Now you know 3
that Hermogenes is a conscientious man and would
be ashamed to take a favour from you without
making a return. Yet surely it is worth many
servants to have a willing, loyal, staunch subordi-
nate, capable of doing what he is told, and not only
so, but able to make himself useful unbidden, to
think clearly and give advice. Good householders, 4
you know, say that the right time to buy is when a
valuable article can be bought at a low price; and
in these times the circumstances afford an opportunity of acquiring good friends very cheap."

"Thank you, Socrates," said Diodorus, "pray bid 5
Hermogenes call on me."

"No, indeed I won't," said he; "for in my
opinion it is at least as good for you to go to him
yourself as to invite him to come to you, and you
have quite as much to gain as he by doing so."

The consequence was that Diodorus set off to visit 6
Hermogenes; and in return for a small sum he
acquired a friend who made a point of thinking how
he could help and please him either by word or
deed.

BOOK III

Γ

I. Ὅτι δὲ τοὺς ὀρεγομένους τῶν καλῶν ἐπιμελεῖς ὧν ὀρέγοιντο ποιῶν ὠφέλει, νῦν τοῦτο διηγήσομαι. ἀκούσας γάρ ποτε Διονυσόδωρον εἰς τὴν πόλιν ἥκειν ἐπαγγελλόμενον στρατηγεῖν διδάξειν, ἔλεξε πρός τινα τῶν συνόντων, ὃν ἠσθάνετο βουλόμενον τῆς τιμῆς ταύτης ἐν τῇ πόλει

2 τυχεῖν· Αἰσχρὸν μέντοι, ὦ νεανία, τὸν βουλόμενον ἐν τῇ πόλει στρατηγεῖν, ἐξὸν τοῦτο μαθεῖν, ἀμελῆσαι αὐτοῦ· καὶ δικαίως ἂν οὗτος ὑπὸ τῆς πόλεως ζημιοῖτο πολὺ μᾶλλον ἢ εἴ τις ἀνδριάντας

3 ἐργολαβοίη μὴ μεμαθηκὼς ἀνδριαντοποιεῖν. ὅλης γὰρ τῆς πόλεως ἐν τοῖς πολεμικοῖς κινδύνοις ἐπιτρεπομένης τῷ στρατηγῷ, μεγάλα τά τε ἀγαθὰ κατορθοῦντος αὐτοῦ καὶ τὰ κακὰ διαμαρτάνοντος εἰκὸς γίγνεσθαι. πῶς οὖν οὐκ ἂν δικαίως ὁ τοῦ μὲν μανθάνειν τοῦτο ἀμελῶν, τοῦ δὲ αἱρεθῆναι ἐπιμελόμενος ζημιοῖτο;

Τοιαῦτα μὲν δὴ λέγων ἔπεισεν αὐτὸν ἐλθόντα

4 μανθάνειν. ἐπεὶ δὲ μεμαθηκὼς ἧκε, προσέπαιζεν αὐτῷ λέγων· Οὐ δοκεῖ ὑμῖν, ὦ ἄνδρες, ὥσπερ Ὅμηρος τὸν Ἀγαμέμνονα γεραρὸν ἔφη εἶναι, καὶ ὅδε στρατηγεῖν μαθὼν γεραρώτερος φαίνεσθαι; καὶ γὰρ ὥσπερ ὁ κιθαρίζειν μαθὼν καὶ ἐὰν μὴ κιθαρίζῃ, κιθαριστής ἐστι καὶ ὁ μαθὼν ἰᾶσθαι κἂν μὴ ἰατρεύῃ, ὅμως ἰατρός ἐστιν, οὕτω καὶ ὅδε ἀπὸ τοῦδε τοῦ χρόνου διατελεῖ στρατηγὸς ὤν, κἂν μηδεὶς αὐτὸν ἕληται. ὁ δὲ μὴ ἐπιστάμενος

BOOK III

I. I WILL now explain how he helped those who were eager to win distinction by making them qualify themselves for the honours they coveted.

He once heard that Dionysodorus had arrived at Athens, and gave out that he was going to teach generalship. Being aware that one of his companions wished to obtain the office of general from the state, he addressed him thus: "Young man, 2 surely it would be disgraceful for one who wishes to be a general in the state to neglect the opportunity of learning the duties, and he would deserve to be punished by the state much more than one who carved statues without having learned to be a sculptor. For in the dangerous times of war the 3 whole state is in the general's hands, and great good may come from his success and great evil from his failure. Therefore anyone who exerts himself to gain the votes, but neglects to learn the business, deserves punishment."

This speech persuaded the man to go and learn. When he had learnt his lesson and returned, Soc- 4 rates chaffed him. "Don't you think, sirs," he said, "that our friend looks more 'majestic,' as Homer called Agamemnon, now that he has learnt generalship? For just as he who has learnt to play the harp is a harper even when he doesn't play, and he who has studied medicine is a doctor even though he doesn't practise, so our friend will be a general for ever, even if no one votes for him. But your

οὔτε στρατηγὸς οὔτε ἰατρός ἐστιν, οὐδ' ἐὰν ὑπὸ
5 πάντων ἀνθρώπων αἱρεθῇ. ἀτάρ, ἔφη, ἵνα καὶ
ἐὰν ἡμῶν τις ἢ ταξιαρχῇ ἢ λοχαγῇ σοι, ἐπι-
στημονέστεροι τῶν πολεμικῶν ὦμεν, λέξον ἡμῖν,
πόθεν ἤρξατό σε διδάσκειν τὴν στρατηγίαν.

Καὶ ὅς, Ἐκ τοῦ αὐτοῦ, ἔφη, εἰς ὅπερ καὶ
ἐτελεύτα· τὰ γὰρ τακτικὰ ἐμέ γε καὶ ἄλλο οὐδὲν
ἐδίδαξεν.

6 Ἀλλὰ μήν, ἔφη ὁ Σωκράτης, τοῦτό γε
πολλοστὸν μέρος ἐστὶ στρατηγίας. καὶ γὰρ
παρασκευαστικὸν τῶν εἰς τὸν πόλεμον τὸν
στρατηγὸν εἶναι χρὴ καὶ ποριστικὸν τῶν ἐπιτηδείων τοῖς στρατιώταις καὶ μηχανικὸν καὶ ἐργαστι-
κὸν καὶ ἐπιμελῆ καὶ καρτερικὸν καὶ ἀγχίνουν καὶ
φιλόφρονά τε καὶ ὠμὸν καὶ ἁπλοῦν τε καὶ
ἐπίβουλον καὶ φυλακτικόν τε καὶ κλέπτην
καὶ προετικὸν καὶ ἅρπαγα καὶ φιλόδωρον καὶ
πλεονέκτην καὶ ἀσφαλῆ καὶ ἐπιθετικόν, καὶ ἄλλα
πολλὰ καὶ φύσει καὶ ἐπιστήμῃ δεῖ τὸν εὖ
7 στρατηγήσοντα ἔχειν. καλὸν δὲ καὶ τὸ τακτικὸν
εἶναι· πολὺ γὰρ διαφέρει στράτευμα τεταγμένον
ἀτάκτου, ὥσπερ λίθοι τε καὶ πλίνθοι καὶ ξύλα
καὶ κέραμος ἀτάκτως μὲν ἐρριμμένα οὐδὲν
χρήσιμά ἐστιν, ἐπειδὰν δὲ ταχθῇ κάτω μὲν καὶ
ἐπιπολῆς τὰ μήτε σηπόμενα μήτε τηκόμενα, οἵ
τε λίθοι καὶ ὁ κέραμος, ἐν μέσῳ δὲ αἵ τε πλίνθοι
καὶ τὰ ξύλα, ὥσπερ ἐν οἰκοδομίᾳ συντίθενται,
τότε γίγνεται πολλοῦ ἄξιον κτῆμα οἰκία.

8 Ἀλλὰ πάνυ, ἔφη ὁ νεανίσκος, ὅμοιον, ὦ
Σώκρατες, εἴρηκας. καὶ γὰρ ἐν τῷ πολέμῳ τοὺς
ἀρίστους πρώτους δεῖ τάττειν καὶ τελευταίους, ἐν

ignoramus is neither general nor doctor, even if he gets every vote. But," he continued, " in order that 5 any one of us who may happen to command a regiment or platoon under you may have a better knowledge of warfare, tell us the first lesson he gave you in generalship."

" The first was like the last," he replied; " he taught me tactics—nothing else."

" But then that is only a small part of generalship. 6 For a general must also be capable of furnishing military equipment and providing supplies for the men;[1] he must be resourceful, active, careful, hardy and quick-witted; he must be both gentle and brutal, at once straightforward and designing, capable of both caution and surprise, lavish and rapacious, generous and mean, skilful in defence and attack; and there are many other qualifications, some natural, some acquired, that are necessary to one who would succeed as a general. It is well to 7 understand tactics too; for there is a wide difference between right and wrong disposition of the troops,[2] just as stones, bricks, timber and tiles flung together anyhow are useless, whereas when the materials that neither rot nor decay, that is, the stones and tiles, are placed at the bottom and the top, and the bricks and timber are put together in the middle, as in building, the result is something of great value, a house, in fact."

" Your analogy is perfect, Socrates," said the 8 youth; "for in war one must put the best men in the van and the rear,[3] and the worst in the centre,

---

[1] *Cyropaedia*, I. vi. 14. [2] *Ibid.*, VI. iii. 25.
[3] *Ibid.*, VII. v. 4.

μέσῳ δὲ τοὺς χειρίστους, ἵνα ὑπὸ μὲν τῶν
ἄγωνται, ὑπὸ δὲ τῶν ὠθῶνται.

9   Εἰ μὲν τοίνυν, ἔφη, καὶ διαγιγνώσκειν σε τοὺς
ἀγαθοὺς καὶ τοὺς κακοὺς ἐδίδαξεν· εἰ δὲ μή, τί
σοι ὄφελος ὧν ἔμαθες; οὐδὲ γὰρ εἴ σε ἀργύριον
ἐκέλευσε πρῶτον μὲν καὶ τελευταῖον τὸ κάλλιστον
τάττειν, ἐν μέσῳ δὲ τὸ χείριστον, μὴ διδάξας διαγιγνώσκειν τό τε καλὸν καὶ τὸ κίβδηλον, οὐδὲν ἄν
σοι ὄφελος ἦν.

'Αλλὰ μὰ Δί', ἔφη, οὐκ ἐδίδαξεν· ὥστε αὐτοὺς
ἂν ἡμᾶς δέοι τούς τε ἀγαθοὺς καὶ τοὺς κακοὺς
κρίνειν.

10   Τί οὖν οὐ σκοποῦμεν, ἔφη, πῶς ἂν αὐτῶν μὴ
διαμαρτάνοιμεν;

Βούλομαι, ἔφη ὁ νεανίσκος.

Οὐκοῦν, ἔφη, εἰ μὲν ἀργύριον δέοι ἁρπάζειν,
τοὺς φιλαργυρωτάτους πρώτους καθιστάντες
ὀρθῶς ἂν τάττοιμεν;

Ἔμοιγε δοκεῖ.

Τί δὲ τοὺς κινδυνεύειν μέλλοντας; ἆρα τοὺς
φιλοτιμοτάτους προτακτέον;

Οὗτοι γοῦν εἰσιν, ἔφη, οἱ ἕνεκα ἐπαίνου κινδυνεύειν ἐθέλοντες. οὐ τοίνυν οὗτοί γε ἄδηλοι, ἀλλ'
ἐπιφανεῖς πανταχοῦ ὄντες εὐεύρετοι ἂν εἶεν.

11   'Ατάρ, ἔφη, πότερά σε τάττειν μόνον ἐδίδαξεν
ἢ καὶ ὅπῃ καὶ ὅπως χρηστέον ἑκάστῳ τῶν
ταγμάτων;

Οὐ πάνυ, ἔφη.

Καὶ μὴν πολλά γ' ἐστί, πρὸς ἃ οὔτε τάττειν
οὔτε ἄγειν ὡσαύτως προσήκει.

'Αλλὰ μὰ Δί', ἔφη, οὐ διεσαφήνιζε ταῦτα.

that they may be led by the van and driven forward
by the rearguard."

"Well and good, provided that he taught you also 9
to distinguish the good and the bad men. If not,
what have you gained by your lessons? No more
than you would have gained if he had ordered you
to put the best money at the head and tail, and the
worst in the middle, without telling you how to
distinguish good from base coin."

"I assure you he didn't; so we should have to
judge for ourselves which are the good men and
which are the bad."

"Then we had better consider how we may avoid 10
mistaking them."

"I want to do so," said the youth.

"Well now," said Socrates, "if we had to lay
hands on a sum of money, would not the right
arrangement be to put the most covetous men in
the front?"

"I think so."

"And what should we do with those who are
going to face danger? Should our first line consist
of the most ambitious?'

"Oh yes: they are the men who will face danger
for the sake of glory. About these, now, there is
no mystery: they are conspicuous everywhere, and
so it is easy to find them."

"But," said Socrates, "did he teach you only the 11
disposition of an army, or did he include where and
how to use each formation?"

"Not at all."

"And yet there are many situations that call for
a modification of tactics and strategy."

"I assure you he didn't explain that."

Νὴ Δί', ἔφη, πάλιν τοίνυν ἐλθὼν ἐπανερώτα·
ἢν γὰρ ἐπίστηται καὶ μὴ ἀναιδὴς ᾖ, αἰσχυνεῖται
ἀργύριον εἰληφὼς ἐνδεᾶ σε ἀποπέμψασθαι.

II. Ἐντυχὼν δέ ποτε στρατηγεῖν ᾑρημένῳ τῳ,
Τοῦ ἕνεκεν, ἔφη, Ὅμηρον οἴει τὸν Ἀγαμέμνονα
προσαγορεῦσαι ποιμένα λαῶν; ἆρά γε ὅτι ὥσπερ
τὸν ποιμένα δεῖ ἐπιμελεῖσθαι, ὅπως σῶαί τε
ἔσονται αἱ οἶες καὶ τὰ ἐπιτήδεια ἕξουσι, καὶ οὗ
ἕνεκα τρέφονται, τοῦτο ἔσται, οὕτω καὶ τὸν
στρατηγὸν ἐπιμελεῖσθαι δεῖ, ὅπως σῶοί τε οἱ
στρατιῶται ἔσονται καὶ τὰ ἐπιτήδεια ἕξουσι, καὶ
οὗ ἕνεκα στρατεύονται, τοῦτο ἔσται; στρατεύονται
δέ, ἵνα κρατοῦντες τῶν πολεμίων εὐδαιμονέστεροι
2 ὦσιν. ἢ τί δήποτε οὕτως ἐπῄνεσε τὸν Ἀγαμέμνονα εἰπών·

Ἀμφότερον, βασιλεύς τ' ἀγαθὸς κρατερός τ'
αἰχμητής;

ἆρά γε ὅτι αἰχμητής τε κρατερὸς ἂν εἴη, οὐκ εἰ
μόνος αὐτὸς εὖ ἀγωνίζοιτο πρὸς τοὺς πολεμίους,
ἀλλ' εἰ καὶ παντὶ τῷ στρατοπέδῳ τούτου αἴτιος
εἴη, καὶ βασιλεὺς ἀγαθός, οὐκ εἰ μόνου τοῦ
ἑαυτοῦ βίου καλῶς προεστήκοι, ἀλλ' εἰ καὶ ὧν
3 βασιλεύοι, τούτοις εὐδαιμονίας αἴτιος εἴη; καὶ
γὰρ βασιλεὺς αἱρεῖται οὐχ ἵνα ἑαυτοῦ καλῶς
ἐπιμελῆται, ἀλλ' ἵνα καὶ οἱ ἑλόμενοι δι' αὐτὸν εὖ
πράττωσι· καὶ στρατεύονται δὲ πάντες, ἵνα ὁ
βίος αὐτοῖς ὡς βέλτιστος ᾖ, καὶ στρατηγοὺς
αἱροῦνται τούτου ἕνεκα, ἵνα πρὸς τοῦτο αὐτοῖς
4 ἡγεμόνες ὦσι. δεῖ οὖν τὸν στρατηγοῦντα τοῦτο
παρασκευάζειν τοῖς ἑλομένοις αὐτὸν στρατηγόν·

"Then pray go back and ask him. If he knows and has a conscience, he will be ashamed to send you home ill-taught, after taking your money."

II. One day when he met a man who had been chosen general, he asked him,[1] "For what reason, think you, is Agamemnon dubbed 'Shepherd of the people' by Homer?[2] Is it because a shepherd must see that his sheep are safe and are fed, and that the object for which they are kept is attained, and a general must see that his men are safe and are fed, and that the object for which they fight is attained, or, in other words, that victory over the enemy may add to their happiness? Or what reason 2 can Homer have for praising Agamemnon as 'both a good king and a doughty warrior too'?[3] Is it that he would be 'a doughty warrior too' not if he alone were a good fighter, but if he made all his men like himself; and 'a good king' not if he merely ordered his own life aright, but if he made his subjects happy as well? Because a king is chosen, not to take 3 good care of himself, but for the good of those who have chosen him;[4] and all men fight in order that they may get the best life possible, and choose generals to guide them to it. Therefore it is the 4 duty of a commander to contrive this for those who have chosen him for general. For anything more

---

[1] *Cyropaedia*, VIII. xi. 14.   [2] *Iliad*, ii. 243.
[3] *Ibid.*, iii. 179.   [4] *Cyropaedia*, I. vi. 8.

καὶ γὰρ οὔτε κάλλιον τούτου ἄλλο ῥᾴδιον εὑρεῖν
οὔτε αἴσχιον τοῦ ἐναντίου.

Καὶ οὕτως ἐπισκοπῶν, τίς εἴη ἀγαθοῦ ἡγεμόνος
ἀρετή, τὰ μὲν ἄλλα περιῄρει, κατέλειπε δὲ τὸ
εὐδαίμονας ποιεῖν ὧν ἂν ἡγῆται.

III. Καὶ ἱππαρχεῖν δέ τινι ᾑρημένῳ οἶδά ποτε
αὐτὸν τοιάδε διαλεχθέντα·

Ἔχοις ἄν, ἔφη, ὦ νεανία, εἰπεῖν ἡμῖν, ὅτου
ἕνεκα ἐπεθύμησας ἱππαρχεῖν; οὐ γὰρ δὴ τοῦ
πρῶτος τῶν ἱππέων ἐλαύνειν· καὶ γὰρ οἱ
ἱπποτοξόται τούτου γε ἀξιοῦνται· προελαύνουσι
γοῦν καὶ τῶν ἱππάρχων.

Ἀληθῆ λέγεις, ἔφη.

Ἀλλὰ μὴν οὐδὲ τοῦ γνωσθῆναί γε· ἐπεὶ καὶ
οἱ μαινόμενοί γε ὑπὸ πάντων γιγνώσκονται.

Ἀληθές, ἔφη, καὶ τοῦτο λέγεις.

2 Ἀλλ' ἄρα ὅτι τὸ ἱππικὸν οἴει ἂν τῇ πόλει
βέλτιον ποιήσας παραδοῦναι, καὶ εἴ τις χρεία
γίγνοιτο ἱππέων, τούτων ἡγούμενος ἀγαθοῦ τινος
αἴτιος γενέσθαι τῇ πόλει;

Καὶ μάλα, ἔφη.

Καὶ ἔστι γε νὴ Δί', ἔφη ὁ Σωκράτης, καλόν,
ἐὰν δύνῃ ταῦτα ποιῆσαι. ἡ δὲ ἀρχή που, ἐφ' ἣν
ᾕρησαι, ἵππων τε καὶ ἀμβατῶν ἐστιν.

Ἔστι γὰρ οὖν, ἔφη.

3 Ἴθι δὴ λέξον ἡμῖν τοῦτο πρῶτον, ὅπως διανοῇ
τοὺς ἵππους βελτίους ποιῆσαι;

Καὶ ὅς, Ἀλλὰ τοῦτο μέν, ἔφη, οὐκ ἐμὸν οἶμαι
τὸ ἔργον εἶναι, ἀλλὰ ἰδίᾳ ἕκαστον δεῖν τοῦ
ἑαυτοῦ ἵππου ἐπιμελεῖσθαι.

4 Ἐὰν οὖν, ἔφη ὁ Σωκράτης, παρέχωνταί σοι
τοὺς ἵππους οἱ μὲν οὕτως κακόποδας ἢ κακο-

honourable than that is not easy to find, or anything more disgraceful than its opposite."

By these reflections on what constitutes a good leader he stripped away all other virtues, and left just the power to make his followers happy.

III. Again, when someone had been chosen a leader of cavalry, I remember that Socrates conversed with him in the following manner:

"Young man," he said, "can you tell us why you hankered after a cavalry command? I presume it was not to be first of the cavalry in the charge; for that privilege belongs to the mounted archers; at any rate they ride ahead of their commanders even."

"True."

"Nor was it to get yourself known either. Even madmen are known to everyone."

"True again."

"But perhaps you think you can hand over the 2 cavalry in better condition to the state when you retire, and can do something for the good of the state as a cavalry leader, in case there is any occasion to employ that arm?"

"Yes, certainly," said he.

"Yes," said Socrates, "and no doubt it is a fine thing if you can do that. The command, I presume, for which you have been chosen, is the command of horses and riders."

"Indeed it is."

"Come then, tell us first how you propose to 3 improve the horses."

"Oh, but I don't think that is my business. Every man must look after his own horse."

"Then if some of your men appear on parade with 4 their horses ailing or suffering from bad feet or sore

σκελεῖς ἢ ἀσθενεῖς, οἱ δὲ οὕτως ἀτρόφους, ὥστε
μὴ δύνασθαι ἀκολουθεῖν, οἱ δὲ οὕτως ἀναγώγους,
ὥστε μὴ μένειν ὅπου ἂν σὺ τάξῃς, οἱ δὲ οὕτως
λακτιστάς, ὥστε μηδὲ τάξαι δυνατὸν εἶναι, τί σοι
τοῦ ἱππικοῦ ὄφελος ἔσται; ἢ πῶς δυνήσῃ τοιούτων ἡγούμενος ἀγαθόν τι ποιῆσαι τὴν πόλιν;

Καὶ ὅς, Ἀλλὰ καλῶς τε λέγεις, ἔφη, καὶ
πειράσομαι τῶν ἵππων εἰς τὸ δυνατὸν ἐπιμελεῖσθαι.

5   Τί δέ; τοὺς ἱππέας οὐκ ἐπιχειρήσεις, ἔφη,
βελτίονας ποιῆσαι;

Ἔγωγ', ἔφη.

Οὐκοῦν πρῶτον μὲν ἀναβατικωτέρους ἐπὶ τοὺς
ἵππους ποιήσεις αὐτούς;

Δεῖ γοῦν, ἔφη· καὶ γὰρ εἴ τις αὐτῶν καταπέσοι,
μᾶλλον ἂν οὕτω σῴζοιτο.

6   Τί γάρ; ἐάν που κινδυνεύειν δέῃ, πότερον
ἐπάγειν τοὺς πολεμίους ἐπὶ τὴν ἄμμον κελεύσεις,
ἔνθαπερ εἰώθατε ἱππεύειν, ἢ πειράσῃ τὰς μελέτας
ἐν τοιούτοις ποιεῖσθαι χωρίοις, ἐν οἷσπερ οἱ
πόλεμοι γίγνονται;

Βέλτιον γοῦν, ἔφη.

7   Τί γάρ; τοῦ βάλλειν ὡς πλείστους ἀπὸ τῶν
ἵππων ἐπιμέλειάν τινα ποιήσει;

Βέλτιον γοῦν, ἔφη, καὶ τοῦτο.

Θήγειν δὲ τὰς ψυχὰς τῶν ἱππέων καὶ ἐξοργίζειν
πρὸς τοὺς πολεμίους, ἅπερ ἀλκιμωτέρους ποιεῖ,
διανενόησαι;

Εἰ δὲ μή, ἀλλὰ νῦν γε πειράσομαι, ἔφη.

8   Ὅπως δέ σοι πείθωνται οἱ ἱππεῖς, πεφρόντικάς
τι; ἄνευ γὰρ δὴ τούτου οὔτε ἵππων οὔτε ἱππέων
ἀγαθῶν καὶ ἀλκίμων οὐδὲν ὄφελος.

178

legs, others with underfed animals that can't go the pace, others with restive brutes that won't keep in line, others with such bad kickers that it is impossible to line them up at all, what will you be able to make of your cavalry? how will you be able to do the state any good with a command like that?"

"I am much obliged to you," he replied, "and I will try to look after the horses carefully."

"Won't you also try to improve the men?" said 5 Socrates.

"I will."

"Then will you first train them to mount better?"

"Oh yes, I must, so that if anyone is thrown he may have a better chance of saving himself."

"Further, when there is some danger before you, 6 will you order them to draw the enemy into the sandy ground where your manœuvres are held, or will you try to carry out your training in the kind of country that the enemy occupy?"

"Oh yes, that is the better way."

"And again, will you pay much attention to 7 bringing down as many of the enemy as possible without dismounting?"

"Oh yes, that too is the better way."

"Have you thought of fostering a keen spirit among the men and hatred of the enemy, so as to make them more gallant in action?"

"Well, at any rate, I will try to do so now."

"And have you considered how to make the men 8 obey you? Because without that horses and men, however good and gallant, are of no use."

Ἀληθῆ λέγεις, ἔφη· ἀλλὰ πῶς ἄν τις μάλιστα, ὦ Σώκρατες, ἐπὶ τοῦτο αὐτοὺς προτρέψαιτο ;

9 Ἐκεῖνο μὲν δήπου οἶσθα, ὅτι ἐν παντὶ πράγματι οἱ ἄνθρωποι τούτοις μάλιστα ἐθέλουσι πείθεσθαι, οὓς ἂν ἡγῶνται βελτίστους εἶναι. καὶ γὰρ ἐν νόσῳ ὃν ἂν ἡγῶνται ἰατρικώτατον εἶναι, τούτῳ μάλιστα πείθονται, καὶ ἐν πλῷ ὃν ἂν κυβερνητικώτατον, καὶ ἐν γεωργίᾳ ὃν ἂν γεωργικώτατον.

Καὶ μάλα, ἔφη.

Οὐκοῦν εἰκός, ἔφη, καὶ ἐν ἱππικῇ ὃς ἂν μάλιστα εἰδὼς φαίνηται ἃ δεῖ ποιεῖν, τούτῳ μάλιστα ἐθέλειν τοὺς ἄλλους πείθεσθαι.

10 Ἐὰν οὖν, ἔφη, ἐγώ, ὦ Σώκρατες, βέλτιστος ὢν αὐτῶν δῆλος ὦ, ἀρκέσει μοι τοῦτο εἰς τὸ πείθεσθαι αὐτοὺς ἐμοί ;

Ἐάν γε πρὸς τούτῳ, ἔφη, διδάξῃς αὐτούς, ὡς τὸ πείθεσθαί σοι κάλλιόν τε καὶ σωτηριώτερον αὐτοῖς ἔσται.

Πῶς οὖν, ἔφη, τοῦτο διδάξω ;

Πολὺ νὴ Δί’, ἔφη, ῥᾷον ἢ εἴ σοι δέοι διδάσκειν, ὡς τὰ κακὰ τῶν ἀγαθῶν ἀμείνω καὶ λυσιτελέστερά ἐστι.

11 Λέγεις, ἔφη, σὺ τὸν ἵππαρχον πρὸς τοῖς ἄλλοις ἐπιμελεῖσθαι δεῖν καὶ τοῦ λέγειν δύνασθαι ;

Σὺ δ’ ᾤου, ἔφη, χρῆναι σιωπῇ ἱππαρχεῖν ; ἢ οὐκ ἐντεθύμησαι, ὅτι ὅσα τε νόμῳ μεμαθήκαμεν κάλλιστα ὄντα, δι’ ὧν γε ζῆν ἐπιστάμεθα, ταῦτα πάντα διὰ λόγου ἐμάθομεν καὶ εἴ τι ἄλλο καλὸν μανθάνει τις μάθημα, διὰ λόγου μανθάνει καὶ οἱ ἄριστα διδάσκοντες μάλιστα λόγῳ χρῶνται καὶ οἱ τὰ σπουδαιότατα μάλιστα ἐπιστάμενοι κάλ-

" True, but what is the best way of encouraging them to obey, Socrates?"

" Well, I suppose you know that under all con- 9 ditions human beings are most willing to obey those whom they believe to be the best.[1]   Thus in sickness they most readily obey the doctor, on board ship the pilot, on a farm the farmer, whom they think to be most skilled in his business."

" Yes, certainly."

" Then it is likely that in horsemanship too, one who clearly knows best what ought to be done will most easily gain the obedience of the others."

" If then, Socrates, I am plainly the best horse- 10 man among them, will that suffice to gain their obedience?"

" Yes, if you also show them that it will be safer and more honourable for them to obey you."

" How, then, shall I show that?"

" Well, it's far easier than if you had to show them that bad is better than good and more profitable."

" Do you mean that in addition to his other 11 duties a cavalry leader must take care to be a good speaker?"

" Did you suppose that a commander of cavalry should be mum?   Did you never reflect that all the best we learned according to custom—the learning, I mean, that teaches us how to live—we learned by means of words, and that every other good lesson to be learned is learned by means of words; that the best teachers rely most on the spoken word and those with the deepest knowledge of the greatest

---

[1] *Cyropaedia*, iii. i. 20.

12 λιστα διαλέγονται; ἢ τόδε οὐκ ἐντεθύμησαι, ὡς
ὅταν γε χορὸς εἷς ἐκ τῆσδε τῆς πόλεως γίγνηται,
ὥσπερ ὁ εἰς Δῆλον πεμπόμενος, οὐδεὶς ἄλλοθεν
οὐδαμόθεν τούτῳ ἐφάμιλλος γίγνεται οὐδὲ εὐανδρία
ἐν ἄλλῃ πόλει ὁμοία τῇ ἐνθάδε συνάγεται;
Ἀληθῆ λέγεις, ἔφη.

13 Ἀλλὰ μὴν οὔτε εὐφωνίᾳ τοσοῦτον διαφέρουσιν
Ἀθηναῖοι τῶν ἄλλων οὔτε σωμάτων μεγέθει καὶ
ῥώμῃ ὅσον φιλοτιμίᾳ, ἥπερ μάλιστα παροξύνει
πρὸς τὰ καλὰ καὶ ἔντιμα.
Ἀληθές, ἔφη, καὶ τοῦτο.

14 Οὐκοῦν οἴει, ἔφη, καὶ τοῦ ἱππικοῦ τοῦ ἐνθάδε
εἴ τις ἐπιμεληθείη, πολὺ ἂν καὶ τούτῳ διενεγκεῖν
τῶν ἄλλων ὅπλων τε καὶ ἵππων παρασκευῇ καὶ
εὐταξίᾳ καὶ τῷ ἑτοίμως κινδυνεύειν πρὸς τοὺς
πολεμίους, εἰ νομίσειαν ταῦτα ποιοῦντες ἐπαίνου
καὶ τιμῆς τεύξεσθαι;
Εἰκός γε, ἔφη.

15 Μὴ τοίνυν ὄκνει, ἔφη, ἀλλὰ πειρῶ τοὺς ἄνδρας
ἐπὶ ταῦτα προτρέπειν, ἀφ' ὧν αὐτός τε ὠφελήσῃ
καὶ οἱ ἄλλοι πολῖται διὰ σέ.
Ἀλλὰ νὴ Δία πειράσομαι, ἔφη.

IV. Ἰδὼν δέ ποτε Νικομαχίδην ἐξ ἀρχαιρεσιῶν
ἀπιόντα ἤρετο· Τίνες, ὦ Νικομαχίδη, στρατηγοὶ
ᾕρηνται;

Καὶ ὅς, Οὐ γάρ, ἔφη, ὦ Σώκρατες, τοιοῦτοί
εἰσιν Ἀθηναῖοι, ὥστε ἐμὲ μὲν οὐχ εἵλοντο, ὃς ἐκ
καταλόγου στρατευόμενος κατατέτριμμαι καὶ
λοχαγῶν καὶ ταξιαρχῶν καὶ τραύματα ὑπὸ τῶν
πολεμίων τοσαῦτα ἔχω· ἅμα δὲ τὰς οὐλὰς τῶν
τραυμάτων ἀπογυμνούμενος ἐπεδείκνυεν· Ἀντισθένην δέ, ἔφη, εἵλοντο, τὸν οὔτε ὁπλίτην πω

subjects are the best talkers? Did you never reflect 12
that, whenever one chorus is selected from the
citizens of this state—for instance, the chorus that
is sent to Delos—no choir from any other place can
compare with it, and no state can collect so goodly
a company?"

"True."

"And yet the reason is that Athenians excel all 13
others not so much in singing or in stature or in
strength, as in love of honour, which is the strongest
incentive to deeds of honour and renown."

"True again."

"Then don't you think that if one took the same 14
pains with our cavalry, they too would greatly excel
others in arms and horses and discipline and readi-
ness to face the enemy, if they thought that they
would win glory and honour by it?"

"I expect so."

"Don't hesitate then, but try to encourage this 15
keenness among the men: both you and your fellow-
citizens will benefit by the results of your efforts."

"Most certainly I will try."

IV. Once on seeing Nicomachides returning from
the elections, he asked, "Who have been chosen
generals, Nicomachides?"

"Isn't it like the Athenians?" replied he; "they
haven't chosen me after all the hard work I have
done, since I was called up, in the command of
company or regiment, though I have been so often
wounded in action" (and here he uncovered and
showed his scars); "yet they have chosen Antisthenes, who has never served in a marching regiment

στρατευσάμενον ἔν τε τοῖς ἱππεῦσιν οὐδὲν
περίβλεπτον ποιήσαντα ἐπιστάμενόν τε ἄλλο
οὐδὲν ἢ χρήματα συλλέγειν ;

2 Οὐκοῦν, ἔφη ὁ Σωκράτης, τοῦτο μὲν ἀγαθόν,
εἴ γε τοῖς στρατιώταις ἱκανὸς ἔσται τὰ ἐπιτήδεια
πορίζειν ;

Καὶ γὰρ οἱ ἔμποροι, ἔφη ὁ Νικομαχίδης,
χρήματα συλλέγειν ἱκανοί εἰσιν· ἀλλ' οὐχ ἕνεκα
τούτου καὶ στρατηγεῖν δύναιντ' ἄν.

3 Καὶ ὁ Σωκράτης ἔφη· 'Αλλὰ καὶ φιλόνικος
'Αντισθένης ἐστίν, ὃ στρατηγῷ προσεῖναι ἐπιτήδειόν ἐστιν· οὐχ ὁρᾷς, ὅτι καὶ ὁσάκις κεχο-
ρήγηκε, πᾶσι τοῖς χοροῖς νενίκηκε ;

Μὰ Δί', ἔφη ὁ Νικομαχίδης, ἀλλ' οὐδὲν ὅμοιόν
ἐστι χοροῦ τε καὶ στρατεύματος προεστάναι.

4 Καὶ μήν, ἔφη ὁ Σωκράτης, οὐδὲ ᾠδῆς γε ὁ
'Αντισθένης οὐδὲ χορῶν διδασκαλίας ἔμπειρος
ὢν ὅμως ἐγένετο ἱκανὸς εὑρεῖν τοὺς κρατίστους
ταῦτα.

Καὶ ἐν τῇ στρατιᾷ οὖν, ἔφη ὁ Νικομαχίδης,
ἄλλους μὲν εὑρήσει τοὺς τάξοντας ἀνθ' ἑαυτοῦ,
ἄλλους δὲ τοὺς μαχουμένους.

5 Οὐκοῦν, ἔφη ὁ Σωκράτης, ἐάν γε καὶ ἐν τοῖς
πολεμικοῖς τοὺς κρατίστους, ὥσπερ ἐν τοῖς
χορικοῖς, ἐξευρίσκῃ τε καὶ προαιρῆται, εἰκότως
ἂν καὶ τούτου νικηφόρος εἴη· καὶ δαπανᾶν δ'
αὐτὸν εἰκὸς μᾶλλον ἂν ἐθέλειν εἰς τὴν σὺν ὅλῃ
τῇ πόλει τῶν πολεμικῶν νίκην ἢ εἰς τὴν σὺν τῇ
φυλῇ τῶν χορικῶν.

6 Λέγεις σύ, ἔφη, ὦ Σώκρατες, ὡς τοῦ αὐτοῦ
ἀνδρός ἐστι χορηγεῖν τε καλῶς καὶ στρατηγεῖν ;

Λέγω ἔγωγ', ἔφη, ὡς ὅτου ἄν τις προστατεύῃ,

nor distinguished himself in the cavalry and understands nothing but money-making."

"Isn't that a recommendation," said Socrates, 2 " supposing he proves capable of supplying the men's needs?"

"Why," retorted Nicomachides, "merchants too are capable of making money, but that doesn't make them fit to command an army."

"But," cried Socrates, "Antisthenes also is eager 3 for victory, and that is a good point in a general.[1] Whenever he has been choragus, you know, his choir has always won."

"No doubt," said Nicomachides, "but there is no analogy between the handling of a choir and of an army."

"But, you see," said Socrates, "though Antis- 4 thenes knows nothing about music or choir training, he showed himself capable of finding the best experts in these."

"In the army too, then," said Nicomachides, "he will find others to command for him, and others to do the fighting."

"And therefore," said Socrates, "if he finds out 5 and prefers the best men in warfare as in choir training it is likely that he will be victorious in that too ; and probably he will be more ready to spend on winning a battle with the whole state than on winning a choral competition with his tribe."

"Do you mean to say, Socrates, that the man 6 who succeeds with a chorus will also succeed with an army?"

"I mean that, whatever a man controls, if he

---

[1] *Cyropaedia*, I. vi. 18.

ἐὰν γιγνώσκῃ τε ὧν δεῖ καὶ ταῦτα πορίζεσθαι δύνηται, ἀγαθὸς ἂν εἴη προστάτης, εἴτε χοροῦ εἴτε οἴκου εἴτε πόλεως εἴτε στρατεύματος προστατεύοι.

7 Καὶ ὁ Νικομαχίδης. Μὰ Δί', ἔφη, ὦ Σώκρατες, οὐκ ἄν ποτε ᾤμην ἐγώ σου ἀκοῦσαι, ὡς οἱ ἀγαθοὶ οἰκονόμοι ἀγαθοὶ στρατηγοὶ ἂν εἶεν.

Ἴθι δή, ἔφη, ἐξετάσωμεν τὰ ἔργα ἑκατέρου αὐτῶν, ἵνα εἰδῶμεν, πότερον τὰ αὐτά ἐστιν ἢ διαφέρει τι.

Πάνυ γε, ἔφη.

8 Οὐκοῦν, ἔφη, τὸ μὲν τοὺς ἀρχομένους κατηκόους τε καὶ εὐπειθεῖς ἑαυτοῖς παρασκευάζειν ἀμφοτέρων ἐστὶν ἔργον ;

Καὶ μάλα, ἔφη.

Τί δέ ; τὸ προστάττειν ἕκαστα τοῖς ἐπιτηδείοις πράττειν ;

Καὶ τοῦτ', ἔφη.

Καὶ μὴν τὸ τοὺς κακοὺς κολάζειν καὶ τοὺς ἀγαθοὺς τιμᾶν ἀμφοτέροις οἶμαι προσήκειν.

Πάνυ μὲν οὖν, ἔφη.

9 Τὸ δὲ τοὺς ὑπηκόους εὐμενεῖς ποιεῖσθαι πῶς οὐ καλὸν ἀμφοτέροις ;

Καὶ τοῦτ', ἔφη.

Συμμάχους δὲ καὶ βοηθοὺς προσάγεσθαι δοκεῖ σοι συμφέρειν ἀμφοτέροις ἢ οὔ ;

Πάνυ μὲν οὖν, ἔφη.

Ἀλλὰ φυλακτικοὺς τῶν ὄντων οὐκ ἀμφοτέρους εἶναι προσήκει ;

Σφόδρα γ', ἔφη.

Οὐκοῦν καὶ ἐπιμελεῖς καὶ φιλοπόνους ἀμφοτέρους εἶναι προσήκει περὶ τὰ αὑτῶν ἔργα ;

knows what he wants and can get it he will be a good controller, whether he control a chorus, an estate, a city or an army."

" Really, Socrates," cried Nicomachides, " I should 7 never have thought to hear you say that a good business man would make a good general."

" Come then, let us review the duties of each that we may know whether they are the same or different."

" By all means."

" Is it not the duty of both to make their sub- 8 ordinates willing and obedient ? "

" Decidedly."

" And to put the right man in the right place ? " [1]

" That is so."

" I suppose, moreover, that both should punish the bad and reward the good."

" Yes, certainly."

" Of course both will do well to win the goodwill 9 of those under them ? "

" That is so."

" Do you think that it is to the interest of both to attract allies and helpers ? "

" Yes, certainly."

" And should not both be able to keep what they have got ? "

" They should indeed."

" And should not both be strenuous and industrious in their own work ? " [2]

---

[1] *Cyropaedia*, I. vi. 20.   [2] *Ibid.*, 8.

10 Ταῦτα μέν, ἔφη, πάντα ὁμοίως ἀμφοτέρων
ἐστίν, ἀλλὰ τὸ μάχεσθαι οὐκέτι ἀμφοτέρων.
᾿Αλλ᾽ ἐχθροί γέ τοι ἀμφοτέροις γίγνονται ;
Καὶ μάλα, ἔφη, τοῦτό γε.
Οὐκοῦν τὸ περιγενέσθαι τούτων ἀμφοτέροις
συμφέρει ;

11 Πάνυ γ᾽, ἔφη· ἀλλ᾽ ἐκεῖνο παρίης, ἂν δέῃ
μάχεσθαι, τί ὠφελήσει ἡ οἰκονομική ;
᾿Ενταῦθα δήπου καὶ πλεῖστον, ἔφη· ὁ γὰρ
ἀγαθὸς οἰκονόμος, εἰδὼς ὅτι οὐδὲν οὕτω λυσιτελές
τε καὶ κερδαλέον ἐστὶν ὡς τὸ μαχόμενον τοὺς
πολεμίους νικᾶν οὐδὲ οὕτως ἀλυσιτελές τε καὶ
ζημιῶδες ὡς τὸ ἡττᾶσθαι, προθύμως μὲν τὰ πρὸς
τὸ νικᾶν συμφέροντα ζητήσει καὶ παρασκευάσεται,
ἐπιμελῶς δὲ τὰ πρὸς τὸ ἡττᾶσθαι φέροντα
σκέψεται καὶ φυλάξεται, ἐνεργῶς δ᾽, ἂν τὴν
παρασκευὴν ὁρᾷ νικητικὴν οὖσαν, μαχεῖται, οὐχ
ἥκιστα δὲ τούτων, ἐὰν ἀπαράσκευος ᾖ, φυλάξεται
12 συνάπτειν μάχην. μὴ καταφρόνει, ἔφη, ὦ
Νικομαχίδη, τῶν οἰκονομικῶν ἀνδρῶν· ἡ γὰρ
τῶν ἰδίων ἐπιμέλεια πλήθει μόνον διαφέρει τῆς
τῶν κοινῶν, τὰ δ᾽ ἄλλα παραπλήσια ἔχει, τὸ
<δὲ>[1] μέγιστον, ὅτι οὔτε ἄνευ ἀνθρώπων οὐδετέρα
γίγνεται οὔτε δι᾽ ἄλλων μὲν ἀνθρώπων τὰ ἴδια
πράττεται, δι᾽ ἄλλων δὲ τὰ κοινά· οὐ γὰρ ἄλλοις
τισὶν ἀνθρώποις οἱ τῶν κοινῶν ἐπιμελόμενοι
χρῶνται ἢ οἷσπερ οἱ τὰ ἴδια οἰκονομοῦντες· οἷς
οἱ ἐπιστάμενοι χρῆσθαι καὶ τὰ ἴδια καὶ τὰ κοινὰ
καλῶς πράττουσιν, οἱ δὲ μὴ ἐπιστάμενοι
ἀμφοτέρωθι πλημμελοῦσι.

V. Περικλεῖ δέ ποτε τῷ τοῦ πάνυ Περικλέους
υἱῷ διαλεγόμενος, ᾿Εγώ τοι, ἔφη, ὦ Περίκλεις,

188

"All these are common to both; but fighting 10 is not."

"But surely both are bound to find enemies?"

"Oh yes, they are."

"Then is it not important for both to get the better of them?"

"Undoubtedly; but you don't say how business 11 capacity will help when it comes to fighting."

"That is just where it will be most helpful. For the good business man, through his knowledge that nothing profits or pays like a victory in the field, and nothing is so utterly unprofitable and entails such heavy loss as a defeat, will be eager to seek and furnish all aids to victory, careful to consider and avoid what leads to defeat, prompt to engage the enemy if he sees he is strong enough to win, and, above all, will avoid an engagement when he is not ready. Don't look down on business men, 12 Nicomachides. For the management of private concerns differs only in point of number from that of public affairs. In other respects they are much alike, and particularly in this, that neither can be carried on without men, and the men employed in private and public transactions are the same. For those who take charge of public affairs employ just the same men when they attend to their own; and those who understand how to employ them are successful directors of public and private concerns, and those who do not, fail in both."

V. Once when talking with the son of the great Pericles, he said: "For my part, Pericles, I feel

---

¹ δὲ added by Castalio : Sauppe omits.

ἐλπίδα ἔχω σοῦ στρατηγήσαντος ἀμείνω τε καὶ
ἐνδοξοτέραν τὴν πόλιν εἰς τὰ πολεμικὰ ἔσεσθαι
καὶ τῶν πολεμίων κρατήσειν.

Καὶ ὁ Περικλῆς, Βουλοίμην ἄν, ἔφη, ὦ
Σώκρατες, ἃ λέγεις· ὅπως δὲ ταῦτα γένοιτ᾽ ἄν,
οὐ δύναμαι γνῶναι.

Βούλει οὖν, ἔφη ὁ Σωκράτης, διαλογιζόμενοι
περὶ αὐτῶν ἐπισκοπῶμεν, ὅπου ἤδη τὸ δυνατόν
ἐστι;

Βούλομαι, ἔφη.

2 Οὐκοῦν οἶσθα, ἔφη, ὅτι πλήθει μὲν οὐδὲν
μείους εἰσὶν Ἀθηναῖοι Βοιωτῶν;

Οἶδα γάρ, ἔφη.

Σώματα δὲ ἀγαθὰ καὶ καλὰ πότερον ἐκ
Βοιωτῶν οἴει πλείω ἂν ἐκλεχθῆναι ἢ ἐξ Ἀθηναίων;

Οὐδὲ ταύτῃ μοι δοκοῦσι λείπεσθαι.

Εὐμενεστέρους δὲ ποτέρους ἑαυτοῖς εἶναι
νομίζεις;

Ἀθηναίους ἔγωγε· Βοιωτῶν μὲν γὰρ πολλοὶ
πλεονεκτούμενοι ὑπὸ Θηβαίων δυσμενῶς αὐτοῖς
ἔχουσιν, Ἀθήνησι δὲ οὐδὲν ὁρῶ τοιοῦτον.

3 Ἀλλὰ μὴν φιλοτιμότατοί γε καὶ μεγαλο-
φρονέστατοι πάντων εἰσίν· ἅπερ οὐχ ἥκιστα
παροξύνει κινδυνεύειν ὑπὲρ εὐδοξίας τε καὶ
πατρίδος.

Οὐδὲ ἐν τούτοις Ἀθηναῖοι μεμπτοί.

Καὶ μὴν προγόνων γε καλὰ ἔργα οὐκ ἔστιν οἷς
μείζω καὶ πλείω ὑπάρχει ἢ Ἀθηναίοις· ᾧ πολλοὶ
ἐπαιρόμενοι προτρέπονταί τε ἀρετῆς ἐπιμελεῖσθαι
καὶ ἄλκιμοι γίγνεσθαι.

4 Ταῦτα μὲν ἀληθῆ λέγεις πάντα, ὦ Σώκρατες·

hopeful that, now you have become general, our city will be more efficient and more famous in the art of war, and will defeat our enemies."

"I could wish," answered Pericles, "that it might be as you say, Socrates; but how these changes are to come about I cannot see."

"Should you like to discuss them with me, then," said Socrates, "and consider how they can be brought about?"

"I should."

"Do you know then, that in point of numbers the 2 Athenians are not inferior to the Boeotians?"

"Yes, I know."

"Do you think that the larger number of fine, well-developed men could be selected from among the Boeotians or the Athenians?"

"In that matter too they seem to be at no disadvantage."

"Which do you think are the more united?"

"The Athenians, I should say, for many of the Boeotians resent the selfish behaviour of the Thebans. At Athens I see nothing of that sort."

"And again, the Athenians are more ambitious 3 and more high-minded than other peoples; and these qualities are among the strongest incentives to heroism and patriotic self-sacrifice."

"Yes, in these respects too the Athenians need not fear criticism."

"And besides, none have inherited a past more crowded with great deeds; and many are heartened by such a heritage and encouraged to care for virtue and prove their gallantry."

"All you have said is true, Socrates. But, you 4

ἀλλ' ὁρᾷς, ὅτι ἀφ' οὗ ἥ τε σὺν Τολμίδῃ τῶν
χιλίων ἐν Λεβαδείᾳ συμφορὰ ἐγένετο καὶ ἡ μεθ'
Ἱπποκράτους ἐπὶ Δηλίῳ, ἐκ τούτων τεταπείνωται
μὲν ἡ τῶν Ἀθηναίων δόξα πρὸς τοὺς Βοιωτούς,
ἐπῆρται δὲ τὸ τῶν Θηβαίων φρόνημα πρὸς τοὺς
Ἀθηναίους, ὥστε Βοιωτοὶ μὲν οἱ πρόσθεν οὐδ' ἐν
τῇ ἑαυτῶν τολμῶντες Ἀθηναίοις ἄνευ Λακε-
δαιμονίων τε καὶ τῶν ἄλλων Πελοποννησίων
ἀντιτάττεσθαι νῦν ἀπειλοῦσιν αὐτοὶ καθ' αὑτοὺς
ἐμβαλεῖν εἰς τὴν Ἀττικήν, Ἀθηναῖοι δὲ οἱ
πρότερον [1] πορθοῦντες τὴν Βοιωτίαν φοβοῦνται,
μὴ Βοιωτοὶ δῃώσωσι τὴν Ἀττικήν.

5 Καὶ ὁ Σωκράτης, Ἀλλ' αἰσθάνομαι μέν, ἔφη,
ταῦτα οὕτως ἔχοντα· δοκεῖ δέ μοι ἀνδρὶ ἀγαθῷ
ἄρχοντι νῦν εὐαρεστοτέρως διακεῖσθαι ἡ πόλις.
τὸ μὲν γὰρ θάρρος ἀμέλειάν τε καὶ ῥᾳθυμίαν καὶ
ἀπείθειαν ἐμβάλλει, ὁ δὲ φόβος προσεκτικωτέρους
τε καὶ εὐπειθεστέρους καὶ εὐτακτοτέρους ποιεῖ.

6 τεκμήραιο δ' ἂν τοῦτο καὶ ἀπὸ τῶν ἐν ταῖς
ναυσίν· ὅταν μὲν γὰρ δήπου μηδὲν φοβῶνται,
μεστοί εἰσιν ἀταξίας, ἔστ' ἂν δὲ ἢ χειμῶνα ἢ
πολεμίους δείσωσιν, οὐ μόνον τὰ κελευόμενα
πάντα ποιοῦσιν, ἀλλὰ καὶ σιγῶσι καραδοκοῦντες
τὰ προσταχθησόμενα, ὥσπερ χορευταί.

7 Ἀλλὰ μήν, ἔφη ὁ Περικλῆς, εἴ γε νῦν μάλιστα
πείθοιντο, ὥρα ἂν εἴη λέγειν, πῶς ἂν αὐτοὺς
προτρεψαίμεθα πάλιν ἀνερασθῆναι τῆς ἀρχαίας
ἀρετῆς τε καὶ εὐκλείας καὶ εὐδαιμονίας.

8 Οὐκοῦν, ἔφη ὁ Σωκράτης, εἰ μὲν ἐβουλόμεθα
χρημάτων αὐτοὺς ὧν οἱ ἄλλοι εἶχον ἀντιποιεῖσθαι,

---

[1] Sauppe adds with the MSS., ὅτε Βοιωτοὶ μόνοι ἐγένοντο
which was removed by Cobet.

see, since the disasters sustained by Tolmides and the Thousand at Lebadea [1] and by Hippocrates at Delium, [2] the relations of the Athenians and Boeotians are changed : the glory of the Athenians is brought low, the pride of the Thebans is exalted ; and now the Boeotians, who formerly would not venture, even in their own country, to face the Athenians without help from Sparta and the rest of the Peloponnese, threaten to invade Attica by themselves, and the Athenians, who formerly overran Boeotia, fear that the Boeotians may plunder Attica."

"Ah, I am aware of that," answered Socrates ; 5 " but the disposition of our city is now more to a good ruler's liking. For confidence breeds carelessness, slackness, disobedience : fear makes men more attentive, more obedient, more amenable to discipline. The behaviour of sailors is a case in point. So long 6 as they have nothing to fear, they are, I believe, an unruly lot, but when they expect a storm or an attack, they not only carry out all orders, but watch in silence for the word of command like choristers."

"Well," exclaimed Pericles, "if they are now in 7 the mood for obedience, it seems time to say how we can revive in them a longing for the old virtue and fame and happiness."

"If then," said Socrates, "we wanted them to 8 claim money that others held, the best way of egging

---

[1] At the battle of Coronea (or Lebadea) in 446 B.C., the Boeotians defeated and destroyed the Athenian army and gained independence (Thucydides, I. 113).

[2] The Athenians were heavily defeated by the Boeotians at Delium in 424 B.C. (*Ibid.*, IV. 96 f.).

ἀποδεικνύντες αὐτοῖς ταῦτα πατρῷά τε ὄντα καὶ
προσήκοντα μάλιστ᾽ ἂν οὕτως αὐτοὺς ἐξορμῷμεν
ἀντέχεσθαι τούτων· ἐπεὶ δὲ τοῦ μετ᾽ ἀρετῆς
πρωτεύειν αὐτοὺς ἐπιμελεῖσθαι βουλόμεθα, τοῦτ᾽
αὖ δεικτέον ἐκ παλαιοῦ μάλιστα προσῆκον αὐτοῖς
καὶ ὡς τούτου ἐπιμελόμενοι πάντων ἂν εἶεν
κράτιστοι.

9   Πῶς οὖν ἂν τοῦτο διδάσκοιμεν ;

Οἶμαι μέν, εἰ τούς γε παλαιοτάτους ὧν ἀκούομεν
προγόνους αὐτῶν ἀναμιμνήσκοιμεν αὐτοὺς ἀκη-
κοότας ἀρίστους γεγονέναι.

10   Ἄρα λέγεις τὴν τῶν θεῶν κρίσιν, ἣν οἱ περὶ
Κέκροπα δι᾽ ἀρετὴν ἔκριναν ;

Λέγω γάρ, καὶ τὴν Ἐρεχθέως γε τροφὴν καὶ
γένεσιν καὶ τὸν πόλεμον τὸν ἐπ᾽ ἐκείνου γενόμενον
πρὸς τοὺς ἐκ τῆς ἐχομένης ἠπείρου πάσης καὶ
τὸν ἐφ᾽ Ἡρακλειδῶν πρὸς τοὺς ἐν Πελοποννήσῳ
καὶ πάντας τοὺς ἐπὶ Θησέως πολεμηθέντας, ἐν
οἷς πᾶσιν ἐκεῖνοι δῆλοι γεγόνασι τῶν καθ᾽ ἑαυτοὺς
11   ἀνθρώπων ἀριστεύσαντες· εἰ δὲ βούλει, ἃ ὕστερον
οἱ ἐκείνων μὲν ἀπόγονοι, οὐ πολὺ δὲ πρὸ ἡμῶν
γεγονότες ἔπραξαν, τὰ μὲν αὐτοὶ καθ᾽ αὑτοὺς
ἀγωνιζόμενοι πρὸς τοὺς κυριεύοντας τῆς τε Ἀσίας
πάσης καὶ τῆς Εὐρώπης μέχρι Μακεδονίας καὶ
πλείστην τῶν προγεγονότων δύναμιν καὶ ἀφορμὴν
κεκτημένους καὶ μέγιστα ἔργα κατειργασμένους,
τὰ δὲ καὶ μετὰ Πελοποννησίων ἀριστεύοντες καὶ
κατὰ γῆν καὶ κατὰ θάλατταν· οἳ δὴ καὶ λέγονται
πολὺ διενεγκεῖν τῶν καθ᾽ αὑτοὺς ἀνθρώπων.

---

[1] *i.e.* between Poseidon and Athena for the possession of
Attica.

them on to seize it would be to show them that it was their fathers' money and belongs to them. As we want them to strive for pre-eminence in virtue, we must show that this belonged to them in old days, and that by striving for it they will surpass all other men."

"How then can we teach this?" 9

"I think by reminding them that their earliest ancestors of whom we have any account were, as they themselves have been told, the most valiant."

"Do you refer to the judgment of the gods,[1] which 10 Cecrops delivered in his court because of his virtue?"

"Yes, and the care and birth of Erectheus,[2] and the war waged in his day with all the adjacent country, and the war between the sons of Heracles [3] and the Peloponnesians, and all the wars waged in the days of Theseus,[4] in all of which it is manifest that they were champions among the men of their time. You may add the victories of their descend- 11 ants,[5] who lived not long before our own day: some they gained unaided in their struggle with the lords of all Asia and of Europe as far as Macedonia, the owners of more power and wealth than the world had ever seen, who had wrought deeds that none had equalled; in others they were fellow-champions with the Peloponnesians both on land and sea. These men, like their fathers, are reported to have been far superior to all other men of their time."

---

[2] *Iliad*, II. 547. Ἐρεχθῆος μεγαλήτορος οὔ ποτ' Ἀθήνη θρέψε Διὸς θυγάτηρ, τέκε δὲ ζείδωρος Ἄρουρα.

[3] The Athenians claimed that it was through their assistance that the sons of Heracles gained the victory (Herodotus, ix. 27). [4] Against the Amazons and Thracians.

[5] In the great Persian wars.

Λέγονται γάρ, ἔφη.

12 Τοιγαροῦν πολλῶν μὲν μεταναστάσεων ἐν τῇ Ἑλλάδι γεγονυιῶν διέμειναν ἐν τῇ ἑαυτῶν, πολλοὶ δὲ ὑπὲρ δικαίων ἀντιλέγοντες ἐπέτρεπον ἐκείνοις, πολλοὶ δὲ ὑπὸ κρειττόνων ὑβριζόμενοι κατέφευγον πρὸς ἐκείνους.

13 Καὶ ὁ Περικλῆς, Καὶ θαυμάζω γ᾽, ἔφη, ὦ Σώκρατες, ἡ πόλις ὅπως ποτ᾽ ἐπὶ τὸ χεῖρον ἔκλινεν.

Ἐγὼ μέν, ἔφη, οἶμαι, ὁ Σωκράτης, ὥσπερ καὶ ἀθληταί τινες διὰ τὸ πολὺ ὑπερενεγκεῖν καὶ κρατιστεῦσαι καταρραθυμήσαντες ὑστερίζουσι τῶν ἀντιπάλων, οὕτω καὶ Ἀθηναίους πολὺ διενεγκόντας ἀμελῆσαι ἑαυτῶν καὶ διὰ τοῦτο χείρους γεγονέναι.

14 Νῦν οὖν, ἔφη, τί ἂν ποιοῦντες ἀναλάβοιεν τὴν ἀρχαίαν ἀρετήν;

Καὶ ὁ Σωκράτης· Οὐδὲν ἀπόκρυφον δοκεῖ μοι εἶναι, ἀλλ᾽ εἰ μὲν ἐξευρόντες τὰ τῶν προγόνων ἐπιτηδεύματα μηδὲν χεῖρον ἐκείνων ἐπιτηδεύοιεν, οὐδὲν ἂν χείρους ἐκείνων γενέσθαι· εἰ δὲ μή, τούς γε νῦν πρωτεύοντας μιμούμενοι καὶ τούτοις τὰ αὐτὰ ἐπιτηδεύοντες, ὁμοίως μὲν τοῖς αὐτοῖς χρώμενοι οὐδὲν ἂν χείρους ἐκείνων εἶεν, εἰ δ᾽ ἐπιμελέστερον, καὶ βελτίους.

15 Λέγεις, ἔφη, πόρρω που εἶναι τῇ πόλει τὴν καλοκἀγαθίαν. πότε γὰρ οὕτως Ἀθηναῖοι ὥσπερ Λακεδαιμόνιοι ἢ πρεσβυτέρους αἰδέσονται, οἳ ἀπὸ τῶν πατέρων ἄρχονται καταφρονεῖν τῶν γεραιτέρων, ἢ σωμασκήσουσιν οὕτως, οἳ οὐ μόνον αὐτοὶ εὐεξίας ἀμελοῦσιν, ἀλλὰ καὶ τῶν ἐπιμελο-
16 μένων καταγελῶσι; πότε δὲ οὕτω πείσονται τοῖς

196

"Yes, that is the report of them."

"Therefore, though there have been many migra- 12 tions in Greece, these continued to dwell in their own land: many referred to them their rival claims, many found a refuge with them from the brutality of the oppressor."

"Yes, Socrates," cried Pericles, "and I wonder 13 how our city can have become so degenerate."

"My own view," replied Socrates, "is that the Athenians, as a consequence of their great superiority, grew careless of themselves, and have thus become degenerate, much as athletes who are in a class by themselves and win the championship easily are apt to grow slack and drop below their rivals.

"How, then, can they now recover their old 14 virtue?"

"There is no mystery about it, as I think. If they find out the customs of their ancestors and practise them as well as they did, they will come to be as good as they were; or failing that, they need but to imitate those who now have the pre-eminence and to practise their customs, and if they are equally careful in observing them, they will be as good as they, and, if more careful, even better."

"That means that it is a long march for our city 15 to perfection. For when will Athenians show the Lacedaemonian reverence for age, seeing that they despise all their elders, beginning with their own fathers? When will they adopt the Lacedaemonian system of training, seeing that they not only neglect to make themselves fit, but mock at those who take the trouble to do so? When will they 16

ἄρχουσιν, οἳ καὶ ἀγάλλονται ἐπὶ τῷ καταφρονεῖν
τῶν ἀρχόντων, ἢ πότε οὕτως ὁμονοήσουσιν, οἵ γε
ἀντὶ μὲν τοῦ συνεργεῖν ἑαυτοῖς τὰ συμφέροντα
ἐπηρεάζουσιν ἀλλήλοις καὶ φθονοῦσιν ἑαυτοῖς
μᾶλλον ἢ τοῖς ἄλλοις ἀνθρώποις, μάλιστα δὲ
πάντων ἔν τε ταῖς ἰδίαις συνόδοις καὶ ταῖς κοιναῖς
διαφέρονται· καὶ πλείστας δίκας ἀλλήλοις δικά-
ζονται καὶ προαιροῦνται μᾶλλον οὕτω κερδαίνειν
ἀπ' ἀλλήλων ἢ συνωφελοῦντες αὑτούς, τοῖς δὲ
κοινοῖς ὥσπερ ἀλλοτρίοις χρώμενοι περὶ τούτων
αὖ μάχονται καὶ ταῖς εἰς τὰ τοιαῦτα δυνάμεσι
17 μάλιστα χαίρουσιν; ἐξ ὧν πολλὴ μὲν ἀτηρία
καὶ κακία τῇ πόλει ἐμφύεται, πολλὴ δὲ ἔχθρα
καὶ μῖσος ἀλλήλων τοῖς πολίταις ἐγγίγνεται, δι'
ἃ ἔγωγε μάλα φοβοῦμαι ἀεί, μή τι μεῖζον ἢ ὥστε
φέρειν δύνασθαι κακὸν τῇ πόλει συμβῇ.

18 Μηδαμῶς, ἔφη ὁ Σωκράτης, ὦ Περίκλεις, οὕτως
ἡγοῦ ἀνηκέστῳ πονηρίᾳ νοσεῖν Ἀθηναίους. οὐχ
ὁρᾷς, ὡς εὔτακτοι μέν εἰσιν ἐν τοῖς ναυτικοῖς,
εὐτάκτως δ' ἐν τοῖς γυμνικοῖς ἀγῶσι πείθονται
τοῖς ἐπιστάταις, οὐδένων δὲ καταδεέστερον ἐν
τοῖς χοροῖς ὑπηρετοῦσι τοῖς διδασκάλοις;

19 Τοῦτο γάρ τοι, ἔφη, καὶ θαυμαστόν ἐστι, τὸ
τοὺς μὲν τοιούτους πειθαρχεῖν τοῖς ἐφεστῶσι,
τοὺς δὲ ὁπλίτας καὶ τοὺς ἱππεῖς, οἳ δοκοῦσι καλοκἀγαθίᾳ προκεκρίσθαι τῶν πολιτῶν, ἀπειθεστά-
τους εἶναι πάντων.

20 Καὶ ὁ Σωκράτης ἔφη· Ἡ δὲ ἐν Ἀρείῳ πάγῳ
βουλή, ὦ Περίκλεις, οὐκ ἐκ τῶν δεδοκιμασμένων
καθίσταται;

Καὶ μάλα, ἔφη.

Οἶσθα οὖν τινας, ἔφη, κάλλιον ἢ νομιμώτερον

reach that standard of obedience to their rulers, seeing that they make contempt of rulers a point of honour? Or when will they attain that harmony, seeing that, instead of working together for the general good,[1] they are more envious and bitter against one another than against the rest of the world, are the most quarrelsome of men in public and private assemblies, most often go to law with one another, and would rather make profit of one another so than by mutual service, and while regarding public affairs as alien to themselves, yet fight over them too, and find their chief enjoyment in having the means to carry on such strife? So it comes about that mischief and evil grow apace in the city, enmity and mutual hatred spring up among the people, so that I am always dreading that some evil past bearing may befall the city."

"No, no, Pericles, don't think the wickedness of the Athenians so utterly past remedy. Don't you see what good discipline they maintain in their fleets, how well they obey the umpires in athletic contests, how they take orders from the choir-trainers as readily as any?"

"Ah yes, and strange indeed it is that such men submit themselves to their masters, and yet the infantry and cavalry, who are supposed to be the pick of the citizens for good character, are the most insubordinate."

Then Socrates asked, "But what of the Court of the Areopagus, Pericles? Are not its members persons who have won approval?"

"Certainly."

"Then do you know of any who decide the cases

---

[1] *Cyropaedia*, VIII. i. 2.

ἢ σεμνότερον ἢ δικαιότερον τάς τε δίκας δικάζοντας καὶ τἆλλα πάντα πράττοντας ;

Οὐ μέμφομαι, ἔφη, τούτοις.

Οὐ τοίνυν, ἔφη, δεῖ ἀθυμεῖν ὡς οὐκ εὐτάκτων ὄντων Ἀθηναίων.

21 Καὶ μὴν ἔν γε τοῖς στρατιωτικοῖς, ἔφη, ἔνθα μάλιστα δεῖ σωφρονεῖν τε καὶ εὐτακτεῖν καὶ πειθαρχεῖν, οὐδενὶ τούτων προσέχουσιν.

Ἴσως γάρ, ἔφη ὁ Σωκράτης, ἐν τούτοις οἱ ἥκιστα ἐπιστάμενοι ἄρχουσιν αὐτῶν. οὐχ ὁρᾷς, ὅτι κιθαριστῶν μὲν καὶ χορευτῶν καὶ ὀρχηστῶν οὐδὲ εἷς ἐπιχειρεῖ ἄρχειν μὴ ἐπιστάμενος οὐδὲ παλαιστῶν οὐδὲ παγκρατιαστῶν ; ἀλλὰ πάντες οἱ τούτων ἄρχοντες ἔχουσι δεῖξαι, ὁπόθεν ἔμαθον ταῦτα, ἐφ' οἷς ἐφεστᾶσι· τῶν δὲ στρατηγῶν οἱ πλεῖστοι

22 αὐτοσχεδιάζουσιν. οὐ μέντοι σέ γε τοιοῦτον ἐγὼ νομίζω εἶναι, ἀλλ' οἶμαί σε οὐδὲν ἧττον ἔχειν εἰπεῖν, ὁπότε στρατηγεῖν ἢ ὁπότε παλαίειν ἤρξω μανθάνειν· καὶ πολλὰ μὲν οἶμαί σε τῶν πατρῴων στρατηγημάτων παρειληφότα διασῴζειν, πολλὰ δὲ πανταχόθεν συνηχέναι, ὁπόθεν οἷόν τε ἦν

23 μαθεῖν τι ὠφέλιμον εἰς στρατηγίαν. οἶμαι δέ σε πολλὰ μεριμνᾶν, ὅπως μὴ λάθῃς σεαυτὸν ἀγνοῶν τι τῶν εἰς στρατηγίαν ὠφελίμων, καὶ ἐάν τι τοιοῦτον αἴσθῃ σεαυτὸν μὴ εἰδότα, ζητεῖν τοὺς ἐπισταμένους ταῦτα, οὔτε δώρων οὔτε χαρίτων φειδόμενον, ὅπως μάθῃς παρ' αὐτῶν ἃ μὴ ἐπίστασαι καὶ συνεργοὺς ἀγαθοὺς ἔχῃς.

24 Καὶ ὁ Περικλῆς, Οὐ λανθάνεις με, ὦ Σώκρατες, ἔφη, ὅτι οὐδ' οἰόμενός με τούτων ἐπιμελεῖσθαι ταῦτα λέγεις, ἀλλ' ἐγχειρῶν με διδάσκειν, ὅτι τὸν μέλλοντα στρατηγεῖν τούτων ἁπάντων

that come before them and perform all their other functions more honourably, more in accordance with law, with more dignity and justice?"

"I am not finding fault with the Areopagus."

"Then you must not despair of Athenian discipline."

"But, you see, in the army, where good conduct, 21 discipline, submission are most necessary, our people pay no attention to these things."

"This may be due to the incompetence of the officers. You must have noticed that no one attempts to exercise authority over our harpists, choristers and dancers, if he is incompetent, nor over wrestlers or wrestlers who also box? All who have authority over them can tell where they learned their business; but most of our generals are improvisors. However, I don't suppose you are one 22 of this sort. I suppose you can say when you began to learn strategy as well as when you began wrestling. Many of the principles, I think, you have inherited from your father, and many others you have gathered from every source from which you could learn anything useful to a general. I think, too, that you 23 take much trouble that you may not unconsciously lack any knowledge useful to a general; and if you find that you don't know anything, you seek out those who have the knowledge, grudging neither gifts nor thanks, that you may learn what you don't know from them and may have the help of good coaching."

"I can see, Socrates, that in saying this you don't 24 really think I study these things, but you are trying to show me that one who is going to command an

ἐπιμελεῖσθαι δεῖ. ὁμολογῶ μέντοι κἀγώ σοι
ταῦτα.

25 Τοῦτο δ', ἔφη, ὦ Περίκλεις, κατανενόηκας, ὅτι
κρόκειται τῆς χώρας ἡμῶν ὄρη μεγάλα, καθήκοντα
ἐπὶ τὴν Βοιωτίαν, δι' ὧν εἰς τὴν χώραν εἴσοδοι
στεναί τε καὶ προσάντεις εἰσί, καὶ ὅτι μέση διέζω-
σται ὄρεσιν ἐρυμνοῖς;

Καὶ μάλα, ἔφη.

26 Τί δέ; ἐκεῖνο ἀκήκοας, ὅτι Μυσοὶ καὶ Πισίδαι
ἐν τῇ βασιλέως χώρᾳ κατέχοντες ἐρυμνὰ πάνυ
χωρία καὶ κούφως ὡπλισμένοι δύνανται πολλὰ
μὲν τὴν βασιλέως χώραν καταθέοντες κακοποιεῖν,
αὐτοὶ δὲ ζῆν ἐλεύθεροι;

27 Καὶ τοῦτό γ', ἔφη, ἀκούω.

Ἀθηναίους δ' οὐκ ἂν οἴει, ἔφη, μέχρι τῆς
ἐλαφρᾶς ἡλικίας ὡπλισμένους κουφοτέροις ὅπλοις
καὶ τὰ προκείμενα τῆς χώρας ὄρη κατέχοντας
βλαβεροὺς μὲν τοῖς πολεμίοις εἶναι, μεγάλην δὲ
προβολὴν τοῖς πολίταις τῆς χώρας κατεσκευά-
σθαι;

Καὶ ὁ Περικλῆς, Πάντ' οἶμαι, ἔφη, ὦ Σώκρατες,
καὶ ταῦτα χρήσιμα εἶναι.

28 Εἰ τοίνυν, ἔφη ὁ Σωκράτης, ἀρέσκει σοι ταῦτα,
ἐπιχείρει αὐτοῖς, ὦ ἄριστε· ὅ, τι μὲν γὰρ ἂν
τούτων καταπράξῃς, καὶ σοὶ καλὸν ἔσται καὶ τῇ
πόλει ἀγαθόν· ἐὰν δέ τι αὐτῶν ἀδυνατῇς, οὔτε
τὴν πόλιν βλάψεις οὔτε σαυτὸν καταισχυνεῖς.

VI. Γλαύκωνα δὲ τὸν Ἀρίστωνος, ὅτ' ἐπεχείρει δημηγορεῖν, ἐπιθυμῶν προστατεύειν τῆς πόλεως οὐδέπω εἴκοσιν ἔτη γεγονώς, τῶν ἄλλων
οἰκείων τε καὶ φίλων οὐδεὶς ἐδύνατο παῦσαι
ἑλκόμενόν τε ἀπὸ τοῦ βήματος καὶ καταγέλαστον

army must study all of them; and of course I admit that you are right."

"Have you observed, Pericles, that our frontier is 25 protected by great mountains extending to Boeotia, through which there are steep and narrow passes leading into our land, and that the interior is cut across by rugged mountains?"

"Certainly."

"Further, have you heard that the Mysians and 26 Pisidians, occupying very rugged country in the Great King's territory and lightly armed, contrive to overrun and damage the King's territory and to preserve their own freedom?"[1]

"Yes, I have heard so."

"And don't you think that active young Athenians, 27 more lightly armed and occupying the mountains that protect our country, would prove a thorn in the side of the enemy and a strong bulwark of defence to our people?"

"Socrates," replied Pericles, "I think all these suggestions too have a practical value."

"Then, since you like them, adopt them, my 28 good fellow. Any part of them that you carry out will bring honour to you and good to the state; and should you fail in part, you will neither harm the state nor disgrace yourself."

VI. Ariston's son, Glaucon, was attempting to become an orator and striving for headship in the state, though he was less than twenty years old; and none of his friends or relations could check him, though he would get himself dragged from the platform and make himself a laughing-stock. Only

[1] *Anabasis*, II. v. 13.

ὄντα· Σωκράτης δὲ εὔνους ὢν αὐτῷ διά τε Χαρμίδην τὸν Γλαύκωνος καὶ διὰ Πλάτωνα μόνος
ἔπαυσεν.

2   Ἐντυχὼν γὰρ αὐτῷ πρῶτον μὲν εἰς τὸ ἐθελῆ-
σαι ἀκούειν τοιάδε λέξας κατέσχεν· Ὦ Γλαύκων,
ἔφη, προστατεύειν ἡμῖν διανενόησαι τῆς πόλεως ;

Ἔγωγ᾽, ἔφη, ὦ Σώκρατες.

Νὴ Δί᾽, ἔφη, καλὸν γάρ, εἴπερ τι καὶ ἄλλο τῶν
ἐν ἀνθρώποις. δῆλον γάρ, ὅτι ἐὰν τοῦτο δια-
πράξῃ, δυνατὸς μὲν ἔσῃ αὐτὸς τυγχάνειν ὅτου ἂν
ἐπιθυμῇς, ἱκανὸς δὲ τοὺς φίλους ὠφελεῖν, ἐπαρεῖς
δὲ τὸν πατρῷον οἶκον, αὐξήσεις δὲ τὴν πατρίδα,
ὀνομαστὸς δ᾽ ἔσῃ πρῶτον μὲν ἐν τῇ πόλει, ἔπειτα
ἐν τῇ Ἑλλάδι, ἴσως δὲ ὥσπερ Θεμιστοκλῆς καὶ
ἐν τοῖς βαρβάροις· ὅπου δ᾽ ἂν ᾖς, πανταχοῦ περί-
βλεπτος ἔσῃ.

3   Ταῦτ᾽ οὖν ἀκούων ὁ Γλαύκων ἐμεγαλύνετο καὶ
ἡδέως παρέμενε.

Μετὰ δὲ ταῦτα ὁ Σωκράτης, Οὐκοῦν, ἔφη,
τοῦτο μέν, ὦ Γλαύκων, δῆλον, ὅτι εἴπερ τιμᾶσθαι
βούλει, ὠφελητέα σοι ἡ πόλις ἐστί ;

Πάνυ μὲν οὖν, ἔφη.

Πρὸς θεῶν, ἔφη, μὴ τοίνυν ἀποκρύψῃ, ἀλλ᾽
εἰπὸν ἡμῖν, ἐκ τίνος ἄρξῃ τὴν πόλιν εὐεργετεῖν.

4   Ἐπεὶ δὲ ὁ Γλαύκων διεσιώπησεν, ὡς ἂν τότε
σκοπῶν, ὁπόθεν ἄρχοιτο, Ἄρ᾽, ἔφη ὁ Σωκράτης,

Socrates, who took an interest in him for the sake of Plato and Glaucon's[1] son Charmides, managed to check him.

For once on meeting him, he stopped him and 2 contrived to engage his attention by saying: "Glaucon, have you made up your mind to be our chief man in the state?"

"I have, Socrates."

"Well, upon my word there's no more honourable ambition in the world; for obviously, if you gain your object, you will be able to get whatever you want, and you will have the means of helping your friends: you will lift up your father's house and exalt your fatherland; and you will make a name for yourself first at home, later on in Greece, and possibly, like Themistocles, in foreign lands as well; wherever you go, you will be a man of mark."

When Glaucon heard this, he felt proud and 3 gladly lingered.

Next Socrates asked, "Well, Glaucon, as you want to win honour, is it not obvious that you must benefit your city?"

"Most certainly."

"Pray don't be reticent, then; but tell us how you propose to begin your services to the state."

As Glaucon remained dumb, apparently consider- 4 ing for the first time how to begin, Socrates said:

[1] *i.e.* the elder Glaucon.

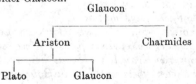

ὥσπερ φίλου οἶκον εἰ αὐξῆσαι βούλοιο, πλουσιώτερον αὐτὸν ἐπιχειροίης ἂν ποιεῖν, οὕτω καὶ
τὴν πόλιν πειράσῃ πλουσιωτέραν ποιῆσαι;

Πάνυ μὲν οὖν, ἔφη.

5   Οὐκοῦν πλουσιωτέρα γ᾽ ἂν εἴη προσόδων αὐτῇ
πλειόνων γενομένων;

Εἰκὸς γοῦν, ἔφη.

Λέξον δή, ἔφη, ἐκ τίνων νῦν αἱ πρόσοδοι τῇ
πόλει καὶ πόσαι τινές εἰσι; δῆλον γάρ, ὅτι
ἔσκεψαι, ἵνα εἰ μέν τινες αὐτῶν ἐνδεῶς ἔχουσιν,
ἐκπληρώσῃς, εἰ δὲ παραλείπονται, προσπορίσῃς.

Ἀλλὰ μὰ Δί᾽, ἔφη ὁ Γλαύκων, ταῦτά γε οὐκ
ἐπέσκεμμαι.

6   Ἀλλ᾽ εἰ τοῦτο, ἔφη, παρέλιπες, τάς γε δαπάνας
τῆς πόλεως ἡμῖν εἰπέ· δῆλον γάρ, ὅτι καὶ τούτων
τὰς περιττὰς ἀφαιρεῖν διανοεῖ.

Ἀλλὰ μὰ τὸν Δί᾽, ἔφη, οὐδὲ πρὸς ταῦτά πω
ἐσχόλασα.

Οὐκοῦν, ἔφη, τὸ μὲν πλουσιωτέραν τὴν πόλιν
ποιεῖν ἀναβαλούμεθα· πῶς γὰρ οἷόν τε μὴ εἰδότα
γε τὰ ἀναλώματα καὶ τὰς προσόδους ἐπιμεληθῆναι
τούτων;

7   Ἀλλ᾽, ὦ Σώκρατες, ἔφη ὁ Γλαύκων, δυνατόν
ἐστι καὶ ἀπὸ πολεμίων τὴν πόλιν πλουτίζειν.

Νὴ Δία σφόδρα γ᾽, ἔφη ὁ Σωκράτης, ἐάν τις
αὐτῶν κρείττων ᾖ· ἥττων δὲ ὢν καὶ τὰ ὄντα
προσαποβάλοι ἄν.

Ἀληθῆ λέγεις, ἔφη.

8   Οὐκοῦν, ἔφη, τόν γε βουλευσόμενον, πρὸς
οὕστινας δεῖ πολεμεῖν, τήν τε τῆς πόλεως δύναμιν
καὶ τὴν τῶν ἐναντίων εἰδέναι δεῖ, ἵνα ἐὰν μὲν ᾖ
τῆς πόλεως κρείττων ᾖ, συμβουλεύῃ ἐπιχειρεῖν

"If you wanted to add to a friend's fortune, you would set about making him richer. Will you try, then, to make your city richer?"

"Certainly."

"Would she not be richer if she had a larger 5 revenue?"

"Oh yes, presumably."

"Now tell me, from what sources are the city's revenues at present derived and what is their total? No doubt you have gone into this matter, in order to raise the amount of any that are deficient and supply any that are lacking."

"Certainly not," exclaimed Glaucon, "I haven't gone into that."

"Well, if you have left that out, tell us the 6 expenditure of the city. No doubt you intend to cut down any items that are excessive."

"The fact is, I haven't had time yet for that either."

"Oh, then we will postpone the business of making the city richer; for how is it possible to look after income and expenditure without knowing what they are?"

"Well, Socrates, one can make our enemies con- 7 tribute to the city's wealth."

"Yes, of course, provided he is stronger than they; but if he be weaker, he may lose what she has got instead."

"True."

"Therefore, in order to advise her whom to fight, 8 it is necessary to know the strength of the city and of the enemy, so that, if the city be stronger, one

τῷ πολέμῳ, ἐὰν δὲ ἡ τῶν ἐναντίων, εὐλαβεῖσθαι
πείθῃ.

Ὀρθῶς λέγεις, ἔφη.

9 Πρῶτον μὲν τοίνυν, ἔφη, λέξον ἡμῖν τῆς πόλεως
τήν τε πεζικὴν καὶ τὴν ναυτικὴν δύναμιν, εἶτα
τὴν τῶν ἐναντίων.

Ἀλλὰ μὰ τὸν Δί᾿, ἔφη, οὐκ ἂν ἔχοιμί σοι οὕτω
γε ἀπὸ στόματος εἰπεῖν.

Ἀλλ᾿ εἰ γέγραπταί σοι, ἔνεγκε, ἔφη· πάνυ γὰρ
ἡδέως ἂν τοῦτο ἀκούσαιμι.

Ἀλλὰ μὰ τὸν Δί᾿, ἔφη, οὐδὲ γέγραπταί μοί
πω.

10 Οὐκοῦν, ἔφη, καὶ περὶ πολέμου συμβουλεύειν
τήν γε πρώτην ἐπισχήσομεν· ἴσως γὰρ καὶ διὰ
τὸ μέγεθος αὐτῶν ἄρτι ἀρχόμενος τῆς προστατείας
οὔπω ἐξήτακας. ἀλλά τοι περί γε φυλακῆς τῆς
χώρας οἶδ᾿ ὅτι σοι ἤδη μεμέληκε καὶ οἶσθα, ὁπόσαι τε φυλακαὶ ἐπίκαιροί εἰσι καὶ ὁπόσαι μὴ καὶ
ὁπόσοι τε φρουροὶ ἱκανοί εἰσι καὶ ὁπόσοι μή εἰσι·
καὶ τὰς μὲν ἐπικαίρους φυλακὰς συμβουλεύσεις
μείζονας ποιεῖν, τὰς δὲ περιττὰς ἀφαιρεῖν.

11 Νὴ Δί᾿, ἔφη ὁ Γλαύκων, ἁπάσας μὲν οὖν ἔγωγε
ἕνεκά γε τοῦ οὕτως αὐτὰς φυλάττεσθαι, ὥστε
κλέπτεσθαι τὰ ἐκ τῆς χώρας.

Ἐὰν δέ τις ἀφέλῃ γ᾿, ἔφη, τὰς φυλακάς, οὐκ
οἴει καὶ ἁρπάζειν ἐξουσίαν ἔσεσθαι τῷ βουλομένῳ; ἀτάρ, ἔφη, πότερον ἐλθὼν αὐτὸς ἐξήτακας
τοῦτο ἢ πῶς οἶσθα, ὅτι κακῶς φυλάττονται;

Εἰκάζω, ἔφη.

Οὐκοῦν, ἔφη, καὶ περὶ τούτων, ὅταν μηκέτι
εἰκάζωμεν, ἀλλ᾿ ἤδη εἰδῶμεν, τότε συμβουλεύσο-
μεν;

may recommend her to go to war, but if weaker than the enemy, may persuade her to beware."

"You are right."

"First, then, tell us the naval and military 9 strength of our city, and then that of her enemies."

"No, of course I can't tell you out of my head."

"Well, if you have made notes, fetch them, for I should greatly like to hear this."

"But, I tell you, I haven't yet made any notes either."

"Then we will postpone offering advice about war 10 too for the present. You are new to power, and perhaps have not had time to investigate such big problems. But the defence of the country, now, I feel sure you have thought about that, and know how many of the garrisons are well placed and how many are not, and how many of the guards are efficient and how many are not; and you will propose to strengthen the well-placed garrisons and to do away with those that are superfluous."

"No, no; I shall propose to do away with them 11 all, for the only effect of maintaining them is that our crops are stolen."

"But if you do away with the garrisons, don't you think that anyone will be at liberty to rob us openly? However, have you been on a tour of inspection, or how do you know that they are badly maintained?"

"By guess-work."

"Then shall we wait to offer advice on this question too until we really know, instead of merely guessing?"

Ἴσως, ἔφη ὁ Γλαύκων, βέλτιον.

12 Εἴς γε μήν, ἔφη, τἀργύρεια οἶδ᾽ ὅτι οὐκ ἀφῖξαι, ὥστ᾽ ἔχειν εἰπεῖν, διότι νῦν ἐλάττω ἢ πρόσθεν προσέρχεται αὐτόθεν.

Οὐ γὰρ οὖν ἐλήλυθα, ἔφη.

Καὶ γὰρ νὴ Δί᾽, ἔφη ὁ Σωκράτης, λέγεται βαρὺ τὸ χωρίον εἶναι, ὥστε ὅταν περὶ τούτου δέῃ συμβουλεύειν, αὕτη σοι ἡ πρόφασις ἀρκέσει.

Σκώπτομαι, ἔφη ὁ Γλαύκων.

13 Ἀλλ᾽ ἐκείνου γέ τοι, ἔφη, οἶδ᾽ ὅτι οὐκ ἠμέληκας, ἀλλ᾽ ἔσκεψαι, πόσον χρόνον ἱκανός ἐστιν ὁ ἐκ τῆς χώρας γιγνόμενος σῖτος διατρέφειν τὴν πόλιν καὶ πόσου εἰς τὸν ἐνιαυτὸν προσδεῖται, ἵνα μὴ τούτου γε λάθῃ σέ ποτε ἡ πόλις ἐνδεὴς γενομένη, ἀλλ᾽ εἰδὼς ἔχῃς ὑπὲρ τῶν ἀναγκαίων συμβουλεύων τῇ πόλει βοηθεῖν τε καὶ σώζειν αὐτήν.

Λέγεις, ἔφη ὁ Γλαύκων, παμμέγεθες πρᾶγμα, εἴ γε καὶ τῶν τοιούτων ἐπιμελεῖσθαι δεήσει.

14 Ἀλλὰ μέντοι, ἔφη ὁ Σωκράτης, οὐδ᾽ ἂν τὸν ἑαυτοῦ ποτε οἶκον καλῶς τις οἰκήσειεν, εἰ μὴ πάντα μὲν εἴσεται ὧν προσδεῖται, πάντων δὲ ἐπιμελόμενος ἐκπληρώσει. ἀλλ᾽ ἐπεὶ ἡ μὲν πόλις ἐκ πλειόνων ἢ μυρίων οἰκιῶν συνέστηκε, χαλεπὸν δ᾽ ἐστὶν ἅμα τοσούτων οἴκων ἐπιμελεῖσθαι, πῶς οὐχ ἕνα τὸν τοῦ θείου πρῶτον ἐπειράθης αὐξῆσαι; δεῖται δέ. κἂν μὲν τοῦτον δύνῃ, καὶ πλείοσιν ἐπιχειρήσεις· ἕνα δὲ μὴ δυνάμενος ὠφελῆσαι πῶς ἂν πολλούς γε δυνηθείης; ὥσπερ εἴ τις ἓν τάλαντον μὴ δύναιτο φέρειν, πῶς οὐ φανερόν, ὅτι πλείω γε φέρειν οὐδ᾽ ἐπιχειρητέον αὐτῷ;

15 Ἀλλ᾽ ἔγωγ᾽, ἔφη ὁ Γλαύκων, ὠφελοίην ἂν τὸν τοῦ θείου οἶκον, εἴ μοι ἐθέλοι πείθεσθαι.

210

" Perhaps it would be better."

" Now for the silver mines. I am sure you have 12
not visited them, and so cannot tell why the amount
derived from them has fallen."

" No, indeed, I have not been there."

" To be sure : the district is considered unhealthy,
and so when you have to offer advice on the problem,
this excuse will serve."

" You're chaffing me."

" Ah, but there's one problem I feel sure you 13
haven't overlooked : no doubt you have reckoned
how long the corn grown in the country will maintain the population, and how much is needed
annually, so that you may not be caught napping,
should the city at any time be short, and may come
to the rescue and relieve the city by giving expert
advice about food."

" What an overwhelming task, if one has got
to include such things as that in one's duties !"

" But, you know, no one will ever manage even 14
his own household successfully unless he knows all
its needs and sees that they are all supplied. Seeing that our city contains more than ten thousand
houses, and it is difficult to look after so many
families at once, you must have tried to make a
start by doing something for one, I mean your
uncle's ? It needs it ; and if you succeed with
that one, you can set to work on a larger number.
But if you can't do anything for one, how are you
going to succeed with many ? If a man can't carry
one talent, it's absurd for him to try to carry more
than one, isn't it ? "

" Well, I could do something for uncle's house- 15
hold if only he would listen to me."

XENOPHON

Εἶτα, ἔφη ὁ Σωκράτης, τὸν θεῖον οὐ δυνάμενος πείθειν Ἀθηναίους πάντας μετὰ τοῦ θείου νομίζεις
16 δυνήσεσθαι ποιῆσαι πείθεσθαί σοι; φυλάττου, ἔφη, ὦ Γλαύκων, ὅπως μὴ τοῦ εὐδοξεῖν ἐπιθυμῶν εἰς τοὐναντίον ἔλθῃς. ἢ οὐχ ὁρᾷς, ὡς σφαλερόν ἐστι τὸ ἃ μὴ οἶδέ τις, ταῦτα ἢ λέγειν ἢ πράττειν; ἐνθυμοῦ δὲ τῶν ἄλλων, ὅσους οἶσθα τοιούτους, οἷοι φαίνονται καὶ λέγοντες ἃ μὴ ἴσασι καὶ πράττοντες, πότερά σοι δοκοῦσιν ἐπὶ τοῖς τοιούτοις ἐπαίνου μᾶλλον ἢ ψόγου τυγχάνειν καὶ πότερον
17 θαυμάζεσθαι μᾶλλον ἢ καταφρονεῖσθαι· ἐνθυμοῦ δὲ καὶ τῶν εἰδότων ὅ τι τε λέγουσι καὶ ὅ τι ποιοῦσι, καί, ὡς ἐγὼ νομίζω, εὑρήσεις ἐν πᾶσιν ἔργοις τοὺς μὲν εὐδοκιμοῦντάς τε καὶ θαυμαζομένους ἐκ τῶν μάλιστα ἐπισταμένων ὄντας, τοὺς δὲ κακοδοξοῦντάς τε καὶ καταφρονουμένους ἐκ
18 τῶν ἀμαθεστάτων. εἰ οὖν ἐπιθυμεῖς εὐδοκιμεῖν τε καὶ θαυμάζεσθαι ἐν τῇ πόλει, πειρῶ κατεργάσασθαι ὡς μάλιστα τὸ εἰδέναι ἃ βούλει πράττειν· ἐὰν γὰρ τούτῳ διενεγκὼν τῶν ἄλλων ἐπιχειρῇς τὰ τῆς πόλεως πράττειν, οὐκ ἂν θαυμάσαιμι, εἰ πάνυ ῥᾳδίως τύχοις ὧν ἐπιθυμεῖς.

VII. Χαρμίδην δὲ τὸν Γλαύκωνος ὁρῶν ἀξιόλογον μὲν ἄνδρα ὄντα καὶ πολλῷ δυνατώτερον τῶν τὰ πολιτικὰ τότε πραττόντων, ὀκνοῦντα δὲ προσιέναι τῷ δήμῳ καὶ τῶν τῆς πόλεως πραγμάτων ἐπιμελεῖσθαι, Εἰπέ μοι, ἔφη, ὦ Χαρμίδη, εἴ τις ἱκανὸς ὢν τοὺς στεφανίτας ἀγῶνας νικᾶν καὶ διὰ τοῦτο αὐτός τε τιμᾶσθαι καὶ τὴν πατρίδα ἐν τῇ Ἑλλάδι εὐδοκιμωτέραν ποιεῖν μὴ θέλοι ἀγωνίζεσθαι, ποῖόν τινα τοῦτον νομίζοις ἂν τὸν ἄνδρα εἶναι;

" What? You can't persuade your uncle, and yet you suppose you will be able to persuade all the Athenians, including your uncle, to listen to you? 16 Pray take care, Glaucon, that your daring ambition doesn't lead to a fall! Don't you see how risky it is to say or do what you don't understand? Think of others whom you know to be the sort of men who say and do what they obviously don't understand. Do you think they get praise or blame by it? And 17 think of those who understand what they say and what they do. You will find, I take it, that the men who are famous and admired always come from those who have the widest knowledge, and the infamous and despised from the most ignorant. Therefore, if you want to win fame and admiration 18 in public life, try to get a thorough knowledge of what you propose to do. If you enter on a public career with this advantage over others, I should not be surprised if you gained the object of your ambition quite easily."

VII. Seeing that Glaucon's son, Charmides, was a respectable man and far more capable than the politicians of the day, and nevertheless shrank from speaking in the assembly and taking a part in politics, he said: " Tell me, Charmides, what would you think of a man who was capable of gaining a victory in the great games and consequently of winning honour for himself and adding to his country's fame in the Greek world, and yet refused to compete? "

Δῆλον ὅτι, ἔφη, μαλακόν τε καὶ δειλόν.

2 Εἰ δέ τις, ἔφη, δυνατὸς ὢν τῶν τῆς πόλεως πραγμάτων ἐπιμελόμενος τήν τε πόλιν αὔξειν καὶ αὐτὸς διὰ τοῦτο τιμᾶσθαι ὀκνοίη δὴ τοῦτο πράττειν, οὐκ ἂν εἰκότως δειλὸς νομίζοιτο ;

Ἴσως, ἔφη· ἀτὰρ πρὸς τί με ταῦτ᾽ ἐρωτᾷς ;

Ὅτι, ἔφη, οἶμαί σε δυνατὸν ὄντα ὀκνεῖν ἐπιμελεῖσθαι, καὶ ταῦτα ὧν ἀνάγκη σοι μετέχειν πολίτῃ γε ὄντι.

3 Τὴν δὲ ἐμὴν δύναμιν, ἔφη ὁ Χαρμίδης, ἐν ποίῳ ἔργῳ καταμαθὼν ταῦτά μου καταγιγνώσκεις ;

Ἐν ταῖς συνουσίαις, ἔφη, αἷς σύνει τοῖς τὰ τῆς πόλεως πράττουσι· καὶ γὰρ ὅταν τι ἀνακοινῶνταί σοι, ὁρῶ σε καλῶς συμβουλεύοντα καὶ ὅταν τι ἁμαρτάνωσιν, ὀρθῶς ἐπιτιμῶντα.

4 Οὐ ταὐτόν ἐστιν, ἔφη, ὦ Σώκρατες, ἰδίᾳ τε διαλέγεσθαι καὶ ἐν τῷ πλήθει ἀγωνίζεσθαι.

Καὶ μήν, ἔφη, ὅ γε ἀριθμεῖν δυνάμενος οὐδὲν ἧττον ἐν τῷ πλήθει ἢ μόνος ἀριθμεῖ καὶ οἱ κατὰ μόνας ἄριστα καθαρίζοντες οὗτοι καὶ ἐν τῷ πλήθει κρατιστεύουσιν.

5 Αἰδῶ δὲ καὶ φόβον, ἔφη, οὐχ ὁρᾷς ἔμφυτά τε ἀνθρώποις ὄντα καὶ πολλῷ μᾶλλον ἐν τοῖς ὄχλοις ἢ ἐν ταῖς ἰδίαις ὁμιλίαις παριστάμενα ;

Καὶ σέ γε διδάξων, ἔφη, ὥρμημαι, ὅτι οὔτε τοὺς φρονιμωτάτους αἰδούμενος οὔτε τοὺς ἰσχυροτάτους φοβούμενος ἐν τοῖς ἀφρονεστάτοις τε καὶ

6 ἀσθενεστάτοις αἰσχύνει λέγειν. πότερον γὰρ τοὺς κναφεῖς αὐτῶν ἢ τοὺς σκυτεῖς ἢ τοὺς τέκτονας ἢ τοὺς χαλκεῖς ἢ τοὺς γεωργοὺς ἢ τοὺς ἐμπόρους ἢ τοὺς ἐν τῇ ἀγορᾷ μεταβαλλομένους καὶ φροντίζοντας ὅ τι ἐλάττονος πριάμενοι

" I should think him a poltroon and a coward, of course."

" Then if a man were to shrink from state busi- 2 ness though capable of discharging it with advantage to the state and honour to himself, wouldn't it be reasonable to think him a coward ? "

" Perhaps ; but why ask me that ? "

" Because I fancy that you shrink from work that is within your powers, work in which it is your duty as a citizen to take a hand."

" What makes you think so ? In what sort of 3 work have you discovered my powers ? "

" In your intercourse with public men. Whenever they take counsel with you, I find that you give excellent advice, and whenever they make a mistake, your criticism is sound."

" A private conversation is a very different thing 4 from a crowded debate, Socrates."

" But, you know, a man who is good at figures counts as well in a crowd as in solitude ; and those who play the harp best in private excel no less in a crowd."

" But surely you see that bashfulness and timidity 5 come natural to a man, and affect him far more powerfully in the presence of a multitude than in private society ? "

" Yes, and I mean to give you a lesson. The wisest do not make you bashful, and the strongest do not make you timid ; yet you are ashamed to address an audience of mere dunces and weaklings. Who are they that make you ashamed ? The fullers 6 or the cobblers or the builders or the smiths or the farmers or the merchants, or the traffickers in the market-place who think of nothing but buying cheap

πλείονος ἀποδῶνται αἰσχύνει; ἐκ γὰρ τούτων
7 ἁπάντων ἡ ἐκκλησία συνίσταται. τί δὲ οἴει διαφέρειν ὃ σὺ ποιεῖς ἢ τῶν ἀσκητῶν ὄντα κρείττω
τοὺς ἰδιώτας φοβεῖσθαι; σὺ γὰρ τοῖς πρωτεύου-
σιν ἐν τῇ πόλει, ὧν ἔνιοι καταφρονοῦσί σου,
ῥᾳδίως διαλεγόμενος καὶ τῶν ἐπιμελομένων τοῦ
τῇ πόλει διαλέγεσθαι πολὺ περιὼν ἐν τοῖς μηδε-
πώποτε φροντίσασι τῶν πολιτικῶν μηδὲ σοῦ
καταπεφρονηκόσιν ὀκνεῖς λέγειν δεδιώς, μὴ κατα-
γελασθῇς.

8 Τί δ'; ἔφη, οὐ δοκοῦσί σοι πολλάκις οἱ ἐν τῇ
ἐκκλησίᾳ τῶν ὀρθῶς λεγόντων καταγελᾶν;

Καὶ γὰρ οἱ ἕτεροι, ἔφη· διὸ καὶ θαυμάζω σου,
εἰ ἐκείνους, ὅταν τοῦτο ποιῶσι, ῥᾳδίως χειρού-
μενος τούτοις μηδένα τρόπον οἴει δυνήσεσθαι
9 προσενεχθῆναι. ὠγαθέ, μὴ ἀγνόει σεαυτὸν μηδὲ
ἁμάρτανε ἃ οἱ πλεῖστοι ἁμαρτάνουσιν· οἱ γὰρ
πολλοὶ ὡρμηκότες ἐπὶ τὸ σκοπεῖν τὰ τῶν ἄλλων
πράγματα οὐ τρέπονται ἐπὶ τὸ ἑαυτοὺς ἐξετάζειν.
μὴ οὖν ἀπορρᾳθύμει τούτου, ἀλλὰ διατείνου
μᾶλλον πρὸς τὸ σαυτῷ προσέχειν· καὶ μὴ ἀμέλει
τῶν τῆς πόλεως, εἴ τι δυνατόν ἐστι διὰ σὲ βέλτιον
ἔχειν. τούτων γὰρ καλῶς ἐχόντων οὐ μόνον οἱ
ἄλλοι πολῖται, ἀλλὰ καὶ οἱ σοὶ φίλοι καὶ αὐτὸς
σὺ οὐκ ἐλάχιστα ὠφελήσῃ.

VIII. Ἀριστίππου δὲ ἐπιχειροῦντος ἐλέγχειν
τὸν Σωκράτην, ὥσπερ αὐτὸς ὑπ' ἐκείνου τὸ πρότερον ἠλέγχετο, βουλόμενος τοὺς συνόντας ὠφελεῖν ὁ Σωκράτης ἀπεκρίνατο οὐχ ὥσπερ οἱ
φυλαττόμενοι, μή πῃ ὁ λόγος ἐπαλλαχθῇ, ἀλλ'
ὡς ἂν πεπεισμένοι μάλιστα πράττειν τὰ δέοντα.

2 Ὁ μὲν γὰρ αὐτὸν ἤρετο, εἴ τι εἰδείη ἀγαθόν,

and selling dear? For these are the people who
make up the Assembly. You behave like a man who 7
can beat trained athletes and is afraid of amateurs!
You are at your ease when you talk with the first
men in the state, some of whom despise you, and
you are a far better talker than the ordinary run of
politicians; and yet you are shy of addressing men
who never gave a thought to public affairs and
haven't learnt to despise you—all because you fear
ridicule!"

"Well, don't you think the Assembly often laughs 8
at sound argument?"

"Yes, and so do the others; and that's why I am
surprised that you, who find it easy to manage them
when they do it, think you will be quite unable to
deal with the Assembly. My good man, don't be 9
ignorant of yourself: don't fall into the common
error. For so many are in such a hurry to pry into
other people's business that they never turn aside to
examine themselves. Don't refuse to face this duty
then: strive more earnestly to pay heed to yourself;
and don't neglect public affairs, if you have the
power to improve them. If they go well, not only
the people, but your friends and you yourself at least
as much as they will profit."

VIII. When Aristippus attempted to cross-examine
Socrates in the same fashion as he had been cross-
examined by him in their previous encounter, Socrates, wishing to benefit his companions, answered
like a man who is resolved to do what is right, and
not like a debater guarding against any distortion of
the argument.

Aristippus asked if he knew of anything good, in 2

ἵνα εἴ τι εἴποι τῶν τοιούτων, οἷον ἢ σιτίον ἢ ποτὸν
ἢ χρήματα ἢ ὑγίειαν ἢ ῥώμην ἢ τόλμαν, δεικνύοι
δὴ τοῦτο κακὸν ἐνίοτε ὄν. ὁ δὲ εἰδώς, ὅτι ἐάν τι
ἐνοχλῇ ἡμᾶς, δεόμεθα τοῦ παύσοντος, ἀπεκρίνατο
3 ᾗπερ καὶ ποιεῖν κράτιστον· Ἆρά γε, ἔφη, ἐρωτᾷς
με, εἴ τι οἶδα πυρετοῦ ἀγαθόν ;

Οὐκ ἔγωγ', ἔφη.

Ἀλλ' ὀφθαλμίας ;

Οὐδὲ τοῦτο.

Ἀλλὰ λιμοῦ ;

Οὐδὲ λιμοῦ.

Ἀλλὰ μήν, ἔφη, εἴ γ' ἐρωτᾷς με, εἴ τι ἀγαθὸν
οἶδα ὃ μηδενὸς ἀγαθόν ἐστιν, οὔτ' οἶδα, ἔφη, οὔτε
δέομαι.

4   Πάλιν δὲ τοῦ Ἀριστίππου ἐρωτῶντος αὐτόν,
εἴ τι εἰδείη καλόν, Καὶ πολλά, ἔφη.

Ἆρ' οὖν, ἔφη, πάντα ὅμοια ἀλλήλοις ;

Ὡς οἷόν τε μὲν οὖν, ἔφη, ἀνομοιότατα ἔνια.

Πῶς οὖν, ἔφη, τὸ τῷ καλῷ ἀνόμοιον καλὸν ἂν
εἴη ;

Ὅτι νὴ Δί', ἔφη, ἔστι μὲν τῷ καλῷ πρὸς δρόμον
ἀνθρώπῳ ἄλλος ἀνόμοιος καλὸς πρὸς πάλην, ἔστι
δὲ ἀσπὶς καλὴ πρὸς τὸ προβάλλεσθαι ὡς ἔνι
ἀνομοιοτάτη τῷ ἀκοντίῳ καλῷ πρὸς τὸ σφόδρα
τε καὶ ταχὺ φέρεσθαι.

5   Οὐδὲν διαφερόντως, ἔφη, ἀποκρίνῃ μοι ἢ ὅτε
σε ἠρώτησα, εἴ τι ἀγαθὸν εἰδείης.

Σὺ δ' οἴει, ἔφη, ἄλλο μὲν ἀγαθόν, ἄλλο δὲ
καλὸν εἶναι ; οὐκ οἶσθ', ὅτι πρὸς ταὐτὰ πάντα
καλά τε κἀγαθά ἐστι ; πρῶτον μὲν γὰρ ἡ ἀρετὴ
οὐ πρὸς ἄλλα μὲν ἀγαθόν, πρὸς ἄλλα δὲ καλόν
ἐστιν· ἔπειτα οἱ ἄνθρωποι τὸ αὐτό τε καὶ πρὸς

order that if Socrates mentioned some good thing, such as food, drink, money, health, strength, or daring, he might show that it is sometimes bad. But he, knowing that when anything troubles us we need what will put an end to the trouble, gave the best answer: "Are you asking me," he said, 3 "whether I know of anything good for a fever?"

"No, not that."

"For ophthalmia?"

"No, nor that."

"For hunger?"

"No, not for hunger either."

"Well, but if you are asking me whether I know of anything good in relation to nothing, I neither know nor want to know."

Again Aristippus asked him whether he knew of 4 anything beautiful: "Yes, many things," he replied.

"All like one another?"

"On the contrary, some are as unlike as they can be."

"How then can that which is unlike the beautiful be beautiful?"

"The reason, of course, is that a beautiful wrestler is unlike a beautiful runner, a shield beautiful for defence is utterly unlike a javelin beautiful for swift and powerful hurling."

"That is the same answer as you gave to my 5 question whether you knew of anything good."

"You think, do you, that good is one thing and beautiful another? Don't you know that all things are both beautiful and good in relation to the same things? In the first place, Virtue is not a good thing in relation to some things and a beautiful thing in relation to others. Men, again, are called

τὰ αὐτὰ καλοί τε κἀγαθοὶ λέγονται· πρὸς τὰ
αὐτὰ δὲ καὶ τὰ σώματα τῶν ἀνθρώπων καλά τε
κἀγαθὰ φαίνεται, πρὸς ταὐτὰ δὲ καὶ τἆλλα
πάντα, οἷς ἄνθρωποι χρῶνται, καλά τε κἀγαθὰ
νομίζεται, πρὸς ἅπερ ἂν εὔχρηστα ᾖ.

6 Ἆρ᾽ οὖν, ἔφη, καὶ κόφινος κοπροφόρος καλόν
ἐστι ;

Νὴ Δί᾽, ἔφη, καὶ χρυσῆ γε ἀσπὶς αἰσχρόν, ἐὰν
πρὸς τὰ ἑαυτῶν ἔργα ὁ μὲν καλῶς πεποιημένος
ᾖ, ἡ δὲ κακῶς.

Λέγεις σύ, ἔφη, καλά τε καὶ αἰσχρὰ τὰ αὐτὰ
εἶναι ;

7 Καὶ νὴ Δί᾽ ἔγωγ᾽, ἔφη, ἀγαθά τε καὶ κακά·
πολλάκις γὰρ τό τε λιμοῦ ἀγαθὸν πυρετοῦ κακόν
ἐστι καὶ τὸ πυρετοῦ ἀγαθὸν λιμοῦ κακόν ἐστι·
πολλάκις δὲ τὸ μὲν πρὸς δρόμον καλὸν πρὸς
πάλην αἰσχρόν, τὸ δὲ πρὸς πάλην καλὸν πρὸς
δρόμον αἰσχρόν· πάντα γὰρ ἀγαθὰ μὲν καὶ καλά
ἐστι πρὸς ἃ ἂν εὖ ἔχῃ, κακὰ δὲ καὶ αἰσχρὰ πρὸς
ἃ ἂν κακῶς.

8 Καὶ οἰκίας δὲ λέγων τὰς αὐτὰς καλάς τε εἶναι
καὶ χρησίμους παιδεύειν ἔμοιγ᾽ ἐδόκει, οἵας χρὴ
οἰκοδομεῖσθαι.

Ἐπεσκόπει δὲ ὧδε· Ἆρά γε τὸν μέλλοντα
οἰκίαν οἵαν χρὴ ἔχειν τοῦτο δεῖ μηχανᾶσθαι,
ὅπως ἡδίστη τε ἐνδιαιτᾶσθαι καὶ χρησιμωτάτη
ἔσται ;

9 Τούτου δὲ ὁμολογουμένου, Οὐκοῦν ἡδὺ μὲν
θέρους ψυχεινὴν ἔχειν, ἡδὺ δὲ χειμῶνος ἀλε-
εινήν ;

Ἐπειδὴ δὲ καὶ τοῦτο συμφαῖεν, Οὐκοῦν ἐν ταῖς
πρὸς μεσημβρίαν βλεπούσαις οἰκίαις τοῦ μὲν

'beautiful and good' in the same respect and in relation to the same things: it is in relation to the same things that men's bodies look beautiful and good and that all other things men use are thought beautiful and good, namely, in relation to those things for which they are useful."

"Is a dung basket beautiful then?" 6

"Of course, and a golden shield is ugly, if the one is well made for its special work and the other badly."

"Do you mean that the same things are both beautiful and ugly?"

"Of course—and both good and bad. For what 7 is good for hunger is often bad for fever, and what is good for fever bad for hunger; what is beautiful for running is often ugly for wrestling, and what is beautiful for wrestling ugly for running. For all things are good and beautiful in relation to those purposes for which they are well adapted, bad and ugly in relation to those for which they are ill adapted."

Again his dictum about houses, that the same 8 house is both beautiful and useful, was a lesson in the art of building houses as they ought to be.

He approached the problem thus:

"When one means to have the right sort of house, must he contrive to make it as pleasant to live in and as useful as can be?"

And this being admitted, "Is it pleasant," he 9 asked, "to have it cool in summer and warm in winter?"

And when they agreed with this also, "Now in houses with a south aspect, the sun's rays penetrate

χειμῶνος ὁ ἥλιος εἰς τὰς παστάδας ὑπολάμπει,
τοῦ δὲ θέρους ὑπὲρ ἡμῶν αὐτῶν καὶ τῶν στεγῶν
πορευόμενος σκιὰν παρέχει. οὐκοῦν εἴ γε καλῶς
ἔχει ταῦτα οὕτω γίγνεσθαι, οἰκοδομεῖν δεῖ ὑψη-
λότερα μὲν τὰ πρὸς μεσημβρίαν, ἵνα ὁ χειμερινὸς
ἥλιος μὴ ἀποκλείηται, χθαμαλώτερα δὲ τὰ πρὸς
ἄρκτον, ἵνα οἱ ψυχροὶ μὴ ἐμπίπτωσιν ἄνεμοι·
10 ὡς δὲ συνελόντι εἰπεῖν, ὅποι πάσας ὥρας αὐτός
τε ἂν ἥδιστα καταφεύγοι καὶ τὰ ὄντα ἀσφαλέ-
στατα τίθοιτο, αὕτη ἂν εἰκότως ἡδίστη τε καὶ
καλλίστη οἴκησις εἴη. γραφαὶ δὲ καὶ ποικιλίαι
πλείονας εὐφροσύνας ἀποστεροῦσιν ἢ παρέχουσι.

Ναοῖς γε μὴν καὶ βωμοῖς χώραν ἔφη εἶναι
πρεπωδεστάτην, ἥτις ἐμφανεστάτη οὖσα ἀστι-
βεστάτη εἴη· ἡδὺ μὲν γὰρ ἰδόντας προσεύξασθαι,
ἡδὺ δὲ ἁγνῶς ἔχοντας προσιέναι.

IX. Πάλιν δὲ ἐρωτώμενος, ἡ ἀνδρεία πότερον
εἴη διδακτὸν ἢ φυσικόν, Οἶμαι μέν, ἔφη, ὥσπερ
σῶμα σώματος ἰσχυρότερον πρὸς τοὺς πόνους
φύεται, οὕτω καὶ ψυχὴν ψυχῆς ἐρρωμενεστέραν
πρὸς τὰ δεινὰ φύσει γίγνεσθαι. ὁρῶ γὰρ ἐν τοῖς
αὐτοῖς νόμοις τε καὶ ἔθεσι τρεφομένους πολὺ δια-
2 φέροντας ἀλλήλων τόλμῃ. νομίζω μέντοι πᾶσαν
φύσιν μαθήσει καὶ μελέτῃ πρὸς ἀνδρείαν αὔξεσθαι.
δῆλον μὲν γάρ, ὅτι Σκύθαι καὶ Θρᾷκες οὐκ ἂν
τολμήσειαν ἀσπίδας καὶ δόρατα λαβόντες Λακεδαιμονίοις διαμάχεσθαι· φανερὸν δέ, ὅτι Λακεδαιμόνιοι οὔτ' ἂν Θρᾳξὶ πέλταις καὶ ἀκοντίοις
οὔτε Σκύθαις τόξοις ἐθέλοιεν ἂν διαγωνίζεσθαι.
3 ὁρῶ δ' ἔγωγε καὶ ἐπὶ τῶν ἄλλων πάντων ὁμοίως
καὶ φύσει διαφέροντας ἀλλήλων τοὺς ἀνθρώπους
καὶ ἐπιμελείᾳ πολὺ ἐπιδιδόντας. ἐκ δὲ τούτων

into the porticoes in winter, but in summer the path of the sun is right over our heads and above the roof, so that there is shade. If, then, this is the best arrangement, we should build the south side loftier to get the winter sun and the north side lower to keep out the cold winds. To put it shortly, 10 the house in which the owner can find a pleasant retreat at all seasons and can store his belongings safely is presumably at once the pleasantest and the most beautiful. As for paintings and decorations, they rob one of more delights than they give."

For temples and altars the most suitable position, he said, was a conspicuous site remote from traffic; for it is pleasant to breathe a prayer at the sight of them, and pleasant to approach them filled with holy thoughts.

IX. When asked again whether Courage could be taught or came by nature, he replied: "I think that just as one man's body is naturally stronger than another's for labour, so one man's soul is naturally braver than another's in danger. For I notice that men brought up under the same laws and customs differ widely in daring. Nevertheless, I think that 2 every man's nature acquires more courage by learning and practice. Of course Scythians and Thracians would not dare to take bronze shield and spear and fight Lacedaemonians; and of course Lacedaemonians would not be willing to face Thracians with leather shields and javelins, nor Scythians with bows for weapons. And similarly in all other points, I 3 find that human beings naturally differ one from another and greatly improve by application. Hence

δῆλόν ἐστιν, ὅτι πάντας χρὴ καὶ τοὺς εὐφυεστέ-
ρους καὶ τοὺς ἀμβλυτέρους τὴν φύσιν ἐν οἷς
ἂν ἀξιόλογοι βούλωνται γενέσθαι, ταῦτα καὶ
μανθάνειν καὶ μελετᾶν.

4   Σοφίαν δὲ καὶ σωφροσύνην οὐ διώριζεν, ἀλλὰ
τὸν [1] τὰ μὲν καλά τε κἀγαθὰ γιγνώσκοντα
χρῆσθαι αὐτοῖς καὶ τὸν τὰ αἰσχρὰ εἰδότα εὐλαβεῖσθαι σοφόν τε καὶ σώφρονα ἔκρινε. προσε-
ρωτώμενος δέ, εἰ τοὺς ἐπισταμένους μὲν ἃ δεῖ
πράττειν, ποιοῦντας δὲ τἀναντία σοφούς τε καὶ
ἐγκρατεῖς εἶναι νομίζοι, Οὐδέν γε μᾶλλον, ἔφη,
ἢ ἀσόφους τε καὶ ἀκρατεῖς· πάντας γὰρ οἶμαι
προαιρουμένους ἐκ τῶν ἐνδεχομένων ἃ οἴονται
συμφορώτατα αὐτοῖς εἶναι, ταῦτα πράττειν.
νομίζω οὖν τοὺς μὴ ὀρθῶς πράττοντας οὔτε
5 σοφοὺς οὔτε σώφρονας εἶναι. ἔφη δὲ καὶ τὴν
δικαιοσύνην καὶ τὴν ἄλλην πᾶσαν ἀρετὴν σοφίαν
εἶναι. τά τε γὰρ δίκαια καὶ πάντα, ὅσα ἀρετῇ
πράττεται, καλά τε καὶ ἀγαθὰ εἶναι· καὶ οὔτ᾽
ἂν τοὺς ταῦτα εἰδότας ἄλλο ἀντὶ τούτων οὐδὲν
προελέσθαι οὔτε τοὺς μὴ ἐπισταμένους δύνασθαι
πράττειν, ἀλλὰ καὶ ἐὰν ἐγχειρῶσιν, ἁμαρτάνειν.
οὕτω καὶ τὰ καλά τε καὶ ἀγαθὰ τοὺς μὲν σοφοὺς
πράττειν, τοὺς δὲ μὴ σοφοὺς οὐ δύνασθαι, ἀλλὰ
καὶ ἐὰν ἐγχειρῶσιν, ἁμαρτάνειν. ἐπεὶ οὖν τά τε
δίκαια καὶ τἄλλα καλά τε καὶ ἀγαθὰ πάντα
ἀρετῇ πράττεται, δῆλον εἶναι, ὅτι καὶ δικαιοσύνη
6 καὶ ἡ ἄλλη πᾶσα ἀρετὴ σοφία ἐστί. μανίαν
γε μὴν ἐναντίον μὲν ἔφη εἶναι σοφίᾳ, οὐ μέντοι
γε τὴν ἀνεπιστημοσύνην μανίαν ἐνόμιζε. τὸ δὲ
ἀγνοεῖν ἑαυτὸν καὶ ἃ μὴ οἶδε δοξάζειν τε καὶ

it is clear that all men, whatever their natural gifts, the talented and the dullards alike, must learn and practise what they want to excel in."

Between Wisdom and Prudence he drew no dis- 4 tinction; but if a man knows and practises what is beautiful and good, knows and avoids what is base,[1] that man he judged to be both wise and prudent. When asked further whether he thought that those who know what they ought to do and yet do the opposite are at once wise and vicious, he answered: "No; not so much that, as both unwise and vicious. For I think that all men have a choice between various courses, and choose and follow the one which they think conduces most to their advantage. Therefore I hold that those who follow the wrong course are neither wise nor prudent."

He said that Justice and every other form of 5 Virtue is Wisdom. "For just actions and all forms of virtuous activity are beautiful and good. He who knows the beautiful and good will never choose anything else, he who is ignorant of them cannot do them, and even if he tries, will fail. Hence the wise do what is beautiful and good, the unwise cannot and fail if they try. Therefore since just actions and all other forms of beautiful and good activity are virtuous actions, it is clear that Justice and every other form of Virtue is Wisdom."

Madness, again, according to him, was the opposite 6 of Wisdom. Nevertheless he did not identify Ignorance with Madness; but not to know yourself, and

---

[1] The Greek text is corrupt, but the sense is clear.

[1] The MSS. vary between τὸ and τὸν here and in the words following. Sauppe prints τῷ twice after Heindorf.

οἴεσθαι γιγνώσκειν ἐγγυτάτω μανίας ἐλογίζετο
εἶναι. τοὺς μέντοι πολλοὺς ἔφη ἃ μὲν οἱ πλεῖστοι
ἀγνοοῦσι, τοὺς διημαρτηκότας τούτων οὐ φάσκειν
μαίνεσθαι, τοὺς δὲ διημαρτηκότας ὧν οἱ πολλοὶ
7 γιγνώσκουσι μαινομένους καλεῖν· ἐάν τε γάρ τις
μέγας οὕτως οἴηται εἶναι, ὥστε κύπτειν τὰς
πύλας τοῦ τείχους διεξιών, ἐάν τε οὕτως ἰσχυρός,
ὥστ' ἐπιχειρεῖν οἰκίας αἴρεσθαι ἢ ἄλλῳ τῳ ἐπιτίθεσθαι τῶν πᾶσι δήλων ὅτι ἀδύνατά ἐστι, τοῦτον
μαίνεσθαι φάσκειν· τοὺς δὲ μικρῶν διαμαρτά-
νοντας οὐ δοκεῖν τοῖς πολλοῖς μαίνεσθαι, ἀλλ'
ὥσπερ τὴν ἰσχυρὰν ἐπιθυμίαν ἔρωτα καλοῦσιν,
οὕτω καὶ τὴν μεγάλην παράνοιαν μανίαν αὐτοὺς
καλεῖν.

8 Φθόνον δὲ σκοπῶν ὅ τι εἴη λύπην μέν τινα
ἐξεύρισκεν αὐτὸν ὄντα, οὔτε μέντοι τὴν ἐπὶ φίλων
ἀτυχίαις οὔτε τὴν ἐπ' ἐχθρῶν εὐτυχίαις γιγνο-
μένην, ἀλλὰ μόνους ἔφη φθονεῖν τοὺς ἐπὶ ταῖς
τῶν φίλων εὐπραξίαις ἀνιωμένους. θαυμαζόντων
δέ τινων, εἴ τις φιλῶν τινα ἐπὶ τῇ εὐπραξίᾳ
αὐτοῦ λυποῖτο, ὑπεμίμνησκεν, ὅτι πολλοὶ οὕτω
πρός τινας ἔχουσιν, ὥστε κακῶς μὲν πράττοντας
μὴ δύνασθαι περιορᾶν, ἀλλὰ βοηθεῖν ἀτυχοῦσιν,
εὐτυχούντων δὲ λυπεῖσθαι. τοῦτο μέντοι φρονίμῳ
μὲν ἀνδρὶ οὐκ ἂν συμβῆναι, τοὺς ἠλιθίους δὲ ἀεὶ
πάσχειν αὐτό.

9 Σχολὴν δὲ σκοπῶν τί εἴη ποιοῦντας μέν τι
τοὺς πλείστους εὑρίσκειν ἔφη· καὶ γὰρ τοὺς
πεττεύοντας καὶ τοὺς γελωτοποιοῦντας ποιεῖν τι,
πάντας δὲ τούτους ἔφη σχολάζειν· ἐξεῖναι γὰρ

---

[1] The last sentence cannot imply that Socrates thought
self-ignorance "a slight error," but must be merely a further

to assume and think that you know what you do
not, he put next to Madness. "Most men, however," he declared, "do not call those mad who err
in matters that lie outside the knowledge of ordinary
people : madness is the name they give to errors in
matters of common knowledge. For instance, if a 7
man imagines himself to be so tall as to stoop when
he goes through the gateways in the Wall, or so
strong as to try to lift houses or to perform any
other feat that everybody knows to be impossible,
they say he's mad. They don't think a slight error
implies madness, but just as they call strong desire
love, so they name a great delusion madness." [1]

Considering the nature of Envy, he found it to be 8
a kind of pain, not, however, at a friend's misfortune,
nor at an enemy's good fortune, but the envious are
those only who are annoyed at their friends' suc-
cesses. Some expressed surprise that anyone who
loves another should be pained at his success, but
he reminded them that many stand in this relation
towards others, that they cannot disregard them in
time of trouble, but aid them in their misfortune,
and yet they are pained to see them prospering.
This, however, could not happen to a man of sense,
but it is always the case with fools.

Considering the nature of Leisure, he said his 9
conclusion was that almost all men do something.
Even draught-players and jesters do something,
but all these are at leisure, for they might [2] go and

elucidation of popular nomenclature. But it comes very
awkwardly here.

[2] Or, if with Stobaeus we omit ἐξεῖναι γὰρ αὐτοῖς, "have
leisure to go."

αὐτοῖς ἰέναι πράξοντας τὰ βελτίω τούτων. ἀπὸ
μέντοι τῶν βελτιόνων ἐπὶ τὰ χείρω ἰέναι οὐδένα
σχολάζειν· εἰ δέ τις ἴοι, τοῦτον ἀσχολίας αὐτῷ
οὔσης κακῶς ἔφη τοῦτο πράττειν.

10 Βασιλεῖς δὲ καὶ ἄρχοντας οὐ τοὺς τὰ σκῆπτρα
ἔχοντας ἔφη εἶναι οὐδὲ τοὺς ὑπὸ τῶν τυχόντων
αἱρεθέντας οὐδὲ τοὺς κλήρῳ λαχόντας οὐδὲ τοὺς
βιασαμένους οὐδὲ τοὺς ἐξαπατήσαντας, ἀλλὰ τοὺς
11 ἐπισταμένους ἄρχειν. ὁπότε γάρ τις ὁμολογήσειε
τοῦ μὲν ἄρχοντος εἶναι τὸ προστάττειν ὅ τι χρὴ
ποιεῖν, τοῦ δὲ ἀρχομένου τὸ πείθεσθαι, ἐπεδείκνυεν ἔν τε νηὶ τὸν μὲν ἐπιστάμενον ἄρχοντα,
τὸν δὲ ναύκληρον καὶ τοὺς ἄλλους τοὺς ἐν τῇ
νηὶ πάντας πειθομένους τῷ ἐπισταμένῳ, καὶ ἐν
γεωργίᾳ τοὺς κεκτημένους ἀγροὺς καὶ ἐν νόσῳ
τοὺς νοσοῦντας καὶ ἐν σωμασκίᾳ τοὺς σωμα-
σκοῦντας καὶ τοὺς ἄλλους πάντας, οἷς ὑπάρχει
τι ἐπιμελείας δεόμενον, ἂν μὲν αὐτοὶ ἡγῶνται
ἐπίστασθαι ἐπιμελεῖσθαι· εἰ δὲ μή, τοῖς ἐπισταμένοις οὐ μόνον παροῦσι πειθομένους ἀλλὰ καὶ
ἀπόντας μεταπεμπομένους, ὅπως ἐκείνοις πειθόμενοι τὰ δέοντα πράττωσιν· ἐν δὲ ταλασίᾳ καὶ
τὰς γυναῖκας ἐπεδείκνυεν ἀρχούσας τῶν ἀνδρῶν
διὰ τὸ τὰς μὲν εἰδέναι, ὅπως χρὴ ταλασιουργεῖν,
τοὺς δὲ μὴ εἰδέναι.

12 Εἰ δέ τις πρὸς ταῦτα λέγοι, ὅτι τῷ τυράννῳ
ἔξεστι μὴ πείθεσθαι τοῖς ὀρθῶς λέγουσι, Καὶ
πῶς ἄν, ἔφη, ἐξείη μὴ πείθεσθαι, ἐπικειμένης γε
ζημίας, ἐάν τις τῷ εὖ λέγοντι μὴ πείθηται; ἐν
ᾧ γὰρ ἄν τις πράγματι μὴ πείθηται τῷ εὖ
λέγοντι, ἁμαρτήσεται δήπου, ἁμαρτάνων δὲ
ζημιωθήσεται.

do something better. But nobody has leisure to go from a better to a worse occupation. If anyone does so, he acts wrongly, having no leisure.[1]

Kings and rulers, he said, are not those who hold 10 the sceptre, nor those who are chosen by the multitude, nor those on whom the lot falls, nor those who owe their power to force or deception; but those who know how to rule.[2] For once it was granted that it is 11 the business of the ruler to give orders and of the ruled to obey, he went on to show that on a ship the one who knows, rules, and the owner and all the others on board obey the one who knows: in farming the landowners, in illness the patients, in training those who are in training, in fact everybody concerned with anything that needs care, look after it themselves if they think they know how, but, if not, they obey those who know, and not only when such are present, but they even send for them when absent, that they may obey them and do the right thing. In spinning wool, again, he would point out, the women govern the men because they know how to do it and men do not.

If anyone objected that a despot may refuse to 12 obey a good counsellor, "How can he refuse," he would ask, "when a penalty waits on disregard of good counsel? All disregard of good counsel is bound surely to result in error, and his error will not go unpunished."

---

[1] Or, omitting κακῶς ἔφη with Stobaeus, "he does it in spite of want of leisure."

[2] *Cyropaedia*, I. i. 3.

13 Εἰ δὲ φαίη τις τῷ τυράννῳ ἐξεῖναι καὶ ἀποκτεῖναι τὸν εὖ φρονοῦντα, Τὸν δὲ ἀποκτείναντα, ἔφη, τοὺς κρατίστους τῶν συμμάχων οἴει ἀζήμιον γίγνεσθαι ἢ ὡς ἔτυχε ζημιοῦσθαι; πότερα γὰρ ἂν μᾶλλον οἴει σῴζεσθαι τὸν τοῦτο ποιοῦντα ἢ οὕτω καὶ τάχιστ' ἂν ἀπολέσθαι;

14 Ἐρομένου δέ τινος αὐτόν, τί δοκοίη αὐτῷ κράτιστον ἀνδρὶ ἐπιτήδευμα εἶναι, ἀπεκρίνατο Εὐπραξία. ἐρομένου δὲ πάλιν, εἰ καὶ τὴν εὐτυχίαν ἐπιτήδευμα νομίζοι εἶναι, Πᾶν μὲν οὖν τοὐναντίον ἔγωγ', ἔφη, τύχην καὶ πρᾶξιν ἡγοῦμαι· τὸ μὲν γὰρ μὴ ζητοῦντα ἐπιτυχεῖν τινι τῶν δεόντων εὐτυχίαν οἶμαι εἶναι, τὸ δὲ μαθόντα τε καὶ μελετήσαντά τι εὖ ποιεῖν εὐπραξίαν νομίζω, καὶ οἱ τοῦτο ἐπιτηδεύοντες δοκοῦσί μοι εὖ

15 πράττειν. καὶ ἀρίστους δὲ καὶ θεοφιλεστάτους ἔφη εἶναι ἐν μὲν γεωργίᾳ τοὺς τὰ γεωργικὰ εὖ πράττοντας, ἐν δ' ἰατρείᾳ τοὺς τὰ ἰατρικά, ἐν δὲ πολιτείᾳ τοὺς τὰ πολιτικά· τὸν δὲ μηδὲν εὖ πράττοντα οὔτε χρήσιμον οὐδὲν ἔφη εἶναι οὔτε θεοφιλῆ.

X. Ἀλλὰ μὴν καὶ εἴ ποτε τῶν τὰς τέχνας ἐχόντων καὶ ἐργασίας ἕνεκα χρωμένων αὐταῖς διαλέγοιτό τινι, καὶ τούτοις ὠφέλιμος ἦν.

Εἰσελθὼν μὲν γάρ ποτε πρὸς Παρράσιον τὸν ζωγράφον καὶ διαλεγόμενος αὐτῷ, Ἆρα, ἔφη, ὦ Παρράσιε, γραφική ἐστιν εἰκασία τῶν ὁρωμένων; τὰ γοῦν κοῖλα καὶ τὰ ὑψηλὰ καὶ τὰ σκοτεινὰ καὶ τὰ φωτεινὰ καὶ τὰ σκληρὰ καὶ τὰ μαλακὰ καὶ τὰ τραχέα καὶ τὰ λεῖα καὶ τὰ νέα καὶ τὰ παλαιὰ σώματα διὰ τῶν χρωμάτων ἀπεικάζοντες ἐκμιμεῖσθε.

If anyone said that a despot can kill a loyal 13
subject, "Do you think," he retorted, "that he who
kills the best of his allies suffers no loss, or that his
loss is trifling? Do you think that this conduct
brings him safety, or rather swift destruction?"

When someone asked him what seemed to him 14
the best pursuit for a man, he answered: "Doing
well." Questioned further, whether he thought
good luck a pursuit, he said: "On the contrary,
I think luck and doing are opposite poles. To hit
on something right by luck without search I call
good luck, to do something well after study and
practice I call doing well; and those who pursue
this seem to me to do well. And the best men and 15
dearest to the gods," he added, "are those who do
their work well; if it is farming, as good farmers;
if medicine, as good doctors; if politics, as good
politicians. He who does nothing well is neither
useful in any way nor dear to the gods."

X. Then again, whenever he talked with artists
who followed their art as a business, he was as useful
to them as to others.

Thus, on entering the house of Parrhasius the
painter one day, he asked in the course of a conversation with him: "Is painting a representation of
things seen, Parrhasius? Anyhow, you painters
with your colours represent and reproduce figures
high and low, in light and in shadow, hard and soft,
rough and smooth, young and old."

Ἀληθῆ λέγεις, ἔφη.

2 Καὶ μὴν τά γε καλὰ εἴδη ἀφομοιοῦντες, ἐπειδὴ οὐ ῥᾴδιον ἑνὶ ἀνθρώπῳ περιτυχεῖν ἄμεμπτα πάντα ἔχοντι, ἐκ πολλῶν συνάγοντες τὰ ἐξ ἑκάστου κάλλιστα οὕτως ὅλα τὰ σώματα καλὰ ποιεῖτε φαίνεσθαι.

3 Ποιοῦμεν γάρ, ἔφη, οὕτω.

Τί γάρ; ἔφη, τὸ πιθανώτατον καὶ ἥδιστον καὶ φιλικώτατον καὶ ποθεινότατον καὶ ἐρασμιώτατον ἀπομιμεῖσθε τῆς ψυχῆς ἦθος; ἢ οὐδὲ μιμητόν ἐστι τοῦτο;

Πῶς γὰρ ἄν, ἔφη, μιμητὸν εἴη, ὦ Σώκρατες, ὃ μήτε συμμετρίαν μήτε χρῶμα μήτε ὧν σὺ εἶπας ἄρτι μηδὲν ἔχει μηδὲ ὅλως ὁρατόν ἐστιν;

4 Ἆρ᾽ οὖν, ἔφη, γίγνεται ἐν ἀνθρώπῳ τό τε φιλοφρόνως καὶ τὸ ἐχθρῶς βλέπειν πρός τινας;

Ἔμοιγε δοκεῖ, ἔφη.

Οὐκοῦν τοῦτό γε μιμητὸν ἐν τοῖς ὄμμασι;

Καὶ μάλα, ἔφη.

Ἐπὶ δὲ τοῖς τῶν φίλων ἀγαθοῖς καὶ τοῖς κακοῖς ὁμοίως σοι δοκοῦσιν ἔχειν τὰ πρόσωπα οἵ τε φροντίζοντες καὶ οἱ μή[1];

Μὰ Δί᾽ οὐ δῆτα, ἔφη· ἐπὶ μὲν γὰρ τοῖς ἀγαθοῖς φαιδροί, ἐπὶ δὲ τοῖς κακοῖς σκυθρωποὶ γίγνονται.

Οὐκοῦν, ἔφη, καὶ ταῦτα δυνατὸν ἀπεικάζειν;

Καὶ μάλα, ἔφη.

5 Ἀλλὰ μὴν καὶ τὸ μεγαλοπρεπές τε καὶ ἐλευθέριον καὶ τὸ ταπεινόν τε καὶ ἀνελεύθερον καὶ τὸ σωφρονικόν τε καὶ φρόνιμον καὶ τὸ ὑβριστικόν τε καὶ ἀπειρόκαλον καὶ διὰ τοῦ προσώπου καὶ διὰ τῶν σχημάτων καὶ ἑστώτων καὶ κινουμένων ἀνθρώπων διαφαίνει.

"True."

"And further, when you copy types of beauty, it 2 is so difficult to find a perfect model that you combine the most beautiful details of several, and thus contrive to make the whole figure look beautiful."

"Yes, we do!" 3

"Well now, do you also reproduce the character of the soul, the character that is in the highest degree captivating, delightful, friendly, fascinating, lovable? Or is it impossible to imitate that?"

"Oh no, Socrates; for how could one imitate that which has neither shape nor colour nor any of the qualities you mentioned just now, and is not even visible?"

"Do human beings commonly express the feelings 4 of sympathy and aversion by their looks?"

"I think so."

"Then cannot thus much be imitated in the eyes?"

"Undoubtedly."

"Do you think that the joys and sorrows of their friends produce the same expression on men's faces, whether they really care or not?"

"Oh no, of course not: they look radiant at their joys, downcast at their sorrows."

"Then is it possible to represent these looks too?"

"Undoubtedly."

"Moreover, nobility and dignity, self-abasement 5 and servility, prudence and understanding, insolence and vulgarity, are reflected in the face and in the attitudes of the body whether still or in motion."

---

[1] οἵ τε . . . μή perhaps spurious, as Hartman holds.

Ἀληθῆ λέγεις, ἔφη.

Οὐκοῦν καὶ ταῦτα μιμητά;

Καὶ μάλα, ἔφη.

Πότερον οὖν, ἔφη, νομίζεις ἥδιον ὁρᾶν τοὺς ἀνθρώπους δι' ὧν τὰ καλά τε καὶ ἀγαθὰ καὶ ἀγαπητὰ ἤθη φαίνεται ἢ δι' ὧν τὰ αἰσχρά τε καὶ πονηρὰ καὶ μισητά;

Πολὺ νὴ Δί', ἔφη, διαφέρει, ὦ Σώκρατες.

6 Πρὸς δὲ Κλείτωνα τὸν ἀνδριαντοποιὸν εἰσελθών ποτε καὶ διαλεγόμενος αὐτῷ, Ὅτι μέν, ἔφη, ὦ Κλείτων, καλοὶ οὖς[1] ποιεῖς δρομεῖς τε καὶ παλαιστὰς καὶ πύκτας καὶ παγκρατιαστάς, ὁρῶ τε καὶ οἶδα· ὃ δὲ μάλιστα ψυχαγωγεῖ διὰ τῆς ὄψεως τοὺς ἀνθρώπους, τὸ ζωτικὸν φαίνεσθαι, πῶς τοῦτο ἐνεργάζῃ τοῖς ἀνδριᾶσιν;

7 Ἐπεὶ δὲ ἀπορῶν ὁ Κλείτων οὐ ταχὺ ἀπεκρίνατο, Ἆρ', ἔφη, τοῖς τῶν ζώντων εἴδεσιν ἀπεικάζων τὸ ἔργον ζωτικωτέρους ποιεῖς φαίνεσθαι τοὺς ἀνδριάντας;

Καὶ μάλα, ἔφη.

Οὐκοῦν τά τε ὑπὸ τῶν σχημάτων κατασπώμενα καὶ τἀνασπώμενα ἐν τοῖς σώμασι καὶ τὰ συμπιεζόμενα καὶ τὰ διελκόμενα καὶ τὰ ἐντεινόμενα καὶ τὰ ἀνιέμενα ἀπεικάζων ὁμοιότερά τε τοῖς ἀληθινοῖς καὶ πιθανώτερα ποιεῖς φαίνεσθαι;

Πάνυ μὲν οὖν, ἔφη.

8 Τὸ δὲ καὶ τὰ πάθη τῶν ποιούντων τι σωμάτων ἀπομιμεῖσθαι οὐ ποιεῖ τινα τέρψιν τοῖς θεωμένοις;

---

[1] καλοὶ οὖς Dindorf: ἀλλοίους Sauppe with MSS. and Stobaeus.

"True."

"Then these, too, can be imitated, can they not?"

"Undoubtedly."

"Now which do you think the more pleasing sight, one whose features and bearing reflect a beautiful and good and lovable character, or one who is the embodiment of what is ugly and depraved and hateful?"

"No doubt there is a great difference, Socrates."

On another occasion he visited Cleiton the 6 sculptor, and while conversing with him said: "Cleiton, that your statues of runners, wrestlers, boxers and fighters are beautiful I see and know. But how do you produce in them that illusion of life which is their most alluring charm to the beholder?"

As Cleiton was puzzled and did not reply at once, 7 "Is it," he added, "by faithfully representing the form of living beings that you make your statues look as if they lived?"

"Undoubtedly."

"Then is it not by accurately representing the different parts of the body as they are affected by the pose—the flesh wrinkled or tense, the limbs compressed or outstretched, the muscles taut or loose —that you make them look more like real members and more convincing?"

"Yes, certainly."

"Does not the exact imitation of the feelings that 8 affect bodies in action also produce a sense of satisfaction in the spectator?"

Εἰκὸς γοῦν, ἔφη.

Οὐκοῦν καὶ τῶν μὲν μαχομένων ἀπειλητικὰ τὰ ὄμματα ἀπεικαστέον, τῶν δὲ νενικηκότων εὐφραινομένων ἡ ὄψις μιμητέα;

Σφόδρα γ᾽, ἔφη.

Δεῖ ἄρα, ἔφη, τὸν ἀνδριαντοποιὸν τὰ τῆς ψυχῆς ἔργα τῷ εἴδει προσεικάζειν.

9 Πρὸς δὲ Πιστίαν τὸν θωρακοποιὸν εἰσελθών, ἐπιδείξαντος αὐτοῦ τῷ Σωκράτει θώρακας εὖ εἰργασμένους, Νὴ τὴν Ἥραν, ἔφη, καλόν γε, ὦ Πιστία, τὸ εὕρημα τὸ τὰ μὲν δεόμενα σκέπης τοῦ ἀνθρώπου σκεπάζειν τὸν θώρακα, ταῖς δὲ 0 χερσὶ μὴ κωλύειν χρῆσθαι. ἀτάρ, ἔφη, λέξον μοι, ὦ Πιστία, διὰ τί οὔτ᾽ ἰσχυροτέρους οὔτε πολυτελεστέρους τῶν ἄλλων ποιῶν τοὺς θώρακας πλείονος πωλεῖς;

Ὅτι, ἔφη, ὦ Σώκρατες, εὐρυθμοτέρους ποιῶ.

Τὸν δὲ ῥυθμόν, ἔφη, πότερα μέτρῳ ἢ σταθμῷ ἀποδεικνύων πλείονος τιμᾷ; οὐ γὰρ δὴ ἴσους γε πάντας οὐδὲ ὁμοίους οἶμαί σε ποιεῖν, εἴ γε ἁρμόττοντας ποιεῖς.

Ἀλλὰ νὴ Δί᾽, ἔφη, ποιῶ· οὐδὲν γὰρ ὄφελός ἐστι θώρακος ἄνευ τούτου.

11 Οὐκοῦν, ἔφη, σώματά γε ἀνθρώπων τὰ μὲν εὔρυθμά ἐστι, τὰ δὲ ἄρρυθμα;

Πάνυ μὲν οὖν, ἔφη.

Πῶς οὖν, ἔφη, τῷ ἀρρύθμῳ σώματι ἁρμόττοντα τὸν θώρακα εὔρυθμον ποιεῖς;

Ὥσπερ καὶ ἁρμόττοντα, ἔφη· ὁ ἁρμόττων γάρ ἐστιν εὔρυθμος.

12 Δοκεῖς μοι, ἔφη ὁ Σωκράτης, τὸ εὔρυθμον οὐ

" Oh yes, presumably."

" Then must not the threatening look in the eyes of fighters be accurately represented, and the triumphant expression on the face of conquerors be imitated?"

" Most certainly."

" It follows, then, that the sculptor must represent in his figures the activities of the soul."

On visiting Pistias the armourer, who showed him 9 some well-made breastplates, Socrates exclaimed: " Upon my word, Pistias, it's a beautiful invention, for the breastplate covers the parts that need protection without impeding the use of the hands. But 10 tell me, Pistias," he added, " why do you charge more for your breastplates than any other maker, though they are no stronger and cost no more to make?"

" Because the proportions of mine are better, Socrates."

" And how do you show their proportions when you ask a higher price—by weight or measure? For I presume you don't make them all of the same weight or the same size, that is, if you make them to fit."

" Fit? Why, of course! a breastplate is of no use without that!"

" Then are not some human bodies well, others 11 ill proportioned?"

" Certainly."

" Then if a breastplate is to fit an ill-proportioned body, how do you make it well-proportioned?"

" By making it fit; for if it is a good fit it is well-proportioned."

" Apparently you mean well-proportioned not 12

καθ' ἑαυτὸ λέγειν, ἀλλὰ πρὸς τὸν χρώμενον·
ὥσπερ ἂν εἰ φαίης ἀσπίδα, ᾧ ἂν ἁρμόττῃ, τούτῳ
εὔρυθμον εἶναι, καὶ χλαμύδα καὶ τἆλλα ὡσαύτως
13 ἔοικεν ἔχειν τῷ σῷ λόγῳ. ἴσως δὲ καὶ ἄλλο τι
οὐ μικρὸν ἀγαθὸν τῷ ἁρμόττειν πρόσεστι.

Δίδαξον, ἔφη, ὦ Σώκρατες, εἴ τι ἔχεις.

῏Ηττον, ἔφη, τῷ βάρει πιέζουσιν οἱ ἁρμόττοντες
τῶν ἀναρμόστων τὸν αὐτὸν σταθμὸν ἔχοντες. οἱ
μὲν γὰρ ἀνάρμοστοι ἢ ὅλοι ἐκ τῶν ὤμων κρεμά-
μενοι ἢ καὶ ἄλλο τι τοῦ σώματος σφόδρα
πιέζοντες δύσφοροι καὶ χαλεποὶ γίγνονται· οἱ
δὲ ἁρμόττοντες, διειλημμένοι τὸ βάρος τὸ μὲν
ὑπὸ τῶν κλειδῶν καὶ ἐπωμίδων, τὸ δ' ὑπὸ τῶν
ὤμων, τὸ δὲ ὑπὸ τοῦ στήθους, τὸ δὲ ὑπὸ τοῦ
νώτου, τὸ δὲ ὑπὸ τῆς γαστρός, ὀλίγου δεῖν οὐ
φορήματι, ἀλλὰ προσθήματι ἐοίκασιν.

14 Εἴρηκας, ἔφη, αὐτό, δι' ὅπερ ἔγωγε τὰ ἐμὰ ἔργα
πλείστου ἄξια νομίζω εἶναι· ἔνιοι μέντοι τοὺς
ποικίλους καὶ τοὺς ἐπιχρύσους θώρακας μᾶλλον
ὠνοῦνται.

Ἀλλὰ μήν, ἔφη, εἴ γε διὰ ταῦτα μὴ ἁρμόττοντας ὠνοῦνται, κακὸν ἔμοιγε δοκοῦσι ποικίλον
15 τε καὶ ἐπίχρυσον ὠνεῖσθαι. ἀτάρ, ἔφη, τοῦ
σώματος μὴ μένοντος, ἀλλὰ τοτὲ μὲν κυρτουμένου,
τοτὲ δὲ ὀρθουμένου, πῶς ἂν ἀκριβεῖς θώρακες
ἁρμόττοιεν;

Οὐδαμῶς, ἔφη.

Λέγεις, ἔφη, ἁρμόττειν οὐ τοὺς ἀκριβεῖς, ἀλλὰ
τοὺς μὴ λυποῦντας ἐν τῇ χρείᾳ.

Αὐτός, ἔφη, τοῦτο λέγεις, ὦ Σώκρατες, καὶ
πάνυ ὀρθῶς ἀποδέχῃ.

XI. Γυναικὸς δέ ποτε οὔσης ἐν τῇ πόλει καλῆς,

238

absolutely, but in relation to the wearer, as you might call a shield well-proportioned for the man whom it fits, or a military cape—and this seems to apply to everything according to you. And per- 13 haps there is another important advantage in a good fit."

"Tell it me, if you know, Socrates."

"The good fit is less heavy to wear than the misfit, though both are of the same weight. For the misfit, hanging entirely from the shoulders, or pressing on some other part of the body, proves uncomfortable and irksome; but the good fit, with its weight distributed over the collar-bone and shoulder-blades, the shoulders, chest, back and belly, may almost be called an accessory rather than an encumbrance."

"The advantage you speak of is the very one 14 which I think makes my work worth a big price. Some, however, prefer to buy the ornamented and the gold-plated breastplates."

"Still, if the consequence is that they buy misfits, it seems to me they buy ornamented and gold-plated trash. However, as the body is not rigid, but 15 now bent, now straight, how can tight breastplates fit?"

"They can't."

"You mean that the good fits are not the tight ones, but those that don't chafe the wearer?"

"That is your own meaning, Socrates, and you have hit the right nail on the head."

XI. At one time there was in Athens a beautiful

ἧ ὄνομα ἦν Θεοδότη, καὶ οἴας συνεῖναι τῷ πεί-
θοντι, μνησθέντος αὐτῆς τῶν παρόντων τινὸς καὶ
εἰπόντος, ὅτι κρεῖττον εἴη λόγου τὸ κάλλος τῆς
γυναικός, καὶ ζωγράφους φήσαντος εἰσιέναι πρὸς
αὐτὴν ἀπεικασομένους, οἷς ἐκείνην ἐπιδεικνύειν
ἑαυτῆς ὅσα καλῶς ἔχοι, Ἰτέον ἂν εἴη θεασομέ-
νους, ἔφη ὁ Σωκράτης· οὐ γὰρ δὴ ἀκούσαί γε
τὸ λόγου κρεῖττον ἔστι καταμαθεῖν.

2   Καὶ ὁ διηγησάμενος, Οὐκ ἂν φθάνοιτ᾽, ἔφη,
ἀκολουθοῦντες. οὕτω μὲν δὴ πορευθέντες πρὸς
τὴν Θεοδότην καὶ καταλαβόντες ζωγράφῳ τινὶ
παρεστηκυῖαν ἐθεάσαντο.

Παυσαμένου δὲ τοῦ ζωγράφου, Ὦ ἄνδρες, ἔφη
ὁ Σωκράτης, πότερον ἡμᾶς δεῖ μᾶλλον Θεοδότῃ
χάριν ἔχειν, ὅτι ἡμῖν τὸ κάλλος ἑαυτῆς ἐπέδειξεν,
ἢ ταύτην ἡμῖν, ὅτι ἐθεασάμεθα; ἆρ᾽ εἰ μὲν
ταύτῃ ὠφελιμωτέρα ἐστὶν ἡ ἐπίδειξις, ταύτην
ἡμῖν χάριν ἑκτέον, εἰ δὲ ἡμῖν ἡ θέα, ἡμᾶς
ταύτῃ;

3   Εἰπόντος δέ τινος, ὅτι δίκαια λέγοι, Οὐκοῦν,
ἔφη, αὕτη μὲν ἤδη τε τὸν παρ᾽ ἡμῶν ἔπαινον
κερδαίνει καὶ ἐπειδὰν εἰς πλείους διαγγείλωμεν,
πλείω ὠφελήσεται· ἡμεῖς δὲ ἤδη τε ὧν ἐθεασάμεθα ἐπιθυμοῦμεν ἅψασθαι καὶ ἄπιμεν ὑποκνιζό-
μενοι καὶ ἀπελθόντες ποθήσομεν. ἐκ δὲ τούτων
εἰκὸς ἡμᾶς μὲν θεραπεύειν, ταύτην δὲ θεραπεύεσθαι. καὶ ἡ Θεοδότη, Νὴ Δί᾽, ἔφη, εἰ τοίνυν
ταῦθ᾽ οὕτως ἔχει, ἐμὲ ἂν δέοι ὑμῖν τῆς θέας
χάριν ἔχειν.

4   Ἐκ δὲ τούτου ὁ Σωκράτης ὁρῶν αὐτήν τε
πολυτελῶς κεκοσμημένην καὶ μητέρα παροῦσαν
αὐτῇ ἐν ἐσθῆτι καὶ θεραπείᾳ οὐ τῇ τυχούσῃ καὶ

woman named Theodoté, who was ready to keep
company with anyone who pleased her. One of the
bystanders mentioned her name, declaring that
words failed him to describe the lady's beauty, and
adding that artists visited her to paint her portrait,
and she showed them as much as decency allowed.
" We had better go and see her," cried Socrates;
" of course what beggars description can't very well
be learned by hearsay."

" Come with me at once," returned his informant. 2
So off they went to Theodoté's house, where they
found her posing before a painter, and looked on.

When the painter had finished, Socrates said:
" My friends, ought we to be more grateful to
Theodoté for showing us her beauty, or she to us
for looking at it? Does the obligation rest with her,
if she profits more by showing it, but with us, if we
profit more by looking?"

When someone answered that this was a fair way 3
of putting it, " Well now," he went on, " she already
has our praise to her credit, and when we spread
the news, she will profit yet more; whereas we
already long to touch what we have seen, and we
shall go away excited and shall miss her when
we are gone. The natural consequence is that
we become her adorers, she the adored."

" Then, if that is so," exclaimed Theodoté, " of
course I ought to be grateful to you for looking."

At this point Socrates noticed that she was sump- 4
tuously dressed, and that her mother at her side
was wearing fine clothes and jewellery; and she had

θεραπαίνας πολλὰς καὶ εὐειδεῖς καὶ οὐδὲ ταύτας
ἠμελημένως ἐχούσας καὶ τοῖς ἄλλοις τὴν οἰκίαν
ἀφθόνως κατεσκευασμένην, Εἰπέ μοι, ἔφη, ὦ
Θεοδότη, ἔστι σοι ἀγρός;

Οὐκ ἔμοιγ', ἔφη.

Ἀλλ' ἄρα οἰκία προσόδους·ἔχουσα;

Οὐδὲ οἰκία, ἔφη.

Ἀλλὰ μὴ χειροτέχναι τινές;

Οὐδὲ χειροτέχναι, ἔφη.

Πόθεν οὖν, ἔφη, τἀπιτήδεια ἔχεις;

Ἐάν τις, ἔφη, φίλος μοι γενόμενος εὖ ποιεῖν
ἐθέλῃ, οὗτός μοι βίος ἐστί.

5 Νὴ τὴν Ἥραν, ἔφη, ὦ Θεοδότη, καλόν γε τὸ
κτῆμα καὶ πολλῷ κρεῖττον ἢ οἰῶν τε καὶ αἰγῶν
καὶ βοῶν φίλων ἀγέλην κεκτῆσθαι. ἀτάρ, ἔφη,
πότερον τῇ τύχῃ ἐπιτρέπεις, ἐάν τίς σοι φίλος
ὥσπερ μυῖα πρόσπτηται, ἢ καὶ αὐτή τι μηχανᾷ;

6 Πῶς δ' ἄν, ἔφη, ἐγὼ τούτου μηχανὴν εὕροιμι;

Πολὺ νὴ Δί', ἔφη, προσηκόντως μᾶλλον ἢ αἱ
φάλαγγες· οἶσθα γάρ, ὡς ἐκεῖναι θηρῶσι τὰ
πρὸς τὸν βίον· ἀράχνια γὰρ δήπου λεπτὰ ὑφηνά-
μεναι ὅ τι ἂν ἐνταῦθα ἐμπέσῃ, τούτῳ τροφῇ
χρῶνται.

7 Καὶ ἐμοὶ οὖν, ἔφη, συμβουλεύεις ὑφήνασθαί τι
θήρατρον;

Οὐ γὰρ δὴ οὕτως γε ἀτέχνως οἴεσθαι χρὴ τὸ
πλεῖστον ἄξιον ἄγρευμα φίλους θηράσειν. οὐχ
ὁρᾷς, ὅτι καὶ τὸ μικροῦ ἄξιον τοὺς λαγῶς θηρῶντες
8 πολλὰ τεχνάζουσιν; ὅτι μὲν γὰρ τῆς νυκτὸς
νέμονται, κύνας νυκτερευτικὰς πορισάμενοι ταύ-
ταις αὐτοὺς θηρῶσιν· ὅτι δὲ μεθ' ἡμέραν ἀποδι-
δράσκουσιν, ἄλλας κτῶνται κύνας, αἵτινες ᾗ ἂν

many pretty maids, who also were well cared for, and her house was lavishly furnished.

"Tell me, Theodoté," he said, "have you a farm?"

"Not I," she answered.

"Or a house, perhaps, that brings in money?"

"No, nor a house."

"Some craftsmen, possibly?"

"No, none."

"Then where do you get your supplies from?"

"I live on the generosity of any friend I pick up."

"A fine property, upon my word, Theodoté, and 5 much better than abundance of sheep and goats and oxen. But," he went on, "do you trust to luck, waiting for friends to settle on you like flies, or have you some contrivance of your own?"

"How could I invent a contrivance for that?" 6

"Much more conveniently, I assure you, than the spiders. For you know how they hunt for a living: they weave a thin web, I believe, and feed on anything that gets into it."

"And do you advise me, then, to weave a trap of 7 some sort?"

"Of course not. Don't suppose you are going to hunt friends, the noblest game in the world, by such crude methods. Don't you notice that many tricks are employed even for hunting such a poor thing as the hare?[1] Since hares feed by night, 8 hounds specially adapted for night work are provided to hunt them; and since they run away at daybreak, another pack of hounds is obtained for tracking

---

[1] *Cyropaedia*, I. vi. 40.

ἐκ τῆς νομῆς εἰς τὴν εὐνὴν ἀπέλθωσι, τῇ ὀσμῇ
αἰσθανόμεναι εὑρίσκουσιν αὐτούς· ὅτι δὲ πο-
δώκεις εἰσίν, ὥστε καὶ ἐκ τοῦ φανεροῦ τρέχοντες
ἀποφεύγειν, ἄλλας αὖ κύνας ταχείας παρασκευά-
ζονται, ἵνα κατὰ πόδας ἁλίσκωνται· ὅτι δὲ καὶ
ταύτας αὐτῶν τινες ἀποφεύγουσι, δίκτυα ἱστᾶσιν
εἰς τὰς ἀτραπούς, ᾗ φεύγουσιν, ἵν' εἰς ταῦτα
ἐμπίπτοντες συμποδίζωνται.

9   Τίνι οὖν, ἔφη, τοιούτῳ φίλους ἂν ἐγὼ θηρῴην ;
Ἐὰν νὴ Δί', ἔφη, ἀντὶ κυνὸς κτήσῃ ὅστις σοι
ἰχνεύων μὲν τοὺς φιλοκάλους καὶ πλουσίους
εὑρήσει, εὑρὼν δὲ μηχανήσεται, ὅπως ἐμβάλῃ
αὐτοὺς εἰς τὰ σὰ δίκτυα.

10   Καὶ ποῖα, ἔφη, ἐγὼ δίκτυα ἔχω ;
Ἓν μὲν δήπου, ἔφη, καὶ μάλα εὖ περιπλεκό-
μενον, τὸ σῶμα· ἐν δὲ τούτῳ ψυχήν, ᾗ καταμανθάνεις καὶ ὡς ἂν ἐμβλέπουσα χαρίζοιο καὶ
ὅ τι ἂν λέγουσα εὐφραίνοις καὶ ὅτι δεῖ τὸν μὲν
ἐπιμελόμενον ἀσμένως ὑποδέχεσθαι, τὸν δ' ἐντρυ-
φῶντα ἀποκλείειν καὶ ἀρρωστήσαντός γε φίλου
φροντιστικῶς ἐπισκέψασθαι καὶ καλόν τι πράξαντος σφόδρα συνησθῆναι καὶ τῷ σφόδρα σοῦ
φροντίζοντι ὅλῃ τῇ ψυχῇ κεχαρίσθαι. φιλεῖν
γε μὴν εὖ οἶδ' ὅτι ἐπίστασαι οὐ μόνον μαλακῶς,
ἀλλὰ καὶ εὐνοϊκῶς· καὶ ὅτι ἀρεστοί σοί εἰσιν οἱ
φίλοι, οἶδ' ὅτι οὐ λόγῳ ἀλλ' ἔργῳ ἀναπείθεις.
Μὰ τὸν Δί', ἔφη ἡ Θεοδότη, ἐγὼ τούτων οὐδὲν
μηχανῶμαι.

11   Καὶ μήν, ἔφη, πολὺ διαφέρει τὸ κατὰ φύσιν τε
καὶ ὀρθῶς ἀνθρώπῳ προσφέρεσθαι. καὶ γὰρ δὴ

them by the scent along the run from the feeding ground to the form; and since they are so nimble that once they are off they actually escape in the open, yet a third pack of speedy hounds is formed to catch them by hot pursuit; and as some escape even so, nets are set up in the tracks where they escape, that they may be driven into them and stopped dead."

"Then can I adapt this plan to the pursuit of 9 friends?"

"Of course you can, if for the hound you substitute an agent who will track and find rich men with an eye for beauty, and will then contrive to chase them into your nets."

"Nets! What nets have I got?" 10

"One, surely, that clips close enough—your body! And inside it you have a soul that teaches you what glance will please, what words delight, and tells you that your business is to give a warm welcome to an eager suitor, but to slam the door upon a coxcomb; yes, and when a friend has fallen sick, to show your anxiety by visiting him; and when he has had a stroke of good fortune, to congratulate him eagerly; and if he is eager in his suit, to put yourself at his service heart and soul. As for loving, you know how to do that, I am sure, both tenderly and truly; and that your friends give you satisfaction, you convince them, I know, not by words but by deeds."

"Upon my word," said Theodoté, "I don't contrive one of these things."

"Nevertheless," he continued, "it is very im- 11 portant that your behaviour to a man should be both natural and correct. For assuredly you can neither

βίᾳ μὲν οὔτ᾽ ἂν ἕλοις οὔτε κατάσχοις φίλον,
εὐεργεσίᾳ δὲ καὶ ἡδονῇ τὸ θηρίον τοῦτο ἀλώσιμόν
τε καὶ παραμόνιμόν ἐστιν.

Ἀληθῆ λέγεις, ἔφη.

12 Δεῖ τοίνυν, ἔφη, πρῶτον μὲν τοὺς φροντίζοντάς
σου τοιαῦτα ἀξιοῦν, οἷα ποιοῦσιν αὐτοῖς μικρό-
τατα μελήσει· ἔπειτα δὲ αὐτὴν ἀμείβεσθαι χαρι-
ζομένην τὸν αὐτὸν τρόπον. οὕτω γὰρ ἂν μάλιστα
φίλοι γίγνοιντο καὶ πλεῖστον χρόνον φιλοῖεν καὶ
13 μέγιστα εὐεργετοῖεν. χαρίζοιο δ᾽ ἂν μάλιστα, εἰ
δεομένοις δωροῖο τὰ παρὰ σεαυτῆς. ὁρᾷς γάρ,
ὅτι καὶ τῶν βρωμάτων τὰ ἥδιστα, ἐὰν μέν τις
προσφέρῃ πρὶν ἐπιθυμεῖν, ἀηδῆ φαίνεται, κεκορεσμένοις δὲ καὶ βδελυγμίαν παρέχει· ἐὰν δέ τις
προσφέρῃ λιμὸν ἐμποιήσας, κἂν φαυλότερα ᾖ,
πάνυ ἡδέα φαίνεται.

14 Πῶς οὖν ἄν, ἔφη, ἐγὼ λιμὸν ἐμποιεῖν τῳ τῶν
παρ᾽ ἐμοὶ δυναίμην;

Εἰ νὴ Δί᾽, ἔφη, πρῶτον μὲν τοῖς κεκορεσμένοις
μήτε προσφέροις μήτε ὑπομιμνήσκοις, ἕως ἂν τῆς
πλησμονῆς παυσάμενοι πάλιν δέωνται, ἔπειτα
τοὺς δεομένους ὑπομιμνήσκοις ὡς κοσμιωτάτῃ τε
ὁμιλίᾳ καὶ τῷ μὴ φαίνεσθαι βουλομένη χαρίζεσθαι
καὶ διαφεύγουσα, ἕως ἂν ὡς μάλιστα δεηθῶσι·
τηνικαῦτα γὰρ πολὺ διαφέρει τὰ αὐτὰ δῶρα ἢ
πρὶν ἐπιθυμῆσαι διδόναι.

15 Καὶ ἡ Θεοδότη, Τί . οὖν οὐ σύ μοι, ἔφη, ὦ
Σώκρατες, ἐγένου συνθηρατὴς τῶν φίλων;

Ἐάν γε νὴ Δί᾽, ἔφη, πείθῃς με σύ.

Πῶς οὖν ἄν, ἔφη, πείσαιμί σε;

catch a friend nor keep him by violence;[1] it is kindness and sweetness that catch the creature and hold him fast."

"True," she said.

"First, then, you must ask such favours of your suitors as they will grant without a moment's hesitation; and next you must repay their favours in the same coin; for in this way they will prove most sincerely your friends, most constant in their affection and most generous. And they will appreciate your favours most highly if you wait till they ask for them. The sweetest meats, you see, if served before they are wanted, seem sour, and to those who have had enough they are positively nauseating; but even poor fare is very welcome when offered to a hungry man."

"And how can I make them hunger for my fare?"

"Why, in the first place, you must not offer it to them when they have had enough, nor prompt them until they have thrown off the surfeit and are beginning to want more; then, when they feel the want, you must prompt them by behaving as a model of propriety, by a show of reluctance to yield, and by holding back until they are as keen as can be; for then the same gifts are much more to the recipient than when they are offered before they are desired."

"Then, Socrates," exclaimed Theodoté, "why don't you become my partner in the pursuit of friends?"

"By all means—if you persuade me."

"And how am I to persuade you?"

---

[1] *Cyropaedia*, VIII. vii. 13.

Ζητήσεις, ἔφη, τοῦτο αὐτὴ καὶ μηχανήσῃ, ἐάν τί μου δέῃ.

Εἴσιθι τοίνυν, ἔφη, θαμινά.

16 Καὶ ὁ Σωκράτης ἐπισκώπτων τὴν αὑτοῦ ἀπραγμοσύνην, Ἀλλ᾽, ὦ Θεοδότη, ἔφη, οὐ πάνυ μοι ῥᾴδιόν ἐστι σχολάσαι· καὶ γὰρ ἴδια πράγματα πολλὰ καὶ δημόσια παρέχει μοι ἀσχολίαν· εἰσὶ δὲ καὶ φίλαι μοι, αἳ οὔτε ἡμέρας οὔτε νυκτὸς ἀφ᾽ αὑτῶν ἐάσουσί με ἀπιέναι φίλτρα τε μανθάνουσαι παρ᾽ ἐμοῦ καὶ ἐπῳδάς.

17 Ἐπίστασαι γάρ, ἔφη, καὶ ταῦτα, ὦ Σώκρατες; Ἀλλὰ διὰ τί οἴει, ἔφη, Ἀπολλόδωρόν τε τόνδε καὶ Ἀντισθένην οὐδέποτέ μου ἀπολείπεσθαι; διὰ τί δὲ καὶ Κέβητα καὶ Σιμμίαν Θήβηθεν παραγίγνεσθαι; εὖ ἴσθι, ὅτι ταῦτα οὐκ ἄνευ πολλῶν φίλτρων τε καὶ ἐπῳδῶν καὶ ἰύγγων ἐστί.

18 Χρῆσον τοίνυν μοι, ἔφη, τὴν ἴυγγα, ἵνα ἐπὶ σοὶ πρῶτον ἕλκω αὐτήν.

Ἀλλὰ μὰ Δί᾽, ἔφη, οὐκ αὐτὸς ἕλκεσθαι πρὸς σὲ βούλομαι, ἀλλὰ σὲ πρὸς ἐμὲ πορεύεσθαι.

Ἀλλὰ πορεύσομαι, ἔφη· μόνον ὑποδέχου.

Ἀλλ᾽ ὑποδέξομαί σε, ἔφη, ἐὰν μή τις φιλωτέρα σου ἔνδον ᾖ.

XII. Ἐπιγένην δὲ τῶν συνόντων τινά, νέον τε ὄντα καὶ τὸ σῶμα κακῶς ἔχοντα, ἰδών, Ὡς ἰδιωτικῶς, ἔφη, τὸ σῶμα ἔχεις, ὦ Ἐπίγενες.

Καὶ ὅς, Ἰδιώτης γάρ, ἔφη, εἰμί, ὦ Σώκρατες.

Οὐδέν γε μᾶλλον, ἔφη, τῶν ἐν Ὀλυμπίᾳ μελλόντων ἀγωνίζεσθαι· ἢ δοκεῖ σοι μικρὸς εἶναι ὁ περὶ τῆς ψυχῆς πρὸς τοὺς πολεμίους ἀγών, ὃν

"That you will find out and contrive for yourself, if you want my help."

"Come and see me often, then."

"Ah!" said Socrates, making fun of his own 16 leisurely habits, "it's not so easy for me to find time. For I have much business to occupy me, private and public; and I have the dear girls, who won't leave me day or night; they are studying potions with me and spells."

"Indeed! do you understand these things too, 17 Socrates?"

"Why, what is the reason that master Apollodorus and Antisthenes never leave me, do you suppose? And why do Cebes and Simmias come to me from Thebes? I assure you these things don't happen without the help of many potions and spells and magic wheels."

"Do lend me your wheel, that I may turn it first 18 to draw you."

"But of course I don't want to be drawn to you: I want you to come to me."

"Oh, I'll come: only mind you welcome me."

"Oh, you shall be welcome—unless there's a dearer girl with me!"

XII. On noticing that Epigenes, one of his companions, was in poor condition, for a young man, he said: "You look as if you need exercise,[1] Epigenes."

"Well," he replied, "I'm not an athlete, Socrates."

"Just as much as the competitors entered for Olympia," he retorted. "Or do you count the life and death struggle with their enemies, upon which,

---

[1] ἰδιώτης is one who is ignorant of any profession or occupation: ἰδιωτικῶς ἔχειν here means to be ignorant of athletic training.

2 Ἀθηναῖοι θήσουσιν, ὅταν τύχωσι; καὶ μὴν οὐκ ὀλίγοι μὲν διὰ τὴν τοῦ σώματος καχεξίαν ἀποθνήσκουσί τε ἐν τοῖς πολεμικοῖς κινδύνοις καὶ αἰσχρῶς σώζονται· πολλοὶ δὲ δι' αὐτὸ τοῦτο ζῶντές τε ἁλίσκονται καὶ ἁλόντες ἤτοι δουλεύουσι τὸν λοιπὸν βίον, ἐὰν οὕτω τύχωσι, τὴν χαλεπωτάτην δουλείαν, ἢ εἰς τὰς ἀνάγκας τὰς ἀλγεινοτάτας ἐμπεσόντες καὶ ἐκτίσαντες ἐνίοτε πλείω τῶν ὑπαρχόντων αὐτοῖς τὸν λοιπὸν βίον ἐνδεεῖς τῶν ἀναγκαίων ὄντες καὶ κακοπαθοῦντες διαζῶσι· πολλοὶ δὲ δόξαν αἰσχρὰν κτῶνται διὰ τὴν τοῦ

3 σώματος ἀδυναμίαν δοκοῦντες ἀποδειλιᾶν. ἢ καταφρονεῖς τῶν ἐπιτιμίων τῆς καχεξίας τούτων καὶ ῥᾳδίως ἂν οἴει φέρειν τὰ τοιαῦτα; καὶ μὴν οἶμαί γε πολλῷ ῥᾴω καὶ ἡδίω τούτων εἶναι ἃ δεῖ ὑπομένειν τὸν ἐπιμελόμενον τῆς τοῦ σώματος εὐεξίας· ἢ ὑγιεινότερόν τε καὶ εἰς τἆλλα χρησιμώτερον νομίζεις εἶναι τὴν καχεξίαν τῆς εὐεξίας; ἢ τῶν διὰ τὴν εὐεξίαν γιγνομένων

4 καταφρονεῖς; καὶ μὴν πάντα γε τἀναντία συμβαίνει τοῖς εὖ τὰ σώματα ἔχουσιν ἢ τοῖς κακῶς. καὶ γὰρ ὑγιαίνουσιν οἱ τὰ σώματα εὖ ἔχοντες καὶ ἰσχύουσι· καὶ πολλοὶ μὲν διὰ τοῦτο ἐκ τῶν πολεμικῶν ἀγώνων σώζονταί τε εὐσχημόνως καὶ τὰ δεινὰ πάντα διαφεύγουσι, πολλοὶ δὲ φίλοις τε βοηθοῦσι καὶ τὴν πατρίδα εὐεργετοῦσι καὶ διὰ ταῦτα χάριτός τε ἀξιοῦνται καὶ δόξαν μεγάλην κτῶνται καὶ τιμῶν καλλίστων τυγχάνουσι καὶ διὰ ταῦτα[1] τόν τε λοιπὸν βίον ἥδιον καὶ κάλλιον διαζῶσι καὶ τοῖς ἑαυτῶν παισὶ καλλίους ἀφορμὰς εἰς τὸν βίον καταλείπουσιν.

5 Οὔτοι χρὴ ὅτι ἡ πόλις οὐκ ἀσκεῖ δημοσίᾳ τὰ

it may be, the Athenians will enter, but a small thing? Why, many, thanks to their bad condition, 2 lose their life in the perils of war or save it disgracefully: many, just for this same cause, are taken prisoners, and then either pass the rest of their days, perhaps, in slavery of the hardest kind, or, after meeting with cruel sufferings and paying, sometimes, more than they have, live on, destitute and in misery. Many, again, by their bodily weakness earn infamy, being thought cowards. Or do you despise these, 3 the rewards of bad condition, and think that you can easily endure such things? And yet I suppose that what has to be borne by anyone who takes care to keep his body in good condition is far lighter and far pleasanter than these things. Or is it that you think bad condition healthier and generally more serviceable than good, or do you despise the effects of good condition? And yet the results of physical 4 fitness are the direct opposite of those that follow from unfitness. The fit are healthy and strong; and many, as a consequence, save themselves decorously on the battle-field and escape all the dangers of war; many help friends and do good to their country and for this cause earn gratitude; get great glory and gain very high honours, and for this cause live henceforth a pleasanter and better life, and leave to their children better means of winning a livelihood.

"I tell you, because military training is not 5

---

[1] The Latin version of Bessario (Rome, 1521) omits διὰ ταῦτα, which is bracketed by Sauppe as spurious.

πρὸς τὸν πόλεμον, διὰ τοῦτο καὶ ἰδίᾳ ἀμελεῖν,
ἀλλὰ μηδὲν ἧττον ἐπιμελεῖσθαι. εὖ γὰρ ἴσθι,
ὅτι οὐδὲ ἐν ἄλλῳ οὐδενὶ ἀγῶνι οὐδὲ ἐν πράξει
οὐδεμιᾷ μεῖον ἕξεις διὰ τὸ βέλτιον τὸ σῶμα
παρεσκευάσθαι· πρὸς πάντα γάρ, ὅσα πράττουσιν
ἄνθρωποι, χρήσιμον τὸ σῶμά ἐστιν· ἐν πάσαις δὲ
ταῖς τοῦ σώματος χρείαις πολὺ διαφέρει ὡς
6 βέλτιστα τὸ σῶμα ἔχειν· ἐπεὶ καὶ ἐν ᾧ δοκεῖς
ἐλαχίστην σώματος χρείαν εἶναι, ἐν τῷ διανοεῖσθαι, τίς οὐκ οἶδεν, ὅτι καὶ ἐν τούτῳ πολλοὶ
μεγάλα σφάλλονται διὰ τὸ μὴ ὑγιαίνειν τὸ σῶμα;
καὶ λήθη δὲ καὶ ἀθυμία καὶ δυσκολία καὶ μανία
πολλάκις πολλοῖς διὰ τὴν τοῦ σώματος καχεξίαν
εἰς τὴν διάνοιαν ἐμπίπτουσιν οὕτως, ὥστε καὶ τὰς
7 ἐπιστήμας ἐκβάλλειν. τοῖς δὲ τὰ σώματα εὖ
ἔχουσι πολλὴ ἀσφάλεια καὶ οὐδεὶς κίνδυνος διά
γε τὴν τοῦ σώματος καχεξίαν τοιοῦτόν τι παθεῖν,
εἰκὸς δὲ μᾶλλον πρὸς τὰ ἐναντία τῶν διὰ τὴν
καχεξίαν γιγνομένων τὴν εὐεξίαν χρήσιμον εἶναι.
καίτοι τῶν γε τοῖς εἰρημένοις ἐναντίων ἕνεκα τί
οὐκ ἄν τις νοῦν ἔχων ὑπομείνειεν;

8 Αἰσχρὸν δὲ καὶ τὸ διὰ τὴν ἀμέλειαν γηρᾶναι,
πρὶν ἰδεῖν ἑαυτὸν ποῖος ἂν κάλλιστος καὶ
κράτιστος τῷ σώματι γένοιτο. ταῦτα δὲ οὐκ
ἔστιν ἰδεῖν ἀμελοῦντα· οὐ γὰρ ἐθέλει αὐτόματα
γίγνεσθαι.

XIII. Ὀργιζομένου δέ ποτέ τινος, ὅτι προσ-
ειπών τινα χαίρειν οὐκ ἀντιπροσερρήθη, Γελοῖον,
ἔφη, τὸ εἰ μὲν τὸ σῶμα κάκιον ἔχοντι ἀπήντησάς

publicly recognised by the state, you must not make that an excuse for being a whit less careful in attending to it yourself. For you may rest assured that there is no kind of struggle, apart from war, and no undertaking in which you will be worse off by keeping your body in better fettle. For in everything that men do the body is useful; and in all uses of the body it is of great importance to be in as high a state of physical efficiency as possible. 6 Why, even in the process of thinking, in which the use of the body seems to be reduced to a minimum, it is matter of common knowledge that grave mistakes may often be traced to bad health. And because the body is in a bad condition, loss of memory, depression, discontent, insanity often assail the mind so violently as to drive whatever knowledge it contains clean out of it. But a sound and healthy body 7 is a strong protection to a man, and at least there is no danger then of such a calamity happening to him through physical weakness: on the contrary, it is likely that his sound condition will serve to produce effects the opposite of those that arise from bad condition. And surely a man of sense would submit to anything to obtain the effects that are the opposite of those mentioned in my list.

"Besides, it is a disgrace to grow old through 8 sheer carelessness before seeing what manner of man you may become by developing your bodily strength and beauty to their highest limit. But you cannot see that, if you are careless; for it will not come of its own accord."

XIII. On a man who was angry because his greeting was not returned: "Ridiculous!" he exclaimed; "you would not have been angry if you

τῳ, μὴ ἂν ὀργίζεσθαι, ὅτι δὲ τὴν ψυχὴν
ἀγροικοτέρως διακειμένῳ περιέτυχες, τοῦτό σε
λυπεῖν.

2 Ἄλλου δὲ λέγοντος, ὅτι ἀηδῶς ἐσθίοι, ᾿Ακου-
μενός, ἔφη, τούτου φάρμακον ἀγαθὸν διδάσκει.
ἐρομένου δέ, Ποῖον; Παύσασθαι ἐσθίοντα, ἔφη·
καὶ ἥδιόν τε καὶ εὐτελέστερον καὶ ὑγιεινότερον
διάξειν παυσάμενον.

3 Ἄλλου δ' αὖ λέγοντος, ὅτι θερμὸν εἴη παρ'
ἑαυτῷ τὸ ὕδωρ, ὃ πίνοι, Ὅταν ἄρ', ἔφη, βούλῃ
θερμῷ λούσασθαι, ἕτοιμον ἔσται σοι.

Ἀλλὰ ψυχρόν, ἔφη, ἐστὶν ὥστε λούσασθαι.

Ἆρ' οὖν, ἔφη, καὶ οἱ οἰκέται σου ἄχθονται
πίνοντές τε αὐτὸ καὶ λούμενοι αὐτῷ;

Μὰ τὸν Δί', ἔφη· ἀλλὰ καὶ πολλάκις τεθαύμακα, ὡς ἡδέως αὐτῷ πρὸς ἀμφότερα ταῦτα
χρῶνται.

Πότερον δέ, ἔφη, τὸ παρὰ σοὶ ὕδωρ θερμότερον
πιεῖν ἐστιν ἢ τὸ ἐν Ἀσκληπιοῦ;

Τὸ ἐν Ἀσκληπιοῦ, ἔφη.

Πότερον δὲ λούσασθαι ψυχρότερον, τὸ παρὰ
σοὶ ἢ τὸ ἐν Ἀμφιαράου;

Τὸ ἐν Ἀμφιαράου, ἔφη.

Ἐνθυμοῦ οὖν, ἔφη, ὅτι κινδυνεύεις δυσαρεστό-
τερος εἶναι τῶν τε οἰκετῶν καὶ τῶν ἀρρωστούντων.

4 Κολάσαντος δέ τινος ἰσχυρῶς ἀκόλουθον, ἤρετο,
τί χαλεπαίνοι τῷ θεράποντι.

Ὅτι, ἔφη, ὀψοφαγίστατός τε ὢν βλακότατός
ἐστι καὶ φιλαργυρώτατος ὢν ἀργότατος.

had met a man in worse health; and yet you are annoyed because you have come across someone with ruder manners!"

On another who declared that he found no 2 pleasure in eating: "Acumenus," he said, "has a good prescription for that ailment." And when asked "What?" he answered, "Stop eating; and you will then find life pleasanter, cheaper, and healthier."

On yet another who complained that the drinking 3 water at home was warm: "Consequently," he said, "when you want warm water to wash in, you will have it at hand."

"But it's too cold for washing," objected the other.

"Then do your servants complain when they use it both for drinking and washing?"

"Oh no: indeed I have often felt surprised that they are content with it for both these purposes."

"Which is the warmer to drink, the water in your house or Epidaurus water?" [1]

"Epidaurus water."

"And which is the colder to wash in, yours or Oropus water?" [2]

"Oropus water."

"Then reflect that you are apparently harder to please than servants and invalids."

When someone punished his footman severely, he 4 asked why he was angry with his man.

"Because he's a glutton and he's a fool," said the other: "he's rapacious and he's lazy."

---

[1] The hot spring in the precincts of Asclepius' temple at Epidaurus.

[2] The spring by the temple of Amphiaraus at Oropus in Boeotia.

Ἤδη ποτὲ οὖν ἐπεσκέψω, πότερος πλειόνων πληγῶν δεῖται, σὺ ἢ ὁ θεράπων;

5 Φοβουμένου δέ τινος τὴν εἰς Ὀλυμπίαν ὁδόν, Τί, ἔφη, φοβῇ τὴν πορείαν; οὐ καὶ οἴκοι σχεδὸν ὅλην τὴν ἡμέραν περιπατεῖς; καὶ ἐκεῖσε πορευόμενος περιπατήσας ἀριστήσεις, περιπατήσας δειπνήσεις καὶ ἀναπαύσῃ. οὐκ οἶσθα, ὅτι εἰ ἐκτείναις τοὺς περιπάτους, οὓς ἐν πέντε ἢ ἓξ ἡμέραις περιπατεῖς, ῥᾳδίως ἂν Ἀθήνηθεν εἰς Ὀλυμπίαν ἀφίκοιο; χαριέστερον δὲ καὶ προεξορμᾶν ἡμέρᾳ μιᾷ μᾶλλον ἢ ὑστερίζειν. τὸ μὲν γὰρ ἀναγκάζεσθαι περαιτέρω τοῦ μετρίου μηκύνειν τὰς ὁδοὺς χαλεπόν, τὸ δὲ μιᾷ ἡμέρᾳ πλείονας πορευθῆναι πολλὴν ῥᾳστώνην παρέχει. κρεῖττον οὖν ἐν τῇ ὁρμῇ σπεύδειν ἢ ἐν τῇ ὁδῷ.

6 Ἄλλου δὲ λέγοντος, ὡς παρετάθη μακρὰν ὁδὸν πορευθείς, ἤρετο αὐτόν, εἰ καὶ φορτίον ἔφερε.

Μὰ Δί᾽ οὐκ ἔγωγ᾽, ἔφη, ἀλλὰ τὸ ἱμάτιον.

Μόνος δ᾽ ἐπορεύου, ἔφη, ἢ καὶ ἀκόλουθός σοι ἠκολούθει;

Ἠκολούθει, ἔφη.

Πότερον κενός, ἔφη, ἢ φέρων τι;

Φέρων νὴ Δί᾽, ἔφη, τά τε στρώματα καὶ τἆλλα σκεύη.

Καὶ πῶς, ἔφη, ἀπήλλαχεν ἐκ τῆς ὁδοῦ;

Ἐμοὶ μὲν δοκεῖν, ἔφη, βέλτιον ἐμοῦ.

Τί οὖν; ἔφη, εἰ τὸ ἐκείνου φορτίον ἔδει σε φέρειν, πῶς ἂν οἴει διατεθῆναι;

Κακῶς νὴ Δί᾽, ἔφη· μᾶλλον δὲ οὐδ᾽ ἂν ἠδυνήθην κομίσαι.

Τὸ οὖν τοσούτῳ ἧττον τοῦ παιδὸς δύνασθαι πονεῖν πῶς ἠσκημένου δοκεῖ σοι ἀνδρὸς εἶναι;

" Have you ever considered, then, which deserves the more stripes, the master or the man ? "

When someone was afraid of the journey to 5 Olympia, he said :

" Why do you fear the distance ? When you are at home, don't you spend most of the day in walking about ? on your way there you will take a walk before lunch, and another before dinner, and then take a rest. Don't you know that if you put together the walks you take in five or six days, you can easily cover the distance from Athens to Olympia ? It is more comfortable, too, to start a day early rather than a day late, since to be forced to make the stages of the journey unduly long is unpleasant ; but to take a day extra on the way makes easy going. So it is better to hurry over the start than on the road."

When another said that he was worn out after a 6 long journey, he asked him whether he had carried a load.

" Oh no," said the man ; " only my cloak."

" Were you alone, or had you a footman with you ? "

" I had."

" Empty-handed or carrying anything ? "

" He carried the rugs and the rest of the baggage, of course."

" And how has he come out of the journey ? "

" Better than I, so far as I can tell."

" Well then, if you had been forced to carry his load, how would you have felt, do you suppose ? "

" Bad, of course ; or rather, I couldn't have done it."

" Indeed ! do you think a trained man ought to be so much less capable of work than his slave ? "

XIV. Ὁπότε δὲ τῶν συνιόντων ἐπὶ δεῖπνον οἱ μὲν μικρὸν ὄψον, οἱ δὲ πολὺ φέροιεν, ἐκέλευεν ὁ Σωκράτης τὸν παῖδα τὸ μικρὸν ἢ εἰς τὸ κοινὸν τιθέναι ἢ διανέμειν ἑκάστῳ τὸ μέρος. οἱ οὖν τὸ πολὺ φέροντες ᾐσχύνοντο τό τε μὴ κοινωνεῖν τοῦ εἰς τὸ κοινὸν τιθεμένου καὶ τὸ μὴ ἀντιτιθέναι τὸ ἑαυτῶν. ἐτίθεσαν οὖν καὶ τὸ ἑαυτῶν εἰς τὸ κοινόν· καὶ ἐπεὶ οὐδὲν πλέον εἶχον τῶν μικρὸν φερομένων, ἐπαύοντο πολλοῦ ὀψωνοῦντες.

2 Καταμαθὼν δέ ποτε τῶν συνδειπνούντων τινὰ τοῦ μὲν σίτου πεπαυμένον, τὸ δὲ ὄψον αὐτὸ καθ’ αὑτὸ ἐσθίοντα, λόγου ὄντος περὶ ὀνομάτων, ἐφ’ οἵῳ ἔργῳ ἕκαστον εἴη, Ἔχοιμεν ἄν, ἔφη, ὦ ἄνδρες, εἰπεῖν, ἐπὶ ποίῳ ποτὲ ἔργῳ ἄνθρωπος ὀψοφάγος καλεῖται; ἐσθίουσι μὲν γὰρ δὴ πάντες ἐπὶ τῷ σίτῳ ὄψον, ὅταν παρῇ· ἀλλ’ οὐκ οἶμαί πω ἐπὶ τούτῳ γε ὀψοφάγοι καλοῦνται.

Οὐ γὰρ οὖν, ἔφη τις τῶν παρόντων.

3 Τί γάρ; ἔφη, ἐάν τις ἄνευ τοῦ σίτου τὸ ὄψον αὐτὸ ἐσθίῃ μὴ ἀσκήσεως, ἀλλ’ ἡδονῆς ἕνεκα, πότερον ὀψοφάγος εἶναι δοκεῖ ἢ οὔ;

Σχολῇ γ’ ἄν, ἔφη, ἄλλος τις ὀψοφάγος εἴη.

Καί τις ἄλλος τῶν παρόντων, Ὁ δὲ μικρῷ σίτῳ, ἔφη, πολὺ ὄψον ἐπεσθίων;

Ἐμοὶ μέν, ἔφη ὁ Σωκράτης, καὶ οὗτος δοκεῖ δικαίως ἂν ὀψοφάγος καλεῖσθαι· καὶ ὅταν γε οἱ ἄλλοι ἄνθρωποι τοῖς θεοῖς εὔχωνται πολυκαρπίαν, εἰκότως ἂν οὗτος πολυοψίαν εὔχοιτο.

4 Ταῦτα δὲ τοῦ Σωκράτους εἰπόντος, νομίσας ὁ

---

¹ ὄψον, literally a tit-bit eaten with bread; Lat. *pulmentum.*

XIV. Whenever some of the members of a dining-club brought more meat [1] than others, Socrates would tell the waiter either to put the small contribution into the common stock or to portion it out equally among the diners. So the high batteners felt obliged not only to take their share of the pool, but to pool their own supplies in return; and so they put their own supplies also into the common stock. And since they thus got no more than those who brought little with them, they gave up spending much on meat.

He observed on one occasion that one of the 2 company at dinner had ceased to take bread, and ate the meat by itself. Now the talk was of names and the actions to which they are properly applied. " Can we say, my friends," said Socrates, " what is the nature of the action for which a man is called greedy? For all, I presume, eat meat with their bread when they get the chance : but I don't think there is so far any reason for calling them greedy? "

" No, certainly not," said one of the company.

" Well, suppose he eats the meat alone, without 3 the bread, not because he's in training, but to tickle his palate, does he seem a greedy fellow or not? "

" If not, it's hard to say who does," was the reply.

Here another of the company queried, " And he who eats a scrap of bread with a large helping of meat? "

" He too seems to me to deserve the epithet," said Socrates. " Aye, and when others pray for a good wheat harvest, he, presumably, would pray for a good meat supply."

The young man, guessing that these remarks of 4

νεανίσκος εἰς αὑτὸν εἰρῆσθαι τὰ λεχθέντα τὸ μὲν
ὄψον οὐκ ἐπαύσατο ἐσθίων, ἄρτον δὲ προσέλαβε.
καὶ ὁ Σωκράτης καταμαθών, Παρατηρεῖτ᾽,
ἔφη, τοῦτον οἱ πλησίον, ὁπότερα τῷ σίτῳ ὄψῳ ἢ
τῷ ὄψῳ σίτῳ χρήσεται.

5 Ἄλλον δέ ποτε τῶν συνδείπνων ἰδὼν ἐπὶ τῷ
ἑνὶ ψωμῷ πλειόνων ὄψων γευόμενον, Ἄρα γένοιτ᾽
ἄν, ἔφη, πολυτελεστέρα ὀψοποιία ἢ μᾶλλον τὰ
ὄψα λυμαινομένη ἢ ἣν ὀψοποιεῖται ὁ ἅμα πολλὰ
ἐσθίων καὶ ἅμα παντοδαπὰ ἡδύσματα εἰς τὸ
στόμα λαμβάνων; πλείω μέν γε τῶν ὀψοποιῶν
συμμιγνύων πολυτελέστερα ποιεῖ· ἃ δὲ ἐκεῖνοι μὴ
συμμιγνύουσιν ὡς οὐχ ἁρμόττοντα, ὁ συμμιγνύων,
εἴπερ ἐκεῖνοι ὀρθῶς ποιοῦσιν, ἁμαρτάνει τε καὶ
6 καταλύει τὴν τέχνην αὐτῶν. καίτοι πῶς οὐ
γελοῖόν ἐστι παρασκευάζεσθαι μὲν ὀψοποιοὺς
τοὺς ἄριστα ἐπισταμένους, αὐτὸν δὲ μηδ᾽
ἀντιποιούμενον τῆς τέχνης ταύτης τὰ ὑπ᾽ ἐκείνων
ποιούμενα μετατιθέναι; καὶ ἄλλο δέ τι προσ-
γίγνεται τῷ ἅμα πολλὰ ἐσθίειν ἐθισθέντι· μὴ
παρόντων γὰρ πολλῶν μειονεκτεῖν ἄν τι δοκοίη
ποθῶν τὸ σύνηθες· ὁ δὲ συνεθισθεὶς τὸν ἕνα
ψωμὸν ἑνὶ ὄψῳ προπέμπειν, ὅτε μὴ παρείη
πολλά, δύναιτ᾽ ἂν ἀλύπως τῷ ἑνὶ χρῆσθαι.

7 Ἔλεγε δὲ καὶ ὡς τὸ εὐωχεῖσθαι ἐν τῇ Ἀθηναίων
γλώττῃ ἐσθίειν καλοῖτο· τὸ δὲ εὖ προσκεῖσθαι
ἔφη ἐπὶ τῷ ταῦτα ἐσθίειν, ἃ μήτε τὴν ψυχὴν
μήτε τὸ σῶμα λυποίη μηδὲ δυσεύρετα εἴη· ὥστε
καὶ τὸ εὐωχεῖσθαι τοῖς κοσμίως διαιτωμένοις
ἀνετίθει.

Socrates applied to him, did not stop eating his meat, but took some bread with it. When Socrates observed this, he cried: "Watch the fellow, you who are near him, and see whether he treats the bread as his meat or the meat as his bread."

On another occasion he noticed one of the com- 5 pany at dinner tasting several dishes with each bite of bread. "Can you imagine," he asked, "a meal more extravagant and more ruinous to the victuals than his who eats many things together, and crams all sorts of sauces into his mouth at once? At any rate by mixing more ingredients than the cooks, he adds to the cost, and since he mixes ingredients that they regard as unsuitable in a mixture, if they are right, then he is wrong and is ruining their art. Yet it is surely ridiculous for a master to obtain 6 highly skilled cooks, and then, though he claims no knowledge of the art, to alter their confections? There's another drawback, too, attaching to the habit of eating many things together. For if many dishes are not provided, one seems to go short because one misses the usual variety: whereas he who is accustomed to take one kind of meat along with one bit of bread can make the best of one dish when more are not forthcoming."

He used to say too that the term "good feeding" 7 in Attic was a synonym for "eating." The "good" in the compound implied the eating of food that could harm neither body nor soul and was not hard to come by. Thus he attributed even good feeding to sober livers.

BOOK IV

Δ.

I. Οὕτω δὲ Σωκράτης ἦν ἐν παντὶ πράγματι καὶ πάντα τρόπον ὠφέλιμος, ὥστε σκοπουμένῳ τῷ καὶ μετρίως αἰσθανομένῳ φανερὸν εἶναι, ὅτι οὐδὲν ὠφελιμώτερον ἦν τοῦ Σωκράτει συνεῖναι καὶ μετ᾽ ἐκείνου διατρίβειν ὁπουοῦν καὶ ἐν ὁτῳοῦν πράγματι· ἐπεὶ καὶ τὸ ἐκείνου μεμνῆσθαι μὴ παρόντος οὐ μικρὰ ὠφέλει τοὺς εἰωθότας τε αὐτῷ συνεῖναι καὶ ἀποδεχομένους ἐκεῖνον. καὶ γὰρ παίζων οὐδὲν ἧττον ἢ σπουδάζων ἐλυσιτέλει τοῖς συνδιατρίβουσι.

2 Πολλάκις γὰρ ἔφη μὲν ἄν τινος ἐρᾶν, φανερὸς δ᾽ ἦν οὐ τῶν τὰ σώματα πρὸς ὥραν, ἀλλὰ τῶν τὰς ψυχὰς πρὸς ἀρετὴν εὖ πεφυκότων ἐφιέμενος. ἐτεκμαίρετο δὲ τὰς ἀγαθὰς φύσεις ἐκ τοῦ ταχύ τε μανθάνειν οἷς προσέχοιεν καὶ μνημονεύειν ἃ μάθοιεν καὶ ἐπιθυμεῖν τῶν μαθημάτων πάντων, δι᾽ ὧν ἔστιν οἶκόν[1] τε καλῶς οἰκεῖν καὶ πόλιν καὶ τὸ ὅλον ἀνθρώποις τε καὶ τοῖς ἀνθρωπίνοις πράγμασιν εὖ χρῆσθαι· τοὺς γὰρ τοιούτους ἡγεῖτο παιδευθέντας οὐκ ἂν μόνον αὐτούς τε εὐδαίμονας εἶναι καὶ τοὺς ἑαυτῶν οἴκους καλῶς οἰκεῖν, ἀλλὰ καὶ ἄλλους ἀνθρώπους καὶ πόλεις

3 δύνασθαι εὐδαίμονας ποιεῖν. οὐ τὸν αὐτὸν δὲ τρόπον ἐπὶ πάντας ᾔει, ἀλλὰ τοὺς μὲν οἰομένους φύσει ἀγαθοὺς εἶναι, μαθήσεως δὲ καταφρονοῦντας ἐδίδασκεν, ὅτι αἱ ἄρισται δοκοῦσαι εἶναι φύσεις

---

[1] οἶκόν Hirschig: οἰκίαν Sauppe with MSS. and Stobaeus.

BOOK IV

I. SOCRATES was so useful in all circumstances and in all ways, that any observer gifted with ordinary perception can see that nothing was more useful than the companionship of Socrates, and time spent with him in any place and in any circumstances. The very recollection of him in absence brought no small good to his constant companions and followers; for even in his light moods they gained no less from his society than when he was serious.

Thus he would often say he was "in love"; but 2 clearly his heart was set not on those who were fair to outward view, but on those whose souls excelled in goodness. These excellent beings he recognised by their quickness to learn whatever subject they studied, ability to remember what they learned, and desire for every kind of knowledge on which depend good management of a household and estate and tactful dealing with men and the affairs of men. For education would make such beings not only happy in themselves, and successful in the management of their households, but capable of conferring happiness on their fellow-men and on states alike. His method of approach varied. To those who 3 thought themselves possessed of natural endowments and despised learning, he explained that the greater

μάλιστα παιδείας δέονται, ἐπιδεικνύων τῶν τε
ἵππων τοὺς εὐφυεστάτους θυμοειδεῖς τε καὶ
σφοδροὺς ὄντας, εἰ μὲν ἐκ νέων δαμασθεῖεν,
εὐχρηστοτάτους καὶ ἀρίστους γιγνομένους, εἰ δὲ
ἀδάμαστοι γένοιντο, δυσκαθεκτοτάτους καὶ
φαυλοτάτους, καὶ τῶν κυνῶν τῶν εὐφυεστάτων,
φιλοπόνων τε οὐσῶν καὶ ἐπιθετικῶν τοῖς θηρίοις,
τὰς μὲν καλῶς ἀχθείσας ἀρίστας γίνεσθαι πρὸς
τὰς θήρας καὶ χρησιμωτάτας, ἀναγώγους δὲ
γιγνομένας ματαίους τε καὶ μανιώδεις καὶ
4 δυσπειθεστάτας. ὁμοίως δὲ καὶ τῶν ἀνθρώπων
τοὺς εὐφυεστάτους, ἐρρωμενεστάτους τε ταῖς
ψυχαῖς ὄντας καὶ ἐξεργαστικωτάτους ὧν ἂν
ἐγχειρῶσι, παιδευθέντας μὲν καὶ μαθόντας ἃ δεῖ
πράττειν ἀρίστους τε καὶ ὠφελιμωτάτους
γίγνεσθαι· πλεῖστα γὰρ καὶ μέγιστα ἀγαθὰ
ἐργάζεσθαι· ἀπαιδεύτους δὲ καὶ ἀμαθεῖς γενο-
μένους κακίστους τε καὶ βλαβερωτάτους
γίγνεσθαι· κρίνειν γὰρ οὐκ ἐπισταμένους ἃ δεῖ
πράττειν πολλάκις πονηροῖς ἐπιχειρεῖν πράγμασι,
μεγαλείους δὲ καὶ σφοδροὺς ὄντας δυσκαθέκτους
τε καὶ δυσαποτρέπτους εἶναι· διὸ πλεῖστα καὶ
μέγιστα κακὰ ἐργάζεσθαι.

5 Τοὺς δ' ἐπὶ πλούτῳ μέγα φρονοῦντας καὶ
νομίζοντας οὐδὲν προσδεῖσθαι παιδείας, ἐξαρκέσειν
δὲ σφίσι τὸν πλοῦτον οἰομένους πρὸς τὸ δια-
πράττεσθαί τε ὅ τι ἂν βούλωνται καὶ τιμᾶσθαι
ὑπὸ τῶν ἀνθρώπων, ἐφρένου λέγων, ὅτι μῶρος
μὲν εἴη εἴ τις οἴεται μὴ μαθὼν τά τε ὠφέλιμα καὶ
τὰ βλαβερὰ τῶν πραγμάτων διαγνώσεσθαι,
μῶρος δ' εἴ τις μὴ διαγιγνώσκων μὲν ταῦτα, διὰ
δὲ τὸν πλοῦτον ὅ τι ἂν βούληται ποριζόμενος

the natural gifts, the greater is the need of education ;
pointing out that thoroughbreds by their spirit and
mettle develop into serviceable and splendid creatures, if they are broken in as colts, but if unbroken,
prove intractable and sorry jades ; and high-bred
puppies, keen workers and good tacklers of game,
make first-rate hounds and useful dogs, if well trained,
but, if untrained, turn out stupid, crazy, disobedient
brutes. It is the same with human beings. The 4
most highly gifted, the youths of ardent soul, capable
of doing whatever they attempt, if educated and
taught their duty grow into excellent and useful
men ; for manifold and great are their good deeds.
But untrained and untaught, these same become
utterly evil and mischievous ; for without knowledge
to discern their duty, they often put their hand to
vile deeds, and through the very grandeur and vehe-
mence of their nature, they are uncontrollable and
intractable : therefore manifold and great are their
evil deeds.[1]

Those who prided themselves on riches and 5
thought they had no need of education, supposing
that their wealth would suffice them for gaining the
objects of their wishes and winning honour among
men, he admonished thus. "Only a fool," he said,
"can think it possible to distinguish between things
useful and things harmful without learning : only a
fool can think that without distinguishing these he
will get all he wants by means of his wealth and be

---

[1] Is Alcibiades in his mind?

οἴεται δυνήσεσθαι τὰ συμφέροντα πράττειν,
ἠλίθιος δ' εἴ τις μὴ δυνάμενος τὰ συμφέροντα
πράττειν εὖ τε πράττειν οἴεται καὶ τὰ πρὸς τὸν
βίον αὑτῷ ἢ καλῶς ἢ ἱκανῶς παρεσκευάσθαι,
ἠλίθιος δὲ καὶ εἴ τις οἴεται διὰ τὸν πλοῦτον μηδὲν
ἐπιστάμενος δόξειν τι ἀγαθὸς εἶναι ἢ μηδὲν
ἀγαθὸς εἶναι δοκῶν εὐδοκιμήσειν.

II. Τοῖς δὲ νομίζουσι παιδείας τε τῆς ἀρίστης
τετυχηκέναι καὶ μέγα φρονοῦσιν ἐπὶ σοφίᾳ ὡς
προσεφέρετο, νῦν διηγήσομαι. καταμαθὼν γὰρ
Εὐθύδημον τὸν καλὸν γράμματα πολλὰ συνειλεγ-
μένον ποιητῶν τε καὶ σοφιστῶν τῶν εὐδοκιμω-
τάτων καὶ ἐκ τούτων ἤδη τε νομίζοντα διαφέρειν
τῶν ἡλικιωτῶν ἐν σοφίᾳ καὶ μεγάλας ἐλπίδας
ἔχοντα παντων διοίσειν τῷ δύνασθαι λέγειν τε
καὶ πράττειν πρῶτον μὲν, αἰσθανόμενος αὐτὸν
διὰ νεότητα οὔπω εἰς τὴν ἀγορὰν εἰσιόντα, εἰ
δέ τι βούλοιτο διαπράξασθαι, καθίζοντα εἰς
ἡνιοποιεῖόν τι τῶν ἐγγὺς τῆς ἀγορᾶς, εἰς τοῦτο
καὶ αὐτὸς ᾔει τῶν μεθ' ἑαυτοῦ τινας ἔχων.

2   Καὶ πρῶτον μὲν πυνθανομένου τινός, πότερον
Θεμιστοκλῆς διὰ συνουσίαν τινὸς τῶν σοφῶν ἢ
φύσει τοσοῦτον διήνεγκε τῶν πολιτῶν, ὥστε πρὸς
ἐκεῖνον ἀποβλέπειν τὴν πόλιν, ὁπότε σπουδαίου
ἀνδρὸς δεηθείη, ὁ Σωκράτης βουλόμενος κινεῖν
τὸν Εὐθύδημον εὔηθες ἔφη εἶναι τὸ οἴεσθαι τὰς
μὲν ὀλίγου ἀξίας τέχνας μὴ γίγνεσθαι σπουδαίους
ἄνευ διδασκάλων ἱκανῶν, τὸ δὲ προεστάναι
πόλεως, πάντων ἔργων μέγιστον ὄν, ἀπὸ ταὐτο-
μάτου παραγίγνεσθαι τοῖς ἀνθρώποις.

able to do what is expedient: only a simpleton can think that without the power to do what is expedient he is doing well and has made good or sufficient provision for his life: only a simpleton can think that by his wealth alone without knowledge he will be reputed good at something, or will enjoy a good reputation without being reputed good at anything in particular.

II. I will now show his method of dealing with those who thought they had received the best education, and prided themselves on wisdom. He was informed that Euthydemus, the handsome, had formed a large collection of the works of celebrated poets and professors, and therefore supposed himself to be a prodigy of wisdom for his age, and was confident of surpassing all competitors in power of speech and action. At present, Socrates observed, he did not enter the Market-place owing to his youth, but when he wanted to get anything done, he would be found sitting in a saddler's shop near the Market. So, to make an opening, Socrates went to this shop with some of his companions.

At the first visit, one of them asked: "Was it by 2 constant intercourse with some wise man or by natural ability that Themistocles stood out among his fellow-citizens as the man to whom the people naturally looked when they felt the want of a great leader?"

In order to set Euthydemus thinking, Socrates said:

"If in the minor arts great achievement is impossible without competent masters, surely it is absurd to imagine that the art of statesmanship, the greatest of all accomplishments, comes to a man of its own accord."

3 Πάλιν δέ ποτε παρόντος τοῦ Εὐθυδήμου, ὁρῶν
αὐτὸν ἀποχωροῦντα τῆς συνεδρίας καὶ φυλαττόμενον, μὴ δόξῃ τὸν Σωκράτην θαυμάζειν ἐπὶ σοφίᾳ,
Ὅτι μέν, ἔφη, ὦ ἄνδρες, Εὐθύδημος οὑτοσὶ ἐν
ἡλικίᾳ γενόμενος, τῆς πόλεως λόγον περί τινος
προτιθείσης, οὐκ ἀφέξεται τοῦ συμβουλεύειν,
εὔδηλόν ἐστιν ἐξ ὧν ἐπιτηδεύει· δοκεῖ δέ μοι καλὸν
προοίμιον τῶν δημηγοριῶν παρασκευάσασθαι
φυλαττόμενος, μὴ δόξῃ μανθάνειν τι παρά του.
δῆλον γὰρ ὅτι λέγειν ἀρχόμενος ὧδε προοιμιάσεται·
4 Παρ' οὐδενὸς μὲν πώποτε, ὦ ἄνδρες Ἀθηναῖοι,
οὐδὲν ἔμαθον οὐδ' ἀκούων τινὰς εἶναι λέγειν τε καὶ
πράττειν ἱκανοὺς ἐζήτησα τούτοις ἐντυχεῖν οὐδ'
ἐπεμελήθην τοῦ διδάσκαλόν τινά μοι γενέσθαι
τῶν ἐπισταμένων, ἀλλὰ καὶ τἀναντία· διατετέλεκα
γὰρ φεύγων οὐ μόνον τὸ μανθάνειν τι παρά τινος,
ἀλλὰ καὶ τὸ δόξαι. ὅμως δὲ ὅ τι ἂν ἀπὸ ταὐτο-
μάτου ἐπίῃ μοι, συμβουλεύσω ὑμῖν.
5 Ἁρμόσειε δ' ἂν οὕτω προοιμιάζεσθαι καὶ τοῖς
βουλομένοις παρὰ τῆς πόλεως ἰατρικὸν ἔργον
λαβεῖν· ἐπιτήδειόν γ' ἂν αὐτοῖς εἴη τοῦ λόγου
ἄρχεσθαι ἐντεῦθεν·

Παρ' οὐδενὸς μὲν πώποτε, ὦ ἄνδρες Ἀθηναῖοι,
τὴν ἰατρικὴν τέχνην ἔμαθον οὐδ' ἐζήτησα διδάσκαλον ἐμαυτῷ γενέσθαι τῶν ἰατρῶν οὐδένα· διατετέλεκα γὰρ φυλαττόμενος οὐ μόνον τὸ μαθεῖν τι
παρὰ τῶν ἰατρῶν, ἀλλὰ καὶ τὸ δόξαι μεμαθηκέναι
τὴν τέχνην ταύτην. ὅμως δέ μοι τὸ ἰατρικὸν ἔργον
δότε· πειράσομαι γὰρ ἐν ὑμῖν ἀποκινδυνεύων
μανθάνειν.

Πάντες οὖν οἱ παρόντες ἐγέλασαν ἐπὶ τῷ προ-
οιμίῳ.

Some time afterwards, meeting Euthydemus again, **3** he saw that he was reluctant to join the circle and anxious not to betray any admiration for the wisdom of Socrates: "Well, gentlemen," said he, "when our friend Euthydemus has attained his full powers, and some question of policy is before the Assembly, he won't be backward in offering advice: that is obvious from his behaviour. I fancy he has prepared a noble exordium to his addresses, with due care not to give the impression that he is indebted to anyone for his knowledge. No doubt he will begin his speech with this introduction:

"'Men of Athens, I have never yet learnt any- **4** thing from anyone, nor when I have been told of any man's ability in speech and in action, have I sought to meet him, nor have I been at pains to find a teacher among the men who know. On the contrary, I have constantly avoided learning anything of anyone, and even the appearance of it. Nevertheless I shall recommend to your consideration anything that comes into my head.'

"This exordium might be adapted so as to suit **5** candidates for the office of public physician. They might begin their speeches in this strain:

"'Men of Athens, I have never yet studied medicine, nor sought to find a teacher among our physicians; for I have constantly avoided learning anything from the physicians, and even the appearance of having studied their art. Nevertheless I ask you to appoint me to the office of a physician, and I will endeavour to learn by experimenting on you.'"

The exordium set all the company laughing.

6 Ἐπεὶ δὲ φανερὸς ἦν ὁ Εὐθύδημος ἤδη μὲν οἷς ὁ Σωκράτης λέγοι προσέχων, ἔτι δὲ φυλαττόμενος αὐτός τι φθέγγεσθαι καὶ νομίζων τῇ σιωπῇ σωφροσύνης δόξαν περιβάλλεσθαι, τότε ὁ Σωκράτης βουλόμενος αὐτὸν παῦσαι τούτου, Θαυμαστὸν γάρ, ἔφη, τί ποτε οἱ βουλόμενοι κιθαρίζειν ἢ αὐλεῖν ἢ ἱππεύειν ἢ ἄλλο τι τῶν τοιούτων ἱκανοὶ γενέσθαι πειρῶνται ὡς συνεχέστατα ποιεῖν ὅ τι ἂν βούλωνται δυνατοὶ γενέσθαι καὶ·οὐ καθ' ἑαυτούς, ἀλλὰ παρὰ τοῖς ἀρίστοις δοκοῦσιν εἶναι, πάντα ποιοῦντες καὶ ὑπομένοντες ἕνεκα τοῦ μηδὲν ἄνευ τῆς ἐκείνων γνώμης ποιεῖν, ὡς οὐκ ἂν ἄλλως ἀξιόλογοι γενόμενοι, τῶν δὲ βουλομένων δυνατῶν γενέσθαι λέγειν τε καὶ πράττειν τὰ πολιτικὰ νομίζουσί τινες ἄνευ παρασκευῆς καὶ ἐπιμελείας αὐτόματοι ἐξαίφνης δυνατοὶ ταῦτα ποιεῖν ἔσεσθαι.

7 καίτοι γε τοσούτῳ ταῦτα ἐκείνων δυσκατεργαστότερα φαίνεται, ὅσῳπερ πλειόνων περὶ ταῦτα πραγματευομένων ἐλάττους οἱ κατεργαζόμενοι γίγνονται. δῆλον οὖν ὅτι καὶ ἐπιμελείας δέονται πλείονος καὶ ἰσχυροτέρας οἱ τούτων ἐφιέμενοι ἢ οἱ ἐκείνων.

8 Κατ' ἀρχὰς μὲν οὖν ἀκούοντος Εὐθυδήμου τοιούτους λόγους ἔλεγε Σωκράτης· ὡς δ' ᾔσθετο αὐτὸν ἑτοιμότερον ὑπομένοντα, ὅτε διαλέγοιτο, καὶ προθυμότερον ἀκούοντα, μόνος ἦλθεν εἰς τὸ ἡνιοποιεῖον· παρακαθεζομένου δ' αὐτῷ τοῦ Εὐθυδήμου, Εἰπέ μοι, ἔφη, ὦ Εὐθύδημε, τῷ ὄντι, ὥσπερ ἐγὼ ἀκούω, πολλὰ γράμματα συνῆχας τῶν λεγομένων σοφῶν ἀνδρῶν γεγονέναι;

Καὶ ὁ Εὐθύδημος, Νὴ τὸν Δί', ἔφη, ὦ Σώκρατες· καὶ ἔτι γε συνάγω, ἕως ἂν κτήσωμαι ὡς ἂν δύνωμαι πλεῖστα.

Now when it became evident that Socrates had 6
gained the attention of Euthydemus, but that
Euthydemus still avoided breaking silence himself,
and thought that he assumed an air of prudence by
remaining dumb, Socrates wanted to put an end to
that affectation. "How strange it is," he said, "that
those who want to play the harp or the flute, or to
ride or to get skill in any similar accomplishment,
work hard at the art they mean to master, and not
by themselves but under the tuition of the most
eminent professors, doing and bearing anything in
their anxiety to do nothing without their teachers'
guidance, just because that is the only way to
become proficient : and yet, among those who want
to shine as speakers in the Assembly and as statesmen, there are some who think that they will be
able to do so on a sudden, by instinct, without
training or study. Yet surely these arts are much 7
the harder to learn ; for many more are interested
in them and far fewer succeed. Clearly then these
arts demand a longer and more intense application
than the others."

For a time, then, Socrates continued to talk in 8
this strain, while Euthydemus listened. But on
finding him more tolerant of his conversation and
more attentive, Socrates went alone to the saddler's ;
and when Euthydemus had taken a seat beside him,
he said : "Tell me, Euthydemus, am I rightly informed that you have a large collection of books
written by the wise men of the past, as they are
called ? "

"By Zeus, yes, Socrates," answered he, "and I
am still adding to it, to make it as complete as
possible."

9 Νὴ τὴν Ἥραν, ἔφη ὁ Σωκράτης, ἄγαμαί γέ
σου, διότι οὐκ ἀργυρίου καὶ χρυσίου προείλου
θησαυροὺς κεκτῆσθαι μᾶλλον ἢ σοφίας· δῆλον
γὰρ ὅτι νομίζεις ἀργύριον καὶ χρυσίον οὐδὲν
βελτίους ποιεῖν τοὺς ἀνθρώπους, τὰς δὲ τῶν
σοφῶν ἀνδρῶν γνώμας ἀρετῇ πλουτίζειν τοὺς
κεκτημένους.

Καὶ ὁ Εὐθύδημος ἔχαιρεν ἀκούων ταῦτα, νομίζων δοκεῖν τῷ Σωκράτει ὀρθῶς μετιέναι τὴν
10 σοφίαν. ὁ δὲ καταμαθὼν αὐτὸν ἡσθέντα τῷ
ἐπαίνῳ τούτῳ, Τί δὲ δὴ βουλόμενος ἀγαθὸς γενέσθαι, ἔφη, ὦ Εὐθύδημε, συλλέγεις τὰ γράμματα;

Ἐπεὶ δὲ διεσιώπησεν ὁ Εὐθύδημος σκοπῶν, ὅ
τι ἀποκρίναιτο, πάλιν ὁ Σωκράτης. Ἆρα μὴ
ἰατρός; ἔφη· πολλὰ γὰρ καὶ ἰατρῶν ἐστι
συγγράμματα.

Καὶ ὁ Εὐθύδημος, Μὰ Δί', ἔφη, οὐκ ἔγωγε.

Ἀλλὰ μὴ ἀρχιτέκτων βούλει γενέσθαι; γνω-
μονικοῦ γὰρ ἀνδρὸς καὶ τοῦτο δεῖ.

Οὔκουν ἔγωγ', ἔφη.

Ἀλλὰ μὴ γεωμέτρης ἐπιθυμεῖς, ἔφη, γενέσθαι
ἀγαθός, ὥσπερ ὁ Θεόδωρος;

Οὐδὲ γεωμέτρης, ἔφη.

Ἀλλὰ μὴ ἀστρολόγος, ἔφη, βούλει γενέσθαι;

Ὡς δὲ καὶ τοῦτο ἠρνεῖτο, Ἀλλὰ μὴ ῥαψῳδός;
ἔφη· καὶ γὰρ τὰ Ὁμήρου σέ φασιν ἔπη πάντα
κεκτῆσθαι.

Μὰ Δί' οὐκ ἔγωγ', ἔφη· τοὺς γάρ τοι ῥαψῳδοὺς
οἶδα τὰ μὲν ἔπη ἀκριβοῦντας, αὐτοὺς δὲ πάνυ
ἠλιθίους ὄντας.

"By Hera," retorted Socrates,[1] "I do admire you 9 for valuing the treasures of wisdom above gold and silver. For you are evidently of opinion that, while gold and silver cannot make men better, the thoughts of the wise enrich their possessors with virtue."

Now Euthydemus was glad to hear this, for he guessed that in the opinion of Socrates he was on the road to wisdom. But Socrates, aware that he 10 was pleased with his approbation, went on to say : " Tell me, Euthydemus, what kind of goodness do you want to get by collecting these books ? "

And as Euthydemus was silent, considering what answer to give, " Possibly you want to be a doctor ? " he guessed : " Medical treatises alone make a large collection."

" Oh no, not at all."

" But perhaps you wish to be an architect? One needs a well-stored mind for that too."

" No, indeed I don't."

" Well, perhaps you want to be a good mathematician, like Theodorus ? "[2]

" No, not that either."

" Well, perhaps you want to be an astronomer ? " And as he again said no, " Perhaps a rhapsodist, then ? They tell me you have a complete copy of Homer."

" Oh no, not at all ; for your rhapsodists, I know, are consummate as reciters, but they are very silly fellows themselves."

---

[1] νὴ τὴν Ἥραν, a favourite oath of Socrates, is not rendered literally elsewhere ; but here it seems to be intended to cap νὴ τὸν Δία.

[2] Theodorus of Cyrene, who is one of the characters in the *Theaetetus* of Plato.

11 Καὶ ὁ Σωκράτης ἔφη· Οὐ δήπου, ὦ Εὐθύδημε,
ταύτης τῆς ἀρετῆς ἐφίεσαι, δι' ἣν ἄνθρωποι
πολιτικοὶ γίγνονται καὶ οἰκονομικοὶ καὶ ἄρχειν
ἱκανοὶ καὶ ὠφέλιμοι τοῖς τε ἄλλοις ἀνθρώποις καὶ
ἑαυτοῖς ;

Καὶ ὁ Εὐθύδημος, Σφόδρα γ', ἔφη, ὦ Σώκρατες,
ταύτης τῆς ἀρετῆς δέομαι.

Νὴ Δί', ἔφη ὁ Σωκράτης, τῆς καλλίστης ἀρετῆς
καὶ μεγίστης ἐφίεσαι τέχνης· ἔστι γὰρ τῶν
βασιλέων αὕτη καὶ καλεῖται βασιλική. ἀτάρ,
ἔφη, κατανενόηκας, εἰ οἷόν τέ ἐστι μὴ ὄντα
δίκαιον ἀγαθὸν ταῦτα γενέσθαι ;

Καὶ μάλα, ἔφη, καὶ οὐχ οἷόν τέ γε ἄνευ δικαιοσύνης ἀγαθὸν πολίτην γενέσθαι.

12 Τί οὖν ; ἔφη, σὺ δὴ τοῦτο κατείργασαι ;

Οἶμαί γ', ἔφη, ὦ Σώκρατες, οὐδενὸς ἂν ἧττον
φανῆναι δίκαιος.

Ἆρ' οὖν, ἔφη, τῶν δικαίων ἔστιν ἔργα ὥσπερ
τῶν τεκτόνων ;

Ἔστι μέντοι, ἔφη.

Ἆρ' οὖν, ἔφη, ὥσπερ οἱ τέκτονες ἔχουσι τὰ
ἑαυτῶν ἔργα ἐπιδεῖξαι, οὕτως οἱ δίκαιοι τὰ αὑτῶν
ἔχοιεν ἂν διεξηγήσασθαι ;

Μὴ οὖν, ἔφη ὁ Εὐθύδημος, οὐ δύνωμαι ἐγὼ τὰ
τῆς δικαιοσύνης ἔργα ἐξηγήσασθαι ; καὶ νὴ Δί'
ἔγωγε τὰ τῆς ἀδικίας· ἐπεὶ οὐκ ὀλίγα ἔστι καθ'
ἑκάστην ἡμέραν τοιαῦτα ὁρᾶν τε καὶ ἀκούειν.

13 Βούλει οὖν, ἔφη ὁ Σωκράτης, γράψωμεν ἐνταυθὶ μὲν δέλτα, ἐνταυθὶ δὲ ἄλφα ; εἶτα ὅ τι
μὲν ἂν δοκῇ ἡμῖν τῆς δικαιοσύνης ἔργον εἶναι,
πρὸς τὸ δέλτα θῶμεν, ὅ τι δ' ἂν τῆς ἀδικίας,
πρὸς τὸ ἄλφα ;

Then Socrates exclaimed : " Surely, Euthydemus, 11 you don't covet the kind of excellence that makes good statesmen and managers, competent rulers and benefactors of themselves and mankind in general ? "

" Yes, I do, Socrates," answered Euthydemus, " that kind of excellence I greatly desire."

" Why," cried Socrates, " it is the noblest kind of excellence, the greatest of arts that you covet, for it belongs to kings and is dubbed ' kingly.' However," he added, " have you reflected whether it be possible to excel in these matters without being a just man ? "

" Yes, certainly ; and it is, in fact, impossible to be a good citizen without justice."

" Then tell me, have you got that ? " 12

" Yes, Socrates, I think I can show myself to be as just as any man."

" And have just men, like carpenters, their works ? "

" Yes, they have."

" And as carpenters can point out their works, should just men be able to rehearse theirs ? "

" Do you suppose," retorted Euthydemus, " that I am unable to rehearse the works of justice ? Of course I can,—and the works of injustice too, since there are many opportunities of seeing and hearing of them every day."

" I propose, then, that we write J in this column 13 and I in that, and then proceed to place under these letters, J and I, what we take to be the works of justice and injustice respectively."

Εἴ τί σοι δοκεῖ, ἔφη, προσδεῖν τούτων, ποίει ταῦτα.

14 Καὶ ὁ Σωκράτης γράψας ὥσπερ εἶπεν, Οὐκοῦν, ἔφη, ἔστιν ἐν ἀνθρώποις τὸ ψεύδεσθαι ;

Ἔστι μέντοι, ἔφη.

Ποτέρωσε οὖν, ἔφη, θῶμεν τοῦτο ;

Δῆλον, ἔφη, ὅτι πρὸς τὴν ἀδικίαν.

Οὐκοῦν, ἔφη, καὶ τὸ ἐξαπατᾶν ἔστι ;

Καὶ μάλα, ἔφη.

Τοῦτο οὖν ποτέρωσε θῶμεν ;

Καὶ τοῦτο δῆλον ὅτι, ἔφη, πρὸς τὴν ἀδικίαν.

Τί δὲ τὸ κακουργεῖν ;

Καὶ τοῦτο, ἔφη.

Τὸ δὲ ἀνδραποδίζεσθαι ;

Καὶ τοῦτο.

Πρὸς δὲ τῇ δικαιοσύνῃ οὐδὲν ἡμῖν τούτων κείσεται, ὦ Εὐθύδημε ;

Δεινὸν γὰρ ἂν εἴη, ἔφη.

15 Τί δ᾽ ; ἐάν τις στρατηγὸς αἱρεθεὶς ἄδικόν τε καὶ ἐχθρὰν πόλιν ἐξανδραποδίσηται, φήσομεν τοῦτον ἀδικεῖν ;

Οὐ δῆτα, ἔφη.

Δίκαια δὲ ποιεῖν οὐ φήσομεν ;

Καὶ μάλα.

Τί δ᾽ ; ἐὰν ἐξαπατᾷ πολεμῶν αὐτοῖς ;

Δίκαιον, ἔφη, καὶ τοῦτο.

Ἐὰν δὲ κλέπτῃ τε καὶ ἁρπάζῃ τὰ τούτων, οὐ δίκαια ποιήσει ;

Καὶ μάλα, ἔφη, ἀλλ᾽ ἐγώ σε τὸ πρῶτον ὑπελάμβανον πρὸς τοὺς φίλους μόνον ταῦτα ἐρωτᾶν.

" Do so, if you think it helps at all "

Having written down the letters as he proposed, Socrates went on : " Lying occurs among men, does 14 it not ? "

" Yes, it does."

" Under which heading, then, are we to put that ? "

" Under the heading of injustice, clearly."

" Deceit, too, is found, is it not ? "

" Certainly."

" Under which heading will that go ? "

" Under injustice again, of course."

" What about doing mischief ? "

" That too."

" Selling into slavery ? "

" That too."

" Then we shall assign none of these things to justice, Euthydemus ? "

" No, it would be monstrous to do so."

" Now suppose a man who has been elected 15 general enslaves an unjust and hostile city, shall we say that he acts unjustly ? "

" Oh no ! "

" We shall say that his actions are just, shall we not ? "

" Certainly."

" And what if he deceives the enemy when at war ? "[1]

" That too is just."

" And if he steals and plunders their goods, will not his actions be just ? "

" Certainly ; but at first I assumed that your questions had reference only to friends."

---

[1] *Cyropaedia*, I. vi. 31, VI. i. 55.

Οὐκοῦν, ἔφη, ὅσα πρὸς τῇ ἀδικίᾳ ἐθήκαμεν, ταῦτα καὶ πρὸς τῇ δικαιοσύνῃ θετέον ἂν εἴη ; Ἔοικεν, ἔφη.

16 Βούλει οὖν, ἔφη, ταῦτα οὕτω θέντες διορισώμεθα πάλιν πρὸς μὲν τοὺς πολεμίους δίκαιον εἶναι τὰ τοιαῦτα ποιεῖν, πρὸς δὲ τοὺς φίλους ἄδικον, ἀλλὰ δεῖν πρός γε τούτους ὡς ἀπλούστατον εἶναι ; Πάνυ μὲν οὖν, ἔφη ὁ Εὐθύδημος.

17 Τί οὖν ; ἔφη ὁ Σωκράτης, ἐάν τις στρατηγὸς ὁρῶν ἀθύμως ἔχον τὸ στράτευμα ψευσάμενος φήσῃ συμμάχους προσιέναι καὶ τῷ ψεύδει τούτῳ παύσῃ τῆς ἀθυμίας τοὺς στρατιώτας, ποτέρωθι τὴν ἀπάτην ταύτην θήσομεν ; Δοκεῖ μοι, ἔφη, πρὸς τὴν δικαιοσύνην.

Ἐὰν δέ τις υἱὸν ἑαυτοῦ δεόμενον φαρμακείας καὶ μὴ προσιέμενον φάρμακον ἐξαπατήσας ὡς σιτίον τὸ φάρμακον δῷ καὶ τῷ ψεύδει χρησάμενος οὕτως ὑγιᾶ ποιήσῃ, ταύτην αὖ τὴν ἀπάτην ποῖ θετέον ; Δοκεῖ μοι, ἔφη, καὶ ταύτην εἰς τὸ αὐτό.

Τί δ' ; ἐάν τις, ἐν ἀθυμίᾳ ὄντος φίλου, δείσας, μὴ διαχρήσηται ἑαυτόν, κλέψῃ ἢ ἁρπάσῃ ἢ ξίφος ἢ ἄλλο τι τοιοῦτον, τοῦτο αὖ ποτέρωσε θετέον ; Καὶ τοῦτο νὴ Δί', ἔφη, πρὸς τὴν δικαιοσύνην.

18 Λέγεις, ἔφη, σὺ οὐδὲ πρὸς τοὺς φίλους ἅπαντα δεῖν ἁπλοΐζεσθαι ; Μὰ Δί' οὐ δῆτα, ἔφη· ἀλλὰ μετατίθεμαι τὰ εἰρημένα, εἴπερ ἔξεστι.

Δεῖ γέ τοι, ἔφη ὁ Σωκράτης, ἐξεῖναι πολὺ 19 μᾶλλον ἢ μὴ ὀρθῶς τιθέναι. τῶν δὲ δὴ τοὺς φίλους ἐξαπατώντων ἐπὶ βλάβῃ, ἵνα μηδὲ τοῦ-

"Then everything that we assigned to injustice should be assigned to justice also?"

"Apparently."

"Then I propose to revise our classification, and 16 to say: It is just to do such things to enemies, but it is unjust to do them to friends, towards whom one's conduct should be scrupulously honest."

"By all means."

"Now suppose that a general, seeing that his 17 army is downhearted, tells a lie and says that reinforcements are approaching, and by means of this lie checks discouragement among the men, under which heading shall we put this deception?"

"Under justice, I think."

"Suppose, again, that a man's son refuses to take a dose of medicine when he needs it, and the father induces him to take it by pretending that it is food, and cures him by means of this lie, where shall we put this deception?"

"That too goes on the same side, I think."

"And again, suppose one has a friend suffering from depression, and, for fear that he may make away with himself, one takes away his sword or something of the sort, under which heading shall we put that now?"

"That too goes under justice, of course."

"You mean, do you, that even with friends 18 straightforward dealing is not invariably right?"

"It isn't, indeed! I retract what I said before, if you will let me."

"Why, I'm bound to let you; it's far better than getting our lists wrong. But now, consider 19 deception practised on friends to their detriment: we mustn't overlook that either. Which is the

τὸ παραλίπωμεν ἄσκεπτον, πότερος ἀδικώτερός
ἐστιν, ὁ ἑκὼν ἢ ὁ ἄκων ;

Ἀλλ', ὦ Σώκρατες, οὐκέτι μὲν ἔγωγε πιστεύω
οἷς ἀποκρίνομαι· καὶ γὰρ τὰ πρόσθεν πάντα νῦν
ἄλλως ἔχειν δοκεῖ μοι ἢ ὡς ἐγὼ τότε ᾤμην· ὅμως
δὲ εἰρήσθω μοι, ἀδικώτερον εἶναι τὸν ἑκόντα
ψευδόμενον τοῦ ἄκοντος.

20   Δοκεῖ δέ σοι μάθησις καὶ ἐπιστήμη τοῦ δικαίου
εἶναι ὥσπερ τῶν γραμμάτων ;

Ἔμοιγε.

Πότερον δὲ γραμματικώτερον κρίνεις, ὃς ἂν
ἑκὼν μὴ ὀρθῶς γράφῃ καὶ ἀναγιγνώσκῃ ἢ ὃς ἂν
ἄκων ;

Ὃς ἂν ἑκών, ἔγωγε· δύναιτο γὰρ ἄν, ὁπότε
βούλοιτο, καὶ ὀρθῶς αὐτὰ ποιεῖν.

Οὐκοῦν ὁ μὲν ἑκὼν μὴ ὀρθῶς γράφων γραμ-
ματικὸς ἂν εἴη, ὁ δὲ ἄκων ἀγράμματος ;

Πῶς γὰρ οὔ ;

Τὰ δίκαια δὲ πότερον ὁ ἑκὼν ψευδόμενος καὶ
ἐξαπατῶν οἶδεν ἢ ὁ ἄκων ;

Δῆλον ὅτι ὁ ἑκών.

Οὐκοῦν γραμματικώτερον μὲν τὸν ἐπιστάμενον
γράμματα τοῦ μὴ ἐπισταμένου φῂς εἶναι ;

Ναί.

Δικαιότερον δὲ τὸν ἐπιστάμενον τὰ δίκαια τοῦ
μὴ ἐπισταμένου ;

Φαίνομαι· δοκῶ δέ μοι καὶ ταῦτα οὐκ οἶδ' ὅπως
λέγειν.

21   Τί δὲ δή, ὃς ἂν βουλόμενος τἀληθῆ λέγειν
μηδέποτε τὰ αὐτὰ περὶ τῶν αὐτῶν λέγῃ, ἀλλ'
ὁδόν τε φράζων τὴν αὐτὴν τοτὲ μὲν πρὸς ἕω, τοτὲ

more unjust deception in that case, the intentional or unintentional?"

"Nay, Socrates, I have lost all confidence in my answers; for all the opinions that I expressed before seem now to have taken an entirely different form. Still I venture to say that the intentional deception is more unjust than the unintentional."

"Do you think there is a doctrine and science of the just, as there is of letters?" 20

"Yes."

"Which, in your judgment, is the more literate, the man who intentionally blunders in writing and reading, or the man who blunders unintentionally?"

"The one who blunders intentionally, I presume; for he can always be accurate when he chooses."

"May we not say, then, that the intentional blunderer is literate and the unintentional is illiterate?"

"Indeed we must."

"And which knows what is just, the intentional liar and deceiver, or the unintentional?"

"The intentional, clearly."

"You say, then, as I understand, that he who knows letters is more literate than he who is ignorant of them?"

"Yes"

"And he who knows what is just is more just than he who does not know?"

"Apparently; but here again I don't feel sure of my own meaning."

"Now come, what do you think of the man who wants to tell the truth, but never sticks to what he says; when he shows you the way, tells you first 21

δὲ πρὸς ἑσπέραν φράζῃ καὶ λογισμὸν ἀποφαινόμενος τὸν αὐτὸν τοτὲ μὲν πλείω, τοτὲ δ' ἐλάττω
ἀποφαίνηται, τί σοι δοκεῖ ὁ τοιοῦτος ;

Δῆλος νὴ Δί' εἶναι ὅτι ἃ ᾤετο εἰδέναι οὐκ
οἶδεν.

22 Οἶσθα δέ τινας ἀνδραποδώδεις καλουμένους ;
Ἔγωγε.

Πότερον διὰ σοφίαν ἢ δι' ἀμαθίαν ;
Δῆλον ὅτι δι' ἀμαθίαν.

Ἀρ' οὖν διὰ τὴν τοῦ χαλκεύειν ἀμαθίαν τοῦ
ὀνόματος τούτου τυγχάνουσιν ;
Οὐ δῆτα.

Ἀλλ' ἄρα διὰ τὴν τοῦ τεκταίνεσθαι ;
Οὐδὲ διὰ ταύτην.

Ἀλλὰ διὰ τὴν τοῦ σκυτεύειν ;
Οὐδὲ δι' ἓν τούτων, ἔφη, ἀλλὰ καὶ τοὐναντίον·
οἱ γὰρ πλεῖστοι τῶν γε τὰ τοιαῦτα ἐπισταμένων
ἀνδραποδώδεις εἰσίν.

Ἀρ' οὖν τῶν τὰ καλὰ καὶ ἀγαθὰ καὶ δίκαια μὴ
εἰδότων τὸ ὄνομα τοῦτ' ἐστίν ;
Ἔμοιγε δοκεῖ, ἔφη.

23 Οὐκοῦν δεῖ παντὶ τρόπῳ διατειναμένους φεύγειν,
ὅπως μὴ ἀνδράποδα ὦμεν.

Ἀλλὰ νὴ τοὺς θεούς, ἔφη, ὦ Σώκρατες, πάνυ
ᾤμην φιλοσοφεῖν φιλοσοφίαν, δι' ἧς ἂν μάλιστα
ἐνόμιζον παιδευθῆναι τὰ προσήκοντα ἀνδρὶ καλοκἀγαθίας ὀρεγομένῳ· νῦν δὲ πῶς οἴει με ἀθύμως
ἔχειν ὁρῶντα ἐμαυτὸν διὰ μὲν τὰ προπεπονη-
μένα οὐδὲ τὸ ἐρωτώμενον ἀποκρίνεσθαι δυνάμενον
ὑπὲρ ὧν μάλιστα χρὴ εἰδέναι, ἄλλην δὲ ὁδὸν
οὐδεμίαν ἔχοντα, ἣν ἂν πορευόμενος βελτίων
γενοίμην ;

that the road runs east, then that it runs west ; and when he casts up figures, makes the total now larger, now smaller ? "

" Why, I think he shows that he doesn't know what he thought he knew."

" Are you aware that some people are called 22 slavish ? "

" Yes."

" To what do they owe the name, to knowledge or to ignorance ? "

" To ignorance, obviously."

" To ignorance of the smiths' trade, shall we say ? "

" Certainly not."

" Ignorance of carpentry perhaps ? "

" No, not to that either."

" Of cobbling ? "

" No, to none of these : on the contrary, those who are skilled in such trades are for the most part slavish."

" Then is this name given to those who are ignorant of the beautiful and good and just ? "

" That is my opinion."

" Then we must strain every nerve to escape being 23 slaves."

" Upon my word, Socrates, I did feel confident that I was a student of a philosophy that would provide me with the best education in all things needful to one who would be a gentleman. But you can imagine my dismay when I realise that in spite of all my pains I am even incapable of answering a question about things that one is bound to know, and yet find no other way that will lead to my improvement."

24 Καὶ ὁ Σωκράτης, Εἰπέ μοι, ἔφη, ὦ Εὐθύδημε, εἰς Δελφοὺς δὲ ἤδη πώποτε ἀφίκου ;

Καὶ δίς γε νὴ Δί', ἔφη.

Κατέμαθες οὖν πρὸς τῷ ναῷ που γεγραμμένον τὸ Γνῶθι σαυτόν ;

Ἔγωγε.

Πότερον οὖν οὐδέν σοι τοῦ γράμματος ἐμέλησεν ἢ προσέσχες τε καὶ ἐπεχείρησας σαυτὸν ἐπισκοπεῖν, ὅστις εἴης ;

Μὰ Δί' οὐ δῆτα, ἔφη. καὶ γὰρ δὴ πάνυ τοῦτό γε ᾤμην εἰδέναι· σχολῇ γὰρ ἂν ἄλλο τι ᾔδειν, εἴ γε μηδ' ἐμαυτὸν ἐγίγνωσκον.

25 Πότερα δέ σοι δοκεῖ γιγνώσκειν ἑαυτὸν ὅστις τοὔνομα τὸ ἑαυτοῦ μόνον οἶδεν ἢ ὅστις, ὥσπερ οἱ τοὺς ἵππους ὠνούμενοι οὐ πρότερον οἴονται γιγνώσκειν ὃν ἂν βούλωνται γνῶναι, πρὶν ἂν ἐπισκέψωνται, πότερον εὐπειθής ἐστιν ἢ δυσπειθὴς καὶ πότερον ἰσχυρός ἐστιν ἢ ἀσθενὴς καὶ πότερον ταχὺς ἢ βραδὺς καὶ τἆλλα τὰ πρὸς τὴν τοῦ ἵππου χρείαν ἐπιτήδειά τε καὶ ἀνεπιτήδεια ὅπως ἔχει, οὕτως ὁ ἑαυτὸν ἐπισκεψάμενος, ὁποῖός ἐστι πρὸς τὴν ἀνθρωπίνην χρείαν, ἔγνωκε τὴν αὑτοῦ δύναμιν ;

Οὕτως ἔμοιγε δοκεῖ, ἔφη, ὁ μὴ εἰδὼς τὴν αὑτοῦ δυναμιν ἀγνοεῖν ἑαυτόν.

26 Ἐκεῖνο δὲ οὐ φανερόν, ἔφη, ὅτι διὰ μὲν τὸ εἰδέναι ἑαυτοὺς πλεῖστα ἀγαθὰ πάσχουσιν ἄνθρωποι, διὰ δὲ τὸ ἐψεῦσθαι ἑαυτῶν πλεῖστα κακά ; οἱ μὲν γὰρ εἰδότες ἑαυτοὺς τά τε ἐπιτήδεια ἑαυτοῖς ἴσασι καὶ διαγιγνώσκουσιν ἅ τε δύνανται καὶ ἃ μή· καὶ ἃ μὲν ἐπίστανται πράττοντες πορίζονταί τε ὧν δέονται καὶ εὖ πράττουσιν, ὧν δὲ

Hereupon Socrates exclaimed : "Tell me, Euthy- 24 demus, have you ever been to Delphi?"

"Yes, certainly ; twice."

"Then did you notice somewhere on the temple the inscription 'Know thyself'?"

"I did."

"And did you pay no heed to the inscription, or did you attend to it and try to consider who you were?"

"Indeed I did not; because I felt sure that I knew that already ; for I could hardly know anything else if I did not even know myself."

"And what do you suppose a man must know to 25 know himself, his own name merely? Or must he consider what sort of a creature he is for human use and get to know his own powers; just as those who buy horses don't think that they know the beast they want to know until they have considered whether he is docile or stubborn, strong or weak, fast or slow, and generally how he stands in all that makes a useful or a useless horse?"

"That leads me to think that he who does not know his own powers is ignorant of himself."

"Is it not clear too that through self-knowledge 26 men come to much good, and through self-deception to much harm? For those who know themselves, know what things are expedient for themselves and discern their own powers and limitations. And by doing what they understand, they get what they want and prosper : by refraining from attempting

μὴ ἐπίστανται ἀπεχόμενοι ἀναμάρτητοι γίγνονται
καὶ διαφεύγουσι τὸ κακῶς πράττειν· διὰ τοῦτο
δὲ καὶ τοὺς ἄλλους ἀνθρώπους δυνάμενοι δοκιμάζειν καὶ διὰ τῆς τῶν ἄλλων χρείας τά τε ἀγαθὰ
27 πορίζονταί καὶ τὰ κακὰ φυλάττονται. οἱ δὲ μὴ
εἰδότες, ἀλλὰ διεψευσμένοι τῆς ἑαυτῶν δυνάμεως
πρός τε τοὺς ἄλλους ἀνθρώπους καὶ τἆλλα ἀν-
θρώπινα πράγματα ὁμοίως διάκεινται καὶ οὔτε
ὧν δέονται ἴσασιν οὔτε ὅ τι πράττουσιν οὔτε οἷς
χρῶνται, ἀλλὰ πάντων τούτων διαμαρτάνοντες
τῶν τε ἀγαθῶν ἀποτυγχάνουσι καὶ τοῖς κακοῖς
28 περιπίπτουσι. καὶ οἱ μὲν εἰδότες ὅ τι ποιοῦσιν
ἐπιτυγχάνοντες ὧν πράττουσιν εὔδοξοί τε καὶ
τίμιοι γίγνονται· καὶ οἵ τε ὅμοιοι τούτοις ἡδέως
χρῶνται οἵ τε ἀποτυγχάνοντες τῶν πραγμάτων
ἐπιθυμοῦσι τούτους ὑπὲρ αὑτῶν βουλεύεσθαι καὶ
προΐστασθαί γε[1] αὑτῶν τούτους καὶ τὰς ἐλπίδας
τῶν ἀγαθῶν ἐν τούτοις ἔχουσι καὶ διὰ πάντα
29 ταῦτα πάντων μάλιστα τούτους ἀγαπῶσιν. οἱ
δὲ μὴ εἰδότες ὅ τι ποιοῦσι, κακῶς δὲ αἱρούμενοι
καὶ οἷς ἂν ἐπιχειρήσωσιν ἀποτυγχάνοντες οὐ
μόνον ἐν αὐτοῖς τούτοις ζημιοῦνταί τε καὶ κολά-
ζονται, ἀλλὰ καὶ ἀδοξοῦσι διὰ ταῦτα καὶ κατα-
γέλαστοι γίγνονται καὶ καταφρονούμενοι καὶ
ἀτιμαζόμενοι ζῶσιν.

Ὁρᾷς δὲ καὶ τῶν πόλεων ὅτι ὅσαι ἂν ἀγνο-
ήσασαι τὴν ἑαυτῶν δύναμιν κρείττοσι πολεμή-
σωσιν, αἱ μὲν ἀνάστατοι γίγνονται, αἱ δ᾽ ἐξ
ἐλευθέρων δοῦλαι.

30 Καὶ ὁ Εὐθύδημος, Ὡς πάνυ μοι δοκοῦν, ἔφη,
ὦ Σώκρατες, περὶ πολλοῦ ποιητέον εἶναι τὸ
ἑαυτὸν γιγνώσκειν, οὕτως ἴσθι· ὁπόθεν δὲ χρὴ

what they do not understand, they make no mistakes and avoid failure. And consequently through their power of testing other men too, and through their intercourse with others, they get what is good and shun what is bad. Those who do not know 27 and are deceived in their estimate of their own powers, are in the like condition with regard to other men and other human affairs. They know neither what they want, nor what they do, nor those with whom they have intercourse; but mistaken in all these respects, they miss the good and stumble into the bad. Furthermore, those who know what 28 they do win fame and honour by attaining their ends. Their equals are glad to have dealings with them; and those who miss their objects look to them for counsel, look to them for protection, rest on them their hopes of better things, and for all these reasons love them above all other men. But 29 those who know not what they do, choose amiss, fail in what they attempt and, besides incurring direct loss and punishment thereby, they earn contempt through their failures, make themselves ridiculous and live in dishonour and humiliation.

"And the same is true of communities. You find that whenever a state, in ignorance of its own power, goes to war with a stronger people, it is exterminated or loses its liberty."

"Socrates," answered Euthydemus, "you may 30 rest assured that I fully appreciate the importance of knowing oneself. But where should the process

---

[1] γε Stephanus : τε Sauppe with the MSS. and Stobaeus.

ἄρξασθαι ἐπισκοπεῖν ἑαυτόν, τοῦτο πρὸς σὲ
ἀποβλέπω εἴ μοι ἐθελήσαις ἂν ἐξηγήσασθαι.

31 Οὐκοῦν, ἔφη ὁ Σωκράτης, τὰ μὲν ἀγαθὰ καὶ τὰ
κακὰ ὁποῖά ἐστι, πάντως που γιγνώσκεις.

Νὴ Δί', ἔφη· εἰ γὰρ μηδὲ ταῦτα οἶδα, καὶ τῶν
ἀνδραπόδων φαυλότερος ἂν εἴην.

Ἴθι δή, ἔφη, καὶ ἐμοὶ ἐξήγησαι αὐτά.

Ἀλλ' οὐ χαλεπόν, ἔφη· πρῶτον μὲν γὰρ αὐτὸ
τὸ ὑγιαίνειν ἀγαθὸν εἶναι νομίζω, τὸ δὲ νοσεῖν
κακόν, ἔπειτα καὶ τὰ αἴτια ἑκατέρου αὐτῶν καὶ
ποτὰ καὶ βρωτὰ καὶ ἐπιτηδεύματα τὰ μὲν πρὸς
τὸ ὑγιαίνειν φέροντα ἀγαθά, τὰ δὲ πρὸς τὸ νοσεῖν
κακά.

32 Οὐκοῦν, ἔφη, καὶ τὸ ὑγιαίνειν καὶ τὸ νοσεῖν,
ὅταν μὲν ἀγαθοῦ τινος αἴτια γίγνηται, ἀγαθὰ ἂν
εἴη, ὅταν δὲ κακοῦ, κακά.

Πότε δ' ἄν, ἔφη, τὸ μὲν ὑγιαίνειν κακοῦ αἴτιον
γένοιτο, τὸ δὲ νοσεῖν ἀγαθοῦ ;

Ὅταν νὴ Δί', ἔφη, στρατείας τε αἰσχρᾶς καὶ
ναυτιλίας βλαβερᾶς καὶ ἄλλων πολλῶν τοιούτων
οἱ μὲν διὰ ῥώμην μετασχόντες ἀπόλωνται, οἱ δὲ
δι' ἀσθένειαν ἀπολειφθέντες σωθῶσιν.

Ἀληθῆ λέγεις· ἀλλ' ὁρᾷς, ἔφη, ὅτι καὶ τῶν
ὠφελίμων οἱ μὲν διὰ ῥώμην μετέχουσιν, οἱ δὲ
δι' ἀσθένειαν ἀπολείπονται.

Ταῦτα οὖν, ἔφη, ποτὲ μὲν ὠφελοῦντα, ποτὲ δὲ
βλάπτοντα μᾶλλον ἀγαθὰ ἢ κακά ἐστιν ;

Οὐδὲν μὰ Δία φαίνεται κατά γε τοῦτον τὸν
λόγον.

33 Ἀλλ' ἤ γέ τοι σοφία, ὦ Σώκρατες, ἀναμφι-
σβητήτως ἀγαθόν ἐστιν· ποῖον γὰρ ἄν τις πρᾶγμα
οὐ βέλτιον πράττοι σοφὸς ὢν ἢ ἀμαθής ;

of self-examination begin? I look to you for a statement, please."

"Well," said Socrates, "I may assume, I take it, 31 that you know what things are good and what are evil?"

"Of course, for if I don't know so much as that, I must be worse than a slave."

"Come then, state them for my benefit."

"Well, that's a simple matter. First health in itself is, I suppose, a good, sickness an evil. Next the various causes of these two conditions—meat, drink, habits—are good or evil according as they promote health or sickness."

"Then health and sickness too must be good when 32 their effect is good, and evil when it is evil."

"But when can health possibly be the cause of evil, or sickness of good?"

"Why, in many cases; for instance, a disastrous campaign or a fatal voyage: the able-bodied who go are lost, the weaklings who stay behind are saved."

"True; but you see, in the successful adventures too the able-bodied take part, the weaklings are left behind."

"Then since these bodily conditions sometimes lead to profit, and sometimes to loss, are they any more good than evil?"

"No, certainly not; at least so it appears from the argument. But wisdom now, Socrates,—that 33 at any rate is indisputably a good thing; for what is there that a wise man would not do better than a fool?"

Τί δαί; τὸν Δαίδαλον, ἔφη, οὐκ ἀκήκοας ὅτι ληφθεὶς ὑπὸ Μίνω διὰ τὴν σοφίαν ἠναγκάζετο ἐκείνῳ δουλεύειν καὶ τῆς τε πατρίδος ἅμα καὶ τῆς ἐλευθερίας ἐστερήθη καὶ ἐπιχειρῶν ἀποδιδράσκειν μετὰ τοῦ υἱοῦ τόν τε παῖδα ἀπώλεσε καὶ αὐτὸς οὐκ ἠδυνήθη σωθῆναι, ἀλλ' ἀπενεχθεὶς εἰς τοὺς βαρβάρους πάλιν ἐκεῖ ἐδούλευε;

Λέγεται νὴ Δί', ἔφη, ταῦτα.

Τὰ δὲ Παλαμήδους οὐκ ἀκήκοας πάθη; τοῦτον γὰρ δὴ πάντες ὑμνοῦσιν ὡς διὰ σοφίαν φθονηθεὶς ὑπὸ τοῦ Ὀδυσσέως ἀπόλλυται.

Λέγεται καὶ ταῦτα, ἔφη.

Ἄλλους δὲ πόσους οἴει διὰ σοφίαν ἀνασπάστους πρὸς βασιλέα γεγονέναι καὶ ἐκεῖ δουλεύειν;

34 Κινδυνεύει, ἔφη, ὦ Σώκρατες, ἀναμφιλογώτατον ἀγαθὸν εἶναι τὸ εὐδαιμονεῖν.

Εἴ γε μή τις αὐτό, ἔφη, ὦ Εὐθύδημε, ἐξ ἀμφιλόγων ἀγαθῶν συντιθείη.

Τί δ' ἄν, ἔφη, τῶν εὐδαιμονικῶν ἀμφίλογον εἴη;

Οὐδέν, ἔφη, εἴ γε μὴ προσθήσομεν αὐτῷ κάλλος ἢ ἰσχὺν ἢ πλοῦτον ἢ δόξαν ἢ καί τι ἄλλο τῶν τοιούτων.

Ἀλλὰ νὴ Δία προσθήσομεν, ἔφη· πῶς γὰρ ἂν τις ἄνευ τούτων εὐδαιμονοίη;

35 Νὴ Δί', ἔφη, προσθήσομεν ἄρα, ἐξ ὧν πολλὰ καὶ χαλεπὰ συμβαίνει τοῖς ἀνθρώποις· πολλοὶ μὲν γὰρ διὰ τὸ κάλλος ὑπὸ τῶν ἐπὶ τοῖς ὡραίοις παρακεκινηκότων διαφθείρονται, πολλοὶ δὲ διὰ τὴν ἰσχὺν μείζοσιν ἔργοις ἐπιχειροῦντες οὐ μικροῖς κακοῖς περιπίπτουσι, πολλοὶ δὲ διὰ τὸν πλοῦτον διαθρυπτόμενοί τε καὶ ἐπιβουλευόμενοι

"Indeed! have you not heard how Daedalus was seized by Minos because of his wisdom, and was forced to be his slave, and was robbed of his country and his liberty, and essaying to escape with his son, lost the boy and could not save himself, but was carried off to the barbarians and again lived as a slave there?"

"That is the story, of course."

"And have you not heard the story of Palamedes? Surely, for all the poets sing of him, how that he was envied for his wisdom and done to death by Odysseus."

"Another well-known tale!"

"And how many others, do you suppose, have been kidnapped on account of their wisdom, and haled off to the great King's court, and live in slavery there?"

"Happiness seems to be unquestionably a good, 34 Socrates."

"It would be so, Euthydemus, were it not made up of goods that are questionable."

"But what element in happiness can be called in question?"

"None, provided we don't include in it beauty or strength or wealth or glory or anything of the sort."

"But of course we shall do that. For how can anyone be happy without them?"

"Then of course we shall include the sources of 35 much trouble to mankind. For many are ruined by admirers whose heads are turned at the sight of a pretty face; many are led by their strength to attempt tasks too heavy for them, and meet with serious evils: many by their wealth are corrupted,

ἀπόλλυνται, πολλοὶ δὲ διὰ δόξαν καὶ πολιτικὴν
δύναμιν μεγάλα κακὰ πεπόνθασιν.

36 Ἀλλὰ μήν, ἔφη, εἴ γε μηδὲ τὸ εὐδαιμονεῖν
ἐπαινῶν ὀρθῶς λέγω, ὁμολογῶ μηδ' ὅ τι πρὸς
τοὺς θεοὺς εὔχεσθαι χρὴ εἰδέναι.

Ἀλλὰ ταῦτα μέν, ἔφη ὁ Σωκράτης, ἴσως
διὰ τὸ σφόδρα πιστεύειν εἰδέναι οὐδ' ἔσκεψαι·
ἐπεὶ δὲ πόλεως δημοκρατουμένης παρασκευάζῃ
προεστάναι, δῆλον ὅτι δημοκρατίαν γε οἶσθα τί
ἐστι.

Πάντως δήπου, ἔφη.

37 Δοκεῖ οὖν σοι δυνατὸν εἶναι δημοκρατίαν εἰδέναι
μὴ εἰδότα δῆμον ;

Μὰ Δί' οὐκ ἔμοιγε.

Καὶ δῆμον ἄρ' οἶσθα τί ἐστιν ;

Οἶμαι ἔγωγε.

Καὶ τί νομίζεις δῆμον εἶναι ;

Τοὺς πένητας τῶν πολιτῶν ἔγωγε.

Καὶ τοὺς πένητας ἄρα οἶσθα ;

Πῶς γὰρ οὔ ;

Ἆρ' οὖν καὶ τοὺς πλουσίους οἶσθα ;

Οὐδέν γε ἧττον ἢ καὶ τοὺς πένητας.

Ποίους δὲ πένητας καὶ ποίους πλουσίους
καλεῖς ;

Τοὺς μέν, οἶμαι, μὴ ἱκανὰ ἔχοντας εἰς ἃ δεῖ
τελεῖν πένητας, τοὺς δὲ πλείω τῶν ἱκανῶν
πλουσίους.

38 Καταμεμάθηκας οὖν, ὅτι ἐνίοις μὲν πάνυ ὀλίγα
ἔχουσιν οὐ μόνον ἀρκεῖ ταῦτα, ἀλλὰ καὶ περιποι-
οῦνται ἀπ' αὐτῶν, ἐνίοις δὲ πάνυ πολλὰ οὐχ
ἱκανά ἐστι ;

Καὶ νὴ Δί', ἔφη ὁ Εὐθύδημος, ὀρθῶς γάρ με

and fall victims to conspiracies; many through glory
and political power have suffered great evils."

" Well now, if I am at fault in praising even 36
happiness, I confess I know not what one should ask
for in one's prayers."

" But perhaps you never even thought about these
things, because you felt so confident that you knew
them. However, as the state you are preparing
yourself to direct is governed by the people, no
doubt you know what popular government is?"

" I think so, certainly."

" Then do you suppose it possible to know popular 37
government without knowing the people?"

" Indeed I don't."

" And do you know, then, what the people
consists of?"

" I think so."

" Of what do you suppose it to consist?"

"The poorer classes, I presume."

" You know the poor, then?"

" Of course I do."

" And you know the rich too?"

" Yes, just as well as the poor."

" What kind of men do you call poor and rich
respectively?"

" The poor, I imagine, are those who have not
enough to pay for what they want; the rich those
who have more than enough."

" Have you observed, then, that some who have 38
very little not only find it enough, but even manage
to save out of it, whereas others cannot live within
their means, however large?"

" Yes, certainly—thanks for reminding me—I

XENOPHON

ἀναμιμνήσκεις, οἶδα[1] καὶ τυράννους τινάς, οἳ
δι' ἔνδειαν ὥσπερ οἱ ἀπορώτατοι ἀναγκάζονται
ἀδικεῖν.

39 Οὐκοῦν, ἔφη ὁ Σωκράτης, εἴ γε ταῦτα οὕτως
ἔχει, τοὺς μὲν τυράννους εἰς τὸν δῆμον θήσομεν,
τοὺς δὲ ὀλίγα κεκτημένους, ἐὰν οἰκονομικοὶ ὦσιν,
εἰς τοὺς πλουσίους.

Καὶ ὁ Εὐθύδημος ἔφη· Ἀναγκάζει με καὶ
ταῦτα ὁμολογεῖν δῆλον ὅτι ἡ ἐμὴ φαυλότης·
καὶ φροντίζω, μὴ κράτιστον ᾖ μοι σιγᾶν· κινδυνεύω γὰρ ἁπλῶς οὐδὲν εἰδέναι. καὶ πάνυ
ἀθύμως ἔχων ἀπῆλθε καὶ καταφρονήσας ἑαυτοῦ
καὶ νομίσας τῷ ὄντι ἀνδράποδον εἶναι.

40 Πολλοὶ μὲν οὖν τῶν οὕτω διατεθέντων ὑπὸ
Σωκράτους οὐκέτι αὐτῷ προσῄεσαν, οὓς καὶ
βλακοτέρους ἐνόμιζεν· ὁ δὲ Εὐθύδημος ὑπέλαβεν
οὐκ ἂν ἄλλως ἀνὴρ ἀξιόλογος γενέσθαι, εἰ μὴ ὅτι
μάλιστα Σωκράτει συνείη· καὶ οὐκ ἀπελείπετο
ἔτι αὐτοῦ, εἰ μή τι ἀναγκαῖον εἴη· ἔνια δὲ καὶ
ἐμιμεῖτο ὧν ἐκεῖνος ἐπετήδευεν. ὁ δ' ὡς ἔγνω
αὐτὸν οὕτως ἔχοντα, ἥκιστα μὲν διετάραττεν,
ἁπλούστατα δὲ καὶ σαφέστατα ἐξηγεῖτο ἅ τε
ἐνόμιζεν εἰδέναι δεῖν καὶ ἐπιτηδεύειν κράτιστα
εἶναι.

III. Τὸ μὲν οὖν λεκτικοὺς καὶ πρακτικοὺς καὶ
μηχανικοὺς γίγνεσθαι τοὺς συνόντας οὐκ ἔσπευδεν,
ἀλλὰ πρότερον τούτων ᾤετο χρῆναι σωφροσύνην
αὐτοῖς ἐγγενέσθαι. τοὺς γὰρ ἄνευ τοῦ σωφρονεῖν
ταῦτα δυναμένους ἀδικωτέρους τε καὶ δυνατω-
τέρους κακουργεῖν ἐνόμιζεν εἶναι.

2 Πρῶτον μὲν δὴ περὶ θεοὺς ἐπειρᾶτο σώφρονας
ποιεῖν τοὺς συνόντας. ἄλλοι μὲν οὖν αὐτῷ πρὸς

know, in fact, of some despots even who are driven to crime by poverty, just like paupers."

"Therefore, if that is so, we will include despots 39 in the people, and men of small means, if they are thrifty, in the rich."

"I am forced to agree once more," cried Euthydemus, "evidently by my stupidity. I am inclined to think I had better hold my tongue, or I shall know nothing at all presently." And so he went away very dejected, disgusted with himself and convinced that he was indeed a slave.

Now many of those who were brought to this pass 40 by Socrates, never went near him again and were regarded by him as mere blockheads. But Euthydemus guessed that he would never be of much account unless he spent as much time as possible with Socrates. Henceforward, unless obliged to absent himself, he never left him, and even began to adopt some of his practices. Socrates, for his part, seeing how it was with him, avoided worrying him, and began to expound very plainly and clearly the knowledge that he thought most needful and the practices that he held to be most excellent.

III. Skill in speaking and efficiency in affairs, therefore, and ingenuity, were not the qualities that he was eager to foster in his companions. He held that they needed first to acquire prudence. For he believed that those faculties, unless accompanied by prudence, increased in their possessors injustice and power for mischief.

In the first place, then, he tried to make his com- 2 panions prudent towards the gods. Accordingly he

---

[1] οἶδα Stobaeus : οἶδα γὰρ Sauppe with MSS.

ἄλλους οὕτως ὁμιλοῦντι παραγενόμενοι διηγοῦντο·
ἐγὼ δέ, ὅτε πρὸς Εὐθύδημον τοιάδε διελέγετο,
παρεγενόμην.

3 Εἰπέ μοι, ἔφη, ὦ Εὐθύδημε, ἤδη ποτέ σοι
ἐπῆλθεν ἐνθυμηθῆναι, ὡς ἐπιμελῶς οἱ θεοὶ ὧν
οἱ ἄνθρωποι δέονται κατεσκευάκασι;

Καὶ ὅς, Μὰ τὸν Δί', ἔφη, οὐκ ἔμοιγε.

Ἀλλ' οἶσθά γ', ἔφη, ὅτι πρῶτον μὲν φωτὸς
δεόμεθα, ὃ ἡμῖν οἱ θεοὶ παρέχουσι;

Νὴ Δί', ἔφη, ὅ γ' εἰ μὴ εἴχομεν, ὅμοιοι τοῖς
τυφλοῖς ἂν ἦμεν ἕνεκά γε τῶν ἡμετέρων
ὀφθαλμῶν.

Ἀλλὰ μὴν καὶ ἀναπαύσεώς γε δεομένοις ἡμῖν
νύκτα παρέχουσι κάλλιστον ἀναπαυτήριον.

Πάνυ γ', ἔφη, καὶ τοῦτο χάριτος ἄξιον.

4 Οὐκοῦν καὶ ἐπειδὴ ὁ μὲν ἥλιος φωτεινὸς ὢν
τάς τε ὥρας τῆς ἡμέρας ἡμῖν καὶ τἆλλα πάντα
σαφηνίζει, ἡ δὲ νὺξ διὰ τὸ σκοτεινὴ εἶναι
ἀσαφεστέρα ἐστίν, ἄστρα ἐν τῇ νυκτὶ ἀνέφηναν,
ἃ ἡμῖν τὰς ὥρας τῆς νυκτὸς ἐμφανίζει, καὶ διὰ
τοῦτο πολλὰ ὧν δεόμεθα πράττομεν;

Ἔστι ταῦτα, ἔφη.

Ἀλλὰ μὴν ἥ γε σελήνη οὐ μόνον τῆς νυκτός,
ἀλλὰ καὶ τοῦ μηνὸς τὰ μέρη φανερὰ ἡμῖν ποιεῖ.

Πάνυ μὲν οὖν, ἔφη.

5 Τὸ δ', ἐπεὶ τροφῆς δεόμεθα, ταύτην ἡμῖν ἐκ τῆς
γῆς ἀναδιδόναι καὶ ὥρας ἁρμοττούσας πρὸς τοῦτο
παρέχειν, αἳ ἡμῖν οὐ μόνον ὧν δεόμεθα πολλὰ καὶ
παντοῖα παρασκευάζουσιν, ἀλλὰ καὶ οἷς εὐφραι-
νόμεθα;

Πάνυ, ἔφη, καὶ ταῦτα φιλάνθρωπα.

Τὸ δὲ καὶ ὕδωρ ἡμῖν παρέχειν οὕτω πολλοῦ

discoursed on this topic at various times, as those who were present used to relate. The following conversation between him and Euthydemus I heard myself.

"Tell me, Euthydemus," he began, "has it ever 3 occurred to you to reflect on the care the gods have taken to furnish man with what he needs?"

"No, indeed it has not," replied Euthydemus.

"Well, no doubt you know that our first and foremost need is light, which is supplied to us by the gods?"

"Of course; since without light our eyes would be as useless as if we were blind."

"And again, we need rest; and therefore the gods grant us the welcome respite of night."

"Yes, for that too we owe them thanks."

"And since the night by reason of her darkness is 4 dim, whereas the sun by his brightness illuminates the hours of the day and all things else, have they not made stars to shine in the night, that mark the watches of night for us, and do we not thereby satisfy many of our needs?"

"That is so."

"Moreover, the moon reveals to us not only the divisions of the night, but of the month too."

"Certainly."

"Now, seeing that we need food, think how they 5 make the earth to yield it, and provide to that end appropriate seasons which furnish in abundance the diverse things that minister not only to our wants but to our enjoyment."

"Truly these things too show loving-kindness."

"Think again of their precious gift of water, that 6

ἄξιον, ὥστε συμφύειν τε καὶ συναύξειν τῇ γῇ καὶ
ταῖς ὥραις πάντα τὰ χρήσιμα ἡμῖν, συντρέφειν
δὲ καὶ αὐτοὺς ἡμᾶς, καὶ μιγνύμενον πᾶσι τοῖς
τρέφουσιν ἡμᾶς εὐκατεργαστότερά τε καὶ ὠφελιμώτερα καὶ ἡδίω ποιεῖν αὐτὰ καὶ ἐπειδὴ πλείστου
δεόμεθα τούτου, ἀφθονέστατον αὐτὸ παρέχειν
ἡμῖν ;

Καὶ τοῦτο, ἔφη, προνοητικόν.

7   Τὸ δὲ καὶ τὸ πῦρ πορίσαι ἡμῖν ἐπίκουρον μὲν
ψύχους, ἐπίκουρον δὲ σκότους, συνεργὸν δὲ πρὸς
πᾶσαν τέχνην καὶ πάντα, ὅσα ὠφελείας ἕνεκα
ἄνθρωποι κατασκευάζονται ; ὡς γὰρ συνελόντι
εἰπεῖν, οὐδὲν ἀξιόλογον ἄνευ πυρὸς ἄνθρωποι τῶν
πρὸς τὸν βίον χρησίμων κατασκευάζονται.

Ὑπερβάλλει, ἔφη, καὶ τοῦτο φιλανθρωπίᾳ.

8   Τὸ δὲ τὸν ἥλιον, ἐπειδὰν ἐν χειμῶνι τράπηται,
προσιέναι τὰ μὲν ἁδρύνοντα, τὰ δὲ ξηραίνοντα,
ὧν καιρὸς διελήλυθε, καὶ ταῦτα διαπραξάμενον
μηκέτι ἐγγυτέρω προσιέναι, ἀλλ᾽ ἀποτρέπεσθαι
φυλαττόμενον, μή τι ἡμᾶς μᾶλλον τοῦ δέοντος
θερμαίνων βλάψῃ, καὶ ὅταν αὖ πάλιν ἀπιὼν
γένηται, ἔνθα καὶ ἡμῖν δῆλόν ἐστιν ὅτι εἰ προσω-
τέρω ἄπεισιν, ἀποπαγησόμεθα ὑπὸ τοῦ ψύχους,
πάλιν αὖ τρέπεσθαι καὶ προσχωρεῖν καὶ ἐνταῦθα
τοῦ οὐρανοῦ ἀναστρέφεσθαι, ἔνθα μάλιστ᾽ ἂν
ἡμᾶς ὠφελοίη ;

Νὴ τὸν Δί᾽, ἔφη, καὶ ταῦτα παντάπασιν ἔοικεν
ἀνθρώπων ἕνεκα γιγνομένοις.

9   Τὸ δ᾽, ἐπειδὴ καὶ τοῦτο φανερόν, ὅτι οὐκ ἂν
ὑπενέγκοιμεν οὔτε τὸ καῦμα οὔτε τὸ ψῦχος, εἰ
ἐξαπίνης γίγνοιτο, οὕτω μὲν κατὰ μικρὸν προσιέναι τὸν ἥλιον, οὕτω δὲ κατὰ μικρὸν ἀπιέναι, ὥστε

aids the earth and the seasons to give birth and
increase to all things useful to us and itself helps
to nourish our bodies, and mingling with all that
sustains us, makes it more digestible, more whole-
some, and more palatable : and how, because we need
so much of it, they supply it without stint."

"That too shows design at work."

"Think again of the blessing of fire, our defence 7
against cold and against darkness, our helpmate in
every art and all that man contrives for his service.
In fact, to put it shortly, nothing of any account that
is useful to the life of man is contrived without the
aid of fire."

"This too is a signal token of loving-kindness."

"Think again how the sun, when past the winter 8
solstice, approaches, ripening some things and
withering others, whose time is over ; and having
accomplished this, approaches no nearer, but turns
away, careful not to harm us by excess of heat ; and
when once again in his retreat he reaches the point
where it is clear to ourselves, that if he goes further
away, we shall be frozen with the cold, back he turns
once more and draws near and revolves in that region
of the heavens where he can best serve us."

"Yes, verily, these things do seem to be done for
the sake of mankind."

"And again, since it is evident that we could not 9
endure the heat or the cold if it came suddenly,[1]
the sun's approach and retreat are so gradual that

---

[1] *Cyropaedia*, VI. ii. 29.

λανθάνειν ἡμᾶς εἰς ἑκάτερα τὰ ἰσχυρότατα καθι-
σταμένους ;

Ἐγὼ μέν, ἔφη ὁ Εὐθύδημος, ἤδη τοῦτο σκοπῶ,
εἰ ἄρα τί ἐστι τοῖς θεοῖς ἔργον ἢ ἀνθρώπους
θεραπεύειν· ἐκεῖνο δὲ μόνον ἐμποδίζει με, ὅτι καὶ
τἆλλα ζῷα τούτων μετέχει.

10 Οὐ γὰρ καὶ τοῦτ', ἔφη ὁ Σωκράτης, φανερόν,
ὅτι καὶ ταῦτα ἀνθρώπων ἕνεκα γίγνεταί τε καὶ
ἀνατρέφεται ; τί γὰρ ἄλλο ζῷον αἰγῶν τε καὶ
οἰῶν καὶ βοῶν καὶ ἵππων καὶ ὄνων καὶ τῶν ἄλλων
ζῴων τοσαῦτα ἀγαθὰ ἀπολαύει ὅσα ἄνθρωποι ;
ἐμοὶ μὲν γὰρ δοκεῖ πλείω ἢ τῶν φυτῶν· τρέφονται γοῦν καὶ χρηματίζονται οὐδὲν ἧττον ἀπὸ τούτων ἢ ἀπ' ἐκείνων· πολὺ δὲ γένος ἀνθρώπων τοῖς
μὲν ἐκ τῆς γῆς φυομένοις εἰς τροφὴν οὐ χρῆται,
ἀπὸ δὲ βοσκημάτων γάλακτι καὶ τυρῷ καὶ κρέασι
τρεφόμενοι ζῶσι· πάντες δὲ τιθασεύοντες καὶ
δαμάζοντες τὰ χρήσιμα τῶν ζῴων εἴς τε πόλεμον
καὶ εἰς ἄλλα πολλὰ συνεργοῖς χρῶνται.

Ὁμογνωμονῶ σοι καὶ τοῦτ', ἔφη· ὁρῶ γὰρ αὐτῶν
καὶ τὰ πολὺ ἰσχυρότερα ἡμῶν οὕτως ὑποχείρια
γιγνόμενα τοῖς ἀνθρώποις, ὥστε χρῆσθαι αὐτοῖς
ὅ τι ἂν βούλωνται.

11 Τὸ δ', ἐπειδὴ πολλὰ μὲν καλὰ καὶ ὠφέλιμα,
διαφέροντα δὲ ἀλλήλων ἐστί προσθεῖναι τοῖς
ἀνθρώποις αἰσθήσεις ἁρμοττούσας πρὸς ἕκαστα,
δι' ὧν ἀπολαύομεν πάντων τῶν ἀγαθῶν· τὸ δὲ καὶ
λογισμὸν ἡμῖν ἐμφῦσαι, ᾧ περὶ ὧν αἰσθανόμεθα
λογιζόμενοί τε καὶ μνημονεύοντες καταμανθάνο-
μεν, ὅπῃ ἕκαστα συμφέρει, καὶ πολλὰ μηχανώ-
μεθα, δι' ὧν τῶν τε ἀγαθῶν ἀπολαύομεν καὶ τὰ
12 κακὰ ἀλεξόμεθα· τὸ δὲ καὶ ἑρμηνείαν δοῦναι, δι'

we arrive at the one or the other extreme imperceptibly."

"For myself," exclaimed Euthydemus, "I begin to doubt whether after all the gods are occupied in any other work than the service of man. The one difficulty I feel is that the lower animals also enjoy these blessings."

"Yes," replied Socrates, " and is it not evident 10 that they too receive life and food for the sake of man? For what creature reaps so many benefits as man from goats and sheep and horses and oxen and asses and the other animals? He owes more to them, in my opinion, than to the fruits of the earth. At the least they are not less valuable to him for food and commerce ; in fact a large portion of mankind does not use the products of the earth for food, but lives on the milk and cheese and flesh they get from live stock. Moreover, all men tame and domesticate the useful kinds of animals, and make them their fellow-workers in war and many other undertakings."

"There too I agree with you, seeing that animals far stronger than man become so entirely subject to him that he puts them to any use he chooses."

"Think again of the multitude of things beautiful 11 and useful and their infinite variety, and how the gods have endowed man with senses adapted for the perception of every kind, so that there is nothing good that we cannot enjoy ; and again, how they have implanted in us the faculty of reasoning, whereby we are able to reason about the objects of our perceptions and to commit them to memory, and so come to know what advantage every kind can yield, and devise many means of enjoying the good and driving away the bad ; and think of the power 12

XENOPHON

ἧς πάντων τῶν ἀγαθῶν μεταδίδομέν τε ἀλλήλοις διδάσκοντες καὶ κοινωνοῦμεν καὶ νόμους τιθέμεθα καὶ πολιτευόμεθα ;

Παντάπασιν ἐοίκασιν, ὦ Σώκρατες, οἱ θεοὶ πολλὴν τῶν ἀνθρώπων ἐπιμέλειαν ποιεῖσθαι.

Τὸ δὲ καὶ εἰ ἀδυνατοῦμεν τὰ συμφέροντα προνοεῖσθαι ὑπὲρ τῶν μελλόντων, ἡμῖν αὐτοὺς συνεργεῖν διὰ μαντικῆς τοῖς πυνθανομένοις φράζοντας τὰ ἀποβησόμενα καὶ διδάσκοντας, ᾗ ἂν ἄριστα γίγνοιτο ;

Σοὶ δ᾽, ἔφη, ὦ Σώκρατες, ἐοίκασιν ἔτι φιλικώτερον ἢ τοῖς ἄλλοις χρῆσθαι, εἴ γε μηδὲ ἐπερωτώμενοι ὑπὸ σοῦ προσημαίνουσί σοι ἅ τε χρὴ ποιεῖν καὶ ἃ μή.

13 Ὅτι δὲ ἀληθῆ λέγω, καὶ σὺ γνώσῃ, ἂν μὴ ἀναμένῃς, ἕως ἂν τὰς μορφὰς τῶν θεῶν ἴδῃς, ἀλλ᾽ ἐξαρκῇ σοι τὰ ἔργα αὐτῶν ὁρῶντι σέβεσθαι καὶ τιμᾶν τοὺς θεούς. ἐννόει δέ, ὅτι καὶ αὐτοὶ οἱ θεοὶ οὕτως ὑποδεικνύουσιν· οἵ τε γὰρ ἄλλοι ἡμῖν τἀγαθὰ διδόντες οὐδὲν τούτων εἰς τοὐμφανὲς ἰόντες διδόασι καὶ ὁ τὸν ὅλον κόσμον συντάττων τε καὶ συνέχων, ἐν ᾧ πάντα καλὰ καὶ ἀγαθά ἐστι, καὶ ἀεὶ μὲν χρωμένοις ἀτριβῆ τε καὶ ὑγιᾶ καὶ ἀγήρατα παρέχων, θᾶττον δὲ νοήματος ὑπηρετοῦντα ἀναμαρτήτως, οὗτος τὰ μέγιστα μὲν πράττων ὁρᾶται, τάδε δὲ οἰκονομῶν ἀόρατος ἡμῖν 14 ἐστιν. ἐννόει δ᾽, ὅτι καὶ ὁ πᾶσι φανερὸς δοκῶν εἶναι ἥλιος οὐκ ἐπιτρέπει τοῖς ἀνθρώποις ἑαυτὸν ἀκριβῶς ὁρᾶν, ἀλλ᾽ ἐάν τις αὐτὸν ἀναιδῶς ἐγχειρῇ θεᾶσθαι, τὴν ὄψιν ἀφαιρεῖται. καὶ τοὺς ὑπηρέτας δὲ τῶν θεῶν εὑρήσεις ἀφανεῖς ὄντας· κεραυνός τε γὰρ ὅτι μὲν ἄνωθεν ἀφίεται δῆλον

of expression, which enables us to impart to one
another all good things by teaching and to take our
share of them, to enact laws and to administer states."

"Truly, Socrates, it does appear that the gods
devote much care to man."

"Yet again, in so far as we are powerless of
ourselves to foresee what is expedient for the future,[1]
the gods lend us their aid, revealing the issues by
divination to inquirers, and teaching them how to
obtain the best results."

"With you, Socrates, they seem to deal even more
friendly than with other men, if it is true that, even
unasked, they warn you by signs what to do and
what not to do."

"Yes, and you will realise the truth of what I say 13
if, instead of waiting for the gods to appear to you
in bodily presence, you are content to praise and
worship them because you see their works. Mark
that the gods themselves give the reason for doing
so ; for when they bestow on us their good gifts, not
one of them ever appears before us gift in hand ; and
especially he who co-ordinates and holds together the
universe, wherein all things are fair and good, and
presents them ever unimpaired and sound and ageless
for our use,[2] and quicker than thought to serve us
unerringly, is manifest in his supreme works, and yet
is unseen by us in the ordering of them. Mark that 14
even the sun, who seems to reveal himself to all,
permits not man to behold him closely, but if any
attempts to gaze recklessly upon him, blinds their
eyes. And the gods' ministers too you will find to
be invisible. That the thunderbolt is hurled from

---

[1] *Cyropaedia*, I. vi. 46.
[2] *Ibid.*, VIII. vii. 22.

καὶ ὅτι οἷς ἂν ἐντύχῃ πάντων κρατεῖ· ὁρᾶται δ'
οὔτ' ἐπιὼν οὔτε κατασκήψας οὔτε ἀπιών· καὶ
ἄνεμοι αὐτοὶ μὲν οὐχ ὁρῶνται, ἃ δὲ ποιοῦσι
φανερὰ ἡμῖν ἐστι καὶ προσιόντων αὐτῶν αἰσθανόμεθα. ἀλλὰ μὴν καὶ ἀνθρώπου γε ψυχή, ἣ εἴπερ
τι καὶ ἄλλο τῶν ἀνθρωπίνων τοῦ θείου μετέχει,
ὅτι μὲν βασιλεύει ἐν ἡμῖν φανερόν, ὁρᾶται δὲ οὐδ'
αὐτή.

Ἃ χρὴ κατανοοῦντα μὴ καταφρονεῖν τῶν ἀορά-
των, ἀλλ' ἐκ τῶν γιγνομένων τὴν δύναμιν αὐτῶν
καταμανθάνοντα τιμᾶν τὸ δαιμόνιον.

15 Ἐγὼ μέν, ὦ Σώκρατες, ἔφη ὁ Εὐθύδημος, ὅτι
μὲν οὐδὲ μικρὸν ἀμελήσω τοῦ δαιμονίου, σαφῶς
οἶδα· ἐκεῖνο δὲ ἀθυμῶ, ὅτι μοι δοκεῖ τὰς τῶν θεῶν
εὐεργεσίας οὐδ' ἂν εἷς ποτε ἀνθρώπων ἀξίαις
χάρισιν ἀμείβεσθαι.

16 Ἀλλὰ μὴ τοῦτο ἀθύμει, ἔφη, ὦ Εὐθύδημε· ὁρᾶς
γάρ, ὅτι ὁ ἐν Δελφοῖς θεός, ὅταν τις αὐτὸν
ἐπερωτᾷ, πῶς ἂν τοῖς θεοῖς χαρίζοιτο, ἀποκρίνεται
Νόμῳ πόλεως. νόμος δὲ δήπου πανταχοῦ ἐστι
κατὰ δύναμιν ἱεροῖς θεοὺς ἀρέσκεσθαι.

Πῶς οὖν ἄν τις κάλλιον καὶ εὐσεβέστερον τιμῴη
17 θεοὺς ἢ ὡς αὐτοὶ κελεύουσιν, οὕτω ποιῶν; ἀλλὰ
χρὴ τῆς μὲν δυνάμεως μηδὲν ὑφίεσθαι· ὅταν γάρ
τις τοῦτο ποιῇ, φανερὸς δήπου ἐστὶ τότε οὐ τιμῶν
θεούς. χρὴ οὖν μηδὲν ἐλλείποντα κατὰ δύναμιν
τιμᾶν τοὺς θεοὺς θαρρεῖν τε καὶ ἐλπίζειν τὰ
μέγιστα ἀγαθά· οὐ γὰρ παρ' ἄλλων γ' ἄν τις
μείζω ἐλπίζων σωφρονοίη ἢ παρὰ τῶν τὰ μέγιστα
ὠφελεῖν δυναμένων οὐδ' ἂν ἄλλως μᾶλλον ἢ εἰ

heaven, and that he overwhelms all on whom he falls, is evident, but he is seen neither coming nor striking nor going. And the winds are themselves invisible, yet their deeds are manifest to us, and we perceive their approach. Moreover, the soul of man, which more than all else that is human partakes of the divine, reigns manifestly within us, and yet is itself unseen.

"For these reasons it behoves us not to despise the things that are unseen, but, realising their power in their manifestations, to honour the godhead."

"Socrates," replied Euthydemus, "that I will in 15 no wise be heedless of the godhead I know of a surety. But my heart fails me when I think that no man can ever render due thanks to the gods for their benefits."

"Nay, be not down-hearted, Euthydemus; for you 16 know that to the inquiry, 'How am I to please the gods?' the Delphic god replies, 'Follow the custom of the state'; and everywhere, I suppose, it is the custom that men propitiate the gods with sacrifices according to their power. How then can a man honour the gods more excellently and more devoutly than by doing as they themselves ordain? Only he 17 must fall no whit short of his power. For when he does that, it is surely plain that he is not then honouring the gods. Therefore it is by coming no whit short of his power in honouring the gods that he is to look with confidence for the greatest blessings.[1] For there are none from whom a man of prudence would hope for greater things than those who can confer the greatest benefits, nor can he show his prudence more clearly than by pleasing them.

[1] *Cyropaedia*, I. vi. 4.

τούτοις ἀρέσκοι. ἀρέσκοι δὲ πῶς ἂν μᾶλλον ἢ εἰ
ὡς μάλιστα πείθοιτο αὐτοῖς ;

8 Τοιαῦτα μὲν δὴ λέγων τε καὶ αὐτὸς ποιῶν
εὐσεβεστέρους τε καὶ σωφρονεστέρους τοὺς συνόντας παρεσκεύαζεν.

IV. Ἀλλὰ μὴν καὶ περὶ τοῦ δικαίου γε οὐκ
ἀπεκρύπτετο ἣν εἶχε γνώμην, ἀλλὰ καὶ ἔργῳ
ἀπεδείκνυτο, ἰδίᾳ τε πᾶσι νομίμως τε καὶ ὠφελί-
μως χρώμενος καὶ κοινῇ ἄρχουσί τε ἃ οἱ νόμοι
προστάττοιεν πειθόμενος καὶ κατὰ πόλιν καὶ ἐν
ταῖς στρατείαις οὕτως, ὥστε διάδηλος εἶναι παρὰ
2 τοὺς ἄλλους εὐτακτῶν, καὶ ὅτε ἐν ταῖς ἐκκλησίαις
ἐπιστάτης γενόμενος οὐκ ἐπέτρεψε τῷ δήμῳ παρὰ
τοὺς νόμους ψηφίσασθαι, ἀλλὰ σὺν τοῖς νόμοις
ἠναντιώθη τοιαύτῃ ὁρμῇ τοῦ δήμου, ἣν οὐκ ἂν
3 οἶμαι ἄλλον οὐδένα ἄνθρωπον ὑπομεῖναι· καὶ ὅτε
οἱ τριάκοντα προσέταττον αὐτῷ παρὰ τοὺς νόμους
τι, οὐκ ἐπείθετο· τοῖς τε γὰρ νέοις ἀπαγορευόν-
των αὐτῶν μὴ διαλέγεσθαι καὶ προσταξάντων
ἐκείνῳ τε καὶ ἄλλοις τισὶ τῶν πολιτῶν ἀγαγεῖν
τινα ἐπὶ θανάτῳ, μόνος οὐκ ἐπείσθη διὰ τὸ παρὰ
4 τοὺς νόμους αὐτῷ προστάττεσθαι· καὶ ὅτε τὴν
ὑπὸ Μελήτου γραφὴν ἔφευγε, τῶν ἄλλων εἰωθότων ἐν τοῖς δικαστηρίοις πρὸς χάριν τε τοῖς
δικασταῖς διαλέγεσθαι καὶ κολακεύειν καὶ δεῖσθαι
παρὰ τοὺς νόμους καὶ διὰ τὰ τοιαῦτα πολλῶν
πολλάκις ὑπὸ τῶν δικαστῶν ἀφιεμένων, ἐκεῖνος
οὐδὲν ἠθέλησε τῶν εἰωθότων ἐν τῷ δικαστηρίῳ
παρὰ τοὺς νόμους ποιῆσαι, ἀλλὰ ῥᾳδίως ἂν ἀφε-
θεὶς ὑπὸ τῶν δικαστῶν, εἰ καὶ μετρίως τι τούτων
ἐποίησε, προείλετο μᾶλλον τοῖς νόμοις ἐμμένων
ἀποθανεῖν ἢ παρανομῶν ζῆν.

And how can he please them better than by obeying them strictly?"

Thus by precept and by example alike he strove 18 to increase in his companions Piety and Prudence.

IV. Again, concerning Justice he did not hide his opinion, but proclaimed it by his actions. All his private conduct was lawful and helpful: to public authority he rendered such scrupulous obedience in all that the laws required, both in civil life and in military service, that he was a pattern of good discipline to all. When chairman in the Assemblies 2 he would not permit the people to record an illegal vote, but, upholding the laws, resisted a popular impulse that might even have overborne any but himself. And when the Thirty laid a command on 3 him that was illegal, he refused to obey. Thus he disregarded their repeated injunction not to talk with young men; and when they commanded him and certain other citizens to arrest a man on a capital charge, he alone refused, because the command laid on him was illegal.[1] Again, when he was tried on 4 the charge brought by Meletus, whereas it is the custom of defendants to curry favour with the jury and to indulge in flattery and illegal appeals, and many by such means have been known to gain a verdict of acquittal, he rejected utterly the familiar chicanery of the courts; and though he might easily have gained a favourable verdict by even a moderate indulgence in such stratagems, he chose to die through his loyalty to the laws rather than to live through violating them.

---

[1] Alluding to the famous case of Leon.

5 Καὶ ἔλεγε δὲ οὕτως καὶ πρὸς ἄλλους μὲν πολλάκις,[1] οἶδα δέ ποτε αὐτὸν καὶ πρὸς Ἱππίαν τὸν
Ἠλεῖον περὶ τοῦ δικαίου τοιάδε διαλεχθέντα.
διὰ χρόνου γὰρ ἀφικόμενος ὁ Ἱππίας Ἀθήναζε
παρεγένετο τῷ Σωκράτει λέγοντι πρός τινας, ὡς
θαυμαστὸν εἴη τὸ εἰ μέν τις βούλοιτο σκυτέα
διδάξασθαί τινα ἢ τέκτονα ἢ χαλκέα ἢ ἱππέα, μὴ
ἀπορεῖν, ὅποι ἂν πέμψας τούτου τύχοι· [φασὶ δέ
τινες, καὶ ἵππον καὶ βοῦν τῷ βουλομένῳ δικαίους
ποιήσασθαι πάντα μεστὰ εἶναι τῶν διδαξόντων·]
ἐὰν δέ τις βούληται ἢ αὐτὸς μαθεῖν τὸ δίκαιον ἢ
υἱὸν ἢ οἰκέτην διδάξασθαι, μὴ εἰδέναι ὅποι ἂν
ἐλθὼν τύχοι τούτου.

6 Καὶ ὁ μὲν Ἱππίας ἀκούσας ταῦτα ὥσπερ ἐπισκώπτων αὐτόν, Ἔτι γὰρ σύ, ἔφη, ὦ Σώκρατες,
ἐκεῖνα τὰ αὐτὰ λέγεις, ἃ ἐγὼ πάλαι ποτέ σου
ἤκουσα ;

Καὶ ὁ Σωκράτης, Ὃ δέ γε τούτου δεινότερον,
ἔφη, ὦ Ἱππία, οὐ μόνον ἀεὶ τὰ αὐτὰ λέγω, ἀλλὰ
καὶ περὶ τῶν αὐτῶν· σὺ δ᾽ ἴσως διὰ τὸ πολυ-
μαθὴς εἶναι περὶ τῶν αὐτῶν οὐδέποτε τὰ αὐτὰ
λέγεις.

Ἀμέλει, ἔφη, πειρῶμαι καινόν τι λέγειν ἀεί.

7 Πότερον, ἔφη, καὶ περὶ ὧν ἐπίστασαι, οἷον
περὶ γραμμάτων ἐάν τις ἔρηταί σε, πόσα καὶ ποῖα
Σωκράτους ἐστίν, ἄλλα μὲν πρότερον, ἄλλα δὲ νῦν
πειρᾷ λέγειν ; ἢ περὶ ἀριθμῶν τοῖς ἐρωτῶσιν, εἰ
τὰ δὶς πέντε δέκα ἐστίν, οὐ τὰ αὐτὰ νῦν ἃ καὶ
πρότερον ἀποκρίνῃ ;

Περὶ μὲν τούτων, ἔφη, ὦ Σώκρατες, ὥσπερ
σὺ καὶ ἐγὼ ἀεὶ τὰ αὐτὰ λέγω· περὶ μέντοι τοῦ

Such views frequently found expression in his conversations with different persons; I recollect the substance of one that he had with Hippias of Elis concerning Justice. Hippias, who had not been in Athens for a considerable time, found Socrates talking: he was saying that if you want to have a man taught cobbling or building or smithing or riding, you know where to send him to learn the craft: some indeed declare that if you want to train up a horse or an ox in the way he should go, teachers abound. And yet, strangely enough, if you want to learn Justice yourself, or to have your son or servant taught it, you know not where to go for a teacher.

When Hippias heard this, "How now?" he cried in a tone of raillery, "still the same old sentiments, Socrates, that I heard from you so long ago?"

"Yes, Hippias," he replied, "always the same, and—what is more astonishing—on the same topics too! You are so learned that I daresay you never say the same thing on the same subjects."

"I certainly try to say something fresh every time."

"Do you mean, about what you know? For example, in answer to the question, 'How many letters are there in "Socrates" and how do you spell it?' do you try to say something different now from what you said before? Or take figures: suppose you are asked if twice five are ten, don't you give the same answer now as you gave before?"

"About letters and figures, Socrates, I always say the same thing, just like you. As for Justice, I feel

---

[1] Ch. IV. § 1-5, ἄλλους μὲν πολλάκις, are bracketed by Sauppe, and many others as spurious; but see the analysis in the Introduction.

δικαίου πάνυ οἶμαι νῦν ἔχειν εἰπεῖν, πρὸς ἃ οὔτε
σὺ οὔτ' ἂν ἄλλος οὐδεὶς δύναιτ' ἀντειπεῖν.

8   Νὴ τὴν Ἥραν, ἔφη, μέγα λέγεις ἀγαθὸν εὑρηκέναι, εἰ παύσονται μὲν οἱ δικασταὶ δίχα ψηφιζό-
μενοι, παύσονται δὲ οἱ πολῖται περὶ τῶν δικαίων
ἀντιλέγοντές τε καὶ ἀντιδικοῦντες καὶ στασιά-
ζοντες, παύσονται δὲ αἱ πόλεις διαφερόμεναι περὶ
τῶν δικαίων καὶ πολεμοῦσαι. καὶ ἐγὼ μὲν οὐκ
οἶδ' ὅπως ἂν ἀπολειφθείην σου πρὸ τοῦ ἀκοῦσαι
τηλικούτου ἀγαθὸν εὑρηκότος.

9   Ἀλλὰ μὰ Δί', ἔφη, οὐκ ἀκούσῃ, πρίν γ' ἂν
αὐτὸς ἀποφήνῃ, ὅ τι νομίζεις τὸ δίκαιον εἶναι.
ἀρκεῖ γὰρ, ὅτι τῶν ἄλλων καταγελᾷς ἐρωτῶν μὲν
καὶ ἐλέγχων πάντας, αὐτὸς δ' οὐδενὶ θέλων
ὑπέχειν λόγον οὐδὲ γνώμην ἀποφαίνεσθαι περὶ
οὐδενός.

10   Τί δέ; ὦ Ἱππία, ἔφη, οὐκ ᾔσθησαι, ὅτι ἐγὼ ἃ
δοκεῖ μοι δίκαια εἶναι οὐδὲν παύομαι ἀποδεικνύ-
μενος;

Καὶ ποῖος δή σοι, ἔφη, οὗτος ὁ λόγος ἐστίν;

Εἰ δὲ μὴ λόγῳ, ἔφη, ἀλλ' ἔργῳ ἀποδείκνυμαι·
ἢ οὐ δοκεῖ σοι ἀξιοτεκμαρτότερον τοῦ λόγου τὸ
ἔργον εἶναι;

Πολύ γε νὴ Δί', ἔφη· δίκαια μὲν γὰρ λέγοντες
πολλοὶ ἄδικα ποιοῦσι, δίκαια δὲ πράττων οὐδ' ἂν
εἷς ἄδικος εἴη.

11   Ἤισθησαι οὖν πώποτέ μου ἢ ψευδομαρτυροῦν-
τος ἢ συκοφαντοῦντος ἢ φίλους ἢ πόλιν εἰς
στάσιν ἐμβάλλοντος ἢ ἄλλο τι ἄδικον πράττοντος;

Οὐκ ἔγωγ', ἔφη.

Τὸ δὲ τῶν ἀδίκων ἀπέχεσθαι οὐ δίκαιον ἡγῇ;

confident that I can now say that which neither you nor anyone else can contradict."

"Upon my word, you mean to say that you have 8 made a great discovery, if jurymen are to cease from voting different ways, citizens from disputing and litigation, and wrangling about the justice of their claims, cities from quarrelling about their rights and making war; and for my part, I don't see how to tear myself away from you till I have heard about your great discovery."

"But I vow you shall not hear unless you first 9 declare your own opinion about the nature of Justice; for it's enough that you mock at others, questioning and examining everybody, and never willing to render an account yourself or to state an opinion about anything."

"Indeed, Hippias! Haven't you noticed that I 10 never cease to declare my notions of what is just?"

"And how can you call that an account?"

"I declare them by my deeds, anyhow, if not by my words. Don't you think that deeds are better evidence than words?"

"Yes, much better, of course; for many say what is just and do what is unjust; but no one who does what is just can be unjust."

"Then have you ever found me dealing in perjury 11 or calumny, or stirring up strife between friends or fellow-citizens, or doing any other unjust act?"

"I have not."

"To abstain from what is unjust is just, don't you think?"

Δῆλος εἶ, ἔφη, ὦ Σώκρατες, καὶ νῦν διαφεύγειν
ἐγχειρῶν τὸ ἀποδείκνυσθαι γνώμην, ὅ τι νομίζεις
τὸ δίκαιον· οὐ γὰρ ἃ πράττουσιν οἱ δίκαιοι, ἀλλ᾽
ἃ μὴ πράττουσι, ταῦτα λέγεις.

12 ᾿Αλλ᾽ ᾤμην ἔγωγ᾽, ἔφη ὁ Σωκράτης, τὸ μὴ
θέλειν ἀδικεῖν ἱκανὸν δικαιοσύνης ἐπίδειγμα εἶναι.
εἰ δέ σοι μὴ δοκεῖ, σκέψαι, ἐὰν τόδε σοι μᾶλλον
ἀρέσκῃ· φημὶ γὰρ ἐγὼ τὸ νόμιμον δίκαιον εἶναι.
᾿Αρα τὸ αὐτὸ λέγεις, ὦ Σώκρατες, νόμιμόν τε
καὶ δίκαιον εἶναι;

13 ῎Εγωγε, ἔφη.
Οὐ γὰρ αἰσθάνομαί σου, ὁποῖον νόμιμον ἢ ποῖον
δίκαιον λέγεις.
Νόμους δὲ πόλεως, ἔφη, γιγνώσκεις;
῎Εγωγε, ἔφη.
Καὶ τίνας τούτους νομίζεις;
῝Α οἱ πολῖται, ἔφη, συνθέμενοι ἅ τε δεῖ ποιεῖν
καὶ ὧν ἀπέχεσθαι ἐγράψαντο.
Οὐκοῦν, ἔφη, νόμιμος μὲν ἂν εἴη ὁ κατὰ ταῦτα
πολιτευόμενος, ἄνομος δὲ ὁ ταῦτα παραβαίνων;
Πάνυ μὲν οὖν, ἔφη.
Οὐκοῦν καὶ δίκαια μὲν ἂν πράττοι ὁ τούτοις
πειθόμενος, ἄδικα δ᾽ ὁ τούτοις ἀπειθῶν;
Πάνυ μὲν οὖν.
Οὐκοῦν ὁ μὲν τὰ δίκαια πράττων δίκαιος, ὁ δὲ
τὰ ἄδικα ἄδικος;
Πῶς γὰρ οὔ;
῾Ο μὲν ἄρα νόμιμος δίκαιός ἐστιν, ὁ δὲ ἄνομος
ἄδικος.

14 Καὶ ὁ ῾Ιππίας, Νόμους δ᾽, ἔφη, ὦ Σώκρατες,

---

¹ *Cyropaedia*, I. iii. 17.

" Even now, Socrates, you are clearly endeavouring to avoid stating what you think Justice to be. You are saying not what the just do, but what they don't do."

" Well, I thought that unwillingness to do injustice 12 was sufficient proof of Justice. But, if you don't think so, see whether you like this better: I say that what is lawful is just." [1]

" Do you mean, Socrates, that lawful and just are the same thing ? "

" I do."

" Because I don't see what you mean by lawful or 13 what you mean by just."

" Does the expression ' laws of a state ' convey a meaning to you ? "

" It does."

" And what do you think they are ? "

" Covenants made by the citizens whereby they have enacted what ought to be done and what ought to be avoided."

" Then would not that citizen who acts in accordance with these act lawfully, and he who transgresses them act unlawfully ? "

" Yes, certainly."

" And would not he who obeys them do what is just, and he who disobeys them do what is unjust ? "

" Certainly."

" Then would not he who does what is just be just, and he who does what is unjust be unjust ? "

" Of course."

" Consequently he who acts lawfully is just, and he who acts unlawfully is unjust."

" Laws," said Hippias, " can hardly be thought of 14

πῶς ἄν τις ἡγήσαιτο σπουδαῖον πρᾶγμα εἶναι ἢ
τὸ πείθεσθαι αὐτοῖς, οὕς γε πολλάκις αὐτοὶ οἱ
θέμενοι ἀποδοκιμάσαντες μετατίθενται ;

Καὶ γὰρ πόλεμον, ἔφη ὁ Σωκράτης, πολλάκις
ἀράμεναι αἱ πόλεις πάλιν εἰρήνην ποιοῦνται.

Καὶ μάλα, ἔφη.

Διάφορον οὖν τι οἴει ποιεῖν, ἔφη, τοὺς τοῖς
νόμοις πειθομένους φαυλίζων, ὅτι καταλυθεῖεν ἂν
οἱ νόμοι, ἢ εἰ τοὺς ἐν τοῖς πολέμοις εὐτακτοῦντας
ψέγοις, ὅτι γένοιτ' ἂν εἰρήνη ; ἢ καὶ τοὺς ἐν τοῖς
πολέμοις ταῖς πατρίσι προθύμως βοηθοῦντας
μέμφῃ ;

15 Μὰ Δί' οὐκ ἔγωγ', ἔφη.

Λυκοῦργον δὲ τὸν Λακεδαιμόνιον, ἔφη ὁ Σωκράτης, καταμεμάθηκας ὅτι οὐδὲν ἂν διάφορον τῶν
ἄλλων πόλεων τὴν Σπάρτην ἐποίησεν, εἰ μὴ τὸ
πείθεσθαι τοῖς νόμοις μάλιστα ἐνειργάσατο αὐτῇ ;
τῶν δὲ ἀρχόντων ἐν ταῖς πόλεσιν οὐκ οἶσθα ὅτι
οἵτινες ἂν τοῖς πολίταις αἰτιώτατοι ὦσι τοῦ τοῖς
νόμοις πείθεσθαι, οὗτοι ἄριστοί εἰσι καὶ πόλις,
ἐν ᾗ μάλιστα οἱ πολῖται τοῖς νόμοις πείθονται, ἐν
εἰρήνῃ τε ἄριστα διάγει καὶ ἐν πολέμῳ ἀνυπόστα-
16 τός ἐστιν ; ἀλλὰ μὴν καὶ ὁμόνοιά γε μέγιστόν τε
ἀγαθὸν δοκεῖ ταῖς πόλεσιν εἶναι καὶ πλειστάκις
ἐν αὐταῖς αἵ τε γερουσίαι καὶ οἱ ἄριστοι ἄνδρες
παρακελεύονται τοῖς πολίταις ὁμονοεῖν, καὶ πανταχοῦ ἐν τῇ Ἑλλάδι νόμος κεῖται τοὺς πολίτας
ὀμνύναι ὁμονοήσειν, καὶ πανταχοῦ ὀμνύουσι τὸν
ὅρκον τοῦτον· οἶμαι δ' ἐγὼ ταῦτα γίγνεσθαι οὐχ
ὅπως τοὺς αὐτοὺς χοροὺς κρίνωσιν οἱ πολῖται οὐδ'
ὅπως τοὺς αὐτοὺς αὐλητὰς ἐπαινῶσιν οὐδ' ὅπως
τοὺς αὐτοὺς ποιητὰς αἱρῶνται οὐδ' ἵνα τοῖς αὐτοῖς

much account, Socrates, or observance of them, seeing that the very men who passed them often reject and amend them."

"Yes," said Socrates, "and after going to war, cities often make peace again."

"To be sure."

"Then is there any difference, do you think, between belittling those who obey the laws on the ground that the laws may be annulled, and blaming those who behave well in the wars on the ground that peace may be made? Or do you really censure those who are eager to help their fatherland in the wars?"

"No, of course not."

"Lycurgus the Lacedaemonian now—have you 15 realised that he would not have made Sparta to differ from other cities in any respect, had he not established obedience to the laws most securely in her? Among rulers in cities, are you not aware that those who do most to make the citizens obey the laws are the best, and that the city in which the citizens are most obedient to the laws has the best time in peace and is irresistible in war? And again, agreement is 16 deemed the greatest blessing for cities: their senates and their best men constantly exhort the citizens to agree, and everywhere in Greece there is a law that the citizens shall promise under oath to agree, and everywhere they take this oath. The object of this, in my opinion, is not that the citizens may vote for the same choirs, not that they may praise the same flute-players, not that they may select the same poets, not that they may like the same things, but that

ἥδωνται, ἀλλ' ἵνα τοῖς νόμοις πείθωνται. τούτοις
γὰρ τῶν πολιτῶν ἐμμενόντων, αἱ πόλεις ἰσχυρό-
ταταί τε καὶ εὐδαιμονέσταται γίγνονται· ἄνευ δὲ
ὁμονοίας οὔτ' ἂν πόλις εὖ πολιτευθείη οὔτ' οἶκος
17 καλῶς οἰκηθείη. ἰδίᾳ δὲ πῶς μὲν ἄν τις ἧττον
ὑπὸ πόλεως ζημιοῖτο, πῶς δ' ἂν μᾶλλον τιμῷτο
ἢ εἰ τοῖς νόμοις πείθοιτο; πῶς δ' ἂν ἧττον ἐν
τοῖς δικαστηρίοις ἡττῷτο ἢ πῶς ἂν μᾶλλον νικῴη;
τίνι δ' ἄν τις μᾶλλον πιστεύσειε παρακαταθέσθαι
ἢ χρήματα ἢ υἱοὺς ἢ θυγατέρας; τίνα δ' ἂν ἡ
πόλις ὅλη ἀξιοπιστότερον ἡγήσαιτο τοῦ νομίμου;
παρὰ τίνος δ' ἂν μᾶλλον τῶν δικαίων τύχοιεν ἢ
γονεῖς ἢ οἰκεῖοι ἢ οἰκέται ἢ φίλοι ἢ πολῖται ἢ
ξένοι; τίνι δ' ἂν μᾶλλον πολέμιοι πιστεύσειαν
ἢ ἀνοχὰς ἢ σπονδὰς ἢ συνθήκας περὶ εἰρήνης;
τίνι δ' ἂν μᾶλλον ἢ τῷ νομίμῳ σύμμαχοι ἐθέλοιεν
γίγνεσθαι; τῷ δ' ἂν μᾶλλον οἱ σύμμαχοι πιστεύσειαν ἢ ἡγεμονίαν ἢ φρουραρχίαν ἢ πόλεις; τίνα
δ' ἄν τις εὐεργετήσας ὑπολάβοι χάριν κομιεῖσθαι
μᾶλλον ἢ τὸν νόμιμον; ἢ τίνα μᾶλλον ἄν τις
εὐεργετήσειεν ἢ παρ' οὗ χάριν ἀπολήψεσθαι
νομίζει; τῷ δ' ἄν τις βούλοιτο μᾶλλον φίλος εἶναι
ἢ τῷ τοιούτῳ ἢ τῷ ἧττον ἐχθρός; τῷ δ' ἄν τις
ἧττον πολεμήσειεν ἢ ᾧ μάλιστα μὲν φίλος εἶναι
βούλοιτο, ἥκιστα δ' ἐχθρὸς καὶ ᾧ πλεῖστοι μὲν
φίλοι καὶ σύμμαχοι βούλοιντο εἶναι, ἐλάχιστοι
δ' ἐχθροὶ καὶ πολέμιοι;
18 Ἐγὼ μὲν οὖν, ὦ Ἱππία, τὸ αὐτὸ ἀποδείκνυμαι
νόμιμόν τε καὶ δίκαιον εἶναι· σὺ δ' εἰ τἀναντία
γιγνώσκεις, δίδασκε.

Καὶ ὁ Ἱππίας, Ἀλλὰ μὰ τὸν Δί', ἔφη, ὦ Σώκρατες, οὔ μοι δοκῶ τἀναντία γιγνώσκειν οἷς
εἴρηκας περὶ τοῦ δικαίου.

they may obey the laws. For those cities whose citizens abide by them prove strongest and enjoy most happiness; but without agreement no city can be made a good city, no house can be made a prosperous house. And how is the individual citizen less likely 17 to incur penalties from the state, and more certain to gain honour than by obeying the laws? How less likely to be defeated in the courts or more certain to win? Whom would anyone rather trust as guardian of his money or sons or daughters? Whom would the whole city think more trustworthy than the man of lawful conduct? From whom would parents or kinsfolk or servants or friends or fellow-citizens or strangers more surely get their just rights? Whom would enemies rather trust in the matter of a truce or treaty or terms of peace? Whom would men rather choose for an ally? And to whom would allies rather entrust leadership or command of a garrison, or cities? Whom would anyone more confidently expect to show gratitude for benefits received? Or whom would one rather benefit than him from whom he thinks he will receive due gratitude? Whose friendship would anyone desire, or whose enmity would he avoid more earnestly? Whom would anyone less willingly make war on than him whose friendship he covets and whose enmity he is fain to avoid, who attracts the most friends and allies, and the fewest opponents and enemies?

"So, Hippias, I declare lawful and just to be the 18 same thing. If you are of the contrary opinion, tell me."

"Upon my word, Socrates," answered Hippias, "I don't think my opinion is contrary to what you have said about Justice."

Ἀγράφους δέ τινας οἶσθα, ἔφη, ὦ Ἱππία, νόμους;

Τούς γ᾽ ἐν πάσῃ, ἔφη, χώρᾳ κατὰ ταὐτὰ νομιζομένους.

Ἔχοις ἂν οὖν εἰπεῖν, ἔφη, ὅτι οἱ ἄνθρωποι αὐτοὺς ἔθεντο;

Καὶ πῶς ἄν, ἔφη, οἵ γε οὔτε συνελθεῖν ἅπαντες ἂν δυνηθεῖεν οὔτε ὁμόφωνοί εἰσι;

Τίνας οὖν, ἔφη, νομίζεις τεθεικέναι τοὺς νόμους τούτους;

Ἐγὼ μέν, ἔφη, θεοὺς οἶμαι τοὺς νόμους τούτους τοῖς ἀνθρώποις θεῖναι· καὶ γὰρ παρὰ πᾶσιν ἀνθρώποις πρῶτον νομίζεται θεοὺς σέβειν.

20 Οὐκοῦν καὶ γονέας τιμᾶν πανταχοῦ νομίζεται;

Καὶ τοῦτο, ἔφη.

Οὐκοῦν καὶ μήτε γονέας παισὶ μίγνυσθαι μήτε παῖδας γονεῦσιν;

Οὐκέτι μοι δοκεῖ, ἔφη, ὦ Σώκρατες, οὗτος θεοῦ νόμος εἶναι.

Τί δή; ἔφη.

Ὅτι, ἔφη, αἰσθάνομαί τινας παραβαίνοντας αὐτόν.

21 Καὶ γὰρ ἄλλα πολλά, ἔφη, παρανομοῦσιν· ἀλλὰ δίκην γέ τοι διδόασιν οἱ παραβαίνοντες τοὺς ὑπὸ τῶν θεῶν κειμένους νόμους, ἣν οὐδενὶ τρόπῳ δυνατὸν ἀνθρώπῳ διαφυγεῖν, ὥσπερ τοὺς ὑπ᾽ ἀνθρώπων κειμένους νόμους ἔνιοι παραβαίνοντες διαφεύγουσι τὸ δίκην διδόναι, οἱ μὲν λανθάνοντες, οἱ δὲ βιαζόμενοι.

22 Καὶ ποίαν, ἔφη, δίκην, ὦ Σώκρατες, οὐ δύνανται διαφεύγειν γονεῖς τε παισὶ καὶ παῖδες γονεῦσι μιγνύμενοι;

" Do you know what is meant by ' unwritten laws,' 19 Hippias ? "

" Yes, those that are uniformly observed in every country."

" Could you say that men made them ? "

" Nay, how could that be, seeing that they cannot all meet together and do not speak the same language ? "

" Then by whom have these laws been made, do you suppose ? "

" I think that the gods made these laws for men. For among all men the first law is to fear the gods."

" Is not the duty of honouring parents another 20 universal law ? "

" Yes, that is another."

" And that parents shall not have sexual inter- course with their children nor children with their parents ? " [1]

" No, I don't think that is a law of God."

" Why so ? "

" Because I notice that some transgress it."

" Yes, and they do many other things contrary to 21 the laws. But surely the transgressors of the laws ordained by the gods pay a penalty that a man can in no wise escape, as some, when they transgress the laws ordained by man, escape punishment, either by concealment or by violence."

" And pray what sort of penalty is it, Socrates, 22 that may not be avoided by parents and children who have intercourse with one another ? "

---

[1] *Cyropaedia*, v. i. 10.

Τὴν μεγίστην νὴ Δί', ἔφη· τί γὰρ ἂν μεῖζον πάθοιεν ἄνθρωποι τεκνοποιούμενοι τοῦ κακῶς τεκνοποιεῖσθαι ;

23 Πῶς ἔϕη, ἔϕη, κακῶς οὗτοι τεκνοποιοῦνται, οὕς γε οὐδὲν κωλύει ἀγαθοὺς αὐτοὺς ὄντας ἐξ ἀγαθῶν παιδοποιεῖσθαι ;

῞Οτι νὴ Δί', ἔϕη, οὐ μόνον ἀγαθοὺς δεῖ τοὺς ἐξ ἀλλήλων παιδοποιουμένους εἶναι, ἀλλὰ καὶ ἀκμά- ζοντας τοῖς σώμασιν· ἢ δοκεῖ σοι ὅμοια τὰ σπέρ- ματα εἶναι τὰ τῶν ἀκμαζόντων τοῖς τῶν μήπω ἀκμαζόντων ἢ τῶν παρηκμακότων ;

Ἀλλὰ μὰ Δί', ἔϕη, οὐκ εἰκὸς ὅμοια εἶναι.

Πότερα οὖν, ἔϕη, βελτίω ;

Δῆλον ὅτι, ἔϕη, τὰ τῶν ἀκμαζόντων.

Τὰ τῶν μὴ ἀκμαζόντων ἄρα οὐ σπουδαῖα ;

Οὐκ εἰκὸς μὰ Δί', ἔϕη.

Οὐκοῦν οὕτω γε οὐ δεῖ παιδοποιεῖσθαι ;

Οὐ γὰρ οὖν, ἔϕη.

Οὐκοῦν οἵ γε οὕτω παιδοποιούμενοι ὡς οὐ δεῖ παιδοποιοῦνται ;

῎Εμοιγε δοκεῖ, ἔϕη.

Τίνες οὖν ἄλλοι, ἔϕη, κακῶς ἂν παιδοποιοῖντο, εἴ γε μὴ οὗτοι ;

Ὁμογνωμονῶ σοι, ἔϕη, καὶ τοῦτο.

24 Τί δέ ; τοὺς εὖ ποιοῦντας ἀντευεργετεῖν οὐ πανταχοῦ νόμιμόν ἐστι ;

Νόμιμον, ἔϕη· παραβαίνεται δὲ καὶ τοῦτο.

Οὐκοῦν καὶ οἱ τοῦτο παραβαίνοντες δίκην δι- δόασι φίλων μὲν ἀγαθῶν ἔρημοι γιγνόμενοι, τοὺς δὲ μισοῦντας ἑαυτοὺς ἀναγκαζόμενοι διώκειν· ἢ οὐχ οἱ μὲν εὖ ποιοῦντες τοὺς χρωμένους ἑαυτοῖς

"The greatest, of course. For what greater penalty can men incur when they beget children than begetting them badly?"

"How do they beget children badly then, if, as 23 may well happen, the fathers are good men and the mothers good women?"

"Surely because it is not enough that the two parents should be good. They must also be in full bodily vigour: unless you suppose that those who are in full vigour are no more efficient as parents than those who have not yet reached that condition or have passed it."

"Of course that is unlikely."

"Which are the better then?"

"Those who are in full vigour, clearly."

"Consequently those who are not in full vigour are not competent to become parents?"

"It is improbable, of course."

"In that case then, they ought not to have children?"

"Certainly not."

"Therefore those who produce children in such circumstances produce them wrongly?"

"I think so."

"Who then will be bad fathers and mothers, if not they?"

"I agree with you there too."

"Again, is not the duty of requiting benefits 24 universally recognised by law?"

"Yes, but this law too is broken."

"Then does not a man pay forfeit for the breach of that law too, in the gradual loss of good friends and the necessity of hunting those who hate him? Or is it not true that, whereas those who benefit an

ἀγαθοὶ φίλοι εἰσίν, οἱ δὲ μὴ ἀντευεργετοῦντες
τοὺς τοιούτους διὰ μὲν τὴν ἀχαριστίαν μισοῦνται
ὑπ' αὐτῶν, διὰ δὲ τὸ μάλιστα λυσιτελεῖν τοῖς
τοιούτοις χρῆσθαι τούτους μάλιστα διώκουσι;

Νὴ τὸν Δί', ὦ Σώκρατες, ἔφη, θείοις ταῦτα
πάντα ἔοικε· τὸ γὰρ τοὺς νόμους αὐτοὺς τοῖς
παραβαίνουσι τὰς τιμωρίας ἔχειν βελτίονος ἢ
κατ' ἄνθρωπον νομοθέτου δοκεῖ μοι εἶναι.

25 Πότερον οὖν, ὦ Ἱππία, τοὺς θεοὺς ἡγῇ τὰ
δίκαια νομοθετεῖν ἢ ἄλλα τῶν δικαίων;

Οὐκ ἄλλα μὰ Δί', ἔφη· σχολῇ γὰρ ἂν ἄλλος
γέ τις τὰ δίκαια νομοθετήσειεν εἰ μὴ θεός.

Καὶ τοῖς θεοῖς ἄρα, ὦ Ἱππία, τὸ αὐτὸ δίκαιόν
τε καὶ νόμιμον εἶναι ἀρέσκει.

Τοιαῦτα λέγων τε καὶ πράττων δικαιοτέρους
ἐποίει τοὺς πλησιάζοντας.

V. Ὡς δὲ καὶ πρακτικωτέρους ἐποίει τοὺς
συνόντας ἑαυτῷ, νῦν αὖ τοῦτο λέξω. νομίζων
γὰρ ἐγκράτειαν ὑπάρχειν ἀγαθὸν εἶναι τῷ μέλλοντι καλόν τι πράξειν, πρῶτον μὲν αὐτὸς φανερὸς ἦν τοῖς συνοῦσιν ἠσκηκὼς αὐτὸν μάλιστα
πάντων ἀνθρώπων, ἔπειτα διαλεγόμενος προετρέ-
πετο πάντων μάλιστα τοὺς συνόντας πρὸς
2 ἐγκράτειαν. ἀεὶ μὲν οὖν περὶ τῶν πρὸς ἀρετὴν
χρησίμων αὐτός τε διετέλει μεμνημένος καὶ τοὺς
συνόντας πάντας ὑπομιμνήσκων· οἶδα δέ ποτε
αὐτὸν καὶ πρὸς Εὐθύδημον περὶ ἐγκρατείας τοιάδε
διαλεχθέντα·

Εἰπέ μοι, ἔφη, ὦ Εὐθύδημε, ἆρα καλὸν καὶ
μεγαλεῖον νομίζεις εἶναι καὶ ἀνδρὶ καὶ πόλει
κτῆμα ἐλευθερίαν;

acquaintance are good friends to him, he is hated by them for his ingratitude, if he makes no return, and then, because it is most profitable to enjoy the acquaintance of such men, he hunts them most assiduously?"

"Assuredly, Socrates, all this does suggest the work of the gods. For laws that involve in themselves punishment meet for those who break them, must, I think, be framed by a better legislator than man."

"Then, Hippias, do you think that the gods 25 ordain what is just or what is otherwise?"

"Not what is otherwise—of course not; for if a god ordains not that which is just, surely no other legislator can do so."

"Consequently, Hippias, the gods too accept the identification of just and lawful."

By such words and actions he encouraged Justice in those who resorted to his company.

V. He did also try to make his companions efficient in affairs, as I will now show. For holding that it is good for anyone who means to do honourable work to have self-control, he made it clear to his companions, in the first place, that he had been assiduous in self-discipline;[1] moreover, in his conversation he exhorted his companions to cultivate self-control above all things. Thus he bore in mind 2 continually the aids to virtue, and put all his companions in mind of them. I recall in particular the substance of a conversation that he once had with Euthydemus on self-control.

"Tell me, Euthydemus," he said, "do you think that freedom is a noble and splendid possession both for individuals and for communities?"

---

[1] *Cyropaedia*, VIII. i. 32.

Ὡς οἷόν τέ γε μάλιστα, ἔφη.

3 Ὅστις οὖν ἄρχεται ὑπὸ τῶν διὰ τοῦ σώματος
ἡδονῶν καὶ διὰ ταύτας μὴ δύναται πράττειν τὰ
βέλτιστα, νομίζεις τοῦτον ἐλεύθερον εἶναι ;

Ἥκιστα, ἔφη.

Ἴσως γὰρ ἐλευθέριον φαίνεταί σοι τὸ πράττειν
τὰ βέλτιστα, εἶτα τὸ ἔχειν τοὺς κωλύσοντας τὰ
τοιαῦτα ποιεῖν ἀνελεύθερον νομίζεις ;

Παντάπασί γ᾿, ἔφη.

4 Παντάπασιν ἄρα σοι δοκοῦσιν οἱ ἀκρατεῖς
ἀνελεύθεροι εἶναι ;

Νὴ τὸν Δί᾿ εἰκότως.

Πότερα δέ σοι δοκοῦσιν οἱ ἀκρατεῖς κωλύεσθαι
μόνον τὰ κάλλιστα πράττειν ἢ καὶ ἀναγκάζεσθαι
τὰ αἴσχιστα ποιεῖν ;

Οὐδὲν ἧττον ἔμοιγ᾿, ἔφη, δοκοῦσι ταῦτα ἀναγκάζεσθαι ἢ ἐκεῖνα κωλύεσθαι.

5 Ποίους δέ τινας δεσπότας ἡγῇ τοὺς τὰ μὲν
ἄριστα κωλύοντας, τὰ δὲ κάκιστα ἀναγκάζοντας ;

Ὡς δυνατὸν νὴ Δί᾿, ἔφη, κακίστους.

Δουλείαν δὲ ποίαν κακίστην νομίζεις εἶναι ;

Ἐγὼ μέν, ἔφη, τὴν παρὰ τοῖς κακίστοις δεσπόταις.

Τὴν κακίστην ἄρα δουλείαν οἱ ἀκρατεῖς δου-
λεύουσιν ;

Ἔμοιγε δοκεῖ, ἔφη.

6 Σοφίαν δὲ τὸ μέγιστον ἀγαθὸν οὐ δοκεῖ σοι
ἀπείργουσα τῶν ἀνθρώπων ἡ ἀκρασία εἰς τοὐναντίον αὐτοὺς ἐμβάλλειν ; ἢ οὐ δοκεῖ σοι προσέ-
χειν τε τοῖς ὠφελοῦσι καὶ καταμανθάνειν αὐτὰ
κωλύειν ἀφέλκουσα ἐπὶ τὰ ἡδέα καὶ πολλάκις
αἰσθανομένους τῶν ἀγαθῶν τε καὶ τῶν κακῶν

" Yes, I think it is, in the highest degree."

" Then do you think that the man is free who is 3 ruled by bodily pleasures and is unable to do what is best because of them ? "

" By no means."

" Possibly, in fact, to do what is best appears to you to be freedom, and so you think that to have masters who will prevent such activity is bondage ? "

" I am sure of it."

" You feel sure then that the incontinent are bond 4 slaves ? "

" Of course, naturally."

" And do you think that the incontinent are merely prevented from doing what is most honourable, or are also forced to do what is most dishonourable ? "

" I think that they are forced to do that just as much as they are prevented from doing the other."

" What sort of masters are they, in your opinion, 5 who prevent the best and enforce the worst ? "

" The worst possible, of course."

" And what sort of slavery do you believe to be the worst ? "

" Slavery to the worst masters, I think."

" The worst slavery, therefore, is the slavery endured by the incontinent ? "

" I think so."

" As for Wisdom, the greatest blessing, does not 6 incontinence exclude it and drive men to the opposite ? Or don't you think that incontinence prevents them from attending to useful things and understanding them, by drawing them away to things pleasant, and often so stuns their perception

ἐκπλήξασα ποιεῖν τὸ χεῖρον ἀντὶ τοῦ βελτίονος
αἱρεῖσθαι;

7   Γίγνεται τοῦτ', ἔφη.

Σωφροσύνης δέ, ὦ Εὐθύδημε, τίνι ἂν φαίημεν
ἧττον ἢ τῷ ἀκρατεῖ προσήκειν; αὐτὰ γὰρ δήπου
τὰ ἐναντία σωφροσύνης καὶ ἀκρασίας ἔργα ἐστίν.

Ὁμολογῶ καὶ τοῦτο, ἔφη.

Τοῦ δ' ἐπιμελεῖσθαι ὧν προσήκει οἴει τι κωλυ-
τικώτερον εἶναι ἀκρασίας;

Οὔκουν ἔγωγ', ἔφη.

Τοῦ δὲ ἀντὶ τῶν ὠφελούντων τὰ βλάπτοντα
προαιρεῖσθαι ποιοῦντος καὶ τούτων μὲν ἐπιμελεῖσθαι, ἐκείνων δὲ ἀμελεῖν πείθοντος καὶ τοῖς
σωφρονοῦσι τὰ ἐναντία ποιεῖν ἀναγκάζοντος οἴει
τι ἀνθρώπῳ κάκιον εἶναι;

Οὐδέν, ἔφη.

8   Οὔκουν τὴν ἐγκράτειαν τῶν ἐναντίων ἢ τὴν
ἀκρασίαν εἰκὸς τοῖς ἀνθρώποις αἰτίαν εἶναι;

Πάνυ μὲν οὖν, ἔφη.

Οὔκουν καὶ τῶν ἐναντίων τὸ αἴτιον εἰκὸς
ἄριστον εἶναι;

Εἰκὸς γάρ, ἔφη.

Ἔοικεν ἄρ', ἔφη, ὦ Εὐθύδημε, ἄριστον ἀνθρώπῳ
ἐγκράτεια εἶναι;

Εἰκότως γάρ, ἔφη, ὦ Σώκρατες.

9   Ἐκεῖνο δέ, ὦ Εὐθύδημε, ἤδη πώποτε ἐνεθυ-
μήθης;

Ποῖον; ἔφη.

Ὅτι καὶ ἐπὶ τὰ ἡδέα, ἐφ' ἅπερ μόνα δοκεῖ ἡ
ἀκρασία τοὺς ἀνθρώπους ἄγειν, αὐτὴ μὲν οὐ
δύναται ἄγειν, ἡ δ' ἐγκράτεια πάντων μάλιστα
ἥδεσθαι ποιεῖ.

of good and evil that they choose the worse instead
of the better?"

"That does happen."

"With Prudence, Euthydemus, who, shall we say, 7
has less to do than the incontinent? For I presume that the actions prompted by prudence and
incontinence are exact opposites?"

"I agree with that too."

"To caring for what is right is there any stronger
hindrance, do you think, than incontinence?"

"Indeed I do not."

"And do you think there can be aught worse for
a man than that which causes him to choose the
harmful rather than the useful, and persuades him
to care for the one and to be careless of the other,
and forces him to do the opposite of what prudence
dictates?"

"Nothing."

"And is it not likely that self-control causes 8
actions the opposite of those that are due to
incontinence?"

"Certainly."

"Then is not the cause of the opposite actions
presumably a very great blessing?"

"Yes, presumably."

"Consequently we may presume, Euthydemus,
that self-control is a very great blessing to a man?"

"We may presume so, Socrates."

"Has it ever occurred to you, Euthydemus——?" 9

"What?"

"That though pleasure is the one and only goal
to which incontinence is thought to lead men, she
herself cannot bring them to it, whereas nothing
produces pleasure so surely as self-control?"

Πῶς ; ἔφη.

Ὥσπερ ἡ μὲν ἀκρασία οὐκ ἐῶσα καρτερεῖν
οὔτε λιμὸν οὔτε δίψαν οὔτε ἀφροδισίων ἐπιθυμίαν
οὔτε ἀγρυπνίαν, δι' ὧν μόνων ἔστιν ἡδέως μὲν
φαγεῖν τε καὶ πιεῖν καὶ ἀφροδισιάσαι, ἡδέως δ'
ἀναπαύσασθαί τε καὶ κοιμηθῆναι, καὶ περιμεί-
ναντας καὶ ἀνασχομένους, ἕως ἂν ταῦτα ὡς ἔνι
ἥδιστα γένηται, κωλύει τοῖς ἀναγκαιοτάτοις τε
καὶ συνεχεστάτοις ἀξιολόγως ἥδεσθαι· ἡ δ' ἐγκράτεια μόνη ποιοῦσα καρτερεῖν τὰ εἰρημένα μόνη
καὶ ἥδεσθαι ποιεῖ ἀξίως μνήμης ἐπὶ τοῖς εἰρημένοις.

Παντάπασιν, ἔφη, ἀληθῆ λέγεις.

10 Ἀλλὰ μὴν τοῦ μαθεῖν τι καλὸν καὶ ἀγαθὸν
καὶ τοῦ ἐπιμεληθῆναι τῶν τοιούτων τινός, δι' ὧν
ἄν τις καὶ τὸ ἑαυτοῦ σῶμα καλῶς διοικήσειε καὶ
τὸν ἑαυτοῦ οἶκον καλῶς οἰκονομήσειε καὶ φίλοις
καὶ πόλει ὠφέλιμος γένοιτο καὶ ἐχθροὺς κρατή-
σειεν, ἀφ' ὧν οὐ μόνον ὠφέλειαι, ἀλλὰ καὶ ἡδοναὶ
μέγισται γίγνονται, οἱ μὲν ἐγκρατεῖς ἀπολαύουσι
πράττοντες αὐτά, οἱ δ' ἀκρατεῖς οὐδενὸς μετέ-
χουσι. τῷ γὰρ ἂν ἧττον φήσαιμεν τῶν τοιούτων
προσήκειν ἢ ᾧ ἥκιστα ἔξεστι ταῦτα πράττειν,
κατεχομένῳ ἐπὶ τῷ σπουδάζειν περὶ τὰς ἐγγυτάτω ἡδονάς ;

11 Καὶ ὁ Εὐθύδημος, Δοκεῖς μοι, ἔφη, ὦ Σώκρατες,
λέγειν, ὡς ἀνδρὶ ἥττονι τῶν διὰ τοῦ σώματος
ἡδονῶν πάμπαν οὐδεμιᾶς ἀρετῆς προσήκει.

Τί γὰρ διαφέρει, ἔφη, ὦ Εὐθύδημε, ἄνθρωπος
ἀκρατὴς θηρίου τοῦ ἀμαθεστάτου ; ὅστις γὰρ τὰ
μὲν κράτιστα μὴ σκοπεῖ, τὰ ἥδιστα δ' ἐκ παντὸς

"How so?"

"Incontinence will not let them endure hunger or thirst or desire or lack of sleep, which are the sole causes of pleasure in eating and drinking and sexual indulgence, and in resting and sleeping, after a time of waiting and resistance until the moment comes when these will give the greatest possible satisfaction; and thus she prevents them from experiencing any pleasure worthy to be mentioned in the most elementary and recurrent forms of enjoyment. But self-control alone causes them to endure the sufferings I have named, and therefore she alone causes them to experience any pleasure worth mentioning in such enjoyments."

"What you say is entirely true."

"Moreover, the delights of learning something 10 good and excellent, and of studying some of the means whereby a man knows how to regulate his body well and manage his household successfully, to be useful to his friends and city and to defeat his enemies—knowledge that yields not only very great benefits but very great pleasures—these are the delights of the self-controlled; but the incontinent have no part in them. For who, should we say, has less concern with these than he who has no power of cultivating them because all his serious purposes are centred in the pleasures that lie nearest?"

"Socrates," said Euthydemus, "I think you mean 11 that he who is at the mercy of the bodily pleasures has no concern whatever with virtue in any form."

"Yes, Euthydemus; for how can an incontinent man be any better than the dullest beast? How can he who fails to consider the things that matter most, and strives by every means to do the things

τρόπου ζητεῖ ποιεῖν, τί ἂν διαφέροι τῶν ἀφρονε
στάτων βοσκημάτων ; ἀλλὰ τοῖς ἐγκρατέσι μόνοις
ἔξεστι σκοπεῖν τὰ κράτιστα τῶν πραγμάτων καὶ
λόγῳ καὶ ἔργῳ διαλέγοντας κατὰ γένη τὰ μὲν
ἀγαθὰ προαιρεῖσθαι, τῶν δὲ κακῶν ἀπέχεσθαι.

12   Καὶ οὕτως ἔφη ἀρίστους τε καὶ εὐδαιμονεστά
τους ἄνδρας γίγνεσθαι καὶ διαλέγεσθαι δυνατωτά
τους. ἔφη δὲ καὶ τὸ διαλέγεσθαι ὀνομασθῆναι
ἐκ τοῦ συνιόντας κοινῇ βουλεύεσθαι διαλέγοντας
κατὰ γένη τὰ πράγματα· δεῖν οὖν πειρᾶσθαι ὅτι
μάλιστα πρὸς τοῦτο ἑαυτὸν ἕτοιμον παρασκευά
ζειν καὶ τούτου μάλιστα ἐπιμελεῖσθαι· ἐκ τούτου
γὰρ γίγνεσθαι ἄνδρας ἀρίστους τε καὶ ἡγεμονικω
τάτους καὶ διαλεκτικωτάτους.

VI. Ὡς δὲ καὶ διαλεκτικωτέρους ἐποίει τοὺς
συνόντας, πειράσομαι καὶ τοῦτο λέγειν. Σωκρά
της γὰρ τοὺς μὲν εἰδότας, τί ἕκαστον εἴη τῶν
ὄντων, ἐνόμιζε καὶ τοῖς ἄλλοις ἂν ἐξηγεῖσθαι
δύνασθαι· τοὺς δὲ μὴ εἰδότας οὐδὲν ἔφη θαυμασ
τὸν εἶναι αὐτούς τε σφάλλεσθαι καὶ ἄλλους
σφάλλειν· ὧν ἕνεκα σκοπῶν σὺν τοῖς συνοῦσι,
τί ἕκαστον εἴη τῶν ὄντων, οὐδέποτ’ ἔληγε.

Πάντα μὲν οὖν ᾗ διωρίζετο πολὺ ἔργον ἂν εἴη
διεξελθεῖν· ἐν ὅσοις δὲ τὸν τρόπον τῆς ἐπισκέψεως
δηλώσειν οἶμαι, τοσαῦτα λέξω.

2   Πρῶτον δὲ περὶ εὐσεβείας ὧδέ πως ἐσκόπει.

Εἰπέ μοι, ἔφη, ὦ Εὐθύδημε, ποῖόν τι νομίζεις
εὐσέβειαν εἶναι ;

Καὶ ὅς, Κάλλιστον νὴ Δί’, ἔφη.

Ἔχεις οὖν εἰπεῖν, ὁποῖός τις ὁ εὐσεβής ἐστιν ;

Ἐμοὶ μὲν δοκεῖ, ἔφη, ὁ τοὺς θεοὺς τιμῶν.

that are most pleasant, be better than the stupidest of creatures? No, only the self-controlled have power to consider the things that matter most, and, sorting them out after their kind, by word and deed alike to prefer the good and reject the evil."

And thus, he said, men become supremely good 12 and happy and skilled in discussion. The very word "discussion," according to him, owes its name to the practice of meeting together for common deliberation, *sorting, discussing* [1] things after their kind: and therefore one should be ready and prepared for this and be zealous for it; for it makes for excellence, leadership and skill in discussion.

VI. I will try also to show how he encouraged his companions to become skilled in discussion. Socrates held that those who know what any given thing is can also expound it to others; on the other hand, those who do not know are misled themselves and mislead others. For this reason he never gave up considering with his companions what any given thing is.

To go through all his definitions would be an arduous task. I will say only enough to indicate his method of analysis.

His analysis of Piety—to take that first—was 2 more or less as follows:

"Tell me, Euthydemus, what sort of thing is Piety, in your opinion?"

"A very excellent thing, to be sure," he replied.

"Can you say what sort of man is pious?"

"He who worships the gods, I think."

---

[1] The etymological point, διαλέγω, "classify," implying διαλέγομαι, "discuss," is lost in the English.

Ἔξεστι δὲ ὃν ἄν τις βούληται τρόπον τους
θεοὺς τιμᾶν;

Οὐκ ἀλλὰ νόμοι εἰσί, καθ᾽ οὓς δεῖ τοὺς θεοὺς
τιμᾶν.

3 Οὐκοῦν ὁ τοὺς νόμους τούτους εἰδὼς εἰδείη ἄν,
ὡς δεῖ τοὺς θεοὺς τιμᾶν;

Οἶμαι ἔγωγ᾽, ἔφη.

Ἆρ᾽ οὖν ὁ εἰδώς, ὡς δεῖ τοὺς θεοὺς τιμᾶν, οὐκ
ἄλλως οἴεται δεῖν τοῦτο ποιεῖν ἢ ὡς οἶδεν;

Οὐ γὰρ οὖν, ἔφη.

Ἄλλως δέ τις θεοὺς τιμᾷ ἢ ὡς οἴεται δεῖν;

4 Οὐκ οἶμαι, ἔφη.

Ὁ ἄρα τὰ περὶ τοὺς θεοὺς νόμιμα εἰδὼς
νομίμως ἂν τοὺς θεοὺς τιμῴη;

Πάνυ μὲν οὖν.

Οὐκοῦν ὅ γε νομίμως τιμῶν ὡς δεῖ τιμᾷ;

Πῶς γὰρ οὔ;

Ὁ δέ γε ὡς δεῖ τιμῶν εὐσεβής ἐστι;

Πάνυ μὲν οὖν, ἔφη.

Ὁ ἄρα τὰ περὶ τοὺς θεοὺς νόμιμα εἰδὼς ὀρθῶς
ἂν ἡμῖν εὐσεβὴς ὡρισμένος εἴη;

Ἐμοὶ γοῦν, ἔφη, δοκεῖ.

5 Ἀνθρώποις δὲ ἄρα ἔξεστιν ὃν ἄν τις τρόπον
βούληται χρῆσθαι;

Οὐκ ἀλλὰ καὶ περὶ τούτους ἐστί[1] νόμιμα.[2]

Οὐκοῦν οἱ κατὰ ταῦτα χρώμενοι ἀλλήλοις ὡς
δεῖ χρῶνται;

Πῶς γὰρ οὔ;

---

[1] ἐστι Hirschig: ὁ εἰδὼς & Sauppe with MSS. and Stobaeus.
[2] After νόμιμα Sauppe has καθ᾽ ἃ δεῖ πρὸς ἀλλήλους χρῆσθαι,
νόμιμος ἂν εἴη with MSS. Stobaeus omits the last three
words, and Gilbert regards all after νόμιμα as spurious.

" May a man worship the gods according to his own will and pleasure?"

" No, there are laws to be observed in worshipping the gods!"

" Then will not he who knows these laws know 3 how he must worship the gods?"

" I think so."

" Then does he who knows how he must worship the gods think that he must do so according to his knowledge, and not otherwise?"

" He does indeed."

" And does everyone worship the gods as he thinks he ought, and not otherwise?"

" I think so."

" Then will he who knows what is lawful about 4 the gods worship the gods lawfully?"

" Certainly."

" Then does not he who worships lawfully worship as he ought?"

" Of course."

" Yes, but he who worships as he ought is pious?"

" Certainly."

" Shall we therefore rightly define the pious man as one who knows what is lawful concerning the gods?"

" I at any rate think so."

" In dealing with men, again, may one do as one 5 chooses?"

" No, in the case of men too there are laws of conduct."

" Then do not those who observe them in their dealings with one another behave as they ought?"

" Of course."

335

Οὐκοῦν οἵ γε ὡς δεῖ χρώμενοι καλῶς χρῶνται ;

Πάνυ μὲν οὖν, ἔφη.

Οὐκοῦν οἵ γε τοῖς ἀνθρώποις καλῶς χρώμενοι καλῶς πράττουσι τἀνθρώπεια πράγματα ;

Εἰκός γ᾽, ἔφη.

Οὐκοῦν οἱ τοῖς νόμοις πειθόμενοι δίκαια οὗτοι ποιοῦσι ;

Πάνυ μὲν οὖν, ἔφη.

6 Δίκαια δέ, ἔφη, οἶσθα ὁποῖα καλεῖται ;

Ἃ οἱ νόμοι κελεύουσιν, ἔφη.

Οἱ ἄρα ποιοῦντες ἃ οἱ νόμοι κελεύουσι δίκαιά τε ποιοῦσι καὶ ἃ δεῖ ;

Πῶς γὰρ οὔ ;

Οὐκοῦν οἵ γε τὰ δίκαια ποιοῦντες δίκαιοί εἰσιν ;

Οἶμαι ἔγωγ᾽, ἔφη.

Οἴει οὖν τινας πείθεσθαι τοῖς νόμοις μὴ εἰδότας ἃ οἱ νόμοι κελεύουσιν ;

Οὐκ ἔγωγ᾽, ἔφη.

Εἰδότας δὲ ἃ δεῖ ποιεῖν οἴει τινὰς οἴεσθαι δεῖν μὴ ταῦτα ποιεῖν ;

Οὐκ οἶμαι, ἔφη.

Οἶσθα δέ τινας ἄλλα ποιοῦντας ἢ ἃ οἴονται δεῖν ;

Οὐκ ἔγωγ᾽, ἔφη.

Οἱ ἄρα τὰ περὶ ἀνθρώπους νόμιμα εἰδότες οὗτοι τὰ δίκαια ποιοῦσι ;

Πάνυ μὲν οὖν, ἔφη.

Οὐκοῦν οἵ γε τὰ δίκαια ποιοῦντες δίκαιοί εἰσι ;

Τίνες γὰρ ἄλλοι ; ἔφη.

Ὀρθῶς ἄν ποτε ἄρα ὁριζοίμεθα ὁριζόμενοι δικαίους εἶναι τοὺς εἰδότας τὰ περὶ ἀνθρώπους νόμιμα ;

"And do not they who behave as they ought behave well?"

"Certainly."

"And do not they who behave well towards men act well in human affairs?"

"Presumably."

"And do not those who obey the laws do what is just?"

"Certainly."

"Do you know what sort of things are called just?" 6

"The things that the laws command."

"Consequently those who do what the laws command do both what is just and what they must do?"

"Of course."

"And are not they who do what is just, just men?"

"I think so."

"Do you think then, that any obey the laws without knowing what the laws command?"

"I do not."

"And knowing what they must do, do you suppose that any think they must not do it?"

"I don't think so."

"Do you know of any who do, not what they think they must do, but something else?"

"I do not."

"Consequently those who know what is lawful concerning men do what is just?"

"Certainly."

"But are not they who do what is just, just men?"

"Exactly."

"At last, then, we may rightly define just men as those who know best what is just concerning men?"

Ἐμοιγε δοκεῖ, ἔφη.

7 Σοφίαν δὲ τί ἂν φήσαιμεν εἶναι; εἰπέ μοι, πότερά σοι δοκοῦσιν οἱ σοφοὶ ἃ ἐπίστανται, ταῦτα σοφοὶ εἶναι ἢ εἰσί τινες ἃ μὴ ἐπίστανται σοφοί;

Ἃ ἐπίστανται δῆλον ὅτι, ἔφη. πῶς γὰρ ἄν τις ἅ γε μὴ ἐπίσταιτο, ταῦτα σοφὸς εἴη;

Ἆρ᾽ οὖν οἱ σοφοὶ ἐπιστήμῃ σοφοί εἰσι;

Τίνι γὰρ ἄν, ἔφη, ἄλλῳ τις εἴη σοφὸς εἴ γε μὴ ἐπιστήμῃ;

Ἄλλο δέ τι σοφίαν οἴει εἶναι ἢ ᾧ σοφοί εἰσιν;

Οὐκ ἔγωγε.

Ἐπιστήμη ἄρα σοφία ἐστίν;

Ἔμοιγε δοκεῖ.

Ἆρ᾽ οὖν δοκεῖ σοι ἀνθρώπῳ δυνατὸν εἶναι τὰ ὄντα πάντα ἐπίστασθαι;

Οὐδὲ μὰ Δί᾽ ἔμοιγε πολλοστὸν μέρος αὐτῶν.

Πάντα μὲν ἄρα σοφὸν οὐχ οἷόν τε ἄνθρωπον εἶναι;

Μὰ Δί᾽ οὐ δῆτα, ἔφη.

Ὃ ἄρα ἐπίσταται ἕκαστος, τοῦτο καὶ σοφός ἐστιν;

Ἔμοιγε δοκεῖ.

8 Ἆρ᾽ οὖν, ὦ Εὐθύδημε, καὶ τἀγαθὸν οὕτω ζητητέον ἐστί;

Πῶς; ἔφη.

Δοκεῖ σοι τὸ αὐτὸ πᾶσιν ὠφέλιμον εἶναι;

Οὐκ ἔμοιγε.

Τί δέ; τὸ ἄλλῳ ὠφέλιμον οὐ δοκεῖ σοι ἐνίοτε ἄλλῳ βλαβερὸν εἶναι;

Καὶ μάλα, ἔφη.

Ἄλλο δ᾽ ἄν τι φαίης ἀγαθὸν εἶναι ἢ τὸ ὠφέλιμον;

" I think so."

" And what of Wisdom? How shall we describe 7 it? Tell me, does it seem to you that the wise are wise about what they know, or are some wise about what they do not know?"

" About what they know, obviously; for how can a man be wise about the things he doesn't know?"

" The wise, then, are wise by knowledge?"

" How else can a man be wise if not by knowledge?"

" Do you think that wisdom is anything but that by which men are wise?"

" No."

" It follows that Wisdom is Knowledge?"

" I think so."

" Then do you think it possible for a man to know all things?"

" Of course not—nor even a fraction of them."

" So an all-wise man is an impossibility?"

" Of course, of course."

" Consequently everyone is wise just in so far as he knows?"

" I think so."

" Now to seek the Good, Euthydemus: is this 8 the way?"

" What do you mean?"

" Does it seem to you that the same thing is useful to everyone?"

" No."

" In fact, what is useful to one may sometimes be hurtful to another, don't you think?"

" Assuredly."

" Should you call anything good except what is useful?"

Οὐκ ἔγωγ᾽, ἔφη.

Τὸ ἄρα ὠφέλιμον ἀγαθόν ἐστιν ὅτῳ ἂν ὠφέλιμον ᾖ;

Δοκεῖ μοι, ἔφη.

9 Τὸ δὲ καλὸν ἔχοιμεν ἄν πως ἄλλως εἰπεῖν ἢ ὀνομάζεις καλὸν ἢ σῶμα ἢ σκεῦος ἢ ἄλλ᾽ ὁτιοῦν, ὃ οἶσθα πρὸς πάντα καλὸν ὄν;

Μὰ Δί᾽ οὐκ ἔγωγ᾽, ἔφη.

Ἆρ᾽ οὖν πρὸς ὃ ἂν ἕκαστον χρήσιμον ᾖ, πρὸς τοῦτο ἑκάστῳ καλῶς ἔχει χρῆσθαι;

Πάνυ μὲν οὖν, ἔφη.

Καλὸν δὲ πρὸς ἄλλο τι ἐστιν ἕκαστον ἢ πρὸς ὃ ἑκάστῳ καλῶς ἔχει χρῆσθαι;

Οὐδὲ πρὸς ἓν ἄλλο, ἔφη.

Τὸ χρήσιμον ἄρα καλόν ἐστι πρὸς ὃ ἂν ᾖ χρήσιμον;

Ἔμοιγε δοκεῖ, ἔφη.

10 Ἀνδρείαν δέ, ὦ Εὐθύδημε, ἆρα τῶν καλῶν νομίζεις εἶναι;

Κάλλιστον μὲν οὖν ἔγωγ᾽, ἔφη.

Χρήσιμον ἄρα οὐ πρὸς τὰ ἐλάχιστα νομίζεις τὴν ἀνδρείαν;

Νὴ Δί᾽, ἔφη, πρὸς τὰ μέγιστα μὲν οὖν.

Ἆρ᾽ οὖν δοκεῖ σοι πρὸς τὰ δεινά τε καὶ ἐπικίνδυνα χρήσιμον εἶναι τὸ ἀγνοεῖν αὐτά;

Ἥκιστά γ᾽, ἔφη.

Οἱ ἄρα μὴ φοβούμενοι τὰ τοιαῦτα διὰ τὸ μὴ εἰδέναι, τί ἐστιν, οὐκ ἀνδρεῖοί εἰσι;

Νὴ Δί᾽, ἔφη· πολλοὶ γὰρ ἂν οὕτω γε τῶν τε μαινομένων καὶ τῶν δειλῶν ἀνδρεῖοι εἶεν.

" No."

" Consequently what is useful is good for him to whom it is useful?"

" I think so."

" Consider the Beautiful: can we define it in any other way? Or is it possible to name a beautiful body, for instance, or vessel, or anything else that you know to be beautiful for all purposes?"

" Of course not."

" Then does the beauty in using anything consist in using it for just that purpose for which that particular thing is useful?"

" Certainly."

" And is a thing beautiful for any other purpose than that for which it is beautiful to use that particular thing?"

" For no other purpose whatever."

" The useful, then, is beautiful for any purpose for which it is useful?"

" I think so."

" Next comes Courage, Euthydemus. Do you think it a beautiful thing?"

" I prefer to say very beautiful."

" So you think Courage useful for no mean purposes?"

" Of course—or rather, for the greatest."

" Then do you think that in the pressure of terrors and dangers it is useful to be ignorant of them?"

" By no means."

" So those who feel no fear of such things because they are ignorant of them are not courageous?"

" Of course not, for in that case many madmen and cowards would be courageous."

341

Τί δὲ οἱ καὶ τὰ μὴ δεινὰ δεδοικότες ;

Ἔτι γε νὴ Δία, ἔφη, ἧττον.

Ἆρ' οὖν τοὺς μὲν ἀγαθοὺς πρὸς τὰ δεινὰ καὶ ἐπικίνδυνα ὄντας ἀνδρείους ἡγῇ εἶναι, τοὺς δὲ κακοὺς δειλούς ;

Πάνυ μὲν οὖν, ἔφη.

11 Ἀγαθοὺς δὲ πρὸς τὰ τοιαῦτα νομίζεις ἄλλους τινὰς ἢ τοὺς δυναμένους αὐτοῖς καλῶς χρῆσθαι ;

Οὐκ ἀλλὰ τούτους, ἔφη.

Κακοὺς δὲ ἄρα τοὺς οἵους τούτοις κακῶς χρῆσθαι ;

Τίνας γὰρ ἄλλους ; ἔφη.

Ἆρ' οὖν ἕκαστοι χρῶνται ὡς οἴονται δεῖν ;

Πῶς γὰρ ἄλλως ; ἔφη.

Ἆρ' οὖν οἱ μὴ δυνάμενοι καλῶς χρῆσθαι ἴσασιν, ὡς δεῖ χρῆσθαι ;

Οὐ δήπου γε, ἔφη.

Οἱ ἄρα εἰδότες, ὡς δεῖ χρῆσθαι, οὗτοι καὶ δύνανται ;

Μόνοι γ', ἔφη.

Τί δὲ οἱ μὴ διημαρτηκότες, ἆρα κακῶς χρῶνται τοῖς τοιούτοις ;

Οὐκ οἶμαι, ἔφη.

Οἱ ἄρα κακῶς χρώμενοι διημαρτήκασιν ;

Εἰκός γ', ἔφη.

Οἱ μὲν ἄρα ἐπιστάμενοι τοῖς δεινοῖς τε καὶ ἐπικινδύνοις καλῶς χρῆσθαι ἀνδρεῖοί εἰσιν, οἱ δὲ διαμαρτάνοντες τούτου δειλοί ;

Ἔμοιγε δοκοῦσιν, ἔφη.

12 Βασιλείαν δὲ καὶ τυραννίδα ἀρχὰς μὲν ἀμφοτέρας ἡγεῖτο εἶναι, διαφέρειν δὲ ἀλλήλων ἐνόμιζε.

" What of those who are afraid when there is no ground for fear?"

" Still less, of course."

" Then do you think that those who are good in the presence of terrors and dangers are courageous, and those who are bad are cowards?"

" Certainly."

" And do you think that any are good in the 11 presence of such things, except those who can deal with them well?"

" None but these."

" And bad, except such as deal badly with them?"

" These and none others."

" Then do both classes behave as they think they must?"

" How can they behave otherwise?"

" Then do those who cannot behave well know how they must behave?"

" Surely not."

" So those who know how they must behave are just those who can?"

" Yes, only they."

" Well now, do those who are not utterly mistaken deal badly with such things?"

" I think not."

" So those who behave badly are utterly mistaken?"

" Presumably."

" It follows that those who know how to deal well with terrors and dangers are courageous, and those who utterly mistake the way are cowards?"

" That is my opinion."

Kingship and despotism, in his judgment, were 12 both forms of government, but he held that they

τὴν μὲν γὰρ ἑκόντων τε τῶν ἀνθρώπων καὶ κατὰ
νόμους τῶν πόλεων ἀρχὴν βασιλείαν ἡγεῖτο, τὴν
δὲ ἀκόντων τε καὶ μὴ κατὰ νόμους, ἀλλ᾽ ὅπως ὁ
ἄρχων βούλοιτο, τυραννίδα. καὶ ὅπου μὲν ἐκ
τῶν τὰ νόμιμα ἐπιτελούντων αἱ ἀρχαὶ καθίσταν-
ται, ταύτην μὲν τὴν πολιτείαν ἀριστοκρατίαν
ἐνόμιζεν εἶναι, ὅπου δ᾽ ἐκ τιμημάτων, πλουτοκρα-
τίαν, ὅπου δ᾽ ἐκ πάντων, δημοκρατίαν.

13   Εἰ δέ τις αὐτῷ περί του ἀντιλέγοι μηδὲν ἔχων
σαφὲς λέγειν, ἀλλ᾽ ἄνευ ἀποδείξεως ἤτοι σοφώ-
τερον φάσκων εἶναι ὃν αὐτὸς λέγοι ἢ πολιτικώ-
τερον ἢ ἀνδρειότερον ἢ ἄλλο τι τῶν τοιούτων,
ἐπὶ τὴν ὑπόθεσιν ἐπανῆγεν ἂν πάντα τὸν λόγον
ὧδέ πως·

14   Φῂς σὺ ἀμείνω πολίτην εἶναι ὃν σὺ ἐπαινεῖς ἢ
ὃν ἐγώ ;

Φημὶ γὰρ οὖν.

Τί οὖν οὐκ ἐκεῖνο πρῶτον ἐπεσκεψάμεθα, τί
ἐστιν ἔργον ἀγαθοῦ πολίτου ;

Ποιῶμεν τοῦτο.

Οὐκοῦν ἐν μὲν χρημάτων διοικήσει κρατοίη ἂν
ὁ χρήμασιν εὐπορωτέραν τὴν πόλιν ποιῶν ;

Πάνυ μὲν οὖν, ἔφη.

Ἐν δέ γε πολέμῳ ὁ καθυπερτέραν τῶν ἀντιπάλων ;

Πῶς γὰρ οὔ ;

Ἐν δὲ πρεσβείᾳ ἆρ᾽ ὃς ἂν φίλους ἀντὶ πολεμίων παρασκευάζῃ ;

Εἰκός γε.

Οὐκοῦν καὶ ἐν δημηγορίᾳ ὁ στάσεις τε παύων
καὶ ὁμόνοιαν ἐμποιῶν ;

Ἔμοιγε δοκεῖ.

differed. For government of men with their consent and in accordance with the laws of the state was kingship; while government of unwilling subjects and not controlled by laws, but imposed by the will of the ruler, was despotism. And where the officials are chosen among those who fulfil the requirements of the laws, the constitution is an aristocracy: where rateable property is the qualification for office, you have a plutocracy: where all are eligible, a democracy.

Whenever anyone argued with him on any point 13 without being able to make himself clear, asserting but not proving, that so and so was wiser or an abler politician or braver or what not, he would lead the whole discussion back to the definition required, much in this way:

" Do you say that your man is a better citizen 14 than mine?"

" I do indeed."

" Then why didn't we first consider what is the function of a good citizen?"

" Let us do so."

" In financial administration, then, is not the better man he who makes the city wealthier?"

" Certainly."

" And in war he who makes her stronger than her rivals?"

" Of course."

" And on an embassy he who turns enemies into friends?"

" Presumably."

" And in debate he who puts down strife and produces harmony?"

" I think so."

Οὕτω δὲ τῶν λόγων ἐπαναγομένων καὶ τοῖς
ἀντιλέγουσιν αὐτοῖς φανερὸν ἐγίγνετο τἀληθές.
15 ὁπότε δὲ αὐτός τι τῷ λόγῳ διεξίοι, διὰ τῶν
μάλιστα ὁμολογουμένων ἐπορεύετο, νομίζων ταύτην ἀσφάλειαν εἶναι λόγου. τοιγαροῦν πολὺ
μάλιστα ὧν ἐγὼ οἶδα, ὅτε λέγοι, τοὺς ἀκούοντας
ὁμολογοῦντας παρεῖχε. ἔφη δὲ καὶ Ὅμηρον τῷ
Ὀδυσσεῖ ἀναθεῖναι τὸ ἀσφαλῆ ῥήτορα εἶναι,
ὡς ἱκανὸν αὐτὸν ὄντα διὰ τῶν δοκούντων τοῖς
ἀνθρώποις ἄγειν τοὺς λόγους.

VII. Ὅτι μὲν οὖν ἁπλῶς τὴν ἑαυτοῦ γνώμην
ἀπεφαίνετο Σωκράτης πρὸς τοὺς ὁμιλοῦντας
αὐτῷ, δοκεῖ μοι δῆλον ἐκ τῶν εἰρημένων εἶναι·
ὅτι δὲ καὶ τοῦ [1] αὐτάρκεις ἐν ταῖς προσηκούσαις
πράξεσιν αὐτοὺς εἶναι ἐπεμελεῖτο, νῦν τοῦτο
λέξω. πάντων μὲν γὰρ ὧν ἐγὼ οἶδα μάλιστα
ἔμελεν αὐτῷ εἰδέναι, ὅτου τις ἐπιστήμων εἴη τῶν
συνόντων αὐτῷ· ὧν δὲ προσήκει ἀνδρὶ καλῷ
κἀγαθῷ εἰδέναι, ὅ τι μὲν αὐτὸς εἰδείη, πάντων
προθυμότατα ἐδίδασκεν· ὅτου δὲ αὐτὸς ἀπειρό-
τερος εἴη, πρὸς τοὺς ἐπισταμένους ἦγεν αὐτούς.
2 ἐδίδασκε δὲ καὶ μέχρι ὅτου δέοι ἔμπειρον εἶναι
ἑκάστου πράγματος τὸν ὀρθῶς πεπαιδευμένον.

Αὐτίκα γεωμετρίαν μέχρι μὲν τούτου ἔφη δεῖν
μανθάνειν, ἕως ἱκανός τις γένοιτο, εἴ ποτε δεήσειε,
γῆν μέτρῳ ὀρθῶς ἢ παραλαβεῖν ἢ παραδοῦναι ἢ
διανεῖμαι ἢ ἔργον ἀποδείξασθαι. οὕτω δὲ τοῦτο
ῥᾴδιον εἶναι μαθεῖν, ὥστε τὸν προσέχοντα τὸν
νοῦν τῇ μετρήσει ἅμα τήν τε γῆν ὁπόση ἐστὶν
3 εἰδέναι καὶ ὡς μετρεῖται ἐπιστάμενον ἀπιέναι. τὸ

---

[1] τοῦ B : Sauppe omits.

By this process of leading back the argument even his adversary came to see the truth clearly. When- 15 ever he himself argued out a question, he advanced by steps that gained general assent, holding this to be the only sure method. Accordingly, whenever he argued, he gained a greater measure of assent from his hearers than any man I have known. He said that Homer gave Odysseus the credit of being "a safe speaker"[1] because he had a way of leading the discussion from one acknowledged truth to another.

VII. I think that I have said enough to show that Socrates stated his own opinion plainly to those who consorted with him : I will now show that he also took pains to make them independent in doing the work that they were fitted for. For I never knew a man who was so careful to discover what each of his companions knew. Whatever it befits a gentleman to know he taught most zealously, so far as his own knowledge extended ; if he was not entirely familiar with a subject, he took them to those who knew. He also taught them how far a well-educated 2 man should make himself familiar with any given subject.

For instance, he said that the study of geometry should be pursued until the student was competent to measure a parcel of land accurately in case he wanted to take over, convey or divide it, or to compute the yield ; and this knowledge was so easy to acquire, that anyone who gave his mind to mensuration knew the size of the piece and carried away a knowledge of the principles of land measurement. He was 3

---

[1] *Odyssey*, viii. 171.

δὲ μέχρι τῶν δυσσυνέτων διαγραμμάτων γεωμετρίαν μανθάνειν ἀπεδοκίμαζεν. ὅ τι μὲν γὰρ
ὠφελοίη ταῦτα, οὐκ ἔφη ὁρᾶν· καίτοι οὐκ ἄπειρός
γε αὐτῶν ἦν. ἔφη δὲ ταῦτα ἱκανὰ εἶναι ἀνθρώπου
βίον κατατρίβειν καὶ ἄλλων πολλῶν τε καὶ ὠφελίμων μαθημάτων ἀποκωλύειν.

4 Ἐκέλευε δὲ καὶ ἀστρολογίας ἐμπείρους γίγνεσθαι, καὶ ταύτης μέντοι μέχρι τοῦ νυκτός τε
ὥραν καὶ μηνὸς καὶ ἐνιαυτοῦ δύνασθαι γιγνώσκειν ἕνεκα τοῦ[1] πορείας τε καὶ πλοῦ καὶ φυλακῆς καὶ ὅσα ἄλλα ἢ νυκτὸς ἢ μηνὸς ἢ ἐνιαυτοῦ
πράττεται, πρὸς ταῦτ᾽ ἔχειν τεκμηρίοις χρῆσθαι
τὰς ὥρας τῶν εἰρημένων διαγιγνώσκοντας. καὶ
ταῦτα δὲ ῥᾴδια εἶναι μαθεῖν παρά τε νυκτοθηρῶν
καὶ κυβερνητῶν καὶ ἄλλων πολλῶν, οἷς ἐπιμελὲς
5 ταῦτα εἰδέναι. τὸ δὲ μέχρι τούτου ἀστρονομίαν
μανθάνειν, μέχρι τοῦ καὶ τὰ μὴ ἐν τῇ αὐτῇ περι-
φορᾷ ὄντα καὶ τοὺς πλάνητάς τε καὶ ἀσταθμή-
τους ἀστέρας γνῶναι καὶ τὰς ἀποστάσεις αὐτῶν
ἀπὸ τῆς γῆς καὶ τὰς περιόδους · καὶ τὰς αἰτίας
αὐτῶν ζητοῦντας κατατρίβεσθαι, ἰσχυρῶς ἀπέ-
τρεπεν. ὠφέλειαν μὲν γὰρ οὐδεμίαν οὐδ᾽ ἐν
τούτοις ἔφη ὁρᾶν· καίτοι οὐδὲ τούτων γε ἀνήκοος
ἦν· ἔφη δὲ καὶ ταῦτα ἱκανὰ εἶναι κατατρίβειν
ἀνθρώπου βίον καὶ πολλῶν καὶ ὠφελίμων ἀποκωλύειν.

6 Ὅλως δὲ τῶν οὐρανίων, ᾗ ἕκαστα ὁ θεὸς μηχα-
νᾶται, φροντιστὴν γίγνεσθαι ἀπέτρεπεν· οὔτε
γὰρ εὑρετὰ ἀνθρώποις αὐτὰ ἐνόμιζεν εἶναι οὔτε
χαρίζεσθαι θεοῖς ἂν ἡγεῖτο τὸν ζητοῦντα ἃ ἐκεῖνοι
σαφηνίσαι οὐκ ἐβουλήθησαν. κινδυνεῦσαι δ᾽ ἂν

---

[1] τοῦ B : Sauppe omits.

against carrying the study of geometry so far as to include the more complicated figures, on the ground that he could not see the use of them. Not that he was himself unfamiliar with them, but he said that they were enough to occupy a lifetime, to the complete exclusion of many other useful studies.

Similarly he recommended them to make them- 4 selves familiar with astronomy, but only so far as to be able to find the time of night, month and year, in order to use reliable evidence when planning a journey by land or sea, or setting the watch, and in all other affairs that are done in the night or month or year, by distinguishing the times and seasons aforesaid. This knowledge, again, was easily to be had from night hunters and pilots and others who made it their business to know such things. But he 5 strongly deprecated studying astronomy so far as to include the knowledge of bodies revolving in different courses, and of planets and comets, and wearing oneself out with the calculation of their distance from the earth, their periods of revolution and the causes of these. Of such researches, again he said that he could not see what useful purpose they served. He had indeed attended lectures on these subjects too; but these again, he said, were enough to occupy a lifetime to the complete exclusion of many useful studies.

In general, with regard to the phenomena of the 6 heavens, he deprecated curiosity to learn how the deity contrives them: he held that their secrets could not be discovered by man, and believed that any attempt to search out what the gods had not chosen to reveal must be displeasing to them. He

ἔφη καὶ παραφρονῆσαι τὸν ταῦτα μεριμνῶντα
οὐδὲν ἧττον ἢ Ἀναξαγόρας παρεφρόνησεν ὁ μέγιστον φρονήσας ἐπὶ τῷ τὰς τῶν θεῶν μηχανὰς
ἐξηγεῖσθαι.

7 Ἐκεῖνος γὰρ λέγων μὲν τὸ αὐτὸ εἶναι πῦρ τε
καὶ ἥλιον ἠγνόει, ὅτι τὸ μὲν πῦρ οἱ ἄνθρωποι
ῥᾳδίως καθορῶσιν, εἰς δὲ τὸν ἥλιον οὐ δύνανται
ἀντιβλέπειν καὶ ὑπὸ μὲν τοῦ ἡλίου καταλαμπό-
μενοι τὰ χρώματα μελάντερα ἔχουσιν, ὑπὸ δὲ
τοῦ πυρὸς οὔ· ἠγνόει δὲ καὶ ὅτι τῶν ἐκ τῆς γῆς
φυομένων ἄνευ μὲν ἡλίου αὐγῆς οὐδὲν δύναται
καλῶς αὔξεσθαι, ὑπὸ δὲ τοῦ πυρὸς θερμαινόμενα
πάντα ἀπόλλυται· φάσκων δὲ τὸν ἥλιον λίθον
διάπυρον εἶναι καὶ τοῦτο ἠγνόει, ὅτι λίθος μὲν
ἐν πυρὶ ὢν οὔτε λάμπει οὔτε πολὺν χρόνον
ἀντέχει, ὁ δὲ ἥλιος τὸν πάντα χρόνον πάντων
λαμπρότατος ὢν διαμένει.

8 Ἐκέλευε δὲ καὶ λογισμοὺς μανθάνειν· καὶ τούτων δὲ ὁμοίως τοῖς ἄλλοις ἐκέλευε φυλάττεσθαι
τὴν μάταιον πραγματείαν, μέχρι δὲ τοῦ ὠφελίμου
πάντα καὶ αὐτὸς συνεσκόπει καὶ συνδιεξῄει τοῖς
συνοῦσι.

9 Προέτρεπε δὲ σφόδρα καὶ ὑγιείας ἐπιμελεῖσθαι
τοὺς συνόντας παρά τε τῶν εἰδότων μανθάνοντας
ὁπόσα ἐνδέχοιτο καὶ ἑαυτῷ ἕκαστον προσέχοντα
διὰ παντὸς τοῦ βίου, τί βρῶμα ἢ τί πῶμα ἢ ποῖος
πόνος συμφέροι αὐτῷ καὶ πῶς τούτοις χρώμενος
ὑγιεινότατ' ἂν διάγοι. τοῦ γὰρ οὕτω προσέχον-
τος ἑαυτῷ ἔργον ἔφη εἶναι εὑρεῖν ἰατρὸν τὰ πρὸς
ὑγίειαν συμφέροντα αὐτῷ μᾶλλον διαγιγνώ-
σκοντα.

10 Εἰ δέ τις μᾶλλον ἢ κατὰ τὴν ἀνθρωπίνην

said that he who meddles with these matters runs the risk of losing his sanity as completely as Anaxagoras, who took an insane pride in his explanation of the divine machinery.

For that sage, in declaring the sun to be fire, 7 ignored the facts than men can look at fire without inconvenience, but cannot gaze steadily at the sun; that their skin is blackened by the sun's rays, but not by fire. Further, he ignored the fact that sunlight is essential to the health of all vegetation, whereas if anything is heated by fire it withers. Again, when he pronounced the sun to be a red-hot stone, he ignored the fact that a stone in fire neither glows nor can resist it long, whereas the sun shines with unequalled brilliance for ever.

He also recommended the study of arithmetic. 8 But in this case as in the others he recommended avoidance of vain application; and invariably, whether theories or ascertained facts formed the subject of his conversation, he limited it to what was useful.

He also strongly urged his companions to take 9 care of their health. "You should find out all you can," he said, "from those who know. Everyone should watch himself throughout his life, and notice what sort of meat and drink and what form of exercise suit his constitution, and how he should regulate them in order to enjoy good health. For by such attention to yourselves you can discover better than any doctor what suits your constitution."

When anyone was in need of help that human 10

σοφίαν ὠφελεῖσθαι βούλοιτο, συνεβούλευε μαντικῆς ἐπιμελεῖσθαι. τὸν γὰρ εἰδότα, δι᾿ ὧν οἱ
θεοὶ τοῖς ἀνθρώποις περὶ τῶν πραγμάτων σημαί-
νουσιν, οὐδέποτ᾿ ἔρημον ἔφη γίγνεσθαι συμβουλῆς
θεῶν.

VIII. Εἰ δέ τις, ὅτι φάσκοντος αὐτοῦ τὸ δαιμόνιον ἑαυτῷ προσημαίνειν ἅ τε δέοι καὶ ἃ μὴ δέοι
ποιεῖν ὑπὸ τῶν δικαστῶν κατεγνώσθη θάνατος,
οἴεται αὐτὸν ἐλέγχεσθαι περὶ τοῦ δαιμονίου
ψευδόμενον, ἐννοησάτω πρῶτον μέν, ὅτι οὕτως
ἤδη τότε πόρρω τῆς ἡλικίας ἦν, ὥστ᾿ εἰ καὶ μὴ
τότε, οὐκ ἂν πολλῷ ὕστερον τελευτῆσαι τὸν βίον·
εἶτα ὅτι τὸ μὲν ἀχθεινότατον τοῦ βίου καὶ ἐν ᾧ
πάντες τὴν διάνοιαν μειοῦνται ἀπέλιπεν, ἀντὶ δὲ
τούτου τῆς ψυχῆς τὴν ῥώμην ἐπιδειξάμενος
εὔκλειαν προσεκτήσατο τήν τε δίκην πάντων
ἀνθρώπων ἀληθέστατα καὶ ἐλευθεριώτατα καὶ
δικαιότατα εἰπὼν καὶ τὴν κατάγνωσιν τοῦ θανά-
2 του πρᾳότατα καὶ ἀνδρωδέστατα ἐνεγκών. ὁμολογεῖται γὰρ οὐδένα πω τῶν μνημονευομένων
ἀνθρώπων κάλλιον θάνατον ἐνεγκεῖν. ἀνάγκη
μὲν γὰρ ἐγένετο αὐτῷ μετὰ τὴν κρίσιν τριάκοντα
ἡμέρας βιῶναι διὰ τὸ Δήλια μὲν ἐκείνου τοῦ
μηνὸς εἶναι, τὸν δὲ νόμον μηδένα ἐᾶν δημοσίᾳ
ἀποθνήσκειν, ἕως ἂν ἡ θεωρία ἐκ Δήλου ἐπαν-
έλθῃ, καὶ τὸν χρόνον τοῦτον ἅπασι τοῖς συνήθεσι
φανερὸς ἐγένετο οὐδὲν ἀλλοιότερον διαβιοὺς ἢ τὸν
ἔμπροσθεν χρόνον· καίτοι τὸν ἔμπροσθέν γε
πάντων ἀνθρώπων μάλιστα ἐθαυμάζετο ἐπὶ τῷ
3 εὐθύμως τε καὶ εὐκόλως ζῆν. καὶ πῶς ἄν τις
κάλλιον ἢ οὕτως ἀποθάνοι; ἢ ποῖος ἂν εἴη
θάνατος καλλίων ἢ ὃν κάλλιστά τις ἀποθάνοι;

wisdom was unable to give he advised him to resort to divination ; for he who knew the means whereby the gods give guidance to men concerning their affairs never lacked divine counsel.

VIII. As for his claim that he was forewarned by "the deity" what he ought to do and what not to do, some may think that it must have been a delusion because he was condemned to death. But they should remember two facts. First, he had already reached such an age, that had he not died then, death must have come to him soon after. Secondly, he escaped the most irksome stage of life and the inevitable diminution of mental powers, and instead won glory by the moral strength revealed in the wonderful honesty and frankness and probity of his defence, and in the equanimity and manliness with which he bore the sentence of death.

In fact it is admitted that there is no record of 2 death more nobly borne. For he was forced to live for thirty days after the verdict was given, because it was the month of the Dêlia,[1] and the law did not allow any public execution to take place until the sacred embassy had returned from Delos. During this interval, as all his intimate acquaintances could see, he continued to live exactly as before ; and, in truth, before that time he had been admired above all men for his cheerfulness and serenity. How, 3 then, could man die more nobly? Or what death could be nobler than the death most nobly faced?

[1] See Plato, *Phaedo*, p. 58 b. The festival was held in the month Thargelion, our May.

ποῖος δ' ἂν γένοιτο θάνατος εὐδαιμονέστερος τοῦ
καλλίστου ; ἢ ποῖος θεοφιλέστερος τοῦ εὐδαιμονε-
στάτου ; ¹

4 Λέξω δὲ καὶ ἃ Ἑρμογένους τοῦ Ἱππονίκου
ἤκουσα περὶ αὐτοῦ. ἔφη γάρ, ἤδη Μελήτου
γεγραμμένου αὐτὸν τὴν γραφήν, αὐτὸς ἀκούων
αὐτοῦ πάντα μᾶλλον ἢ περὶ τῆς δίκης διαλεγομένου λέγειν αὐτῷ, ὡς χρὴ σκοπεῖν, ὅ τι ἀπολογή-
σεται. τὸν δὲ τὸ μὲν πρῶτον εἰπεῖν· Οὐ γὰρ
δοκῶ σοι τοῦτο μελετῶν διαβεβιωκέναι ; ἐπεὶ δὲ
αὐτὸν ἤρετο, ὅπως, εἰπεῖν αὐτόν, ὅτι οὐδὲν ἄλλο
ποιῶν διαγεγένηται ἢ διασκοπῶν μὲν τά τε δίκαια
καὶ τὰ ἄδικα, πράττων δὲ τὰ δίκαια καὶ τῶν
ἀδίκων ἀπεχόμενος, ἥνπερ νομίζοι καλλίστην
5 μελέτην ἀπολογίας εἶναι. αὐτὸς δὲ πάλιν εἰπεῖν·
Οὐχ ὁρᾷς, ὦ Σώκρατες, ὅτι οἱ Ἀθήνησι δικασταὶ
πολλοὺς μὲν ἤδη μηδὲν ἀδικοῦντας λόγῳ παραχθέντες ἀπέκτειναν, πολλοὺς δὲ ἀδικοῦντας ἀπέλυσαν ; Ἀλλὰ νὴ τὸν Δία, φάναι αὐτόν, ὦ
Ἑρμόγενες, ἤδη μου ἐπιχειροῦντος φροντίσαι τῆς
πρὸς τοὺς δικαστὰς ἀπολογίας ἠναντιώθη τὸ
δαιμόνιον. καὶ αὐτὸς εἰπεῖν· Θαυμαστὰ λέγεις.
6 τὸν δέ, Θαυμάζεις, φάναι, εἰ τῷ θεῷ δοκεῖ βέλτιον
εἶναι ἐμὲ τελευτᾶν τὸν βίον ἤδη ; οὐκ οἶσθ', ὅτι
μέχρι μὲν τοῦδε τοῦ χρόνου ἐγὼ οὐδενὶ ἀνθρώπων
ὑφείμην ἂν οὔτε βέλτιον οὔθ' ἥδιον ἐμοῦ βεβιωκέναι ; ἄριστα μὲν γὰρ οἶμαι ζῆν τοὺς ἄριστα
ἐπιμελομένους τοῦ ὡς βελτίστους γίγνεσθαι,
ἥδιστα δὲ τοὺς μάλιστα αἰσθανομένους, ὅτι
7 βελτίους γίγνονται. ἃ ἐγὼ μέχρι τοῦδε τοῦ χρόνου
ἠσθανόμην ἐμαυτῷ συμβαίνοντα καὶ τοῖς ἄλλοις
ἀνθρώποις ἐντυγχάνων καὶ πρὸς τοὺς ἄλλους

What death more blessed than the noblest? Or what dearer to the gods than the most blessed?

I will repeat what Hermogenes, son of Hipponicus, 4 told me about him. "When Meletus had actually formulated his indictment," he said, "Socrates talked freely in my presence, but made no reference to the case. I told him that he ought to be thinking about his defence. His first remark was, 'Don't you think that I have been preparing for it all my life?' And when I asked him how, he said that he had been constantly occupied in the consideration of right and wrong, and in doing what was right and avoiding what was wrong, which he regarded as the best preparation for a defence. Then I said, 'Don't 5 you see, Socrates, that the juries in our courts are apt to be misled by argument, so that they often put the innocent to death, and acquit the guilty?' 'Ah, yes, Hermogenes,' he answered, 'but when I did try to think out my defence to the jury, the deity at once resisted.' 'Strange words,' said I; and he, 6 'Do you think it strange, if it seems better to God that I should die now? Don't you see that to this day I never would acknowledge that any man had lived a better or a pleasanter life than I? For they live best, I think, who strive best to become as good as possible: and the pleasantest life is theirs who are conscious that they are growing in goodness. And to this day that has been my experience; and 7 mixing with others and closely comparing myself

---

[1] § 3 is regarded as spurious by Sauppe.

ἀνθρώπους[1] παραθεωρῶν ἐμαυτὸν οὕτω διατετέλεκα περὶ ἐμαυτοῦ γιγνώσκων· καὶ οὐ μόνον ἐγώ,
ἀλλὰ καὶ οἱ ἐμοὶ φίλοι οὕτως ἔχοντες περὶ ἐμοῦ
διατελοῦσιν, οὐ διὰ τὸ φιλεῖν ἐμέ, καὶ γὰρ οἱ τοὺς
ἄλλους φιλοῦντες οὕτως ἂν εἶχον πρὸς τοὺς
ἑαυτῶν φίλους, ἀλλὰ διόπερ καὶ αὐτοὶ ἂν οἴονται
8 ἐμοὶ συνόντες βέλτιστοι γίγνεσθαι. εἰ δὲ βιώσο-
μαι πλείω χρόνον, ἴσως ἀναγκαῖον ἔσται τὰ τοῦ
γήρως ἐπιτελεῖσθαι καὶ ὁρᾶν τε καὶ ἀκούειν ἧττον
καὶ διανοεῖσθαι χεῖρον καὶ δυσμαθέστερον ἀπο-
βαίνειν καὶ ἐπιλησμονέστερον καὶ ὧν πρότερον
βελτίων ἦν, τούτων χείρω γίγνεσθαι. ἀλλὰ μὴν
ταῦτά γε μὴ αἰσθανομένῳ μὲν ἀβίωτος ἂν εἴη ὁ
βίος, αἰσθανόμενον δὲ πῶς οὐκ ἀνάγκη χεῖρόν τε
καὶ ἀηδέστερον ζῆν;
9 Ἀλλὰ μὴν εἴ γε ἀδίκως ἀποθανοῦμαι, τοῖς
μὲν ἀδίκως ἐμὲ ἀποκτείνασιν αἰσχρὸν ἂν εἴη
τοῦτο· εἰ γὰρ τὸ ἀδικεῖν αἰσχρόν ἐστι, πῶς οὐκ
αἰσχρὸν καὶ τὸ ἀδίκως ὁτιοῦν ποιεῖν;[2] ἐμοὶ δὲ
τί αἰσχρὸν τὸ ἑτέρους μὴ δύνασθαι περὶ ἐμοῦ τὰ
10 δίκαια μήτε γνῶναι μήτε ποιῆσαι; ὁρῶ δ' ἔγωγε
καὶ τὴν δόξαν τῶν προγεγονότων ἀνθρώπων ἐν
τοῖς ἐπιγιγνομένοις οὐχ ὁμοίαν καταλειπομένην
τῶν τε ἀδικησάντων καὶ τῶν ἀδικηθέντων. οἶδα
δέ, ὅτι καὶ ἐγὼ ἐπιμελείας τεύξομαι ὑπ' ἀνθρώπων, καὶ ἐὰν νῦν ἀποθάνω, οὐχ ὁμοίως τοῖς ἐμὲ
ἀποκτείνασιν· οἶδα γὰρ ἀεὶ μαρτυρήσεσθαί μοι,
ὅτι ἐγὼ ἠδίκησα μὲν οὐδένα πώποτε ἀνθρώπων
οὐδὲ χείρω ἐποίησα, βελτίους δὲ ποιεῖν ἐπειρώμην ἀεὶ τοὺς ἐμοὶ συνόντας.
11 Τοιαῦτα μὲν πρὸς Ἑρμογένην τε διελέχθη καὶ
πρὸς τοὺς ἄλλους. τῶν δὲ Σωκράτην γιγνωσκόν-

with them, I have held without ceasing to this opinion of myself. And not I only, but my friends cease not to feel thus towards me, not because of their love for me (for why does not love make others feel thus towards their friends?), but because they think that they too would rise highest in goodness by being with me. But if I am to live on, haply 8 I may be forced to pay the old man's forfeit—to become sand-blind and deaf and dull of wit, slower to learn, quicker to forget, outstripped now by those who were behind me. Nay, but even were I unconscious of the change, life would be a burden to me ; and if I knew, misery and bitterness would surely be my lot.

"'But now, if I am to die unjustly, they who 9 unjustly kill me will bear the shame of it. For if to do injustice is shameful, whatever is unjustly done must surely bring shame. But to me what shame is it that others fail to decide and act justly concerning me? I see that posterity judges differently of the 10 dead according as they did or suffered injustice. I know that men will remember me too, and, if I die now, not as they will remember those who took my life. For I know that they will ever testify of me that I wronged no man at any time, nor corrupted any man, but strove ever to make my companions better.'"

This was the tenor of his conversation with 11 Hermogenes and with the others. All who knew

---

[1] ἀνθρώπους B : Sauppe omits.
[2] εἰ γὰρ . . . ποιεῖν is regarded as spurious by Sauppe.

τῶν οἷος ἦν οἱ ἀρετῆς ἐφιέμενοι πάντες ἔτι καὶ νῦν
διατελοῦσι πάντων μάλιστα ποθοῦντες ἐκεῖνον,
ὡς ὠφελιμώτατον ὄντα πρὸς ἀρετῆς ἐπιμέλειαν.
ἐμοὶ μὲν δὴ τοιοῦτος ὤν, οἷον ἐγὼ διήγημαι,
εὐσεβὴς μὲν οὕτως, ὥστε μηδὲν ἄνευ τῆς τῶν
θεῶν γνώμης ποιεῖν, δίκαιος δέ, ὥστε βλάπτειν
μὲν μηδὲ μικρὸν μηδένα, ὠφελεῖν δὲ τὰ μέγιστα
τοὺς χρωμένους αὐτῷ, ἐγκρατὴς δέ, ὥστε μηδέποτε προαιρεῖσθαι τὸ ἥδιον ἀντὶ τοῦ βελτίονος,
φρόνιμος δέ, ὥστε μὴ διαμαρτάνειν κρίνων τὰ
βελτίω καὶ τὰ χείρω μηδὲ ἄλλου προσδεῖσθαι,
ἀλλ' αὐτάρκης εἶναι πρὸς τὴν τούτων γνῶσιν,
ἱκανὸς δὲ καὶ λόγῳ εἰπεῖν τε καὶ διορίσασθαι
τὰ τοιαῦτα, ἱκανὸς δὲ καὶ ἄλλους δοκιμάσαι τε
καὶ ἁμαρτάνοντας ἐλέγξαι καὶ προτρέψασθαι
ἐπ' ἀρετὴν καὶ καλοκἀγαθίαν, ἐδόκει τοιοῦτος
εἶναι, οἷος ἂν εἴη ἄριστός τε ἀνὴρ καὶ εὐδαιμο-
νέστατος. εἰ δέ τῳ μὴ ἀρέσκει ταῦτα, παρα-
βάλλων τὸ ἄλλων ἦθος πρὸς ταῦτα οὕτω
κρινέτω.

what manner of man Socrates was and who seek after virtue continue to this day to miss him beyond all others, as the chief of helpers in the quest of virtue. For myself, I have described him as he was: so religious that he did nothing without counsel from the gods; so just that he did no injury, however small, to any man, but conferred the greatest benefits on all who dealt with him; so self-controlled that he never chose the pleasanter rather than the better course; so wise that he was unerring in his judgment of the better and the worse, and needed no counsellor, but relied on himself for his knowledge of them; masterly in expounding and defining such things; no less masterly in putting others to the test, and convincing them of error and exhorting them to follow virtue and gentleness. To me then he seemed to be all that a truly good and happy man must be. But if there is any doubter, let him set the character of other men beside these things; then let him judge.

THE OECONOMICUS

ΞΕΝΟΦΩΝΤΟΣ ΟΙΚΟΝΟΜΙΚΟΣ

I. Ἤκουσα δέ ποτε αὐτοῦ καὶ περὶ οἰκονομίας τοιάδε διαλεγομένου. Εἰπέ μοι, ἔφη, ὦ Κριτόβουλε, ἆρά γε ἡ οἰκονομία ἐπιστήμης τινὸς ὄνομά ἐστιν, ὥσπερ ἡ ἰατρικὴ καὶ καλκευτικὴ καὶ τεκτονική;

Ἔμοιγε δοκεῖ, ἔφη ὁ Κριτόβουλος.

2 Ἦ καὶ ὥσπερ τούτων τῶν τεχνῶν ἔχοιμεν ἂν εἰπεῖν ὅ τι ἔργον ἑκάστης, οὕτω καὶ τῆς οἰκονομίας δυνάμεθα εἰπεῖν ὅ τι ἔργον αὐτῆς ἐστι;

Δοκεῖ γοῦν, ἔφη ὁ Κριτόβουλος, οἰκονόμου ἀγαθοῦ εἶναι εὖ οἰκεῖν τὸν ἑαυτοῦ οἶκον.

3 Ἦ καὶ τὸν ἄλλου δὲ οἶκον, ἔφη ὁ Σωκράτης, εἰ ἐπιτρέποι τις αὐτῷ, οὐκ ἂν δύναιτο, εἰ βούλοιτο, εὖ οἰκεῖν, ὥσπερ καὶ τὸν ἑαυτοῦ; ὁ μὲν γὰρ τεκτονικὴν ἐπιστάμενος ὁμοίως ἂν καὶ ἄλλῳ δύναιτο ἐργάζεσθαι ὅτιπερ καὶ ἑαυτῷ, καὶ ὁ οἰκονομικός γ' ἂν ὡσαύτως.

Ἔμοιγε δοκεῖ, ὦ Σώκρατες.

4 Ἔστιν ἄρα, ἔφη ὁ Σωκράτης, τὴν τέχνην ταύτην ἐπισταμένῳ, καὶ εἰ μὴ αὐτὸς τύχοι χρήματα ἔχων, τὸν ἄλλου οἶκον οἰκονομοῦντα ὥσπερ καὶ οἰκοδομοῦντα μισθοφορεῖν;

Νὴ Δία καὶ πολύν γε μισθόν, ἔφη ὁ Κριτόβουλος, φέροιτ' ἄν, εἰ δύναιτο οἶκον παραλαβὼν τελεῖν τε ὅσα δεῖ καὶ περιουσίαν ποιῶν αὔξειν τὸν οἶκον.

THE OECONOMICUS

A DISCUSSION ON ESTATE MANAGEMENT

I. I once heard him discuss the subject of estate management in the following manner.

"Tell me, Critobulus, is estate management the name of a branch of knowledge, like medicine, smithing and carpentry?"

"I think so," replied Critobulus.

"And can we say what the function of estate 2 management is, just as we can say what is the function of each of these arts?"

"Well, I suppose that the business of a good estate manager is to manage his own estate well."

"Yes, and in case he were put in charge of 3 another man's estate, could he not, if he chose, manage it as well as he manages his own? Anyone who understands carpentry can do for another exactly the same work as he does for himself; and so, I presume, can a good estate manager."

"I think so, Socrates."

"Is it possible, then, for one who understands this 4 art, even if he has no property of his own, to earn money by managing another man's estate, just as he might do by building him a house?"

"Yes, of course; and he would get a good salary if, after taking over an estate, he continued to pay all outgoings, and to increase the estate by showing a balance."

5 Οἶκος δὲ δὴ τί δοκεῖ ἡμῖν εἶναι; ἆρα ὅπερ οἰκία ἢ καὶ ὅσα τις ἔξω τῆς οἰκίας κέκτηται, πάντα τοῦ οἴκου ταῦτά ἐστιν;

Ἐμοὶ γοῦν, ἔφη ὁ Κριτόβουλος, δοκεῖ καὶ εἰ μηδ᾽ ἐν τῇ αὐτῇ πόλει εἴη τῷ κεκτημένῳ, πάντα τοῦ οἴκου εἶναι, ὅσα τις κέκτηται.

6 Οὔκουν καὶ ἐχθροὺς κέκτηταί τινες;

Νὴ Δία καὶ πολλούς γε ἔνιοι.

Ἦ καὶ κτήματα αὐτῶν φήσομεν εἶναι τοὺς ἐχθρούς;

Γελοῖον μεντἂν εἴη, ἔφη ὁ Κριτόβουλος, εἰ ὁ τοὺς ἐχθροὺς αὔξων προσέτι καὶ μισθὸν τούτου φέροι.

7 Ὅτι τοι ἡμῖν ἐδόκει οἶκος ἀνδρὸς εἶναι ὅπερ κτῆσις.

Νὴ Δί᾽, ἔφη ὁ Κριτόβουλος, ὅ τι γέ τις ἀγαθὸν κέκτηται· οὐ μὰ Δί᾽ οὐκ εἴ τι κακόν, τοῦτο κτῆμα ἐγὼ καλῶ.

Σὺ δ᾽ ἔοικας τὰ ἑκάστῳ ὠφέλιμα κτήματα καλεῖν.

Πάνυ μὲν οὖν, ἔφη· τὰ δέ γε βλάπτοντα ζημίαν ἔγωγε νομίζω μᾶλλον ἢ χρήματα.

8 Κἂν ἄρα γέ τις ἵππον πριάμενος μὴ ἐπίστηται αὐτῷ χρῆσθαι, ἀλλὰ καταπίπτων ἀπ᾽ αὐτοῦ κακὰ λαμβάνῃ, οὐ χρήματα αὐτῷ ἐστιν ὁ ἵππος;

Οὔκ, εἴπερ τὰ χρήματά γ᾽ ἐστὶν ἀγαθόν.

Οὐδ᾽ ἄρα γε ἡ γῆ ἀνθρώπῳ ἐστὶ χρήματα, ὅστις οὕτως ἐργάζεται αὐτήν, ὥστε ζημιοῦσθαι ἐργαζόμενος;

Οὐδὲ ἡ γῆ μέντοι χρήματά ἐστιν, εἴπερ ἀντὶ τοῦ τρέφειν πεινῆν παρασκευάζει.

9 Οὐκοῦν καὶ τὰ πρόβατα ὡσαύτως, εἴ τις διὰ

" But what do we mean now by an estate? Is it 5 the same thing as a house, or is all property that one possesses outside the house also part of the estate? "

" Well, I think that even if the property is situated in different cities, everything a man possesses is part of his estate."

" Do not some men possess enemies? " 6

" Of course ; some in fact possess many."

" Shall we include their enemies in their possessions ? "

" It would be ridiculous, surely, if one actually received a salary for increasing the number of a man's enemies ! "

" Because, you know, we supposed a man's estate 7 to be the same as his property."

" To be sure—meaning thereby the good things that he possesses. No, of course I don't call any bad thing that he may possess property."

" You seem to use the word property of whatever is profitable to its owner."

" Certainly ; but what is harmful I regard as loss rather than wealth."

" Yes, and consequently if a man buys a horse and 8 doesn't know how to manage it, and so keeps on getting thrown and injuring himself by trying to ride it, the horse is not wealth to him, I presume? "

" No, if we assume that wealth is a good thing."

" It follows that land is not wealth either to a man who works it in such a way that his work results in loss."

" To be sure : even land is not wealth if it makes us starve instead of supporting us."

" And the same will hold good of sheep, will it not? 9

τὸ μὴ ἐπίστασθαι προβάτοις χρῆσθαι ζημιοῖτο,
οὐδὲ τὰ πρόβατα χρήματα τούτῳ εἴη ἄν;

Οὔκουν ἔμοιγε δοκεῖ.

Σὺ ἄρα, ὡς ἔοικε, τὰ μὲν ὠφελοῦντα χρήματα
ἡγῇ, τὰ δὲ βλάπτοντα οὐ χρήματα.

Οὕτως.

10   Ταὐτὰ ἄρα ὄντα τῷ μὲν ἐπισταμένῳ χρῆσθαι
αὐτῶν ἑκάστοις χρήματά ἐστι, τῷ δὲ μὴ ἐπισταμένῳ οὐ χρήματα· ὥσπερ γε αὐλοὶ τῷ μὲν
ἐπισταμένῳ ἀξίως λόγου αὐλεῖν χρήματά εἰσι,
τῷ δὲ μὴ ἐπισταμένῳ οὐδὲν μᾶλλον ἢ ἄχρηστοι
λίθοι.

Εἰ μὴ ἀποδίδοιτό γε αὐτούς.[1]

11   Τοῦτ᾽ αὖ φαίνεται ἡμῖν, ἀποδιδομένοις μὲν οἱ
αὐλοὶ χρήματα, μὴ ἀποδιδομένοις δέ, ἀλλὰ
κεκτημένοις οὔ, τοῖς μὴ ἐπισταμένοις αὐτοῖς
χρῆσθαι.

Καὶ ὁμολογουμένως γε, ὦ Σώκρατες, ὁ λόγος
ἡμῖν χωρεῖ, ἐπείπερ εἴρηται τὰ ὠφελοῦντα χρήματα εἶναι. μὴ πωλούμενοι μὲν γὰρ οὐ χρήματά
εἰσιν οἱ αὐλοί· οὐδὲν γὰρ χρήσιμοί εἰσι· πωλούμενοι δὲ χρήματα.

12   Πρὸς ταῦτα δ᾽ ὁ Σωκράτης εἶπεν· Ἢν ἐπίστη-
ταί γε πωλεῖν. εἰ δὲ πωλοίη αὖ πρὸς τοῦτο,
ᾧ μὴ ἐπίσταιτο χρῆσθαι, οὐδὲ πωλούμενοί εἰσι
χρήματα κατά γε τὸν σὸν λόγον.

Λέγειν ἔοικας, ὦ Σώκρατες, ὅτι οὐδὲ τὸ ἀργύ-
ριόν ἐστι χρήματα, εἰ μή τις ἐπίσταιτο χρῆσθαι
αὐτῷ.

13   Καὶ σὺ δέ μοι δοκεῖς οὕτω συνομολογεῖν, ἀφ᾽
ὧν τις ὠφελεῖσθαι δύναται χρήματα εἶναι. εἰ
γοῦν τις χρῷτο τῷ ἀργυρίῳ, ὥστε πριάμενος οἷον

if a man loses through ignorance of sheep farming, his sheep too will not be wealth to him?"

"I think not."

"It seems, then, that your view is this: what is profitable is wealth, what is harmful is not wealth."

"Quite so."

"That is to say, the same things are wealth and 10 not wealth, according as one understands or does not understand how to use them. A flute, for example, is wealth to one who is competent to play it, but to an incompetent person it is no better than useless stones."

"True—unless he sells it."

"We now see that to persons who don't understand 11 its use, a flute is wealth if they sell it, but not wealth if they keep it instead of selling."

"Yes, Socrates, and our argument runs consistently, since we have said that what is profitable is wealth. For a flute, if not put up for sale, is not wealth, because it is useless: if put up for sale it becomes wealth."

"Yes," commented Socrates, "provided he knows 12 how to sell; but again, in case he sells it for something he doesn't know how to use, even then the sale doesn't convert it into wealth, according to you."

"You imply, Socrates, that even money isn't wealth to one who doesn't know how to use it."

"And you, I think, agree with me to this extent, 13 that wealth is that from which a man can derive profit. At any rate, if a man uses his money to buy a

---

[1] 10-11. The distribution between the speakers as correctly arranged by Thalheim. Previously this sentence was assigned to Socrates, and the first sentence of §11 to Critobulus.

367

ἑταίραν διὰ ταύτην κάκιον μὲν τὸ σῶμα ἔχοι,
κάκιον δὲ τὴν ψυχήν, κάκιον δὲ τὸν οἶκον, πῶς
ἂν ἔτι τὸ ἀργύριον αὐτῷ ὠφέλιμον εἴη ;

Οὐδαμῶς, εἰ μή πέρ γε καὶ τὸν ὑοσκύαμον
καλούμενον χρήματα εἶναι φήσομεν, ὑφ' οὗ οἱ
φαγόντες αὐτὸν παραπλῆγες γίγνονται.

14   Τὸ μὲν δὴ ἀργύριον, εἰ μή τις ἐπίσταιτο αὐτῷ
χρῆσθαι, οὕτω πόρρω ἀπωθείσθω, ὦ Κριτόβουλε,
ὥστε μηδὲ χρήματα εἶναι. οἱ δὲ φίλοι, ἤν τις
ἐπίστηται αὐτοῖς χρῆσθαι ὥστε ὠφελεῖσθαι ἀπ'
αὐτῶν, τί φήσομεν αὐτοὺς εἶναι ;

Χρήματα νὴ Δί', ἔφη ὁ Κριτόβουλος, καὶ πολύ
γε μᾶλλον ἢ τοὺς βοῦς, ἢν ὠφελιμώτεροί γε ὦσι
τῶν βοῶν.

15   Καὶ οἱ ἐχθροί γε ἄρα κατά γε τὸν σὸν λόγον
χρήματά εἰσι τῷ δυναμένῳ ἀπὸ τῶν ἐχθρῶν
ὠφελεῖσθαι.

Ἐμοὶ γοῦν δοκεῖ.

Οἰκονόμου ἄρα ἐστὶν ἀγαθοῦ καὶ τοῖς ἐχθροῖς
ἐπίστασθαι χρῆσθαι ὥστε ὠφελεῖσθαι ἀπὸ τῶν
ἐχθρῶν.

Ἰσχυρότατά γε.

Καὶ γὰρ δὴ ὁρᾷς, ἔφη, ὦ Κριτόβουλε, ὅσοι
μὲν δὴ οἶκοι ἰδιωτῶν ηὐξημένοι εἰσὶν ἀπὸ πολέμου,
ὅσοι δὲ τυράννων.

16   Ἀλλὰ γὰρ τὰ μὲν καλῶς ἔμοιγε δοκεῖ λέγεσθαι,
ὦ Σώκρατες, ἔφη ὁ Κριτόβουλος· ἐκεῖνο δ' ἡμῖν
τί φαίνεται, ὁπόταν ὁρῶμέν τινας ἐπιστήμας μὲν
ἔχοντας καὶ ἀφορμάς, ἀφ' ὧν δύνανται ἐργαζόμενοι αὔξειν τοὺς οἴκους, αἰσθανώμεθα δὲ αὐτοὺς
ταῦτα μὴ θέλοντας ποιεῖν καὶ διὰ τοῦτο ὁρῶμεν
ἀνωφελεῖς οὔσας αὐτοῖς τὰς ἐπιστήμας ; ἄλλο

mistress who makes him worse off in body and soul
and estate, how can his money be profitable to him
then?"

"By no means, unless we are ready to maintain
that the weed called nightshade, which drives you
mad if you eat it, is wealth."

"Then money is to be kept at a distance, 14
Critobulus, if one doesn't know how to use it, and not
to be included in wealth. But how about friends?
If one knows how to make use of them so as to profit
by them, what are they to be called?"

"Wealth, of course, and much more so than cattle,
if it be true that they are more profitable than cattle."

"Yes, and it follows from what you say that enemies 15
too are wealth to anyone who can derive profit from
them."

"Well, that is my opinion."

"Consequently it is the business of a good estate
manager to know how to deal with enemies so as to
derive profit from them too."

"Most decidedly."

"In fact, Critobulus, you cannot fail to notice that
many private persons have been indebted to war for
the increase of their estates, and many princes too."

"Yes, so far so good, Socrates. But sometimes we 16
come across persons possessed of knowledge and means
whereby they can increase their estates if they work,
and we find that they are unwilling to do so; and
consequently we see that their knowledge profits them
nothing. What are we to make of that? In these

τι ἢ τούτοις αὖ οὔτε αἱ ἐπιστῆμαι χρήματά εἰσιν
οὔτε τὰ κτήματα ;

17 Περὶ δούλων μοι, ἔφη ὁ Σωκράτης, ἐπιχειρεῖς,
ὦ Κριτόβουλε, διαλέγεσθαι ;

Οὐ μὰ Δί, ἔφη, οὐκ ἔγωγε, ἀλλὰ καὶ πάνυ
εὐπατριδῶν ἐνίων γε δοκούντων εἶναι, οὓς ἐγὼ
ὁρῶ τοὺς μὲν καὶ πολεμικάς, τοὺς δὲ καὶ εἰρηνικὰς
ἐπιστήμας ἔχοντας, ταύτας δὲ οὐκ ἐθέλοντας
ἐργάζεσθαι, ὡς μὲν ἐγὼ οἶμαι, δι' αὐτὸ τοῦτο ὅτι
δεσπότας οὐκ ἔχουσιν.

18 Καὶ πῶς ἄν, ἔφη ὁ Σωκράτης, δεσπότας οὐκ
ἔχοιεν, εἰ εὐχόμενοι εὐδαιμονεῖν καὶ ποιεῖν βουλόμενοι ἀφ' ὧν ἔχοιεν ἀγαθὰ ἔπειτα κωλύονται
ποιεῖν ταῦτα ὑπὸ τῶν ἀρχόντων ;

Καὶ τίνες δὴ οὗτοί εἰσιν, ἔφη ὁ Κριτόβουλος,
οἳ ἀφανεῖς ὄντες ἄρχουσιν αὐτῶν ;

19 Ἀλλὰ μὰ Δί, ἔφη ὁ Σωκράτης, οὐκ ἀφανεῖς
εἰσιν, ἀλλὰ καὶ πάνυ φανεροί. καὶ ὅτι πονηρό-
τατοί γέ εἰσιν οὐδὲ σὲ λανθάνουσιν, εἴπερ πονη-
ρίαν γε νομίζεις ἀργίαν τ' εἶναι καὶ μαλακίαν
20 ψυχῆς καὶ ἀμέλειαν. καὶ ἄλλαι δ' εἰσὶν ἀπα-
τηλαί τινες δέσποιναι προσποιούμεναι ἡδοναὶ
εἶναι, κυβεῖαί τε καὶ ἀνωφελεῖς ἀνθρώπων ὁμι-
λίαι, αἳ προϊόντος τοῦ χρόνου καὶ αὐτοῖς τοῖς
ἐξαπατηθεῖσι καταφανεῖς γίγνονται ὅτι λῦπαι
ἄρα ἦσαν ἡδοναῖς περιπεπεμμέναι, αἳ διακωλύου-
σιν αὐτοὺς ἀπὸ τῶν ὠφελίμων ἔργων κρατοῦσαι.

21 Ἀλλὰ καὶ ἄλλοι, ἔφη, ὦ Σώκρατες, ἐργάζεσθαι
μὲν οὐ κωλύονται ὑπὸ τούτων, ἀλλὰ καὶ πάνυ
σφοδρῶς πρὸς τὸ ἐργάζεσθαι ἔχουσι καὶ μηχανᾶσθαι προσόδους· ὅμως δὲ καὶ τοὺς οἴκους
κατατρίβουσι καὶ ἀμηχανίαις συνέχονται.

cases, surely, neither their knowledge nor their property is wealth ? "

"Are you trying to raise a discussion about slaves, 17 Critobulus ? "

"Oh no, not at all: I am referring to persons of whom some, at any rate, are considered men of the highest lineage. I observe that there are persons skilled in the arts of war or peace, as the case may be, who are unwilling to practise them, and the reason, I think, is just this, that they have no master over them."

"What, no master over them, when, in spite of 18 their prayers for prosperity and their desire to do what will bring them good, they are thwarted in their intentions by the powers that rule them ? "

"And who, pray, may these unseen rulers be ? " 19

"No, not unseen, but open and undisguised, surely ! And very vicious rulers they are too, as you yourself must see, if at least you regard idleness and moral cowardice and negligence as vice. Aye, and 20 then there is a set of deceitful mistresses that pretend to be pleasures—such as gambling and consorting with bad companions : even the victims of their deception find as time goes on that these, after all, are really pains concealed beneath a thin veneer of pleasures, and that they are hindering them from all profitable work by their influence over them."

"But there are other men, Socrates, whose energy 21 is not hindered by these influences, in fact they have an eager desire to work and to make an income : nevertheless they exhaust their estates and are beset with difficulties."

22 Δοῦλοι γάρ εἰσι καὶ οὗτοι, ἔφη ὁ Σωκράτης, καὶ πάνυ γε χαλεπῶν δεσποτῶν,[1] οἱ μὲν λιχνειῶν, οἱ δὲ λαγνειῶν, οἱ δὲ οἰνοφλυγιῶν, οἱ δὲ φιλοτι- μιῶν τινων μώρων καὶ δαπανηρῶν, ἃ οὕτω χαλε- πῶς ἄρχει τῶν ἀνθρώπων, ὧν ἂν ἐπικρατήσωσιν, ὥσθ' ἕως μὲν ἂν ὁρῶσιν ἡβῶντας αὐτοὺς καὶ δυναμένους ἐργάζεσθαι, ἀναγκάζουσι φέρειν ἃ ἂν αὐτοὶ ἐργάσωνται καὶ τελεῖν εἰς τὰς αὑτῶν ἐπι- θυμίας, ἐπειδὰν δὲ αὐτοὺς ἀδυνάτους αἴσθωνται ὄντας ἐργάζεσθαι διὰ τὸ γῆρας, ἀπολείπουσι τούτους κακῶς γηράσκειν, ἄλλοις δ' αὖ πειρῶνται 23 δούλοις χρῆσθαι. ἀλλὰ δεῖ, ὦ Κριτόβουλε, πρὸς ταῦτα οὐχ ἧττον διαμάχεσθαι περὶ τῆς ἐλευθερίας ἢ πρὸς τοὺς σὺν ὅπλοις πειρωμένους καταδου- λοῦσθαι. πολέμιοι γοῦν ἤδη ὅταν καλοὶ κἀγαθοὶ ὄντες καταδουλώσωνταί τινας, πολλοὺς δὴ βελ- τίους ἠνάγκασαν εἶναι σωφρονίσαντες καὶ ῥᾷον βιοτεύειν τὸν λοιπὸν χρόνον ἐποίησαν· αἱ δὲ τοιαῦται δέσποιναι αἰκιζόμεναι τὰ σώματα τῶν ἀνθρώπων καὶ τὰς ψυχὰς καὶ τοὺς οἴκους οὔποτε λήγουσιν, ἔστ' ἂν ἄρχωσιν αὐτῶν.

II. Ὁ οὖν Κριτόβουλος ἐκ τούτων ὧδέ πως εἶπεν· Ἀλλὰ περὶ μὲν τῶν τοιούτων ἀρκούντως πάνυ μοι δοκῶ τὰ λεγόμενα ὑπὸ σοῦ ἀκηκοέναι· αὐτὸς δ' ἐμαυτὸν ἐξετάζων δοκῶ μοι εὑρίσκειν ἐπιεικῶς τῶν τοιούτων ἐγκρατῆ ὄντα, ὥστ' εἴ μοι συμβουλεύοις, ὅ τι ἂν ποιῶν αὔξοιμι τὸν οἶκον, οὐκ ἄν μοι δοκῶ ὑπό γε τούτων ὧν σὺ δεσποινῶν καλεῖς κωλύεσθαι· ἀλλὰ θαρρῶν συμ- βούλευε ὅ τι ἔχεις ἀγαθόν· ἢ κατέγνωκας ἡμῶν, ὦ Σώκρατες, ἱκανῶς πλουτεῖν καὶ οὐδὲν δοκούμέν σοι προσδεῖσθαι χρημάτων ;

" Yes, they too are slaves, and hard indeed are their 22
masters : some are in bondage to gluttony, some to
lechery, some to drink, and some to foolish and
costly ambitions. And so hard is the rule of these
passions over every man who falls into their clutches,
that so long as they see that he is strong and capable
of work, they force him to pay over all the profits of
his toil, and to spend it on their own desires ; but no
sooner do they find that he is too old to work, than
they leave him to an old age of misery, and try to
fasten the yoke on other shoulders. Ah, Critobulus, 23
we must fight for our freedom against these tyrants
as persistently as if they were armed men trying to
enslave us. Indeed, open enemies may be gentlemen, and when they enslave us, may, by chastening,
purge us of our faults and cause us to live better
lives in future. But such mistresses as these never
cease to plague men in body and soul and estate all
the time that they have dominion over them."

II. The word was now with Critobulus, who continued thus :

" Well, I think you have told me quite enough
about such passions as these, and when I examine
myself I find, I think, that I have them fairly well
under control ; and therefore, if you will advise me
what I should do to increase my estate, I don't think
those mistresses, as you call them, are likely to hinder
me. So do not hesitate to give me any good advice
you can : unless, indeed, you have made up your
mind that we are rich enough already, Socrates, and
think we have no need of more money ? "

---

[1] Weiske's δεσποινῶν, mistresses, and Hirschig's αἲ . .
ἄρχουσι for ἃ ἄρχει are highly probable.

2 Οὔκουν ἔγωγε, ἔφη ὁ Σωκράτης, εἰ καὶ περὶ
ἐμοῦ λέγεις, οὐδέν μοι δοκῶ προσδεῖσθαι χρημάτων, ἀλλ᾽ ἱκανῶς πλουτεῖν· σὺ μέντοι, ὦ
Κριτόβουλε, πάνυ μοι δοκεῖς πένεσθαι, καὶ ναὶ
μὰ Δί᾽ ἔστιν ὅτε καὶ πάνυ οἰκτείρω σε ἐγώ.

3 Καὶ ὁ Κριτόβουλος γελάσας εἶπε, Καὶ πόσον
ἂν πρὸς τῶν θεῶν οἴει, ὦ Σώκρατες, ἔφη, εὑρεῖν
τὰ σὰ κτήματα πωλούμενα, πόσον δὲ τὰ ἐμά ;
Ἐγὼ μὲν οἶμαι, ἔφη ὁ Σωκράτης, εἰ ἀγαθοῦ
ὠνητοῦ ἐπιτύχοιμι, εὑρεῖν ἄν μοι σὺν τῇ οἰκίᾳ
καὶ τὰ ὄντα πάντα πάνυ ῥᾳδίως πέντε μνᾶς·[1] τὰ
μέντοι σὰ ἀκριβῶς οἶδα ὅτι πλέον ἂν εὕροι ἢ
ἑκατονταπλάσια τούτου.

4 Κᾆτα οὕτως ἐγνωκὼς σὺ μὲν οὐχ ἡγῇ προσδεῖσθαι χρημάτων, ἐμὲ δὲ οἰκτείρεις ἐπὶ τῇ πενίᾳ ;
Τὰ μὲν γὰρ ἐμά, ἔφη, ἱκανά ἐστιν ἐμοὶ παρέχειν
τὰ ἐμοὶ ἀρκοῦντα· εἰς δὲ τὸ σὸν σχῆμα, ὃ σὺ
περιβέβλησαι, καὶ τὴν σὴν δόξαν οὐδ᾽ εἰ τρὶς
ὅσα νῦν κέκτησαι προσγένοιτό σοι, οὐδ᾽ ὡς ἂν
ἱκανά μοι δοκεῖ εἶναί σοι.

5 Πῶς δὴ τοῦτ᾽ ; ἔφη ὁ Κριτόβουλος.
[Ἀπεφήνατο ὁ Σωκράτης·] Ὅτι πρῶτον μὲν ὁρῶ
σοι ἀνάγκην οὖσαν θύειν πολλά τε καὶ μεγάλα ἢ
οὔτε θεοὺς οὔτε ἀνθρώπους οἶμαί σε ἂν ἀνασχέσθαι·[2]
ἔπειτα ξένους προσήκει σοι πολλοὺς δέχεσθαι
καὶ τούτους μεγαλοπρεπῶς· ἔπειτα δὲ πολίτας
δειπνίζειν καὶ εὖ ποιεῖν ἢ ἔρημον συμμάχων εἶναι.

6 ἔτι δὲ καὶ τὴν πόλιν αἰσθάνομαι τὰ μὲν ἤδη σοι
προστάττουσαν μεγάλα τελεῖν, ἱπποτροφίας τε
καὶ χορηγίας καὶ γυμνασιαρχίας καὶ προστατείας,

---

[1] A little more than £20.

[2] It is unlikely that προστατείας is used here for προστασίας,

"Oh, if you mean to include me, I certainly think 2
I have no need of more money and am rich enough.
But you seem to me to be quite poor, Critobulus,
and at times, I assure you, I feel quite sorry for
you."

"And how much, pray," asked Critobulus, laugh- 3
ing, "would your property fetch at a sale, do you
suppose, Socrates, and how much would mine?"

"Well, if I found a good buyer, I think the whole
of my goods and chattels, including the house, might
readily sell for five minae.[1]   Yours, I feel sure, would
fetch more than a hundred times that sum."

"And in spite of that estimate, you really think 4
you have no need of money and pity me for my
poverty?"

"Yes, because my property is sufficient to satisfy
my wants, but I don't think you would have enough
to keep up the style you are living in and to support
your reputation, even if your fortune were three times
what it is."

"How can that be?" exclaimed Critobulus.   5

"Because, in the first place," explained Socrates,
"I notice that you are bound to offer many large
sacrifices; else, I fancy, you would get into trouble
with gods and men alike.   Secondly, it is your duty
to entertain many strangers, on a generous scale too.
Thirdly, you have to give dinners and play the benefactor to the citizens, or you lose your following.
Moreover, I observe that already the state is exact- 6
ing heavy contributions from you : you must needs
keep horses, pay for choruses and gymnastic com-
petitions, and accept presidencies;[2] and if war

the charge of resident aliens, since there is no proof that
this duty involved expense to the patron.

ἢν δὲ δὴ πόλεμος γένηται, οἶδ᾽ ὅτι καὶ τριηραρχίας
[μισθοὺς] καὶ εἰσφορὰς τοσαύτας σοι προστά-
ξουσιν, ὅσας σὺ οὐ ῥᾳδίως ὑποίσεις. ὅπου δ᾽ ἂν
ἐνδεῶς δόξῃς τι τούτων ποιεῖν, οἶδ᾽ ὅτι σε τιμω-
ρήσονται Ἀθηναῖοι οὐδὲν ἧττον ἢ εἰ τὰ αὑτῶν
7 λάβοιεν κλέπτοντα. πρὸς δὲ τούτοις ὁρῶ σε
οἰόμενον πλουτεῖν καὶ ἀμελῶς μὲν ἔχοντα πρὸς
τὸ μηχανᾶσθαι χρήματα, παιδικοῖς δὲ πράγμασι
προσέχοντα τὸν νοῦν, ὥσπερ ἐξόν σοι. ὧν ἕνεκα
οἰκτείρω σε, μή τι ἀνήκεστον κακὸν πάθῃς καὶ
8 εἰς πολλὴν ἀπορίαν καταστῇς. καὶ ἐμοὶ μέν, εἴ
τι καὶ προσδεηθείην, οἶδ᾽ ὅτι καὶ σὺ γιγνώσκεις,
ὡς εἰσὶν οἳ καὶ ἐπαρκέσειαν ἄν, ὥστε πάνυ μικρὰ
πορίσαντες κατακλύσειαν ἂν ἀφθονίᾳ τὴν ἐμὴν
δίαιταν· οἱ δὲ σοὶ φίλοι πολὺ ἀρκοῦντα σοῦ
μᾶλλον ἔχοντες τῇ ἑαυτῶν κατασκευῇ ἢ σὺ τῇ
σῇ ὅμως ὡς παρὰ σοῦ ὠφελησόμενοι ἀποβλέπουσι.
9 Καὶ ὁ Κριτόβουλος εἶπεν· Ἐγὼ τούτοις, ὦ
Σώκρατες, οὐκ ἔχω ἀντιλέγειν· ἀλλ᾽ ὥρα σοι
προστατεύειν ἐμοῦ, ὅπως μὴ τῷ ὄντι οἰκτρὸς
γένωμαι.

Ἀκούσας οὖν ὁ Σωκράτης εἶπε· Καὶ οὐ θαυμαστὸν δοκεῖς, ὦ Κριτόβουλε, τοῦτο σαυτῷ
ποιεῖν, ὅτι ὀλίγῳ μὲν πρόσθεν, ὅτε ἐγὼ ἔφην
πλουτεῖν, ἐγέλασας ἐπ᾽ ἐμοὶ ὡς οὐδὲ εἰδότι, ὅ τι
εἴη πλοῦτος, καὶ πρότερον οὐκ ἐπαύσω πρὶν ἐξή-
λεγξάς με καὶ ὁμολογεῖν ἐποίησας μηδὲ ἑκατοστὸν
μέρος τῶν σῶν κεκτῆσθαι, νῦν δὲ κελεύεις προστατεύειν μέ σου καὶ ἐπιμελεῖσθαι, ὅπως ἂν μὴ
παντάπασιν ἀληθῶς πένης γένοιο;

10 Ὁρῶ γάρ σε, ἔφη, ὦ Σώκρατες, ἕν τι πλουτηρὸν
ἔργον ἐπιστάμενον περιουσίαν ποιεῖν. τὸν οὖν
376

breaks out, I know they will require you to maintain
a ship and pay taxes that will nearly crush you.
Whenever you seem to fall short of what is expected
of you, the Athenians will certainly punish you as
though they had caught you robbing them. Besides 7
all this, I notice that you imagine yourself to be a
rich man ; you are indifferent to money, and yet go
courting minions, as though the cost were nothing to
you. And that is why I pity you, and fear that you
may come to grief and find yourself reduced to penury.
Now, if I ran short of money, no doubt you know as 8
well as I do that I should not lack helpers who
would need to contribute very little to fill my cup
to overflowing. But your friends, though far better
supplied with means to support their establishment
than you, yet look to receive help from you."

"I cannot dispute this, Socrates," said Critobulus, 9
"but it is time for you to take me in hand, and see
that I don't become a real object of pity."

At this Socrates exclaimed, "What, don't you
think it strange, Critobulus, that a little while ago,
when I said I was rich, you laughed at me, as though
I did not even know the meaning of riches, and
would not cease until you had proved me wrong and
made me own that my possessions were less than
one-hundredth part of yours, and yet now you bid
me take you in hand and see that you don't become
in literal truth a poor man?"

"Well, Socrates, I see that you understand one 10
process by which wealth is created—how to create a

ἀπ᾽ ὀλίγων περιποιοῦντα ἐλπίζω ἀπὸ πολλῶν γ᾽
ἂν πάνυ ῥᾳδίως πολλὴν περιουσίαν ποιῆσαι.

11   Οὔκουν μέμνησαι ἀρτίως ἐν τῷ λόγῳ, ὅτε οὐδ᾽
ἀναγρύζειν μοι ἐξουσίαν ἐποίησας λέγων, ὅτι τῷ
μὴ ἐπισταμένῳ ἵπποις χρῆσθαι οὐκ εἴη χρήματα
οἱ ἵπποι οὐδὲ ἡ γῆ οὐδὲ τὰ πρόβατα οὐδὲ ἀργύριον
οὐδὲ ἄλλο οὐδέν, ὅτῳ τις μὴ ἐπίσταιτο χρῆσθαι;
εἰσὶ μὲν οὖν αἱ πρόσοδοι ἀπὸ τῶν τοιούτων· ἐμὲ
δὲ πῶς τινι τούτων οἴει ἂν ἐπιστηθῆναι χρῆσθαι,
ᾧ τὴν ἀρχὴν οὐδὲν πώποτ᾽ ἐγένετο τούτων;

12   Ἀλλ᾽ ἐδόκει ἡμῖν, καὶ εἰ μὴ χρήματά τις τύχοι
ἔχων, ὅμως εἶναί τις ἐπιστήμη οἰκονομίας. τί
οὖν κωλύει καὶ σὲ ἐπίστασθαι;

Ὅπερ νὴ Δία καὶ αὐλεῖν ἂν κωλύσειεν ἄνθρωπον ἐπίστασθαι, εἰ μήτε αὐτὸς πώποτε κτή-
σαιτο αὐλοὺς μήτε ἄλλος αὐτῷ παράσχοι ἐν τοῖς
13 αὑτοῦ μανθάνειν· οὕτω δὴ καὶ ἐμοὶ ἔχει περὶ τῆς
οἰκονομίας. οὔτε γὰρ αὐτὸς ὄργανα χρήματα
ἐκεκτήμην, ὥστε μανθάνειν, οὔτε ἄλλος πώποτέ
μοι παρέσχε τὰ ἑαυτοῦ διοικεῖν ἀλλ᾽ ἢ σὺ νυνὶ
ἐθέλεις παρέχειν. οἱ δὲ δήπου τὸ πρῶτον μανθάνοντες κιθαρίζειν καὶ τὰς λύρας λυμαίνονται· καὶ
ἐγὼ δὴ εἰ ἐπιχειρήσαιμι ἐν τῷ σῷ οἴκῳ μανθάνειν
οἰκονομεῖν, ἴσως ἂν καταλυμηναίμην ἄν σου τὸν
οἶκον.

14   Πρὸς ταῦτα ὁ Κριτόβουλος εἶπε· Προθύμως
γε, ὦ Σώκρατες, ἀποφεύγειν μοι πειρᾷ μηδέν
με συνωφελῆσαι εἰς τὸ ῥᾷον ὑποφέρειν τὰ ἐμοὶ
ἀναγκαῖα πράγματα. Οὐ μὰ Δί᾽, ἔφη ὁ Σωκράτης, οὐκ ἔγωγε, ἀλλ᾽ ὅσα ἔχω καὶ πάνυ προθύμως
15 ἐξηγήσομαί σοι. οἶμαι δ᾽ ἂν καὶ εἰ ἐπὶ πῦρ

balance. So a man who saves on a small income can, I suppose, very easily show a large surplus with a large one."

"Then don't you remember saying just now in our 11 conversation, when you wouldn't give me leave to utter a syllable, that if a man doesn't know how to manage horses, his horses are not wealth to him, nor his land, sheep, money or anything else, if he doesn't know how to manage them? Now these are the sources from which income is derived : and how do you suppose that I can possibly know how to manage any of these things, seeing that I never yet possessed any one of them?"

"Still we held that, even if a man happens to 12 have no wealth, there is such a thing as a science of household management. Then what reason is there why you should not know it?"

"Exactly the same reason, of course, that a man would have for not knowing how to play on the flute if he had never possessed one himself and had never borrowed one to learn on. That is just my case 13 with regard to estate management ; for never having possessed wealth myself, I have not had an opportunity of learning on an instrument of my own, and nobody has ever let me handle his, until you made your offer. Beginners, I fancy, are apt to spoil the lyres they learn on ; and if I attempted to learn to manage estates by practising on yours, possibly I might spoil it entirely for you."

"Ah, Socrates!" rejoined Critobulus, "I see you 14 are eager to avoid giving me any help towards lightening the weight of my troublesome duties."

"Not at all, not at all," said Socrates, "I am all eagerness to tell you all I know. Suppose that you 15

ἐλθόντος σου καὶ μὴ ὄντος παρ᾽ ἐμοί, εἰ ἄλλοσε
ἡγησάμην ὁπόθεν σοι εἴη λαβεῖν, οὐκ ἂν ἐμέμφου
μοι, καὶ εἰ ὕδωρ παρ᾽ ἐμοῦ αἰτοῦντί σοι αὐτὸς μὴ
ἔχων ἄλλοσε καὶ ἐπὶ τοῦτο ἤγαγον, οἶδ᾽ ὅτι οὐδ᾽
ἂν τοῦτό μοι ἐμέμφου, καὶ εἰ βουλομένου μουσικὴν
μαθεῖν σου παρ᾽ ἐμοῦ δείξαιμί σοι πολὺ δεινοτέρους ἐμοῦ περὶ μουσικὴν καί σοι χάριν ἂν
εἰδότας, εἰ ἐθέλοις παρ᾽ αὐτῶν μανθάνειν, τί ἂν
ἔτι μοι ταῦτα ποιοῦντι μέμφοιο;

Οὐδὲν ἂν δικαίως γε, ὦ Σώκρατες.

16 Ἐγὼ τοίνυν σοι δείξω, ὦ Κριτόβουλε, ὅσα νῦν
λιπαρεῖς παρ᾽ ἐμοῦ μανθάνειν, πολὺ ἄλλους ἐμοῦ
δεινοτέρους περὶ ταῦτα. ὁμολογῶ δὲ μεμεληκέναι
μοι, οἵτινες ἕκαστα ἐπιστημονέστατοί εἰσι τῶν ἐν
17 τῇ πόλει. καταμαθὼν γάρ ποτε ἀπὸ τῶν αὐτῶν
ἔργων τοὺς μὲν πάνυ ἀπόρους ὄντας, τοὺς δὲ πάνυ
πλουσίους ἀπεθαύμασα καὶ ἔδοξέ μοι ἄξιον εἶναι
ἐπισκέψεως, ὅ τι εἴη τοῦτο. καὶ εὗρον ἐπισκοπῶν
18 πάνυ οἰκείως ταῦτα γιγνόμενα. τοὺς μὲν γὰρ
εἰκῇ ταῦτα πράττοντας ζημιουμένους ἑώρων, τοὺς
δὲ γνώμῃ συντεταμένῃ ἐπιμελουμένους καὶ θᾶττον καὶ ῥᾷον καὶ κερδαλεώτερον κατέγνων πράττοντας. παρ᾽ ὧν ἂν καὶ σὲ οἶμαι, εἰ βούλοιο,
μαθόντα, εἴ σοι ὁ θεὸς μὴ ἐναντιοῖτο, πάνυ ἂν
δεινὸν χρηματιστὴν γενέσθαι.

III. Ἀκούσας ταῦτα ὁ Κριτόβουλος εἶπε, Νῦν
τοι, ἔφη, ἐγώ σε οὐκέτι ἀφήσω, ὦ Σώκρατες, πρὶν
ἄν μοι ἃ ὑπέσχησαι ἐναντίον τῶν φίλων τουτωνὶ
ἀποδείξῃς.

had come to me for fire, and I, having none by me, had taken you to some place where you could get it ; you would not, I think, have found fault with me : or, if you had asked for water, and I, having none myself, had brought you to some other place for it, I feel sure that you would not have found fault with me for that either : or, suppose you wanted to learn music with me and I directed you to persons far more skilled in music than I am, who would be grateful to you for taking lessons with them, what fault could you find with me for doing so?"

"None, if I were fair, Socrates." 16

"Well then, Critobulus, I will direct you to others far more skilled than I in the things you now seek to learn from me. I confess that I have made a point of finding out who are the greatest masters of various sciences to be found in Athens. For observ- 17 ing once that the same pursuits lead in one case to great poverty and in another to great riches, I was filled with amazement, and thought it worth while to consider what this could mean. And on consider- ation I found that these things happen quite naturally. For I saw that those who follow these pursuits care- 18 lessly suffer loss, and I discovered that those who devote themselves earnestly to them accomplish them more quickly, more easily and with more profit. I think that if you would elect to learn from these, you too with God's favour would turn out a clever man of business."

III. "Socrates," exclaimed Critobulus on hearing this, "I don't intend to let you go now, until you have proved to my satisfaction what you have promised in the presence of our friends here to prove."

Τί οὖν, ἔφη ὁ Σωκράτης, ὦ Κριτόβουλε, ἤν σοι ἀποδεικνύω πρῶτον μὲν οἰκίας τοὺς μὲν ἀπὸ πολλοῦ ἀργυρίου ἀχρήστους οἰκοδομοῦντας, τοὺς δὲ ἀπὸ πολὺ ἐλάττονος πάντα ἐχούσας ὅσα δεῖ, ἢ δόξω ἔν τί σοι τοῦτο τῶν οἰκονομικῶν ἔργων ἐπιδεικνύαι;

Καὶ πάνυ γ᾽, ἔφη ὁ Κριτόβουλος.

2 Τί δ᾽ ἦν τὸ τούτου ἀκόλουθον μετὰ τοῦτό σοι ἐπιδεικνύω, τοὺς μὲν πάνυ πολλὰ καὶ παντοῖα κεκτημένους ἔπιπλα καὶ τούτοις, ὅταν δέωνται, μὴ ἔχοντας χρῆσθαι μηδὲ εἰδότας, εἰ σῶά ἐστιν αὐτοῖς, καὶ διὰ ταῦτα πολλὰ μὲν αὐτοὺς ἀνιωμένους, πολλὰ δ᾽ ἀνιῶντας τοὺς οἰκέτας· τοὺς δὲ οὐδὲν πλέον, ἀλλὰ καὶ μείονα τούτων κεκτημένους ἔχοντας εὐθὺς ἕτοιμα ὅτων ἂν δέωνται χρῆσθαι;

3 Ἀλλὰ τί οὖν τούτων ἐστίν, ὦ Σώκρατες, αἴτιον ἢ ὅτι τοῖς μὲν ὅποι ἔτυχεν ἕκαστον καταβέβληται, τοῖς δὲ ἐν χώρᾳ ἕκαστα τεταγμένα κεῖται;

Ναὶ μὰ Δί᾽, ἔφη ὁ Σωκράτης· καὶ οὐδ᾽ ἐν χώρᾳ γε, ἐν ᾗ ἔτυχεν, ἀλλὰ ἔνθα προσήκει, ἕκαστα διατέτακται.

Λέγειν τί μοι δοκεῖς, ἔφη, καὶ τοῦτο, ὁ Κριτόβουλος, τῶν οἰκονομικῶν.

4 Τί οὖν, ἤν σοι, ἔφη, καὶ οἰκέτας αὖ ἐπιδεικνύω ἔνθα μὲν πάντας ὡς εἰπεῖν δεδεμένους καὶ τούτους θαμινὰ ἀποδιδράσκοντας, ἔνθα δὲ λελυμένους καὶ ἐθέλοντάς τε ἐργάζεσθαι καὶ παραμένειν, οὐ καὶ τοῦτό σοι δόξω ἀξιοθέατον τῆς οἰκονομίας ἔργον ἐπιδεικνύαι;

Ναὶ μὰ Δί᾽, ἔφη ὁ Κριτόβουλος, καὶ σφόδρα γε.

" Well then," said Socrates, " what if I prove to your satisfaction, Critobulus, to begin with, that some men spend large sums in building houses that are useless, while others build houses perfect in all respects for much less? Will you think that I am putting before you one of the operations that constitute estate management?"

" Yes, certainly."

" And what if I show you next the companion to 2 this—that some possess many costly belongings and cannot use them at need, and do not even know whether they are safe and sound, and so are continually worried themselves and worrying their servants, whereas others, though they possess not more, but even less, have whatever they want ready for use?"

" What is the reason of this, then, Socrates? Is it 3 not simply this, that the former stow their things away anywhere and the latter have everything neatly arranged in some place?"

" Yes, of course, arranged carefully in the proper place, not just anywhere."

" Your point, I take it, is that this too is an element in estate management."

" Then what if I show you besides that in some 4 households nearly all the servants are in fetters and yet continually try to run away, whereas in others they are under no restraint and are willing to work and to stay at their posts? Won't you think that here too I am pointing out to you a notable effect of estate management?"

" Yes, of course; very much so."

5 Ἦν δὲ καὶ παραπλησίους γεωργίας γεωργοῦντας τοὺς μὲν ἀπολωλέναι φάσκοντας ὑπὸ γεωργίας καὶ ἀποροῦντας, τοὺς δὲ ἀφθόνως καὶ καλῶς πάντα ἔχοντας, ὅσων δέονται, ἀπὸ τῆς γεωργίας;

Ναὶ μὰ Δί’, ἔφη ὁ Κριτόβουλος. ἴσως γὰρ ἀναλίσκουσιν οὐκ εἰς ἃ δεῖ μόνον, ἀλλὰ καὶ εἰς ἃ βλάβην φέρει αὐτῷ καὶ τῷ οἴκῳ.

6 Εἰσὶ μέν τινες ἴσως, ἔφη ὁ Σωκράτης, καὶ τοιοῦτοι. ἀλλ’ ἐγὼ οὐ τούτους λέγω, ἀλλ’ οἳ οὐδ’ εἰς τἀναγκαῖα ἔχουσι δαπανᾶν, γεωργεῖν φάσκοντες.

Καὶ τί ἂν εἴη τούτου αἴτιον, ὦ Σώκρατες;

Ἐγώ σε ἄξω καὶ ἐπὶ τούτους, ἔφη ὁ Σωκράτης· σὺ δὲ θεώμενος δήπου καταμαθήσῃ.

Νὴ Δί’, ἔφη, ἢν δύνωμαί γε.

7 Οὐκοῦν χρὴ θεώμενον σαυτοῦ ἀποπειρᾶσθαι εἰ γνώσῃ. νῦν δ’ ἐγώ σε σύνοιδα ἐπὶ μὲν κωμῳδῶν θέαν καὶ πάνυ πρωὶ ἀνιστάμενον καὶ πάνυ μακρὰν ὁδὸν βαδίζοντα καὶ ἐμὲ ἀναπείθοντα προθύμως συνθεᾶσθαι· ἐπὶ δὲ τοιοῦτον οὐδέν με πώποτε ἔργον παρεκάλεσας.

Οὐκοῦν γελοῖός σοι φαίνομαι εἶναι, ὦ Σώκρατες.

8 Σαυτῷ δὲ πολὺ νὴ Δί’, ἔφη, γελοιότερος. ἢν δὲ καὶ ἀφ’ ἱππικῆς σοι ἐπιδεικνύω τοὺς μὲν εἰς ἀπορίαν τῶν ἐπιτηδείων ἐληλυθότας, τοὺς δὲ διὰ τὴν ἱππικὴν καὶ πάνυ εὐπόρους ὄντας καὶ ἅμα ἀγαλλομένους ἐπὶ τῷ κέρδει;

Οὐκοῦν τούτους μὲν καὶ ἐγὼ ὁρῶ καὶ οἶδα ἑκατέρους καὶ οὐδέν τι μᾶλλον τῶν κερδαινόντων γίγνομαι.

9 Θεᾷ γὰρ αὐτοὺς ᾗπερ τοὺς τραγῳδούς τε καὶ κωμῳδούς, οὐχ ὅπως ποιητὴς οἴομαι γένῃ, ἀλλ’

384

" And that when men farm the same kind of land, 5
some are poverty-stricken and declare that they are
ruined by farming, and others do well with the farm
and have all they want in abundance ? "

" Yes, of course ; for maybe some spend money
not on necessary purposes only but on what brings
harm to the owner and the estate."

" Perhaps there are such people.   But I am refer- 6
ring rather to those who haven't the money to meet
even the necessary expenses, though professing to be
farmers."

" Now what can be the reason of that, Socrates ? "

" I will take you to these too ; and when you
watch them, you will find out, I fancy."

" Of course ; that is, if I can."

" Then you must watch, and try by experiment 7
whether you are capable of understanding.   At
present I observe that when a comedy is to be
seen, you get up very early and walk a very long
way and press me eagerly to go to the play with
you.   But you have never yet invited me to see
a drama of real life like this."

" You think me ridiculous, don't you, Socrates ? "

" You think yourself far more so, I am sure.   And 8
suppose I show you that some have been brought
to penury by keeping horses, while others prosper
by doing so, and moreover glory in their gain ? "

" Well, I too see and know instances of both ; I
am not one of the gainers for all that."

" The fact is you watch them just as you watch 9
the actors in tragedy or comedy, not, I suppose, to

ὅπως ἡσθῇς ἰδών τι ἢ ἀκούσας· καὶ ταῦτα μὲν
ἴσως οὕτως ὀρθῶς ἔχει, οὐ γὰρ ποιητὴς βούλει
γενέσθαι, ἱππικῇ δ' ἀναγκαζόμενος χρῆσθαι οὐ
μῶρος οἴει εἶναι, εἰ μὴ σκοπεῖς, ὅπως μὴ ἰδιώτης
ἔσῃ τούτου τοῦ ἔργου, ἄλλως τε καὶ τῶν αὐτῶν
ἵππων [1] ἀγαθῶν εἴς τε τὴν χρῆσιν καὶ κερδαλέων
εἰς πώλησιν ὄντων ;

10 Πωλοδαμνεῖν με κελεύεις, ὦ Σώκρατες ;

Οὐ μὰ Δι' οὐδέν τι μᾶλλον ἢ καὶ γεωργοὺς ἐκ
παιδίων ὠνούμενον κατασκευάζειν, ἀλλ' εἶναί
τινές μοι δοκοῦσιν ἡλικίαι καὶ ἵππων καὶ ἀνθρώπων, αἳ εὐθύς τε χρήσιμαί εἰσι καὶ ἐπὶ τὸ
βέλτιον ἐπιδιδόασιν. ἔχω δ' ἐπιδεῖξαι καὶ γυναιξὶ
ταῖς γαμεταῖς τοὺς μὲν οὕτω χρωμένους, ὥστε
συνεργοὺς ἔχειν αὐτὰς εἰς τὸ συναύξειν τοὺς
οἴκους, τοὺς δὲ ᾗ [2] ὡς πλεῖστα λυμαίνονται.

11 Καὶ τούτου πότερα χρή, ὦ Σώκρατες, τὸν ἄνδρα
αἰτιᾶσθαι ἢ τὴν γυναῖκα ;

Πρόβατον μέν, ἔφη ὁ Σωκράτης, ὡς ἐπὶ τὸ
πολὺ ἢν κακῶς ἔχῃ, τὸν νομέα αἰτιώμεθα, καὶ
ἵππος ὡς ἐπὶ τὸ πολὺ ἢν κακουργῇ, τὸν ἱππέα
κακίζομεν· τῆς δὲ γυναικός, εἰ μὲν διδασκομένη
ὑπὸ τοῦ ἀνδρὸς τἀγαθὰ κακοποιεῖ, ἴσως δικαίως
ἂν ἡ γυνὴ τὴν αἰτίαν ἔχοι· εἰ δὲ μὴ διδάσκων τὰ
καλὰ κἀγαθὰ ἀνεπιστήμονι τούτων χρῷτο, ἆρ' οὐ
12 δικαίως ἂν ὁ ἀνὴρ τὴν αἰτίαν ἔχοι ; πάντως δ',
ἔφη, ὦ Κριτόβουλε, φίλοι γάρ ἐσμεν οἱ παρόντες,
ἀπαλήθευσον [3] πρὸς ἡμᾶς. ἔστιν ὅτῳ ἄλλῳ τῶν
σπουδαίων πλείω ἐπιτρέπεις ἢ τῇ γυναικί ;

---

[1] ἵππων Graux : ὄντων Sauppe with the MSS.
[2] ὡς πλεῖστα Stephanus : οἱ πλεῖστοι Sauppe with most MSS.
[3] ἀπαλήθευσον Stephanus : ἀπαληθεῦσαι Sauppe with the MSS.

become a playwright, but for the pleasure of seeing
and hearing something. And perhaps there is no
harm in that, because you don't want to write plays;
but seeing that you are forced to meddle with
horses, don't you think that common-sense requires
you to see that you are not ignorant of the business,
the more so as the self-same horses are both good
to use and profitable to sell?"

"Would you have me break in colts, Socrates?" 10

"Of course not, no more than I would have you
buy children to train as agricultural labourers; but
horses and human beings alike, I think, on reaching
a certain age forthwith become useful and go on
improving. I can also show you that husbands differ
widely in their treatment of their wives, and some
succeed in winning their co-operation and thereby
increase their estates, while others bring utter ruin
on their houses by their behaviour to them."

"And ought one to blame the husband or the 11
wife for that, Socrates?"

"When a sheep is ailing," said Socrates, "we
generally blame the shepherd, and when a horse is
vicious, we generally find fault with his rider. In
the case of a wife, if she receives instruction in the
right way from her husband and yet does badly,
perhaps she should bear the blame; but if the
husband does not instruct his wife in the right way of
doing things, and so finds her ignorant, should he
not bear the blame himself? Anyhow, Critobulus, 12
you should tell us the truth, for we are all friends
here. Is there anyone to whom you commit more
affairs of importance than you commit to your
wife?"

Οὐδενί, ἔφη.

Ἔστι δὲ ὅτῳ ἐλάττονα διαλέγῃ ἢ τῇ γυναικί ;
Εἰ δὲ μή, οὐ πολλοῖς γε, ἔφη.

13 Ἔγημας δὲ αὐτὴν παῖδα νέαν μάλιστα καὶ
ὡς ἠδύνατο ἐλάχιστα ἑωρακυῖαν καὶ ἀκηκουῖαν ;
Μάλιστα.

Οὐκοῦν πολὺ θαυμαστότερον, εἴ τι ὧν δεῖ
λέγειν ἢ πράττειν ἐπίσταιτο ἢ εἰ ἐξαμαρτάνοι.

14 Οἷς δὲ σὺ λέγεις ἀγαθὰς εἶναι γυναῖκας, ὦ
Σώκρατες, ἢ αὐτοὶ ταύτας ἐπαίδευσαν ;

Οὐδὲν οἷον τὸ ἐπισκοπεῖσθαι. συστήσω δέ
σοι ἐγὼ καὶ Ἀσπασίαν, ἣ ἐπιστημονέστερον
15 ἐμοῦ σοι ταῦτα πάντα ἐπιδείξει. νομίζω δὲ
γυναῖκα κοινωνὸν ἀγαθὴν οἴκου οὖσαν πάνυ
ἀντίρροπον εἶναι τῷ ἀνδρὶ ἐπὶ τὸ ἀγαθόν. ἔρχεται μὲν γὰρ εἰς τὴν οἰκίαν διὰ τῶν τοῦ ἀνδρὸς
πράξεων τὰ κτήματα ὡς ἐπὶ τὸ πολύ, δαπανᾶται δὲ
διὰ τῶν τῆς γυναικὸς ταμιευμάτων τὰ πλεῖστα·
καὶ εὖ μὲν τούτων γιγνομένων αὔξονται οἱ οἶκοι,
κακῶς δὲ τούτων πραττομένων οἱ οἶκοι μειοῦνται.

16 οἶμαι δέ σοι καὶ τῶν ἄλλων ἐπιστημῶν τοὺς
ἀξίως λόγου ἑκάστην ἐργαζομένους ἔχειν ἂν ἐπι-
δεῖξαί σοι, εἴ τι προσδεῖσθαι νομίζεις.

IV. Ἀλλὰ πάσας μὲν τί σε δεῖ ἐπιδεικνύναι, ὦ
Σώκρατες ; ἔφη ὁ Κριτόβουλος· οὔτε γὰρ κτήσασθαι πασῶν τῶν τεχνῶν ἐργάτας ῥάδιον οἵους
δεῖ οὔτε ἔμπειρον γενέσθαι αὐτῶν οἷόν τε, ἀλλ᾽
αἳ δοκοῦσι κάλλισται τῶν ἐπιστημῶν καὶ ἐμοὶ
πρέποι ἂν μάλιστα ἐπιμελομένῳ, ταύτας μοι καὶ
αὐτὰς ἐπιδείκνυε καὶ τοὺς πράττοντας αὐτὰς
καὶ αὐτὸς δὲ ὅ τι δύνασαι συνωφέλει εἰς ταῦτα
διδάσκων.

" There is not."

" Is there anyone with whom you talk less ? "

" There are few or none, I confess."

" And you married her when she was a mere 13
child and had seen and heard almost nothing ? "

" Certainly."

" Then it would be far more surprising if she
understood what she should say or do than if she
made mistakes."

" But what of the husbands who, as you say, have 14
good wives, Socrates ? Did they train them
themselves ? "

" There's nothing like investigation. I will in-
troduce Aspasia to you, and she will explain the
whole matter to you with more knowledge than I
possess. I think that the wife who is a good 15
partner in the household contributes just as much as
her husband to its good ; because the incomings
for the most part are the result of the husband's
exertions, but the outgoings are controlled mostly
by the wife's dispensation. If both do their part
well, the estate is increased ; if they act incom-
petently, it is diminished. If you think you want 16
to know about other branches of knowledge, I fancy
I can show you people who acquit themselves
creditably in any one of them."

IV. " Surely, Socrates, there is no need to go
through the whole list. For it is not easy to get
workmen who are skilled in all the arts, nor is it
possible to become an expert in them. Pray select
the branches of knowledge that seem the noblest
and would be most suitable for me to cultivate :
show me these, and those who practise them ; and
give me from your own knowledge any help you can
towards learning them."

2 Ἀλλὰ καλῶς, ἔφη, λέγεις, ὦ Κριτόβουλε. καὶ γὰρ αἵ γε βαναυσικαὶ καλούμεναι καὶ ἐπίρρητοί τέ εἰσι καὶ εἰκότως μέντοι πάνυ ἀδοξοῦνται πρὸς τῶν πόλεων. καταλυμαίνονται γὰρ τὰ σώματα τῶν τε ἐργαζομένων καὶ τῶν ἐπιμελομένων ἀναγκάζουσαι καθῆσθαι καὶ σκιατραφεῖσθαι, ἔνιαι δὲ καὶ πρὸς πῦρ ἡμερεύειν. τῶν δὲ σωμάτων θηλυνομένων καὶ αἱ ψυχαὶ πολὺ ἀρρωστότεραι 3 γίγνονται. καὶ ἀσχολίας δὲ μάλιστα ἔχουσι καὶ φίλων καὶ πόλεως συνεπιμελεῖσθαι αἱ βαναυσικαὶ καλούμεναι. ὥστε οἱ τοιοῦτοι δοκοῦσι κακοὶ καὶ φίλοις χρῆσθαι καὶ ταῖς πατρίσιν ἀλεξητῆρες εἶναι. καὶ ἐν ἐνίαις μὲν τῶν πόλεων, μάλιστα δὲ ἐν ταῖς εὐπολέμοις δοκούσαις εἶναι οὐδ' ἔξεστι τῶν πολιτῶν οὐδενὶ βαναυσικὰς τέχνας ἐργάζεσθαι.

4 Ἡμῖν δὲ δὴ ποίαις συμβουλεύεις, ὦ Σώκρατες, χρῆσθαι;

Ἆρα, ἔφη ὁ Σωκράτης, μὴ αἰσχυνθῶμεν τὸν Περσῶν βασιλέα μιμήσασθαι; ἐκεῖνον γάρ φασιν ἐν τοῖς καλλίστοις τε καὶ ἀναγκαιοτάτοις ἡγούμενον εἶναι ἐπιμελήμασι γεωργίαν τε καὶ τὴν πολεμικὴν τέχνην τούτων ἀμφοτέρων ἰσχυρῶς ἐπιμελεῖσθαι.

5 Καὶ ὁ Κριτόβουλος ἀκούσας ταῦτα εἶπε, Καὶ τοῦτο, ἔφη, πιστεύεις, ὦ Σώκρατες, βασιλέα τὸν Περσῶν γεωργίας τι συνεπιμελεῖσθαι;

Ὧδ' ἄν, ἔφη ὁ Σωκράτης, ἐπισκοποῦντες, ὦ Κριτόβουλε, ἴσως ἂν καταμάθοιμεν, εἴ τι συνεπιμελεῖται. τῶν μὲν γὰρ πολεμικῶν ἔργων ὁμολογοῦμεν αὐτὸν ἰσχυρῶς ἐπιμελεῖσθαι, ὅτι ἐξ ὁπόσωνπερ ἐθνῶν δασμοὺς λαμβάνει, τέταχε τῷ

"Very good, Critobulus; for, to be sure, the 2 illiberal arts, as they are called, are spoken against, and are, naturally enough, held in utter disdain in our states. For they spoil the bodies of the workmen and the foremen, forcing them to sit still and live indoors, and in some cases to spend the day at the fire. The softening of the body involves a serious weakening of the mind. Moreover, these 3 so-called illiberal arts leave no spare time for attention to one's friends and city, so that those who follow them are reputed bad at dealing with friends [1] and bad defenders of their country. In fact, in some of the states, and especially in those reputed warlike, it is not even lawful for any of the citizens to work at illiberal arts."

"But what arts, pray, do you advise us to follow, 4 Socrates?"

"Need we be ashamed of imitating the king of the Persians? For they say that he pays close attention to husbandry and the art of war, holding that these are two of the noblest and most necessary pursuits."

"And do you really believe, Socrates," exclaimed 5 Critobulus on hearing this, "that the king of the Persians includes husbandry among his occupations?"

"Perhaps, Critobulus, the following considerations will enable us to discover whether he does so. We allow that he pays close attention to warfare, because he has given a standing order to every governor of the nations from which he receives tribute, to supply

---

[1] Or, less probably, "bad for friends to deal with."

391

ἄρχοντι ἑκάστῳ, εἰς ὁπόσους δεῖ διδόναι τροφὴν
ἱππέας καὶ τοξότας καὶ σφενδονήτας καὶ γερ-
ροφόρους, οἵτινες τῶν τε ὑπ' αὐτοῦ ἀρχομένων
ἱκανοὶ ἔσονται κρατεῖν καὶ ἢν πολέμιοι ἐπίωσιν,

6 ἀρήξουσι τῇ χώρᾳ, χωρὶς δὲ τούτων φύλακας ἐν
ταῖς ἀκροπόλεσι τρέφει· καὶ τὴν μὲν τροφὴν τοῖς
φρουροῖς δίδωσιν ὁ ἄρχων, ᾧ τοῦτο προστέτακται,
βασιλεὺς δὲ κατ' ἐνιαυτὸν ἐξέτασιν ποιεῖται τῶν
μισθοφόρων καὶ τῶν ἄλλων, οἷς ὡπλίσθαι προστέτακται, καὶ πάντας ἅμα συνάγων πλὴν τοὺς
ἐν ταῖς ἀκροπόλεσιν ἔνθα δὴ ὁ σύλλογος καλεῖ-
ται· καὶ τοὺς μὲν ἀμφὶ τὴν ἑαυτοῦ οἴκησιν αὐτὸς
ἐφορᾷ, τοὺς δὲ πρόσω ἀποικοῦντας πιστοὺς

7 πέμπει ἐπισκοπεῖν· καὶ οἳ μὲν ἂν φαίνωνται
τῶν φρουράρχων καὶ τῶν χιλιάρχων καὶ τῶν
σατραπῶν τὸν ἀριθμὸν τὸν τεταγμένον ἔκπλεων
ἔχοντες καὶ τούτους δοκίμοις ἵπποις τε καὶ ὅπλοις
κατεσκευασμένους παρέχωσι, τούτους μὲν τοὺς
ἄρχοντας καὶ ταῖς τιμαῖς αὔξει καὶ δώροις μεγάλοις
καταπλουτίζει, οὓς δ' ἂν εὕρῃ τῶν ἀρχόντων ἢ
καταμελοῦντας τῶν φρουρῶν ἢ κατακερδαίνοντας,
τούτους χαλεπῶς κολάζει καὶ παύων τῆς ἀρχῆς
ἄλλους ἐπιμελητὰς καθίστησι. τῶν μὲν δὴ
πολεμικῶν ἔργων ταῦτα ποιῶν δοκεῖ ἡμῖν
ἀναμφιλόγως ἐπιμελεῖσθαι.

8 Ἔτι δὲ ὁπόσην μὲν τῆς χώρας διελαύνων ἐφορᾷ
αὐτὸς καὶ δοκιμάζει, ὁπόσην δὲ μὴ αὐτὸς ἐφορᾷ,
πέμπων πιστοὺς ἐπισκοπεῖται. καὶ οὓς μὲν ἂν
αἰσθάνηται τῶν ἀρχόντων συνοικουμένην τε τὴν
χώραν παρεχομένους καὶ ἐνεργὸν οὖσαν τὴν γῆν
καὶ πλήρη δένδρων τε ὧν ἑκάστη φέρει καὶ καρπῶν, τούτοις μὲν χώραν τε ἄλλην προστίθησι

maintenance for a specified number of horsemen and
archers and slingers and light infantry, that they
may be strong enough to control his subjects and to
protect the country in the event of an invasion;
and, apart from these, he maintains garrisons in the 6
citadels. Maintenance for these is supplied by the
governor charged with this duty, and the king
annually reviews the mercenaries and all the other
troops ordered to be under arms, assembling all but
the men in the citadels at the place of muster, as it
is called: he personally inspects the men who are
near his residence, and sends trusted agents to
review those who live far away. The officers, 7
whether commanders of garrisons or of regiments or
viceroys, who turn out with a full complement of
men and parade them equipped with horses and
arms in good condition, he promotes in the scale of
honour and enriches with large grants of money;
but those officers whom he finds to be neglecting
the garrisons or making profit out of them he
punishes severely, and appoints others to take
their office. These actions, then, seem to us to
leave no room for question that he pays attention
to warfare.

"As for the country, he personally examines so 8
much of it as he sees in the course of his progress
through it; and he receives reports from his trusted
agents on the territories that he does not see for
himself. To those governors who are able to show
him that their country is densely populated and
that the land is in cultivation and well stocked with
the trees of the district and with the crops, he
assigns more territory and gives presents, and

καὶ δώροις κοσμεῖ καὶ ἕδραις ἐντίμοις γεραίρει,
οἷς δ' ἂν ὁρᾷ ἀργόν τε τὴν χώραν οὖσαν καὶ
ὀλιγάνθρωπον ἢ διὰ χαλεπότητα ἢ δι' ὕβριν ἢ
δι' ἀμέλειαν, τούτους δὲ κολάζων καὶ παύων τῆς
9 ἀρχῆς ἄρχοντας ἄλλους καθίστησι. ταῦτα ποιῶν
δοκεῖ ἧττον ἐπιμελεῖσθαι, ὅπως ἡ γῆ ἐνεργὸς
ἔσται ὑπὸ τῶν κατοικούντων ἢ ὅπως εὖ φυλάξεται
ὑπὸ τῶν φρουρούντων, καὶ εἰσὶ δ' αὐτῷ οἱ ἄρχοντες διατεταγμένοι ἐφ' ἑκάτερον οὐχ οἱ αὐτοί,
ἀλλ' οἱ μὲν ἄρχουσι τῶν κατοικούντων τε καὶ τῶν
ἐργατῶν καὶ δασμοὺς ἐκ τούτων ἐκλέγουσιν, οἱ δ'
10 ἄρχουσι τῶν ὡπλισμένων τε καὶ τῶν¹ φρουρῶν.
κἂν μὲν ὁ φρούραρχος μὴ ἱκανῶς τῇ χώρᾳ ἀρήγῃ,
ὁ τῶν ἐνοικούντων ἄρχων καὶ τῶν ἔργων ἐπιμελούμενος κατηγορεῖ τοῦ φρουράρχου, ὅτι οὐ
δύνανται ἐργάζεσθαι διὰ τὴν ἀφυλαξίαν, ἢν δὲ
παρέχοντος τοῦ φρουράρχου εἰρήνην τοῖς ἔργοις
ὁ ἄρχων ὀλιγάνθρωπόν τε παρέχηται καὶ ἀργὸν
τὴν χώραν, τούτου αὖ κατηγορεῖ ὁ φρούραρχος.
11 καὶ γὰρ σχεδόν τι οἱ κακῶς τὴν χώραν ἐργαζόμενοι οὔτε τοὺς φρουροὺς τρέφουσιν οὔτε τοὺς
δασμοὺς δύνανται ἀποδιδόναι. ὅπου δ' ἂν σα-
τράπης καθιστῆται, οὗτος ἀμφοτέρων τούτων
ἐπιμελεῖται.

12 Ἐκ τούτων ὁ Κριτόβουλος εἶπεν· Οὐκοῦν εἰ
μὲν δὴ ταῦτα ποιεῖ βασιλεύς, ὦ Σώκρατες, οὐδὲν
ἔμοιγε δοκεῖ ἧττον τῶν γεωργικῶν ἔργων ἐπιμελεῖσθαι ἢ τῶν πολεμικῶν.

13 Ἔτι δὲ πρὸς τούτοις, ἔφη ὁ Σωκράτης, ἐν
ὁπόσαις τε χώραις ἐνοικεῖ καὶ εἰς ὁπόσας ἐπι-
στρέφεται, ἐπιμελεῖται τούτων, ὅπως κῆποι

rewards them with seats of honour.[1]   Those whose
territory he finds uncultivated and thinly populated
either through harsh administration or through contempt or through carelessness, he punishes, and
appoints others to take their office.   By such action, 9
does he seem to provide less for the cultivation of
the land by the inhabitants than for its protection
by the garrisons?   Moreover, each of these duties is
entrusted to a separate class of officers; one class
governs the residents and the labourers, and collects
tribute from them, the other commands the men
under arms and the garrisons.   If the commander of 10
a garrison affords insufficient protection to the
country, the civil governor and controller of agriculture denounces the commander, setting out that
the inhabitants are unable to work the farms for
want of protection.   If, on the other hand, the
commander brings peace to the farms, and the
governor nevertheless causes the land to be sparsely
populated and idle, the commander in turn denounces the governor.   For, roughly speaking, 11
where cultivation is inefficient, the garrisons are
not maintained and the tribute cannot be paid.
Wherever a viceroy is appointed, he attends to
both these matters."

At this point Critobulus said : " Well, Socrates, if 12
the Great King does this, it seems to me that he
pays as much attention to husbandry as to warfare."

" Yet further," continued Socrates, "in all the 13
districts he resides in and visits he takes care that

---

[1] *Cyropaedia*, VIII. i. 39.

[1] τε καὶ τῶν added by Graux : Sauppe omits.

τε ἔσονται οἱ παράδεισοι καλούμενοι πάντων
καλῶν τε κἀγαθῶν μεστοί, ὅσα ἡ γῆ φύειν
θέλει, καὶ ἐν τούτοις αὐτὸς τὰ πλεῖστα διατρίβει,
ὅταν μὴ ἡ ὥρα τοῦ ἔτους ἐξείργῃ.

14 Νὴ Δί', ἔφη ὁ Κριτόβουλος, ἀνάγκη τοίνυν, ὦ
Σώκρατες, ἔνθα γε διατρίβει αὐτός, καὶ ὅπως
ὡς κάλλιστα κατεσκευασμένοι ἔσονται οἱ παράδεισοι ἐπιμελεῖσθαι δένδρεσι καὶ τοῖς ἄλλοις
ἅπασι καλοῖς, ὅσα ἡ γῆ φύει.

15 Φασὶ δέ τινες, ἔφη ὁ Σωκράτης, ὦ Κριτόβουλε,
καὶ ὅταν δῶρα διδῷ ὁ βασιλεύς, πρῶτον μὲν
εἰσκαλεῖν τοὺς πολέμῳ ἀγαθοὺς γεγονότας, ὅτι
οὐδὲν ὄφελος πολλὰ ἀροῦν, εἰ μὴ εἶεν οἱ ἀρή-
ξοντες· δεύτερον δὲ τοὺς κατασκευάζοντας τὰς
χώρας ἄριστα καὶ ἐνεργοὺς ποιοῦντας λέγοντα,
ὅτι οὐδ' ἂν οἱ ἄλκιμοι δύναιντο ζῆν, εἰ μὴ εἶεν

16 οἱ ἐργαζόμενοι. λέγεται δὲ καὶ Κῦρός ποτε,
ὅσπερ εὐδοκιμώτατος δὴ βασιλεὺς γεγένηται,
εἰπεῖν τοῖς ἐπὶ τὰ δῶρα κεκλημένοις, ὅτι αὐτὸς
ἂν δικαίως τὰ ἀμφοτέρων δῶρα λαμβάνοι·
κατασκευάζειν τε γὰρ ἄριστος εἶναι ἔφη χώραν
καὶ ἀρήγειν τοῖς κατεσκευασμένοις.

17 Κῦρος μὲν τοίνυν, ἔφη ὁ Κριτόβουλος, ὦ
Σώκρατες, καὶ ἐπηγάλλετο οὐδὲν ἧττον, εἰ ταῦτα
ἔλεγεν, ἐπὶ τῷ χώρας ἐνεργοὺς ποιεῖν καὶ κατασκευάζειν ἢ ἐπὶ τῷ πολεμικὸς εἶναι.

18 Καὶ ναὶ μὰ Δί', ἔφη ὁ Σωκράτης, Κῦρός γε,
εἰ ἐβίωσεν, ἄριστος ἂν δοκεῖ ἄρχων γενέσθαι,
καὶ τούτου τεκμήρια ἄλλα τε πολλὰ παρέσχηται
καὶ ὁπότε περὶ τῆς βασιλείας τῷ ἀδελφῷ ἐπορεύετο μαχούμενος, παρὰ μὲν Κύρου οὐδεὶς λέγεται
αὐτομολῆσαι πρὸς βασιλέα, παρὰ δὲ βασιλέως

there are 'paradises,' as they call them, full of all the good and beautiful things that the soil will produce, and in this he himself spends most of his time, except when the season precludes it."

"Then it is of course necessary, Socrates, to take 14 care that these paradises in which the king spends his time shall contain a fine stock of trees and all other beautiful things that the soil produces."

"And some say, Critobulus, that when the king 15 makes gifts, he first invites those who have distinguished themselves in war, because it is useless to have broad acres under tillage unless there are men to defend them; and next to them, those who stock and cultivate the land best, saying that even stout-hearted warriors cannot live without the aid of workers. There is a story that Cyrus, lately the 16 most illustrious of princes, once said to the company invited to receive his gifts, 'I myself deserve to receive the gifts awarded in both classes; for I am the best at stocking land and the best at protecting the stock.'"

"Well, if Cyrus said that, Socrates, he took as 17 much pride in cultivating and stocking land as in being a warrior."

"Yes, and, upon my word, if Cyrus had only lived, 18 it seems that he would have proved an excellent ruler. One of the many proofs that he has given of this is the fact that, when he was on his way to fight his brother for the throne, it is said that not a man deserted from Cyrus to the king, whereas tens

19 πολλαὶ μυριάδες πρὸς Κῦρον. ἐγὼ δὲ καὶ τοῦτο
ἡγοῦμαι μέγα τεκμήριον ἄρχοντος ἀρετῆς εἶναι,
ᾧ ἂν ἑκόντες πείθωνται καὶ ἐν τοῖς δεινοῖς παραμένειν ἐθέλωσιν. ἐκείνῳ δὲ [καὶ] οἱ φίλοι ζῶντί
τε συνεμάχοντο καὶ ἀποθανόντι συναπέθανον
πάντες περὶ τὸν νεκρὸν μαχόμενοι πλὴν Ἀριαίου.
Ἀριαῖος δ᾽ ἔτυχεν ἐπὶ τῷ εὐωνύμῳ κέρατι τεταγ-
μένος.

20 Οὗτος τοίνυν ὁ Κῦρος λέγεται Λυσάνδρῳ, ὅτε
ἦλθεν ἄγων αὐτῷ τὰ παρὰ τῶν συμμάχων δῶρα,
ἄλλα τε φιλοφρονεῖσθαι, ὡς αὐτὸς ἔφη ὁ
Λύσανδρος ξένῳ ποτέ τινι ἐν Μεγάροις διηγού-
μενος, καὶ τὸν ἐν Σάρδεσι παράδεισον ἐπιδεικ-
21 νύναι αὐτὸν ἔφη. ἐπεὶ δὲ ἐθαύμαζεν αὐτὸν ὁ
Λύσανδρος, ὡς καλὰ μὲν τὰ δένδρα εἴη, δι᾽ ἴσου
δὲ [τὰ] πεφυτευμένα, ὀρθοὶ δὲ οἱ στίχοι τῶν
δένδρων, εὐγώνια δὲ πάντα καλῶς εἴη, ὀσμαὶ
δὲ πολλαὶ καὶ ἡδεῖαι συμπαρομαρτοῖεν αὐτοῖς
περιπατοῦσι, καὶ ταῦτα θαυμάζων εἶπεν· Ἀλλ᾽
ἐγώ τοι, ὦ Κῦρε, πάντα μὲν ταῦτα θαυμάζω ἐπὶ
τῷ κάλλει, πολὺ δὲ μᾶλλον ἄγαμαι τοῦ κατα-
μετρήσαντός σοι καὶ διατάξαντος ἕκαστα τούτων.
22 ἀκούσαντα δὲ ταῦτα τὸν Κῦρον ἡσθῆναί τε καὶ
εἰπεῖν· Ταῦτα τοίνυν, ὦ Λύσανδρε, ἐγὼ πάντα
καὶ διεμέτρησα καὶ διέταξα, ἔστι δ᾽ αὐτῶν, φάναι,
23 ἃ καὶ ἐφύτευσα αὐτός. καὶ ὁ Λύσανδρος ἔφη,
ἀποβλέψας εἰς αὐτὸν καὶ ἰδὼν τῶν τε ἱματίων
τὸ κάλλος ὧν εἶχε καὶ τῆς ὀσμῆς αἰσθόμενος καὶ
τῶν στρεπτῶν καὶ τῶν ψελίων [τὸ κάλλος] καὶ
τοῦ ἄλλου κόσμου οὗ εἶχεν, εἰπεῖν, Τί λέγεις,
φάναι, ὦ Κῦρε; ἦ γὰρ σὺ ταῖς σαῖς χερσὶ τούτων
24 τι ἐφύτευσας; καὶ τὸν Κῦρον ἀποκρίνασθαι,

of thousands deserted from the king to Cyrus. I **19**
think you have one clear proof of a ruler's excellence,
when men obey him willingly[1] and choose to stand
by him in moments of danger. Now his friends all
fought at his side and fell at his side to a man,
fighting round his body, with the one exception of
Ariaeus, whose place in the battle was, in point of
fact, on the left wing.[2]

"Further, the story goes that when Lysander **20**
came to him bringing the gifts from the allies, this
Cyrus showed him various marks of friendliness, as
Lysander himself related once to a stranger at
Megara, adding besides that Cyrus personally
showed him round his paradise at Sardis. Now **21**
Lysander admired the beauty of the trees in it, the
accuracy of the spacing, the straightness of the
rows, the regularity of the angles and the multitude of the sweet scents that clung round them
as they walked; and for wonder of these things he
cried, 'Cyrus, I really do admire all these lovely
things, but I am far more impressed with your
agent's skill in measuring and arranging everything
so exactly.' Cyrus was delighted to hear this and **22**
said: 'Well, Lysander, the whole of the measurement and arrangement is my own work, and I did
some of the planting myself.' 'What, Cyrus?' **23**
exclaimed Lysander, looking at him, and marking
the beauty and perfume of his robes, and the
splendour of the necklaces and bangles and other
jewels that he was wearing; 'did you really plant
part of this with your own hands?' 'Does that **24**

---

[1] *Mem* III. iii. 9.
[2] *Anabasis*, I. ix. 31. Ariaeus fled when he saw that Cyrus
had fallen.

Θαυμάζεις τοῦτο, φάναι, ὦ Λύσανδρε; ὄμνυμί
σοι τὸν Μίθρην, ὅτανπερ ὑγιαίνω, μηπώποτε
δειπνῆσαι πρὶν ἱδρῶσαι ἢ τῶν πολεμικῶν τι ἢ
τῶν γεωργικῶν ἔργων μελετῶν ἢ ἀεὶ ἕν γέ τι
φιλοτιμούμενος.

25 Καὶ αὐτὸς μέντοι ἔφη ὁ Λύσανδρος ἀκούσας
ταῦτα δεξιώσασθαί τε αὐτὸν καὶ εἰπεῖν· Δικαίως
μοι δοκεῖς, ὦ Κῦρε, εὐδαίμων εἶναι· ἀγαθὸς γὰρ
ὢν ἀνὴρ εὐδαιμονεῖς.

V. Ταῦτα δέ, ὦ Κριτόβουλε, ἐγὼ διηγοῦμαι,
ἔφη ὁ Σωκράτης, ὅτι τῆς γεωργίας οὐδ' οἱ πάνυ
μακάριοι δύνανται ἀπέχεσθαι. ἔοικε γὰρ ἡ ἐπιμέλεια αὐτῆς εἶναι ἅμα τε ἡδυπάθειά τις καὶ οἴκου
αὔξησις καὶ σωμάτων ἄσκησις εἰς τὸ δύνασθαι
2 ὅσα ἀνδρὶ ἐλευθέρῳ προσήκει. πρῶτον μὲν γὰρ
ἀφ' ὧν ζῶσιν οἱ ἄνθρωποι, ταῦτα ἡ γῆ φέρει ἐργαζομένοις, καὶ ἀφ' ὧν τοίνυν ἡδυπαθοῦσι προσεπι-
3 φέρει· ἔπειτα δὲ ὅσα κοσμοῦσι βωμοὺς καὶ
ἀγάλματα καὶ οἷς αὐτοὶ κοσμοῦνται, καὶ ταῦτα
μετὰ ἡδίστων ὀσμῶν καὶ θεαμάτων παρέχει·
ἔπειτα δὲ ὄψα πολλὰ τὰ μὲν φύει, τὰ δὲ τρέφει·
καὶ γὰρ ἡ προβατευτικὴ τέχνη συνῆπται τῇ
γεωργίᾳ, ὥστε ἔχειν καὶ θεοὺς ἐξαρέσκεσθαι
4 θύοντας καὶ αὐτοὺς χρῆσθαι. παρέχουσα δ'
ἀφθονώτατα ἀγαθὰ οὐκ ἐᾷ ταῦτα μετὰ μαλακίας
λαμβάνειν, ἀλλὰ ψύχῃ τε χειμῶνος καὶ θάλπῃ
θέρους ἐθίζει καρτερεῖν. καὶ τοὺς μὲν αὐτουργοὺς
διὰ τῶν χειρῶν γυμνάζουσα ἰσχὺν αὐτοῖς προστίθησι, τοὺς δὲ τῇ ἐπιμελείᾳ γεωργοῦντας ἀνδρίζει
πρωΐ τε ἐγείρουσα καὶ πορεύεσθαι σφοδρῶς ἀναγ-
κάζουσα. καὶ γὰρ ἐν τῷ χώρῳ καὶ ἐν τῷ ἄστει
ἀεὶ ἐν ὥρᾳ αἱ ἐπικαιριώταται πράξεις εἰσίν.

surprise you, Lysander?' asked Cyrus in reply. 'I swear by the Sun-god that I never yet sat down to dinner when in sound health, without first working hard at some task of war or agriculture, or exerting myself somehow.'

"Lysander himself declared, I should add, that on 25 hearing this, he congratulated him in these words: 'I think you deserve your happiness, Cyrus, for you earn it by your virtues.'"

V. "Now I tell you this," continued Socrates, "because even the wealthiest cannot hold aloof from husbandry. For the pursuit of it is in some sense a luxury as well as a means of increasing one's estate and of training the body in all that a free man should be able to do. For, in the first place, the 2 earth yields to cultivators the food by which men live; she yields besides the luxuries they enjoy. Secondly, she supplies all the things with which 3 they decorate altars and statues and themselves, along with most pleasant sights and scents. Thirdly, she produces or feeds the ingredients of many delicate dishes; for the art of breeding stock is closely linked with husbandry; so that men have victims for propitiating the gods with sacrifice and cattle for their own use. And though she supplies good 4 things in abundance, she suffers them not to be won without toil, but accustoms men to endure winter's cold and summer's heat. She gives increased strength through exercise to the men that labour with their own hands, and hardens the overseers of the work by rousing them early and forcing them to move about briskly. For on a farm no less than in a town the most important operations have their

5 ἔπειτα ἤν τε σὺν ἵππῳ ἀρήγειν τις τῇ πόλει
βούληται, τὸν ἵππον ἱκανωτάτη ἡ γεωργία συντρέφειν, ἤν τε πεζῇ, σφοδρὸν τὸ σῶμα παρέχει·
θήραις τε ἐπιφιλοπονεῖσθαι συνεπαίρει τι ἡ
γῆ καὶ κυσὶν εὐπέτειαν τροφῆς παρέχουσα καὶ
6 θηρία συμπαρατρέφουσα. ὠφελούμενοι δὲ καὶ
οἱ ἵπποι καὶ αἱ κύνες ἀπὸ τῆς γεωργίας ἀντωφε-
λοῦσι τὸν χῶρον, ὁ μὲν ἵππος πρωί τε κομίζων
τὸν κηδόμενον εἰς τὴν ἐπιμέλειαν καὶ ἐξουσίαν
παρέχων ὀψὲ ἀπιέναι, αἱ δὲ κύνες τά τε θηρία
ἀπερύκουσαι ἀπὸ λύμης καρπῶν καὶ προβάτων
καὶ τῇ ἐρημίᾳ τὴν ἀσφάλειαν συμπαρέχουσαι.
7 παρορμᾷ δέ τι καὶ εἰς τὸ ἀρήγειν σὺν ὅπλοις τῇ
χώρᾳ καὶ ἡ γῆ τοὺς γεωργοὺς ἐν τῷ μέσῳ τοὺς
καρποὺς τρέφουσα τῷ κρατοῦντι λαμβάνειν.
8 καὶ δραμεῖν δὲ καὶ βαλεῖν καὶ πηδῆσαι τίς ἱκανω-
τέρους τέχνη γεωργίας παρέχεται; τίς δὲ τοῖς
ἐργαζομένοις πλείω τέχνη ἀντιχαρίζεται; τίς δὲ
ἥδιον τὸν ἐπιμελόμενον δέχεται, προτείνουσα
προσιόντι λαβεῖν ὅ τι χρῄζει; τίς δὲ ξένους
9 ἀφθονώτερον δέχεται; χειμάσαι δὲ πυρὶ ἀφθόνῳ
καὶ θερμοῖς λουτροῖς ποῦ πλείων εὐμάρεια ἢ ἐν
χώρῳ τῳ; ποῦ δὲ ἥδιον θερίσαι ὕδασί τε καὶ πνεύ-
10 μασι καὶ σκιαῖς ἢ κατ' ἀγρόν; τίς δὲ ἄλλη θεοῖς
ἀπαρχὰς πρεπωδεστέρας παρέχει ἢ ἑορτὰς πλη-
ρεστέρας ἀποδεικνύει; τίς δὲ οἰκέταις προσφι-
λεστέρα ἢ γυναικὶ ἡδίων ἢ τέκνοις ποθεινοτέρα
11 ἢ φίλοις εὐχαριστοτέρα; ἐμοὶ μὲν θαυμαστὸν
δοκεῖ εἶναι, εἴ τις ἐλεύθερος ἄνθρωπος ἢ κτῆμά
τι τούτου ἥδιον κέκτηται ἢ ἐπιμέλειαν ἡδίω τινὰ
ταύτης εὕρηκεν ἢ ὠφελιμωτέραν εἰς τὸν βίον.

fixed times. Again, if a man wants to serve in the 5
cavalry, farming is his most efficient partner in
furnishing keep for his horse; if on foot, it makes
his body brisk. And the land helps in some measure
to arouse a liking for the toil of hunting, since it
affords facilities for keeping hounds and at the same
time supplies food for the wild game that preys on the
land. And if husbandry benefits horses and hounds, 6
they benefit the farm no less, the horses by carrying
the overseer early to the scene of his duties and
enabling him to leave it late, the hounds by keeping
the wild animals from injuring crops and sheep, and
by helping to give safety to solitude. The land also 7
stimulates armed protection of the country on the
part of the husbandmen, by nourishing her crops in
the open for the strongest to take. And what art 8
produces better runners, throwers and jumpers than
husbandry? What art rewards the labourer more
generously? What art welcomes her follower more
gladly, inviting him to come and take whatever
he wants? What art entertains strangers more
generously? Where is there greater facility for 9
passing the winter comforted by generous fire and
warm baths, than on a farm? Where is it pleasanter
to spend the summer enjoying the cool waters and
breezes and shade, than in the country? What 10
other art yields more seemly first-fruits for the gods,
or gives occasion for more crowded festivals? What
art is dearer to servants, or pleasanter to a wife, or
more delightful to children, or more agreeable to
friends? To me indeed it seems strange, if any free 11
man has come by a possession pleasanter than this,
or has found out an occupation pleasanter than this
or more useful for winning a livelihood.

12 Ἔτι δὲ ἡ γῆ θέλουσα[1] τοὺς δυναμένους καταμανθάνειν καὶ δικαιοσύνην διδάσκει· τοὺς γὰρ ἄριστα θεραπεύοντας αὐτὴν πλεῖστα ἀγαθὰ ἀντιποιεῖ.

13 ἐὰν δ' ἄρα καὶ ὑπὸ πλήθους ποτὲ στρατευμάτων τῶν ἔργων στερηθῶσιν οἱ ἐν τῇ γεωργίᾳ ἀναστρεφόμενοι καὶ σφοδρῶς καὶ ἀνδρικῶς παιδευόμενοι, οὗτοι εὖ παρεσκευασμένοι καὶ τὰς ψυχὰς καὶ τὰ σώματα, ἢν μὴ θεὸς ἀποκωλύῃ, δύνανται ἰόντες εἰς τὰς τῶν ἀποκωλυόντων λαμβάνειν ἀφ' ὧν θρέψονται. πολλάκις δ' ἐν τῷ πολέμῳ καὶ ἀσφαλέστερόν ἐστι σὺν τοῖς ὅπλοις τὴν τροφὴν μαστεύειν ἢ σὺν τοῖς γεωργικοῖς ὀργάνοις.

14 Συμπαιδεύει δὲ καὶ εἰς τὸ ἐπαρκεῖν ἀλλήλοις ἡ γεωργία. ἐπί τε γὰρ τοὺς πολεμίους σὺν ἀνθρώποις δεῖ ἰέναι τῆς τε γῆς σὺν ἀνθρώποις ἐστὶν ἡ

15 ἐργασία. τὸν οὖν μέλλοντα εὖ γεωργήσειν δεῖ τοὺς ἐργαστῆρας καὶ προθύμους παρασκευάζειν καὶ πείθεσθαι θέλοντας· τὸν δὲ ἐπὶ πολεμίους ἄγοντα ταὐτὰ δεῖ μηχανᾶσθαι δωρούμενόν τε τοῖς ποιοῦσιν ἃ δεῖ ποιεῖν τοὺς ἀγαθοὺς καὶ κολάζοντα

16 τοὺς ἀτακτοῦντας. καὶ παρακελεύεσθαι δὲ πολλάκις οὐδὲν ἧττον δεῖ τοῖς ἐργάταις τὸν γεωργὸν ἢ τὸν στρατηγὸν τοῖς στρατιώταις· καὶ ἐλπίδων δὲ ἀγαθῶν οὐδὲν ἧττον οἱ δοῦλοι τῶν ἐλευθέρων δέονται, ἀλλὰ καὶ μᾶλλον, ὅπως μένειν ἐθέλωσι.

17 καλῶς δὲ κἀκεῖνος εἶπεν, ὃς ἔφη τὴν γεωργίαν τῶν ἄλλων τεχνῶν μητέρα καὶ τροφὸν εἶναι. εὖ μὲν γὰρ φερομένης τῆς γεωργίας ἔρρωνται καὶ αἱ ἄλλαι τέχναι ἅπασαι, ὅπου δ' ἂν ἀναγκασθῇ ἡ γῆ χερσεύειν, ἀποσβέννυνται καὶ αἱ ἄλλαι τέχναι σχεδόν τι καὶ κατὰ γῆν καὶ κατὰ θάλατταν.

18 Ἀκούσας δὲ ταῦτα ὁ Κριτόβουλος εἶπεν· Ἀλλὰ

" Yet again, the earth willingly [1] teaches righteous- 12
ness to those who can learn ; for the better she is
served, the more good things she gives in return.
And if haply those who are occupied in farming, and 13
are receiving a rigorous and manly teaching, are
forced at any time to quit their lands by great
armies, they, as men well-found in mind and in body,
can enter the country of those who hinder them, and
take sufficient for their support.   Often in time of
war it is safer to go armed in search of food than to
gather it with farming implements.

" Moreover, husbandry helps to train men for cor- 14
porate effort.   For men are essential to an expedition
against an enemy, and the cultivation of the soil
demands the aid of men.   Therefore nobody can be 15
a good farmer unless he makes his labourers both
eager and obedient ; and the captain who leads men
against an enemy must contrive to secure the same
results by rewarding those who act as brave men
should act and punishing the disobedient.   And it 16
is no less necessary for a farmer to encourage his
labourers often, than for a general to encourage his
men.   And slaves need the stimulus of good hopes
no less, nay, even more than free men, to make
them steadfast.   It has been nobly said that hus- 17
bandry is the mother and nurse of the other arts.
For when húsbandry flourishes, all the other arts are
in good fettle ; but whenever the land is compelled
to lie waste, the other arts of landsmen and mariners
alike well-nigh perish."

" Well, Socrates," replied Critobulus to this, " I 18

---

[1] Or θεὸς οὖσα, "is a goddess and."

---

[1] θεὸς οὖσα Stobaeus, probably rightly.

XENOPHON

ταῦτα μὲν ἔμοιγε, ὦ Σώκρατες, καλῶς δοκεῖς
λέγειν· ὅτι δὲ τῆς γεωργικῆς τὰ πλεῖστά ἐστιν
ἀνθρώπῳ ἀδύνατα προνοῆσαι[1] . . . καὶ γὰρ χάλα-
ζαι καὶ πάχναι ἐνίοτε καὶ αὐχμοὶ καὶ ὄμβροι
ἐξαίσιοι καὶ ἐρυσῖβαι καὶ ἄλλα πολλάκις τὰ
καλῶς ἐγνωσμένα καὶ πεποιημένα ἀφαιροῦνται·
καὶ πρόβατα δ' ἐνίοτε κάλλιστα τεθραμμένα
νόσος ἐλθοῦσα κάκιστα ἀπώλεσεν.

19 Ἀκούσας δὲ ταῦτα ὁ Σωκράτης εἶπεν· Ἀλλ'
ᾤμην ἔγωγέ σε, ὦ Κριτόβουλε, εἰδέναι, ὅτι οἱ θεοὶ
οὐδὲν ἧττόν εἰσι κύριοι τῶν ἐν τῇ γεωργίᾳ ἔργων
ἢ τῶν ἐν τῷ πολέμῳ. καὶ τοὺς μὲν ἐν τῷ πολέμῳ
ὁρᾷς οἶμαι πρὸ τῶν πολεμικῶν πράξεων ἐξαρεσκο-
μένους τοὺς θεοὺς καὶ ἐπερωτῶντας θυσίαις καὶ
20 οἰωνοῖς, ὅ τι τε χρὴ ποιεῖν καὶ ὅ τι μή. περὶ δὲ
τῶν γεωργικῶν πράξεων ἧττον οἴει δεῖν τοὺς θεοὺς
ἱλάσκεσθαι; εὖ γὰρ ἴσθι, ἔφη, ὅτι οἱ σώφρονες
καὶ ὑπὲρ ὑγρῶν καὶ ξηρῶν καρπῶν καὶ βοῶν καὶ
ἵππων καὶ προβάτων καὶ ὑπὲρ πάντων γε δὴ τῶν
κτημάτων τοὺς θεοὺς θεραπεύουσιν.

VI. Ἀλλὰ ταῦτα μέν, ἔφη, ὦ Σώκρατες, καλῶς
μοι δοκεῖς λέγειν κελεύων πειρᾶσθαι σὺν τοῖς
θεοῖς ἄρχεσθαι παντὸς ἔργου, ὡς τῶν θεῶν κυρίων
ὄντων οὐδὲν ἧττον τῶν εἰρηνικῶν ἢ τῶν πολεμικῶν
ἔργων. ταῦτα μὲν οὖν πειρασόμεθα οὕτω ποιεῖν.
σὺ δ' ἡμῖν ἔνθεν λέγων περὶ τῆς οἰκονομίας ἀπέ-
λιπες, πειρῶ τὰ τούτων ἐχόμενα διεκπεραίνειν, ὡς
καὶ νῦν μοι δοκῶ ἀκηκοὼς ὅσα εἶπες μᾶλλόν τι
ἤδη διορᾶν ἢ πρόσθεν, ὅ τι χρὴ ποιοῦντα
βιοτεύειν.

2 Τί οὖν, ἔφη ὁ Σωκράτης, ἆρα, εἰ πρῶτον μὲν
ἐπανέλθοιμεν ὅσα μὲν ὁμολογοῦντες διεληλύθαμεν,

think you are right so far. But in husbandry a man can rely very little on forecast. For hailstorms and frosts sometimes, and droughts and rains and blight ruin schemes well planned and well carried out; and sometimes well-bred stock is miserably destroyed by an outbreak of disease."

"Well," said Socrates in reply,[1] "I thought you 19 knew, Critobulus, that the operations of husbandry no less than those of war are in the hands of the gods. And you observe, I suppose, that men engaged in war try to propitiate the gods before taking action; and with sacrifices and omens seek to know what they ought to do and what they ought not to do; and for the business of husbandry do you think 20 it less necessary to ask the blessing of the gods? Know of a surety that right-minded men offer prayer for fruits and crops and cattle and horses and sheep, aye and for all that they possess."

VI. "Well, Socrates, I think you are right when you bid me try to begin every undertaking with the gods' help, since the gods control the works of peace no less than of war. We will try, then, to do so. But now go back to the point where you broke off in your talk about estate management, and try to expound the subject completely step by step, since after hearing what you have said so far, I seem even now to discern rather more clearly than before what I must do to earn my living."

"I suggest then," resumed Socrates, "that we 2 should first recapitulate those points of our discussion on which we have already reached agreement, in

---

[1] *Mem.* I. iv. 15; IV. iii. 12. *Cyrop.* I. vi. 46.

---

[1] Reisig saw that something is lost after προνοῆσαι.

ἵν᾽, ἤν πως δυνώμεθα, πειραθῶμεν οὕτω καὶ τὰ λοιπὰ διεξιέναι συνομολογοῦντες ;

3 Ἡδὺ γοῦν ἐστιν, ἔφη ὁ Κριτόβουλος, ὥσπερ καὶ χρημάτων κοινωνήσαντας ἀναμφιλόγως διελθεῖν, οὕτω καὶ λόγων κοινωνοῦντας περὶ ὧν ἂν διαλεγώμεθα συνομολογοῦντας διεξιέναι.

4 Οὐκοῦν, ἔφη ὁ Σωκράτης, ἐπιστήμης μέν τινος ἔδοξεν ἡμῖν ὄνομα εἶναι ἡ οἰκονομία, ἡ δὲ ἐπιστήμη αὕτη ἐφαίνετο, ᾗ οἴκους δύνανται αὔξειν ἄνθρωποι, οἶκος δ᾽ ἡμῖν ἐφαίνετο ὅπερ κτῆσις ἡ σύμπασα, κτῆσιν δὲ τοῦτο ἔφαμεν εἶναι, ὅ τι ἑκάστῳ εἴη ὠφέλιμον εἰς τὸν βίον, ὠφέλιμα δὲ ὄντα εὑρίσκετο πάντα, ὁπόσοις τις ἐπίσταιτο 5 χρῆσθαι. πάσας μὲν οὖν τὰς ἐπιστήμας οὔτε μαθεῖν οἷόν τε ἡμῖν ἐδόκει συναποδοκιμάζειν τε ταῖς πόλεσι τὰς βαναυσικὰς καλουμένας τέχνας, ὅτι καὶ τὰ σώματα καταλυμαίνεσθαι δοκοῦσι καὶ 6 τὰς ψυχὰς καταγνύουσι. τεκμήριον δὲ σαφέστατον γενέσθαι ἂν τούτου ἔφαμεν, εἰ πολεμίων εἰς τὴν χώραν ἰόντων διακαθίσας τις τοὺς γεωργοὺς καὶ τοὺς τεχνίτας χωρὶς ἑκατέρους ἐπερωτῴη, πότερα δοκεῖ ἀρήγειν τῇ χώρᾳ ἢ ὑφεμένους 7 τῆς γῆς τὰ τείχη διαφυλάττειν. οὕτως γὰρ ἂν τοὺς μὲν ἀμφὶ γῆν ἔχοντας ᾠόμεθ᾽ ἂν ψηφίζεσθαι ἀρήγειν, τοὺς δὲ τεχνίτας μὴ μάχεσθαι, ἀλλ᾽ ὅπερ πεπαίδευνται καθῆσθαι μήτε πονοῦντας μήτε 8 κινδυνεύοντας. ἐδοκιμάσαμεν δὲ ἀνδρὶ καλῷ τε κἀγαθῷ ἐργασίαν εἶναι καὶ ἐπιστήμην κρατίστην γεωργίαν, ἀφ᾽ ἧς τὰ ἐπιτήδεια ἄνθρωποι πορί- 9 ζονται. αὕτη γὰρ ἡ ἐργασία μαθεῖν τε ῥᾴστη

---

[1] Nothing to this effect occurs in c. iv.

order that we may try to agree as thoroughly, if possible, when we go through the remaining steps."

"O yes; when several are jointly interested in 3 money, it is pleasant to have no disagreement in going over the accounts; and it is equally pleasant for us, as the interested parties in a discussion, to agree as we go over the several steps."

"Well now, we thought that estate management is 4 the name of a branch of knowledge, and this knowledge appeared to be that by which men can increase estates, and an estate appeared to be identical with the total of one's property, and we said that property is that which is useful for supplying a livelihood, and useful things turned out to be all those things that one knows how to use. Now we thought that it is im- 5 possible to learn all the sciences, and we agreed with our states in rejecting the so-called illiberal arts, because they seem to spoil the body and unnerve the mind. We said [1] that the clearest proof 6 of this would be forthcoming, if in the course of a hostile invasion the husbandmen and craftsmen were made to sit apart, and each group were asked whether they voted for defending the country or withdrawing from the open and guarding the fortresses. We 7 thought that in these circumstances the men who have to do with the land would give their vote for defending it, the craftsmen for not fighting, but sitting still, as they have been brought up to do, aloof from toil and danger. We came to the con- 8 clusion that for a gentleman the best occupation and the best science is husbandry, from which men obtain what is necessary to them. For this occupation 9 seemed to be the easiest to learn and the pleasantest

ἐδόκει εἶναι καὶ ἡδίστη ἐργάζεσθαι καὶ τὰ σώματα
κάλλιστά τε καὶ εὐρωστότατα παρέχεσθαι καὶ
ταῖς ψυχαῖς ἥκιστα ἀσχολίαν παρέχειν φίλων τε
10 καὶ πόλεως συνεπιμελεῖσθαι.   συμπαροξύνειν δέ
τι ἐδόκει ἡμῖν καὶ εἰς τὸ ἀλκίμους εἶναι ἡ γεωργία
ἔξω τῶν ἐρυμάτων τὰ ἐπιτήδεια φύουσά τε καὶ
τρέφουσα τοὺς ἐργαζομένους.   διὰ ταῦτα δὲ καὶ
εὐδοξοτάτη εἶναι πρὸς τῶν πόλεων αὕτη ἡ βιοτεία,
ὅτι καὶ πολίτας ἀρίστους καὶ εὐνουστάτους παρέχεσθαι δοκεῖ τῷ κοινῷ.

11   Καὶ ὁ Κριτόβουλος, Ὅτι μέν, ὦ Σώκρατες, ἔφη,
κάλλιστόν τε καὶ ἄριστον καὶ ἥδιστον ἀπὸ γεωργίας τὸν βίον ποιεῖσθαι, πάνυ μοι δοκῶ πεπεῖσθαι
ἱκανῶς· ὅτι δὲ ἔφησθα καταμαθεῖν τὰ αἴτια τῶν
τε οὕτω γεωργούντων, ὥστε ἀπὸ τῆς γεωργίας
ἀφθόνως ἔχειν ὧν δέονται καὶ τῶν οὕτως ἐργαζομένων, ὡς μὴ λυσιτελεῖν αὐτοῖς τὴν γεωργίαν, καὶ
ταῦτ' ἄν μοι δοκῶ ἡδέως ἑκάτερα ἀκούειν σου,
ὅπως ἃ μὲν ἀγαθά ἐστι ποιῶμεν, ἃ δὲ βλαβερὰ
μὴ ποιῶμεν.

12   Τί οὖν, ἔφη ὁ Σωκράτης, ὦ Κριτόβουλε, ἤν σοι
ἐξ ἀρχῆς διηγήσωμαι, ὡς συνεγενόμην ποτὲ ἀνδρί,
ὃς ἐμοὶ ἐδόκει εἶναι τῷ ὄντι τούτων τῶν ἀνδρῶν,
ἐφ' οἷς τοῦτο τὸ ὄνομα δικαίως ἐστίν, ὁ καλεῖται
καλός τε κἀγαθὸς ἀνήρ;

    Πάνυ ἄν, ἔφη ὁ Κριτόβουλος, βουλοίμην ἂν
οὕτως ἀκούειν, ὡς καὶ ἔγωγε ἐρῶ τούτου τοῦ
13 ὀνόματος ἄξιος γενέσθαι.   Λέξω τοίνυν σοι, ἔφη ὁ
Σωκράτης, ὡς καὶ ἦλθον ἐπὶ τὴν σκέψιν αὐτοῦ.
τοὺς μὲν γὰρ ἀγαθοὺς τέκτονας, ἀγαθοὺς [1] χαλ-
κέας, ἀγαθοὺς ζωγράφους, ἀγαθοὺς ἀνδριαντο-
ποιοὺς καὶ τὰ ἄλλα τὰ τοιαῦτα πάνυ ὀλίγος μοι

to work at, to give to the body the greatest measure
of strength and beauty, and to leave to the mind
the greatest amount of spare time for attending to
the interests of one's friends and city. Moreover, 10
since the crops grow and the cattle on a farm
graze outside the walls, husbandry seemed to us to
help in some measure to make the workers valiant.
And so this way of making a living appeared to be
held in the highest estimation by our states, because
it seems to turn out the best citizens and most loyal
to the community."

"I have already heard enough, I think, Socrates, 11
to convince me that it is in the highest degree
honourable, good and pleasant to get a living by
husbandry. But you told me that you have discovered the reasons why some farmers are so successful that husbandry yields them all they need in
abundance, and others are so inefficient that they find
farming unprofitable. I should like to hear the
reasons in each case, in order that we may do what
is good and avoid what is harmful."

"Well then, Critobulus, I propose to give you a 12
complete account of an interview I once had with a
man whom I took to be really one of those who are
justly styled 'gentlemen.'"

"I should greatly like to hear it, Socrates, for I
long to deserve that title myself."

"Then I will tell you how I came to take note of 13
him. For it took me a very little time to visit our good
builders, good smiths, good painters, good sculptors,

---

¹ ἀγαθούς Stobaeus : Sauppe omits with the MSS.

χρόνος ἐγένετο ἱκανὸς περιελθεῖν τε καὶ θεάσασθαι τὰ δεδοκιμασμένα καλὰ ἔργα αὐτοῖς εἶναι.

14 ὅπως δὲ δὴ καὶ τοὺς ἔχοντας τὸ σεμνὸν ὄνομα τοῦτο τὸ καλός τε κἀγαθὸς ἐπισκεψαίμην, τί ποτ᾽ ἐργαζόμενοι τοῦτ᾽ ἀξιοῖντο καλεῖσθαι, πάνυ μου ἡ

15 ψυχὴ ἐπεθύμει αὐτῶν τινι συγγενέσθαι. καὶ πρῶτον μὲν ὅτι προσέκειτο τὸ καλὸς τῷ ἀγαθῷ, ὄντινα ἴδοιμι καλόν, τούτῳ προσῄειν καὶ ἐπειρώμην καταμανθάνειν, εἴπου ἴδοιμι προσηρτημένον

16 τῷ καλῷ τὸ ἀγαθόν. ἀλλ᾽ οὐκ ἄρα εἶχεν οὕτως, ἀλλὰ ἐνίους ἐδόκουν καταμανθάνειν τῶν καλῶν τὰς μορφὰς πάνυ μοχθηροὺς ὄντας τὰς ψυχάς. ἔδοξεν οὖν μοι ἀφέμενον τῆς καλῆς ὄψεως ἐπ᾽ αὐτῶν τινα ἐλθεῖν τῶν καλουμένων καλῶν τε

17 κἀγαθῶν. ἐπεὶ οὖν τὸν Ἰσχόμαχον ἤκουον πρὸς πάντων καὶ ἀνδρῶν καὶ γυναικῶν καὶ ξένων καὶ ἀστῶν καλόν τε κἀγαθὸν ἐπονομαζόμενον, ἔδοξέ μοι τούτῳ πειραθῆναι συγγενέσθαι.

VII. Ἰδὼν οὖν ποτε αὐτὸν ἐν τῇ τοῦ Διὸς τοῦ ἐλευθερίου στοᾷ καθήμενον, ἐπεί μοι ἔδοξε σχολάζειν, προσῆλθον αὐτῷ καὶ παρακαθιζόμενος εἶπον·

Τί, ὦ Ἰσχόμαχε, οὐ μάλα εἰωθὼς σχολάζειν κάθησαι; ἐπεὶ τά γε πλεῖστα ἢ πράττοντά τι ὁρῶ σε ἢ οὐ πάνυ σχολάζοντα ἐν τῇ ἀγορᾷ.

2 Οὐδὲ ἄν γε νῦν, ἔφη ὁ Ἰσχόμαχος, ὦ Σώκρατες, ἑώρας, εἰ μὴ ξένους τινὰς συνεθέμην ἀναμένειν ἐνθάδε.

Ὅταν δὲ μὴ πράττῃς τι τοιοῦτον, πρὸς τῶν θεῶν, ἔφην ἐγώ, ποῦ διατρίβεις καὶ τί ποιεῖς; ἐγὼ γάρ τοι πάνυ βούλομαί σου πυθέσθαι, τί ποτε πράττων καλός τε κἀγαθὸς κέκλησαι, ἐπεὶ οὐκ ἔνδον γε διατρίβεις οὐδὲ τοιαύτη σου ἡ ἕξις τοῦ σώματος καταφαίνεται.

and other people of the kind, and to inspect those of
their works that are declared to be beautiful; but I 14
felt a desire to meet one of those who are called by
that grand name 'gentleman,' which implies 'beautiful' as well as 'good,' in order to consider what they
did to deserve it. And, first, because the epithet 15
'beautiful' is added to 'good,' I went up to every
person I noticed, and tried to discover whether I
could anywhere see goodness in combination with
beauty. But after all, it was not so: I thought I 16
discovered that some who were beautiful to look
at were thoroughly depraved in their minds. So I
decided to let good looks alone, and to seek out
someone known as 'a gentleman.' Accordingly, 17
since I heard the name applied to Ischomachus by
men, women, citizens and strangers alike, I decided
to meet him, if I could.

VII. "So, happening one day to see him sitting
in the cloister of the temple of Zeus Eleutherius
apparently at leisure, I approached, and sitting
down at his side, said:

"'Why sitting still, Ischomachus? You are not
much in the habit of doing nothing; for generally
when I see you in the market-place you are either
busy or at least not wholly idle.'

"'True, and you would not have seen me so now, 2
Socrates, had I not made an appointment with some
strangers here.'

"'Pray where do you spend your time,' said I,
'and what do you do when you are not engaged in
some such occupation? For I want very much to
learn how you came to be called a gentleman, since
you do not pass your time indoors, and your condition does not suggest that you do so.'

3 Καὶ ὁ Ἰσχόμαχος γελάσας ἐπὶ τῷ τί ποιῶν
καλὸς κἀγαθὸς κέκλησαι καὶ ἡσθείς, ὥς γ᾽ ἐμοὶ
ἔδοξεν, εἶπεν· Ἀλλ᾽ εἰ μὲν ὅταν σοι διαλέγωνται
περὶ ἐμοῦ τινες, καλοῦσί με τοῦτο τὸ ὄνομα, οὐκ
οἶδα· οὐ γὰρ δὴ ὅταν γέ με εἰς ἀντίδοσιν καλῶν-
ται τριηραρχίας ἢ χορηγίας, οὐδείς, ἔφη, ζητεῖ
τὸν καλόν τε κἀγαθόν, ἀλλὰ σαφῶς, ἔφη, ὀνομά-
ζοντές με Ἰσχόμαχον πατρόθεν προσκαλοῦνται.
ἐγὼ μὲν τοίνυν, ἔφη, ὦ Σώκρατες, ὅ με ἐπήρου,
οὐδαμῶς ἔνδον διατρίβω. καὶ γὰρ δή, ἔφη, τά γε
ἐν τῇ οἰκίᾳ μου πάνυ καὶ αὐτὴ ἡ γυνή ἐστιν ἱκανὴ
διοικεῖν.

4 Ἀλλὰ καὶ τοῦτο, ἔφην, ἔγωγε, ὦ Ἰσχόμαχε,
πάνυ ἂν ἡδέως σου πυθοίμην, πότερα αὐτὸς σὺ
ἐπαίδευσας τὴν γυναῖκα, ὥστε εἶναι οἵαν δεῖ, ἢ
ἐπισταμένην ἔλαβες παρὰ τοῦ πατρὸς καὶ τῆς
μητρὸς διοικεῖν τὰ προσήκοντα αὐτῇ.

5 Καὶ τί ἄν, ἔφη, ὦ Σώκρατες, ἐπισταμένην
αὐτὴν παρέλαβον, ἣ ἔτη μὲν οὔπω πεντεκαίδεκα
γεγονυῖα ἦλθε πρὸς ἐμέ, τὸν δ᾽ ἔμπροσθεν χρόνον
ἔζη ὑπὸ πολλῆς ἐπιμελείας, ὅπως ὡς ἐλάχιστα
μὲν ὄψοιτο, ἐλάχιστα δὲ ἀκούσοιτο, ἐλάχιστα δ᾽
6 ἐροίη; οὐ γὰρ ἀγαπητόν σοι δοκεῖ εἶναι, εἰ μόνον
ἦλθεν ἐπισταμένη ἔρια παραλαβοῦσα ἱμάτιον
ἀποδεῖξαι καὶ ἑωρακυῖα, ὡς ἔργα ταλάσια θερα-
παίναις δίδοται; ἐπεὶ τά γε ἀμφὶ γαστέρα, ἔφη,
πάνυ καλῶς, ὦ Σώκρατες, ἦλθε πεπαιδευμένη·
ὅπερ μέγιστον ἔμοιγε δοκεῖ παίδευμα εἶναι καὶ
ἀνδρὶ καὶ γυναικί.

7 Τὰ δ᾽ ἄλλα, ἔφην ἐγώ, ὦ Ἰσχόμαχε, αὐτὸς
ἐπαίδευσας τὴν γυναῖκα ὥστε ἱκανὴν εἶναι ὧν
προσήκει ἐπιμελεῖσθαι;

"Smiling at my question, 'How came you to be 3
called a gentleman?', and apparently well pleased,
Ischomachus answered: 'Well, Socrates, whether
certain persons call me so when they talk to you
about me, I know not. Assuredly when they
challenge me to an exchange of property in order
to escape some public burden, fitting a warship or
providing a chorus, nobody looks for the "gentleman," but the challenge refers to me as plain
"Ischomachus," my father's son. Well now,
Socrates, as you ask the question, I certainly
do not pass my time indoors; for, you know, my
wife is quite capable of looking after the house by
herself.'

"'Ah, Ischomachus,' said I, 'that is just what I 4
want to hear from you. Did you yourself train
your wife to be of the right sort, or did she know
her household duties when you received her from
her parents?'

"'Why, what knowledge could she have had, 5
Socrates, when I took her for my wife? She was
not yet fifteen years old when she came to me, and
up to that time she had lived in leading-strings,
seeing, hearing and saying as little as possible. If 6
when she came she knew no more than how, when
given wool, to turn out a cloak, and had seen only
how the spinning is given out to the maids, is not
that as much as could be expected? For in control
of her appetite, Socrates, she had been excellently
trained; and this sort of training is, in my opinion,
the most important to man and woman alike.'

"'But in other respects did you train your wife 7
yourself, Ischomachus, so that she should be competent to perform her duties?'

415

Οὐ μὰ Δί', ἔφη ὁ Ἰσχόμαχος, οὐ πρίν γε καὶ ἔθυσα καὶ εὐξάμην ἐμέ τε τυγχάνειν διδάσκοντα καὶ ἐκείνην μανθάνουσαν τὰ βέλτιστα ἀμφοτέροις ἡμῖν.

8 Οὐκοῦν, ἔφην ἐγώ, καὶ ἡ γυνή σοι συνέθυε καὶ συνηύχετο ταὐτὰ ταῦτα ;

Καὶ μάλα γ', ἔφη ὁ Ἰσχόμαχος, πολλὰ ὑποσχομένη μὲν . . . [1] πρὸς τοὺς θεοὺς γενέσθαι οἵαν δεῖ, καὶ εὔδηλος ἦν ὅτι οὐκ ἀμελήσει τῶν διδασκομένων.

9 Πρὸς θεῶν, ἔφην ἐγώ, ὦ Ἰσχόμαχε, τί πρῶτον διδάσκειν ἤρχου αὐτήν, διηγοῦ μοι· ὡς ἐγὼ ταῦτ' ἂν ἥδιόν σου διηγουμένου ἀκούοιμι ἢ εἴ μοι γυμνικὸν ἢ ἱππικὸν ἀγῶνα τὸν κάλλιστον διηγοῖο.

10 Καὶ ὁ Ἰσχόμαχος ἀπεκρίνατο, Τί δέ ; ἔφη, ὦ Σώκρατες, ἐπεὶ ἤδη μοι χειροήθης ἦν καὶ ἐτετιθάσευτο ὥστε διαλέγεσθαι, ἠρόμην αὐτήν, ἔφη, ὧδέ πως·

Εἰπέ μοι, ὦ γύναι, ἆρα ἤδη κατενόησας, τίνος ποτὲ ἕνεκα ἐγώ τε σὲ ἔλαβον καὶ οἱ σοὶ γονεῖς 11 ἔδοσάν σε ἐμοί ; ὅτι μὲν γὰρ οὐκ ἀπορία ἦν, μεθ' ὅτου ἄλλου ἐκαθεύδομεν ἄν, οἶδ' ὅτι καὶ σοὶ καταφανὲς τοῦτ' ἐστί. βουλευόμενος δ' ἔγωγε ὑπὲρ ἐμοῦ καὶ οἱ σοὶ γονεῖς ὑπὲρ σοῦ, τίν' ἂν κοινωνὸν βέλτιστον οἴκου τε καὶ τέκνων λάβοιμεν, ἐγώ τε σὲ ἐξελεξάμην καὶ οἱ σοὶ γονεῖς, ὡς ἐοίκασιν, ἐκ 12 τῶν δυνατῶν ἐμέ. τέκνα μὲν οὖν ἢν θεός ποτε διδῷ ἡμῖν γενέσθαι, τότε βουλευσόμεθα περὶ αὐτῶν, ὅπως ὅτι βέλτιστα παιδεύσομεν αὐτά· κοινὸν γὰρ ἡμῖν καὶ τοῦτο ἀγαθόν, συμμάχων καὶ γηροβοσκῶν ὅτι βελτίστων τυγχάνειν· νῦν δὲ δὴ 13 οἶκος ἡμῖν ὅδε κοινός ἐστιν. ἐγώ τε γὰρ ὅσα μοι

"'Oh no, Socrates; not until I had first offered sacrifice and prayed that I might really teach, and she learn what was best for us both.'

"'Did not your wife join with you in these same 8 sacrifices and prayers?'

"'Oh yes, earnestly promising before heaven to behave as she ought to do; and it was easy to see that she would not neglect the lessons I taught her.'

"'Pray tell me, Ischomachus, what was the first 9 lesson you taught her, since I would sooner hear this from your lips than an account of the noblest athletic event or horse-race?'

"'Well, Socrates, as soon as I found her docile 10 and sufficiently domesticated to carry on conversation, I questioned her to this effect:

"'"Tell me, dear, have you realised for what reason I took you and your parents gave you to me? 11 For it is obvious to you, I am sure, that we should have had no difficulty in finding someone else to share our beds. But I for myself and your parents for you considered who was the best partner of home and children that we could get. My choice fell on you, and your parents, it appears, chose me as the best they could find. Now if God grants us children, 12 we will then think out how we shall best train them. For one of the blessings in which we shall share is the acquisition of the very best of allies and the very best of support in old age; but at present we share in this our home. For I am paying into 13

---

[1] Sauppe does not mark a lacuna, but Schenkl saw that something is lost here.

ἔστιν ἅπαντα εἰς τὸ κοινὸν ἀποφαίνω σύ τε ὅσα
ἤνεγκω πάντα εἰς τὸ κοινὸν κατέθηκας. καὶ οὐ
τοῦτο δεῖ λογίζεσθαι, πότερος ἄρα ἀριθμῷ πλείω
συμβέβληται ἡμῶν, ἀλλ᾽ ἐκεῖνο δεῖ εὖ εἰδέναι, ὅτι
ὁπότερος ἂν ἡμῶν βελτίων κοινωνὸς ᾖ, οὗτος τὰ
πλείονος ἄξια συμβάλλεται.

14 Ἀπεκρίνατο δέ μοι, ὦ Σώκρατες, πρὸς ταῦτα ἡ
γυνή, Τί δ᾽ ἂν ἐγώ σοι, ἔφη, δυναίμην συμπρᾶξαι;
τίς δὲ ἡ ἐμὴ δύναμις; ἀλλ᾽ ἐν σοὶ πάντα ἐστίν.
ἐμὸν δ᾽ ἔφησεν ἡ μήτηρ ἔργον εἶναι σωφρονεῖν.

15 Ναὶ μὰ Δί᾽, ἔφην ἐγώ, ὦ γύναι, καὶ γὰρ ἐμοὶ ὁ
πατήρ. ἀλλὰ σωφρόνων τοί ἐστι καὶ ἀνδρὸς καὶ
γυναικὸς οὕτως ποιεῖν, ὅπως τά τε ὄντα ὡς βέλτιστα ἕξει καὶ ἄλλα ὅτι πλεῖστα ἐκ τοῦ καλοῦ τε
καὶ δικαίου προσγενήσεται.

16 Καὶ τί δή, ἔφη, ὁρᾷς, ἡ γυνή, ὅ τι ἂν ἐγὼ
ποιοῦσα συναύξοιμι τὸν οἶκον;
Ναὶ μὰ Δί᾽, ἔφην ἐγώ, ἅ τε οἱ θεοὶ ἔφυσάν σε
δύνασθαι καὶ ὁ νόμος συνεπαινεῖ, ταῦτα πειρῶ
ὡς βέλτιστα ποιεῖν.

17 Καὶ τί δὴ ταῦτά ἐστιν; ἔφη ἐκείνη. Οἶμαι μὲν
ἔγωγε, ἔφην, οὐ τὰ ἐλαχίστου ἄξια, εἰ μή πέρ γε
καὶ ἡ ἐν τῷ σμήνει ἡγεμὼν μέλιττα ἐπ᾽ ἐλαχίστου
18 ἀξίοις ἔργοις ἐφέστηκεν. ἐμοὶ γάρ τοι, ἔφη φάναι,
καὶ οἱ θεοί, ὦ γύναι, δοκοῦσι πολὺ διεσκεμμένως
μάλιστα τὸ ζεῦγος τοῦτο συντεθεικέναι, ὃ καλεῖται θῆλυ καὶ ἄρρεν, ὅπως ὅτι ὠφελιμώτατον ᾖ
19 αὑτῷ εἰς τὴν κοινωνίαν. πρῶτον μὲν γὰρ τοῦ
μὴ ἐκλιπεῖν ζῴων γένη τοῦτο τὸ ζεῦγος κεῖται
μετ᾽ ἀλλήλων τεκνοποιούμενον, ἔπειτα τὸ γηρο-
βοσκοὺς κεκτῆσθαι ἑαυτοῖς ἐκ τούτου τοῦ ζεύγους

the common stock all that I have, and you have put in all that you brought with you. And we are not to reckon up which of us has actually contributed the greater amount, but we should know of a surety that the one who proves the better partner makes the more valuable contribution."

"'My wife's answer was as follows, Socrates: 14 "How can I possibly help you? What power have I? Nay, all depends on you. My duty, as my mother told me, is to be discreet."

"'"Yes, of course, dear," I said, "my father 15 said the same to me. But discretion both in a man and a woman, means acting in such a manner that their possessions shall be in the best condition possible, and that as much as possible shall be added to them by fair and honourable means."

"'"And what do you see that I can possibly do 16 to help in the improvement of our property?" asked my wife.

"'"Why," said I, "of course you must try to do as well as possible what the gods made you capable of doing and the law sanctions."

"'"And pray, what is that?" said she.

"'"Things of no small moment, I fancy," re- 17 plied I, "unless, indeed, the tasks over which the queen bee in the hive presides are of small moment. For it seems to me, dear, that the gods with great 18 discernment have coupled together male and female, as they are called, chiefly in order that they may form a perfect partnership in mutual service. For, 19 in the first place, that the various species of living creatures may not fail, they are joined in wedlock for the production of children. Secondly, offspring to support them in old age is provided by this

τοῖς γοῦν ἀνθρώποις πορίζεται· ἔπειτα δὲ καὶ ἡ
δίαιτα τοῖς ἀνθρώποις οὐχ ὥσπερ τοῖς κτήνεσίν
ἐστιν ἐν ὑπαίθρῳ, ἀλλὰ στεγῶν δεῖται δηλονότι.

20 δεῖ μέντοι τοῖς μέλλουσιν ἀνθρώποις ἕξειν ὅ τι
εἰσφέρωσιν εἰς τὸ στεγνὸν τοῦ ἐργασομένου τὰς
ἐν τῷ ὑπαίθρῳ ἐργασίας. καὶ γὰρ νεατὸς καὶ
σπόρος καὶ φυτεία καὶ νομαὶ ὑπαίθρια ταῦτα
πάντα ἔργα ἐστίν· ἐκ τούτων δὲ τὰ ἐπιτήδεια

21 γίγνεται. δεῖ δ' αὖ, ἐπειδὰν ταῦτα εἰσενεχθῇ εἰς
τὸ στεγνόν, καὶ τοῦ σώσοντος ταῦτα καὶ τοῦ
ἐργασομένου δ' ἃ τῶν στεγνῶν ἔργα δεόμενά ἐστι.
στεγνῶν δὲ δεῖται καὶ ἡ τῶν νεογνῶν τέκνων
παιδοτροφία, στεγνῶν δὲ καὶ αἱ ἐκ τοῦ καρποῦ
σιτοποιίαι δέονται· ὡσαύτως δὲ καὶ ἡ τῆς ἐσθῆ-

22 τος ἐκ τῶν ἐρίων ἐργασία. ἐπεὶ δ' ἀμφότερα
ταῦτα καὶ ἔργων καὶ ἐπιμελείας δεῖται τά τε ἔνδον
καὶ τὰ ἔξω, καὶ τὴν φύσιν, φάναι, εὐθὺς παρε-
σκεύασεν ὁ θεός, ὡς ἐμοὶ δοκεῖ, τὴν μὲν τῆς
γυναικὸς ἐπὶ τὰ ἔνδον ἔργα καὶ ἐπιμελήματα, τὴν
δὲ τοῦ ἀνδρὸς ἐπὶ τὰ ἔξω ἔργα καὶ ἐπιμελήματα.

23 Ῥίγη μὲν γὰρ καὶ θάλπη καὶ ὁδοιπορίας καὶ
στρατείας τοῦ ἀνδρὸς τὸ σῶμα καὶ τὴν ψυχὴν
μᾶλλον δύνασθαι καρτερεῖν κατεσκεύασεν· ὥστε
τὰ ἔξω ἐπέταξεν αὐτῷ ἔργα· τῇ δὲ γυναικὶ ἧττον
τὸ σῶμα δυνατὸν πρὸς ταῦτα φύσας τὰ ἔνδον
ἔργα αὐτῇ, φάναι ἔφη, προστάξαι μοι δοκεῖ ὁ

24 θεός. εἰδὼς δέ, ὅτι τῇ γυναικὶ καὶ ἐνέφυσε καὶ
προσέταξε τὴν τῶν νεογνῶν τέκνων τροφήν, καὶ
τοῦ στέργειν τὰ νεογνὰ βρέφη πλεῖον αὐτῇ ἐδά-

25 σατο ἢ τῷ ἀνδρί. ἐπεὶ δὲ καὶ τὸ φυλάττειν τὰ
εἰσενεχθέντα τῇ γυναικὶ προσέταξε, γιγνώσκων ὁ
θεός, ὅτι πρὸς τὸ φυλάττειν οὐ κάκιόν ἐστι φοβε-

union, to human beings, at any rate. Thirdly, human beings live not in the open air, like beasts, but obviously need shelter. Nevertheless, those 20 who mean to win store to fill the covered place, have need of someone to work at the open-air occupations; since ploughing, sowing, planting and grazing are all such open-air employments; and these supply the needful food. Then again, as soon 21 as this is stored in the covered place, then there is need of someone to keep it and to work at the things that must be done under cover. Cover is needed for the nursing of the infants; cover is needed for the making of the corn into bread, and likewise for the manufacture of clothes from the wool. And since both the indoor and the out- 22 door tasks demand labour and attention, God from the first adapted the woman's nature, I think, to the indoor and man's to the outdoor tasks and cares.

" ' " For he made the man's body and mind more 23 capable of enduring cold and heat, and journeys and campaigns; and therefore imposed on him the out-door tasks. To the woman, since he has made her body less capable of such endurance, I take it that God has assigned the indoor tasks. And knowing 24 that he had created in the woman and had imposed on her the nourishment of the infants, he meted out to her a larger portion of affection for new-born babes than to the man. And since he imposed on 25 the woman the protection of the stores also, knowing that for protection a fearful disposition is no dis-

ρὰν εἶναι τὴν ψυχήν, πλεῖον μέρος καὶ τοῦ φόβου
ἐδάσατο τῇ γυναικὶ ἢ τῷ ἀνδρί. εἰδὼς δέ, ὅτι καὶ
ἀρήγειν αὖ δεήσει, ἐάν τις ἀδικῇ, τὸν τὰ ἔξω ἔργα
ἔχοντα, τούτῳ αὖ πλεῖον μέρος τοῦ θράσους
26 ἐδάσατο. ὅτι δ' ἀμφοτέρους δεῖ καὶ διδόναι καὶ
λαμβάνειν, τὴν μνήμην καὶ τὴν ἐπιμέλειαν εἰς τὸ
μέσον ἀμφοτέροις κατέθηκεν. ὥστε οὐκ ἂν ἔχοις
διελεῖν, πότερα τὸ ἔθνος τὸ θῆλυ ἢ τὸ ἄρρεν τού-
27 των πλεονεκτεῖ. καὶ τὸ ἐγκρατεῖς δὲ εἶναι ὧν δεῖ
εἰς τὸ μέσον ἀμφοτέροις κατέθηκε καὶ ἐξουσίαν
ἐποίησεν ὁ θεός, ὁπότερος ἂν ᾖ βελτίων, εἴθ' ὁ
ἀνὴρ εἴθ' ἡ γυνή, τοῦτον καὶ πλεῖον φέρεσθαι
28 τούτου τοῦ ἀγαθοῦ. διὰ δὲ τὸ τὴν φύσιν μὴ
πρὸς πάντα ταὐτὰ ἀμφοτέρων εὖ πεφυκέναι, διὰ
τοῦτο καὶ δέονται μᾶλλον ἀλλήλων καὶ τὸ ζεῦγος
ὠφελιμώτερον ἑαυτῷ γεγένηται, ἃ τὸ ἕτερον ἐλλεί-
πεται τὸ ἕτερον δυνάμενον.

29 Ταῦτα δέ, ἔφην, δεῖ ἡμᾶς, ὦ γύναι, εἰδότας ἃ
ἑκατέρῳ ἡμῶν προστέτακται ὑπὸ τοῦ θεοῦ, πειρᾶσθαι ὅπως[1] βέλτιστα τὰ προσήκοντα ἑκάτερον
30 ἡμῶν διαπράττεσθαι. συνεπαινεῖ δέ, ἔφη φάναι,
καὶ ὁ νόμος αὐτὰ συζευγνὺς ἄνδρα καὶ γυναῖκα.
καὶ κοινωνοὺς ὥσπερ τῶν τέκνων ὁ θεὸς ἐποίησεν,
οὕτω καὶ ὁ νόμος τοῦ οἴκου κοινωνοὺς[2] καθίστησι.
καὶ καλὰ δὲ εἶναι ὁ νόμος ἀποδείκνυσιν ἃ ὁ θεὸς
ἔφυσεν ἑκάτερον μᾶλλον δύνασθαι. τῇ μὲν γὰρ
γυναικὶ κάλλιον ἔνδον μένειν ἢ θυραυλεῖν, τῷ δὲ
ἀνδρὶ αἴσχιον ἔνδον μένειν ἢ τῶν ἔξω ἐπιμελεῖ-
31 σθαι. εἰ δέ τις παρ' ἃ ὁ θεὸς ἔφυσε ποιεῖ, ἴσως τι
καὶ ἀτακτῶν τοὺς θεοὺς οὐ λήθει καὶ δίκην δίδω-

---

[1] ὅπως ὡς Sauppe with the MSS. : Cobet removed ὡς.

advantage, God meted out a larger share of fear
to the woman than to the man; and knowing that
he who deals with the outdoor tasks will have to be
their defender against any wrong-doer, he meted
out to him again a larger share of courage. But 26
because both must give and take, he granted to
both impartially memory and attention; and so you
could not distinguish whether the male or the
female sex has the larger share of these. And God 27
also gave to both impartially the power to practise
due self-control, and gave authority to whichever is
the better—whether it be the man or the woman—
to win a larger portion of the good that comes from it.
And just because both have not the same aptitudes, 28
they have the more need of each other, and each
member of the pair is the more useful to the other,
the one being competent where the other is deficient.

" ' " Now since we know, dear, what duties have 29
been assigned to each of us by God, we must endeavour, each of us, to do the duties allotted to us
as well as possible. The law, moreover, approves of 30
them, for it joins together man and woman. And
as God has made them partners in their children, so
the law appoints them partners in the home. And
besides, the law declares those tasks to be honourable for each of them wherein God has made the
one to excel the other. Thus, to the woman it is
more honourable to stay indoors than to abide in the
fields, but to the man it is unseemly rather to stay
indoors than to attend to the work outside. If a 31
man acts contrary to the nature God has given him,
possibly his defiance is detected by the gods and he

---

[1] Sauppe brackets κοινωνοὶς as spurious after Hertlein.
This is wrong in principle.

σιν ἀμελῶν τῶν ἔργων τῶν ἑαυτοῦ ἢ πράττων τὰ
32 τῆς γυναικὸς ἔργα. δοκεῖ δέ μοι, ἔφην, καὶ ἡ τῶν
μελιττῶν ἡγεμὼν τοιαῦτα ἔργα ὑπὸ τοῦ θεοῦ
προστεταγμένα διαπονεῖσθαι.

Καὶ ποῖα δή, ἔφη ἐκείνη, ἔργα ἔχουσα ἡ τῶν
μελιττῶν ἡγεμὼν ἐξομοιοῦται τοῖς ἔργοις οἷς ἐμὲ
δεῖ πράττειν ;
33 "Ὅτι, ἔφην ἐγώ, ἐκείνη γε ἐν τῷ σμήνει μένουσα
οὐκ ἐᾷ ἀργοὺς τὰς μελίττας εἶναι, ἀλλ' ἃς μὲν δεῖ
ἔξω ἐργάζεσθαι ἐκπέμπει ἐπὶ τὸ ἔργον καὶ ἃ ἂν
αὐτῶν ἑκάστη εἰσφέρῃ, οἶδέ τε καὶ δέχεται καὶ
σῴζει ταῦτα, ἔστ' ἂν δέῃ χρῆσθαι. ἐπειδὰν δὲ
ἡ ὥρα τοῦ χρῆσθαι ἥκῃ, διανέμει τὸ δίκαιον
34 ἑκάστῃ. καὶ ἐπὶ τοῖς ἔνδον δ' ἐξυφαινομένοις
κηρίοις ἐφέστηκεν, ὡς καλῶς καὶ ταχέως ὑφαίνη-
ται, καὶ τοῦ γιγνομένου τόκου ἐπιμελεῖται ὡς
ἐκτρέφηται· ἐπειδὰν δὲ ἐκτραφῇ καὶ ἀξιοεργοὶ οἱ
νεοττοὶ γένωνται, ἀποικίζει αὐτοὺς σὺν τῶν ἐπι-
γόνων τινὶ ἡγεμόνι.
35 Ἦ καὶ ἐμὲ οὖν, ἔφη ἡ γυνή, δεήσει ταῦτα
ποιεῖν ;
Δεήσει μέντοι σε, ἔφην ἐγώ, ἔνδον τε μένειν καὶ
οἷς μὲν ἂν ἔξω τὸ ἔργον ᾖ τῶν οἰκετῶν, τούτους
36 συνεκπέμπειν, οἷς δ' ἂν ἔνδον ἔργον ἐργαστέον,
τούτων σοι ἐπιστατητέον καὶ τά τε εἰσφερόμενα
ἀποδεκτέον, καὶ ἃ μὲν ἂν αὐτῶν δέῃ δαπανᾶν, σοὶ
διανεμητέον, ἃ δ' ἂν περιττεύειν δέῃ, προνοητέον
καὶ φυλακτέον, ὅπως μὴ ἡ εἰς τὸν ἐνιαυτὸν κειμένη
δαπάνη εἰς τὸν μῆνα δαπανᾶται. καὶ ὅταν ἔρια
εἰσενεχθῇ σοι, ἐπιμελητέον, ὅπως οἷς δεῖ ἱμάτια
γίγνηται. καὶ ὅ γε ξηρὸς σῖτος ὅπως καλῶς
37 ἐδώδιμος γίγνηται, ἐπιμελητέον. ἐν μέντοι τῶν

424

is punished for neglecting his own work, or med- 32
dling with his wife's. I think that the queen bee is
busy about just such other tasks appointed by God."[1]

"'"And pray," said she, "how do the queen
bee's tasks resemble those that I have to do?"

"'"How? she stays in the hive," I answered, 33
"and does not suffer the bees to be idle; but those
whose duty it is to work outside she sends forth to
their work; and whatever each of them brings in,
she knows and receives it, and keeps it till it is
wanted. And when the time is come to use it, she
portions out the just share to each. She likewise 34
presides over the weaving of the combs in the hive,
that they may be well and quickly woven, and cares
for the brood of little ones, that it be duly reared
up. And when the young bees have been duly
reared and are fit for work, she sends them forth
to found a colony, with a leader to guide the young
adventurers."

"'"Then shall I too have to do these things?" 35
said my wife.

"'"Indeed you will," said I; "your duty will be
to remain indoors and send out those servants whose
work is outside, and superintend those who are to
work indoors, and to receive the incomings, and dis- 36
tribute so much of them as must be spent, and watch
over so much as is to be kept in store, and take
care that the sum laid by for a year be not spent in
a month. And when wool is brought to you, you
must see that cloaks are made for those that want
them. You must see too that the dry corn is in
good condition for making food. One of the duties 37

---

[1] *Cyrop.* v. i. 24.

σοὶ προσηκόντων, ἔφην ἐγώ, ἐπιμελημάτων ἴσως
ἀχαριστότερον δόξει εἶναι, ὅτι ὃς ἂν κάμνῃ τῶν
οἰκετῶν, τούτων σοι ἐπιμελητέον πάντων, ὅπως
θεραπεύηται.

Νὴ Δί, ἔφη ἡ γυνή, ἐπιχαριτώτατον μὲν οὖν,
ἢν μέλλωσί γε οἱ καλῶς θεραπευθέντες χάριν
εἴσεσθαι καὶ εὐνούστεροι ἢ πρόσθεν ἔσεσθαι.

38   Καὶ ἐγώ, ἔφη ὁ Ἰσχόμαχος, ἀγασθεὶς αὐτῆς τὴν
ἀπόκρισιν εἶπον· Ἆρά γε, ὦ γύναι, διὰ τοιαύτας
τινὰς προνοίας καὶ τῆς ἐν τῷ σμήνει ἡγεμόνος αἱ
μέλιτται οὕτω διατίθενται πρὸς αὐτήν, ὥστε ὅταν
ἐκείνη ἐκλίπῃ, οὐδεμία οἴεται τῶν μελιττῶν ἀπο-
λειπτέον εἶναι, ἀλλ᾿ ἕπονται πᾶσαι ;

39   Καὶ ἡ γυνή μοι ἀπεκρίνατο, Θαυμάζοιμ᾿ ἄν,
ἔφη, εἰ μὴ πρὸς σὲ μᾶλλον τείνοι τὰ τοῦ ἡγεμόνος
ἔργα ἢ πρὸς ἐμέ. ἡ γὰρ ἐμὴ φυλακὴ τῶν ἔνδον
καὶ διανομὴ γελοία τις ἂν οἶμαι φαίνοιτο, εἰ μὴ
σύγε ἐπιμελοῖο, ὅπως ἔξωθέν τι εἰσφέροιτο.

40   Γελοία δ᾿ αὖ, ἔφην ἐγώ, ἡ ἐμὴ εἰσφορὰ φαίνοιτ᾿
ἄν, εἰ μὴ εἴη ὅστις τὰ εἰσενεχθέντα σώζοι. οὐχ
ὁρᾷς, ἔφην ἐγώ, οἱ εἰς τὸν τετρημένον πίθον ἀντ-
λεῖν λεγόμενοι ὡς οἰκτείρονται, ὅτι μάτην πονεῖν
δοκοῦσι ; ·

Νὴ Δί, ἔφη ἡ γυνή, καὶ γὰρ τλήμονές εἰσιν, εἰ
τοῦτό γε ποιοῦσιν.

41   Ἄλλαι δέ τοι, ἔφην ἐγώ, ἴδιαι ἐπιμέλειαι, ὦ
γύναι, ἡδεῖαί σοι γίγνονται, ὁπόταν ἀνεπιστήμονα
ταλασίας λαβοῦσα ἐπιστήμονα ποιήσῃς καὶ δι-
πλασίου σοι ἀξία γένηται καὶ ὁπόταν ἀνεπιστήμονα ταμιείας καὶ διακονίας παραλαβοῦσα ἐπιστήμονα καὶ πιστὴν καὶ διακονικὴν ποιησαμένη
παντὸς ἀξίαν ἔχῃς καὶ ὁπόταν τοὺς μὲν σώφρονάς

that fall to you, however, will perhaps seem rather thankless : you will have to see that any servant who is ill is cared for.'' *(14)*

" ' " Oh no," cried my wife, "it will be delightful, assuming that those who are well cared for are going to feel grateful and be more loyal than before.''

" ' " Why, my dear," cried I, delighted with her 33 answer, "what makes the bees so devoted to their leader in the hive, that when she forsakes it, they all follow her, and not one thinks of staying behind ? Is it not the result of some such thoughtful acts on her part ? ''

" ' " It would surprise me," answered my wife, "if 39 the leader's activities did not concern you more than me. For my care of the goods indoors and my management would look rather ridiculous, I fancy, if you did not see that something is gathered in from outside.''

" ' " And my ingathering would look ridiculous," 40 I countered, "if there were not someone to keep what is gathered in. Don't you see how they who 'draw water in a leaky jar,' as the saying goes, are pitied, because they seem to labour in vain ? ''

" ' " Of course," she said, " for they are indeed in a miserable plight if they do that.''

" ' " But I assure you, dear, there are other duties 41 peculiar to you that are pleasant to perform. It is delightful to teach spinning to a maid who had no *(5)* knowledge of it when you received her, and to double her worth to you : to take in hand a girl who is ignorant of housekeeping and service, and after *(6)* teaching her and making her trustworthy and serviceable to find her worth any amount : to have the power of rewarding the discreet and useful

τε καὶ ὠφελίμους τῷ σῷ οἴκῳ ἐξῇ σοι εὖ ποιῆσαι,
42 ἐὰν δέ τις πονηρὸς φαίνηται, ἐξῇ σοι κολάσαι. τὸ
δὲ πάντων ἥδιστον, ἐὰν βελτίων ἐμοῦ φανῇς καὶ
ἐμὲ σὸν θεράποντα ποιήσῃ καὶ μὴ δέῃ σε φοβεῖσθαι, μὴ προϊούσης τῆς ἡλικίας ἀτιμοτέρα ἐν τῷ
οἴκῳ γένῃ, ἀλλὰ πιστεύσῃς, ὅτι πρεσβυτέρα γιγνο-
μένη ὅσῳ ἂν καὶ ἐμοὶ κοινωνὸς καὶ παισὶν οἴκου
φύλαξ ἀμείνων γίγνῃ, τοσούτῳ καὶ τιμιωτέρα ἐν
43 τῷ οἴκῳ ἔσῃ. τὰ γὰρ καλά τε κἀγαθά, ἐγὼ ἔφην,
οὐ διὰ τὰς ὡραιότητας, ἀλλὰ διὰ τὰς ἀρετὰς εἰς
τὸν βίον τοῖς ἀνθρώποις ἐπαύξεται.

Τοιαῦτα μέν, ὦ Σώκρατες, δοκῶ μεμνῆσθαι αὐτῇ
τὰ πρῶτα διαλεχθείς.

VIII. Ἦ καὶ ἐπέγνως τι, ὦ Ἰσχόμαχε, ἔφην
ἐγώ, ἐκ τούτων αὐτὴν κεκινημένην μᾶλλον πρὸς
τὴν ἐπιμέλειαν; Ναὶ μὰ Δί᾽, ἔφη ὁ Ἰσχόμαχος,
καὶ δηχθεῖσάν γε οἶδα αὐτὴν καὶ ἐρυθριάσασαν
σφόδρα, ὅτι τῶν εἰσενεχθέντων τι αἰτήσαντος
2 ἐμοῦ οὐκ εἶχέ μοι δοῦναι. καὶ ἐγὼ μέντοι ἰδὼν
ἀχθεσθεῖσαν αὐτὴν εἶπον, Μηδέν τι, ἔφην, ἀθυ-
μήσῃς, ὦ γύναι, ὅτι οὐκ ἔχεις δοῦναι ὅ σε αἰτῶν
τυγχάνω. ἔστι μὲν γὰρ πενία αὕτη σαφής, τὸ
δεόμενόν τινος μὴ ἔχειν χρῆσθαι· ἀλυπυτέρα δὲ
αὕτη ἡ ἔνδεια, τὸ ζητοῦντά τι μὴ δύνασθαι λαβεῖν
ἢ τὴν ἀρχὴν μηδὲ ζητεῖν εἰδότα, ὅτι οὐκ ἔστιν.
ἀλλὰ γάρ, ἔφην ἐγώ, τούτων οὐ σὺ αἰτία, ἀλλ᾽
ἐγὼ οὐ τάξας σοι παρέδωκα, ὅπου χρὴ ἕκαστα
κεῖσθαι, ὅπως εἰδῇς, ὅπου τε δεῖ τιθέναι καὶ
3 ὁπόθεν λαμβάνειν. ἔστι δ᾽ οὐδὲν οὕτως, ὦ γύναι,
οὔτ᾽ εὔχρηστον οὔτε καλὸν ἀνθρώποις ὡς τάξις.
καὶ γὰρ χορὸς ἐξ ἀνθρώπων συγκείμενός ἐστιν·

members of your household, and of punishing anyone who turns out to be a rogue. But the pleasantest 42 experience of all is to prove yourself better than I am, to make me your servant; and, so far from having cause to fear that as you grow older you may be less honoured in the household, to feel confident that with advancing years, the better partner you prove to me and the better housewife to our children, the greater will be the honour paid to you in our home. For it is not through outward 43 comeliness that the sum of things good and beautiful is increased in the world, but by the daily practice of the virtues."

"'Such was the tenor of my earliest talks with her, Socrates, so far as I can recall them.'"

VIII. "'And did you find, Ischomachus, that they acted as a stimulus to her diligence?' I asked.

"'Yes, indeed,' answered Ischomachus, 'and I recollect that she was vexed and blushed crimson, because she could not give me something from the stores when I asked for it. And seeing that she 2 was annoyed, I said: "Don't worry, dear, because you cannot give me what I am asking for. For not to be able to use a thing when you want it is poverty unquestionably; but failure to get the thing that you seek is less grievous than not to seek it at all because you know that it does not exist. The fact is, you are not to blame for this, but I, because I handed over the things to you without giving directions where they were to be put, so that you might know where to put them and where to find them. My dear, there is nothing so convenient or 3 so good for human beings as order. Thus, a chorus is a combination of human beings; but when the

ἀλλ' ὅταν μὲν ποιῶσιν ὅ τι ἂν τύχῃ ἕκαστος,
ταραχή τις φαίνεται καὶ θεᾶσθαι ἀτερπές, ὅταν
δὲ τεταγμένως ποιῶσι καὶ φθέγγωνται, ἅμα οἱ
αὐτοὶ οὗτοι καὶ ἀξιοθέατοι δοκοῦσιν εἶναι καὶ
4 ἀξιάκουστοι. καὶ στρατιά γε, ἔφην ἐγώ, ὦ γύναι,
ἄτακτος μὲν οὖσα ταραχωδέστατον καὶ τοῖς μὲν
πολεμίοις εὐχειρωτότατον, τοῖς δὲ φίλοις ἀγλευ-
κέστατον ὁρᾶν καὶ ἀχρηστότατον, ὄνος ὁμοῦ,
ὁπλίτης, σκευοφόρος, ψιλός, ἱππεύς, ἅμαξα.
πῶς γὰρ ἂν πορευθείησαν, ἐὰν ἔχοντες οὕτως
ἐπικωλύσωσιν ἀλλήλους, ὁ μὲν βαδίζων τὸν τρέ-
χοντα, ὁ δὲ τρέχων τὸν ἑστηκότα, ἡ δὲ ἅμαξα τὸν
ἱππέα, ὁ δὲ ὄνος τὴν ἅμαξαν, ὁ δὲ σκευοφόρος τὸν
5 ὁπλίτην; εἰ δὲ καὶ μάχεσθαι δέοι, πῶς ἂν οὕτως
ἔχοντες μαχέσαιντο; οἷς γὰρ ἀνάγκη αὐτῶν τοὺς
ἐπιόντας φεύγειν, οὗτοι ἱκανοί εἰσι φεύγοντες
6 καταπατῆσαι τοὺς ὅπλα ἔχοντας. τεταγμένη δὲ
στρατιὰ κάλλιστον μὲν ἰδεῖν τοῖς φίλοις, δυσχε-
ρέστατον δὲ τοῖς πολεμίοις. τίς μὲν γὰρ οὐκ ἂν
φίλος ἡδέως θεάσαιτο ὁπλίτας πολλοὺς ἐν τάξει
πορευομένους, τίς δ' οὐκ ἂν θαυμάσειεν ἱππέας
κατὰ τάξεις ἐλαύνοντας, τίς δὲ οὐκ ἂν πολέμιος
φοβηθείη ἰδὼν διευκρινημένους ὁπλίτας, ἱππέας,
πελταστάς, τοξότας, σφενδονήτας καὶ τοῖς ἄρ-
7 χουσι τεταγμένως ἑπομένους; ἀλλὰ καὶ πορευο-
μένων ἐν τάξει, κἂν πολλαὶ μυριάδες ὦσιν, ὁμοίως
ὥσπερ εἷς ἕκαστος καθ' ἡσυχίαν πάντες πορεύον-
ται· εἰς γὰρ τὸ κενούμενον ἀεὶ οἱ ὄπισθεν ἐπέρ-
8 χονται. καὶ τριήρης δέ τοι ἡ σεσαγμένη ἀνθρώπων διὰ τι ἄλλο φοβερόν ἐστι πολεμίοις ἢ φίλοις
ἀξιοθέατον ἢ ὅτι ταχὺ πλεῖ; διὰ τί δὲ ἄλλο
ἄλυποι ἀλλήλοις εἰσὶν οἱ ἐμπλέοντες ἢ διότι ἐν

430

members of it do as they choose, it becomes mere confusion, and there is no pleasure in watching it; but when they act and chant in an orderly fashion, then those same men at once seem worth seeing and worth hearing. Again, my dear, an army in 4 disorder is a confused mass, an easy prey to enemies, a disgusting sight to friends and utterly useless,— donkey, trooper, carrier, light-armed, horseman, chariot, huddled together.[1] For how are they to march in such a plight, when they hamper one another, some walking while others run, some running while others halt, chariot colliding with horseman, donkey with chariot, carrier with trooper? If there is 5 fighting to be done, how can they fight in such a state? For the units that must needs run away when attacked are enough to trample underfoot the heavy infantry. But an army in orderly array is 6 a noble sight to friends, and an unwelcome spectacle to the enemy. What friend would not rejoice as he watches a strong body of troopers marching in order, would not admire cavalry riding in squadrons? And what enemy would not fear troopers, horsemen, light-armed, archers, slingers disposed in serried ranks and following their officers in orderly fashion? Nay, even on the march where order is kept, though 7 they number tens of thousands, all move steadily forward as one man; for the line behind is continually filling up the gap. Or, again, why is a 8 man-of-war laden with men terrible to an enemy and a goodly sight to friends, if not for its speed? Why do the men on board not hamper one another?

---

[1] *Cyropædia*, VI. iii. 25 ; *Mem.* III. i. 7.

τάξει μὲν κάθηνται, ἐν τάξει δὲ προνεύουσιν, ἐν
τάξει δ' ἀναπίπτουσιν, ἐν τάξει δ' ἐμβαίνουσι
9 καὶ ἐκβαίνουσιν; ἡ δ' ἀταξία ὅμοιόν τί μοι δοκεῖ
εἶναι οἶόνπερ εἰ γεωργὸς ὁμοῦ ἐμβάλοι κριθὰς καὶ
πυροὺς καὶ ὄσπρια, κἄπειτα ὁπότε δέοι ἢ μάζης
ἢ ἄρτου ἢ ὄψου, διαλέγειν δέοι αὐτῷ ἀντὶ τοῦ
λαβόντα διευκρινημένοις χρῆσθαι.

10 Καὶ σὺ οὖν, ὦ γύναι, εἰ τοῦ μὲν ταράχου τούτου
μὴ δέοιο, βούλοιο δ' ἀκριβῶς διοικεῖν τὰ ὄντα
εἰδέναι καὶ τῶν ὄντων εὐπόρως λαμβάνουσα ὅτῳ
ἄν δέῃ χρῆσθαι καὶ ἐμοί, ἐάν τι αἰτῶ, ἐν χάριτι
διδόναι, χώραν τε δοκιμάσωμεθα τὴν προσήκουσαν
ἐκάστοις ἔχειν καὶ ἐν ταύτῃ θέντες διδάξωμεν τὴν
διάκονον λαμβάνειν τε ἐντεῦθεν καὶ κατατιθέναι
πάλιν εἰς ταύτην· καὶ οὕτως εἰσόμεθα τά τε σῶα
ὄντα καὶ τὰ μή· ἡ γὰρ χώρα αὐτὴ τὸ μὴ ὂν
ποθήσει καὶ <τὸ>[1] δεόμενον θεραπείας ἐξετάσει
ἡ ὄψις καὶ τὸ εἰδέναι, ὅπου ἔκαστόν ἐστι, ταχὺ
ἐγχειριεῖ, ὥστε μὴ ἀπορεῖν χρῆσθαι.

11 Καλλίστην δέ ποτε καὶ ἀκριβεστάτην ἔδοξα
σκευῶν τάξιν ἰδεῖν, ὦ Σώκρατες, εἰσβὰς ἐπὶ θέαν
εἰς τὸ μέγα πλοῖον τὸ Φοινικικόν. πλεῖστα γὰρ
σκεύη ἐν σμικροτάτῳ ἀγγείῳ διακεχωρισμένα
12 ἐθεασάμην. διὰ πολλῶν μὲν γὰρ δήπου, ἔφη,
ξυλίνων σκευῶν καὶ πλεκτῶν ὁρμίζεται ναῦς καὶ
ἀνάγεται, διὰ πολλῶν δὲ τῶν κρεμαστῶν καλουμένων πλεῖ, πολλοῖς δὲ μηχανήμασιν ἀνθώπλισται
πρὸς τὰ πολέμια πλοῖα, πολλὰ δὲ ὅπλα τοῖς
ἀνδράσι συμπεριάγει, πάντα δὲ σκεύη, ὅσοισπερ
ἐν οἰκίᾳ χρῶνται ἄνθρωποι, τῇ συσσιτίᾳ ἑκάστῃ
κομίζει· γέμει δὲ παρὰ πάντα φορτίων, ὅσα

---

[1] τὸ added by Hirschig : Sauppe omits.

Is it not just because they are seated in order, swing forward and backward in order, embark and disembark in order? If I want a type of disorder, I think 9 of a farmer who has stored barley, wheat and pulse in one bin; and then when he wants a bannock or a loaf or a pudding, must pick out the grain instead of finding it separate and ready for use.

" " " And so, my dear, if you do not want this 10 confusion, and wish to know exactly how to manage our goods, and to find with ease whatever is wanted, and to satisfy me by giving me anything I ask for, let us choose the place that each portion should occupy; and, having put the things in their place, let us instruct the maid to take them from it and put them back again. Thus we shall know what is safe and sound and what is not; for the place itself will miss whatever is not in it, and a glance will reveal anything that wants attention, and the knowledge where each thing is will quickly bring it to hand, so that we can use it without trouble."

" ' Once I had an opportunity of looking over 11 the great Phoenician merchantman, Socrates, and I thought I had never seen tackle so excellently and accurately arranged. For I never saw so many bits of stuff packed away separately in so small a receptacle. As you know, a ship needs a great 12 quantity of wooden and corded implements when she comes into port or puts to sea, much rigging, as it is called, when she sails, many contrivances to protect her against enemy vessels; she carries a large supply of arms for the men, and contains a set of household utensils for each mess. In addition to all this, she is laden with cargo which the skipper

433

13 ναύκληρος κέρδους ἕνεκα ἄγεται. καὶ ὅσα λέγω,
ἔφη, ἐγώ, πάντα οὐκ ἐν πολλῷ τινι μείζονι χώρᾳ
ἔκειτο ἢ ἐν δεκακλίνῳ στέγῃ συμμέτρῳ. καὶ
οὕτω κείμενα ἕκαστα κατενόησα, ὡς οὔτε ἄλληλα
ἐμποδίζει οὔτε μαστευτοῦ δεῖται οὔτε ἀσυσκεύαστά
ἐστιν οὔτε δυσλύτως ἔχει, ὥστε διατριβὴν παρ-
14 έχειν, ὅταν τῳ ταχὺ δέῃ χρῆσθαι. τὸν δὲ τοῦ
κυβερνήτου διάκονον, ὃς πρῳρεὺς τῆς νεὼς
καλεῖται, οὕτως εὗρον ἐπιστάμενον ἑκάστην τὴν
χώραν, ὡς καὶ ἀπὼν ἂν εἴποι, ὅπου ἕκαστα
κεῖται καὶ ὁπόσα ἐστὶν οὐδὲν ἧττον ἢ ὁ γράμματα
ἐπιστάμενος εἴποι ἂν Σωκράτους καὶ ὁπόσα
15 γράμματα καὶ ὅπου ἕκαστον τέτακται. εἶδον δέ,
ἔφη ὁ Ἰσχόμαχος, καὶ ἐξετάζοντα τοῦτον αὐτὸν
ἐν τῇ σχολῇ πάντα, ὁπόσοις ἄρα δεῖ ἐν τῷ πλοίῳ[1]
χρῆσθαι. θαυμάσας δέ, ἔφη, τὴν ἐπίσκεψιν
αὐτοῦ ἠρόμην, τί πράττοι. ὁ δ' εἶπεν, Ἐπισκοπῶ,
ἔφη, ὦ ξένε, εἴ τι συμβαίνει γίγνεσθαι, πῶς
κεῖται, ἔφη, τὰ ἐν τῇ νηΐ, ἢ εἴ τι ἀποστατεῖ ἢ
16 εἰ δυστραπέλως τι σύγκειται. οὐ γάρ, ἔφη,
ἐγχωρεῖ, ὅταν χειμάζῃ ὁ θεὸς ἐν τῇ θαλάττῃ,
οὔτε μαστεύειν ὅτου ἂν δέῃ οὔτε δυστραπέλως
ἔχον διδόναι. ἀπειλεῖ γὰρ ὁ θεὸς καὶ κολάζει
τοὺς βλᾶκας. ἐὰν δὲ μόνον μὴ ἀπολέσῃ τοὺς
μὴ ἁμαρτάνοντας, πάνυ ἀγαπητόν· ἐὰν δὲ καὶ
πάνυ καλῶς ὑπηρετοῦντας σώζῃ, πολλὴ χάρις,
ἔφη, τοῖς θεοῖς.
17 Ἐγὼ οὖν κατιδὼν ταύτην τὴν ἀκρίβειαν τῆς
κατασκευῆς ἔλεγον τῇ γυναικί, ὅτι πάνυ ἂν ἡμῶν
εἴη βλακικόν, εἰ οἱ μὲν ἐν τοῖς πλοίοις καὶ

[1] πλῷ Cobet.

carries for profit. And all the things I mention 13
were contained in a chamber of little more than a
hundred square cubits.[1] And I noticed that each
kind of thing was so neatly stowed away that there
was no confusion, no work for a searcher, nothing
out of place, no troublesome untying to cause delay
when anything was wanted for immediate use. I 14
found that the steersman's servant, who is called the
mate, knows each particular section so exactly, that
he can tell even when away where everything is
kept and how much there is of it, just as well as a
man who knows how to spell can tell how many
letters there are in Socrates and in what order they
come. Now I saw this man in his spare time in- 15
specting all the stores that are wanted, as a matter
of course, in the ship.[2] I was surprised to see him
looking over them, and asked what he was doing.
" Sir," he answered, " I am looking to see how the
ship's tackle is stored, in case of accident, or whether
anything is missing or mixed up with other stuff.
For when God sends a storm at sea, there's no time 16
to search about for what you want or to serve it out
if it's in a muddle. For God threatens and punishes
careless fellows, and you're lucky if he merely re-
frains from destroying the innocent; and if he saves
you when you do your work well, you have much
cause to thank heaven."

" ' Now after seeing the ship's tackle in such per- 17
fect order, I told my wife : " Considering that folk
aboard a merchant vessel, even though it be a little

---

[1] δεκάκλινος is literally "having space for ten couches";
but it seems that such compounds of κλίνη ("a couch") were
used to denote a definite measure of size.
[2] Or, more probably, "during the voyage."

μικροῖς οὖσι χώρας εὑρίσκουσι καὶ σαλεύοντες
ἰσχυρῶς ὅμως σώζουσι τὴν τάξιν καὶ ὑπερφο-
βούμενοι ὅμως εὑρίσκουσι τὸ δέον λαμβάνειν,
ἡμεῖς δὲ καὶ διῃρημένων ἑκάστοις θηκῶν ἐν τῇ
οἰκίᾳ μεγάλων καὶ βεβηκυίας τῆς οἰκίας ἐν
δαπέδῳ εἰ μὴ εὑρήσομεν καλὴν καὶ εὐεύρετον
χώραν ἑκάστοις αὐτῶν, πῶς οὐκ ἂν πολλὴ ἡμῶν
ἀσυνεσία εἴη;

18 Ὡς μὲν δὴ ἀγαθὸν τετάχθαι σκευῶν κατασκευὴν
καὶ ὡς ῥᾴδιον χώραν ἑκάστοις αὐτῶν εὑρεῖν ἐν
19 οἰκίᾳ θεῖναι ὡς ἑκάστοις συμφέρει, εἴρηται· ὡς δὲ
καλὸν φαίνεται, ἐπειδὰν ὑποδήματα ἐφεξῆς κέηται,
κἂν ὁποῖα ᾖ, καλὸν δὲ ἱμάτια κεχωρισμένα ἰδεῖν,
κἂν ὁποῖα ᾖ, καλὸν δὲ στρώματα, καλὸν δὲ
χαλκία, καλὸν δὲ τὰ ἀμφὶ τραπέζας, καλὸν δὲ
καὶ ὃ πάντων καταγελάσειεν ἂν μάλιστα οὐχ ὁ
σεμνὸς ἀλλ᾽ ὁ κομψός, ὅτι καὶ χύτρας φημὶ
20 εὔρυθμον φαίνεσθαι εὐκρινῶς κειμένας· τὰ δὲ
ἄλλα ἤδη που ἀπὸ τούτου ἅπαντα καλλίω
φαίνεται κατὰ κόσμον κείμενα· χορὸς γὰρ σκευῶν
ἕκαστα φαίνεται, καὶ τὸ μέσον δὲ τούτων καλὸν
φαίνεται, ἐκποδὼν ἑκάστου κειμένου· ὥσπερ
κύκλιος χορὸς οὐ μόνον αὐτὸς καλὸν θέαμά
ἐστιν, ἀλλὰ καὶ τὸ μέσον αὐτοῦ καλὸν καὶ
καθαρὸν φαίνεται.

21 Εἰ δ᾽ ἀληθῆ ταῦτα λέγω, ἔξεστιν, ἔφην, ὦ
γύναι, καὶ πεῖραν λαμβάνειν αὐτῶν οὔτε τι
ζημιωθέντας οὔτε τι πολλὰ πονήσαντας. ἀλλὰ
μὴν οὐδὲ τοῦτο δεῖ ἀθυμῆσαι, ὦ γύναι, ἔφην ἐγώ,
ὡς χαλεπὸν εὑρεῖν τὸν μαθησόμενόν τε τὰς χώρας
22 καὶ μεμνησόμενον καταχωρίζειν ἕκαστα. ἴσμεν
γὰρ δήπου, ὅτι μυριοπλάσια ἡμῶν ἅπαντα ἔχει ἡ

one, find room for things and keep order, though tossed violently to and fro, and find what they want to get, though terror-stricken, it would be downright carelessness on our part if we, who have large store-rooms in our house to keep everything separate and whose house rests on solid ground, fail to find a good and handy place for everything. Would it not be sheer stupidity on our part?

" ' " How good it is to keep one's stock of utensils 18 in order, and how easy to find a suitable place in a house to put each set in, I have already said. And 19 what a beautiful sight is afforded by boots of all sorts and conditions ranged in rows! How beautiful it is to see cloaks of all sorts and conditions kept separate, or blankets, or brazen vessels, or table furniture! Yes, no serious man will smile when I claim that there is beauty in the order even of pots and pans set out in neat array, however much it may move the laughter of a wit. There is 20 nothing, in short, that does not gain in beauty when set out in order. For each set looks like a troop of utensils, and the space between the sets is beautiful to see, when each set is kept clear of it, just as a troop of dancers about the altar is a beautiful spectacle in itself, and even the free space looks beautiful and unencumbered.

" ' " We can test the truth of what I say, dear, 21 without any inconvenience and with very little trouble. Moreover, my dear, there is no ground for any misgiving that it is hard to find someone who will get to know the various places and remember to put each set in its proper place. For we know, I take it, 22 that the city as a whole has ten thousand times as

437

πᾶσα πόλις, ἀλλ᾽ ὅμως ὁποῖον ἂν τῶν οἰκετῶν
κελεύσῃς πριάμενόν τί σοι ἐξ ἀγορᾶς ἐνεγκεῖν,
οὐδεὶς ἀπορήσει, ἀλλὰ πᾶς εἰδὼς φανεῖται, ὅποι
χρὴ ἐλθόντα λαβεῖν ἕκαστα. τούτου μέντοι,
ἔφην ἐγώ, οὐδὲν ἄλλο αἴτιόν ἐστιν ἢ ὅτι ἐν χώρᾳ
23 ἕκαστον [1] κεῖται τεταγμένῃ. ἄνθρωπον δέ γε
ζητῶν, καὶ ταῦτα ἐνίοτε ἀντιζητοῦντα, πολλάκις
ἄν τις πρότερον πρὶν εὑρεῖν ἀπείποι. καὶ τούτου
αὖ οὐδὲν ἄλλο αἴτιόν ἐστιν ἢ τὸ μὴ εἶναι
τεταγμένον, ὅπου ἕκαστον δεῖ ἀναμένειν.

Περὶ μὲν δὴ τάξεως σκευῶν καὶ χρήσεως
τοιαῦτα αὐτῇ διαλεχθεὶς δοκῶ μεμνῆσθαι.

IX. Καὶ τί δή ; ἡ γυνὴ ἐδόκει σοι, ἔφην ἐγώ,
ὦ Ἰσχόμαχε, πῶς τι ὑπακούειν ὧν σὺ ἐσπούδαζες
διδάσκων ;

Τί δέ, εἰ μὴ ὑπισχνεῖτό γε ἐπιμελήσεσθαι καὶ
φανερὰ ἦν ἡδομένη ἰσχυρῶς, ὥσπερ ἐξ ἀμηχανίας
εὐπορίαν τινὰ εὑρηκυῖα, καὶ ἐδεῖτό μου ὡς τάχιστα
ᾗπερ ἔλεγον διατάξαι.

2 Καὶ πῶς δή, ἔφην ἐγώ, ὦ Ἰσχόμαχε, διέταξας
αὐτῇ ;

Τί δέ, εἰ μὴ τῆς οἰκίας τὴν δύναμιν ἔδοξέ μοι
πρῶτον ἐπιδεῖξαι αὐτῇ. οὐ γὰρ ποικίλμασι
πολλοῖς [2] κεκόσμηται, ὦ Σώκρατες, ἀλλὰ τὰ
οἰκήματα ᾠκοδόμηται πρὸς αὐτὸ τοῦτο ἐσκεμμένα,
ὅπως ἀγγεῖα ὡς συμφορώτατα ᾖ τοῖς μέλλουσιν
ἐν αὐτοῖς ἔσεσθαι, ὥστε αὐτὰ ἐκάλει τὰ πρέποντα
3 εἶναι ἑκάστῳ. ὁ μὲν γὰρ θάλαμος ἐν ὀχυρῷ ὢν
τὰ πλείστου ἄξια καὶ στρώματα καὶ σκεύη
παρεκάλει, τὰ δὲ ξηρὰ τῶν στεγῶν τὸν σῖτον, τὰ

---

[1] ἕκαστον is due to the papyrus fragment.
[2] πολλοῖς is due to the papyrus fragment.

much of everything as we have; and yet you may order any sort of servant to buy something in the market and to bring it home, and he will be at no loss: every one of them is bound to know where he should go to get each article. Now the only reason for this is that everything is kept in a fixed place. But when you are searching for a person, you often 23 fail to find him, though he may be searching for you himself. And for this again the one reason is that no place of meeting has been fixed.''

"'Such is the gist of the conversation I think I remember having with her about the arrangement of utensils and their use.'"

IX. "'And what was the result?' I asked; 'did you think, Ischomachus, that your wife paid any heed to the lessons you tried so earnestly to teach her?'

"'Why, she promised to attend to them, and was evidently pleased beyond measure to feel that she had found a solution of her difficulties, and she begged me to lose no time in arranging things as I had suggested.'

"'And how did you arrange things for her, Ischo- 2 machus?' I asked.

"'Why, I decided first to show her the possibilities of our house. For it contains few elaborate decorations, Socrates; but the rooms are designed simply with the object of providing as convenient receptacles as possible for the things that are to fill them, and thus each room invited just what was suited to it. Thus the store-room by the security of its 3 position called for the most valuable blankets and utensils, the dry covered rooms for the corn, the

XENOPHON

δὲ ψυχεινὰ τὸν οἶνον, τὰ δὲ φανὰ ὅσα φάους
4 δεόμενα ἔργα τε καὶ σκεύη ἐστί. καὶ διαιτητήρια
δὲ τοῖς ἀνθρώποις ἐπεδείκνυον αὐτῇ κεκαλ-
λωπισμένα τοῦ μὲν θέρους ψυχεινά, τοῦ δὲ
χειμῶνος ἀλεεινά. καὶ σύμπασαν δὲ τὴν οἰκίαν
ἐπέδειξα αὐτῇ ὅτι πρὸς μεσημβρίαν ἀναπέπταται,
ὥστε εὔδηλον εἶναι, ὅτι χειμῶνος μὲν εὐήλιός
5 ἐστι, τοῦ δὲ θέρους εὔσκιος. ἔδειξα δὲ καὶ τὴν
γυναικωνῖτιν αὐτῇ, θύρᾳ βαλανωτῇ ὡρισμένην
ἀπὸ τῆς ἀνδρωνίτιδος, ἵνα μήτε ἐκφέρηται ἔνδοθεν
ὅ τι μὴ δεῖ μήτε τεκνοποιῶνται οἱ οἰκέται ἄνευ
τῆς ἡμετέρας γνώμης. οἱ μὲν γὰρ χρηστοὶ
παιδοποιησάμενοι εὐνούστεροι ὡς ἐπὶ τὸ πολύ,
οἱ δὲ πονηροὶ συζυγέντες εὐπορώτεροι πρὸς τὸ
κακουργεῖν γίγνονται.
6 Ἐπεὶ δὲ ταῦτα διήλθομεν, ἔφη, οὕτω δὴ ἤδη κατὰ
φυλὰς διεκρίνομεν τὰ ἔπιπλα. ἠρχόμεθα δὲ πρῶτον, ἔφη, ἀθροίζοντες οἷς ἀμφὶ θυσίας χρώμεθα.
μετὰ ταῦτα κόσμον γυναικὸς τὸν εἰς ἑορτὰς
διῃροῦμεν, ἐσθῆτα ἀνδρὸς τὴν εἰς ἑορτὰς καὶ πόλεμον καὶ στρώματα ἐν γυναικωνίτιδι, στρώματα ἐν
ἀνδρωνίτιδι, ὑποδήματα γυναικεῖα, ὑποδήματα
7 ἀνδρεῖα. ὅπλων ἄλλη φυλή, ἄλλη ταλασιουργικῶν
ὀργάνων, ἄλλη σιτοποιικῶν, ἄλλη ὀψοποιικῶν,
ἄλλη τῶν ἀμφὶ λουτρόν, ἄλλη ἀμφὶ μάκτρας,
ἄλλη ἀμφὶ τραπέζας. καὶ ταῦτα πάντα διεχω-
ρίσαμεν, οἷς τε ἀεὶ δεῖ χρῆσθαι, καὶ τὰ θοινατικά.
8 χωρὶς δὲ καὶ τὰ κατὰ μῆνα δαπανώμενα
ἀφείλομεν, δίχα δὲ καὶ τὰ εἰς ἐνιαυτὸν ἀπο-
λελογισμένα κατέθεμεν. οὕτω γὰρ ἧττον λανθάνει,
ὅπως πρὸς τὸ τέλος ἐκβήσεται. ἐπεὶ δὲ ἐχωρίσα-
μεν πάντα κατὰ φυλὰς τὰ ἔπιπλα, εἰς τὰς χώρας

cool for the wine, the well-lit for those works of
art and vessels that need light. I showed her 4
decorated living-rooms for the family that are cool
in summer and warm in winter.[1] I showed her that
the whole house fronts south, so that it was obvious
that it is sunny in winter and shady in summer. I 5
showed her the women's quarters too, separated by
a bolted door from the men's, so that nothing which
ought not to be moved may be taken out, and that
the servants may not breed without our leave. For
honest servants generally prove more loyal if they
have a family; but rogues, if they live in wedlock,
become all the more prone to mischief.

"'And now that we had completed the list, we 6
forthwith set about separating the furniture tribe
by tribe. We began by collecting together the
vessels we use in sacrificing. After that we put
together the women's holiday finery, and the men's
holiday and war garb, blankets in the women's,
blankets in the men's quarters, women's shoes, men's
shoes. Another tribe consisted of arms, and three 7
others of implements for spinning, for bread-making
and for cooking; others, again, of the things required for washing, at the kneading-trough, and for
table use. All these we divided into two sets, things
in constant use and things reserved for festivities.
We also put by themselves the things consumed 8
month by month, and set apart the supplies calculated to last for a year. For this plan makes it
easier to tell how they will last to the end of the
time. When we had divided all the portable property

---

[1] *Mem.* iii. viii. 9.

9 τὰς προσηκούσας ἕκαστα διηνέγκομεν. μετὰ δὲ τοῦτο ὅσοις μὲν τῶν σκευῶν καθ' ἡμέραν χρῶνται οἱ οἰκέται, οἷον σιτοποιικοῖς, ὀψοποιικοῖς, ταλασιουργικοῖς, καὶ εἴ τι ἄλλο τοιοῦτον, ταῦτα μὲν αὐτοῖς τοῖς χρωμένοις δείξαντες ὅπου δεῖ τιθέναι παρεδώκαμεν καὶ ἐπετάξαμεν σῶα παρέχειν·

10 ὅσοις δ' εἰς ἑορτὰς ἢ ξενοδοχίας χρώμεθα ἢ εἰς τὰς διὰ χρόνου πράξεις, ταῦτα δὲ τῇ ταμίᾳ παρεδώκαμεν καὶ δείξαντες τὰς χώρας αὐτῶν καὶ ἀπαριθμήσαντες καὶ γραψάμενοι ἕκαστα εἴπομεν αὐτῇ διδόναι τούτων ὅτῳ δέοι ἕκαστον, καὶ μεμνῆσθαι ὅ τι ἄν τῳ διδῷ, καὶ ἀπολαμβάνουσαν κατατιθέναι πάλιν ὅθενπερ ἂν ἕκαστα λαμβάνῃ.

11 Τὴν δὲ ταμίαν ἐποιησάμεθα ἐπισκεψάμενοι, ἥτις ἡμῖν ἐδόκει εἶναι ἐγκρατεστάτη καὶ γαστρὸς καὶ οἴνου καὶ ὕπνου καὶ ἀνδρῶν συνουσίας, πρὸς τούτοις δὲ ἢ τὸ μνημονικὸν μάλιστα ἐδόκει ἔχειν καὶ τὸ προνοεῖν, μή τι κακὸν λάβῃ παρ' ἡμῶν ἀμελοῦσα, καὶ σκοπεῖν, ὅπως χαριζομένη τι ἡμῖν

12 ὑφ' ἡμῶν ἀντιτιμήσεται. ἐδιδάσκομεν δὲ αὐτὴν καὶ εὐνοϊκῶς ἔχειν πρὸς ἡμᾶς, ὅτ' εὐφραινοίμεθα, τῶν εὐφροσυνῶν μεταδιδόντες καὶ εἴ τι λυπηρὸν εἴη, εἰς ταῦτα παρακαλοῦντες. καὶ τὸ προθυμεῖσθαι δὲ συναύξειν τὸν οἶκον ἐπαιδεύομεν αὐτὴν ἐπιγιγνώσκειν αὐτὴν ποιοῦντες καὶ τῆς

13 εὐπραγίας αὐτῇ μεταδιδόντες. καὶ δικαιοσύνην δ' αὐτῇ ἐνεποιοῦμεν τιμιωτέρους τιθέντες τοὺς δικαίους τῶν ἀδίκων καὶ ἐπιδεικνύοντες πλουσιώτερον καὶ ἐλευθεριώτερον βιοτεύοντας τῶν ἀδίκων· καὶ αὐτὴν δὲ ἐν ταύτῃ τῇ χώρᾳ κατετάττομεν.

14 Ἐπὶ δὲ τούτοις πᾶσιν εἶπον, ἔφη, ὦ Σώκρατες,

tribe by tribe, we arranged everything in its proper place. After that we showed the servants who have 9 to use them where to keep the utensils they require daily, for baking, cooking, spinning and so forth; handed them over to their care and charged them to see that they were safe and sound. The 10 things that we use only for festivals or entertainments, or on rare occasions, we handed over to the housekeeper, and after showing her their places and counting and making a written list of all the items, we told her to give them out to the right servants, to remember what she gave to each of them, and when receiving them back to put everything in the place from which she took it.

"'In appointing the housekeeper, we chose the 11 woman whom on consideration we judged to be the most temperate in eating and wine drinking and sleeping [1] and the most modest with men, the one, too, who seemed to have the best memory, to be most careful not to offend us by neglecting her duties, and to think most how she could earn some reward by obliging us. We also taught her to be loyal to us 12 by making her a partner in all our joys and calling on her to share our troubles. Moreover, we trained her to be eager for the improvement of our estate, by making her familiar with it and by allowing her to share in our success. And further, we put justice 13 into her, by giving more honour to the just than to the unjust, and by showing her that the just live in greater wealth and freedom than the unjust; and we placed her in that position of superiority.

"'When all this was done, Socrates, I told my 14

---

[1] *Mem.* i. v. 1; *Cyropaedia*, i. vi. 8.

ἐγὼ τῇ γυναικί, ὅτι πάντων τούτων οὐδὲν ὄφελος,
εἰ μὴ αὐτὴ ἐπιμελήσεται, ὅπως διαμένῃ ἑκάστῳ
ἡ τάξις. ἐδίδασκον δὲ αὐτήν, ὅτι καὶ ἐν ταῖς
εὐνομουμέναις πόλεσιν οὐκ ἀρκεῖν δοκεῖ τοῖς
πολίταις, ἢν νόμους καλοὺς γράψωνται, ἀλλὰ καὶ
νομοφύλακας προσαιροῦνται, οἵτινες ἐπισκοποῦντες τὸν μὲν ποιοῦντα τὰ νόμιμα ἐπαινοῦσιν,
ἢν δέ τις παρὰ τοὺς νόμους ποιῇ, ζημιοῦσι.
15 νομίσαι οὖν ἐκέλευον, ἔφη, τὴν γυναῖκα καὶ αὐτὴν
νομοφύλακα τῶν ἐν τῇ οἰκίᾳ εἶναι καὶ ἐξετάζειν
δέ, ὅταν δόξῃ αὐτῇ, τὰ σκεύη, ὥσπερ ὁ φρούραρχος
τὰς φυλακὰς ἐξετάζει, καὶ δοκιμάζειν, εἰ καλῶς
ἕκαστον ἔχει, ὥσπερ ἡ βουλὴ ἵππους καὶ ἱππέας
δοκιμάζει, καὶ ἐπαινεῖν δὲ καὶ τιμᾶν ὥσπερ βασί-
λισσαν τὸν ἄξιον ἀπὸ τῆς παρούσης δυνάμεως
καὶ λοιδορεῖν καὶ κολάζειν τὸν τούτων δεόμενον.
16   Πρὸς δὲ τούτοις ἐδίδασκον αὐτήν, ἔφη, ὡς οὐκ
ἂν ἄχθοιτο δικαίως, εἰ πλείω αὐτῇ πράγματα
προστάττω ἢ τοῖς οἰκέταις περὶ τὰ κτήματα,
ἐπιδεικνύων, ὅτι τοῖς μὲν οἰκέταις μέτεστι τῶν
δεσποσύνων χρημάτων τοσοῦτον, ὅσον φέρειν ἢ
θεραπεύειν ἢ φυλάττειν, χρῆσθαι δὲ οὐδενὶ αὐτῶν
ἔξεστιν, ὅτῳ ἂν μὴ δῷ ὁ κύριος· δεσπότου δὲ
ἅπαντά ἐστιν ᾧ ἂν βούληται ἑκάστῳ[1] χρῆσθαι.
17 ὅτῳ οὖν καὶ σωζομένων μεγίστη ὄνησις καὶ
φθειρομένων μεγίστη βλάβη, τούτῳ καὶ τὴν
ἐπιμέλειαν μάλιστα προσήκουσαν ἀπέφαινον.
18   Τί οὖν; ἔφην ἐγώ, ὦ Ἰσχόμαχε, ταῦτα
ἀκούσασα ἡ γυνή πῶς σοι ὑπήκουε;
    Τί δέ, ἔφη, εἰ μὴ εἶπέ γέ μοι, ὦ Σώκρατες, ὅτι
οὐκ ὀρθῶς γιγνώσκοιμι, εἰ οἰοίμην χαλεπὰ
ἐπιτάττειν διδάσκων, ὅτι ἐπιμελεῖσθαι δεῖ τῶν

wife that all these measures were futile, unless she
saw to it herself that our arrangement was strictly
adhered to in every detail. I explained that in
well-ordered cities the citizens are not satisfied with
passing good laws: they go further, and choose
guardians of the laws, who act as overseers, com-
mending the law-abiding and punishing law-breakers.
So I charged my wife to consider herself guardian of 15
the laws to our household. And just as the commander of a garrison inspects his guards, so must
she inspect the chattels whenever she thought it
well to do so; as the Council scrutinises the cavalry
and the horses, so she was to make sure that everything was in good condition: like a queen, she must
reward the worthy with praise and honour, so far as
in her lay, and not spare rebuke and punishment
when they were called for.

"'Moreover, I taught her that she should not be 16
vexed that I assigned heavier duties to her than to
the servants in respect of our possessions. Servants,
I pointed out, carry, tend and guard their master's
property, and only in this sense have a share in it;
they have no right to use anything except by the
owner's leave; but everything belongs to the master,
to use it as he will. Therefore, I explained, he who 17
gains most by the preservation of the goods and
loses most by their destruction, is the one who is
bound to take most care of them.'

"'Well, now, Ischomachus,' said I, 'was your 18
wife inclined to pay heed to your words?'

"'Why, Socrates,' he cried, 'she just told me
that I was mistaken if I supposed that I was laying
a hard task on her in telling her that she must take

---

[1] ἑκάστῳ Camerarius : ἕκαστα Sauppe with the MSS.

ὄντων. χαλεπώτερον γὰρ ἄν, ἔφη φάναι, εἰ αὐτῇ
ἐπέταττον ἀμελεῖν τῶν ἑαυτῆς ἢ εἰ ἐπιμελεῖσθαι
19 δεήσει τῶν οἰκείων ἀγαθῶν. πεφυκέναι γὰρ
δοκεῖ, ἔφη, ὥσπερ καὶ τέκνων ῥᾷον τὸ ἐπιμελεῖσθαι τῇ σώφρονι τῶν ἑαυτῆς ἢ ἀμελεῖν,
οὕτω καὶ τῶν κτημάτων, ὅσα ἴδια ὄντα εὐφραίνει,
ἥδιον τὸ ἐπιμελεῖσθαι νομίζειν ἔφη εἶναι τῇ
σώφρονι τῶν ἑαυτῆς ἢ ἀμελεῖν.

X. Καὶ ἐγὼ ἀκούσας, ἔφη ὁ Σωκράτης, ἀποκρίνασθαι τὴν γυναῖκα αὐτῷ ταῦτα, εἶπον, Νὴ
τὴν Ἥραν, ἔφην, ὦ Ἰσχόμαχε, ἀνδρικήν γε
ἐπιδεικνύεις τὴν διάνοιαν τῆς γυναικός.

Καὶ ἄλλα τοίνυν, ἔφη ὁ Ἰσχόμαχος, θέλω σοι
πάνυ μεγαλόφρονα αὐτῆς διηγήσασθαι, ἅ μου
ἅπαξ ἀκούσασα ταχὺ ἐπείθετο.

Τὰ ποῖα; ἔφην ἐγώ· λέγε· ὡς ἐμοὶ πολὺ ἥδιον
ζώσης ἀρετὴν γυναικὸς καταμανθάνειν ἢ εἰ
Ζεῦξίς μοι καλὴν εἰκάσας γραφῇ γυναῖκα ἐπεδείκνυεν.

2 Ἐντεῦθεν δὴ λέγει ὁ Ἰσχόμαχος, Ἐγὼ τοίνυν,
ἔφη, ἰδών ποτε αὐτήν, ὦ Σώκρατες, ἐντετριμμένην
πολλῷ μὲν ψιμυθίῳ, ὅπως λευκοτέρα ἔτι δοκοίη
εἶναι ἢ ἦν, πολλῇ δ᾽ ἐγχούσῃ, ὅπως ἐρυθροτέρα
φαίνοιτο τῆς ἀληθείας, ὑποδήματα δ᾽ ἔχουσαν
ὑψηλά, ὅπως μείζων δοκοίη εἶναι ἢ ἐπεφύκει,
3 Εἰπέ μοι, ἔφην, ὦ γύναι, ποτέρως ἄν με κρίναις
ἀξιοφίλητον μᾶλλον εἶναι χρημάτων κοινωνόν,
εἰ σοι αὐτὰ τὰ ὄντα ἀποδεικνύοιμι καὶ μήτε
κομπάζοιμι, ὡς πλείω ἔστι μοι τῶν ὄντων, μήτε
ἀποκρυπτοίμην τι τῶν ὄντων μηδέν, ἢ εἰ ἐπειρώμην
σε ἐξαπατᾶν λέγων τε, ὡς πλείω ἔστι μοι τῶν
ὄντων, ἐπιδεικνύς τε ἀργύριον κίβδηλον καὶ

care of our things. It would have been harder, she said, had I required her to neglect her own possessions, than to have the duty of attending to her own peculiar blessings. The fact is,' he added, 19 'just as it naturally comes easier to a good woman to care for her own children than to neglect them, so, I imagine, a good woman finds it pleasanter to look after her own possessions than to neglect them.'"

X. "Now when I heard that his wife had given him this answer, I exclaimed; 'Upon my word, Ischomachus, your wife has a truly masculine mind by your showing!'

"'Yes,' said Ischomachus, 'and I am prepared to give you other examples of high-mindedness on her part, when a word from me was enough to secure her instant obedience.'

"'Tell me what they are,' I cried; 'for if Zeuxis showed me a fair woman's portrait painted by his own hand, it would not give me half the pleasure I derive from the contemplation of a living woman's virtues.'

"Thereupon Ischomachus took up his parable. 2 'Well, one day, Socrates, I noticed that her face was made up: she had rubbed in white lead in order to look even whiter than she is, and alkanet juice to heighten the rosy colour of her cheeks; and she was wearing boots with thick soles to increase her height. So I said to her, "Tell me, my 3 dear, how should I appear more worthy of your love as a partner in our goods, by disclosing to you our belongings just as they are, without boasting of imaginary possessions or concealing any part of what we have, or by trying to trick you with an exaggerated account, showing you bad money and

ὅρμους ὑποξύλους καὶ πορφυρίδας ἐξιτήλους
φαίην ἀληθινὰς εἶναι ;

4 Καὶ ὑπολαβοῦσα εὐθύς, Εὐφήμει, ἔφη· μὴ
γένοιο σὺ τοιοῦτος· οὐ γὰρ ἂν ἔγωγέ σε δυναίμην, εἰ τοιοῦτος εἴης, ἀσπάσασθαι ἐκ τῆς
ψυχῆς.

Οὐκοῦν, ἔφην ἐγώ, συνεληλύθαμεν, ὦ γύναι,
ὡς καὶ τῶν σωμάτων κοινωνήσοντες ἀλλήλοις ;

Φασὶ γοῦν, ἔφη, οἱ ἄνθρωποι.

5 Ποτέρως ἂν οὖν, ἔφην ἐγώ, τοῦ σώματος αὖ
δοκοίην εἶναι ἀξιοφίλητος μᾶλλον κοινωνός, εἴ
σοι τὸ σῶμα πειρῴμην παρέχειν τὸ ἐμαυτοῦ
ἐπιμελόμενος ὅπως ὑγιαινόν τε καὶ ἐρρωμένον
ἔσται καὶ διὰ ταῦτα τῷ ὄντι εὔχρως σοι ἔσομαι,
ἢ εἴ σοι μίλτῳ ἀλειφόμενος καὶ τοὺς ὀφθαλμοὺς
ὑπαλειφόμενος ἀνδρεικέλῳ ἐπιδεικνύοιμί τε ἐμαυτὸν καὶ συνείην ἐξαπατῶν σε καὶ παρέχων ὁρᾶν
καὶ ἅπτεσθαι μίλτου ἀντὶ τοῦ ἐμαυτοῦ χρωτός ;

6 Ἐγὼ μέν, ἔφη ἐκείνη, οὔτ' ἂν μίλτου ἁπτοίμην
ἥδιον ἢ σοῦ οὔτ' ἂν ἀνδρεικέλου χρῶμα ἥδιον
ὁρῴην ἢ τὸ σὸν οὔτ' ἂν τοὺς ὀφθαλμοὺς
ὑπαληλιμμένους ἥδιον ὁρῴην τοὺς σοὺς ἢ ὑγιαί-
νοντας.

7 Καὶ ἐμὲ τοίνυν νόμιζε, εἰπεῖν ἔφη ὁ Ἰσχόμαχος,
ὦ γύναι, μήτε ψιμυθίου μήτε ἐγχούσης χρώματι
ἥδεσθαι μᾶλλον ἢ τῷ σῷ, ἀλλ' ὥσπερ οἱ θεοὶ
ἐποίησαν ἵπποις μὲν ἵππους, βουσὶ δὲ βοῦς
ἥδιστον, προβάτοις δὲ πρόβατα, οὕτω καὶ οἱ
ἄνθρωποι ἀνθρώπου σῶμα καθαρὸν οἴονται
8 ἥδιστον εἶναι· αἱ δ' ἀπάται αὗται τοὺς μὲν ἔξω
πως δύναιντ' ἂν ἀνεξελέγκτως ἐξαπατᾶν, συνόντας
δὲ ἀεὶ ἀνάγκη ἁλίσκεσθαι, ἂν ἐπιχειρῶσιν ἐξα-

gilt necklaces and describing clothes that will fade as real purple?"

"'"Hush!" she broke in immediately, "pray 4 don't be like that—I could not love you with all my heart if you were like that!"

"'"Then, are we not joined together by another bond of union, dear, to be partners in our bodies?"

"'"The world says so, at any rate."   5

"'"How then should I seem more worthy of your love in this partnership of the body—by striving to have my body hale and strong when I present it to you, and so literally to be of a good countenance in your sight, or by smearing my cheeks with red lead and painting myself under the eyes with rouge before I show myself to you and clasp you in my arms, cheating you and offering to your eyes and hands red lead instead of my real flesh?"

"'"Oh," she cried, "I would sooner touch you 6 than red lead, would sooner see your own colour than rouge, would sooner see your eyes bright than smeared with grease."

"'"Then please assume, my dear, that I do not 7 prefer white paint and dye of alkanet to your real colour; but just as the gods have made horses to delight in horses, cattle in cattle, sheep in sheep, so human beings find the human body undisguised most delightful. Tricks like these may serve to gull 8 outsiders, but people who live together are bound to be found out, if they try to deceive one another.

πατᾶν ἀλλήλους. ἢ γὰρ ἐξ εὐνῆς ἁλίσκονται
ἐξανιστάμενοι πρὶν παρασκευάσασθαι ἢ ὑπὸ
ἱδρῶτος ἐλέγχονται ἢ ὑπὸ δακρύων βασανίζονται
ἢ ὑπὸ λουτροῦ ἀληθινῶς κατωπτεύθησαν.

9   Τί οὖν πρὸς θεῶν, ἔφην ἐγώ, πρὸς ταῦτα
ἀπεκρίνατο ;

Τί δέ, ἔφη, εἰ μὴ τοῦ λοιποῦ τοιοῦτον μὲν
οὐδὲν πώποτε ἐπραγματεύσατο, καθαρὰν δὲ καὶ
πρεπόντως ἔχουσαν ἐπειρᾶτο ἑαυτὴν ἐπιδεικνύναι.
καὶ ἐμὲ μέντοι ἠρώτα, εἴ τι ἔχοιμι συμβουλεῦσαι,
ὡς ἂν τῷ ὄντι καλὴ φαίνοιτο, ἀλλὰ μὴ μόνον
10 δοκοίη. καὶ ἐγὼ μέντοι, ὦ Σώκρατες, ἔφη, συνε-
βούλευον αὐτῇ μὴ δουλικῶς ἀεὶ καθῆσθαι, ἀλλὰ
σὺν τοῖς θεοῖς πειρᾶσθαι δεσποτικῶς πρὸς μὲν
τὸν ἱστὸν προσστᾶσαν ὅ τι μὲν βέλτιον ἄλλου
ἐπίσταιτο ἐπιδιδάξαι, ὅ τι δὲ χεῖρον ἐπιμαθεῖν,
ἐπισκέψασθαι δὲ καὶ τὴν[1] σιτοποιόν, παραστῆναι
δὲ καὶ ἀπομετρούσῃ τῇ ταμίᾳ, περιελθεῖν δ'
ἐπισκοπουμένην καὶ εἰ κατὰ χώραν ἔχει ἣν δεῖ
ἕκαστα. ταῦτα γὰρ ἐδόκει μοι ἅμα ἐπιμέλεια
11 εἶναι καὶ περίπατος. ἀγαθὸν δὲ ἔφην εἶναι
γυμνάσιον καὶ τὸ δεῦσαι καὶ μάξαι καὶ ἱμάτια
καὶ στρώματα ἀνασεῖσαι καὶ συνθεῖναι. γυμνα-
ζομένην δὲ ἔφην οὕτως ἂν καὶ ἐσθίειν ἥδιον καὶ
ὑγιαίνειν μᾶλλον καὶ εὐχρωτέραν φαίνεσθαι τῇ
12 ἀληθείᾳ. καὶ ὄψις δέ, ὁπόταν ἀνταγωνίζηται
διακόνῳ καθαρωτέρα οὖσα πρεπόντως τε μᾶλλον
ἠμφιεσμένη,[2] κινητικὸν γίγνεται, ἄλλως τε καὶ
ὁπόταν τὸ ἑκοῦσαν χαρίζεσθαι προσῇ ἀντὶ τοῦ
13 ἀναγκαζομένην ὑπηρετεῖν. αἱ δ' ἀεὶ καθήμεναι
σεμνῶς πρὸς τὰς κεκοσμημένας καὶ ἐξαπατώσας
κρίνεσθαι παρέχουσιν ἑαυτάς. καὶ νῦν, ἔφη, ὦ

For they are found out while they are dressing in
the morning; they perspire and are lost; a tear
convicts them; the bath reveals them as they
are!'"

"'And, pray, what did she say to that?' I asked. 9

"'Nothing,' he said, 'only she gave up such
practices from that day forward, and tried to let me
see her undisguised and as she should be. Still, she
did ask whether I could advise her on one point:
how she might make herself really beautiful, instead[1]
of merely seeming to be so. And this was my 10
advice, Socrates: "Don't sit about for ever like a
slave, but try, God helping you, to behave as a
mistress: stand before the loom and be ready to
instruct those who know less than you, and to learn
from those who know more: look after the baking-[2]
maid: stand by the housekeeper when she is serving
out stores: go round and see whether everything is
in its place." For I thought that would give her
a walk as well as occupation. I also said it was ex- 11
cellent exercise to mix flour and knead dough; and
to shake and fold cloaks and bedclothes; such exercise would give her a better appetite, improve her
health, and add natural colour to her cheeks.
Besides, when a wife's looks outshine a maid's, and 12
she is fresher and more becomingly dressed, they're
a ravishing sight, especially when the wife is also
willing to oblige, whereas the girl's services are
compulsory. But wives who sit about like fine 13
ladies, expose themselves to comparison with painted
and fraudulent hussies. And now, Socrates, you

---

[1] τὴν is omitted by Sauppe with many MSS.
[2] This passage is wrongly punctuated by Sauppe.

Σώκρατες, οὕτως εὖ ἴσθι ἡ γυνή μου κατε-
σκευασμένη βιοτεύει, ὥσπερ ἐγὼ ἐδίδασκον αὐτὴν
καὶ ὥσπερ νῦν σοι λέγω.

XI. Ἐντεῦθεν δ' ἐγὼ εἶπον· Ὦ Ἰσχόμαχε, τὰ
μὲν δὴ περὶ τῶν τῆς γυναικὸς ἔργων ἱκανῶς μοι
δοκῶ ἀκηκοέναι τὴν πρώτην καὶ ἄξιά γε πάνυ
ἐπαίνου ἀμφοτέρων ὑμῶν. τὰ δ' αὖ σὰ ἔργα,
ἔφην ἐγώ, ἤδη μοι λέγε, ἵνα σύ τε ἐφ' οἷς
εὐδοκιμεῖς διηγησάμενος ἡσθῇς κἀγὼ τὰ τοῦ
καλοῦ κἀγαθοῦ ἀνδρὸς ἔργα τελέως διακούσας
καὶ καταμαθών, ἢν δύνωμαι, πολλήν σοι χάριν
εἰδῶ.

2 Ἀλλὰ νὴ Δί', ἔφη ὁ Ἰσχόμαχος, καὶ πάνυ
ἡδέως σοι, ὦ Σώκρατες, διηγήσομαι ἃ ἐγὼ ποιῶν
διατελῶ, ἵνα καὶ μεταρρυθμίσῃς με, ἐάν τί σοι
δοκῶ μὴ καλῶς ποιεῖν.

3 Ἀλλ' ἐγὼ μὲν δή, ἔφην, πῶς ἂν δικαίως μεταρ-
ρυθμίσαιμι ἄνδρα ἀπειργασμένον καλόν τε κἀγαθόν, καὶ ταῦτα ὢν ἀνὴρ ὃς ἀδολεσχεῖν τε δοκῶ
καὶ ἀερομετρεῖν καὶ τὸ πάντων δὴ ἀνοητότατον
4 δοκοῦν εἶναι ἔγκλημα πένης καλοῦμαι. καὶ πάνυ
μεντἄν, ὦ Ἰσχόμαχε, ἦν ἐν πολλῇ ἀθυμίᾳ τῷ
ἐπικλήματι τούτῳ, εἰ μὴ πρώην ἀπαντήσας τῷ
Νικίου τοῦ ἐπηλύτου ἵππῳ εἶδον πολλοὺς ἀκο-
λουθοῦντας αὐτῷ θεατάς, πολὺν δὲ λόγον ἐχόντων
τινῶν περὶ αὐτοῦ ἤκουον· καὶ δῆτα ἠρόμην προσελθὼν τὸν ἱπποκόμον, εἰ πολλὰ εἴη χρήματα τῷ
5 ἵππῳ. ὁ δὲ προσβλέψας με ὡς οὐδὲ ὑγιαίνοντα
τῷ ἐρωτήματι εἶπε· Πῶς δ' ἂν ἵππῳ χρήματα

---

[1] ἀδολεσχεῖν, ἀερομετρεῖν; these are taunts commonly levelled
at Socrates; thus, for instance, Aristophanes, *Clouds*, 225 :

may be sure, my wife's dress and appearance are in accord with my instructions and with my present description.'"

XI. "At this point I said, 'Ischomachus, I think your account of your wife's occupations is sufficient for the present—and very creditable it is to both of you. But now tell me of your own: thus you will have the satisfaction of stating the reasons why you are so highly respected, and I shall be much beholden to you for a complete account of a gentleman's occupations, and if my understanding serves, for a thorough knowledge of them.'

"'Well then, Socrates,' answered Ischomachus, 2 'it will be a very great pleasure to me to give you an account of my daily occupations, that you may correct me if you think there is anything amiss in my conduct.'

"'As to that,' said I, 'how could I presume to 3 correct a perfect gentleman, I who am supposed to be a mere chatterer with my head in the air,[1] I who am called—the most senseless of all taunts—a poor beggar? I do assure you, Ischomachus, this last 4 imputation would have driven me to despair, were it not that a day or two ago I came upon the horse of Nicias the foreigner.[2] I saw a crowd walking behind the creature and staring, and heard some of them talking volubly about him. Well, I went up to the groom and asked him if the horse had many possessions. The man looked at me as if I must be 5 mad to ask such a question, and asked me how a

[1] "What are you at, Socrates?" "I'm walking the air and pondering on the sun"; and 1480: *Socr.*, "Excuse my silly chatter."

[2] If the text is right, this person cannot be the well-known Nicias.

γένοιτο ; οὕτω δὴ ἐγὼ ἀνέκυψα ἀκούσας, ὅτι ἐστὶν
ἄρα θεμιτὸν καὶ πένητι ἵππῳ ἀγαθῷ γενέσθαι, εἰ
6 τὴν ψυχὴν φύσει ἀγαθὴν ἔχοι. ὡς οὖν θεμιτὸν
καὶ ἐμοὶ ἀγαθῷ ἀνδρὶ γενέσθαι διηγοῦ τελέως τὰ
σὰ ἔργα, ἵνα ὅ τι ἂν δύνωμαι ἀκούων καταμαθεῖν
πειρῶμαι καὶ ἐγώ σε ἀπὸ τῆς αὔριον ἡμέρας ἀρξά-
μενος μιμεῖσθαι. καὶ γὰρ ἀγαθή ἐστιν, ἔφην ἐγώ,
ἡμέρα ὡς ἀρετῆς ἄρχεσθαι.

7 Σὺ μὲν παίζεις, ἔφη ὁ Ἰσχόμαχος, ὦ Σώκρατες,
ἐγὼ δὲ ὅμως σοι διηγήσομαι ἃ ἐγὼ ὅσον δύναμαι
8 πειρῶμαι ἐπιτηδεύων διαπερᾶν τὸν βίον. ἐπεὶ
γὰρ καταμεμαθηκέναι δοκῶ, ὅτι οἱ θεοὶ τοῖς ἀνθρώποις ἄνευ μὲν τοῦ γιγνώσκειν τε ἃ δεῖ ποιεῖν
καὶ ἐπιμελεῖσθαι ὅπως ταῦτα περαίνηται οὐ θεμιτὸν ἐποίησαν εὖ πράττειν, φρονίμοις δ' οὖσι καὶ
ἐπιμελέσι τοῖς μὲν διδόασιν εὐδαιμονεῖν, τοῖς δ'
οὔ, οὕτω δὴ ἐγὼ ἄρχομαι μὲν τοὺς θεοὺς θεραπεύων, πειρῶμαι δὲ ποιεῖν, ὡς ἂν θέμις ᾖ μοι
εὐχομένῳ καὶ ὑγιείας τυγχάνειν καὶ ῥώμης σώματος καὶ τιμῆς ἐν πόλει καὶ εὐνοίας ἐν φίλοις
καὶ ἐν πολέμῳ καλῆς σωτηρίας καὶ πλούτου
καλῶς αὐξομένου.

9 Καὶ ἐγὼ ἀκούσας ταῦτα, Μέλει γὰρ δή σοι, ὦ
Ἰσχόμαχε, ὅπως πλουτῇς καὶ πολλὰ χρήματα
ἔχων πολλὰ ἔχῃς πράγματα τούτων ἐπιμελόμενος ;

Καὶ πάνυ γ', ἔφη ὁ Ἰσχόμαχος, μέλει μοι τούτων ὧν ἐρωτᾷς· ἡδὺ γάρ μοι δοκεῖ, ὦ Σώκρατες,
καὶ θεοὺς μεγαλείως τιμᾶν καὶ φίλους, ἤν τινος
δέωνται, ἐπωφελεῖν καὶ τὴν πόλιν μηδὲν κατ' ἐμὲ
χρήμασιν ἀκόσμητον εἶναι.

10 Καὶ γὰρ καλά, ἔφην ἐγώ, ὦ Ἰσχόμαχε, ἐστὶν

horse could own property. At that I recovered, for
his answer showed that it is possible even for a poor
horse to be a good one, if nature has given him a
good spirit. Assume, therefore, that it is possible 6
for me to be a good man, and give me a complete
account of your occupations, that, so far as my
understanding allows me, I may endeavour to follow
your example from to-morrow morning; for that's
a good day for entering on a course of virtue.'

"'You're joking, Socrates,' said Ischomachus; 7
'nevertheless I will tell you what principles I try
my best to follow consistently in life. For I seem 8
to realise that, while the gods have made it impossible for men to prosper without knowing and
attending to the things they ought to do, to some of
the wise and careful they grant prosperity, and to
some deny it; and therefore I begin by worshipping
the gods, and try to conduct myself in such a way
that I may have health and strength in answer to
my prayers, the respect of my fellow-citizens, the
affection of my friends, safety with honour in war,
and wealth increased by honest means.'

"'What, Ischomachus,' I asked on hearing that, 9
'do you really want to be rich and to have much,
along with much trouble to take care of it?'

"'The answer to your questions,' said he, 'is,
Yes, I do indeed. For I would fain honour the gods
without counting the cost, Socrates, help friends in
need, and look to it that the city lacks no adorn-
ment that my means can supply.'

"'Truly noble aspirations, Ischomachus,' I cried, 10

ἃ σὺ λέγεις καὶ δυνατοῦ γε ἰσχυρῶς ἀνδρός· πῶς
γὰρ οὔ; ὅτε πολλοὶ μὲν εἰσὶν ἄνθρωποι, οἳ οὐ
δύνανται ζῆν ἄνευ τοῦ ἄλλων δεῖσθαι, πολλοὶ δὲ
ἀγαπῶσιν, ἢν δύνωνται τὰ ἑαυτοῖς ἀρκοῦντα
πορίζεσθαι. οἱ δὲ δὴ δυνάμενοι μὴ μόνον τὸν
ἑαυτῶν οἶκον διοικεῖν, ἀλλὰ καὶ περιποιεῖν, ὥστε
καὶ τὴν πόλιν κοσμεῖν καὶ τοὺς φίλους ἐπικου-
φίζειν, πῶς τούτους οὐχὶ βαθεῖς τε καὶ ἐρρω-
11 μένους ἄνδρας χρὴ νομίσαι; ἀλλὰ γὰρ ἐπαινεῖν
μέν, ἔφην ἐγώ, τοὺς τοιούτους πολλοὶ δυνάμεθα·
σὺ δέ μοι λέξον, ὦ Ἰσχόμαχε, ἀφ' ὧνπερ ἤρξω,
πῶς ὑγιείας ἐπιμελῇ; πῶς τῆς τοῦ σώματος
ῥώμης; πῶς θέμις εἶναί σοι καὶ ἐκ πολέμου
καλῶς σῴζεσθαι; τῆς δὲ χρηματίσεως καὶ μετὰ
ταῦτα, ἔφην ἐγώ, ἀρκέσει ἀκούειν.

12 Ἀλλ' ἔστι μέν, ἔφη ὁ Ἰσχόμαχος, ὥς γε ἐμοὶ
δοκεῖ, ὦ Σώκρατες, ἀκόλουθα ταῦτα πάντα ἀλλήλων. ἐπεὶ γὰρ ἐσθίει τις τὰ ἱκανὰ ἔχει, ἐκπονοῦντι μὲν ὀρθῶς μᾶλλον δοκεῖ μοι ἡ ὑγίεια
παραμένειν, ἐκπονοῦντι δὲ μᾶλλον ἡ ῥώμη προσ-
γίγνεσθαι, ἀσκοῦντι δὲ τὰ τοῦ πολέμου κάλλιον
σῴζεσθαι, ὀρθῶς δὲ ἐπιμελομένῳ καὶ μὴ κατα-
μαλακιζομένῳ μᾶλλον εἰκὸς τὸν οἶκον αὔξεσθαι.

13 Ἀλλὰ μέχρι μὲν τούτου ἕπομαι, ἔφην ἐγώ, ὦ
Ἰσχόμαχε, ὅτι ἐκπονοῦντα φὴς καὶ ἐπιμελόμενον
καὶ ἀσκοῦντα ἄνθρωπον μᾶλλον τυγχάνειν τῶν
ἀγαθῶν, ὁποίῳ δὲ πόνῳ χρὴ πρὸς τὴν εὐεξίαν καὶ
ῥώμην καὶ ὅπως ἀσκεῖς τὰ τοῦ πολέμου καὶ ὅπως
ἐπιμελῇ τοῦ περιουσίαν ποιεῖν ὡς καὶ φίλους
ἐπωφελεῖν καὶ πόλιν ἐπισχύειν, ταῦτα ἂν ἡδέως,
ἔφην ἐγώ, πυθοίμην.

14 Ἐγὼ τοίνυν, ἔφη, ὦ Σώκρατες, ὁ Ἰσχόμαχος,
456

' and worthy of a man of means, no doubt ! Seeing that there are many who cannot live without help from others, and many are content if they can get enough for their own needs, surely those who can maintain their own estate and yet have enough left to adorn the city and relieve their friends may well be thought high and mighty men. However,' I 11 added, ' praise of such men is a commonplace among us. Please return to your first statement, Ischomachus, and tell me how you take care of your health and your strength, how you make it possible to come through war with safety and honour. I shall be content to hear about your money-making afterwards.'

" ' Well, Socrates,' replied Ischomachus, ' all 12 these things hang together, so far as I can see. For if a man has plenty to eat, and works off the effects [1] properly, I take it that he both insures his health and adds to his strength. By training himself in the arts of war he is more qualified to save himself honourably, and by due diligence and avoidance of loose habits, he is more likely to increase his estate.'

" ' So far, Ischomachus, I follow you,' I answered. 13 ' You mean that by working after meals, by diligence and by training, a man is more apt to obtain the good things of life. But now I should like you to give me details. By what kind of work do you endeavour to keep your health and strength ? How do you train yourself in the arts of war ? What diligence do you use to have a surplus from which to help friends and strengthen the city ? '

" ' Well now, Socrates,' replied Ischomachus, ' I 14

---

[1] *Cyropaedia* i. ii, 10.

ἀνίστασθαι μὲν ἐξ εὐνῆς εἴθισμαι, ἡνίκ' ἂν ἔτι
ἔνδον καταλαμβάνοιμι, εἴ τινα δεόμενος ἰδεῖν τυγ-
χάνοιμι. κἂν μέν τι κατὰ πόλιν δέῃ πράττειν,
ταῦτα πραγματευόμενος περιπάτῳ τούτῳ χρῶμαι·
15 ἢν δὲ μηδὲν ἀναγκαῖον ᾖ κατὰ πόλιν, τὸν μὲν
ἵππον ὁ παῖς προάγει εἰς ἀγρόν, ἐγὼ δὲ περιπάτῳ
χρῶμαι τῇ εἰς ἀγρὸν ὁδῷ ἴσως ἄμεινον, ὦ Σώ-
16 κρατες, ἢ εἰ ἐν τῷ ξυστῷ περιπατοίην. ἐπειδὰν
δὲ ἔλθω εἰς ἀγρόν, ἤν τέ μοι φυτεύοντες τυγχάνωσιν ἤν τε νειοποιοῦντες ἤν τε σπείροντες ἤν τε
καρπὸν προσκομίζοντες, ταῦτα ἐπισκεψάμενος
ὅπως ἕκαστα γίγνεται μεταρρυθμίζω, ἐὰν ἔχω τι
17 βέλτιον τοῦ παρόντος. μετὰ δὲ ταῦτα ὡς τὰ
πολλὰ ἀναβὰς ἐπὶ τὸν ἵππον ἱππασάμην ἱππα-
σίαν ὡς ἂν ἐγὼ δύνωμαι ὁμοιοτάτην ταῖς ἐν τῷ
πολέμῳ ἀναγκαίαις ἱππασίαις, οὔτε πλαγίου οὔτε
κατάντους οὔτε τάφρου οὔτε ὀχετοῦ ἀπεχόμενος,
ὡς μέντοι δυνατὸν ταῦτα ποιοῦντα ἐπιμέλομαι μὴ
18 ἀποχωλεῦσαι τὸν ἵππον. ἐπειδὰν δὲ ταῦτα γένηται, ὁ παῖς ἐξαλίσας τὸν ἵππον οἴκαδε ἀπάγει,
ἅμα φέρων ἀπὸ χώρου ἤν τι δεώμεθα εἰς ἄστυ.
ἐγὼ δὲ τὰ μὲν βάδην τὰ δὲ ἀποδραμὼν οἴκαδε
ἀπεστλεγγισάμην. εἶτα δὲ ἀριστῶ, ὦ Σώκρατες,
ὅσα μήτε κενὸς μήτε ἄγαν πλήρης διημερεύειν.

19   Νὴ τὴν Ἥραν, ἔφην ἐγώ, ὦ Ἰσχόμαχε, ἀρεσ-
κόντως γέ μοι ταῦτα ποιεῖς. τὸ γὰρ ἐν τῷ αὐτῷ
χρόνῳ συνεσκευασμένως χρῆσθαι τοῖς τε πρὸς τὴν
ὑγίειαν καὶ τοῖς πρὸς τὴν ῥώμην παρασκευάσμασι
καὶ τοῖς εἰς τὸν πόλεμον ἀσκήμασι καὶ ταῖς τοῦ
πλούτου ἐπιμελείαις, ταῦτα πάντα ἀγαστά μοι
20 δοκεῖ εἶναι. καὶ γὰρ ὅτι ὀρθῶς ἑκάστου τούτων
ἐπιμελῇ, ἱκανὰ τεκμήρια παρέχῃ· ὑγιαίνοντά τε

rise from my bed at an hour when, if I want to call on anyone, I am sure to find him still at home. If I have any business to do in town, I make it an opportunity for getting a walk. If there is nothing 15 pressing to be done in town, my servant leads my horse to the farm, and I make my walk by going to it on foot, with more benefit, perhaps, Socrates, than if I took a turn in the arcade. When I reach the 16 farm, I may find planting, clearing, sowing or harvesting in progress. I superintend all the details of the work, and make any improvements in method that I can suggest. After this, I usually mount my 17 horse and go through exercises, imitating as closely as I can the exercises needed in warfare. I avoid neither slope nor steep incline, ditch nor water-course, but I use all possible care not to lame my horse when he takes them. After I have finished, 18 the servant gives the horse a roll and leads him home, bringing with him from the farm anything we happen to want in the city. I divide the return home between walking and running. Arrived, I clean myself with a strigil, and then I have luncheon, Socrates, eating just enough to get through the day neither empty-bellied nor too full.'

" 'Upon my word, Ischomachus,' cried I, 'I am 19 delighted with your activities. For you have a pack of appliances for securing health and strength, of exercises for war and specifics for getting rich, and you use them all at the same time! That does seem to me admirable! And in fact you afford con- 20 vincing proofs that your method in pursuing each of these objects is sound. For we see you generally in

459

γὰρ καὶ ἐρρωμένον ὡς ἐπὶ τὸ πολὺ σὺν τοῖς θεοῖς σε ὁρῶμεν καὶ ἐν τοῖς ἱππικωτάτοις τε καὶ πλουσιωτάτοις λεγόμενόν σε ἐπιστάμεθα.

21 Ταῦτα τοίνυν ἐγὼ ποιῶν, ἔφη, ὦ Σώκρατες, ὑπὸ πολλῶν πάνυ συκοφαντοῦμαι, σὺ δ' ἴσως ᾤου με ἐρεῖν, ὡς ὑπὸ πολλῶν καλὸς κἀγαθὸς κέκλημαι.

22 Ἀλλὰ καὶ ἔμελλον δὲ ἐγώ, ἔφην, ὦ Ἰσχόμαχε, τοῦτο ἐρήσεσθαι, εἴ τινα καὶ τούτου ἐπιμέλειαν ποιῇ, ὅπως δύνῃ λόγον διδόναι καὶ λαμβάνειν, ἤν τινί ποτε δέῃ.

Οὐ γὰρ δοκῶ σοι, ἔφη, ὦ Σώκρατες, αὐτὰ ταῦτα διατελεῖν μελετῶν, ἀπολογεῖσθαι μέν, ὅτι οὐδένα ἀδικῶ, εὖ δὲ ποιῶ πολλοὺς ὅσον ἂν δύνωμαι ; κατηγορεῖν δὲ οὐ δοκῶ σοι μελετᾶν ἀνθρώπων, ἀδικοῦντας μὲν καὶ ἰδίᾳ πολλοὺς καὶ τὴν πόλιν καταμανθάνων τινάς, εὖ δὲ ποιοῦντας οὐδένα ;

23 Ἀλλ' εἰ καὶ ἑρμηνεύειν τοιαῦτα μελετᾷς, τοῦτό μοι, ἔφην ἐγώ, ἔτι, ὦ Ἰσχόμαχε, δήλωσον.

Οὐδὲν μὲν οὖν, ὦ Σώκρατες, παύομαι, ἔφη, λέγειν μελετῶν. ἢ γὰρ κατηγοροῦντός τινος τῶν οἰκετῶν ἢ ἀπολογουμένου ἀκούσας ἐλέγχειν πειρῶμαι ἢ μέμφομαί τινα πρὸς τοὺς φίλους ἢ ἐπαινῶ ἢ διαλλάττω τινὰς τῶν ἐπιτηδείων, πειρώμενος διδάσκειν, ὡς συμφέρει αὐτοῖς φίλους εἶναι μᾶλ-

24 λον ἢ πολεμίους. ἐπιτιμῶμέν τινι στρατηγῷ συμπαρόντες ἢ ἀπολογούμεθα ὑπέρ του, εἴ τις ἀδίκως αἰτίαν ἔχει, ἢ κατηγοροῦμεν πρὸς ἀλλήλους, εἴ τις ἀδίκως τιμᾶται. πολλάκις δὲ καὶ βουλευόμενοι ἃ μὲν ἂν ἐπιθυμῶμεν πράττειν,

the enjoyment of health and strength, thanks to the gods, and we know that you are considered one of our best horsemen and wealthiest citizens.'

" ' And what comes of these activites, Socrates ? 21 Not, as you perhaps expected to hear, that I am generally dubbed a gentleman, but that I am persistently slandered.'

" ' Ah,' said I, ' but I was meaning to ask you, 22 Ischomachus, whether you include in your system ability to conduct a prosecution and defence, in case you have to appear in the courts ? '

" ' Why, Socrates,' he answered, ' do you not see[1] that this is just what I am constantly practising— showing my traducers that I wrong no man and do all the good I can to many ? And do you not think that I practise myself in accusing, by taking careful note of certain persons who are doing wrong to many individuals and to the state, and are doing no good to anyone ? '

" ' But tell me one thing more, Ischomachus,' I 23 said ; ' do you also practise the art of expounding these matters ? '

" ' Why, Socrates,' he replied, ' I assiduously practise the art of speaking. For I get one of the servants to act as prosecutor or defendant, and try to confute him ; or I praise or blame someone before his friends ; or I act as peace-maker between some of my acquaintances by trying to show them that it is to their interest to be friends rather than enemies. I assist at a court-martial and censure a 24 soldier, or take turns in defending a man who is unjustly blamed, or in accusing one who is unjustly honoured. We often sit in counsel and speak in

[1] *Mem.* IV. viii. 4.

ταῦτα ἐπαινοῦμεν, ἃ δ' ἂν μὴ βουλώμεθα πράτ-
25 τειν, ταῦτα μεμφόμεθα. ἤδη δ', ἔφη, ὦ Σώκρατες,
καὶ διειλημμένως πολλάκις ἐκρίθην ὅ τι χρὴ
παθεῖν ἢ ἀποτῖσαι.

Ὑπὸ τοῦ, ἔφην ἐγώ, ὦ Ἰσχόμαχε; ἐμὲ γὰρ δὴ
τοῦτο ἐλάνθανεν.

Ὑπὸ τῆς γυναικός, ἔφη.

Καὶ πῶς δή, ἔφην ἐγώ, ἀγωνίζῃ;

Ὅταν μὲν ἀληθῆ λέγειν συμφέρῃ, πάνυ ἐπι-
εικῶς· ὅταν δὲ ψευδῆ, τὸν ἥττω λόγον, ὦ Σώκρατες, οὐ μὰ τὸν Δί' οὐ δύναμαι κρείττω ποιεῖν.

Καὶ ἐγὼ εἶπον· Ἴσως γάρ, ὦ Ἰσχόμαχε, τὸ
ψεῦδος οὐ δύνασαι ἀληθὲς ποιεῖν.

XII. Ἀλλὰ γάρ, ἔφην ἐγώ, μή σε κατακωλύω,
ὦ Ἰσχόμαχε, ἀπιέναι ἤδη βουλόμενον.

Μὰ Δί', ἔφη, ὦ Σώκρατες· ἐπεὶ οὐκ ἂν ἀπέλ-
θοιμι, πρὶν παντάπασιν ἡ ἀγορὰ λυθῇ.

2 Νὴ Δί', ἔφην ἐγώ, φυλάττῃ γὰρ ἰσχυρῶς, μὴ
ἀποβάλῃς τὴν ἐπωνυμίαν τὸ ἀνὴρ καλὸς κἀγαθὸς
κεκλῆσθαι. νῦν γὰρ πολλῶν σοι ἴσως ὄντων
ἐπιμελείας δεομένων, ἐπεὶ συνέθου τοῖς ξένοις,
ἀναμένεις αὐτούς, ἵνα μὴ ψεύσῃ.

Ἀλλά τοι, ὦ Σώκρατες, ἔφη ὁ Ἰσχόμαχος, οὐδ'
ἐκεῖνά μοι ἀμελεῖται, ἃ σὺ λέγεις· ἔχω γὰρ ἐπιτρόπους ἐν τοῖς ἀγροῖς.

3 Πότερα δέ, ἐγὼ ἔφην ὦ Ἰσχόμαχε, ὅταν δεηθῇς
ἐπιτρόπου, καταμαθών, ἤν που ᾖ ἐπιτροπευτικὸς
ἀνήρ, τοῦτον πειρᾷ ὠνεῖσθαι, ὥσπερ ὅταν τέκτο-
νος δεηθῇς, καταμαθὼν εὖ οἶδ' ὅτι ἤν που ἴδῃς
τεκτονικόν, τοῦτον πειρᾷ κτᾶσθαι, ἢ αὐτὸς παιδεύεις τοὺς ἐπιτρόπους;

4 Αὐτὸς νὴ Δί', ἔφη, ὦ Σώκρατες, πειρῶμαι παι-

support of the course we want to adopt and against
the course we want to avoid. I have often been 25
singled out before now, Socrates, and condemned
to suffer punishment or pay damages.'

"'By whom, Ischomachus?' I asked; 'I am in
the dark about that!'

"'By my wife,' was his answer.

"'And, pray, how do you plead?' said I.

"'Pretty well, when it is to my interest to speak
the truth. But when lying is called for, Socrates, I
can't make the worse cause appear the better—oh
no, not at all.'

"'Perhaps, Ischomachus,' I commented, 'you
can't make the falsehood into the truth!'"

XII. "'But perhaps I am keeping you, Ischomachus,' I continued, 'and you want to get away
now?'

"'Oh no, Socrates,' he answered; 'I should not
think of going before the market empties.'

"'To be sure,' I continued; 'you take the 2
utmost care not to forfeit your right to be called a
gentleman! For I daresay there are many things
claiming your attention now; but, as you have made
an appointment with those strangers, you are
determined not to break it.'

"'But I assure you, Socrates, I am not neglecting
the matters you refer to, either; for I keep bailiffs
on my farms.'

"'And when you want a bailiff, Ischomachus, do 3
you look out for a man qualified for such a post, and
then try to buy him—when you want a builder, I
feel sure you inquire for a qualified man and try
to get him—or do you train your bailiffs yourself?'

"'Of course I try to train them myself, Socrates. 4

463

δεύειν. καὶ γὰρ ὅστις μέλλει ἀρκέσειν, ὅταν ἐγὼ
ἀπῶ, ἀντ' ἐμοῦ ἐπιμελούμενος, τί αὐτὸν καὶ δεῖ
ἄλλο ἐπίστασθαι ἢ ἅπερ ἐγώ; εἴπερ γὰρ ἱκανός
εἰμι τῶν ἔργων προστατεύειν, κἂν ἄλλον δήπου
δυναίμην διδάξαι ἅπερ αὐτὸς ἐπίσταμαι.

5   Οὐκοῦν εὔνοιαν πρῶτον, ἔφην ἐγώ, δεήσει αὐτὸν
ἔχειν σοὶ καὶ τοῖς σοῖς, εἰ μέλλει ἀρκέσειν ἀντὶ
σοῦ παρών· ἄνευ γὰρ εὐνοίας τί ὄφελος καὶ
ὁποίας τινὸς οὖν ἐπιτρόπου ἐπιστήμης γίγνεται;

Οὐδὲν μὰ Δί', ἔφη ὁ Ἰσχόμαχος, ἀλλά τοι τὸ
εὐνοεῖν ἐμοὶ καὶ τοῖς ἐμοῖς ἐγὼ πρῶτον πειρῶμαι
παιδεύειν.

6   Καὶ πῶς, ἐγὼ ἔφην, πρὸς τῶν θεῶν εὔνοιαν
ἔχειν σοὶ καὶ τοῖς σοῖς διδάσκεις ὅντινα ἂν
βούλῃ;

Εὐεργετῶν νὴ Δί', ἔφη ὁ Ἰσχόμαχος, ὅταν τινὸς
ἀγαθοῦ οἱ θεοὶ ἀφθονίαν διδῶσιν ἡμῖν.

7   Τοῦτο οὖν λέγεις, ἔφην ἐγώ, ὅτι οἱ ἀπολαύοντες
τῶν σῶν ἀγαθῶν εὐνοί σοι γίγνονται καὶ ἀγαθόν
τί σε βούλονται πράττειν;

Τοῦτο γὰρ ὄργανον, ὦ Σώκρατες, εὐνοίας
ἄριστον ὁρῶ ὄν.

8   Ἢν δὲ δὴ εὔνους σοι γένηται, ἔφην, ὦ Ἰσχόμαχε, ἦ τούτου ἕνεκα ἱκανὸς ἔσται ἐπιτροπεύειν;
οὐχ ὁρᾷς, ὅτι καὶ ἑαυτοῖς εὖνοι πάντες ὄντες ὡς
εἰπεῖν ἄνθρωποι, πολλοὶ αὐτῶν εἰσὶν οἳ οὐκ
ἐθέλουσιν ἐπιμελεῖσθαι, ὅπως αὐτοῖς ἔσται ταῦτα
ἃ βούλονται εἶναί σφισι τὰ ἀγαθά;

9   Ἀλλὰ ναὶ μὰ Δί', ἔφη ὁ Ἰσχόμαχος, τοιούτους ὅταν ἐπιτρόπους βούλωμαι καθιστάναι, καὶ
ἐπιμελεῖσθαι διδάσκω.

For the man has to be capable of taking charge in my absence; so why need he know anything but what I know myself? For if I am fit to manage the farm, I presume I can teach another man what I know myself.'

" 'Then the first requirement will be that he 5 should be loyal to you and yours, if he is to represent you in your absence. For if a steward is not loyal, what is the good of any knowledge he may possess?'

" 'None, of course; but I may tell you, loyalty to me and to mine is the first lesson I try to teach.'

" 'And how, in heaven's name, do you teach your 6 man to be loyal to you and yours?'

" 'By rewarding him, of course, whenever the gods bestow some good thing on us in abundance.'

" 'You mean, then, that those who enjoy a share 7 of your good things are loyal to you and want you to prosper?'

" 'Yes, Socrates, I find that is the best instrument for producing loyalty.'

" 'But, now, if he is loyal to you, Ischomachus, 8 will that be enough to make him a competent bailiff? Don't you see that though all men, practically, wish themselves well, yet there are many who won't take the trouble to get for themselves the good things they want to have?'

" 'Well, when I want to make bailiffs of such men, 9 of course I teach them also to be careful.'

10 Πῶς, ἔφην ἐγώ, πρὸς τῶν θεῶν ; τοῦτο γὰρ δὴ ἐγὼ παντάπασιν οὐ διδακτὸν ᾤμην εἶναι, τὸ ἐπιμελῆ ποιῆσαι.

Οὐδὲ γάρ ἐστιν, ἔφη, ὦ Σώκρατες, ἐφεξῆς γε οὕτως οἷόν τε πάντας διδάξαι ἐπιμελεῖς εἶναι.

11 Ποίους μὲν δή, ἐγὼ ἔφην, οἷόν τε ; πάντως μοι σαφῶς τούτους διασήμηνον.

Πρῶτον μέν, ἔφη, ὦ Σώκρατες, τοὺς οἴνου ἀκρατεῖς οὐκ ἂν δύναιο ἐπιμελεῖσθαι ποιῆσαι· τὸ γὰρ μεθύειν λήθην ἐμποιεῖ πάντων τῶν πράττεσθαι δεομένων.

12 Οἱ οὖν τούτου ἀκρατεῖς μόνοι, ἐγὼ ἔφην, ἀδύνατοί εἰσιν ἐπιμελεῖσθαι ἢ καὶ ἄλλοι τινές ;

Ναὶ μὰ Δί, ἔφη ὁ Ἰσχόμαχος, καὶ οἵ γε τοῦ ὕπνου· οὔτε γὰρ ἂν αὐτὸς δύναιτο καθεύδων τὰ δέοντα ποιεῖν οὔτε ἄλλους παρέχεσθαι.

13 Τί οὖν ; ἐγὼ ἔφην, οὗτοι αὖ μόνοι ἀδύνατοι ἡμῖν ἔσονται ταύτην τὴν ἐπιμέλειαν διδαχθῆναι ἢ καὶ ἄλλοι τινὲς πρὸς τούτοις ;

Ἔμοιγέ τοι δοκοῦσιν, ἔφη ὁ Ἰσχόμαχος, καὶ οἱ τῶν ἀφροδισίων δυσέρωτες ἀδύνατοι εἶναι διδαχθῆναι ἄλλου τινὸς μᾶλλον ἐπιμελεῖσθαι ἢ τούτου·

14 οὔτε γὰρ ἐλπίδα οὔτ' ἐπιμέλειαν ἡδίονα ῥάδιον εὑρεῖν τῆς τῶν παιδικῶν ἐπιμελείας, οὐδὲ μὴν ὅταν παρῇ τὸ πρακτέον, τιμωρίαν χαλεπωτέραν εὐπετές ἐστι τοῦ ἀπὸ τῶν ἐρωμένων κωλύεσθαι. ὑφίεμαι οὖν καὶ οὓς ἂν τοιούτους γνῶ ὄντας μηδ' ἐπιχειρεῖν ἐπιμελητὰς τούτων τινὰς καθιστάναι.

15 Τί δέ, ἔφην ἐγώ, οἵτινες αὖ ἐρωτικῶς ἔχουσι τοῦ κερδαίνειν, ἢ καὶ οὗτοι ἀδύνατοί εἰσιν εἰς ἐπιμέλειαν τῶν κατ' ἀγρὸν ἔργων παιδεύεσθαι ;

Οὐ μὰ Δί, ἔφη ὁ Ἰσχόμαχος, οὐδαμῶς γε, ἀλλὰ

"'Pray how do you do that? I was under the 10
impression that carefulness is a virtue that can't
possibly be taught.'

"'True, Socrates, it isn't possible to teach everyone you come across to be careful.'

"'Very well; what sort of men can be taught? 11
Point these out to me, at all events.'

"'In the first place, Socrates, you can't make
careful men of hard drinkers; for drink makes them
forget everything they ought to do.'

"'Then are drunkards the only men who will 12
never become careful, or are there others?'

"'Of course there are—sluggards must be included; for you can't do your own business when you
are asleep, nor make others do theirs.'

"'Well then, will these make up the total of 13
persons incapable of learning this lesson, or are there
yet others besides?'

"'I should add that in my opinion a man who
falls desperately in love is incapable of giving more
attention to anything than he gives to the object of
his passion. For it isn't easy to find hope or occupa- 14
tion more delightful than devotion to the darling!
aye, and when the thing to be done presses, no
harder punishment can easily be thought of than
the prevention of intercourse with the beloved!
Therefore I shrink from attempting to make a
manager of that sort of man too.'

"'And what about the men who have a passion 15
for lucre? Are they also incapable of being trained
to take charge of the work of a farm?'

"'Not at all; of course not. In fact, they very

καὶ πάνυ εὐάγωγοί εἰσιν εἰς τὴν τούτων ἐπιμέ-
λειαν· οὐδὲν γὰρ ἄλλο δεῖ ἢ δεῖξαι μόνον αὐτοῖς,
ὅτι κερδαλέον ἐστὶν ἡ ἐπιμέλεια.

16   Τοὺς δὲ ἄλλους, ἔφην ἐγώ, εἰ ἐγκρατεῖς τέ εἰσιν
ὧν σὺ κελεύεις καὶ πρὸς τὸ φιλοκερδεῖς εἶναι
μετρίως ἔχουσιν, πῶς ἐκδιδάσκεις ὧν σὺ βούλει
ἐπιμελεῖς γίγνεσθαι;

      Ἁπλῶς, ἔφη, πάνυ, ὦ Σώκρατες. ὅταν μὲν
γὰρ ἐπιμελουμένους ἴδω, καὶ ἐπαινῶ καὶ τιμᾶν
πειρῶμαι αὐτούς, ὅταν δὲ ἀμελοῦντας, λέγειν τε
πειρῶμαι καὶ ποιεῖν ὁποῖα δήξεται αὐτούς.

17   Ἴθι, ἐγὼ ἔφην, ὦ Ἰσχόμαχε, καὶ τόδε μοι
παρατραπόμενος τοῦ λόγου περὶ τῶν παιδευο-
μένων εἰς τὴν ἐπιμέλειαν δήλωσον περὶ τοῦ παιδεύεσθαι, εἰ οἷόν τέ ἐστιν ἀμελῆ αὐτὸν ὄντα
ἄλλους ποιεῖν ἐπιμελεῖς.

18   Οὐ μὰ Δί᾽, ἔφη ὁ Ἰσχόμαχος, οὐδέν γε μᾶλλον
ἢ ἄμουσον ὄντα αὐτὸν ἄλλους μουσικοὺς ποιεῖν.
χαλεπὸν γὰρ τοῦ διδασκάλου πονηρῶς τι ὑποδεικνύοντος καλῶς τοῦτο ποιεῖν μαθεῖν καὶ ἀμελεῖν
γε ὑποδεικνύοντος τοῦ δεσπότου χαλεπὸν ἐπιμελῆ
19 θεράποντα γενέσθαι. ὡς δὲ συντόμως εἰπεῖν,
πονηροῦ μὲν δεσπότου οἰκέτας οὐ δοκῶ χρηστοὺς
καταμεμαθηκέναι· χρηστοῦ μέντοι πονηροὺς ἤδη
εἶδον, οὐ μέντοι ἀζημίους γε. τὸν δὲ ἐπιμελητι-
κοὺς βουλόμενον ποιήσασθαί τινας καὶ ἐφορα-
τικὸν δεῖ εἶναι τῶν ἔργων καὶ ἐξεταστικὸν καὶ
χάριν θέλοντα τῶν καλῶς τελουμένων ἀποδιδόναι
τῷ αἰτίῳ καὶ δίκην μὴ ὀκνοῦντα τὴν ἀξίαν ἐπιθεῖ-
20 ναι τῷ ἀμελοῦντι. καλῶς δέ μοι δοκεῖ ἔχειν, ἔφη
ὁ Ἰσχόμαχος, καὶ ἡ τοῦ βαρβάρου λεγομένη
ἀπόκρισις, ὅτε βασιλεὺς ἄρα ἵππου ἐπιτυχὼν

easily qualify for the work. It is merely necessary
to point out to them that diligence is profitable.'

" ' And assuming that the others are free from the 16
faults that you condemn and are covetous of gain in
a moderate degree, how do you teach them to be
careful in the affairs you want them to superintend ? '

" ' By a very simple plan, Socrates. Whenever I
notice that they are careful, I commend them and
try to show them honour; but when they appear
careless, I try to say and do the sort of things that
will sting them.'

" ' Turn now, Ischomachus, from the subject of 17
the men in training for the occupation, and tell me
about the system : is it possible for anyone to make
others careful if he is careless himself ? '

" ' Of course not : an unmusical person could as 18
soon teach music. For it is hard to learn to do a
thing well when the teacher prompts you badly;
and when a master prompts a servant to be careless,
it is difficult for the man to become a good servant.
To put it shortly, I don't think I have discovered a 19
bad master with good servants : I have, however,
come across a good master with bad servants—but
they suffered for it ! If you want to make men fit
to take charge, you must supervise their work and
examine it, and be ready to reward work well carried
through, and not shrink from punishing carelessness
as it deserves. I like the answer that is attributed 20
to the Persian. The king, you know, had happened

ἀγαθοῦ παχῦναι αὐτὸν ὡς τάχιστα βουλόμενος
ἤρετο τῶν δεινῶν τινα ἀμφ' ἵππους δοκούντων
εἶναι, τί τάχιστα παχύνει ἵππον· τὸν δ' εἰπεῖν
λέγεται, ὅτι δεσπότου ὀφθαλμός. οὕτω δ', ἔφη,
ὦ Σώκρατες, καὶ τἆλλά μοι δοκεῖ δεσπότου
ὀφθαλμὸς τὰ καλά τε κἀγαθὰ μάλιστα ἐργάζεσθαι.

XIII. Ὅταν δὲ παραστήσῃς τινί, ἔφην ἐγώ,
τοῦτο καὶ πάνυ ἰσχυρῶς, ὅτι δεῖ ἐπιμελεῖσθαι ὧν
ἂν σὺ βούλῃ, ἦ ἱκανὸς ἤδη ἔσται ὁ τοιοῦτος
ἐπιτροπεύειν ἤ τι καὶ ἄλλο προσμαθητέον αὐτῷ
ἔσται, εἰ μέλλει ἐπίτροπος ἱκανὸς ἔσεσθαι ;

2   Ναὶ μὰ Δί', ἔφη ὁ Ἰσχόμαχος, ἔτι μέντοι
λοιπὸν αὐτῷ ἐστι γνῶναι, ὅ τι τε ποιητέον καὶ
ὁπότε καὶ ὅπως, εἰ δὲ μή, τί μᾶλλον ἐπιτρόπου
ἄνευ τούτων ὄφελος ἢ ἰατροῦ, ὃς ἐπιμελοῖτο μὲν
κάμνοντός τινος πρωΐ τε ἰὼν καὶ ὀψέ, ὅ τι δὲ
συμφέρον τῷ κάμνοντι ποιεῖν εἴη, τοῦτο μὴ
εἰδείη ;

3   Ἐὰν δὲ δὴ καὶ τὰ ἔργα μάθῃ ὡς ἔστιν ἐργα-
στέα, ἔτι τινός, ἔφην ἐγώ, προσδεήσεται ἢ ἀποτε-
τελεσμένος ἤδη οὗτός σοι ἔσται ἐπίτροπος ;

Ἄρχειν γε, ἔφη, οἶμαι δεῖν αὐτὸν μαθεῖν τῶν
ἐργαζομένων.

4   Ἦ οὖν, ἔφην ἐγώ, καὶ σὺ ἄρχειν ἱκανοὺς εἶναι
παιδεύεις τοὺς ἐπιτρόπους ;

Πειρῶμαί γε δή, ἔφη ὁ Ἰσχόμαχος.

Καὶ πῶς δή, ἔφην ἐγώ, πρὸς τῶν θεῶν τὸ
ἀρχικοὺς εἶναι ἀνθρώπων παιδεύεις ;

Φαύλως, ἔφη, πάνυ, ὦ Σώκρατες, ὥστε ἴσως
ἂν καὶ καταγελάσαις ἀκούων.

5   Οὐ μὲν δὴ ἄξιόν γ', ἔφην ἐγώ, τὸ πρᾶγμα κατα-

on a good horse, and wanted to fatten him as speedily as possible. So he asked one who was reputed clever with horses what is the quickest way of fattening a horse. "The master's eye," replied the man. I think we may apply the answer generally, Socrates, and say that the master's eye in the main does the good and worthy work.'"

XIII. "'When you have impressed on a man,' I resumed, 'the necessity of careful attention to the duties you assign to him, will he then be competent to act as bailiff, or must he learn something besides, if he is to be efficient?'

"'Of course,' answered Ischomachus, 'he has still 2 to understand what he has to do, and when and how to do it. Otherwise how could a bailiff be of more use than a doctor who takes care to visit a patient early and late, but has no notion of the right way to treat his illness?'

"'Well, but suppose he has learned how farm- 3 work is to be done, will he want something more yet, or will your man now be a perfect bailiff?'

"'I think he must learn to rule the labourers.'

"'And do you train your bailiffs to be competent 4 to rule too?'

"'Yes, I try, anyhow.'

"'And pray tell me how you train them to be rulers of men.'

"'By a childishly easy method, Socrates. I dare-say you'll laugh if I tell you.'

"'Oh, but it is certainly not a laughing matter, 5

γέλωτος, ὦ Ἰσχόμαχε. ὅστις γάρ τοι ἀρχικοὺς
ἀνθρώπων δύναται ποιεῖν, δῆλον ὅτι οὗτος καὶ
δεσποτικοὺς ἀνθρώπων δύναται διδάσκειν, ὅστις
δὲ δεσποτικούς, δύναται ποιεῖν καὶ βασιλικούς.
ὥστε οὐ καταγέλωτός μοι δοκεῖ ἄξιος εἶναι, ἀλλ᾽
ἐπαίνου μεγάλου ὁ τοῦτο δυνάμενος ποιεῖν.

6 Οὐκοῦν, ἔφη, ὦ Σώκρατες, τὰ μὲν ἄλλα ζῷα ἐκ
δυοῖν τούτοιν τὸ πείθεσθαι μανθάνουσιν, ἔκ τε
τοῦ ὅταν ἀπειθεῖν ἐπιχειρῶσι κολάζεσθαι καὶ ἐκ
7 τοῦ ὅταν προθύμως ὑπηρετῶσιν εὖ πάσχειν. οἵ
τε γοῦν πῶλοι μανθάνουσιν ὑπακούειν τοῖς πωλο-
δάμναις τῷ ὅταν μὲν πείθωνται τῶν ἡδέων τι
αὐτοῖς γίγνεσθαι, ὅταν δὲ ἀπειθῶσι πράγματα
ἔχειν, ἔστ᾽ ἂν ὑπηρετήσωσι κατὰ γνώμην τῷ
8 πωλοδάμνῃ· καὶ τὰ κυνίδια δὲ πολὺ τῶν ἀνθρώπων καὶ τῇ γνώμῃ καὶ τῇ γλώττῃ ὑποδεέστερα
ὄντα ὅμως καὶ περιτρέχειν καὶ κυβιστᾶν καὶ ἄλλα
πολλὰ μανθάνει τῷ αὐτῷ τούτῳ τρόπῳ. ὅταν
μὲν γὰρ πείθηται, λαμβάνει τι ὧν δεῖται, ὅταν δὲ
9 ἀμελῇ, κολάζεται. ἀνθρώπους δ᾽ ἔστι πιθανω-
τέρους ποιεῖν καὶ λόγῳ ἐπιδεικνύοντα, ὡς συμφέρει αὐτοῖς πείθεσθαι, τοῖς δὲ δούλοις καὶ ἡ
δοκοῦσα θηριώδης παιδεία εἶναι πάνυ ἐστὶν
ἐπαγωγὸς πρὸς τὸ πείθεσθαι διδάσκειν· τῇ γὰρ
γαστρὶ αὐτῶν ἐπὶ ταῖς ἐπιθυμίαις προσχαριζό-
μενος ἂν πολλὰ ἀνύτοις παρ᾽ αὐτῶν. αἱ δὲ
φιλότιμοι τῶν φύσεων καὶ τῷ ἐπαίνῳ παροξύ-
νονται. πεινῶσι γὰρ τοῦ ἐπαίνου οὐχ ἧττον ἔνιαι
τῶν φύσεων ἢ ἄλλαι τῶν σίτων τε καὶ ποτῶν.
10 ταῦτά [τε] οὖν, ὅσαπερ αὐτὸς ποιῶν οἶμαι πιθανω-
τέροις ἀνθρώποις χρῆσθαι, διδάσκων οὓς ἂν ἐπι-
τοόπους βούλωμαι καταστῆσαι καὶ τάδε συλ-

Ischomachus. For anyone who can make men fit to rule others can also teach them to be masters of others; and if he can make them fit to be masters, he can make them fit to be kings. So anyone who can do that seems to me to deserve high praise rather than laughter.'

"'Well now, Socrates, other creatures learn 6 obedience in two ways—by being punished when they try to disobey, and by being rewarded when they are eager to serve you. Colts, for example, 7 learn to obey the horsebreaker by getting something they like when they are obedient, and suffering inconvenience when they are disobedient, until they carry out the horsebreaker's intentions. Puppies, 8 again, are much inferior to men in intelligence and power of expression; and yet they learn to run in circles and turn somersaults and do many other tricks in the same way; for when they obey they get something that they want, and when they are careless, they are punished. And men can be made 9 more obedient by word of mouth merely, by being shown that it is good for them to obey. But in dealing with slaves the training thought suitable for wild animals is also a very effective way of teaching obedience; for you will do much with them by filling their bellies with the food they hanker after. Those of an ambitious disposition are also spurred on by praise, some natures being hungry for praise as others for meat and drink. Now these are pre- 10 cisely the things that I do myself with a view to making men more obedient; but they are not the only lessons I give to those whom I want to appoint my bailiffs. I have other ways of helping them on.

473

λαμβάνω αὐτοῖς· ἱμάτιά τε γάρ, ἃ δεῖ παρέχειν
ἐμὲ τοῖς ἐργαστῆρσι, καὶ ὑποδήματα οὐχ ὅμοια
πάντα ποιῶ, ἀλλὰ τὰ μὲν χείρω, τὰ δὲ βελτίω,
ἵνα ᾖ τὸν κρείττω τοῖς βελτίοσι τιμᾶν, τῷ δὲ
11 χείρονι τὰ ἥττω διδόναι. πάνυ γάρ μοι δοκεῖ,
ἔφη, ὦ Σώκρατες, ἀθυμία ἐγγίγνεσθαι τοῖς ἀγαθοῖς, ὅταν ὁρῶσι τὰ μὲν ἔργα δι' αὐτῶν κατα-
πραττόμενα, τῶν δὲ ὁμοίων τυγχάνοντας ἑαυτοῖς
τοὺς μήτε πονεῖν μήτε κινδυνεύειν ἐθέλοντας,
12 ὅταν δέῃ. αὐτός τε οὖν οὐδ' ὅπως τι οὖν τῶν
ἴσων ἀξιῶ τοὺς ἀμείνους τοῖς κακίοσι τυγχάνειν
τούς τ' ἐπιτρόπους ὅταν μὲν εἰδῶ διαδεδωκότας
τοῖς πλείστου ἀξίοις τὰ κράτιστα, ἐπαινῶ, ἢν δὲ
ἴδω ἢ κολακεύμασί τινα προτιμώμενον ἢ καὶ ἄλλῃ
τινὶ ἀνωφελεῖ χάριτι, οὐκ ἀμελῶ, ἀλλ' ἐπιπλήτ-
τω καὶ πειρῶμαι διδάσκειν, ὦ Σώκρατες, ὅτι οὐδ'
αὐτῷ σύμφορα ταῦτα ποιεῖ.

XIV. Ὅταν δέ, ὦ Ἰσχόμαχε, ἔφην ἐγώ, καὶ
ἄρχειν ἤδη ἱκανός σοι γένηται, ὥστε πειθομένους
παρέχεσθαι, ἢ ἀποτετελεσμένον τοῦτον ἡγῇ ἐπί-
τροπον ἢ ἔτι τινὸς προσδεῖται ὁ ταῦτα ἔχων ἃ σὺ
εἴρηκας ;

2   Ναὶ μὰ Δί', ἔφη ὁ Ἰσχόμαχος, τοῦ γε ἀπέχεσθαι
τῶν δεσποσύνων καὶ μὴ κλέπτειν. εἰ γὰρ ὁ τοὺς
καρποὺς μεταχειριζόμενος τολμῴη ἀφανίζειν,
ὥστε μὴ λείπειν λυσιτελοῦντας τοῖς ἔργοις, τί ἂν
ὄφελος εἴη τὸ διὰ τῆς τούτου ἐπιμελείας γεωργεῖν ;

3   Ἦ καὶ ταύτην οὖν, ἔφην ἐγώ, τὴν δικαιοσύνην
σὺ ὑποδύῃ διδάσκειν ;

Καὶ πάνυ, ἔφη ὁ Ἰσχόμαχος· οὐ μέντοι γε
πάντας ἐξ ἑτοίμου εὑρίσκω ὑπακούοντας τῆς δι-

For the clothes that I must provide for my work-people and the shoes are not all alike. Some are better than others, some worse, in order that I may reward the better servant with the superior articles, and give the inferior things to the less deserving. For I think it is very disheartening to good servants, 11 Socrates, when they see that they do all the work, and others who are not willing to work hard and run risks when need be, get the same as they. For my 12 part, then, I don't choose to put the deserving on a level with the worthless, and when I know that my bailiffs have distributed the best things to the most deserving, I commend them ; and if I see that flattery or any other futile service wins special favour, I don't overlook it, but reprove the bailiff, and try to show him, Socrates, that such favouritism is not even in his own interest.'"

XIV. "'Now, Ischomachus,' said I, 'when you find your man so competent to rule that he can make them obedient, do you think him a perfect bailiff, or does he want anything else, even with the qualifications you have mentioned?'

"'Of course, Socrates,' returned Ischomachus, 'he 2 must be honest and not touch his master's property. For if the man who handles the crops dares to make away with them, and doesn't leave enough to give a profit on the undertaking, what good can come of farming under his management?'

"'Then do you take it on yourself to teach this 3 kind of justice too?'

"'Certainly : I don't find, however, that all readily

4 δασκαλίας ταύτης. καίτοι τὰ μὲν καὶ ἐκ τῶν
Δράκοντος νόμων, τὰ δὲ καὶ ἐκ τῶν Σόλωνος πειρῶμαι, ἔφη, λαμβάνων ἐμβιβάζειν εἰς τὴν δικαιοσύνην τοὺς οἰκέτας. δοκοῦσι γάρ μοι, ἔφη, καὶ
οὗτοι οἱ ἄνδρες θεῖναι πολλοὺς τῶν νόμων ἐπὶ
5 δικαιοσύνης τῆς τοιαύτης διδασκαλίᾳ. γέγραπται γὰρ ζημιοῦσθαι ἐπὶ τοῖς κλέμμασι καὶ δεδέσθαι, ἤν τις ἁλῷ ποιῶν, καὶ θανατοῦσθαι τοὺς
ἐγχειροῦντας. δῆλον οὖν, ἔφη, ὅτι ἔγραφον αὐτὰ
βουλόμενοι ἀλυσιτελῆ ποιῆσαι τοῖς ἀδίκοις τὴν
6 αἰσχροκέρδειαν. ἐγὼ οὖν, ἔφη, καὶ τούτων [προσφέρων] ἔνια καὶ ἄλλα τῶν βασιλικῶν νόμων προσφερόμενος πειρῶμαι δικαίους περὶ τὰ διαχειριζό-
7 μενα ἀπεργάζεσθαι τοὺς οἰκέτας. ἐκεῖνοι μὲν γὰρ
οἱ νόμοι ζημίαι μόνον εἰσὶ τοῖς ἁμαρτάνουσιν, οἱ
δὲ βασιλικοὶ νόμοι οὐ μόνον ζημιοῦσι τοὺς ἀδικοῦντας, ἀλλὰ καὶ ὠφελοῦσι τοὺς δικαίους· ὥστε
ὁρῶντες πλουσιωτέρους γιγνομένους τοὺς δικαίους
τῶν ἀδίκων πολλοὶ καὶ φιλοκερδεῖς ὄντες εὖ μάλα
8 ἐπιμένουσι τῷ μὴ ἀδικεῖν. οὓς δ' ἂν αἰσθάνωμαι,
ἔφη, ὅμως καὶ εὖ πάσχοντας ἔτι ἀδικεῖν πειρωμένους, τούτους ὡς ἀνηκέστους πλεονέκτας ὄντας
9 ἤδη καὶ τῆς χρήσεως ἀποπαύω. οὓς δ' ἂν αὖ
καταμάθω μὴ τῷ πλέον ἔχειν μόνον διὰ τὴν
δικαιοσύνην ἐπαιρομένους δικαίους εἶναι, ἀλλὰ
καὶ τοῦ ἐπαινεῖσθαι ἐπιθυμοῦντας ὑπ' ἐμοῦ, τούτοις ὥσπερ ἐλευθέροις ἤδη χρῶμαι οὐ μόνον πλουτίζων, ἀλλὰ καὶ τιμῶν ὡς καλούς τε κἀγαθούς.
10 τούτῳ γάρ μοι δοκεῖ, ἔφη, ὦ Σώκρατες, διαφέρειν
ἀνὴρ φιλότιμος ἀνδρὸς φιλοκερδοῦς, τῷ ἐθέλειν
ἐπαίνου καὶ τιμῆς ἕνεκα καὶ πονεῖν ὅπου δεῖ καὶ
κινδυνεύειν καὶ αἰσχρῶν κερδῶν ἀπέχεσθαι.

pay heed to this lesson. Nevertheless I guide the 4
servants into the path of justice with the aid of
maxims drawn from the laws of Draco and Solon.
For it seems to me that these famous men enacted
many of their laws with an eye on this particular
kind of justice. For it is written: "thieves shall 5
be fined for their thefts," and "anyone guilty of
attempt shall be imprisoned if taken in the act, and
put to death." [1] The object of these enactments was
clearly to make covetousness unprofitable to the
offender. By applying some of these clauses and 6
other enactments found in the Persian king's code,
I try to make my servants upright in the matters
that pass through their hands. For while those laws 7
only penalise the wrongdoer,[2] the king's code not
only punishes the guilty, but also benefits the upright. Thus, seeing that the honest grow richer
than the dishonest, many, despite their love of lucre,
are careful to remain free from dishonesty. And if I 8
find any attempting to persist in dishonesty, although
they are well treated, I regard them as incorrigibly
greedy, and have nothing more to do with them.
On the other hand, if I discover that a man is in- 9
clined to be honest not only because he gains by his
honesty, but also from a desire to win my approbation, I treat him like a free man by making him
rich; and not only so, but I honour him as a gentleman. For I think, Socrates, that the difference 10
between ambition and greed consists in this, that
for the sake of praise and honour the ambitious are
willing to work properly, to take risks and refrain
from dishonest gain.'"

---

[1] This is neither a clear nor an exact statement of the law
attributed to Solon in Demosth. *Timocrates*, § 113; and some
suspect a corruption in the text.   [2] *Mem.* III. iv. 8.

XV. Ἀλλὰ μέντοι ἐπειδάν γε ἐμποιήσῃς τινὶ
τὸ βούλεσθαί σοι εἶναι τἀγαθά, ἐμποιήσῃς δὲ τῷ
αὐτῷ τούτῳ <τὸ> [1] ἐπιμελεῖσθαι, ὅπως ταῦτά σοι
ἐπιτελῆται, ἔτι δὲ πρὸς τούτοις ἐπιστήμην κτήσῃ
αὐτῷ, ὡς ἂν ποιούμενα ἕκαστα τῶν ἔργων
ὠφελιμώτερα γίγνοιτο, πρὸς δὲ τούτοις ἄρχειν
ἱκανὸν αὐτὸν ποιήσῃς, ἐπὶ δὲ τούτοις πᾶσιν
ἥδηταί σοι τὰ ἐκ τῆς γῆς ὡραῖα ἀποδεικνύων ὅτι
πλεῖστα ὥσπερ σὺ σαυτῷ, οὐκέτι ἐρήσομαι περὶ
τούτου, εἰ ἔτι τινὸς ὁ τοιοῦτος προσδεῖται· πάνυ
γάρ μοι δοκεῖ ἤδη πολλοῦ ἂν ἄξιος εἶναι ἐπίτροπος
ὢν τοιοῦτος. ἐκεῖνο μέντοι, ἔφην ἐγώ, ὦ Ἰσχόμαχε,
μὴ ἀπολίπῃς, ὃ ἡμῖν ἀργότατα ἐπιδεδράμηται τοῦ
λόγου.

2   Τὸ ποῖον ; ἔφη ὁ Ἰσχόμαχος.

Ἔλεξας δήπου, ἔφην ἐγώ, ὅτι μέγιστον εἴη
μαθεῖν, ὅπως δεῖ ἐξεργάζεσθαι ἕκαστα· εἰ δὲ μή,
οὐδὲ τῆς ἐπιμελείας ἔφησθα ὄφελος οὐδὲν γίγνεσθαι, εἰ μή τις ἐπίσταιτο ἃ δεῖ καὶ ὡς δεῖ ποιεῖν.

3   Ἐνταῦθα δὴ εἶπεν ὁ Ἰσχόμαχος· Τὴν τέχνην
με ἤδη, ὦ Σώκρατες, κελεύεις αὐτὴν διδάσκειν τῆς
γεωργίας ;

Αὕτη γὰρ ἴσως, ἔφην ἐγώ, ἤδη ἐστὶν ἡ ποιοῦσα
τοὺς μὲν ἐπισταμένους αὐτὴν πλουσίους, τοὺς δὲ
μὴ ἐπισταμένους πολλὰ πονοῦντας ἀπόρως
βιοτεύειν.

4   Νῦν τοίνυν, ἔφη, ὦ Σώκρατες, καὶ τὴν φιλαν-
θρωπίαν ταύτης τῆς τέχνης ἀκούσῃ. τὸ γὰρ
ὠφελιμωτάτην οὖσαν καὶ ἡδίστην ἐργάζεσθαι
καὶ καλλίστην καὶ προσφιλεστάτην θεοῖς τε
καὶ ἀνθρώποις ἔτι πρὸς τούτοις καὶ ῥάστην εἶναι
μαθεῖν πῶς οὐχὶ γενναῖόν ἐστι ; γενναῖα δὲ δήπου

478

XV. "'Well, well, I won't go on to ask whether anything more is wanting to your man, after you have implanted in him a desire for your prosperity and have made him also careful to see that you achieve it, and have obtained for him, besides, the knowledge needful to ensure that every piece of work done shall add to the profits, and, further, have made him capable of ruling, and when, besides all this, he takes as much ·delight in producing heavy crops for you in due season as you would take if you did the work yourself. For it seems to me that a man like that would make a very valuable bailiff. Nevertheless, Ischomachus, don't leave a gap in that part of the subject to which we have given the most cursory attention.'

"'Which is it?' asked Ischomachus.

"'You said, you know, that the greatest lesson 2 to learn is how things ought to be done; and added that, if a man is ignorant what to do and how to do it, no good can come of his management.'

"Then he said, 'Socrates, are you insisting now 3 that I should teach the whole art and mystery of agriculture?'

"'Yes,' said I; 'for maybe it is just this that makes rich men of those who understand it, and condemns the ignorant to a life of penury, for all their toil.'

"'Well, Socrates, you shall now hear how kindly 4 a thing is this art. Helpful, pleasant, honourable, dear to gods and men in the highest degree, it is also in the highest degree easy to learn. Noble qualities surely! As you know, we call those crea-

---

[1] τὸ added by Heindorf: Sauppe omits with the MSS.

καλοῦμεν καὶ τῶν ζῴων ὁπόσα καλὰ καὶ μεγάλα
καὶ ὠφέλιμα ὄντα πραέα ἐστὶ πρὸς τοὺς ἀνθρώπους.

5 Ἀλλὰ ταῦτα μὲν ἐγώ, ἔφην, ὦ Ἰσχόμαχε,
ἱκανῶς δοκῶ καταμεμαθηκέναι ᾗ εἶπας, καθὰ δεῖ
διδάσκειν τὸν ἐπίτροπον· καὶ γὰρ ᾗ ἔφησθα
εὔνουν σοι ποιεῖν αὐτὸν μαθεῖν δοκῶ καὶ ᾗ
6 ἐπιμελῆ καὶ ἀρχικὸν καὶ δίκαιον. ὃ δὲ εἶπας ὡς
δεῖ μαθεῖν τὸν μέλλοντα ὀρθῶς γεωργίας ἐπιμελεῖσθαι καὶ ἃ δεῖ ποιεῖν καὶ ὡς δεῖ καὶ ὁπότε
ἕκαστα, ταῦτά μοι δοκοῦμεν, ἔφην ἐγώ, ἀργότερόν
7 πως ἐπιδεδραμηκέναι τῷ λόγῳ· ὥσπερ εἰ εἴποις,
ὅτι δεῖ γράμματα ἐπίστασθαι τὸν μέλλοντα
δυνήσεσθαι τὰ ὑπαγορευόμενα γράφειν καὶ τὰ
γεγραμμένα ἀναγιγνώσκειν. ταῦτα γὰρ ἐγὼ
ἀκούσας, ὅτι μὲν δεῖ γράμματα ἐπίστασθαι
ἠκηκόη ἄν, τοῦτο δὲ εἰδὼς οὐδέν τι οἶμαι μᾶλλον
8 ἂν ἐπισταίμην γράμματα. οὕτω δὲ καὶ νῦν ὅτι
μὲν δεῖ ἐπίστασθαι γεωργίαν τὸν μέλλοντα ὀρθῶς
ἐπιμελεῖσθαι αὐτῆς ῥᾳδίως πέπεισμαι, τοῦτο
μέντοι εἰδὼς οὐδέν τι μᾶλλον ἐπίσταμαι ὅπως δεῖ
9 γεωργεῖν. ἀλλ᾽ εἴ μοι αὐτίκα μάλα δόξειε
γεωργεῖν, ὅμοιος ἄν μοι δοκῶ εἶναι τῷ περιιόντι
ἰατρῷ καὶ ἐπισκοποῦντι τοὺς κάμνοντας, εἰδότι
δὲ οὐδὲν ὅ τι συμφέρει τοῖς κάμνουσιν. ἵν᾽ οὖν
μὴ τοιοῦτος ὦ, ἔφην ἐγώ, δίδασκέ με αὐτὰ τὰ
10 ἔργα τῆς γεωργίας. Ἀλλὰ μήν, ἔφη, ὦ Σώκρατες,
οὐχ ὥσπερ γε τὰς ἄλλας τέχνας κατατριβῆναι
δεῖ μανθάνοντας πρὶν ἄξια τῆς τροφῆς ἐργάζεσθαι
τὸν διδασκόμενον, οὐχ οὕτω καὶ ἡ γεωργία
δύσκολός ἐστι μαθεῖν, ἀλλὰ τὰ μὲν ἰδὼν ἂν
ἐργαζομένους, τὰ δὲ ἀκούσας, εὐθὺς ἂν ἐπίσταιο,

tures noble that are beautiful, great and helpful, and yet gentle towards men.'

"'Ah, but I think, Ischomachus, that I quite 5 understand your account of these matters—I mean how to teach a bailiff; for I think I follow your statement that you make him loyal to you, and careful and capable of ruling and honest. But 6 you said that one who is to be successful in the management of a farm must learn what to do and how and when to do it. That is the subject that we have treated, it seems to me, in a rather cursory fashion, as if you said that anyone who is to be 7 capable of writing from dictation and reading what is written must know the alphabet. For had I been told that, I should have been told, to be sure, that I must know the alphabet, but I don't think that piece of information would help me to know it. So 8 too now; I am easily convinced that a man who is to manage a farm successfully must understand farming, but that knowledge doesn't help me to understand how to farm. Were I to decide this 9 very moment to be a farmer, I think I should be like that doctor who goes round visiting the sick, but has no knowledge of the right way to treat them. Therefore, that I may not be like him, you must teach me the actual operations of farming.'

"'Why, Socrates, farming is not troublesome to 10 learn, like other arts, which the pupil must study till he is worn out before he can earn his keep by his work. Some things you can understand by watching men at work, others by just being told,

ὥστε καὶ ἄλλον, εἰ βούλοιο, διδάσκειν. οἶμαι
δ᾽, ἔφη, πάνυ καὶ λεληθέναι πολλὰ σεαυτὸν
11 ἐπιστάμενον αὐτῆς. καὶ γὰρ δὴ οἱ μὲν ἄλλοι
τεχνῖται ἀποκρύπτονταί πως τὰ ἐπικαιριώτατα
ἧς ἕκαστος ἔχει τέχνης, τῶν δὲ γεωργῶν ὁ
κάλλιστα μὲν φυτεύων μάλιστ᾽ ἂν ἥδοιτο, εἴ τις
αὐτὸν θεῷτο, ὁ κάλλιστα δὲ σπείρων ὡσαύτως·
ὅ τι δὲ ἔροιο τῶν καλῶς πεποιημένων, οὐδὲν ὅ τι
12 ἄν σε ἀποκρύψαιτο ὅπως ἐποίησεν. οὕτω καὶ τὰ
ἤθη, ὦ Σώκρατες, ἔφη, γενναιοτάτους τοὺς αὐτῇ
συνόντας ἡ γεωργία ἔοικε παρέχεσθαι.

13   Ἀλλὰ τὸ μὲν προοίμιον, ἔφην ἐγώ, καλὸν καὶ
οὐχ οἷον ἀκούσαντα ἀποτρέπεσθαι τοῦ ἐρωτή-
ματος· σὺ δὲ ὅτι εὐπετές ἐστι μαθεῖν, διὰ τοῦτο
πολύ μοι μᾶλλον διέξιθι αὐτήν. οὐ γὰρ σοὶ
αἰσχρὸν τὰ ῥᾴδια διδάσκειν ἐστίν, ἀλλ᾽ ἐμοὶ
πολὺ αἴσχιον μὴ ἐπίστασθαι, ἄλλως τε καὶ εἰ
χρήσιμα ὄντα τυγχάνει.

XVI. Πρῶτον μὲν τοίνυν, ἔφη, ὦ Σώκρατες,
τοῦτο ἐπιδεῖξαι βούλομαί σοι, ὡς οὐ χαλεπόν
ἐστιν ὃ λέγουσι ποικιλώτατον τῆς γεωργίας εἶναι
οἱ λόγῳ μὲν ἀκριβέστατα αὐτὴν διεξιόντες, ἥκιστα
2 δὲ ἐργαζόμενοι. φασὶ γὰρ τὸν μέλλοντα ὀρθῶς
γεωργήσειν τὴν φύσιν χρῆναι πρῶτον τῆς γῆς
εἰδέναι.

Ὀρθῶς γε, ἔφην ἐγώ, ταῦτα λέγοντες. ὁ γὰρ
μὴ εἰδώς, ὅ τι δύναται ἡ γῆ φέρειν, οὐδ᾽ ὅ τι
σπείρειν οἶμαι οὐδ᾽ ὅ τι φυτεύειν δεῖ εἰδείη ἄν.

3   Οὐκοῦν, ἔφη ὁ Ἰσχόμαχος, καὶ ἀλλοτρίας γῆς
τοῦτο ἔστι γνῶναι, ὅ τι τε δύναται φέρειν καὶ
ὅ τι μὴ δύναται, ὁρῶντα τοὺς καρποὺς καὶ τὰ
δένδρα. ἐπειδὰν μέντοι γνῷ τις, οὐκέτι συμφέρει

well enough to teach another if you wish. And I
believe that you know a good deal about it yourself,
without being aware of the fact. The truth is 11
that, whereas other artists conceal more or less the
most important points in their own art, the farmer
who plants best is most pleased when he is being
watched, so is he who sows best. Question him
about any piece of work well done : and he will tell
you exactly how he did it. So farming, Socrates, 12
more than any other calling, seems to produce a
generous disposition in its followers.'

"'An excellent preamble,' I cried, 'and not of a 13
sort to damp the hearer's curiosity. Come, describe
it to me, all the more because it is so simple to
learn. For it is no disgrace to you to teach
elementary lessons, but far more a disgrace to me
not to understand them, especially if they are
really useful.'"

XVI. "'First then, Socrates, I want to show you
that what is called the most complicated problem in
agriculture by the authors who write most accurately on the theory of the subject, but are not
practical farmers, is really a simple matter. For 2
they tell us that to be a successful farmer one must
first know the nature of the soil.'

"'Yes, and they are right,' I remarked ; 'for
if you don't know what the soil is capable of growing, you can't know, I suppose, what to plant or
what to sow.'

"'Well then,' said Ischomachus, 'you can tell by 3
looking at the crops and trees on another man's
land what the soil can and what it cannot grow.
But when you have found out, it is useless to fight

θεομαχεῖν. οὐ γὰρ ἂν ὅτου δέοιτο αὐτός, τοῦτο
σπείρων καὶ φυτεύων μᾶλλον ἂν ἔχοι τὰ ἐπιτήδεια
4 ἢ ὅ τι ἡ γῆ ἥδοιτο φύουσα καὶ τρέφουσα. ἦν δ᾽
ἄρα δι᾽ ἀργίαν τῶν ἐχόντων αὐτὴν μὴ ἔχῃ τὴν
ἑαυτῆς δύναμιν ἐπιδεικνύναι, ἔστι καὶ παρὰ
γείτονος τόπου πολλάκις ἀληθέστερα περὶ αὐτῆς
γνῶναι ἢ παρὰ γείτονος ἀνθρώπου πυθέσθαι.
5 καὶ χερσεύουσα δὲ ὅμως ἐπιδείκνυσι τὴν αὑτῆς
φύσιν· ἡ γὰρ τὰ ἄγρια καλὰ φύουσα δύναται
θεραπευομένη καὶ τὰ ἥμερα καλὰ ἐκφέρειν. φύσιν
μὲν δὴ γῆς οὕτως καὶ οἱ μὴ πάνυ ἔμπειροι
γεωργίας ὅμως δύνανται διαγιγνώσκειν.
6   Ἀλλὰ τοῦτο μέν, ἔφην ἐγώ, ὦ Ἰσχόμαχε,
ἱκανῶς ἤδη μοι δοκῶ ἀποτεθαρρηκέναι, ὡς οὐ δεῖ
φοβούμενον, μὴ οὐ γνῶ τῆς γῆς φύσιν, ἀπέχεσθαι
7 γεωργίας. καὶ γὰρ δή, ἔφην, ἀνεμνήσθην τὸ τῶν
ἁλιέων, ὅτι θαλαττουργοὶ ὄντες καὶ οὔτε κατα-
στήσαντες ἐπὶ θέαν οὔθ᾽ ἥσυχοι βαδίζοντες, ἀλλὰ
παρατρέχοντες ἅμα τοὺς ἀγρούς, ὅταν ὁρῶσι
τοὺς καρποὺς ἐν τῇ γῇ, ὅμως οὐκ ὀκνοῦσιν ἀποφαίνεσθαι περὶ τῆς γῆς, ὁποία τε ἀγαθή ἐστι καὶ
ὁποία κακή, ἀλλὰ τὴν μὲν ψέγουσι, τὴν δ᾽
ἐπαινοῦσι. καὶ πάνυ τοίνυν τοῖς ἐμπείροις
γεωργίας ὁρῶ αὐτοὺς τὰ πλεῖστα κατὰ ταὐτὰ
ἀποφαινομένους περὶ τῆς ἀγαθῆς γῆς.
8   Πόθεν οὖν βούλει, ἔφη, ὦ Σώκρατες, ἄρξωμαί
σε τῆς γεωργίας ὑπομιμνήσκειν; οἶδα γὰρ ὅτι
ἐπισταμένῳ σοι πάνυ πολλὰ φράσω ὡς δεῖ
γεωργεῖν.
9   Ἐκεῖνό μοι δοκῶ, ἔφην ἐγώ, ὦ Ἰσχόμαχε,
πρῶτον ἂν ἡδέως μανθάνειν, φιλοσόφου γὰρ
μάλιστά ἐστιν ἀνδρός, ὅπως ἂν ἐγώ, εἰ βουλοίμην,

against the gods. For you are not likely to get a better yield from the land by sowing and planting what you want instead of the crops and trees that the land prefers. If it happens that the land does 4 not declare its own capabilities because the owners are lazy, you can often gather more correct information from a neighbouring plot than from a neighbouring proprietor. Yes, and even if the land lies 5 waste, it reveals its nature. For if the wild stuff growing on the land is of fine quality, then by good farming the soil is capable of yielding cultivated crops of fine quality. So the nature of the soil can be ascertained even by the novice who has no experience of farming.'

" ' Well, I think I am now confident, Ischomachus, 6 that I need not avoid farming from fear of not knowing the nature of the soil. The fact is, I am 7 reminded that fishermen, though their business is in the sea, and they neither stop the boat to take a look nor slow down, nevertheless, when they see the crops as they scud past the farms, do not hesitate to express an opinion about the land, which is the good and which is the bad sort, now condemning, now praising it. And, what is more, I notice that in their opinion about the good land they generally agree exactly with experienced farmers.'

" ' Then, Socrates, let me refresh your memory on 8 the subject of agriculture; but where do you wish me to begin? For I am aware that I shall tell you very much that you know already about the right method of farming.'

" ' First, Ischomachus, I think I should be glad 9 to learn, for this is the philosopher's way, how I am

γῆν ἐργαζόμενος πλείστας κριθὰς καὶ πλείστους πυροὺς λαμβάνοιμι.

10 Οὐκοῦν τοῦτο μὲν οἶσθα, ὅτι τῷ σπόρῳ νεὸν δεῖ ὑπεργάζεσθαι ;

11 Οἶδα γάρ, ἔφην ἐγώ.

Εἰ οὖν ἀρχοίμεθα, ἔφη, ἀροῦν τὴν γῆν χειμῶνος ;

Ἀλλὰ πηλὸς ἂν εἴη, ἐγὼ ἔφην.

Ἀλλὰ τοῦ θέρους σοι δοκεῖ ;

Σκληρά, ἔφην ἐγώ, ἡ γῆ ἔσται κινεῖν τῷ ζεύγει.

12 Κινδυνεύει ἔαρος, ἔφη, εἶναι τούτου τοῦ ἔργου ἀρκτέον.

Εἰκὸς γάρ, ἔφην ἐγώ, ἐστὶ μάλιστα χεῖσθαι τὴν γῆν τηνικαῦτα κινουμένην.

Καὶ τὴν πόαν γε ἀναστρεφομένην, ἔφη, ὦ Σώκρατες, τηνικαῦτα κόπρον μὲν τῇ γῇ ἤδη παρέχειν, καρπὸν δ᾽ οὔπω καταβαλεῖν ὥστε

13 φύεσθαι. οἶμαι γὰρ δὴ καὶ τοῦτό σ᾽ ἔτι γιγνώσκειν, ὅτι εἰ μέλλει ἀγαθὴ ἡ νεὸς ἔσεσθαι, ὕλης τε δεῖ καθαρὰν αὐτὴν εἶναι καὶ ὀπτὴν ὅτι μάλιστα πρὸς τὸν ἥλιον.

Πάνυ γε, ἔφην ἐγώ, καὶ ταῦτα οὕτως ἡγοῦμαι χρῆναι ἔχειν.

14 Ταῦτ᾽ οὖν, ἔφη, σὺ ἄλλως πως νομίζεις μᾶλλον ἂν γίγνεσθαι ἢ εἰ ἐν τῷ θέρει ὅτι πλειστάκις μεταβάλοι τις τὴν γῆν ;

Οἶδα μὲν οὖν, ἔφην, ἀκριβῶς, ὅτι οὐδαμῶς ἂν μᾶλλον ἥ μὲν ὕλη ἐπιπολάζοι καὶ αὐαίνοιτο ὑπὸ τοῦ καύματος, ἡ δὲ γῆ ὀπτῷτο ὑπὸ τοῦ ἡλίου ἢ εἴ τις αὐτὴν ἐν μέσῳ τῷ θέρει καὶ ἐν μέσῃ τῇ ἡμέρᾳ κινοίη τῷ ζεύγει.

to cultivate the land if I want to get the heaviest crops of wheat and barley out of it.'

" 'Well, you know, I take it, that fallow must 10 be prepared for sowing?'

" 'Yes, I know.'

" 'Suppose, then, we start ploughing in winter?' 11

" 'Why, the land will be a bog!'

" 'How about starting in summer?'

" 'The land will be hard to plough up.'

" 'It seems that spring is the season for beginning 12 this work.'

" 'Yes, the land is likely to be more friable if it is broken up then.'

" 'Yes, and the grass turned up is long enough at that season to serve as manure, but, not having shed seed, it will not grow. You know also, I 13 presume, that fallow land can't be satisfactory unless it is clear of weeds and thoroughly baked in the sun?'

" 'Yes, certainly; that is essential, I think.'

" 'Do you think that there is any better way of 14 securing that than by turning the land over as often as possible in summer?'

" 'Nay, I know for certain that if you want the weeds to lie on the surface and wither in the heat, and the land to be baked by the sun, the surest way is to plough it up at midday in midsummer.'

15 Εἰ δὲ ἄνθρωποι σκάπτοντες τὴν νεὸν ποιοῖεν, ἔφη, οὐκ εὔδηλον, ὅτι καὶ τούτους δίχα δεῖ ποιεῖν τὴν γῆν καὶ τὴν ὕλην ;

Καὶ τὴν μέν γε ὕλην, ἔφην ἐγώ, καταβάλλειν, ὡς αὐαίνηται, ἐπιπολῆς, τὴν δὲ γῆν στρέφειν, ὡς ἡ ὠμὴ αὐτῆς ὀπτᾶται.

XVII. Περὶ μὲν τῆς νεοῦ ὁρᾶς, ἔφη, ὦ Σώκρατες, ὡς ἀμφοτέροις ἡμῖν ταυτὰ δοκεῖ.

Δοκεῖ γὰρ οὖν, ἔφην ἐγώ.

Περὶ γε μέντοι τοῦ σπόρου ἄλλο τι, ἔφη, ὦ Σώκρατες, γιγνώσκεις ἢ τὴν ὥραν σπείρειν, ἧς πάντες μὲν οἱ πρόσθεν ἄνθρωποι πεῖραν λαβόντες, πάντες δὲ οἱ νῦν λαμβάνοντες ἐγνώκασι κρατίστην

2 εἶναι ; ἐπειδὰν γὰρ ὁ μετοπωρινὸς χρόνος ἔλθῃ, πάντες που οἱ ἄνθρωποι πρὸς τὸν θεὸν ἀπο-βλέπουσιν, ὁπότε βρέξας τὴν γῆν ἀφήσει αὐτοὺς σπείρειν.

Ἐγνώκασι δή γ᾽, ἔφην ἐγώ, ὦ Ἰσχόμαχε, καὶ τὸ μὴ ἐν ξηρᾷ σπείρειν ἑκόντες εἶναι πάντες ἄνθρωποι, δῆλον ὅτι πολλαῖς ζημίαις παλαίσαντες οἱ πρὶν κελευσθῆναι ὑπὸ τοῦ θεοῦ σπείραντες.

3 Οὐκοῦν ταῦτα μέν, ἔφη ὁ Ἰσχόμαχος, ὁμογνω-μονοῦμεν πάντες οἱ ἄνθρωποι.

Ἃ γὰρ ὁ θεὸς διδάσκει, ἔφην ἐγώ, οὕτω γίγνεται ὁμονοεῖν· οἷον ἅμα πᾶσι δοκεῖ βέλτιον εἶναι ἐν τῷ χειμῶνι παχέα ἱμάτια φορεῖν, ἢν δύνωνται, καὶ πῦρ κάειν ἅμα πᾶσι δοκεῖ, ἢν ξύλα ἔχωσιν.

4 Ἀλλ᾽ ἐν τῷδε, ἔφη ὁ Ἰσχόμαχος, πολλοὶ ἤδη διαφέρονται, ὦ Σώκρατες, περὶ τοῦ σπόρου, πότερον ὁ πρώιμος κράτιστος ἢ ὁ μέσος ἢ ὁ ὀψιμώτατος.

"'And if men prepare the fallow by digging, is 15 it not obvious that they too must separate the weeds from the soil?'

"'Yes, and they must throw the weeds on the surface to wither, and turn up the ground so that the lower spit [1] may be baked.'"

XVII. "'You see, then, Socrates, that we agree about the fallow.'

"'It does seem so, to be sure.'

"'And now as to the time for sowing, Socrates. Is it not your opinion that the time to sow is that which has been invariably found to be the best by past experience, and is universally approved by present practice? For as soon as autumn ends, all 2 men, I suppose, look anxiously to God, to see when he will send rain on the earth and make them free to sow.'

"'Yes, Ischomachus, all men have made up their minds, of course, not to sow in dry ground if they can help it, those who sowed without waiting to be bidden by God having had to wrestle with many losses.'

"'So far, then,' said Ischomachus, 'all the world 3 is of one mind.'

"'Yes,' said I, 'where God is our teacher we all come to think alike. For example, all agree that it is better to wear warm clothes in winter, if they can, and all agree on the desirability of having a fire, if they have wood.'

"'But,' said Ischomachus, 'when we come to the 4 question whether sowing is best done early or very late or at the mid-season, we find much difference of opinion, Socrates.'

---

[1] Literally, the "crude land."

Ἀλλ' ὁ θεός, ἔφην ἐγώ, οὐ τεταγμένως τὸ ἔτος ἄγει, ἀλλὰ τὸ μὲν τῷ πρωίμῳ κάλλιστα, τὸ δὲ τῷ μέσῳ, τὸ δὲ τῷ ὀψιμωτάτῳ.

5 Σὺ οὖν, ἔφη, ὦ Σώκρατες, πότερον ἡγῇ κρεῖττον εἶναι ἑνὶ τούτων τῶν σπόρων χρῆσθαι ἐκλεξάμενον, ἐάν τε πολὺ ἐάν τε ὀλίγον σπέρμα σπείρῃ τις, ἢ ἀρξάμενον ἀπὸ τοῦ πρωιμωτάτου μέχρι τοῦ ὀψιμωτάτου σπείρειν;

6 Καὶ ἐγὼ εἶπον· Ἐμοὶ μέν, ὦ Ἰσχόμαχε, δοκεῖ κράτιστον εἶναι παντὸς μετέχειν τοῦ σπόρου. πολὺ γὰρ νομίζω κρεῖττον εἶναι ἀεὶ ἀρκοῦντα σῖτον λαμβάνειν ἢ ποτὲ μὲν πάνυ πολύν, ποτὲ δὲ μηδ' ἱκανόν.

Καὶ τοῦτο τοίνυν σύγε, ἔφη, ὦ Σώκρατες, ὁμογνωμονεῖς ἐμοὶ ὁ μανθάνων τῷ διδάσκοντι, καὶ ταῦτα πρόσθεν ἐμοῦ τὴν γνώμην ἀποφαινόμενος.

7 Τί γάρ, ἔφην ἐγώ, ἐν τῷ ῥίπτειν τὸ σπέρμα ποικίλη τέχνη ἔνεστι;

Πάντως, ἔφη, ὦ Σώκρατες, ἐπισκεψώμεθα καὶ τοῦτο. ὅτι μὲν γὰρ ἐκ τῆς χειρὸς δεῖ ῥίπτεσθαι τὸ σπέρμα, καὶ σύ που οἶσθα, ἔφη.

Καὶ γὰρ ἑώρακα, ἔφην ἐγώ.

Ῥίπτειν δέ γε, ἔφη, οἱ μὲν ὁμαλῶς δύνανται, οἱ δ' οὔ.

Οὐκοῦν τοῦτο μέν, ἔφην ἐγώ, ἤδη μελέτης δεῖται, ὥσπερ τοῖς κιθαρισταῖς ἡ χείρ, ὅπως δύνηται ὑπηρετεῖν τῇ γνώμῃ.

8 Πάνυ μὲν οὖν, ἔφη· ἢν δέ γε ᾖ, ἔφη, ἡ γῆ ἡ μὲν λεπτοτέρα, ἡ δὲ παχυτέρα;

Τί τοῦτο, ἐγὼ ἔφην, λέγεις; ἆρά γε τὴν μὲν λεπτοτέραν ὅπερ ἀσθενεστέραν, τὴν δὲ παχυτέραν ὅπερ ἰσχυροτέραν;

490

"'And God,' said I, 'does not regulate the year by fixed laws; but in one year it may be advantageous to sow early, in another very late, in another at mid-season.'

"'Then do you think, Socrates, that it is better 5 to select one of these times for sowing, whether you sow much or little, or to begin at the earliest moment and continue sowing to the latest?'

"'For my part, Ischomachus, I think it is best to 6 sow for succession throughout the season. For in my opinion it is much better to get enough food at all times than too much at one time and not enough at another.'

"'Here again, then, Socrates, pupil and teacher are of one opinion; and, moreover, you, the pupil, are first in stating this opinion.'

"'Well now, is casting the seed a complicated 7 problem?'

"'By all means let us take that also into consideration, Socrates. I presume that you know as well as I that the seed must be cast by the hand?'

"'Yes, I have seen it.'

"'Ah,' he said, 'but some men can cast evenly, and some cannot.'

"'Then sowers no less than lyre-players need practice, that the hand may be the servant of the will.'

"'Certainly. But suppose that some of the land 8 is rather light and some rather heavy?'

"'What do you mean by that?' I interrupted. 'By "light" do you mean "weak," and by "heavy," "strong"?'

491

Τοῦτ᾽, ἔφη, λέγω, καὶ ἐρωτῶ γέ σε, πότερον
ἴσον ἂν ἑκατέρᾳ τῇ γῇ σπέρμα διδοίης ἢ ποτέρᾳ
ἂν πλεῖον.

9 Τῷ μὲν οἴνῳ, ἔφην, ἔγωγε νομίζω τῷ ἰσχυροτέρῳ
πλεῖον ἐπιχεῖν ὕδωρ καὶ ἀνθρώπῳ τῷ ἰσχυροτέρῳ
πλεῖον βάρος, ἐὰν δέῃ τι φέρειν, ἐπιτιθέναι, κἂν
δέῃ τρέφεσθαί τινας, τοῖς δυνατωτέροις τρέφειν
ἂν τοὺς πλείους προστάξαιμι. εἰ δὲ ἡ ἀσθενὴς
γῆ ἰσχυροτέρα, ἔφην ἐγώ, γίγνεται, ἤν τις
πλείονα καρπὸν αὐτῇ ἐμβάλῃ, ὥσπερ τὰ ὑποζύγια, τοῦτο σύ με δίδασκε.

10 Καὶ ὁ Ἰσχόμαχος γελάσας εἶπεν, Ἀλλὰ
παίζεις μὲν σύγε, ἔφη, ὦ Σώκρατες. εὖ γε μέντοι,
ἔφη, ἴσθι, ἢν μὲν ἐμβαλὼν τὸ σπέρμα τῇ γῇ
ἔπειτα ἐν ᾧ πολλὴν ἔχει τροφὴν ἡ γῆ ἀπὸ τοῦ
οὐρανοῦ χλόης γενομένης ἀπὸ τοῦ σπέρματος
καταστρέψῃς αὐτὸ πάλιν, τοῦτο γίγνεται σῖτος
τῇ γῇ, καὶ ὥσπερ ὑπὸ κόπρου ἰσχὺς αὐτῇ
ἐγγίγνεται· ἢν μέντοι ἐκτρέφειν ἐᾷς τὴν γῆν διὰ
τέλους τὸ σπέρμα εἰς καρπόν, χαλεπὸν τῇ
ἀσθενεῖ γῇ ἐς τέλος πολὺν καρπὸν ἐκφέρειν. καὶ
συὶ δὲ ἀσθενεῖ χαλεπὸν πολλοὺς ἁδροὺς χοίρους
ἐκτρέφειν.

11 Λέγεις σύ, ἔφην ἐγώ, ὦ Ἰσχόμαχε, τῇ
ἀσθενεστέρᾳ γῇ μεῖον δεῖν τὸ σπέρμα ἐμβαλεῖν;

Ναὶ μὰ Δία, ἔφη, ὦ Σώκρατες, καὶ σύ γε
συνομολογεῖς λέγων, ὅτι νομίζεις τοῖς ἀσθενεστέ-
ροις πᾶσι μείω προστάττειν πράγματα.

12 Τοὺς δὲ δὴ σκαλέας, ἔφην ἐγώ, ὦ Ἰσχόμαχε,
τίνος ἕνεκα ἐμβάλλετε τῷ σίτῳ;

Οἶσθα δήπου, ἔφη, ὅτι ἐν τῷ χειμῶνι πολλὰ
ὕδατα γίγνεται.

" ' Yes, I do; and I ask you whether you would give the same quantity of seed to both kinds, or to which you would give more?'

" ' Well, my principle is this: the stronger the 9 wine, the more water I add; the stronger the bearer, the heavier the burden I put on his back; and if it is necessary to feed others, I should require the richest men to feed the greatest number. But tell me whether weak land, like draught animals, becomes stronger when you put more corn into it.'

" ' Ah, you're joking, Socrates,' he said, laughing, 10 ' but allow me to tell you that, if after putting in the seed you plough it in again as soon as the blade appears when the land is obtaining plenty of nourishment from the sky, it makes food for the soil, and strengthens it like manure. If, on the other hand, you let the seed go on growing on the land until it is bolled, it's hard for weak land to yield much grain in the end. It's hard, you know, for a weak sow to rear a big litter of fine pigs.'

" ' Do you mean, Ischomachus, that the weaker 11 the soil the less seed should be put into it?'

" ' Yes, of course, Socrates; and you agree when you say that your invariable custom is to make the burden light that is to be borne by the weak.'

" ' But the hoers, now, Ischomachus, why do you 12 put them on the corn?'

" ' I presume you know that in winter there is a heavy rainfall?'

Τί γὰρ οὔκ ; ἔφην ἐγώ.

Οὐκοῦν θῶμεν τοῦ σίτου καὶ κατακρυφθῆναί τινα ὑπ' αὐτῶν ἰλύος ἐπιχυθείσης καὶ ψιλωθῆναί τινας ῥίζας ὑπὸ ῥεύματος. καὶ ὕλη δὲ πολλάκις ὑπὸ τῶν ὑδάτων δήπου συνεξορμᾷ τῷ σίτῳ καὶ παρέχει πνιγμὸν αὐτῷ.

13   Πάντα, ἔφην ἐγώ, εἰκὸς ταῦτα γίγνεσθαι.

Οὐκοῦν δοκεῖ σοι, ἔφη, ἐνταῦθα ἤδη ἐπικουρίας τινὸς δεῖσθαι ὁ σῖτος ;

Πάνυ μὲν οὖν, ἔφην ἐγώ.

Τῷ οὖν κατιλυθέντι τί ἂν ποιοῦντες δοκοῦσιν ἄν σοι ἐπικουρῆσαι ;

Ἐπικουφίσαντες, ἔφην ἐγώ, τὴν γῆν.

Τί δέ, ἔφη, τῷ ἐψιλωμένῳ τὰς ῥίζας ;

Ἀντιπροσαμησάμενοι τὴν γῆν ἄν, ἔφην ἐγώ.

14   Τί γάρ, ἔφη, ἣν ὕλη πνίγῃ συνεξορμῶσα τῷ σίτῳ καὶ διαρπάζουσα τοῦ σίτου τὴν τροφήν, ὥσπερ οἱ κηφῆνες διαρπάζουσιν ἄχρηστοι ὄντες τῶν μελιττῶν ἃ ἂν ἐκεῖναι ἐργασάμεναι τροφὴν καταθῶνται ;

Ἐκκόπτειν ἂν νὴ Δία δέοι τὴν ὕλην, ἔφην ἐγώ, ὥσπερ τοὺς κηφῆνας ἐκ τῶν σμηνῶν ἀφαιρεῖν.

15   Οὐκοῦν, ἔφη, εἰκότως σοι δοκοῦμεν ἐμβαλεῖν τοὺς σκαλέας ;

Πάνυ γε. ἀτὰρ ἐνθυμοῦμαι, ἔφην ἐγώ, ὦ Ἰσχόμαχε, οἷόν ἐστι τὸ εὖ τὰς εἰκόνας ἐπάγεσθαι. πάνυ γὰρ σύ με ἐξώργισας πρὸς τὴν ὕλην τοὺς κηφῆνας εἰπών, πολὺ μᾶλλον ἢ ὅτε περὶ αὐτῆς τῆς ὕλης ἔλεγες.

XVIII. Ἀτὰρ οὖν, ἔφην ἐγώ, ἐκ τούτου ἄρα θερίζειν εἰκός. δίδασκε οὖν εἴ τι ἔχεις με καὶ εἰς τοῦτο.

" ' Of course.'

" ' Let us assume, then, that part of the corn is waterlogged and covered with mud, and some of the roots are exposed by flooding. And it often happens, you know, that in consequence of rain weeds spring up among the corn and choke it.'

" ' All these things are likely to happen.'   13

" ' Then don't you think that in such circumstances the corn needs prompt succour ? '

" ' Certainly.'

" ' What should be done, do you think, to succour the part that is under the mud ? '

" ' The soil should be lifted.'

" ' And the part that has its roots exposed ? '

" ' It should be earthed up.'

" ' What if weeds are springing up, choking the 14 corn and robbing it of its food, much as useless drones rob bees of the food they have laid in store by their industry ? '

" ' The weeds must be cut, of course, just as the drones must be removed from the hive.'

" ' Don't you think, then, that we have good 15 reason for putting on men to hoe ? '

" ' No doubt ; but I am reflecting, Ischomachus, on the advantage of bringing in an apt simile. For you roused my wrath against the weeds by mentioning the drones, much more than when you spoke of mere weeds.' "

XVIII. " ' However,' I continued, ' after this comes reaping, I fancy. So give me any information you can with regard to that too.'

Ἢν μή γε φανῇς, ἔφη, καὶ εἰς τοῦτο ταὐτὰ
ἐμοὶ ἐπιστάμενος. ὅτι μὲν οὖν τέμνειν τὸν σῖτον
δεῖ, οἶσθα.

Τί δ᾽ οὐ μέλλω ; ἔφην ἐγώ.

Πότερα οὖν τέμνεις, ἔφη, στὰς ἔνθα πνεῖ ἄνεμος
ἢ ἀντίος ;

Οὐκ ἀντίος, ἔφην, ἔγωγε· χαλεπὸν γὰρ οἶμαι
καὶ τοῖς ὄμμασι καὶ ταῖς χερσὶ γίγνεται ἀντίον
ἀχύρων καὶ ἀθέρων θερίζειν.

2   Καὶ ἀκροτομοίης δ᾽ ἄν, ἔφη, ἢ παρὰ γῆν
τέμνοις ;

Ἢν μὲν βραχὺς ᾖ ὁ κάλαμος τοῦ σίτου, ἔγωγ᾽,
ἔφην, κάτωθεν ἂν τέμνοιμι, ἵνα ἱκανὰ τὰ ἄχυρα
μᾶλλον γίγνηται· ἐὰν δὲ ὑψηλὸς ᾖ, νομίζω ὀρθῶς
ἂν ποιεῖν μεσοτομῶν, ἵνα μήτε οἱ ἁλοῶντες
μοχθῶσι περιττὸν πόνον μήτε οἱ λικμῶντες ὧν
οὐδὲν προσδέονται. τὸ δὲ ἐν τῇ γῇ λειφθὲν ἡγοῦμαι καὶ κατακαυθὲν συνωφελεῖν ἂν τὴν γῆν καὶ
εἰς κόπρον ἐμβληθὲν τὴν κόπρον συμπληθύνειν.

3   Ὁρᾷς, ἔφη, ὦ Σώκρατες, ὡς ἁλίσκῃ ἐπ᾽ αὐτοφώρῳ καὶ περὶ θερισμοῦ εἰδὼς ἅπερ ἐγώ ;

Κινδυνεύω, ἔφην ἐγώ, καὶ βούλομαί γε σκέψα-
σθαι, εἰ καὶ ἀλοᾶν ἐπίσταμαι.

Οὐκοῦν, ἔφη, τοῦτο μὲν οἶσθα, ὅτι ὑποζυγίῳ
ἀλοῶσι τὸν σῖτον.

4   Τί δ᾽ οὐκ, ἔφην ἐγώ, οἶδα ; καὶ ὑποζύγιά γε
καλούμενα πάντα ὁμοίως, βοῦς, ἡμιόνους, ἵππους.

Οὐκοῦν, ἔφη, ταῦτα μὲν ἡγῇ τοσοῦτο μόνον
εἰδέναι, πατεῖν τὸν σῖτον ἐλαυνόμενα ;

Τί γὰρ ἂν ἄλλο, ἔφην ἐγώ, ὑποζύγια εἰδείη ;

5   Ὅπως δὲ τὸ δεόμενον κόψουσι καὶ ὁμαλιεῖται ὁ
ἀλοητός, τίνι τοῦτο, ὦ Σώκρατες ; ἔφη.

" ' Yes—unless I find that you know just what I do about that subject too. You know, then, that the corn must be cut.'

" ' I know that, naturally.'

" ' Are you for standing with your back to the wind when you cut corn, or facing it?'

" ' Not facing it, no! I think it is irritating both to the eyes and to the hands to reap with cornstalks and spikes blowing in your face.'

" ' And would you cut near the top or close to the 2 ground?'

" ' If the stalk is short, I should cut low down, so that the straw may be more useful; but if it is long, I think it would be right to cut in the middle, in order that the threshers and winnowers may not spend needless trouble on what they don't want. I imagine that the stubble may be burnt with advantage to the land, or thrown on the manure heap to increase its bulk.'

" ' Do you notice, Socrates, that you stand con- 3 victed of knowing just what I know about reaping too?'

" ' Yes, it seems so; and I want to know besides whether I understand threshing as well.'

" ' Then you know this much, that draught animals are used in threshing?'

" ' Yes, of course I do; and that the term draught 4 animals includes oxen, mules and horses.'

" ' Then do you not think that all the beasts know is how to trample on the corn as they are driven?'

" ' Why, what more should draught animals know?'

" ' And who sees that they tread out the right 5 corn, and that the threshing is level, Socrates?'

Δῆλον ὅτι, ἔφην ἐγώ, τοῖς ἐπαλώσταις. στρέφοντες γὰρ καὶ ὑπὸ τοὺς πόδας ὑποβάλλοντες τὰ ἄτριπτα ἀεὶ δῆλον ὅτι μάλιστα ὁμαλίζοιεν ἂν τὸν δῖνον καὶ τάχιστα ἀνύτοιεν.

Ταῦτα μὲν τοίνυν, ἔφη, οὐδὲν ἐμοῦ λείπῃ γιγνώσκων.

6 Οὐκοῦν, ἔφην ἐγώ, ὦ Ἰσχόμαχε, ἐκ τούτου δὴ καθαροῦμεν τὸν σῖτον λικμῶντες.

Καὶ λέξον γέ μοι, ὦ Σώκρατες, ἔφη ὁ Ἰσχόμαχος, ἦ οἶσθα, ὅτι ἢν ἐκ τοῦ προσηνέμου μέρους τῆς ἅλω ἄρχῃ, δι' ὅλης τῆς ἅλω οἴσεταί σοι τὰ ἄχυρα ;

Ἀνάγκη γάρ, ἔφην ἐγώ.

7 Οὐκοῦν εἰκὸς καὶ ἐπιπίπτειν, ἔφη, αὐτὰ ἐπὶ τὸν σῖτον.

Πολὺ γάρ ἐστιν, ἔφην ἐγώ, τὸ ὑπερενεχθῆναι τὰ ἄχυρα ὑπὲρ τὸν σῖτον εἰς τὸ κενὸν τῆς ἅλω.

Ἢν δέ τις, ἔφη, λικμᾷ ἐκ τοῦ ὑπηνέμου ἀρχόμενος ;

Δῆλον, ἔφην ἐγώ, ὅτι εὐθὺς ἐν τῇ ἀχυροδόκῃ ἔσται τὰ ἄχυρα.

8 Ἐπειδὰν δὲ καθάρῃς, ἔφη, τὸν σῖτον μέχρι τοῦ ἡμίσεος τῆς ἅλω, πότερον εὐθὺς οὕτω κεχυμένου τοῦ σίτου λικμήσεις τὰ ἄχυρα τὰ λοιπὰ ἢ συνώσας τὸν καθαρὸν πρὸς τὸν πόλον ὡς εἰς στενώτατον ;

Συνώσας νὴ Δί', ἔφην ἐγώ, τὸν καθαρὸν σῖτον, ἵν' ὑπερφέρηταί μοι τὰ ἄχυρα εἰς τὸ κενὸν τῆς ἅλω καὶ μὴ δὶς ταὐτὰ ἄχυρα δέῃ λικμᾶν.

9 Σὺ μὲν δὴ ἄρα, ἔφη, ὦ Σώκρατες, σῖτόν γε ὡς ἂν τάχιστα καθαρὸς γένοιτο κἂν ἄλλον δύναιο διδάσκειν.

498

" ' The threshers, clearly. By continually turning
the untrodden corn and throwing it under the
animal's feet they will, of course, keep it level on
the floor and take least time over the work.'

" ' So far, then, your knowledge is quite as good
as mine.'

" ' Will not our next task be to clean the corn by 6
winnowing, Ischomachus?'

" ' Yes, Socrates; and tell me, do you know that
if you start on the windward side of the floor, you
will find the husks carried right across the floor?'

" ' It must be so.'

" ' Is it not likely, then, that some will fall on 7
the grain?'

" ' Yes, it is a long way for the husks to be blown,
right over the grain to the empty part of the floor.'

" ' But what if you start winnowing against the
wind?'

" ' Clearly the chaff will at once fall in the right
place.'

" ' And as soon as you have cleaned the corn 8
over one half of the floor, will you at once go on
throwing up the rest of the chaff while the corn
lies about just as it is, or will you first sweep the
clean corn towards the edge,[1] so as to occupy the
smallest space?'

" ' Of course I shall first sweep the clean corn up,
so that my chaff may be carried across into the
empty space, and I may not have to throw up the
same chaff twice.'

" ' Well, Socrates, it seems you are capable of 9
teaching the quickest way of cleaning corn.'

---

[1] The meaning of πόλος here is really unknown, I believe.

Ταῦτα τοίνυν, ἔφην ἐγώ, ἐλελήθη ἐμαυτὸν
ἐπιστάμενος. καὶ πάλαι ἐννοῶ ἄρα, εἰ λέληθα
καὶ χρυσοχοεῖν καὶ αὐλεῖν καὶ ζωγραφεῖν ἐπιστάμενος. ἐδίδαξε γὰρ οὔτε ταῦτά με οὐδεὶς οὔτε
γεωργεῖν· ὁρῶ δ᾽ ὥσπερ γεωργοῦντας καὶ τὰς
ἄλλας τέχνας ἐργαζομένους ἀνθρώπους.

10 Οὔκουν, ἔφη ὁ Ἰσχόμαχος, ἔλεγον ἐγώ σοι
πάλαι, ὅτι καὶ ταύτῃ εἴη γενναιοτάτη ἡ γεωργικὴ
τέχνη, ὅτι καὶ ῥᾷστη ἐστὶ μαθεῖν ;

Ἄγε δή, ἔφην ἐγώ, οἶδα, ὦ Ἰσχόμαχε· τὰ μὲν
δὴ ἀμφὶ σπόρον ἐπιστάμενος ἄρα ἐλελήθειν
ἐμαυτὸν ἐπιστάμενος.

XIX. Ἔστιν οὖν, ἔφην ἐγώ, τῆς γεωργικῆς
τέχνης καὶ ἡ τῶν δένδρων φυτεία ;

Ἔστι γὰρ οὖν, ἔφη ὁ Ἰσχόμαχος.

Πῶς ἂν οὖν, ἔφην ἐγώ, τὰ μὲν ἀμφὶ τὸν
σπόρον ἐπισταίμην, τὰ δ᾽ ἀμφὶ τὴν φυτείαν οὐκ
ἐπίσταμαι ;

2 Οὐ γὰρ σύ, ἔφη ὁ Ἰσχόμαχος, ἐπίστασαι ;

Πῶς ; ἐγὼ ἔφην, ὅστις μήτ᾽ ἐν ὁποίᾳ τῇ γῇ δεῖ
φυτεύειν οἶδα μήτε ὁπόσον βάθος ὀρύττειν [1] μήτε
ὁπόσον πλάτος μήτε ὁπόσον μῆκος τὸ φυτὸν
ἐμβάλλειν μήτε ὅπως ἂν ἐν τῇ γῇ κείμενον τὸ
φυτὸν μάλιστ᾽ ἂν βλαστάνοι.

3 Ἴθι δή, ἔφη ὁ Ἰσχόμαχος, μάνθανε ὅ τι μὴ
ἐπίστασαι. βοθύνους μὲν γὰρ οἵους ὀρύττουσι
τοῖς φυτοῖς, οἶδ᾽ ὅτι ἑώρακας, ἔφη.

Καὶ πολλάκις ἔγωγ᾽, ἔφην.

Ἤδη τινὰ οὖν αὐτῶν εἶδες βαθύτερον τριπόδου ;

---

[1] ὀρύττειν τὸ φυτὸν Sauppe with the MSS. : but either
ὀρύττειν τῷ φυτῷ should be read or τὸ φυτὸν should go.

" ' I really wasn't aware that I understood these things ; and so I have been thinking for some time whether my knowledge extends to smelting gold, playing the flute, and painting pictures. For I have never been taught these things any more than I have been taught farming ; but I have watched men working at these arts, just as I have watched them farming.'

" ' And didn't I tell you just now that farming is 10 the noblest art for this among other reasons, because it is the easiest to learn ? '

" ' Enough, Ischomachus ; I know. I understood about sowing, it seems, but I wasn't aware that I understood.' "

XIX. " ' However, is the planting of fruit trees another branch of agriculture ? ' I continued.

" ' It is, indeed,' answered Ischomachus.

" ' Then how can I understand all about sowing, and yet know nothing of planting ? '

" ' What, don't you understand it ? '   2

" ' How can I, when I don't know what kind of soil to plant in, nor how deep a hole to dig, nor how broad, nor how much of the plant should be buried, nor how it must be set in the ground to grow best ? '

" ' Come then, learn whatever you don't know. 3 I am sure you have seen the sort of trenches they dig for plants.'

" ' Yes, often enough.'

" ' Did you ever see one more than three feet deep ? '

Οὐδὲ μὰ Δί᾽ ἔγωγ᾽, ἔφην, πενθημιποδίου.

Τί δὲ τὸ πλάτος ἤδη τινὰ τριπόδου πλέον εἶδες ;

Οὐδὲ μὰ Δί᾽, ἔφην ἐγώ, διπόδου.

4 Ἴθι δή, ἔφη, καὶ τόδε ἀπόκριναί μοι, ἤδη τινὰ εἶδες τὸ βάθος ἐλάττονα ποδιαίου ;

Οὐδὲ μὰ Δί᾽, ἔφην, ἔγωγε τριημιποδίου. καὶ γὰρ ἐξορύττοιτο ἂν σκαπτόμενα, ἔφην ἐγώ, τὰ φυτά, εἰ λίαν γε οὕτως ἐπιπολῆς πεφυτευμένα εἴη.

5 Οὐκοῦν τοῦτο μέν, ἔφη, ὦ Σώκρατες, ἱκανῶς οἶσθα, ὅτι οὔτε βαθύτερον πενθημιποδίου ὀρύττουσιν οὔτε βραχύτερον τριημιποδίου.

᾽Ανάγκη γάρ, ἔφην ἐγώ, τοῦτο ὁρᾶσθαι οὕτω γε καταφανὲς ὄν.

6 Τί δέ, ἔφη, ξηροτέραν καὶ ὑγροτέραν γῆν γιγνώσκεις ὁρῶν ;

Ξηρὰ μὲν γοῦν μοι δοκεῖ, ἔφην ἐγώ, εἶναι ἡ περὶ τὸν Λυκαβηττὸν καὶ ἡ ταύτῃ ὁμοία, ὑγρὰ δὲ ἡ ἐν τῷ Φαληρικῷ ἕλει καὶ ἡ ταύτῃ ὁμοία.

7 Πότερα οὖν, ἔφη, ἐν τῇ ξηρᾷ ἂν βαθὺν ὀρύττοις βόθρον τῷ φυτῷ ἢ ἐν τῇ ὑγρᾷ ;

᾽Εν τῇ ξηρᾷ νὴ Δί᾽, ἔφην ἐγώ· ἐπεὶ ἔν γε τῇ ὑγρᾷ ὀρύττων βαθὺν ὕδωρ ἂν εὑρίσκοις καὶ οὐκ ἂν δύναιο ἔτι ἐν ὕδατι φυτεύειν.

Καλῶς μοι δοκεῖς, ἔφη, λέγειν. οὐκοῦν ἐπειδὰν ὀρωρυγμένοι ὦσιν οἱ βόθροι, ὁπηνίκα δεῖ τιθέναι ἑκάτερα τὰ φυτά, ἤδη εἶδες ;

Μάλιστα, ἔφην ἐγώ.

"'No, of course not—nor more than two and a half.'

"'Well, did you ever see one more than three feet broad?'

"'Of course not, nor more than two feet.'

"'Come then, answer this question too. Did 4 you ever see one less than a foot deep?'

"'Never less than a foot and a half, of course. For the plants would come out of the ground when it is stirred about them if they were put in so much too shallow.'

"'Then you know this well enough, Socrates, 5 that the trenches are never more than two and a half feet deep, nor less than a foot and a half.'

"'A thing so obvious as that can't escape one's eyes.'

"'Again, can you distinguish between dry and 6 wet ground by using your eyes?'

"'Oh, I should think that the land round Lycabettus and any like it is an example of dry ground, and the low-lying land at Phalerum and any like it of wet.'

"'In which then would you dig the hole deep for 7 your plant, in the dry or the wet ground?'

"'In the dry, of course; because if you dug deep in the wet, you would come on water, and water would stop your planting.'

"'I think you are quite right. Now suppose the holes are dug; have you ever noticed how [1] the plants for each kind of soil should be put in?'

"'Oh, yes.'

---

[1] There must be something wrong with the text here. The MSS. give ὁπηνίκα, "just when," but that has nothing to do with the matter in hand. Is something lost?

8 Σὺ οὖν βουλόμενος ὡς τάχιστα φῦναι αὐτὰ πότερον ὑποβαλὼν ἂν τῆς γῆς τῆς εἰργασμένης οἴει τὸν βλαστὸν τοῦ κλήματος θᾶττον χωρεῖν διὰ τῆς μαλακῆς ἢ διὰ τῆς ἀργοῦ εἰς τὸ σκληρόν;

Δῆλον, ἔφην ἐγώ, ὅτι διὰ τῆς εἰργασμένης θᾶττον ἂν ἢ διὰ τῆς ἀργοῦ βλαστάνοι.

9 Οὐκοῦν ὑποβλητέα ἂν εἴη τῷ φυτῷ γῆ.

Τί δ' οὐ μέλλει; ἔφην ἐγώ.

Πότερα δὲ ὅλον τὸ κλῆμα ὀρθὸν τιθεὶς πρὸς τὸν οὐρανὸν βλέπον ἡγῇ μᾶλλον ἂν ῥιζοῦσθαι αὐτὸ ἢ καὶ πλάγιόν τι ὑπὸ τῇ ὑποβεβλημένῃ γῇ θείης ἄν, ὥστε κεῖσθαι ὥσπερ γάμμα ὕπτιον;

10 Οὕτω νὴ Δία· πλείονες γὰρ ἂν οἱ ὀφθαλμοὶ κατὰ γῆς εἶεν· ἐκ δὲ τῶν ὀφθαλμῶν καὶ ἄνω ὁρῶ βλαστάνοντα τὰ φυτά. καὶ τοὺς κατὰ τῆς γῆς οὖν ὀφθαλμοὺς ἡγοῦμαι τὸ αὐτὸ τοῦτο ποιεῖν. πολλῶν δὲ φυομένων βλαστῶν κατὰ τῆς γῆς ταχὺ ἂν καὶ ἰσχυρὸν τὸ φυτὸν ἡγοῦμαι βλαστάνειν.

11 Κατὰ ταὐτὰ τοίνυν, ἔφη, καὶ περὶ τούτων γιγνώσκων ἐμοὶ τυγχάνεις. ἐπαμήσαιο δ' ἂν μόνον, ἔφη, τὴν γῆν ἢ καὶ σάξαις ἂν εὖ μάλα περὶ τὸ φυτόν;

Σάττοιμ' ἄν, ἔφην, νὴ Δί' ἐγώ. εἰ μὲν γὰρ μὴ σεσαγμένον εἴη, ὑπὸ μὲν τοῦ ὕδατος εὖ οἶδ' ὅτι πηλὸς ἂν γίγνοιτο ἡ ἄσακτος γῆ, ὑπὸ δὲ τοῦ ἡλίου ξηρὰ μέχρι βυθοῦ, ὥστε τὰ φυτὰ κίνδυνος ὑπὸ μὲν τοῦ ὕδατος σήπεσθαι μὲν δι' ὑγρότητα, αὐαίνεσθαι δὲ διὰ ξηρότητα, θερμαινομένων τῶν ῥιζῶν.

12 Καὶ περὶ ἀμπέλων ἄρα σύγε, ἔφη, φυτείας, ὦ Σώκρατες, τὰ αὐτὰ ἐμοὶ πάντα γιγνώσκων τυγχάνεις.

"'Then assuming that you want them to grow as 8
quickly as possible, do you think that if you put
some prepared soil under them the cuttings will
strike sooner through soft earth into the hard stuff,
or through unbroken ground?'

"'Clearly, they will form roots more quickly in
prepared soil than in unbroken ground.'

"'Then soil must be placed below the plant?'   9
"'No doubt it must.'

"'And if you set the whole cutting upright,
pointing to the sky, do you think it would take root
better, or would you lay part of it slanting under
the soil that has been put below, so that it lies like
a *gamma* upside down?'

"'Of course I would; for then there would be 10
more buds underground; and I notice that plants
shoot from the buds above ground, so I suppose that
the buds under the ground do just the same; and
with many shoots forming underground, the plant
will make strong and rapid growth, I suppose.'

"'Then it turns out that on these points too 11
your opinion agrees with mine. But would you
merely heap up the earth, or make it firm round
the plant?'

"'I should make it firm, of course; for if it were
not firm, I feel sure that the rain would make mud
of the loose earth, and the sun would dry it up from
top to bottom; so the plants would run the risk of
damping off through too much water, or withering
from too much heat at the roots.'

"'About vine[1] planting then, Socrates, your 12
views are again exactly the same as mine.'

[1] The mention of the vine comes in so abruptly that one
again suspects the loss of something in the text.

Ἦ καὶ συκῆν, ἔφην ἐγώ, οὕτως δεῖ φυτεύειν;

Οἶμαι δ᾽, ἔφη ὁ Ἰσχόμαχος, καὶ τἆλλα ἀκρόδρυα πάντα. τῶν γὰρ ἐν τῇ τῆς ἀμπέλου φυτείᾳ καλῶς ἐχόντων τί ἂν ἀποδοκιμάσαις εἰς τὰς ἄλλας φυτείας;

13 Ἐλαίαν δὲ πῶς, ἔφην ἐγώ, φυτεύσομεν, ὦ Ἰσχόμαχε;

Ἀποπειρᾷ μου καὶ τοῦτο, ἔφη, μάλιστα πάντων ἐπιστάμενος. ὁρᾷς μὲν γὰρ δή, ὅτι βαθύτερος ὀρύττεται τῇ ἐλαίᾳ βόθρος· καὶ γὰρ παρὰ τὰς ὁδοὺς μάλιστα ὀρύττεται· ὁρᾷς δ᾽, ὅτι πρέμνα πᾶσι τοῖς φυτευτηρίοις πρόσεστιν· ὁρᾷς δ᾽, ἔφη, τῶν φυτῶν πηλὸν ταῖς κεφαλαῖς πάσαις ἐπικείμενον καὶ πάντων τῶν φυτῶν ἐστεγασμένον τὸ ἄνω.

14 Ὁρῶ, ἔφην ἐγώ, ταῦτα πάντα.

Καὶ ὁρῶν δή, ἔφη, τί αὐτῶν οὐ γιγνώσκεις; ἢ τὸ ὄστρακον ἀγνοεῖς, ἔφη, ὦ Σώκρατες, πῶς ἂν ἐπὶ τοῦ πηλοῦ ἄνω καταθείης;

Μὰ τὸν Δί᾽, ἔφην ἐγώ, οὐδὲν ὧν εἶπας, ὦ Ἰσχόμαχε, ἀγνοῶ, ἀλλὰ πάλιν ἐννοῶ, τί ποτε, ὅτε πάλαι ἤρου με συλλήβδην εἰ ἐπίσταμαι φυτεύειν, οὐκ ἔφην. οὐ γὰρ ἐδόκουν ἔχειν ἂν εἰπεῖν οὐδέν, ᾗ δεῖ φυτεύειν· ἐπεὶ δέ με καθ᾽ ἓν ἕκαστον ἐπεχείρησας ἐρωτᾶν, ἀποκρίνομαί σοι, ὡς σὺ φῄς, ἅπερ σὺ γιγνώσκεις ὁ δεινὸς λεγόμενος

15 γεωργός. ἆρα, ἔφην, ὦ Ἰσχόμαχε, ἡ ἐρώτησις διδασκαλία ἐστίν; ἄρτι γὰρ δή, ἔφην ἐγώ, καταμανθάνω, ᾗ με ἐπηρώτησας ἕκαστα· ἄγων γάρ με δι᾽ ὧν ἐγὼ ἐπίσταμαι, ὅμοια τούτοις ἐπιδεικνὺς ἃ

"'Does this method of planting apply to the fig too?' I asked.

"'Yes, and to all other fruit trees, I think; for in planting other trees why discard anything that gives good results with the vine?'

"'But the olive—how shall we plant that, 13 Ischomachus?'

"'You know quite well, and are only trying to draw me out again. For I am sure you see that a deeper hole is dug for the olive (it is constantly being done on the roadside); you see also that all the growing shoots have stumps adhering to them; and you see that all the heads of the plants are coated with clay, and the part of the plant that is above ground is wrapped up.'

"'Yes, I see all this.'   14

"'You do! Then what is there in it that you don't understand? Is it that you don't know how to put the crocks on the top of the clay, Socrates?'

"'Of course there is nothing in what you have said that I don't know, Ischomachus. But I am again set thinking what can have made me answer 'No' to the question you put to me a while ago, when you asked me briefly, Did I understand planting? For I thought I should have nothing to say about the right method of planting. But now that you have undertaken to question me in particular, my answers, you tell me, agree exactly with the views of a farmer so famous for his skill as yourself! Can it be that questioning is a kind of teaching, 15 Ischomachus? The fact is, I have just discovered the plan of your series of questions! You lead me by paths of knowledge familiar to me, point out things

οὐκ ἐνόμιζον ἐπίστασθαι ἀναπείθεις οἶμαι, ὡς καὶ
ταῦτα ἐπίσταμαι.

16 Ἆρ' οὖν, ἔφη ὁ Ἰσχόμαχος, καὶ περὶ ἀργυρίου
ἐρωτῶν ἄν σε, πότερον καλὸν ἢ οὔ, δυναίμην ἄν
σε πεῖσαι, ὡς ἐπίστασαι διαδοκιμάζειν τὰ καλὰ
καὶ τὰ κίβδηλα ἀργύρια ; καὶ περὶ αὐλητῶν δὴ
δυναίμην ἀναπεῖσαι, ὡς ἐπίστασαι αὐλεῖν, καὶ
περὶ ζωγράφων καὶ περὶ τῶν ἄλλων τῶν
τοιούτων ;

Ἴσως ἄν, ἔφην ἐγώ, ἐπειδὴ καὶ γεωργεῖν
ἀνέπεισάς με ὡς ἐπιστήμων εἴην, καίπερ εἰδότα,
ὅτι οὐδεὶς πώποτε ἐδίδαξέ με ταύτην τὴν τέχνην.

17 Οὐκ ἔστι ταῦτ', ἔφη, ὦ Σώκρατες· ἀλλ' ἐγὼ
καὶ πάλαι σοι ἔλεγον, ὅτι ἡ γεωργία οὕτω
φιλάνθρωπός ἐστι καὶ πραεῖα τέχνη, ὥστε καὶ
ὁρῶντας καὶ ἀκούοντας ἐπιστήμονας εὐθὺς ἑαυτῆς
18 ποιεῖν. πολλὰ δ', ἔφη, καὶ αὐτὴ διδάσκει, ὡς ἂν
κάλλιστά τις αὐτῇ χρῷτο. αὐτίκα ἄμπελος ἀνα-
βαίνουσα μὲν ἐπὶ τὰ δένδρα, ὅταν ἔχῃ τι πλησίον
δένδρον, διδάσκει ἱστάναι αὑτήν· περιπεταν-
νύουσα δὲ τὰ οἴναρα, ὅταν ἔτι αὐτῇ ἁπαλοὶ οἱ
βότρυες ὦσι, διδάσκει σκιάζειν τὰ ἡλιούμενα
19 ταύτην τὴν ὥραν· ὅταν δὲ καιρὸς ᾖ ὑπὸ τοῦ ἡλίου
ἤδη γλυκαίνεσθαι τὰς σταφυλάς, φυλλορροοῦσα
διδάσκει ἑαυτὴν ψιλοῦν καὶ πεπαίνειν τὴν
ὀπώραν, διὰ πολυφορίαν δὲ τοὺς μὲν πέπονας
δεικνύουσα βότρυς, τοὺς δὲ ἔτι ὠμοτέρους φέρουσα
διδάσκει τρυγᾶν ἑαυτήν, ὥσπερ τὰ σῦκα συκά-
ζουσι, τὸ ὀργῶν ἀεί.

XX. Ἐνταῦθα δὴ ἐγὼ εἶπον· Πῶς οὖν, ὦ
Ἰσχόμαχε, εἰ οὕτω γε καὶ ῥᾴδιά ἐστι μαθεῖν τὰ
περὶ τὴν γεωργίαν καὶ πάντες ὁμοίως ἴσασιν ἃ

like what I know, and bring me to think that I really know things that I thought I had no knowledge of.'

" ' Now suppose I questioned you about money,' 16 said Ischomachus, ' whether it is good or bad, could I persuade you that you know how to distinguish good from false by test? And by putting questions about flute-players could I convince you that you understand flute-playing; and by means of questions about painters and other artists——'

" ' You might, since you have convinced me that I understand agriculture, though I know that I have never been taught this art.'

" ' No, it isn't so, Socrates. I told you a while 17 ago that agriculture is such a humane, gentle art that you have but to see her and listen to her, and she at once makes you understand her. She herself 18 gives you many lessons in the best way of treating her. For instance, the vine climbs the nearest tree, and so teaches you that she wants support. And when her clusters are yet tender, she spreads her leaves about them, and teaches you to shade the exposed parts from the sun's rays during that period. But when it is now time for her grapes to be sweet- 19 ened by the sun, she sheds her leaves, teaching you to strip her and ripen her fruit. And thanks to her teeming fertility, she shows some mellow clusters while she carries others yet sour, so saying to you: Pluck my grapes as men pluck figs,— choose the luscious ones as they come.' "

XX. " And now I asked, ' How is it then, Ischomachus, if the operations of husbandry are so easy to learn and all alike know what must needs

δεῖ ποιεῖν, οὐχὶ καὶ πάντες πράττουσιν ὁμοίως,
ἀλλ' οἱ μὲν αὐτῶν ἀφθόνως τε ζῶσι καὶ περιττὰ
ἔχουσιν, οἱ δ' οὐδὲ τὰ ἀναγκαῖα δύνανται πορίζεσθαι, ἀλλὰ καὶ προσοφείλουσιν ;

2 Ἐγὼ δή σοί γε λέξω, ὦ Σώκρατες, ἔφη ὁ
Ἰσχόμαχος. οὐ γὰρ ἡ ἐπιστήμη οὐδ' ἡ ἀνεπιστη-
μοσύνη τῶν γεωργῶν ἐστιν ἡ ποιοῦσα τοὺς μὲν
3 εὐπορεῖν, τοὺς δὲ ἀπόρους εἶναι· οὐδ' ἂν ἀκούσαις,
ἔφη, λόγου οὕτω διαθέοντος, ὅτι διέφθαρται ὁ
οἶκος, διότι οὐχ ὁμαλῶς ὁ σπορεὺς ἔσπειρεν οὐδ'
ὅτι οὐκ ὀρθῶς τοὺς ὄρχους ἐφύτευσεν οὐδ' ὅτι
ἀγνοήσας τις τὴν [1] φέρουσαν ἀμπέλους ἐν ἀφόρῳ
ἐφύτευσεν οὐδ' ὅτι ἠγνόησέ τις, ὅτι ἀγαθόν ἐστι
τῷ σπόρῳ νεὸν προεργάζεσθαι, οὐδ' ὅτι ἠγνόησέ
4 τις, ὡς ἀγαθόν ἐστι τῇ γῇ κόπρον μιγνύναι· ἀλλὰ
πολὺ μᾶλλον ἔστιν ἀκοῦσαι, ἀνὴρ οὐ λαμβάνει
σῖτον ἐκ τοῦ ἀγροῦ· οὐ γὰρ ἐπιμελεῖται, ὡς αὑτῷ
σπείρηται ἢ ὡς κόπρος γίγνηται. οὐδ' οἶνον
ἔχει ἀνήρ· οὐ γὰρ ἐπιμελεῖται, ὡς φυτεύσῃ
ἀμπέλους οὐδὲ αἱ οὖσαι ὅπως φέρωσιν αὐτῷ.
οὐδὲ ἔλαιον οὐδὲ σῦκα ἔχει ἀνήρ· οὐ γὰρ ἐπι-
5 μελεῖται οὐδὲ ποιεῖ, ὅπως ταῦτα ἔχῃ. τοιαῦτ',
ἔφη, ἐστίν, ὦ Σώκρατες, ἃ διαφέροντες ἀλλήλων
οἱ γεωργοὶ διαφερόντως καὶ πράττουσι πολὺ
μᾶλλον ἢ οἱ δοκοῦντες σοφόν τι εὑρηκέναι εἰς τὰ
6 ἔργα. καὶ οἱ στρατηγοὶ ἔστιν ἐν οἷς τῶν στρατη-
γικῶν ἔργων οὐ γνώμῃ διαφέροντες ἀλλήλων οἱ
μὲν βελτίονες οἱ δὲ χείρονές εἰσιν, ἀλλὰ σαφῶς
ἐπιμελείᾳ. ἃ γὰρ καὶ οἱ στρατηγοὶ γιγνώσκουσι
πάντες καὶ τῶν ἰδιωτῶν οἱ πλεῖστοι, ταῦτα οἱ

---

[1] τὴν γῆν φέρουσαν Sauppe with the MSS.: γῆν was
removed by Jacob.

be done, that all have not the same fortune? How is it that some farmers live in abundance and have more than they want, while others cannot get the bare necessaries of life, and even run into debt?'

"'Oh, I will tell you, Socrates. It is not know- 2 ledge nor want of knowledge on the part of farmers that causes one to thrive while another is needy. You won't hear a story like this running 3 about: The estate has gone to ruin because the sower sowed unevenly, or because he didn't plant the rows straight, or because someone, not knowing the right soil for vines, planted them in barren ground, or because someone didn't know that it is well to prepare the fallow for sowing, or because someone didn't know that it is well to manure the land. No, you are much more likely to hear it said: 4 The man gets no corn from his field because he takes no trouble to see that it is sown or manured. Or, The man has got no wine, for he takes no trouble to plant vines or to make his old stock bear. Or, The man has neither olives nor figs, because he doesn't take the trouble; he does nothing to get them. It is not the farmers reputed to have made 5 some clever discovery in agriculture who differ in fortune from others: it is things of this sort that make all the difference, Socrates. This is true of 6 generals also: there are some branches of strategy in which one is better or worse than another, not because he differs in intelligence, but in point of carefulness, undoubtedly. For the things that all generals know, and most privates, are done by some

7 μὲν ποιοῦσι τῶν ἀρχόντων οἱ δ' οὔ. οἷον καὶ
τόδε γιγνώσκουσιν ἅπαντες, ὅτι διὰ πολεμίας
πορευομένους βέλτιόν ἐστι τεταγμένους πορεύεσθαι οὕτως, ὡς ἂν ἄριστα μάχοιντο, εἰ δέοι.
τοῦτο τοίνυν γιγνώσκοντες οἱ μὲν ποιοῦσιν οὕτως,
8 οἱ δ' οὐ ποιοῦσι. φυλακὰς ἅπαντες ἴσασιν ὅτι
βέλτιόν ἐστι καθιστάναι καὶ ἡμερινὰς καὶ
νυκτερινὰς πρὸ τοῦ στρατοπέδου. ἀλλὰ καὶ
τούτου οἱ μὲν ἐπιμελοῦνται ὡς ἔχῃ οὕτως, οἱ δ'
9 οὐκ ἐπιμελοῦνται. ὅταν τε αὖ διὰ στενοπόρων
ἴωσι, πάνυ χαλεπὸν εὑρεῖν ὅστις οὐ γιγνώσκει,
ὅτι προκαταλαμβάνειν τὰ ἐπίκαιρα κρεῖττον ἢ
μή. ἀλλὰ καὶ τούτου οἱ μὲν ἐπιμελοῦνται οὕτω
10 ποιεῖν, οἱ δ' οὔ. ἀλλὰ καὶ κόπρον λέγουσι μὲν
πάντες ὅτι ἄριστον εἰς γεωργίαν ἐστὶ καὶ ὁρῶσι
δὲ αὐτομάτην γιγνομένην· ὅμως δὲ καὶ ἀκριβοῦντες
ὡς γίγνεται, καὶ ῥᾴδιον ὂν πολλὴν ποιεῖν, οἱ μὲν
καὶ τούτου ἐπιμελοῦνται ὅπως ἀθροίζηται, οἱ δὲ
11 παραμελοῦσι. καίτοι ὕδωρ μὲν ὁ ἄνω θεὸς
παρέχει, τὰ δὲ κοῖλα πάντα τέλματα γίγνεται,
ἡ γῆ δὲ ὕλην παντοίαν παρέχει· καθαίρειν δὲ δεῖ
τὴν γῆν τὸν μέλλοντα σπείρειν· ἃ δ' ἐκποδὼν
ἀναιρεῖται, ταῦτα εἴ τις ἐμβάλλοι εἰς τὸ ὕδωρ, ὁ
χρόνος ἤδη αὐτὸς ἂν ποιοίη οἷς ἡ γῆ ἥδεται.
ποία μὲν γὰρ ὕλη, ποία δὲ γῆ ἐν ὕδατι στασίμῳ
οὐ κόπρος γίγνεται ;
12 Καὶ ὁπόσα δὲ θεραπείας δεῖται ἡ γῆ, ὑγροτέρα
τε οὖσα πρὸς τὸν σπόρον ἢ ἁλμωδεστέρα πρὸς
φυτείαν, καὶ ταῦτα γιγνώσκουσι μὲν πάντες καὶ
ὡς τὸ ὕδωρ ἐξάγεται τάφροις καὶ ὡς ἡ ἅλμη
κολάζεται μιγνυμένη πᾶσι τοῖς ἀνάλμοις [καὶ]
ὑγροῖς τε καὶ ξηροῖς· ἀλλὰ καὶ τούτων ἐπι-

commanders and left undone by others. For example, 7
they all know that when marching through an
enemy's country, the right way is to march in the
formation in which they will fight best, if need
be. Well, knowing this, some observe the rule,
others break it. All know that it is right to post 8
sentries by day and night before the camp; but
this too is a duty that some attend to, while others
neglect it. Again, where will you find the man who 9
does not know that, in marching through a defile,
it is better to occupy the points of vantage first?
Yet this measure of precaution too is duly taken
by some and neglected by others. So, too, every- 10
one will say that in agriculture there is nothing so
good as manure, and their eyes tell them that
nature produces it. All know exactly how it is
produced, and it is easy to get any amount of it;
and yet, while some take care to have it collected,
others care nothing about it. Yet the rain is sent 11
from heaven, and all the hollows become pools of
water, and the earth yields herbage of every kind
which must be cleared off the ground by the sower
before sowing; and the rubbish he removes has but
to be thrown into water, and time of itself will make
what the soil likes. For every kind of vegetation,
every kind of soil in stagnant water turns into manure.

"'And again, all the ways of treating the soil 12
when it is too wet for sowing or too salt for planting
are familiar to all men—how the land is drained by
ditches, how the salt is corrected by being mixed
with saltless substances, liquid or dry. Yet these

13 μελοῦνται οἱ μὲν οἱ δ' οὔ. εἰ δέ τις παντάπασιν
ἀγνὼς εἴη, τί δύναται φέρειν ἡ γῆ, καὶ μήτε ἰδεῖν
ἔχοι καρπὸν μηδὲ φυτὸν αὐτῆς μήτε ὅτου ἀκοῦσαι
τὴν ἀλήθειαν περὶ αὐτῆς ἔχοι, οὐ πολὺ μὲν ῥᾷον
γῆς πεῖραν λαμβάνειν παντὶ ἀνθρώπῳ ἢ ἵππου,
πολὺ δὲ ῥᾷον ἢ ἀνθρώπου; οὐ γὰρ ἔστιν ὅ τι ἐπὶ
ἀπάτῃ δείκνυσιν, ἀλλ' ἁπλῶς ἅ τε δύναται καὶ ἃ
14 μὴ σαφηνίζει τε καὶ ἀληθεύει. δοκεῖ δέ μοι ἡ γῆ
καὶ τοὺς κακούς τε κἀγαθοὺς[1] τῷ εὔγνωστα καὶ
εὐμαθῆ πάντα παρέχειν ἄριστα ἐξετάζειν. οὐ
γὰρ ὥσπερ τὰς ἄλλας τέχνας τοῖς μὴ ἐργαζομένοις ἔστι προφασίσασθαι ὅτι οὐκ ἐπίστανται·
γῆν δὲ πάντες ἴσασιν ὅτι εὖ πάσχουσα εὖ ποιεῖ·
15 ἀλλ' ἡ γεωργία ἐστὶ σαφὴς ψυχῆς κατήγορος
κακῆς. ὡς μὲν γὰρ ἂν δύναιτο ἄνθρωπος ζῆν
ἄνευ τῶν ἐπιτηδείων, οὐδεὶς τοῦτο αὐτὸς αὑτὸν
πείθει· ὁ δὲ μήτε ἄλλην τέχνην χρηματοποιὸν
ἐπιστάμενος μήτε γεωργεῖν ἐθέλων φανερὸν ὅτι
κλέπτων ἢ ἁρπάζων ἢ προσαιτῶν διανοεῖται
βιοτεύειν ἢ παντάπασιν ἀλόγιστός ἐστι.

16 Μέγα δὲ ἔφη διαφέρειν εἰς τὸ λυσιτελεῖν
γεωργίαν καὶ μὴ λυσιτελεῖν, ὅταν ὄντων ἐργαστή-
ρων καὶ πλεόνων ὁ μὲν ἔχῃ τινὰ ἐπιμέλειαν, ὡς
τὴν ὥραν αὐτῷ ἐν τῷ ἔργῳ οἱ ἐργάται ὦσιν, ὁ δὲ
μὴ ἐπιμελῆται τούτου. ῥᾳδίως γὰρ ἀνὴρ εἷς
παρὰ τοὺς δέκα διαφέρει τῷ ἐν ὥρᾳ ἐργάζεσθαι
καὶ ἄλλος γε ἀνὴρ διαφέρει τῷ πρὸ τῆς ὥρας
17 ἀπιέναι. τὸ δὲ δὴ ἐᾶν ῥᾳδιουργεῖν δι' ὅλης τῆς
ἡμέρας τοὺς ἀνθρώπους ῥᾳδίως τὸ ἥμισυ διαφέρει
18 τοῦ ἔργου παντός. ὥσπερ καὶ ἐν ταῖς ὁδοιπο-
ρίαις παρὰ στάδια διακόσια ἔστιν ὅτε τοῖς
ἑκατὸν σταδίοις διήνεγκαν ἀλλήλων ἄνθρωποι

matters, again, do not always receive attention. Suppose a man to be wholly ignorant as to what the 13 land can produce, and to be unable to see crop or tree on it, or to hear from anyone the truth about it, yet is it not far easier for any man to prove a parcel of land than to test a horse or to test a human being? For the land never plays tricks, but reveals frankly and truthfully what she can and what she cannot do. I think that just because she conceals nothing from 14 our knowledge and understanding, the land is the surest tester of good and bad men. For the slothful cannot plead ignorance, as in other arts: land, as all men know, responds to good treatment. Husbandry 15 is the clear accuser of the recreant soul. For no one persuades himself that man could live without bread; therefore if a man will not dig and knows no other profit-earning trade, he is clearly minded to live by stealing or robbery or begging—or he is an utter fool.

"'Farming,' he added, 'may result in profit or in 16 loss; it makes a great difference to the result, even when many labourers are employed, whether the farmer takes care that the men are working during the working hours or is careless about it. For one man in ten by working all the time may easily make a difference, and another by knocking off before the time; and, of course, if the men are allowed to be 17 slack all the day long, the decrease in the work done may easily amount to one half of the whole. Just as two travellers on the road, both young and 18 in good health, will differ so much in pace that one will cover two hundred furlongs to the other's hun-

---

[1] The text is corrupt here.

τῷ τάχει, ἀμφότεροι καὶ νέοι ὄντες καὶ ὑγιαίνοντες,
ὅταν ὁ μὲν πράττῃ ἐφ᾽ ὧπερ ὥρμηται βαδίζων, ὁ
δὲ ῥᾳστωνεύῃ τῇ ψυχῇ καὶ παρὰ κρήναις καὶ ὑπὸ
σκιαῖς ἀναπαυόμενός τε καὶ θεώμενος καὶ αὔρας
19 θηρεύων μαλακάς. οὕτω δὲ καὶ ἐν τοῖς ἔργοις
πολὺ διαφέρουσιν εἰς τὸ ἀνύτειν οἱ πράττοντες
ἐφ᾽ ὧπερ τεταγμένοι εἰσὶ καὶ οἱ μὴ πράττοντες,
ἀλλ᾽ εὑρίσκοντες προφάσεις τοῦ μὴ ἐργάζεσθαι
20 καὶ ἐώμενοι ῥᾳδιουργεῖν. τὸ δὲ δὴ καλῶς ἐργάζεσθαι ἢ κακῶς ἐπιμελεῖσθαι, τοῦτο δὴ τοσοῦτον
διαφέρει ὅσον ἢ ὅλως ἐργάζεσθαι ἢ ὅλως ἀργὸν
εἶναι. ὅταν σκαπτόντων, ἵνα ὕλης καθαραὶ αἱ
ἄμπελοι γένωνται, οὕτω σκάπτωσιν, ὥστε πλείω
καὶ καλλίω τὴν ὕλην γίγνεσθαι, πῶς οὕτως οὐκ
ἀργὸν ἂν φήσαις εἶναι;
21 Τὰ οὖν συντρίβοντα τοὺς οἴκους πολὺ μᾶλλον
ταῦτά ἐστιν ἢ αἱ λίαν ἀνεπιστημοσύναι. τὸ γὰρ
τὰς μὲν δαπάνας χωρεῖν ἐντελεῖς ἐκ τῶν οἴκων,
τὰ δὲ ἔργα μὴ τελεῖσθαι λυσιτελούντως πρὸς τὴν
δαπάνην, ταῦτα οὐκέτι δεῖ θαυμάζειν ἐὰν ἀντὶ τῆς
22 περιουσίας ἔνδειαν παρέχηται. τοῖς γε μέντοι
ἐπιμελεῖσθαι δυναμένοις καὶ συντεταμένως γεωρ-
γοῦσιν ἀνυτικωτάτην χρημάτισιν ἀπὸ γεωργίας
καὶ αὐτὸς ἐπετήδευσε καὶ ἐμὲ ἐδίδαξεν ὁ πατήρ.
οὐδέποτε γὰρ εἴα χῶρον ἐξειργασμένον ὠνεῖσθαι,
ἀλλ᾽ ὅστις ἢ δι᾽ ἀμέλειαν ἢ δι᾽ ἀδυναμίαν τῶν
κεκτημένων καὶ ἀργὸς καὶ ἀφύτευτος εἴη, τοῦτον
23 ὠνεῖσθαι παρῄνει. τοὺς μὲν γὰρ ἐξειργασμένους
ἔφη καὶ πολλοῦ ἀργυρίου γίγνεσθαι καὶ ἐπίδοσιν
οὐκ ἔχειν· τοὺς δὲ μὴ ἔχοντας ἐπίδοσιν οὐδὲ
ἡδονὰς ὁμοίας ἐνόμιζε παρέχειν, ἀλλὰ πᾶν κτῆμα
καὶ θρέμμα τὸ ἐπὶ τὸ βέλτιον ἰὸν τοῦτο καὶ

dred, because the one does what he set out to do, by going ahead, while the other is all for ease, now resting by a fountain or in the shade, now gazing at the view, now wooing the soft breeze; so 19 in farm work there is a vast difference in effectiveness between the men who do the job they are put on to do and those who, instead of doing it, invent excuses for not working and are allowed to be slack. In fact, between good work and dishonest slothfulness there is as wide a difference as between actual 20 work and actual idleness. Suppose the vines are being hoed to clear the ground of weeds: if the hoeing is so badly done that the weeds grow ranker and more abundant, how can you call that anything but idleness?'

"'These, then, are the evils that crush estates far 21 more than sheer lack of knowledge. For the outgoing expenses of the estate are not a penny less; but the work done is insufficient to show a profit on the expenditure; after that there's no need to wonder if the expected surplus is converted into a loss. On the other hand, to a careful man, who 22 works strenuously at agriculture, no business gives quicker returns than farming. My father taught me that and proved it by his own practice. For he never allowed me to buy a piece of land that was well farmed; but pressed me to buy any that was uncultivated and unplanted owing to the owner's neglect or incapacity. "Well farmed land," he would 23 say, " costs a large sum and can't be improved ; " and he held that where there is no room for improvement there is not much pleasure to be got from the land : landed estate and livestock must be continually coming on to give the fullest measure of

εὐφραίνειν μάλιστα ᾤετο. οὐδὲν οὖν ἔχει πλείονα
ἐπίδοσιν ἢ χῶρος ἐξ ἀργοῦ πάμφορος γιγνόμενος.
24 εὖ γὰρ ἴσθι, ἔφη, ὦ Σώκρατες, ὅτι τῆς ἀρχαίας
τιμῆς πολλοὺς πολλαπλασίου χώρους ἀξίους
ἡμεῖς ἤδη ἐποιήσαμεν. καὶ τοῦτο, ὦ Σώκρατες,
ἔφη, οὕτω μὲν πολλοῦ ἄξιον τὸ ἐνθύμημα, οὕτω
δὲ ῥᾴδιον καὶ μαθεῖν, ὥστε νυνὶ ἀκούσας σὺ τοῦτο
ἐμοὶ ὁμοίως ἐπιστάμενος ἄπει. καὶ ἄλλον διδάξεις,
25 ἐὰν βούλῃ. καὶ ὁ ἐμὸς δὲ πατὴρ οὔτε ἔμαθε παρ'
ἄλλου τοῦτο οὔτε μεριμνῶν εὗρεν, ἀλλὰ διὰ τὴν
φιλογεωργίαν καὶ φιλοπονίαν ἐπιθυμῆσαι ἔφη
τοιούτου χώρου, ὅπως ἔχοι ὅ τι ποιοίη ἅμα καὶ
26 ὠφελούμενος ἥδοιτο. ἦν γάρ τοι, ἔφη, ὦ Σώκρατες, φύσει, ὡς ἐμοὶ δοκεῖ, φιλογεωργότατος
Ἀθηναίων ὁ ἐμὸς πατήρ.

Καὶ ἐγὼ μέντοι ἀκούσας τοῦτο ἠρόμην αὐτόν·
Πότερα δέ, ὦ Ἰσχόμαχε, ὁπόσους ἐξειργάσατο
χώρους ὁ πατὴρ πάντας ἐκέκτητο ἢ καὶ ἀπεδίδοτο,
εἰ πολὺ ἀργύριον εὑρίσκοι ;

Καὶ ἀπεδίδοτο νὴ Δί', ἔφη ὁ Ἰσχόμαχος· ἀλλὰ
ἄλλον τοι εὐθὺς ἀντεωνεῖτο, ἀργὸν δέ, διὰ τὴν
φιλεργίαν.

27 Λέγεις, ἔφην ἐγώ, ὦ Ἰσχόμαχε, τῷ ὄντι φύσει
τὸν πατέρα φιλογέωργον εἶναι οὐδὲν ἧττον ἢ οἱ
ἔμποροι φιλόσιτοί εἰσι. καὶ γὰρ οἱ ἔμποροι διὰ
τὸ σφόδρα φιλεῖν τὸν σῖτον ὅπου ἂν ἀκούσωσι
πλεῖστον εἶναι, ἐκεῖσε πλέουσιν ἐπ' αὐτὸν καὶ
Αἰγαῖον καὶ Εὔξεινον καὶ Σικελικὸν πόντον
28 περῶντες· ἔπειτα δὲ λαβόντες ὁπόσον δύνανται
πλεῖστον ἄγουσιν αὐτὸν διὰ τῆς θαλάττης, καὶ
ταῦτα εἰς τὸ πλοῖον ἐνθέμενοι, ἐν ᾧπερ αὐτοὶ
πλέουσι. καὶ ὅταν δεηθῶσιν ἀργυρίου, οὐκ εἰκῇ

satisfaction. Now nothing improves more than a farm that is being transformed from a wilderness into fruitful fields. I assure you, Socrates, that we 24 have often added a hundredfold to the value of a farm. There is so much money in this idea, Socrates, and it is so easy to learn, that no sooner have you heard of it from me than you know as much as I do, and can go home and teach it to someone else, if you like. Moreover, my father did not get his knowledge 25 of it at secondhand, nor did he discover it by much thought; but he would say that, thanks to his love of husbandry and hard work, he had coveted a farm of this sort in order that he might have something to do, and combine profit with pleasure. For I assure 26 you, Socrates, no Athenian, I believe, had such a strong natural love of agriculture as my father.'

"Now on hearing this I asked, 'Did your father keep all the farms that he cultivated, Ischomachus, or did he sell when he could get a good price?'

"'He sold, of course,' answered Ischomachus, 'but, you see, owing to his industrious habits, he would promptly buy another that was out of cultivation.'

"'You mean, Ischomachus, that your father really 27 loved agriculture as intensely as merchants love corn. So deep is their love of corn that on receiving reports that it is abundant anywhere, merchants will voyage in quest of it: they will cross the Aegean, the Euxine, the Sicilian sea; and when they have 28 got as much as possible, they carry it over the sea, and they actually stow it in the very ship in which they sail themselves. And when they want money,

αὐτὸν ὅποι ἂν τύχωσιν ἀπέβαλον, ἀλλ' ὅπου ἂν
ἀκούσωσι τιμᾶσθαί τε μάλιστα τὸν σῖτον καὶ
περὶ πλείστου αὐτὸν ποιῶνται οἱ ἄνθρωποι,
τούτοις αὐτὸν ἄγοντες παραδιδόασι. καὶ ὁ σὸς
δὲ πατὴρ οὕτω πως ἔοικε φιλογέωργος εἶναι.

29 Πρὸς ταῦτα δὲ εἶπεν ὁ Ἰσχόμαχος, Σὺ μὲν
παίζεις, ἔφη, ὦ Σώκρατες· ἐγὼ δὲ καὶ φιλοικοδό-
μους νομίζω οὐδὲν ἧττον οἵτινες ἂν ἀποδιδῶνται
ἐξοικοδομοῦντες τὰς οἰκίας, εἶτ' ἄλλας οἰκοδομῶσι.

Νὴ Δία, ἐγὼ δέ γέ σοι, ἔφην, ὦ Ἰσχόμαχε,
ἐπομόσας λέγω ἦ μὴν πιστεύειν σοι φύσει
[νομίζειν] φιλεῖν ταῦτα πάντας, ἀφ' ὧν ἂν
ὠφελεῖσθαι νομίζωσιν.

XXI. Ἀτὰρ ἐννοῶ γε, ἔφην, ὦ Ἰσχόμαχε, ὡς
εὖ τῇ ὑποθέσει ὅλον τὸν λόγον βοηθοῦντα
παρέσχησαι. ὑπέθου γὰρ τὴν γεωργικὴν τέχνην
πασῶν εἶναι εὐμαθεστάτην, καὶ νῦν ἐγὼ ἐκ
πάντων ὧν εἴρηκας τοῦθ' οὕτως ἔχειν παντάπασιν
ὑπὸ σοῦ ἀναπέπεισμαι.

2 Νὴ Δί', ἔφη ὁ Ἰσχόμαχος, ἀλλὰ τόδε τοι, ὦ
Σώκρατες, τὸ πάσαις κοινὸν ταῖς πράξεσι καὶ
γεωργικῇ καὶ πολιτικῇ καὶ οἰκονομικῇ καὶ
πολεμικῇ τὸ ἀρχικὸν εἶναι, τοῦτο δὴ συνομολογῶ
σοὶ ἐγὼ πολὺ διαφέρειν γνώμῃ τοὺς ἑτέρους τῶν
3 ἑτέρων· οἷον καὶ ἐν τριήρει, ἔφη, ὅταν πελαγίζωσι
καὶ δέῃ περᾶν ἡμερινοὺς πλοῦς ἐλαύνοντας, οἱ
μὲν τῶν κελευστῶν δύνανται τοιαῦτα λέγειν καὶ
ποιεῖν, ὥστε ἀκονᾶν τὰς ψυχὰς τῶν ἀνθρώπων
ἐπὶ τὸ ἐθελοντὰς πονεῖν, οἱ δὲ οὕτως ἀγνώμονές
εἰσιν, ὥστε πλεῖον ἢ ἐν διπλασίῳ χρόνῳ τὸν
αὐτὸν ἀνύτουσι πλοῦν. καὶ οἱ μὲν ἱδροῦντες καὶ
ἐπαινοῦντες ἀλλήλους, ὅ τε κελεύων καὶ οἱ

they don't throw the corn away anywhere at haphazard, but they carry it to the place where they hear that corn is most valued and the people prize it most highly, and deliver it to them there. Yes, your father's love of agriculture seems to be something like that.'

"'You're joking, Socrates,' rejoined Ischomachus; 29 'but I hold that a man has a no less genuine love of building who sells his houses as soon as they are finished and proceeds to build others.'

"'Of course; and I declare, Ischomachus, on my oath that I believe you, that all men naturally love whatever they think will bring them profit.'"

XXI. "'But I am pondering over the skill with which you have presented the whole argument in support of your proposition, Ischomachus. For you stated that husbandry is the easiest of all arts to learn, and after hearing all that you have said, I am quite convinced that this is so.'

"'Of course it is,' cried Ischomachus; 'but I 2 grant you, Socrates, that in respect of aptitude for command, which is common to all forms of business alike—agriculture, politics, estate-management, warfare—in that respect the intelligence shown by different classes of men varies greatly. For example, 3 on a man-of-war, when the ship is on the high seas and the rowers must toil all day to reach port, some boatswains can say and do the right thing to sharpen the men's spirits and make them work with a will, while others are so unintelligent that it takes them more than twice the time to finish the same voyage. Here they land bathed in sweat, with mutual congratulations, boatswain and seamen. There they

πειθόμενοι, ἐκβαίνουσιν, οἱ δὲ ἀνιδρωτὶ ἥκουσι
4 μισοῦντες τὸν ἐπιστάτην καὶ μισούμενοι. καὶ
τῶν στρατηγῶν ταύτῃ διαφέρουσιν, ἔφη, οἱ
ἕτεροι τῶν ἑτέρων· οἱ μὲν γὰρ οὔτε πονεῖν
ἐθέλοντας οὔτε κινδυνεύειν παρέχονται, πείθεσθαί
τε οὐκ ἀξιοῦντας οὐδ' ἐθέλοντας ὅσον ἂν μὴ
ἀνάγκη ᾖ, ἀλλὰ καὶ μεγαλυνομένους ἐπὶ τῷ
ἐναντιοῦσθαι τῷ ἄρχοντι· οἱ δὲ αὐτοὶ οὗτοι υὐδ'
αἰσχύνεσθαι ἐπισταμένους παρέχουσιν, ἤν τι τῶν
5 αἰσχρῶν συμβαίνῃ. οἱ δ' αὖ θεῖοι καὶ ἀγαθοὶ
καὶ ἐπιστήμονες ἄρχοντες τοὺς αὐτοὺς τούτους,
πολλάκις δὲ καὶ ἄλλους παραλαμβάνοντες,
αἰσχυνομένους τε ἔχουσιν αἰσχρόν τι ποιεῖν καὶ
πείθεσθαι οἰομένους βέλτιον εἶναι καὶ ἀγαλλομένους τῷ πείθεσθαι ἕνα ἕκαστον καὶ σύμπαντας,
6 πονεῖν ὅταν δεήσῃ, οὐκ ἀθύμως πονοῦντας. ἀλλ'
ὥσπερ ἰδιώταις ἔστιν οἷς ἐγγίγνεται φιλοπονία[1]
τις, οὕτω καὶ ὅλῳ τῷ στρατεύματι ὑπὸ τῶν
ἀγαθῶν ἀρχόντων ἐγγίγνεται καὶ τὸ φιλοπονεῖν
καὶ τὸ φιλοτιμεῖσθαι ὀφθῆναι καλόν τι ποιοῦντας
7 ὑπὸ τοῦ ἄρχοντος. πρὸς ὅντινα δ' ἂν ἄρχοντα
διατεθῶσιν οὕτως οἱ ἑπόμενοι, οὗτοι δὴ ἐρρωμένοι
γε ἄρχοντες γίγνονται, οὐ μὰ Δί' οὐχ οἳ ἂν
αὐτῶν ἄριστα τὸ σῶμα τῶν στρατιωτῶν ἔχωσι
καὶ ἀκοντίζωσι καὶ τοξεύωσιν ἄριστα καὶ ἵππον
ἄριστον ἔχοντες ὡς ἱππικώτατα ἢ πελταστι-
κώτατα προκινδυνεύωσιν, ἀλλ' οἳ ἂν δύνωνται
ἐμποιῆσαι τοῖς στρατιώταις ἀκολουθητέον εἶναι
8 καὶ διὰ πυρὸς καὶ διὰ παντὸς κινδύνου. τούτους
δὴ δικαίως ἄν τις καλοίη μεγαλογνώμονας, ᾧ ἂν
ταῦτα γιγνώσκοντες πολλοὶ ἕπωνται, καὶ μεγάλῃ
χειρὶ εἰκότως οὗτος λέγοιτο πορεύεσθαι, οὗ ἂν τῇ

arrive with a dry skin ; they hate their master and he hates them. Generals, too, differ from one another 4 in this respect. For some make their men unwilling to work and to take risks, disinclined and unwilling to obey, except under compulsion, and actually proud of defying their commander : aye, and they cause them to have no sense of dishonour when something disgraceful occurs. Contrast the genius, the brave and 5 scientific leader : let him take over the command of these same troops, or of others if you like. What effect has he on them ? They are ashamed to do a disgraceful act, think it better to obey, and take a pride in obedience, working cheerfully, every man and all together, when it is necessary to work. Just 6 as a love of work may spring up in the mind of a private soldier here and there, so a whole army under the influence of a good leader is inspired with love of work and ambition to distinguish itself under the commander's eye. Let this be the feeling of the 7 rank and file for their commander ; and I tell you, he is the strong leader, he, and not the sturdiest soldier, not the best with bow and javelin, not the man who rides the best horse and is foremost in facing danger, not the ideal of knight or targeteer, but he who can make his soldiers feel that they are bound to follow him through fire and in any adventure. Him you may justly call high-minded who 8 has many followers of like mind ; and with reason may he be said to march " with a strong arm " whose

---

[1] ἐθελοπονία Sauppe, after Stephanus.

γνώμῃ πολλαὶ χεῖρες ὑπηρετεῖν ἐθέλωσι, καὶ
μέγας τῷ ὄντι οὗτος ἀνήρ, ὃς ἂν μεγάλα δύνηται
γνώμῃ διαπράξασθαι μᾶλλον ἢ ῥώμῃ.

9 Οὕτω δὲ καὶ ἐν τοῖς ἰδίοις ἔργοις, ἄν τε
ἐπίτροπος ᾖ ὁ ἐφεστηκὼς ἄν τε καὶ ἐπιστάτης,
ὃς ἂν δύνηται προθύμους καὶ ἐντεταμένους παρέχεσθαι εἰς τὸ ἔργον καὶ συνεχεῖς, οὗτοι δὴ οἱ
ἀνύτοντές εἰσιν ἐπὶ τἀγαθὰ καὶ πολλὴν τὴν
10 περιουσίαν ποιοῦντες. τοῦ δὲ δεσπότου ἐπι-
φανέντος, ὦ Σώκρατες, ἔφη, ἐπὶ τὸ ἔργον, ὅστις
δύναται καὶ μέγιστα βλάψαι τὸν κακὸν τῶν
ἐργατῶν καὶ μέγιστα τιμῆσαι τὸν πρόθυμον, εἰ
μηδὲν ἐπίδηλον ποιήσουσιν οἱ ἐργάται, ἐγὼ μὲν
αὐτὸν οὐκ ἂν ἀγαίμην, ἀλλ᾿ ὃν ἂν ἰδόντες
κινηθῶσι καὶ μένος ἑκάστῳ ἐμπέσῃ τῶν ἐργατῶν
καὶ φιλονεικία πρὸς ἀλλήλους καὶ φιλοτιμία
κρατίστη οὖσα ἑκάστῳ, τοῦτον ἐγὼ φαίην ἂν
11 ἔχειν τι ἤθους βασιλικοῦ. καὶ ἔστι τοῦτο
μέγιστον, ὡς ἐμοὶ δοκεῖ, ἐν παντὶ ἔργῳ, ὅπου τι
δι᾿ ἀνθρώπων πράττεται, καὶ ἐν γεωργίᾳ δέ. οὐ
μέντοι μὰ Δία τοῦτό γε ἔτι ἐγὼ λέγω ἰδόντα
μαθεῖν εἶναι οὐδ᾿ ἅπαξ ἀκούσαντα, ἀλλὰ καὶ
παιδείας δεῖν φημι τῷ ταῦτα μέλλοντι δυνήσεσθαι καὶ φύσεως ἀγαθῆς ὑπάρξαι καὶ τὸ
12 μέγιστον δὴ θεῖον γενέσθαι. οὐ γὰρ πάνυ μοι
δοκεῖ ὅλον τουτὶ τὸ ἀγαθὸν ἀνθρώπινον εἶναι,
ἀλλὰ θεῖον, τὸ ἐθελόντων ἄρχειν· σαφῶς δὲ
δίδοται τοῖς ἀληθινῶς σωφροσύνῃ τετελεσμένοις.
τὸ δὲ ἀκόντων τυραννεῖν διδόασιν, ὡς ἐμοὶ δοκεῖ,
οὓς ἂν ἡγῶνται ἀξίους εἶναι βιοτεύειν ὥσπερ ὁ
Τάνταλος ἐν Ἅιδου λέγεται τὸν ἀεὶ χρόνον
διατρίβειν φοβούμενος, μὴ δὶς ἀποθάνῃ.

will many an arm is ready to serve; and truly great
is he who can do great deeds by his will rather than
his strength.

"'So too in private industries, the man in authority 9
—bailiff or manager—who can make the workers
keen, industrious and persevering—he is the man
who gives a lift to the business and swells the surplus. But, Socrates, if the appearance of the master 10
in the field, of the man who has the fullest power to
punish the bad and reward the strenuous workmen,
makes no striking impression on the men at work, I
for one cannot envy him. But if at sight of him
they bestir themselves, and a spirit of determination
and rivalry and eagerness to excel falls on every
workman, then I should say: this man has a touch
of the kingly nature in him. And this, in my judg- 11
ment, is the greatest thing in every operation that
makes any demand on the labour of men, and therefore in agriculture. Mind you, I do not go so far as
to say that this can be learnt at sight or at a single
hearing. On the contrary, to acquire these powers
a man needs education; he must be possessed of
great natural gifts; above all, he must be a genius.
For I reckon this gift is not altogether human, but 12
divine—this power to win willing obedience: it is
manifestly a gift of the gods to the true votaries of
prudence. Despotic rule over unwilling subjects
they give, I fancy, to those whom they judge worthy
to live the life of Tantalus, of whom it is said
that in hell he spends eternity, dreading a second
death.'"

525

THE BANQUET

NOTE

THE basis of the text both of the *Symposium* and
of the *Apologia* is that of Sauppe published by
B. Tauchnitz. Variations from this are indicated in
the footnotes (for which I am indebted in several
places to the *apparatus criticus* of the Oxford text
edited by Marchant), except that I have made a few
unnoted changes in accents and punctuation and
have adopted without comment the better attested
spellings ἀποθνήσκω, ἀποτεῖσαι, ἐβούλετο, ηὐ- in
augmented forms, νεώς, οἰκτίρω, σῴζω, -ττ (-σσ-), φῄς,
Φλειάσιος. In the *Symposium* ii. 3 I am inclined to
think that the reading should be ἐστιώμεθα. On the
difficult phrase πρὸς τὸ ὄπισθεν (*Symp.* iv, 23) I should
like to mention Dakyns' suggestion (based on
Pollux ii, 10) of περὶ τὴν ὑπήνην.

INTRODUCTION

THE adventuresome days of Xenophon's earlier life were over, and though in exile from Athens, he was living peacefully, it would seem, in the western part of the Peloponnese somewhere about the year 380 B.C., at the time when he wrote the *Symposium* or *Banquet* purporting to give an account of an evening in Athens about forty years before.

Although Xenophon begins by stating that he himself attended this banquet, we are led by the fact that he nowhere appears in the ensuing discussion and by the fact of his writing so long after the supposed event to suspect that we must not consider his work as an historical document (though possibly based on an actual occurrence), but rather as an attempt to sketch the revered master, Socrates, in one of his times of social relaxation and enjoyment, and, it may have been, to present a corrective to the loftier but less realistic picture of Socrates at dinner with Agathon as drawn for us by Plato in his *Symposium*. In spite of the possibly fictitious nature of the conversation, however, the personages in the dialogue, with perhaps two exceptions, are all historical. Socrates, the great man who aroused such keen admiration and deep affection in Xenophon, Plato, and a large group of other men of diverse tastes and characters, is the central figure,

around whom appear various lesser contemporaries:
Callias, the giver of the feast, represented by Plato
as a dilettante who patronized the sophists, and by
the comic poets Aristophanes and Eupolis as a dissipated and spendthrift scion of a very wealthy family
that had been prominent at Athens in war, sports,
religion, and politics for nearly two centuries;
Autolycus, the object of Callias's admiration, son of
the politician Lycon (who appeared twenty-two years
later as one of the prosecutors of Socrates), a youth
of great beauty and of some athletic prowess, one of
the prize-winners at the Panathenaic games in this
year (421 B.C.) and the next year subject of a comedy
by Eupolis called the *Autolycus*, finally executed by
the Thirty Tyrants; Antisthenes, follower of Gorgias
the sophist and of Socrates, afterward founder
of the Cynic school of philosophy; Niceratus, son of
the wealthy general Nicias (who perished in the
ill-advised Syracusan expedition about seven years
after the events of this evening), represented here
as newly married to an Athenian girl who, we are
told elsewhere, would not survive her husband when
he was killed by the Thirty Tyrants; Critobulus,
son of Socrates' faithful friend Crito; Hermogenes,
probably the brother of Callias, mentioned by Plato
as having failed to receive his share of the ancestral
wealth; Charmides, uncle of Plato and a favourite
of Socrates; and two persons otherwise unknown to
us, Philip the buffoon and the Syracusan.

Not only are the personages all, or nearly all,
historical, but the setting and the action are circum-
stantial and realistic. The time was the summer
of 421 B.C., just after the greater Panathenaic games,
—an ancient festival to Athena held every year,

but every fourth year with special munificence, comprising contests for various kinds of athletes and musicians, and culminating in the brilliant and stately procession of men and maidens, sacrificial victims, charioteers, and cavalrymen that had been immortalized only a few years before this time by Pheidias and his craftsmen in the magnificent Ionic frieze of the Parthenon. Socrates and his friends are invited by Callias in holiday spirit, on the spur of the moment, to attend a banquet which he is about to give to Autolycus and his father. Everything is informal,—the various rambling remarks and bandied pleasantries, the unceremonious interruption by Philip the jester, the entertainment offered by the Syracusan and his trained troupe, and then the more systematic presentation by each man of his special contribution to the common weal, followed by the pantomime. It is hardly worth while to compare this real and vital scene with the jejune *Banquets* of later men, mere stalking-horses for the philosophical disquisitions of an Epicurus, the miscellanies of a Plutarch or an Athenaeus, or the antiquarian pilferings of a Macrobius ; one rather turns to a work nearer in time and in essence, the *Symposium* of Plato, written apparently about 385 B.C., doubtless only a few years before the work of Xenophon. · As might well have been expected, we do not reach in Xenophon the same exalted level of inspiration and poetical feeling that we do in Plato's representation of the banqueters' discussion of Love, but we feel rather the atmosphere of actual, ordinary disputation among men not keyed up to any high pitch of fervour ; we do not have so well-developed or so formal or so long-sustained philosophical debate, but we enjoy a feeling of reality in the evening's event, of seeing more vividly than in Plato just how an Athenian banquet was conducted. And so, if we desire to supplement and correct the realism of the comedians and see the ordinary Athenians in their times of relaxation, we can hardly do better than view them in these pages of Xenophon. There is an Attic grace and restraint, also, in Xenophon that has made his works charming to ancient and to modern alike.

ΞΕΝΟΦΩΝΤΟΣ ΣΥΜΠΟΣΙΟΝ

I. 'Αλλ' ἐμοὶ δοκεῖ τῶν καλῶν κἀγαθῶν ἀνδρῶν ἔργα οὐ μόνον τὰ μετὰ σπουδῆς πραττόμενα ἀξιομνημόνευτα εἶναι ἀλλὰ καὶ τὰ ἐν ταῖς παιδιαῖς. οἷς δὲ παραγενόμενος ταῦτα γιγνώσκω δηλῶσαι βούλομαι.

2 Ἦν μὲν γὰρ Παναθηναίων τῶν μεγάλων ἱπποδρομία, Καλλίας δὲ ὁ Ἱππονίκου ἐρῶν ἐτύγχανεν Αὐτολύκου παιδὸς ὄντος, καὶ νενικηκότα αὐτὸν παγκράτιον ἧκεν ἄγων ἐπὶ τὴν θέαν. ὡς δὲ ἡ ἱπποδρομία ἔληξεν, ἔχων τόν τε Αὐτόλυκον καὶ τὸν πατέρα αὐτοῦ ἀπῄει εἰς τὴν ἐν Πειραιεῖ οἰκίαν·
3 συνείπετο δὲ αὐτῷ καὶ Νικήρατος. ἰδὼν δὲ ὁμοῦ ὄντας Σωκράτην τε καὶ Κριτόβουλον καὶ Ἑρμογένην καὶ 'Αντισθένην καὶ Χαρμίδην, τοῖς μὲν ἀμφ' Αὐτόλυκον ἡγεῖσθαί τινα ἔταξεν, αὐτὸς δὲ
4 προσῆλθε τοῖς ἀμφὶ Σωκράτην, καὶ εἶπεν· Εἰς καλόν γε ὑμῖν συντετύχηκα· ἑστιᾶν γὰρ μέλλω Αὐτόλυκον καὶ τὸν πατέρα αὐτοῦ. οἶμαι οὖν πολὺ ἂν τὴν κατασκευήν μοι λαμπροτέραν φανῆναι εἰ ἀνδράσιν ἐκκεκαθαρμένοις τὰς ψυχὰς ὥσπερ ὑμῖν ὁ ἀνδρὼν κεκοσμημένος εἴη μᾶλλον ἢ εἰ στρατηγοῖς καὶ ἱππάρχοις καὶ σπουδαρχίαις.

534

XENOPHON'S BANQUET

I. To my mind it is worth while to relate not only the serious acts of great and good men but also what they do in their lighter moods. I should like to narrate an experience of mine that gives me this conviction.

It was on the occasion of the horse-races at the greater Panathenaic games; Callias, Hipponicus' son, was enamoured, as it happened, of the boy Autolycus, and in honour of his victory in the pancratium[1] had brought him to see the spectacle. When the racing was over, Callias proceeded on his way to his house in the Peiraeus with Autolycus and the boy's father; Niceratus also was in his company. But on catching sight of a group comprising Socrates, Critobulus, Hermogenes, Antisthenes, and Charmides, Callias bade one of his servants escort Autolycus and the others, and himself going over to Socrates and his companions, said, "This is an opportune meeting, for I am about to give a dinner in honour of Autolycus and his father; and I think that my entertainment would present a great deal more brilliance if my dining-room were graced with the presence of men like you, whose hearts have undergone philosophy's purification, than it would with generals and cavalry commanders and office-seekers."

---

[1] The pancratium was a severe athletic contest involving a combination of boxing and wrestling, and requiring on the part of the contestants unusual physique and condition. There were separate events open to men and to boys.

5 Καὶ ὁ Σωκράτης εἶπεν· Ἀεὶ σὺ ἐπισκώπτεις
ἡμᾶς καταφρονῶν ὅτι σὺ μὲν Πρωταγόρᾳ τε πολὺ
ἀργύριον δέδωκας ἐπὶ σοφίᾳ καὶ Γοργίᾳ καὶ Προδίκῳ καὶ ἄλλοις πολλοῖς, ἡμᾶς δ᾽ ὁρᾷς αὐτουργούς
τινας τῆς φιλοσοφίας ὄντας.

6 Καὶ ὁ Καλλίας, Καὶ πρόσθεν μέν γε, ἔφη,
ἀπεκρυπτόμην ὑμᾶς ἔχων πολλὰ καὶ σοφὰ λέγειν,
νῦν δέ, ἐὰν παρ᾽ ἐμοὶ ἦτε, ἐπιδείξω ὑμῖν ἐμαυτὸν
πάνυ πολλῆς σπουδῆς ἄξιον ὄντα.

7 Οἱ οὖν ἀμφὶ τὸν Σωκράτην πρῶτον μὲν ὥσπερ
εἰκὸς ἦν ἐπαινοῦντες τὴν κλῆσιν οὐχ ὑπισχνοῦντο
συνδειπνήσειν· ὡς δὲ πάνυ ἀχθόμενος φανερὸς ἦν
εἰ μὴ ἕψοιντο, συνηκολούθησαν. ἔπειτα δὲ αὐτῷ
οἱ μὲν γυμνασάμενοι καὶ χρισάμενοι, οἱ δὲ καὶ
8 λουσάμενοι παρῆλθον. Αὐτόλυκος μὲν οὖν παρὰ
τὸν πατέρα ἐκαθέζετο, οἱ δ᾽ ἄλλοι ὥσπερ εἰκὸς
κατεκλίθησαν.

Εὐθὺς μὲν οὖν ἐννοήσας τις[1] τὰ γιγνόμενα
ἡγήσατ᾽ ἂν φύσει βασιλικόν τι τὸ κάλλος εἶναι,
ἄλλως τε καὶ ἢν μετ᾽ αἰδοῦς καὶ σωφροσύνης
9 καθάπερ Αὐτόλυκος τότε κεκτῆταί τις αὐτό. πρῶτον μὲν γὰρ ὥσπερ ὅταν φέγγος τι ἐν νυκτὶ φανῇ,
πάντων προσάγεται τὰ ὄμματα, οὕτω καὶ τότε
τοῦ Αὐτολύκου τὸ κάλλος πάντων εἷλκε τὰς ὄψεις
πρὸς αὐτόν. ἔπειτα τῶν ὁρώντων οὐδεὶς οὐκ
ἔπασχέ τι τὴν ψυχὴν ὑπ᾽ ἐκείνου· οἱ μέν γε
σιωπηρότεροι ἐγίγνοντο, οἱ δὲ καὶ ἐσχηματίζοντό

---

[1] ἐννοήσας τις Aristeides ; ἐννοήσας MSS.

"You are always quizzing us," replied Socrates; "for you have yourself paid a good deal of money for wisdom to Protagoras, Gorgias, Prodicus, and many others, while you see that we are what you might call amateurs in philosophy; and so you feel supercilious toward us."

"Yes," said Callias, "so far, I admit, I have been keeping you ignorant of my ability at profound and lengthy discourse; but now, if you will favour me with your company, I will prove to you that I am a person of some consequence."

Now at first Socrates and his companions thanked him for the invitation, as might be expected, but would not promise to attend the banquet; when it became clear, however, that he was taking their refusal very much to heart, they went with him. And so his guests arrived, some having first taken their exercise and their rub-down, others with the addition of a bath. Autolycus took a seat by his father's side; the others, of course, reclined.[1]

A person who took note of the course of events would have come at once to the conclusion that beauty is in its essence something regal, especially when, as in the present case of Autolycus, its possessor joins with it modesty and sobriety. For in the first place, just as the sudden glow of a light at night draws all eyes to itself, so now the beauty of Autolycus compelled every one to look at him. And again, there was not one of the onlookers who did not feel his soul strangely stirred by the boy; some of them grew quieter than before, others even

[1] Attic reliefs depicting banquet scenes show that it was customary for the men to recline at table, but for the women and children, if present, to sit.

XENOPHON

10 πως. πάντες μὲν οὖν οἱ ἐκ θεῶν του κατεχόμενοι
ἀξιοθέατοι δοκοῦσιν εἶναι· ἀλλ' οἱ μὲν ἐξ ἄλλων
πρὸς τὸ γοργότεροί τε ὁρᾶσθαι καὶ φοβερώτερον
φθέγγεσθαι καὶ σφοδρότεροι εἶναι φέρονται, οἱ δ'
ὑπὸ τοῦ σώφρονος Ἔρωτος ἔνθεοι τά τε ὄμματα
φιλοφρονεστέρως ἔχουσι καὶ τὴν φωνὴν πραοτέ-
ραν ποιοῦνται καὶ τὰ σχήματα εἰς τὸ ἐλευθεριώ-
τατον ἄγουσιν. ἃ δὴ καὶ Καλλίας τότε διὰ τὸν
Ἔρωτα πράττων ἀξιοθέατος ἦν τοῖς τετελεσμένοις
τούτῳ τῷ θεῷ.

11 Ἐκεῖνοι μὲν οὖν σιωπῇ ἐδείπνουν, ὥσπερ τοῦτο
ἐπιτεταγμένον αὐτοῖς ὑπὸ κρείττονός τινος. Φίλιππος δ' ὁ γελωτοποιὸς κρούσας τὴν θύραν εἶπε
τῷ ὑπακούσαντι εἰσαγγεῖλαι ὅστις τε εἴη καὶ διότι
κατάγεσθαι βούλοιτο· συνεσκευασμένος τε παρεῖναι ἔφη πάντα τἀπιτήδεια—ὥστε δειπνεῖν τἀλ-
λότρια, καὶ τὸν παῖδα δὲ ἔφη πάνυ πιέζεσθαι διά
τε τὸ φέρειν—μηδὲν καὶ διὰ τὸ ἀνάριστον εἶναι.

12 ὁ οὖν Καλλίας ἀκούσας ταῦτα εἶπεν· Ἀλλὰ
μέντοι, ὦ ἄνδρες, αἰσχρὸν στέγης γε φθονῆσαι·
εἰσίτω οὖν. καὶ ἅμα ἀπέβλεψεν εἰς τὸν Αὐτόλυκον, δῆλον ὅτι ἐπισκοπῶν τί ἐκείνῳ δόξειε τὸ

13 σκῶμμα εἶναι. ὁ δὲ στὰς ἐπὶ τῷ ἀνδρῶνι ἔνθα τὸ
δεῖπνον ἦν εἶπεν· Ὅτι μὲν γελωτοποιός εἰμι ἴστε
πάντες· ἥκω δὲ προθύμως νομίσας γελοιότερον
εἶναι τὸ ἄκλητον ἢ τὸ κεκλημένον ἐλθεῖν ἐπὶ τὸ
δεῖπνον. Κατακλίνου τοίνυν, ἔφη ὁ Καλλίας·
καὶ γὰρ οἱ παρόντες σπουδῆς μέν, ὡς ὁρᾷς, μεστοί,
γέλωτος δὲ ἴσως ἐνδεέστεροι.

538

assumed some kind of a pose. Now it is true that all who are under the influence of any of the gods seem well worth gazing at; but whereas those who are possessed of the other gods have a tendency to be sterner of countenance, more terrifying of voice, and more vehement, those who are inspired by chaste Love have a more tender look, subdue their voices to more gentle tones, and assume a supremely noble bearing. Such was the demeanour of Callias at this time under the influence of Love; and therefore he was an object well worth the gaze of those initiated into the worship of this god.

The company, then, were feasting in silence, as though some one in authority had commanded them to do so, when Philip the buffoon knocked at the door and told the porter to announce who he was and that he desired to be admitted; he added that with regard to food he had come all prepared, in all varieties—to dine on some other person's,—and that his servant was in great distress with the load he carried of—nothing, and with having an empty stomach. Hearing this, Callias said, "Well, gentlemen, we cannot decently begrudge him at the least the shelter of our roof; so let him come in." With the words he cast a glance at Autolycus, obviously trying to make out what he had thought of the pleasantry. But Philip, standing at the threshold of the men's hall where the banquet was served, announced: "You all know that I am a jester; and so I have come here with a will, thinking it more of a joke to come to your dinner uninvited than to come by invitation." "Well, then," said Callias, "take a place; for the guests, though well fed, as you observe, on seriousness, are perhaps rather ill supplied with laughter."

14 Δειπνούντων δὲ αὐτῶν ὁ Φίλιππος γελοῖόν τι
εὐθὺς ἐπεχείρει λέγειν, ἵνα δὴ ἐπιτελοίη ὧνπερ
ἕνεκα ἐκαλεῖτο ἑκάστοτε ἐπὶ τὰ δεῖπνα. ὡς δ᾽
οὐκ ἐκίνησε γέλωτα, τότε μὲν ἀχθεσθεὶς φανερὸς
ἐγένετο. αὖθις δ᾽ ὀλίγον ὕστερον ἄλλο τι γελοῖον
ἐβούλετο λέγειν. ὡς δὲ οὐδὲ τότε ἐγέλασαν ἐπ᾽
αὐτῷ, ἐν τῷ μεταξὺ παυσάμενος τοῦ δείπνου
15 συγκαλυψάμενος κατέκειτο. καὶ ὁ Καλλίας, Τί
τοῦτ᾽, ἔφη, ὦ Φίλιππε ; ἀλλ᾽ ἢ ὀδύνη σε εἴληφε ;
καὶ ὃς ἀναστενάξας εἶπε, Ναὶ μὰ Δί᾽, ἔφη, ὦ
Καλλία, μεγάλη γε· ἐπεὶ γὰρ γέλως ἐξ ἀνθρώπων ἀπόλωλεν, ἔρρει τὰ ἐμὰ πράγματα. πρόσθεν
μὲν γὰρ τούτου ἕνεκα ἐκαλούμην ἐπὶ τὰ δεῖπνα
ἵνα εὐφραίνοιντο οἱ συνόντες δι᾽ ἐμὲ γελῶντες· νῦν
δὲ τίνος ἕνεκα καὶ καλεῖ μέ τις ; οὔτε γὰρ ἔγωγε
σπουδάσαι ἂν δυναίμην μᾶλλον ἤπερ ἀθάνατος
γενέσθαι, οὔτε μὴν ὡς ἀντικληθησόμενος καλεῖ
μέ τις, ἐπεὶ πάντες ἴσασιν ὅτι ἀρχὴν οὐδὲ νομίζεται εἰς τὴν ἐμὴν οἰκίαν δεῖπνον εἰσφέρεσθαι. καὶ
ἅμα λέγων ταῦτα ἀπεμύττετό τε καὶ τῇ φωνῇ
16 σαφῶς κλαίειν ἐφαίνετο. πάντες μὲν οὖν παρ-
εμυθοῦντό τε αὐτὸν ὡς αὖθις γελασόμενοι καὶ
δειπνεῖν ἐκέλευον, Κριτόβουλος δὲ καὶ ἐξεκάγχα-
σεν ἐπὶ τῷ οἰκτισμῷ αὐτοῦ. ὁ δ᾽ ὡς ᾔσθετο τοῦ
γέλωτος, ἀνεκαλύψατό τε καὶ τῇ ψυχῇ παρακε-
λευσάμενος θαρρεῖν, ὅτι ἔσονται συμβολαί, πάλιν
ἐδείπνει.

II. Ὡς δ᾽ ἀφῃρέθησαν αἱ τράπεζαι καὶ ἔσπει-

---

[1] Philip puns on the ambiguous συμβολαί, which means
either hostile encounters or a banquet to which the viands

No sooner were they engaged in their dinner than Philip attempted a witticism, with a view to rendering the service that secured him all his dinner engagements; but on finding that he did not excite any laughter, he showed himself, for the time, considerably vexed. A little later, however, he must try another jest; but when they would not laugh at him this time either, he stopped while the dinner was in full swing, covered his head with his cloak, and lay down on his couch. "What does this mean, Philip?" Callias inquired. "Are you seized with a pain?" Philip replied with a groan, "Yes, Callias, by Heaven, with a severe one; for since laughter has perished from the world, my business is ruined. For in times past, the reason why I got invitations to dinner was that I might stir up laughter among the guests and make them merry; but now, what will induce any one to invite me? For I could no more turn serious than I could become immortal; and certainly no one will invite me in the hope of a return invitation, as every one knows that there is not a vestige of tradition of bringing dinner into my house." As he said this, he wiped his nose, and to judge by the sound, he was evidently weeping. All tried to comfort him with the promise that they would laugh next time, and urged him to eat; and Critobulus actually burst out into a guffaw at his lugubrious moaning. The moment Philip heard the laughter he uncovered his head, and exhorting his spirit to be of good courage, in view of approaching engagements,[1] he fell to eating again.

II. When the tables had been removed and the

are contributed by the guests. His exhortation to his spirit is quite Odyssean.

σάν τε καὶ ἐπαιάνισαν, ἔρχεται αὐτοῖς ἐπὶ κῶμον
Συρακόσιός τις¹ ἄνθρωπος, ἔχων τε αὐλητρίδα
ἀγαθὴν καὶ ὀρχηστρίδα τῶν τὰ θαύματα δυναμένων ποιεῖν, καὶ παῖδα πάνυ γε ὡραῖον καὶ πάνυ
καλῶς κιθαρίζοντα καὶ ὀρχούμενον. ταῦτα δὲ καὶ
ἐπιδεικνὺς ὡς ἐν θαύματι ἀργύριον ἐλάμβανεν.
2 ἐπεὶ δὲ αὐτοῖς ἡ αὐλητρὶς μὲν ηὔλησεν, ὁ δὲ παῖς
ἐκιθάρισε, καὶ ἐδόκουν μάλα ἀμφότεροι ἱκανῶς
εὐφραίνειν, εἶπεν ὁ Σωκράτης· Νὴ Δί, ὦ Καλλία, τελέως ἡμᾶς ἑστιᾷς. οὐ γὰρ μόνον δεῖπνον
ἄμεμπτον παρέθηκας, ἀλλὰ καὶ θεάματα καὶ
3 ἀκροάματα ἥδιστα παρέχεις. καὶ ὃς ἔφη, Τί οὖν
εἰ καὶ μύρον τις ἡμῖν ἐνέγκοι, ἵνα καὶ εὐωδίᾳ
ἑστιώμεθα; Μηδαμῶς, ἔφη ὁ Σωκράτης. ὥσπερ
γάρ τοι ἐσθὴς ἄλλη μὲν γυναικί, ἄλλη δὲ ἀνδρὶ
καλή, οὕτω καὶ ὀσμὴ ἄλλη μὲν ἀνδρί, ἄλλη δὲ
γυναικὶ πρέπει. καὶ γὰρ ἀνδρὸς μὲν δήπου ἕνεκα
ἀνὴρ οὐδεὶς μύρῳ χρίεται. αἱ μέντοι γυναῖκες,
ἄλλως τε καὶ ἢν νύμφαι τύχωσιν οὖσαι, ὥσπερ ἡ
Νικηράτου τοῦδε καὶ ἡ Κριτοβούλου, μύρου μὲν
τί καὶ προσδέονται; αὐταὶ γὰρ τούτου ὄζουσιν·
ἐλαίου δὲ τοῦ ἐν γυμνασίοις ὀσμὴ καὶ παροῦσα
ἡδίων ἢ μύρου γυναιξὶ καὶ ἀποῦσα ποθεινοτέρα.
4 καὶ γὰρ δὴ μύρῳ μὲν ὁ ἀλειψάμενος καὶ δοῦλος
καὶ ἐλεύθερος εὐθὺς ἅπας ὅμοιον ὄζει· αἱ δ' ἀπὸ
τῶν ἐλευθερίων μόχθων ὀσμαὶ ἐπιτηδευμάτων τε

---

¹ Sauppe follows one MS. in placing τις after ἔρχεται.

---

¹ For the bride of Niceratus, see Introduction, p. 377.
² Perfumes were used at marriage by both bride and
groom.

guests had poured a libation and sung a hymn, there entered a man from Syracuse, to give them an evening's merriment. He had with him a fine flute-girl, a dancing-girl—one of those skilled in acrobatic tricks,—and a very handsome boy, who was expert at playing the cither and at dancing; the Syracusan made money by exhibiting their performances as a spectacle. They now played for the assemblage, the flute-girl on the flute, the boy on the cither; and it was agreed that both furnished capital amusement. Thereupon Socrates remarked: "On my word, Callias, you are giving us a perfect dinner; for not only have you set before us a feast that is above criticism, but you are also offering us very delightful sights and sounds." "Suppose we go further," said Callias, "and have some one bring us some perfume, so that we may dine in the midst of pleasant odours, also." "No, indeed!" replied Socrates. "For just as one kind of dress looks well on a woman and another kind on a man, so the odours appropriate to men and to women are diverse. No man, surely, ever uses perfume for a man's sake. And as for the women, particularly if they chance to be young brides, like the wives of Niceratus [1] here and Critobulus, how can they want any additional perfume? For that is what they are redolent of, themselves. [2] The odour of the olive oil, on the other hand, that is used in the gymnasium is more delightful when you have it on your flesh than perfume is to women, and when you lack it, the want of it is more keenly felt. Indeed, so far as perfume is concerned, when once a man has anointed himself with it, the scent forthwith is all one whether he be slave or free; but the odours that result from

πρῶτον χρηστῶν¹ καὶ χρόνου πολλοῦ δέονται,
εἰ μέλλουσιν ἡδεῖαί τε καὶ ἐλευθέριοι ἔσεσθαι.

Καὶ ὁ Λύκων εἶπεν· Οὐκοῦν νέοις μὲν ἂν εἴη
ταῦτα· ἡμᾶς δὲ τοὺς μηκέτι γυμναζομένους τίνος
ὄζειν δεήσει ;

Καλοκἀγαθίας νὴ Δί, ἔφη ὁ Σωκράτης.

Καὶ πόθεν ἄν τις τοῦτο τὸ χρῖμα λάβοι ;

Οὐ μὰ Δί, ἔφη, οὐ παρὰ τῶν μυροπωλῶν.

Ἀλλὰ πόθεν δή ;

Ὁ μὲν Θέογνις ἔφη,

Ἐσθλῶν μὲν γὰρ ἀπ᾽ ἐσθλὰ διδάξεαι· ἢν δὲ
κακοῖσι
συμμίσγῃς, ἀπολεῖς καὶ τὸν ἐόντα νόον.

5 Καὶ ὁ Λύκων εἶπεν, Ἀκούεις ταῦτα, ὦ υἱέ ;

Ναὶ μὰ Δί, ἔφη ὁ Σωκράτης, καὶ χρῆταί γε.
ἐπεὶ γοῦν νικηφόρος ἐβούλετο τοῦ παγκρατίου
γενέσθαι, σὺν σοὶ σκεψάμενος . . . σὺν σοὶ
σκεψάμενος² αὖ, ὃς ἂν δοκῇ αὐτῷ ἱκανώτατος
εἶναι εἰς τὸ ταῦτα ἐπιτηδεῦσαι, τούτῳ συνέσται.

6 Ἐνταῦθα δὴ πολλοὶ ἐφθέγξαντο· καὶ ὁ μέν τις
αὐτῶν εἶπε, Ποῦ οὖν εὑρήσει τούτου διδάσκαλον ;
ὁ δέ τις ὡς οὐδὲ διδακτὸν τοῦτο εἴη, ἕτερος δέ
7 τις ὡς εἴπερ τι καὶ ἄλλο καὶ τοῦτο μαθητόν.³ ὁ
δὲ Σωκράτης ἔφη· Τοῦτο μὲν ἐπειδὴ ἀμφίλογόν

---

¹ πρῶτον χρηστῶν Athenaeus ; πρῶτον MSS.
² The MSS. read σὺν σοὶ σκεψάμενος only once. There
is obviously something else lost from the text, for the
approximate sense of which see the translation.
³ μαθητόν Stephanus ; μαθητέον MSS.

the exertions of freemen demand primarily noble pursuits engaged in for many years if they are to be sweet and suggestive of freedom."

"That may do for young fellows," observed Lycon; "but what of us who no longer exercise in the gymnasia? What should be our distinguishing scent?"

"Nobility of soul, surely!" replied Socrates.

"And where may a person get this ointment?"

"Certainly not from the perfumers," said Socrates.

"But where, then?"

"Theognis has said:[1]

'Good men teach good; society with bad
Will but corrupt the good mind that you had.'"

"Do you hear that, my son?" asked Lycon.

"Yes, indeed he does," said Socrates; "and he puts it into practice, too. At any rate, when he desired to become a prize-winner in the pancratium, [he availed himself of your help to discover the champions in that sport and associated with them; and so, if he desires to learn the ways of virtue,][2] he will again with your help seek out the man who seems to him most proficient in this way of life and will associate with him."

Thereupon there was a chorus of voices. "Where will he find an instructor in this subject?" said one. Another maintained that it could not be taught at all. A third asserted that this could be learned if anything could. "Since this is a debatable matter," suggested Socrates, "let us reserve it for another

---

[1] Theognis 35 f. (with μαθήσεαι for διδάξεαι).
[2] The words in brackets are meant to represent approximately the sense of words that have been lost in the manuscripts.

ἐστιν, εἰς αὖθις ἀποθώμεθα· νυνὶ δὲ τὰ προκείμενα ἀποτελῶμεν. ὁρῶ γὰρ ἔγωγε τήνδε τὴν
ὀρχηστρίδα ἐφεστηκυῖαν καὶ τροχούς τινα αὐτῇ
προσφέροντα.

8 Ἐκ τούτου δὴ ηὔλει μὲν αὐτῇ ἡ ἑτέρα, παρεστη-
κὼς δέ τις τῇ ὀρχηστρίδι ἀνεδίδου τοὺς τροχοὺς
μέχρι δώδεκα. ἡ δὲ λαμβάνουσα ἅμα τε ὠρχεῖτο
καὶ ἀνερρίπτει δονουμένους συντεκμαιρομένη ὅσον
ἔδει ῥιπτεῖν ὕψος ὡς ἐν ῥυθμῷ δέχεσθαι αὐτούς.

9 Καὶ ὁ Σωκράτης εἶπεν· Ἐν πολλοῖς μέν, ὦ
ἄνδρες, καὶ ἄλλοις δῆλον καὶ ἐν οἷς δ᾽ ἡ παῖς
ποιεῖ ὅτι ἡ γυναικεία φύσις οὐδὲν χείρων τῆς τοῦ
ἀνδρὸς οὖσα τυγχάνει, γνώμης δὲ καὶ ἰσχύος
δεῖται. ὥστε εἴ τις ὑμῶν γυναῖκα ἔχει, θαρρῶν
διδασκέτω ὅ τι βούλοιτ᾽ ἂν αὐτῇ ἐπισταμένῃ
χρῆσθαι.

10 Καὶ ὁ Ἀντισθένης, Πῶς οὖν, ἔφη, ὦ Σώκρατες,
οὕτω γιγνώσκων οὐ καὶ σὺ παιδεύεις Ξανθίππην,
ἀλλὰ χρῇ γυναικὶ τῶν οὐσῶν, οἶμαι δὲ καὶ τῶν
γεγενημένων καὶ τῶν ἐσομένων, χαλεπωτάτῃ;
Ὅτι, ἔφη, ὁρῶ καὶ τοὺς ἱππικοὺς βουλομένους
γενέσθαι οὐ τοὺς εὐπειθεστάτους ἀλλὰ τοὺς θυμοειδεῖς ἵππους κτωμένους. νομίζουσι γάρ, ἢν
τοὺς τοιούτους δύνωνται κατέχειν, ῥᾳδίως τοῖς γε
ἄλλοις ἵπποις χρήσεσθαι. κἀγὼ δὴ βουλόμενος
ἀνθρώποις χρῆσθαι καὶ ὁμιλεῖν ταύτην κέκτημαι,
εὖ εἰδὼς ὅτι εἰ ταύτην ὑποίσω, ῥᾳδίως τοῖς γε
ἄλλοις ἅπασιν ἀνθρώποις συνέσομαι.

Καὶ οὗτος μὲν δὴ ὁ λόγος οὐκ ἀπὸ [1] τοῦ σκοποῦ
ἔδοξεν εἰρῆσθαι.

---

[1] ἀπο Sauppe.

time; for the present let us finish what we have on hand. For I see that the dancing girl here is standing ready, and that some one is bringing her some hoops."

At that, the other girl began to accompany the dancer on the flute, and a boy at her elbow handed her up the hoops until he had given her twelve. She took these and as she danced kept throwing them whirling into the air, observing the proper height to throw them so as to catch them in a regular rhythm.

As Socrates looked on he remarked: "This girl's feat, gentlemen, is only one of many proofs that woman's nature is really not a whit inferior to man's, except in its lack of judgment and physical strength. So if any one of you has a wife, let him confidently set about teaching her whatever he would like to have her know."

"If that is your view, Socrates," asked Antisthenes, "how does it come that you don't practise what you preach by yourself educating Xanthippe, but live with a wife who is the hardest to get along with of all the women there are—yes, or all that ever were, I suspect, or ever will be?"

"Because," he replied, "I observe that men who wish to become expert horsemen do not get the most docile horses but rather those that are high-mettled, believing that if they can manage this kind, they will easily handle any other. My course is similar. Mankind at large is what I wish to deal and associate with; and so I have got her, well assured that if I can endure her, I shall have no difficulty in my relations with all the rest of human kind."

These words, in the judgment of the guests, did not go wide of the mark.

11 Μετὰ δὲ τοῦτο κύκλος εἰσηνέχθη περίμεστος
ξιφῶν ὀρθῶν. εἰς οὖν ταῦτα ἡ ὀρχηστρὶς ἐκυ-
βίστα τε καὶ ἐξεκυβίστα ὑπὲρ αὐτῶν. ὥστε οἱ
μὲν θεώμενοι ἐφοβοῦντο μή τι πάθῃ, ἡ δὲ θαρ-
ρούντως τε καὶ ἀσφαλῶς ταῦτα διεπράττετο.

12 Καὶ ὁ Σωκράτης καλέσας τὸν Ἀντισθένην εἶπεν·
Οὗτοι τούς γε θεωμένους τάδε ἀντιλέξειν ἔτι
οἴομαι ὡς οὐχὶ καὶ ἡ ἀνδρεία διδακτόν, ὁπότε
αὕτη καίπερ γυνὴ οὖσα οὕτω τολμηρῶς εἰς τὰ
ξίφη ἵεται.

13 Καὶ ὁ Ἀντισθένης εἶπεν· Ἆρ᾽ οὖν καὶ τῷδε τῷ
Συρακοσίῳ κράτιστον ἐπιδείξαντι τῇ πόλει τὴν
ὀρχηστρίδα εἰπεῖν, ἐὰν διδῶσιν αὐτῷ Ἀθηναῖοι
χρήματα, ποιήσειν πάντας Ἀθηναίους τολμᾶν
ὁμόσε ταῖς λόγχαις ἰέναι;

14 Καὶ ὁ Φίλιππος, Νὴ Δί᾽, ἔφη, καὶ μὴν ἔγωγε
ἡδέως ἂν θεῴμην Πείσανδρον τὸν δημηγόρον
μανθάνοντα κυβιστᾶν εἰς τὰς μαχαίρας, ὃς νῦν
διὰ τὸ μὴ δύνασθαι λόγχαις ἀντιβλέπειν οὐδὲ
συστρατεύεσθαι ἐθέλει.

15 Ἐκ τούτου ὁ παῖς ὠρχήσατο. καὶ ὁ Σωκράτης
εἶπεν, Εἴδετ᾽, ἔφη, ὡς καλὸς ὁ παῖς ὢν ὅμως σὺν
τοῖς σχήμασιν ἔτι καλλίων φαίνεται ἢ ὅταν
ἡσυχίαν ἔχῃ;

Καὶ ὁ Χαρμίδης εἶπεν· Ἐπαινοῦντι ἔοικας τὸν
ὀρχηστοδιδάσκαλον.

16 Ναὶ μὰ τὸν Δί᾽, ἔφη ὁ Σωκράτης· καὶ γὰρ ἄλλο

But now there was brought in a hoop set all around with upright swords; over these the dancer turned somersaults into the hoop and out again, to the dismay of the onlookers, who thought that she might suffer some mishap. She, however, went through this performance fearlessly and safely.

Then Socrates, drawing Antisthenes' attention, said: "Witnesses of this feat, surely, will never again deny, I feel sure, that courage, like other things, admits of being taught, when this girl, in spite of her sex, leaps so boldly in among the swords!"

"Well, then," asked Antisthenes, "had this Syracusan not better exhibit his dancer to the city and announce that if the Athenians will pay him for it he will give all the men of Athens the courage to face the spear?"

"Well said!" interjected Philip. "I certainly should like to see Peisander the politician[1] learning to turn somersaults among the knives; for, as it is now, his inability to look spears in the face makes him shrink even from joining the army."

At this point the boy performed a dance, eliciting from Socrates the remark, "Did you notice that, handsome as the boy is, he appears even handsomer in the poses of the dance than when he is at rest?"

"It looks to me," said Charmides, "as if you were puffing the dancing-master."

"Assuredly," replied Socrates; "and I remarked

---

[1] Peisander, a demagogue of some power in the unsettled times of the Peloponnesian War, had a number of weak points, especially his military record, which were exposed by the comic poets Eupolis, Hermippus, Plato, and Aristophanes. Cf. Aristophanes *Birds*, 1553 ff.

τι προσενενόησα, ὅτι οὐδὲν ἀργὸν τοῦ σώματος ἐν τῇ ὀρχήσει ἦν, ἀλλ' ἅμα καὶ τράχηλος καὶ σκέλη καὶ χεῖρες ἐγυμνάζοντο, ὥσπερ χρὴ ὀρχεῖσθαι τὸν μέλλοντα εὐφορώτερον τὸ σῶμα ἕξειν. καὶ ἐγὼ μέν, ἔφη, πάνυ ἂν ἡδέως, ὦ Συρακόσιε, μάθοιμι τὰ σχήματα παρὰ σοῦ.

Καὶ ὅς, Τί οὖν χρήσει αὐτοῖς ; ἔφη.

Ὀρχήσομαι νὴ Δία.

17 Ἐνταῦθα δὴ ἐγέλασαν ἅπαντες. καὶ ὁ Σωκράτης μάλα ἐσπουδακότι τῷ προσώπῳ, Γελᾶτε, ἔφη, ἐπ' ἐμοί ; πότερον ἐπὶ τούτῳ εἰ βούλομαι γυμναζόμενος μᾶλλον ὑγιαίνειν ἢ εἰ ἥδιον ἐσθίειν καὶ καθεύδειν ἢ εἰ τοιούτων γυμνασίων ἐπιθυμῶ, μὴ ὥσπερ οἱ δολιχοδρόμοι τὰ σκέλη μὲν παχύνονται, τοὺς δὲ ὤμους λεπτύνονται, μηδ' ὥσπερ οἱ πύκται τοὺς μὲν ὤμους παχύνονται, τὰ δὲ σκέλη λεπτύνονται, ἀλλὰ παντὶ διαπονῶν τῷ 18 σώματι πᾶν ἰσόρροπον ποιεῖν ; ἢ ἐπ' ἐκείνῳ γελᾶτε ὅτι οὐ δεήσει με συγγυμναστὴν ζητεῖν, οὐδ' ἐν ὄχλῳ πρεσβύτην ὄντα ἀποδύεσθαι, ἀλλ' ἀρκέσει μοι οἶκος ἑπτάκλινος,[1] ὥσπερ καὶ νῦν τῷδε τῷ παιδὶ ἤρκεσε τόδε τὸ οἴκημα ἐνιδρῶσαι, καὶ χειμῶνος μὲν ἐν στέγῃ γυμνάσομαι, ὅταν δὲ 19 ἄγαν καῦμα ᾖ, ἐν σκιᾷ ; ἢ τόδε γελᾶτε, εἰ μείζω τοῦ καιροῦ τὴν γαστέρα ἔχων μετριωτέραν βούλομαι ποιῆσαι αὐτήν ; ἢ οὐκ ἴστε ὅτι ἔναγχος ἕωθεν Χαρμίδης οὑτοσὶ κατέλαβέ με ὀρχούμενον ;

Ναὶ μὰ τὸν Δί', ἔφη ὁ Χαρμίδης· καὶ τὸ μέν γε

---

[1] Literally, *a room of seven couches.* Cf. Xen. *Oec.* VIII, 13.

something else, too,—that no part of his body was idle during the dance, but neck, legs, and hands were all active together. And that is the way a person must dance who intends to increase the suppleness of his body. And for myself," he continued, addressing the Syracusan, "I should be delighted to learn the figures from you."

"What use will you make of them?" the other asked.

"I will dance, forsooth."

This raised a general laugh; but Socrates, with a perfectly grave expression on his face, said: "You are laughing at me, are you? Is it because I want to exercise to better my health? Or because I want to take more pleasure in my food and my sleep? Or is it because I am eager for such exercises as these, not like the long-distance runners, who develop their legs at the expense of their shoulders, nor like the prize-fighters, who develop their shoulders but become thin-legged, but rather with a view to giving my body a symmetrical development by exercising it in every part? Or are you laughing because I shall not need to hunt up a partner to exercise with, or to strip, old as I am, in a crowd, but shall find a moderate-sized room[1] large enough for me (just as but now this room was large enough for the lad here to get up a sweat in), and because in winter I shall exercise under cover, and when it is very hot, in the shade? Or is this what provokes your laughter, that I have an unduly large paunch and wish to reduce it? Don't you know that just the other day Charmides here caught me dancing early in the morning?"

"Indeed I did," said Charmides; "and at first I

πρῶτον ἐξεπλάγην καὶ ἔδεισα μὴ μαίνοιο· ἐπεὶ δέ
σου ἤκουσα ὅμοια οἷς νῦν λέγεις, καὶ αὐτὸς ἐλθὼν
οἴκαδε ὠρχούμην μὲν οὔ, οὐ γὰρ πώποτε τοῦτ'
ἔμαθον, ἐχειρονόμουν δέ· ταῦτα γὰρ ἠπιστάμην.

20 Νὴ Δί', ἔφη ὁ Φίλιππος, καὶ γὰρ οὖν οὕτω τὰ
σκέλη τοῖς ὤμοις φαίνῃ ἰσοφόρα ἔχειν ὥστε δοκεῖς
ἐμοί, κἂν εἰ τοῖς ἀγορανόμοις ἀφισταίης [1] ὥσπερ
ἄρτους τὰ κάτω πρὸς τὰ ἄνω, ἀζήμιος ἂν
γενέσθαι.

Καὶ ὁ Καλλίας εἶπεν· Ὦ Σώκρατες, ἐμὲ μὲν
παρακάλει, ὅταν μέλλῃς μανθάνειν ὀρχεῖσθαι,
ἵνα σοι ἀντιστοιχῶ τε καὶ συμμανθάνω.

21 Ἄγε δή, ἔφη ὁ Φίλιππος, καὶ ἐμοὶ αὐλησάτω,
ἵνα καὶ ἐγὼ ὀρχήσωμαι.

Ἐπειδὴ δ' ἀνέστη, διῆλθε μιμούμενος τήν τε τοῦ
22 παιδὸς καὶ τὴν τῆς παιδὸς ὄρχησιν. καὶ πρῶτον
μὲν ὅτι ἐπῄνεσαν ὡς ὁ παῖς σὺν τοῖς σχήμασιν
ἔτι καλλίων ἐφαίνετο, ἀνταπέδειξεν ὅ τι κινοίη
τοῦ σώματος ἅπαν τῆς φύσεως γελοιότερον· ὅτι δ'
ἡ παῖς εἰς τοὔπισθεν καμπτομένη τροχοὺς ἐμιμεῖτο, ἐκεῖνος ταῦτα εἰς τὸ ἔμπροσθεν ἐπικύπτων
μιμεῖσθαι [2] ἐπειρᾶτο. τέλος δ' ὅτι τὸν παῖδ'
ἐπῄνουν ὡς ἐν τῇ ὀρχήσει ἅπαν τὸ σῶμα γυμνά-
ζοι, κελεύσας τὴν αὐλητρίδα θάττονα ῥυθμὸν
ἐπάγειν ἵει ἅμα πάντα καὶ σκέλη καὶ χεῖρας καὶ
23 κεφαλήν. ἐπειδὴ δὲ ἀπειρήκει, κατακλινόμενος

---

[1] ἀφισταίης Mehler ; ἀφιστῴης MSS.
[2] The MSS. add τροχοὺς, which Bornemann deleted.

---

[1] Since the Athenians were dependent largely on imported
grain, they developed an elaborate system of regulations, ad-
ministered by several sets of officials, to protect the consumers

was dumbfounded and feared that you were going
stark mad; but when I heard you say much the
same thing as you did just now, I myself went home,
and although I did not dance, for I had never learned
how, I practised shadow-boxing, for I knew how to
do that."

"Undoubtedly," said Philip; "at any rate, your legs
appear so nearly equal in weight to your shoulders
that I imagine if you were to go to the market com-
missioners and put your lower parts in the scale
against your upper parts, as if they were loaves of
bread,[1] they would let you off without a fine."

"When you are ready to begin your lessons,
Socrates," said Callias, "pray invite me, so that I
may be opposite you in the figures and may learn
with you."

"Come," said Philip, "let me have some flute
music, so that I may dance too."

So he got up and mimicked in detail the dancing
of both the boy and the girl. To begin with, since
the company had applauded the way the boy's
natural beauty was increased by the grace of the
dancing postures, Philip made a burlesque out of the
performance by rendering every part of his body
that was in motion more grotesque than it naturally
was; and whereas the girl had bent backward until
she resembled a hoop, he tried to do the same by
bending forward. Finally, since they had given
the boy applause for putting every part of his body
into play in the dance, he told the flute girl to hit up
the time faster, and danced away, flinging out legs,
hands, and head all at the same time; and when he

from speculation and extortion. One set of officials controlled
the weight and the price of bread.

εἶπε· Τεκμήριον, ὦ ἄνδρες, ὅτι καλῶς γυμνάζει καὶ τὰ ἐμὰ ὀρχήματα. ἐγὼ γοῦν διψῶ· καὶ ὁ παῖς ἐγχεάτω μοι τὴν μεγάλην φιάλην.

Νὴ Δί᾽, ἔφη ὁ Καλλίας, καὶ ἡμῖν γε, ἐπεὶ καὶ ἡμεῖς διψῶμεν ἐπὶ σοὶ γελῶντες.

24 Ὁ δ᾽ αὖ Σωκράτης εἶπεν· Ἀλλὰ πίνειν μέν, ὦ ἄνδρες, καὶ ἐμοὶ πάνυ δοκεῖ· τῷ γὰρ ὄντι ὁ οἶνος ἄρδων τὰς ψυχὰς τὰς μὲν λύπας ὥσπερ ὁ μανδραγόρας τοὺς ἀνθρώπους κοιμίζει, τὰς δὲ φιλοφρο-
25 σύνας ὥσπερ ἔλαιον φλόγα ἐγείρει. δοκεῖ μέντοι μοι καὶ τὰ τῶν ἀνδρῶν σώματα[1] ταὐτὰ πάσχειν ἅπερ καὶ τὰ τῶν ἐν γῇ φυομένων.[2] καὶ γὰρ ἐκεῖνα, ὅταν μὲν ὁ θεὸς αὐτὰ ἄγαν ἀθρόως ποτίζῃ, οὐ δύναται ὀρθοῦσθαι οὐδὲ ταῖς αὔραις διαπνεῖσθαι· ὅταν δ᾽ ὅσῳ ἥδεται τοσοῦτο πίνῃ, καὶ μάλα ὀρθά τε αὔξεται καὶ θάλλοντα ἀφικνεῖται εἰς τὴν
26 καρπογονίαν. οὕτω δὲ καὶ ἡμεῖς ἢν μὲν ἀθρόον τὸ ποτὸν ἐγχεώμεθα, ταχὺ ἡμῖν καὶ τὰ σώματα καὶ αἱ γνῶμαι σφαλοῦνται, καὶ οὐδὲ ἀναπνεῖν, μὴ ὅτι λέγειν τι δυνησόμεθα· ἢν δὲ ἡμῖν οἱ παῖδες μικραῖς κύλιξι πυκνὰ ἐπιψακάζωσιν, ἵνα καὶ ἐγὼ ἐν Γοργιείοις ῥήμασιν εἴπω, οὕτως οὐ βιαζόμενοι ὑπὸ τοῦ οἴνου μεθύειν ἀλλ᾽ ἀναπειθόμενοι πρὸς τὸ παιγνιωδέστερον ἀφιξόμεθα.

---

[1] σώματα Athenaeus; συμπόσια MSS. and Stobaeus.
[2] τὰ τῶν ἐν γῇ φυομένων MSS.; Sauppe adopted the suggestion τὰ ἐν γῇ φυόμενα.

---

[1] Apparently a reminiscence of Aristophanes' *Knights*, 96, 114.

was quite exhausted, he exclaimed as he laid himself down : " Here is proof, gentlemen, that my style of dancing, also, gives excellent exercise; it has certainly given me a thirst; so let the servant fill me up the big goblet."

"Certainly," replied Callias; "and the same for us, for we are thirsty with laughing at you."

Here Socrates again interposed. "Well, gentlemen," said he, "so far as drinking is concerned, you have my hearty approval; for wine does of a truth ' moisten the soul ' [1] and lull our griefs to sleep just as the mandragora does with men, at the same time awakening kindly feelings as oil quickens a flame. However, I suspect that men's bodies fare the same as those of plants that grow in the ground. When God gives the plants water in floods to drink, they cannot stand up straight or let the breezes blow through them; but when they drink only as much as they enjoy, they grow up very straight and tall and come to full and abundant fruitage. So it is with us. If we pour ourselves immense draughts, it will be no long time before both our bodies and our minds reel, and we shall not be able even to draw breath, much less to speak sensibly; but if the servants frequently ' besprinkle ' us—if I too may use a Gorgian [2] expression—with small cups, we shall thus not be driven on by the wine to a state of intoxication, but instead shall be brought by its gentle persuasion to a more sportive mood."

[2] Gorgias was a famous contemporary orator and teacher of rhetoric, whose speeches, though dazzling to inexperienced audiences, were over-formal and ornate. Some of his metaphors drew the criticism of Aristotle as being far-fetched. Cf. *Rhet.* III, iii, 4 (1406^b 4 ff.).

27 Ἐδόκει μὲν δὴ ταῦτα πᾶσι· προσέθηκε δὲ ὁ
Φίλιππος ὡς χρὴ τοὺς οἰνοχόους μιμεῖσθαι τοὺς
ἀγαθοὺς ἁρματηλάτας, θᾶττον περιελαύνοντας
τὰς κύλικας. οἱ μὲν δὴ οἰνοχόοι οὕτως ἐποίουν.

III. Ἐκ δὲ τούτου συνηρμοσμένη τῇ λύρᾳ πρὸς
τὸν αὐλὸν ἐκιθάρισεν ὁ παῖς καὶ ᾖσεν. ἔνθα δὴ
ἐπῄνεσαν μὲν ἅπαντες· ὁ δὲ Χαρμίδης καὶ εἶπεν·
Ἀλλ᾽ ἐμοὶ μὲν δοκεῖ, ὦ ἄνδρες, ὥσπερ Σωκράτης
ἔφη τὸν οἶνον, οὕτω καὶ αὕτη ἡ κρᾶσις τῶν τε
παίδων τῆς ὥρας καὶ τῶν φθόγγων τὰς μὲν λύπας
κοιμίζειν, τὴν δ᾽ Ἀφροδίτην ἐγείρειν.

2 Ἐκ τούτου δὲ πάλιν εἶπεν ὁ Σωκράτης· Οὗτοι
μὲν δή, ὦ ἄνδρες, ἱκανοὶ τέρπειν ἡμᾶς φαίνονται·
ἡμεῖς δὲ τούτων οἶδ᾽ ὅτι πολὺ βελτίονες οἰόμεθα
εἶναι· οὐκ αἰσχρὸν οὖν εἰ μηδ᾽ ἐπιχειρήσομεν
συνόντες ὠφελεῖν τι ἢ εὐφραίνειν ἀλλήλους ;

Ἐντεῦθεν εἶπον πολλοί, Σὺ τοίνυν ἡμῖν ἐξηγοῦ
ποίων λόγων ἁπτόμενοι μάλιστ᾽ ἂν ταῦτα
ποιοῖμεν.

3 Ἐγὼ μὲν τοίνυν, ἔφη, ἥδιστ᾽ ἂν ἀπολάβοιμι
παρὰ Καλλίου τὴν ὑπόσχεσιν. ἔφη γὰρ δήπου,
εἰ συνδειπνοῖμεν, ἐπιδείξειν τὴν αὑτοῦ σοφίαν.

Καὶ ἐπιδείξω γε, ἔφη, ἐὰν καὶ ὑμεῖς ἅπαντες εἰς
μέσον φέρητε ὅ τι ἕκαστος ἐπίστασθε ἀγαθόν.

Ἀλλ᾽ οὐδείς σοι, ἔφη, ἀντιλέγει τὸ μὴ οὐ
λέξειν ὅ τι ἕκαστος ἡγεῖται πλείστου ἄξιον
ἐπίστασθαι.

4 Ἐγὼ μὲν τοίνυν, ἔφη, λέγω ὑμῖν ἐφ᾽ ᾧ μέγι-

This resolution received a unanimous vote, with an amendment added by Philip to the effect that the wine-pourers should emulate skilful charioteers by driving the cups around with ever increasing speed. This the wine-pourers proceeded to do.

III. After this the boy, attuning his lyre to the flute, played and sang, and won the applause of all; and brought from Charmides the remark, "It seems to me, gentlemen, that, as Socrates said of the wine, so this blending of the young people's beauty and of the notes of the music lulls one's griefs to sleep and awakens the goddess of Love."

Then Socrates resumed the conversation. "These people, gentlemen," said he, "show their competence to give us pleasure; and yet we, I am sure, think ourselves considerably superior to them. Will it not be to our shame, therefore, if we do not make even an attempt, while here together, to be of some service or to give some pleasure one to another?"

At that many spoke up: "You lead the way, then, and tell us what to begin talking about to realize most fully what you have in mind."

"For my part," he answered, "I should like to have Callias redeem his promise; for he said, you remember, that if we would take dinner with him, he would give us an exhibition of his profundity."

"Yes," rejoined Callias; "and I will do so, if the rest of you will also lay before us any serviceable knowledge that you severally possess."

"Well," answered Socrates, "no one objects to telling what he considers the most valuable knowledge in his possession."

"Very well, then," said Callias, "I will now tell

557

στον φρονῶ. ἀνθρώπους γὰρ οἶμαι ἱκανὸς εἶναι βελτίους ποιεῖν.

Καὶ ὁ Ἀντισθένης εἶπε, Πότερον τέχνην τινὰ βαναυσικὴν ἢ καλοκἀγαθίαν διδάσκων;

Εἰ καλοκἀγαθία ἐστὶν ἡ δικαιοσύνη.

Νὴ Δἰ, ἔφη ὁ Ἀντισθένης, ἥ γε ἀναμφιλογωτάτη· ἐπεί τοι ἀνδρεία μὲν καὶ σοφία ἔστιν ὅτε βλαβερὰ καὶ φίλοις καὶ πόλει δοκεῖ εἶναι, ἡ δὲ δικαιοσύνη οὐδὲ καθ᾽ ἓν συμμίγνυται τῇ ἀδικίᾳ.

5 Ἐπειδὰν τοίνυν καὶ ὑμῶν[1] ἕκαστος εἴπῃ ὅ τι ὠφέλιμον ἔχει, τότε κἀγὼ οὐ φθονήσω εἰπεῖν τὴν τέχνην δι᾽ ἧς τοῦτο ἀπεργάζομαι. ἀλλὰ σὺ αὖ, ἔφη, λέγε, ὦ Νικήρατε, ἐπὶ ποίᾳ ἐπιστήμῃ μέγα φρονεῖς.

Καὶ ὃς εἶπεν· Ὁ πατὴρ ἐπιμελούμενος ὅπως ἀνὴρ ἀγαθὸς γενοίμην, ἠνάγκασέ με πάντα τὰ Ὁμήρου ἔπη μαθεῖν· καὶ νῦν δυναίμην ἂν Ἰλιάδα ὅλην καὶ Ὀδύσσειαν ἀπὸ στόματος εἰπεῖν.

6 Ἐκεῖνο δ᾽, ἔφη ὁ Ἀντισθένης, λέληθέ σε ὅτι καὶ οἱ ῥαψῳδοὶ πάντες ἐπίστανται ταῦτα τὰ ἔπη;

Καὶ πῶς ἄν, ἔφη, λελήθοι ἀκροώμενόν γε αὐτῶν ὀλίγου ἂν ἑκάστην ἡμέραν;

Οἶσθά τι οὖν ἔθνος, ἔφη, ἠλιθιώτερον ῥαψῳδῶν;

[1] ὑμῶν Castalio; ἡμῶν MSS.

---

[1] The word δικαιοσύνη, translated here by *righteousness*, is sometimes well represented by *justice* or *honesty*. It is the virtue discussed by Plato in the *Republic* and by Aristotle in the fifth book of his *Ethics*.

you what I take greatest pride in. It is that I believe I have the power to make men better."

"How?" asked Antisthenes. "By teaching them some manual trade, or by teaching nobility of character?"

"The latter, if righteousness [1] is the same thing as nobility."

"Certainly it is," replied Antisthenes, "and the least debatable kind, too; for though courage and wisdom appear at times to work injury both to one's friends and to the state, righteousness and unrighteousness never overlap at a single point."

"Well, then, when every one of you has named the benefit he can confer, I will not begrudge describing the art that gives me the success that I speak of. And so, Niceratus," he suggested, "it is your turn; tell us what kind of knowledge you take pride in."

"My father was anxious to see me develop into a good man," said Niceratus, "and as a means to this end he compelled me to memorize all of Homer; and so even now I can repeat the whole *Iliad* and the *Odyssey* by heart."

"But have you failed to observe," questioned Antisthenes, "that the rhapsodes,[2] too, all know these poems?"

"How could I," he replied, "when I listen to their recitations nearly every day?"

"Well, do you know any tribe of men," went on the other, "more stupid than the rhapsodes?"

[2] These professional reciters of epic poetry are represented as being criticized by Socrates, in much the same way as here, in Xenophon's *Memorabilia*, IV. ii. 10 and in Plato's *Ion.*

Οὐ μὰ τὸν Δί, ἔφη ὁ Νικήρατος, οὔκουν ἔμοιγε δοκεῖ.

Δῆλον γάρ, ἔφη ὁ Σωκράτης, ὅτι τὰς ὑπονοίας οὐκ ἐπίστανται. σὺ δὲ Στησιμβρότῳ τε καὶ Ἀναξιμάνδρῳ καὶ ἄλλοις πολλοῖς πολὺ δέδωκας ἀργύριον, ὥστε οὐδέν σε τῶν πολλοῦ ἀξίων λέ-
7 ληθε. τί γὰρ σύ, ἔφη, ὦ Κριτόβουλε, ἐπὶ τίνι μέγιστον φρονεῖς;

Ἐπὶ κάλλει, ἔφη.

Ἦ οὖν καὶ σύ, ἔφη ὁ Σωκράτης, ἕξεις λέγειν ὅτι τῷ σῷ κάλλει ἱκανὸς εἶ βελτίους ἡμᾶς ποιεῖν;

Εἰ δὲ μή, δῆλόν γε ὅτι φαῦλος φανοῦμαι.
8 Τί γὰρ σύ, εἶπεν, ἐπὶ τίνι μέγα φρονεῖς, ὦ Ἀντίσθενες;

Ἐπὶ πλούτῳ, ἔφη.

Ὁ μὲν δὴ Ἑρμογένης ἀνήρετο εἰ πολὺ εἴη αὐτῷ ἀργύριον. ὁ δὲ ἀπώμοσε μηδὲ ὀβολόν.

Ἀλλὰ γῆν πολλὴν κέκτησαι;

Ἴσως ἄν, ἔφη, Αὐτολύκῳ τούτῳ ἱκανὴ γένοιτο ἐγκονίσασθαι.
9 Ἀκουστέον ἂν εἴη καὶ σοῦ. τί γὰρ σύ, ἔφη, ὦ Χαρμίδη, ἐπὶ τίνι μέγα φρονεῖς;

Ἐγὼ αὖ, ἔφη, ἐπὶ πενίᾳ μέγα φρονῶ.

Νὴ Δί, ἔφη ὁ Σωκράτης, ἐπ᾽ εὐχαρίστῳ γε πράγματι. τοῦτο γὰρ δὴ ἥκιστα μὲν ἐπίφθονον, ἥκιστα δὲ περιμάχητον, καὶ ἀφύλακτον ὂν σώ-ζεται καὶ ἀμελούμενον ἰσχυρότερον γίγνεται.

---

[1] Critobulus seems to imply that beauty is his only resource.

[2] The reference is to the handful or so of dry sand that an athlete put on after oiling his skin.

"No, indeed," answered Niceratus; "not I, I am sure."

"No," said Socrates; "and the reason is clear: they do not know the inner meaning of the poems. But you have paid a good deal of money to Stesimbrotus, Anaximander, and many other Homeric critics, so that nothing of their valuable teaching can have escaped your knowledge. But what about you, Critobulus?" he continued. "What do you take greatest pride in?"

"In beauty," he replied.

"What?" exclaimed Socrates. "Are you too going to be able to maintain that you can make us better, and by means of your beauty?"

"Why, otherwise, it is clear enough that I shall cut but an indifferent figure."[1]

"And you, Antisthenes," said Socrates, "what do you take pride in?"

"In wealth," he replied.

Hermogenes asked him whether he had a large amount of money; he swore that he did not have even a penny.

"You own a great deal of land, then?"

"Well, perhaps it might prove big enough," said he, "for Autolycus here to sand himself in."[2]

"It looks as if we should have to hear from you, too. And how about you, Charmides?" he continued. "What do you take pride in?"

"My pride," said he, "on the contrary, is in my poverty."

"A charming thing, upon my word!" exclaimed Socrates. "It seldom causes envy or is a bone of contention; and it is kept safe without the necessity of a guard, and grows sturdier by neglect!"

10　Σὺ δὲ δή, ἔφη ὁ Καλλίας, ἐπὶ τίνι μέγα φρονεῖς, ὦ Σώκρατες ;

Καὶ ὃς μάλα σεμνῶς ἀνασπάσας τὸ πρόσωπον, Ἐπὶ μαστροπείᾳ, εἶπεν.

Ἐπεὶ δὲ ἐγέλασαν ἐπ' αὐτῷ, Ὑμεῖς μὲν γελᾶτε, ἔφη, ἐγὼ δὲ οἶδ' ὅτι καὶ πάνυ ἂν πολλὰ χρήματα λαμβάνοιμι, εἰ βουλοίμην χρῆσθαι τῇ τέχνῃ.

11　Σύ γε μὴν δῆλον, ἔφη ὁ Λύκων πρὸς τὸν Φίλιππον, ὅτι ἐπὶ τῷ γελωτοποιεῖν μέγα φρονεῖς.

Δικαιότερόν γ', ἔφη, οἶμαι, ἢ Καλλιππίδης ὁ ὑποκριτής, ὃς ὑπερσεμνύνεται ὅτι δύναται πολλοὺς κλαίοντας καθίζειν.

12　Οὐκοῦν καὶ σύ, ἔφη ὁ Ἀντισθένης, λέξεις, ὦ Λύκων, ἐπὶ τίνι μέγα φρονεῖς ;

Καὶ ὃς ἔφη, Οὐ γὰρ ἅπαντες ἴστε, ἔφη, ὅτι[1] ἐπὶ τούτῳ τῷ υἱεῖ ;

Οὗτός γε μήν, ἔφη τις, δῆλον ὅτι ἐπὶ τῷ νικηφόρος εἶναι.

Καὶ ὁ Αὐτόλυκος ἀνερυθριάσας εἶπε, Μὰ Δί' οὐκ ἔγωγε.

13　Ἐπεὶ δὲ ἅπαντες ἡσθέντες ὅτι ἤκουσαν αὐτοῦ φωνήσαντος προσέβλεψαν, ἤρετό τις αὐτόν, Ἀλλ' ἐπὶ τῷ μήν, ὦ Αὐτόλυκε ; ὁ δ' εἶπεν, Ἐπὶ τῷ πατρί, καὶ ἅμα ἐνεκλίθη αὐτῷ.

Καὶ ὁ Καλλίας ἰδών, Ἆρ' οἶσθα, ἔφη, ὦ Λύκων, ὅτι πλουσιώτατος εἶ ἀνθρώπων ;

Μὰ Δί', ἔφη, τοῦτο μέντοι ἐγὼ οὐκ οἶδα.

Ἀλλὰ λανθάνει σε ὅτι οὐκ ἂν δέξαιο τὰ βασιλέως χρήματα ἀντὶ τοῦ υἱοῦ ;

---

[1] ὅτι added by Stephanus.

---

[1] Callippides was regarded at this time and afterward as perhaps the most illustrious tragic actor of his time.

"But what of you, Socrates?" said Callias. "What are you proud of?"

Socrates drew up his face into a very solemn expression, and answered, "The trade of procurer."

After the rest had had a laugh at him, "Very well," said he, "you may laugh, but I know that I could make a lot of money if I cared to follow the trade."

"As for you," said Lycon, addressing Philip, "it is obvious that your pride is in your jesting."

"And my pride is better founded, I think," replied Philip, "than that of Callippides, the actor,[1] who is consumed with vanity because he can fill the seats with audiences that weep."

"Will you also not tell us, Lycon," said Antisthenes, "what it is that you take pride in?"

"Don't you all know," he answered, "that it is in my son here?"

"And as for him," said one, "it is plain that he is proud at having taken a prize."

At this Autolycus blushed and said, "No, indeed, not that."

All looked at him, delighted to hear him speak, and one asked, "What is it, then, Autolycus, that you are proud of?" and he answered, "My father," and with the words nestled close against him.

When Callias saw this, "Do you realize, Lycon," said he, "that you are the richest man in the world?"

"No, indeed," the other replied, "I certainly do not know that."

"Why, are you blind to the fact that you would not part with your son for the wealth of the Great King?"

Ἐπ' αὐτοφώρῳ εἴλημμαι, ἔφη, πλουσιώτατος,
ὡς ἔοικεν, ἀνθρώπων ὤν.

14 Σὺ δέ, ἔφη ὁ Νικήρατος, ὦ Ἑρμόγενες, ἐπὶ τίνι
μάλιστα ἀγάλλῃ ;

Καὶ ὅς, Ἐπὶ φίλων, ἔφη, ἀρετῇ καὶ δυνάμει, καὶ
ὅτι τοιοῦτοι ὄντες ἐμοῦ ἐπιμέλονται.

Ἐνταῦθα τοίνυν πάντες προσέβλεψαν αὐτῷ, καὶ
πολλοὶ ἅμα ἤροντο εἰ καὶ σφίσι δηλώσει αὐτούς,
ὁ δὲ εἶπεν ὅτι οὐ φθονήσει.

IV. Ἐκ τούτου ἔλεξεν ὁ Σωκράτης, Οὐκοῦν
λοιπὸν ἂν εἴη ἡμῖν ἃ ἕκαστος ὑπέσχετο ἀποδεικνύναι ὡς πολλοῦ ἄξιά ἐστιν.

Ἀκούοιτ' ἄν, ἔφη ὁ Καλλίας, ἐμοῦ πρῶτον.
ἐγὼ γὰρ ἐν τῷ χρόνῳ ᾧ ὑμῶν ἀκούω ἀπορούντων
τί τὸ δίκαιον, ἐν τούτῳ δικαιοτέρους τοὺς ἀνθρώπους ποιῶ.

Καὶ ὁ Σωκράτης, Πῶς, ὦ λῷστε ; ἔφη.

Διδοὺς νὴ Δί' ἀργύριον.

2 Καὶ ὁ Ἀντισθένης ἐπαναστὰς μάλα ἐλεγκτικῶς
αὐτὸν ἐπήρετο· Οἱ δὲ ἄνθρωποι, ὦ Καλλία, πότερον ἐν ταῖς ψυχαῖς ἢ ἐν τῷ βαλλαντίῳ τὸ δίκαιόν
σοι δοκοῦσιν ἔχειν ;

Ἐν ταῖς ψυχαῖς, ἔφη.

Κἄπειτα σὺ εἰς τὸ βαλλάντιον διδοὺς ἀργύριον
τὰς ψυχὰς δικαιοτέρας ποιεῖς ;

Μάλιστα.

Πῶς ;

Ὅτι διὰ τὸ εἰδέναι ὡς ἔστιν ὅτου πριάμενοι τὰ
ἐπιτήδεια ἕξουσιν οὐκ ἐθέλουσι κακουργοῦντες
κινδυνεύειν.

3 Ἦ καί σοι, ἔφη, ἀποδιδόασιν ὅ τι ἂν λάβωσι ;

"I am caught," was the answer, "red-handed; it does look as if I were the richest man in the world."

"What about you, Hermogenes?" said Niceratus. "What do you delight in most?"

"In the goodness and the power of my friends," he answered, "and in the fact that with all their excellence they have regard for me."

Thereupon all eyes were turned toward him, and many speaking at once asked him whether he would not discover these friends to them; and he answered that he would not be at all loath to do so.

IV. At this point Socrates said: "I suspect that it remains now for each one of us to prove that what he engaged himself to champion is of real worth."

"You may hear me first," said Callias. "While I listen to your philosophical discussions of what righteousness is, I am all the time actually rendering men more righteous."

"How so, my good friend?" asked Socrates.

"Why, by giving them money."

Then Antisthenes got up and in a very argumentative fashion interrogated him. "Where do you think men harbour their righteousness, Callias, in their souls or in their purses?"

"In their souls," he replied.

"So you make their souls more righteous by putting money into their purses?"

"I surely do."

"How?"

"Because they know that they have the wherewithal to buy the necessities of life, and so they are reluctant to expose themselves to the hazards of crime."

"And do they repay you," he asked, "the money that they get from you?"

Μὰ τὸν Δί', ἔφη, οὐ μὲν δή.

Τί δέ, ἀντὶ τοῦ ἀργυρίου χάριτας ;

Οὐ μὰ τὸν Δί', ἔφη, οὐδὲ τοῦτο, ἀλλ' ἔνιοι καὶ ἐχθίονως ἔχουσιν ἢ πρὶν λαβεῖν.

Θαυμαστά γ', ἔφη ὁ Ἀντισθένης ἅμα εἰσβλέπων ὡς ἐλέγχων αὐτόν, εἰ πρὸς μὲν τοὺς ἄλλους δύνασαι δικαίους ποιεῖν αὐτούς, πρὸς δὲ σαυτὸν οὔ.

4 Καὶ τί τοῦτ', ἔφη ὁ Καλλίας, θαυμαστόν; οὐ καὶ τέκτονάς τε καὶ οἰκοδόμους πολλοὺς ὁρᾷς οἳ ἄλλοις μὲν πολλοῖς ποιοῦσιν οἰκίας, ἑαυτοῖς δὲ οὐ δύνανται ποιῆσαι, ἀλλ' ἐν μισθωταῖς οἰκοῦσι ; καὶ ἀνάσχου μέντοι, ὦ σοφιστά, ἐλεγχόμενος.

5 Νὴ Δί', ἔφη ὁ Σωκράτης, ἀνεχέσθω μέντοι· ἐπεὶ καὶ οἱ μάντεις λέγονται δήπου ἄλλοις μὲν προαγορεύειν τὸ μέλλον, ἑαυτοῖς δὲ μὴ προορᾶν τὸ ἐπιόν.

Οὗτος μὲν δὴ ὁ λόγος ἐνταῦθα ἔληξεν.

6 Ἐκ τούτου δὲ ὁ Νικήρατος, Ἀκούοιτ' ἄν, ἔφη, καὶ ἐμοῦ ἃ ἔσεσθε βελτίονες ἢν ἐμοὶ συνῆτε. ἴστε γὰρ δήπου ὅτι Ὅμηρος ὁ σοφώτατος πεποίηκε σχεδὸν περὶ πάντων τῶν ἀνθρωπίνων. ὅστις ἂν οὖν ὑμῶν βούληται ἢ οἰκονομικὸς ἢ δημηγορικὸς ἢ στρατηγικὸς γενέσθαι ἢ ὅμοιος Ἀχιλλεῖ ἢ Αἴαντι ἢ Νέστορι ἢ Ὀδυσσεῖ, ἐμὲ θεραπευέτω. ἐγὼ γὰρ ταῦτα πάντα ἐπίσταμαι.

Ἦ καὶ βασιλεύειν, ἔφη ὁ Ἀντισθένης, ἐπίστασαι, ὅτι οἶσθα ἐπαινέσαντα αὐτὸν τὸν Ἀγαμέμνονα ὡς βασιλεύς τε εἴη ἀγαθὸς κρατερός τ' αἰχμητής ;

Iliad, iii. 179.

"Heavens, no!" he replied.

"Well, do they substitute thanks for money payment?"

"No, indeed, nor that either," he said. "On the contrary, some of them have an even greater dislike of me than before they got the money."

"It is remarkable," said Antisthenes, looking fixedly at him as though he had him in a corner, "that you can make them righteous toward others but not toward yourself."

"What is there remarkable about that?" asked Callias. "Do you not see plenty of carpenters, also, and architects that build houses for many another person but cannot do it for themselves, but live in rented houses? Come now, my captious friend, take your medicine and own that you are beaten."

"By all means," said Socrates, "let him do so. For even the soothsayers have the reputation, you know, of prophesying the future for others but of not being able to foresee their own fate."

Here the discussion of this point ended.

Then Niceratus remarked: "You may now hear me tell wherein you will be improved by associating with me. You know, doubtless, that the sage Homer has written about practically everything pertaining to man. Any one of you, therefore, who wishes to acquire the art of the householder, the political leader, or the general, or to become like Achilles or Ajax or Nestor or Odysseus, should seek my favour, for I understand all these things."

"Ha!" said Antisthenes; "do you understand how to play the king, too, knowing, as you do, that Homer praised Agamemnon [1] for being 'both goodly king and spearman strong'?"

Καὶ ναὶ μὰ Δί', ἔφη, ἔγωγε ὅτι ἁρματηλατοῦντα δεῖ ἐγγὺς μὲν τῆς στήλης κάμψαι,

αὐτὸν δὲ κλινθῆναι εὐξέστου ἐπὶ δίφρου
ἦκ' ἐπ' ἀριστερὰ τοῖν, ἀτὰρ τὸν δεξιὸν ἵππον
κένσαι ὁμοκλήσαντ' εἶξαί τέ οἱ ἡνία χερσί.

7 καὶ πρὸς τούτοις γε ἄλλο οἶδα, καὶ ὑμῖν αὐτίκα
μάλ' ἔξεστι πειρᾶσθαι. εἶπε γάρ που Ὅμηρος,
Ἐπὶ δὲ κρόμυον ποτῷ ὄψον. ἐὰν οὖν ἐνέγκῃ τις
κρόμμυον, αὐτίκα μάλα τοῦτό γε ὠφελημένοι
ἔσεσθε· ἥδιον γὰρ πίεσθε.

8 Καὶ ὁ Χαρμίδης εἶπεν· Ὦ ἄνδρες, ὁ Νικήρα
τος κρομμύων ὄζων ἐπιθυμεῖ οἴκαδε ἐλθεῖν, ἵν' ἡ
γυνὴ αὐτοῦ πιστεύῃ μηδὲ[1] διανοηθῆναι μηδένα ἂν
φιλῆσαι αὐτόν.

Νὴ Δί', ἔφη ὁ Σωκράτης, ἀλλ' ἄλλην που δόξαν
γελοίαν κίνδυνος ἡμῖν προσλαβεῖν. ὄψον μὲν γὰρ
δὴ ὄντως ἔοικεν εἶναι, ὡς κρόμυόν γε οὐ μόνον
σῖτον ἀλλὰ καὶ ποτὸν ἡδύνει. εἰ δὲ δὴ τοῦτο καὶ
μετὰ δεῖπνον τρωξόμεθα, ὅπως μὴ φήσει τις ἡμᾶς
πρὸς Καλλίαν ἐλθόντας ἡδυπαθεῖν.

9 Μηδαμῶς, ἔφη, ὦ Σώκρατες. εἰς μὲν γὰρ μά
χην ὁρμωμένῳ καλῶς ἔχει κρόμμυον ὑποτρώγειν,
ὥσπερ ἔνιοι τοὺς ἀλεκτρυόνας σκόροδα σιτίσαντες
συμβάλλουσιν· ἡμεῖς δὲ ἴσως βουλευόμεθα ὅπως
φιλήσομέν τινα μᾶλλον ἢ μαχούμεθα.

[1] μηδὲ Mehler ; μὴ MSS.

---

[1] Cf. *Iliad*, xxiii. 323, 334.   [2] *Iliad*, xxiii. 335–337.
[3] *Iliad*, xi. 630.

"Yes, indeed!" said he; "and I know also that in driving a chariot one must run close to the goal-post at the turn [1] and

'Himself lean lightly to the left within
The polished car, the right-hand trace-horse goad,
Urge him with shouts, and let him have the reins.' [2]

And beside this I know something else, which you may test immediately. For Homer says somewhere: 'An onion, too, a relish for the drink.' [3] Now if some one will bring an onion, you will receive this benefit, at any rate, without delay; for you will get more pleasure out of your drinking."

"Gentlemen," said Charmides, "Niceratus is intent on going home smelling of onions to make his wife believe that no one would even have conceived the thought of kissing him."

"Undoubtedly," said Socrates. "But we run the risk of getting a different sort of reputation, one that will bring us ridicule. For though the onion seems to be in the truest sense a relish, since it adds to our enjoyment not only of food, but also of drink, yet if we eat it not only with our dinner but after it as well, take care that some one does not say of us that on our visit to Callias we were merely indulging our appetites."

"Heaven forbid, Socrates!" was the reply. "I grant that when a man is setting out for battle, it is well for him to nibble an onion, just as some people give their game-cocks a feed of garlic before pitting them together in the ring; as for us, however, our plans perhaps look more to getting a kiss from some one than to fighting."

Καὶ οὗτος μὲν δὴ ὁ λόγος οὕτω πως ἐπαύσατο.

10 Ὁ δὲ Κριτόβουλος, Οὐκοῦν αὖ ἐγὼ λέξω, ἔφη,
ἐξ ὧν ἐπὶ τῷ κάλλει μέγα φρονῶ ;

Λέγε, ἔφασαν.

Εἰ μὲν τοίνυν μὴ καλός εἰμι, ὡς οἴομαι, ὑμεῖς
ἂν δικαίως ἀπάτης δίκην ὑπέχοιτε· οὐδενὸς γὰρ
ὁρκίζοντος ἀεὶ ὀμνύοντες καλόν μέ φατε εἶναι.
κἀγὼ μέντοι πιστεύω. καλοὺς γὰρ καὶ ἀγαθοὺς

11 ὑμᾶς ἄνδρας νομίζω. εἰ δ' εἰμί τε τῷ ὄντι καλὸς
καὶ ὑμεῖς τὰ αὐτὰ πρὸς ἐμὲ πάσχετε οἷάπερ ἐγὼ
πρὸς τὸν ἐμοὶ δοκοῦντα καλὸν εἶναι, ὄμνυμι
πάντας θεοὺς μὴ ἑλέσθαι ἂν τὴν βασιλέως ἀρχὴν

12 ἀντὶ τοῦ καλὸς εἶναι. νῦν γὰρ ἐγὼ Κλεινίαν
ἥδιον μὲν θεῶμαι ἢ τἆλλα πάντα τὰ ἐν ἀνθρώποις καλά· τυφλὸς δὲ τῶν ἄλλων ἁπάντων
μᾶλλον δεξαίμην ἂν εἶναι ἢ Κλεινίου[1] ἑνὸς ὄντος·
ἄχθομαι δὲ καὶ νυκτὶ καὶ ὕπνῳ ὅτι ἐκεῖνον οὐχ ὁρῶ,
ἡμέρᾳ δὲ καὶ ἡλίῳ τὴν μεγίστην χάριν οἶδα ὅτι μοι

13 Κλεινίαν ἀναφαίνουσιν. ἄξιόν γε μὴν ἡμῖν τοῖς
καλοῖς καὶ ἐπὶ τοῖσδε μέγα φρονεῖν, ὅτι τὸν μὲν
ἰσχυρὸν πονοῦντα δεῖ κτᾶσθαι τἀγαθὰ καὶ τὸν
ἀνδρεῖον κινδυνεύοντα, τὸν δέ γε σοφὸν λέγοντα·
ὁ δὲ καλὸς καὶ ἡσυχίαν ἔχων πάντ' ἂν διαπράξαι-

14 το. ἐγὼ γοῦν καίπερ εἰδὼς ὅτι χρήματα ἡδὺ
κτῆμα ἥδιον μὲν ἂν Κλεινίᾳ τὰ ὄντα διδοίην ἢ
ἕτερα παρ' ἄλλου λαμβάνοιμι, ἥδιον δ' ἂν δου-
λεύοιμι ἢ ἐλεύθερος εἴην, εἴ μου Κλεινίας ἄρχειν

---

[1] Κλεινίου Diogenes Laërtius ; ἐκείνου or κείνου or ἐκείνου
καὶ MSS.

---

[1] A young cousin of the brilliant and dissipated
Alcibiades.

That was about the way the discussion of this point ended.

Then Critobulus said: "Shall I take my turn now and tell you my grounds for taking pride in my handsomeness?"

"Do," they said.

"Well, then, if I am not handsome, as I think I am, you could fairly be sued for misrepresentation; for though no one asks you for an oath, you are always swearing that I am handsome. And indeed I believe you; for I consider you to be honourable men. But, on the other hand, if I really am handsome and you have the same feelings toward me that I have toward the one who is handsome in my eyes, I swear by all the gods that I would not take the kingdom of Persia in exchange for the possession of beauty. For as it is, I would rather gaze at Cleinias [1] than at all the other beautiful objects in the world. I would rather be blind to all things else than to Cleinias alone. I chafe at both night and sleep because then I do not see him; I feel the deepest gratitude to day and the sun because they reveal Cleinias to me. We handsome people have a right to be proud of this fact, too, that whereas the strong man must get the good things of his desire by toil, and the brave man by adventure, and the wise man by his eloquence, the handsome person can attain all his ends without doing anything. So far as I, at least, am concerned, although I realize that money is a delightful possession, I should take more delight in giving what I have to Cleinias than in adding to my possessions from another person's; and I should take more delight in being a slave than in being a free man, if Cleinias would deign to be my

ἐθέλοι. καὶ γὰρ πονοίην ἂν ῥᾷον ἐκείνῳ ἢ ἀνα-
παυοίμην, καὶ κινδυνεύοιμ' ἂν πρὸ ἐκείνου ἥδιον ἢ
15 ἀκίνδυνος ζῴην. ὥστε εἰ σύ, ὦ Καλλία, μέγα
φρονεῖς ὅτι δικαιοτέρους δύνασαι ποιεῖν, ἐγὼ πρὸς
πᾶσαν ἀρετὴν δικαιότερος σοῦ εἰμι ἄγειν ἀνθρώπους. διὰ γὰρ τὸ ἐμπνεῖν τι ἡμᾶς τοὺς καλοὺς τοῖς
ἐρωτικοῖς ἐλευθεριωτέρους μὲν αὐτοὺς ποιοῦμεν
εἰς χρήματα, φιλοπονωτέρους δὲ καὶ φιλοκαλωτέ-
ρους ἐν τοῖς κινδύνοις, καὶ μὴν αἰδημονεστέρους
τε καὶ ἐγκρατεστέρους, οἵ γε καὶ ὧν δέονται μά-
16 λιστα ταῦτ' αἰσχύνονται. μαίνονται δὲ καὶ οἱ μὴ
τοὺς καλοὺς στρατηγοὺς αἱρούμενοι. ἐγὼ γοῦν μετὰ
Κλεινίου κἂν διὰ πυρὸς ἰοίην· οἶδα δ' ὅτι καὶ ὑμεῖς
μετ' ἐμοῦ. ὥστε μηκέτι ἀπόρει, ὦ Σώκρατες, εἴ τι
17 τοὐμὸν κάλλος ἀνθρώπους ὠφελήσει. ἀλλ' οὐδὲ
μέντοι ταύτῃ γε ἀτιμαστέον τὸ κάλλος ὡς ταχὺ
παρακμάζον, ἐπεὶ ὥσπερ γε παῖς γίγνεται καλός,
οὕτω καὶ μειράκιον καὶ ἀνὴρ καὶ πρεσβύτης.
τεκμήριον δέ· θαλλοφόρους γὰρ τῇ Ἀθηνᾷ τοὺς
καλοὺς γέροντας ἐκλέγονται, ὡς συμπαρομαρ-
18 τοῦντος πάσῃ ἡλικίᾳ τοῦ κάλλους. εἰ δὲ ἡδὺ τὸ
παρ' ἑκόντων διαπράττεσθαι ὧν τις δέοιτο, εὖ οἶδ'
ὅτι καὶ νυνὶ θᾶττον ἂν ἐγὼ καὶ σιωπῶν πείσαιμι
τὸν παῖδα τόνδε καὶ τὴν παῖδα φιλῆσαί με ἢ σύ,
ὦ Σώκρατες, εἰ καὶ πάνυ πολλὰ καὶ σοφὰ λέγοις.
19 Τί τοῦτο; ἔφη ὁ Σωκράτης· ὡς γὰρ καὶ ἐμοῦ
καλλίων ὢν ταῦτα κομπάζεις;

master. For I should find it easier to toil for him than to rest, and it would be more delightful to risk my life for his sake than to live in safety. And so, Callias, if you are proud of your ability to make people more righteous, I have a better 'right' than you to claim that I can influence men toward every sort of virtue. For since we handsome men exert a certain inspiration upon the amorous, we make them more generous in money matters, more strenuous and heroic amid dangers, yes, and more modest and self-controlled also; for they feel abashed about the very things that they want most. Madness is in those people, too, who do not elect the handsome men as generals; I certainly would go through fire with Cleinias, and I know that you would, also, with me. Therefore, Socrates, do not puzzle any more over the question whether or not my beauty will be of any benefit to men. But more than that, beauty is not to be contemned on this ground, either, that it soon passes its prime; for just as we recognize beauty in a boy, so we do in a youth, a full-grown man, or an old man. Witness the fact that in selecting garland-bearers for Athena they choose beautiful old men, thus intimating that beauty attends every period of life. Furthermore, if it is pleasurable to attain one's desires with the good will of the giver, I know very well that at this very moment, without uttering a word, I could persuade this boy or this girl to give me a kiss sooner than you could, Socrates, no matter how long and profoundly you might argue."

"How now?" exclaimed Socrates. "You boast as though you actually thought yourself a handsomer man than me."

Νὴ Δί', ἔφη ὁ Κριτόβουλος, ἢ πάντων Σει-
ληνῶν τῶν ἐν τοῖς σατυρικοῖς αἴσχιστος ἂν εἴην.
Ὁ δὲ Σωκράτης καὶ ἐτύγχανε προσεμφερὴς
τούτοις ὤν.[1]

20 Ἄγε νυν, ἔφη ὁ Σωκράτης, ὅπως μεμνήσει δια-
κριθῆναι περὶ τοῦ κάλλους, ἐπειδὰν οἱ προκείμενοι
λόγοι περιέλθωσι. κρινάτω δ' ἡμᾶς μὴ Ἀλέξαν-
δρος ὁ Πριάμου, ἀλλ' αὐτοὶ οὗτοι οὕσπερ σὺ οἴει
ἐπιθυμεῖν σε φιλῆσαι.

21 Κλεινίᾳ δ', ἔφη, ὦ Σώκρατες, οὐκ ἂν ἐπι-
τρέψαις;
Καὶ ὃς εἶπεν, Οὐ γὰρ παύσῃ σὺ Κλεινίου
μεμνημένος;
Ἢν δὲ μὴ ὀνομάζω, ἧττόν τί με οἴει μεμνῆσθαι
αὐτοῦ; οὐκ οἶσθα ὅτι οὕτω σαφὲς ἔχω εἴδωλον
αὐτοῦ ἐν τῇ ψυχῇ ὡς εἰ πλαστικὸς ἢ ζωγραφικὸς
ἦν, οὐδὲν ἂν ἧττον ἐκ τοῦ εἰδώλου ἢ πρὸς αὐτὸν
ὁρῶν ὅμοιον αὐτῷ ἀπειργασάμην;

22 Καὶ ὁ Σωκράτης ὑπέλαβε, Τί δῆτα οὕτως ὅμοιον
εἴδωλον ἔχων πράγματά μοι παρέχεις ἄγεις τέ μ'[2]
αὐτὸν ὅπου ὄψει;
Ὅτι, ὦ Σώκρατες, ἡ μὲν αὐτοῦ ὄψις εὐφραίνειν
δύναται, ἡ δὲ τοῦ εἰδώλου τέρψιν μὲν οὐ παρέχει,
πόθον δὲ ἐμποιεῖ.

---

[1] Sauppe brackets this sentence as an interpolation.
[2] τέ μ'; τε MSS.

---

[1] This is regarded by some as a comment interpolated in the
text, though doubtless true enough. Plato (*Symp.* 215 A, B,
E; 216 C, D; 221 D, E; cf. 222 D) represents Alcibiades as
likening Socrates to the Sileni and particularly to the Satyr
Marsyas. Vase paintings and statues give an idea of the
Greek conception of their coarse features. They regularly

"Of course," was Critobulus's reply; "otherwise I should be the ugliest of all the Satyrs ever on the stage."

Now Socrates, as fortune would have it, really resembled these creatures.[1]

"Come, come," said Socrates; "see that you remember to enter a beauty contest with me when the discussion now under way has gone the rounds. And let our judges be not Alexander, Priam's son,[2] but these very persons whom you consider eager to give you a kiss."

"Would you not entrust the arbitrament to Cleinias, Socrates?"

"Aren't you ever going to get your mind off Cleinias?" was the rejoinder.

"If I refrain from mentioning his name, do you suppose that I shall have him any the less in mind? Do you not know that I have so clear an image of him in my heart that had I ability as a sculptor or a painter I could produce a likeness of him from this image that would be quite as close as if he were sitting for me in person?"

"Why do you annoy me, then," was Socrates' retort, "and keep taking me about to places where you can see him in person, if you possess so faithful an image of him?"

"Because, Socrates, the sight of him in person has the power to delight one, whereas the sight of the image does not give pleasure, but implants a craving for him."

formed the chorus in the Satyr-plays that were given in connection with tragedies.

[2] Usually called Paris; the judge of beauty when Hera, Athena, and Aphrodite appealed for a decision.

23 Καὶ ὁ Ἑρμογένης εἶπεν· Ἀλλ' ἐγώ, ὦ Σώκρατες,
οὐδὲ πρὸς σοῦ ποιῶ τὸ περιιδεῖν Κριτόβουλον
οὕτως ὑπὸ τοῦ ἔρωτος ἐκπλαγέντα.

Δοκεῖς γάρ, ἔφη ὁ Σωκράτης, ἐξ οὗ ἐμοὶ σύνεστιν
οὕτω διατεθῆναι αὐτόν ;

Ἀλλὰ πότε μήν ;

Οὐχ ὁρᾷς ὅτι τούτῳ μὲν παρὰ τὰ ὦτα ἄρτι
ἴουλος καθέρπει, Κλεινίᾳ δὲ πρὸς τὸ ὄπισθεν ἤδη
ἀναβαίνει ; οὗτος οὖν συμφοιτῶν εἰς ταὐτὰ διδα-
24 σκαλεῖα ἐκείνῳ τότε ἰσχυρῶς προσεκαύθη. ἃ δὴ
αἰσθόμενος ὁ πατὴρ παρέδωκέ μοι αὐτόν, εἴ τι
δυναίμην ὠφελῆσαι. καὶ μέντοι πολὺ βέλτιον
ἤδη ἔχει. πρόσθεν μὲν γὰρ ὥσπερ οἱ τὰς Γοργόνας
θεώμενοι λιθίνως ἔβλεπε πρὸς αὐτὸν καὶ οὐδαμοῦ[1]
ἀπῄει ἀπ' αὐτοῦ· νῦν δὲ δὴ εἶδον αὐτὸν καὶ σκαρδα-
25 μύξαντα. καίτοι νὴ τοὺς θεούς, ὦ ἄνδρες, δοκεῖ
μοί γ', ἔφη, ὡς ἐν ἡμῖν αὐτοῖς εἰρῆσθαι, οὗτος καὶ
πεφιληκέναι τὸν Κλεινίαν· οὗ ἔρωτος οὐδέν ἐστι
δεινότερον ὑπέκκαυμα. καὶ γὰρ ἄπληστον καὶ
26 ἐλπίδας τινὰς γλυκείας παρέχει.[2] οὗ ἕνεκα
ἀφεκτέον ἐγώ φημι εἶναι φιλημάτων ὡραίων τῷ
σωφρονεῖν δυνησομένῳ.

27 Καὶ ὁ Χαρμίδης εἶπεν· Ἀλλὰ τί δή ποτε, ὦ
Σώκρατες, ἡμᾶς μὲν οὕτω τοὺς φίλους μορμολύτ-

---

[1] λιθίνως οὐδαμοῦ MSS. (one omitting οὐδαμοῦ); λίθινος
(after the Aldine ed.) Sauppe ; οὐδαμοῦ L. Dindorf.

[2] The MSS. add here the following sentence (probably an
interpolation): Ἴσως δὲ καὶ διὰ τὸ μόνον πάντων ἔργων τὸ τοῖς
στόμασι [so Wyttenbach for σώμασι of the MSS.] συμψαύειν
ὁμώνυμον εἶναι τῷ ταῖς ψυχαῖς φιλεῖσθαι ἐντιμότερόν ἐστιν.
" Possibly the fact also that of all our acts that of touching
one another with the lips is the only one which goes by a
name equivocal with that expressing heartfelt affection causes

"For my part, Socrates," said Hermogenes, "I do not regard it as at all like you to countenance such a mad passion of love in Critobulus."

"What? Do you suppose," asked Socrates, "that this condition has arisen since he began associating with me?"

"If not, when did it?"

"Do you not notice that the soft down is just beginning to grow down in front of his ears, while that of Cleinias is already creeping up the nape of his neck? Well, then, this hot flame of his was kindled in the days when they used to go to school together. It was the discovery of this that caused his father to put him into my hands, in the hope that I might do him some good. And without question he is already much improved. For awhile ago he was like those who look at the Gorgons—he would gaze at Cleinias with a fixed and stony stare and would never leave his presence; but now I have seen him actually close his eyes in a wink. But to tell you the truth, gentlemen," he continued, "by Heaven! it does look to me—to speak confidentially—as if he had also kissed Cleinias; and there is nothing more terribly potent than this at kindling the fires of passion. For it is insatiable and holds out seductive hopes. For this reason I maintain that one who intends to possess the power of self-control must refrain from kissing those in the bloom of beauty."

"But why in the world, Socrates," Charmides now asked, "do you flourish your bogeys so to frighten

---

it to be held in more esteem than would otherwise be the case." The equivocation lies in the common Greek use of φιλεῖν = either *to love* or *to kiss*.

τῇ ἀπὸ τῶν καλῶν, αὐτὸν δὲ σέ, ἔφη, ἐγὼ εἶδον ναὶ
μὰ τὸν Ἀπόλλω, ὅτε παρὰ τῷ γραμματιστῇ ἐν
τῷ αὐτῷ βιβλίῳ ἀμφότεροι ἐμαστεύετέ τι, τὴν
κεφαλὴν πρὸς τῇ κεφαλῇ καὶ τὸν ὦμον γυμνὸν
πρὸς γυμνῷ τῷ Κριτοβούλου ὤμῳ ἔχοντα;

28   Καὶ ὁ Σωκράτης, Φεῦ, ἔφη, ταῦτ᾽ ἄρα, ἔφη, ἐγὼ
ὥσπερ ὑπὸ θηρίου τινὸς δεδηγμένος τόν τε ὦμον
πλεῖον ἢ πέντε ἡμέρας ὤδαξον καὶ ἐν τῇ καρδίᾳ
ὥσπερ κνῆσμά[1] τι ἐδόκουν ἔχειν. ἀλλὰ νῦν τοί
σοι, ἔφη, ὦ Κριτόβουλε, ἐναντίον τοσούτων
μαρτύρων προαγορεύω μὴ ἅπτεσθαί μου πρὶν ἂν
τὸ γένειον τῇ κεφαλῇ ὁμοίως κομήσῃς.

Καὶ οὗτοι μὲν δὴ οὕτως ἀναμὶξ ἔσκωψάν τε καὶ
ἐσπούδασαν.

29   Ὁ δὲ Καλλίας, Σὸν μέρος, ἔφη, λέγειν, ὦ Χαρμίδη, δι᾽ ὅ τι ἐπὶ πενίᾳ μέγα φρονεῖς.

Οὐκοῦν τόδε μέν, ἔφη, ὁμολογεῖται, κρεῖττον
εἶναι θαρρεῖν ἢ φοβεῖσθαι καὶ ἐλεύθερον εἶναι
μᾶλλον ἢ δουλεύειν καὶ θεραπεύεσθαι μᾶλλον ἢ
θεραπεύειν καὶ πιστεύεσθαι ὑπὸ τῆς πατρίδος
30   μᾶλλον ἢ ἀπιστεῖσθαι. ἐγὼ τοίνυν ἐν τῇδε τῇ
πόλει ὅτε μὲν πλούσιος ἦν πρῶτον μὲν ἐφοβούμην
μή τίς μου τὴν οἰκίαν διορύξας καὶ τὰ χρήματα
λάβοι καὶ αὐτόν τί με κακὸν ἐργάσαιτο· ἔπειτα
δὲ καὶ τοὺς συκοφάντας ἐθεράπευον, εἰδὼς ὅτι
παθεῖν μᾶλλον κακῶς ἱκανὸς εἴην ἢ ποιῆσαι ἐκείνους. καὶ γὰρ δὴ καὶ προσετάττετο μὲν ἀεί τί
μοι δαπανᾶν ὑπὸ τῆς πόλεως, ἀποδημῆσαι δὲ
31   οὐδαμοῖ[2] ἐξῆν. νῦν δ᾽ ἐπειδὴ τῶν ὑπερορίων

---

[1] Sauppe adopts Schneider's emendation κνίσμα.
[2] οὐδαμοῖ L. Dindorf; οὐδαμοῦ MSS.

us, your friends, away from the beauties, when, by Apollo! I have seen you yourself," he continued, "when the two of you were hunting down something in the same book-roll at the school, sitting head to head, with your nude shoulder pressing against Critobulus's nude shoulder?"

"Dear me!" exclaimed Socrates. "So that is what affected me like the bite of a wild animal! And for over five days my shoulder smarted and I felt as if I had something like a sting in my heart. But now, Critobulus," said he, "in the presence of all these witnesses I warn you not to lay a finger on me until you get as much hair on your chin as you have on your head."

Such was the mingled raillery and seriousness that these indulged in.

But Callias now remarked, "It is your turn, Charmides, to tell us why poverty makes you feel proud."

"Very well," said he. "So much, at least, every one admits, that assurance is preferable to fear, freedom to slavery, being the recipient of attention to being the giver of it, the confidence of one's country to its distrust. Now, as for my situation in our commonwealth, when I was rich, I was, to begin with, in dread of some one's digging through the wall of my house and not only getting my money but also doing me a mischief personally; in the next place, I knuckled down to the blackmailers, knowing well enough that my abilities lay more in the direction of suffering injury than of inflicting it on them. Then, too, I was for ever being ordered by the government to undergo some expenditure or other, and I never had the opportunity for foreign travel.

στέρομαι καὶ τὰ ἔγγεια οὐ καρποῦμαι καὶ τὰ ἐκ
τῆς οἰκίας πέπραται, ἡδέως μὲν καθεύδω ἐκτετα-
μένος, πιστὸς δὲ τῇ πόλει γεγένημαι, οὐκέτι δὲ
ἀπειλοῦμαι, ἀλλ' ἤδη ἀπειλῶ ἄλλοις, ὡς ἐλευθέρῳ τε ἔξεστί μοι καὶ ἀποδημεῖν καὶ ἐπιδημεῖν·
ὑπανίστανται δέ μοι ἤδη καὶ θάκων καὶ ὁδῶν
32 ἐξίστανται οἱ πλούσιοι. καὶ εἰμὶ νῦν μὲν τυράννῳ ἐοικώς, τότε δὲ σαφῶς δοῦλος ἦν· καὶ τότε
μὲν ἐγὼ φόρον ἀπέφερον τῷ δήμῳ, νῦν δὲ ἡ πόλις
τέλος φέρουσα τρέφει με. ἀλλὰ καὶ Σωκράτει,
ὅτε μὲν πλούσιος ἦν, ἐλοιδόρουν με ὅτι συνῆν, νῦν
δ' ἐπεὶ πένης γεγένημαι, οὐκέτι οὐδὲν μέλει οὐδενί. καὶ μὴν ὅτε μέν γε πολλὰ εἶχον, ἀεί τι ἀπέ-
βαλλον ἢ ὑπὸ τῆς πόλεως ἢ ὑπὸ τῆς τύχης· νῦν
δὲ ἀποβάλλω μὲν οὐδέν, οὐδὲ γὰρ ἔχω, ἀεὶ δέ τι
λήψεσθαι ἐλπίζω.

33 Οὐκοῦν, ἔφη ὁ Καλλίας, καὶ εὔχῃ μηδέποτε
πλουτεῖν, καὶ ἐάν τι ὄναρ ἀγαθὸν ἴδῃς, τοῖς
ἀποτροπαίοις θύεις;

Μὰ Δία τοῦτο μέντοι, ἔφη, ἐγὼ οὐ ποιῶ, ἀλλὰ
μάλα φιλοκινδύνως ὑπομένω, ἤν ποθέν τι ἐλπίζω
λήψεσθαι.

34 Ἀλλ' ἄγε δή, ἔφη ὁ Σωκράτης, σὺ αὖ λέγε ἡμῖν,
ὦ Ἀντίσθενες, πῶς οὕτω βραχέα ἔχων μέγα
φρονεῖς ἐπὶ πλούτῳ.

Ὅτι νομίζω, ὦ ἄνδρες, τοὺς ἀνθρώπους οὐκ ἐν
τῷ οἴκῳ τὸν πλοῦτον καὶ τὴν πενίαν ἔχειν ἀλλ' ἐν

---

[1] Charmides is apparently drawing the picture of the
independent voter or member of a jury.
[2] The poor relief.

Now, however, since I am stripped of my property over the border and get no income from the property in Attica, and my household effects have been sold, I stretch out and enjoy a sound sleep, I have gained the confidence of the state, I am no longer subjected to threats but do the threatening now myself; and I have the free man's privilege of going abroad or staying here at home as I please. People now actually rise from their seats in deference to me, and rich men obsequiously give me the right of way on the street.[1]   Now I am like a despot; then I was clearly a slave.   Then I paid a revenue to the body politic; now I live on the tribute [2] that the state pays to me. Moreover, people used to vilify me, when I was wealthy, for consorting with Socrates; but now that I have got poor, no one bothers his head about it any longer. Again, when my property was large, either the government or fate was continually making me throw some of it to the winds; but now, far from throwing anything away (for I possess nothing), I am always in expectation of acquiring something."

"Your prayers, also," said Callias, "are doubtless to the effect that you may never be rich; and if you ever have a fine dream you sacrifice, do you not, to the deities who avert disasters?"

"Oh, no!" was the reply; "I don't go so far as that; I hazard the danger with great heroism if I have any expectation of getting something from some one."

"Come, now, Antisthenes," said Socrates, "take your turn and tell us how it is that with such slender means you base your pride on wealth."

"Because, sirs, I conceive that people's wealth and poverty are to be found not in their real estate but

XENOPHON

35 ταῖς ψυχαῖς. ὁρῶ γὰρ πολλοὺς μὲν ἰδιώτας, οἳ
πάνυ πολλὰ ἔχοντες χρήματα οὕτω πένεσθαι
ἡγοῦνται ὥστε πάντα μὲν πόνον, πάντα δὲ κίνδυνον ὑποδύονται ἐφ' ᾧ πλείονα κτήσονται, οἶδα δὲ
καὶ ἀδελφούς, οἳ τὰ ἴσα λαχόντες ὁ μὲν αὐτῶν
τἀρκοῦντα ἔχει καὶ περιττεύοντα τῆς δαπάνης,
36 ὁ δὲ τοῦ παντὸς ἐνδεῖται· αἰσθάνομαι δὲ καὶ
τυράννους τινάς, οἳ οὕτω πεινῶσι χρημάτων ὥστε
ποιοῦσι πολὺ δεινότερα τῶν ἀπορωτάτων· δι'
ἔνδειαν γὰρ δήπου οἱ μὲν κλέπτουσιν, οἱ δὲ
τοιχωρυχοῦσιν, οἱ δὲ ἀνδραποδίζονται· τύραννοι
δ' εἰσί τινες οἳ ὅλους μὲν οἴκους ἀναιροῦσιν,
ἀθρόους δ' ἀποκτείνουσι, πολλάκις δὲ καὶ ὅλας
37 πόλεις χρημάτων ἕνεκα ἐξανδραποδίζονται. τούτους μὲν οὖν ἔγωγε καὶ πάνυ οἰκτίρω τῆς ἄγαν
χαλεπῆς νόσου. ὅμοια γάρ μοι δοκοῦσι πάσχειν
ὥσπερ εἴ τις πολλὰ ἔχων καὶ πολλὰ ἐσθίων
μηδέποτε ἐμπίπλαιτο. ἐγὼ δὲ οὕτω μὲν πολλὰ
ἔχω ὡς μόλις αὐτὰ καὶ ἐγὼ αὐτὸς εὑρίσκω· ὅμως
δὲ περίεστί μοι καὶ ἐσθίοντι ἄχρι τοῦ μὴ πεινῆν
ἀφικέσθαι καὶ πίνοντι μέχρι τοῦ μὴ διψῆν καὶ
ἀμφιέννυσθαι ὥστε ἔξω μὲν μηδὲν μᾶλλον Καλ-
38 λίου τούτου τοῦ πλουσιωτάτου ῥιγῶν· ἐπειδάν
γε μὴν ἐν τῇ οἰκίᾳ γένωμαι, πάνυ μὲν ἀλεεινοὶ
χιτῶνες οἱ τοῖχοί μοι δοκοῦσιν εἶναι, πάνυ δὲ
παχεῖαι ἐφεστρίδες οἱ ὄροφοι, στρωμνήν γε μὴν
οὕτως ἀρκοῦσαν ἔχω ὥστ' ἔργον μέ γ' ἐστὶ καὶ
ἀνεγεῖραι. ἢν δέ ποτε καὶ ἀφροδισιάσαι τὸ σῶμά
μου δεηθῇ, οὕτω μοι τὸ παρὸν ἀρκεῖ ὥστε αἷς ἂν

582

in their hearts. For I see many persons, not in office, who though possessors of large resources, yet look upon themselves as so poor that they bend their backs to any toil, any risk, if only they may increase their holdings; and again I know of brothers, with equal shares in their inheritance, where one of them has plenty, and more than enough to meet expenses, while the other is in utter want. Again, I am told of certain despots, also, who have such a greedy appetite for riches that they commit much more dreadful crimes than they who are afflicted with the direst poverty. For it is of course their want that makes some people steal, others commit burglary, others follow the slave trade; but there are some despots who destroy whole families, kill men wholesale, oftentimes enslave even entire cities, for the sake of money. As for such men, I pity them deeply for their malignant disease; for in my eyes their malady resembles that of a person who possessed abundance but though continually eating could never be satisfied. For my own part, my possessions are so great that I can hardly find them myself; yet I have enough so that I can eat until I reach a point where I no longer feel hungry and drink until I do not feel thirsty and have enough clothing so that when out of doors I do not feel the cold any more than my superlatively wealthy friend Callias here, and when I get into the house I look on my walls as exceedingly warm tunics and the roofs as exceptionally thick mantles; and the bedding that I own is so satisfactory that it is actually a hard task to get me awake in the morning. If I ever feel a natural desire for converse with women, I am so well satisfied with whatever chance puts in my way that those to whom

583

προσέλθω ὑπερασπάζονταί με διὰ τὸ μηδένα ἄλ-
39 λον αὐταῖς ἐθέλειν προσιέναι. καὶ πάντα τοίνυν
ταῦτα οὕτως ἡδέα μοι δοκεῖ εἶναι ὡς μᾶλλον μὲν
ἥδεσθαι ποιῶν ἕκαστα αὐτῶν οὐκ ἂν εὐξαίμην,
ἧττον δέ· οὕτω μοι δοκεῖ ἔνια αὐτῶν ἡδίω εἶναι
40 τοῦ συμφέροντος. πλείστου δ' ἄξιον κτῆμα ἐν τῷ
ἐμῷ πλούτῳ λογίζομαι εἶναι ἐκεῖνο, ὅτι εἴ μού τις
καὶ τὰ νῦν ὄντα παρέλοιτο, οὐδὲν οὕτως ὁρῶ
φαῦλον ἔργον ὁποῖον οὐκ ἀρκοῦσαν ἂν τροφὴν
41 ἐμοὶ παρέχοι. καὶ γὰρ ὅταν ἡδυπαθῆσαι βου-
ληθῶ, οὐκ ἐκ τῆς ἀγορᾶς τὰ τίμια ὠνοῦμαι, πολυ-
τελῆ γὰρ γίγνεται, ἀλλ' ἐκ τῆς ψυχῆς ταμιεύομαι.
καὶ πολὺ πλεῖον διαφέρει πρὸς ἡδονήν, ὅταν ἀνα-
μείνας τὸ δεηθῆναι προσφέρωμαι ἢ ὅταν τινὶ τῶν
τιμίων χρῶμαι, ὥσπερ καὶ νῦν τῷδε τῷ Θασίῳ
42 οἴνῳ ἐντυχὼν οὐ διψῶν πίνω αὐτόν. ἀλλὰ μὴν
καὶ πολὺ δικαιοτέρους γε εἰκὸς εἶναι τοὺς εὐτέλειαν μᾶλλον ἢ πολυχρηματίαν σκοποῦντας. οἷς
γὰρ μάλιστα τὰ παρόντα ἀρκεῖ ἥκιστα τῶν ἀλλο-
43 τρίων ὀρέγονται. ἄξιον δ' ἐννοῆσαι ὡς καὶ
ἐλευθερίους ὁ τοιοῦτος πλοῦτος παρέχεται. Σωκράτης τε γὰρ οὗτος, παρ' οὗ ἐγὼ τοῦτον
ἐκτησάμην, οὔτ' ἀριθμῷ οὔτε σταθμῷ ἐπήρκει
μοι, ἀλλ' ὁπόσον ἐδυνάμην φερεσθαι, τοσοῦτόν
μοι παρεδίδου· ἐγώ τε νῦν οὐδενὶ φθονῶ, ἀλλὰ
πᾶσι τοῖς φίλοις καὶ ἐπιδεικνύω τὴν ἀφθονίαν καὶ
μεταδίδωμι τῷ βουλομένῳ τοῦ ἐν τῇ ἐμῇ ψυχῇ

I make my addresses are more than glad to welcome me because they have no one else who wants to consort with them. In a word, all these items appeal to me as being so conducive to enjoyment that I could not pray for greater pleasure in performing any one of them, but could pray rather for less—so much more pleasurable do I regard some of them than is good for one. But the most valuable parcel of my wealth I reckon to be this, that even though some one were to rob me of what I now possess, I see no occupation so humble that it would not give me adequate fare. For whenever I feel an inclination to indulge my appetite, I do not buy fancy articles at the market (for they come high), but I draw on the store-house of my soul. And it goes a long way farther toward producing enjoyment when I take food only after awaiting the craving for it than when I partake of one of these fancy dishes, like this fine Thasian wine that fortune has put in my way and I am drinking without the promptings of thirst. Yes, and it is natural that those whose eyes are set on frugality should be more honest than those whose eyes are fixed on money-making. For those who are most contented with what they have are least likely to covet what belongs to others. And it is worth noting that wealth of this kind makes people generous, also. My friend Socrates here and I are examples. For Socrates, from whom I acquired this wealth of mine, did not come to my relief with limitation of number and weight, but made over to me all that I could carry. And as for me, I am now niggardly to no one, but both make an open display of my abundance to all my friends and share my spiritual wealth with any one of them that desires it.

44 πλούτου. καὶ μὴν καὶ τὸ ἁβρότατόν γε κτῆμα
τὴν σχολὴν ἀεὶ ὁρᾶτέ μοι παροῦσαν, ὥστε καὶ
θεᾶσθαι τὰ ἀξιοθέατα καὶ ἀκούειν τὰ ἀξιάκουστα
καὶ ὃ πλείστου ἐγὼ τιμῶμαι, Σωκράτει σχολάζων
συνδιημερεύειν. καὶ οὗτος δὲ οὐ τοὺς πλεῖστον
ἀριθμοῦντας χρυσίον θαυμάζει, ἀλλ᾽ οἳ ἂν αὐτῷ
ἀρέσκωσι τούτοις συνὼν διατελεῖ.

45 Οὗτος μὲν οὖν οὕτως εἶπεν. ὁ δὲ Καλλίας, Νὴ
τὴν Ἥραν, ἔφη, τά τε ἄλλα ζηλῶ σε τοῦ πλούτου
καὶ ὅτι οὔτε ἡ πόλις σοι ἐπιτάττουσα ὡς δούλῳ
χρῆται οὔτε οἱ ἄνθρωποι, ἢν μὴ δανείσῃς,
ὀργίζονται.

Ἀλλὰ μὰ Δί᾽, ἔφη ὁ Νικήρατος, μὴ ζήλου· ἐγὼ
γὰρ ἥξω παρ᾽ αὐτοῦ δανεισόμενος τὸ μηδενὸς
προσδεῖσθαι, οὕτω πεπαιδευμένος ὑπὸ Ὁμήρου
ἀριθμεῖν

ἑπτ᾽ ἀπύρους τρίποδας, δέκα δὲ χρυσοῖο τά-
λαντα,
αἴθωνας δὲ λέβητας ἐείκοσι, δώδεκα δ᾽ ἵππους,

σταθμῷ καὶ ἀριθμῷ, ὡς πλείστου πλούτου ἐπιθυμῶν οὐ παύομαι· ἐξ ὧν ἴσως καὶ φιλοχρηματώτε-
ρός τισι δοκῶ εἶναι.

Ἔνθα δὴ ἀνεγέλασαν ἅπαντες, νομίζοντες τὰ
ὄντα εἰρηκέναι αὐτόν.

46 Ἐκ τούτου εἶπέ τις· Σὸν ἔργον, ὦ Ἑρμόγενες,
λέγειν τε τοὺς φίλους οἵτινές εἰσι καὶ ἐπιδεικνύναι
ὡς μέγα τε δύνανται καὶ σοῦ ἐπιμέλονται, ἵνα
δοκῇς δικαίως ἐπ᾽ αὐτοῖς μέγα φρονεῖν.

---

[1] *Il.* ix, 122 f., 264 f.

But—most exquisite possession of all!—you observe that I always have leisure, with the result that I can go and see whatever is worth seeing, and hear whatever is worth hearing and—what I prize highest—pass the whole day, untroubled by business, in Socrates' company. Like me, he does not bestow his admiration on those who count the most gold, but spends his time with those who are congenial to him."

Such was the thesis maintained by Antisthenes. "So help me Hera," commented Callias, "among the numerous reasons I find for congratulating you on your wealth, one is that the government does not lay its commands on you and treat you as a slave, another is that people do not feel resentful at your not making them a loan."

" Do not be congratulating him," said Niceratus; "because I am about to go and get him to make me a loan—of his contentment with his lot, schooled as I am by Homer to count

‘ Sev'n pots unfired, ten talents' weight of gold,
    A score of gleaming cauldrons, chargers twelve,’[1]

weighing and calculating until I am never done with yearning for vast riches; as a result, some people perhaps regard me as just a bit fond of lucre."

A burst of laughter from the whole company greeted this admission; for they considered that he had told nothing more than the truth.

" Hermogenes, it devolves on you," some one now remarked, "to mention who your friends are and to demonstrate their great power and their solicitude for you, so that your pride in them may appear justified."

XENOPHON

47 Οὐκοῦν ὡς μὲν καὶ Ἕλληνες καὶ βάρβαροι τοὺς θεοὺς ἡγοῦνται πάντα εἰδέναι τά τε ὄντα καὶ τὰ μέλλοντα εὔδηλον. πᾶσαι γοῦν αἱ πόλεις καὶ πάντα τὰ ἔθνη διὰ μαντικῆς ἐπερωτῶσι τοὺς θεοὺς τί τε χρὴ καὶ τί οὐ χρὴ ποιεῖν. καὶ μὴν ὅτι νομίζομέν γε δύνασθαι αὐτοὺς καὶ εὖ καὶ κακῶς ποιεῖν καὶ τοῦτο σαφές. πάντες γοῦν αἰτοῦνται τοὺς θεοὺς τὰ μὲν φαῦλα ἀποτρέπειν,

48 τἀγαθὰ δὲ διδόναι. οὗτοι τοίνυν οἱ πάντα μὲν εἰδότες πάντα δὲ δυνάμενοι θεοὶ οὕτω μοι φίλοι εἰσὶν ὥστε διὰ τὸ ἐπιμελεῖσθαί μου οὔποτε λήθω αὐτοὺς οὔτε νυκτὸς οὔθ' ἡμέρας οὔθ' ὅποι ἂν ὁρμῶμαι οὔθ' ὅ τι ἂν μέλλω πράττειν. διὰ δὲ τὸ προειδέναι καὶ ὅ τι ἐξ ἑκάστου ἀποβήσεται σημαίνουσί μοι πέμποντες ἀγγέλους φήμας καὶ ἐνύπνια καὶ οἰωνοὺς ἅ τε δεῖ καὶ ἃ οὐ χρὴ ποιεῖν, οἷς ἐγὼ ὅταν μὲν πείθωμαι, οὐδέποτέ μοι μεταμέλει· ἤδη δέ ποτε καὶ ἀπιστήσας ἐκολάσθην.

49 Καὶ ὁ Σωκράτης εἶπεν· Ἀλλὰ τούτων μὲν οὐδὲν ἄπιστον. ἐκεῖνο μέντοι ἔγωγε ἡδέως ἂν πυθοίμην, πῶς αὐτοὺς θεραπεύων οὕτω φίλους ἔχεις.

Ναὶ μὰ τὸν Δί', ἔφη ὁ Ἑρμογένης, καὶ μάλα εὐτελῶς. ἐπαινῶ τε γὰρ αὐτοὺς οὐδὲν δαπανῶν, ὧν τε διδόασιν ἀεὶ αὖ παρέχομαι, εὐφημῶ τε ὅσα ἂν δύνωμαι καὶ ἐφ' οἷς ἂν αὐτοὺς μάρτυρας ποιήσωμαι ἑκὼν οὐδὲν ψεύδομαι.

Νὴ Δί', ἔφη ὁ Σωκράτης, εἰ ἄρα τοιοῦτος ὢν φίλους αὐτοὺς ἔχεις, καὶ οἱ θεοί, ὡς ἔοικε, καλοκἀγαθίᾳ ἥδονται.

Οὗτος μὲν δὴ ὁ λόγος οὕτως ἐσπουδαιολογήθη.

"Very well; in the first place, it is clear as day that both Greeks and barbarians believe that the gods know everything both present and to come; at any rate, all cities and all races ask the gods, by the diviner's art, for advice as to what to do and what to avoid. Second, it is likewise manifest that we consider them able to work us good or ill; at all events, every one prays the gods to avert evil and grant blessings. Well, these gods, omniscient and omnipotent, feel so friendly toward me that their watchfulness over me never lets me out of their ken night or day, no matter where I am going or what business I have in view. They know the results also that will follow any act; and so they send me as messengers omens of sounds, dreams, and birds, and thus indicate what I ought to do and what I ought not to do. And when I do their bidding, I never regret it; on the other hand, I have before now disregarded them and have been punished for it."

"None of these statements," said Socrates, "is incredible. But what I should like very much to know is how you serve them to keep them so friendly."

"A very economical service it is, I declare!" responded Hermogenes. "I sound their praises,— which costs nothing; I always restore them part of what they give me; I avoid profanity of speech as far as I can; and I never wittingly lie in matters wherein I have invoked them to be my witnesses."

"Truly," said Socrates, "if it is conduct like this that gives you their friendship, then the gods also, it would seem, take delight in nobility of soul!"

Such was the serious turn given to the discussion of this topic.

50 Ἐπειδὴ δὲ εἰς τὸν Φίλιππον ἧκον, ἠρώτων αὐτὸν
τί ὁρῶν ἐν τῇ γελωτοποιίᾳ μέγα ἐπ' αὐτῇ
φρονοίη.

Οὐ γὰρ ἄξιον, ἔφη, ὁπότε γε πάντες εἰδότες ὅτι
γελωτοποιός εἰμι, ὅταν μέν τι ἀγαθὸν ἔχωσι, πα-
ρακαλοῦσί με ἐπὶ ταῦτα προθύμως, ὅταν δέ τι
κακὸν λάβωσι, φεύγουσιν ἀμεταστρεπτί, φοβούμενοι μὴ καὶ ἄκοντες γελάσωσι ;

51 Καὶ ὁ Νικήρατος εἶπε· Νὴ Δία, σὺ τοίνυν
δικαίως μέγα φρονεῖς. ἐμοὶ γὰρ αὖ τῶν φίλων
οἱ μὲν εὖ πράττοντες ἐκποδὼν ἀπέρχονται, οἱ δ'
ἂν κακόν τι λάβωσι, γενεαλογοῦσι τὴν συγγένειαν
καὶ οὐδέποτέ μου ἀπολείπονται.

52 Εἶεν· σὺ δὲ δή, ἔφη ὁ Χαρμίδης, ὦ Συρακόσιε,
ἐπὶ τῷ μέγα φρονεῖς ; ἢ δῆλον ὅτι ἐπὶ τῷ παιδί ;

Μὰ τὸν Δί', ἔφη, οὐ μὲν δή· ἀλλὰ καὶ δέδοικα
περὶ αὐτοῦ ἰσχυρῶς. αἰσθάνομαι γάρ τινας
ἐπιβουλεύοντας διαφθεῖραι αὐτόν.

53 Καὶ ὁ Σωκράτης ἀκούσας, Ἡράκλεις, ἔφη, τί
τοσοῦτον νομίζοντες ἠδικῆσθαι ὑπὸ τοῦ σοῦ παιδὸς
ὥστε ἀποκτεῖναι αὐτὸν βούλεσθαι ;

Ἀλλ' οὗτοι, ἔφη, ἀποκτεῖναι βούλονται, ἀλλὰ
πεῖσαι αὐτὸν συγκαθεύδειν αὐτοῖς.

Σὺ δ', ὡς ἔοικας, εἰ τοῦτο γένοιτο, νομίζεις ἂν
διαφθαρῆναι αὐτόν ;

Ναὶ μὰ Δί', ἔφη, παντάπασί γε.

54 Οὐδ' αὐτὸς ἄρ', ἔφη, συγκαθεύδεις αὐτῷ ;

Νὴ Δί' ὅλας γε καὶ πάσας τὰς νύκτας.

When they got around to Philip, they asked him what he saw in the jester's profession to feel proud of it.

"Have I not a right to be proud," said he, "when all know that I am a jester, and so whenever they have a bit of good fortune, give me hearty invitations to come and join them, but when they suffer some reverse, run from me with never a glance behind, in dread that they may be forced to laugh in spite of themselves?"

"Your pride is abundantly justified," said Niceratus. "In my case, on the contrary, those friends who enjoy success keep out of my way, but those that run into some mishap reckon up their kinship to me on the family tree, and I can't get rid of them."

"No doubt," said Charmides; and then, turning to the Syracusan, "What is it that you are proud of? The boy, I suppose?"

"Quite the contrary," was the reply; "I am instead in extreme apprehension about him. For I understand that there are certain persons plotting his undoing."

On receiving this information, "Good Heavens!" exclaimed Socrates; "what wrong do they imagine your lad has done them that is grave enough to make them wish to kill him?"

Syr. "It is not killing him that they desire; oh, no! but to persuade him to sleep with them."

Soc. "Your belief, then, if I mistake not, is that if this happened, he would be undone?"

Syr. "Aye, utterly!"

Soc. "Do you not then sleep in his bed yourself?"

Syr. "Most certainly, all night and every night."

591

Νὴ τὴν ῞Ηραν, ἔφη ὁ Σωκράτης, εὐτύχημά γέ
σου μέγα τὸ τὸν χρῶτα τοιοῦτον φῦναι ἔχοντα
ὥστε μόνον μὴ διαφθείρειν τοὺς συγκαθεύδοντας.
ὥστε σοί γε εἰ μὴ ἐπ' ἄλλῳ ἀλλ' ἐπὶ τῷ χρωτὶ
ἄξιον μέγα φρονεῖν.

55 ᾽Αλλὰ μὰ Δί', ἔφη, οὐκ ἐπὶ τούτῳ μέγα φρονῶ.
᾽Αλλ' ἐπὶ τῷ μήν;
᾽Επὶ νὴ Δία τοῖς ἄφροσιν. οὗτοι γὰρ τὰ ἐμὰ
νευρόσπαστα θεώμενοι τρέφουσί με.

Ταῦτα γάρ, ἔφη ὁ Φίλιππος, καὶ πρῴην ἐγώ
σου ἤκουον εὐχομένου πρὸς τοὺς θεοὺς ὅπου ἂν ᾖς
διδόναι καρποῦ μὲν ἀφθονίαν, φρενῶν δὲ ἀφορίαν.

56 Εἶεν, ἔφη ὁ Καλλίας· σὺ δὲ δή, ὦ Σώκρατες,
τί ἔχεις εἰπεῖν ὡς ἄξιόν σοί ἐστι μέγα φρονεῖν ἐφ'
ᾗ εἶπας οὕτως ἀδόξῳ οὔσῃ τέχνῃ;

Καὶ ὃς εἶπεν· ῾Ομολογησώμεθα πρῶτον ποῖά
ἐστιν ἔργα τοῦ μαστροποῦ· καὶ ὅσα ἂν ἐρωτῶ μὴ
ὀκνεῖτε ἀποκρίνεσθαι, ἵνα εἰδῶμεν ὅσα ἂν συνομο-
λογῶμεν. καὶ ὑμῖν οὕτω δοκεῖ; ἔφη.

Πάνυ μὲν οὖν, ἔφασαν. ὡς δ' ἅπαξ εἶπον Πάνυ
μὲν οὖν, τοῦτο πάντες ἐκ τοῦ λοιποῦ ἀπεκρίναντο.

57 Οὐκοῦν ἀγαθοῦ μέν, ἔφη, ὑμῖν δοκεῖ μαστροποῦ
ἔργον εἶναι ἢν ἂν ᾖ ὃν ἂν μαστροπεύῃ ἀρέσκοντα
τοῦτον ἀποδεικνύναι οἷς ἂν συνῇ;

Πάνυ μὲν οὖν, ἔφασαν.

Οὐκοῦν ἓν μέν τί ἐστιν εἰς τὸ ἀρέσκειν ἐκ τοῦ
πρέπουσαν ἔχειν σχέσιν καὶ τριχῶν καὶ ἐσθῆτος;

Πάνυ μὲν οὖν, ἔφασαν.

58 Οὐκοῦν καὶ τόδε ἐπιστάμεθα ὅτι ἔστιν ἀνθρώπῳ

Soc. "Marry, you are in great luck to be formed of such flesh that you are unique in not corrupting those that sleep with you. And so you have a right to be proud of your flesh if of nothing else."

Syr. "And yet that is not the basis of my pride."

Soc. "What is, then?"

Syr. "Fools, in faith. They give me a livelihood by coming to view my marionettes."

"Ah!" ejaculated Philip; "that explains the prayer I heard you uttering the other day, that wherever you were the gods would grant you an abundant harvest of grain but a crop-failure of wits!"

"Good!" said Callias. "And now, Socrates, what can you advance in support of your pride in that disreputable profession that you mentioned?"

"Let us first," said he, "come to an understanding on the functions that belong to the procurer. Do not hesitate to answer all the questions I ask you, so that we may know our points of agreement. Is that your pleasure?" he asked.

"Certainly," was their reply; and when they had once started with "certainly," that was the regular answer they all made to his questions thereafter.

Soc. "Well, then, you consider it the function of a good procurer to render the man or the woman whom he is serving attractive to his or her associates?"

All. "Certainly."

Soc. "Now, one thing that contributes to rendering a person attractive is a comely arrangement of hair and clothing, is it not?"

All. "Certainly."

"This, also, we know, do we not, that it is in a

τοῖς αὐτοῖς ὄμμασι καὶ φιλικῶς καὶ ἐχθρῶς πρός τινας βλέπειν ;

Πάνυ μὲν οὖν.

Τί δέ ; τῇ αὐτῇ φωνῇ ἔστι καὶ αἰδημόνως καὶ θρασέως φθέγγεσθαι ;

Πάνυ μὲν οὖν.

Τί δέ ; λόγοι οὐκ εἰσὶ μέν τινες ἀπεχθανόμενοι, εἰσὶ δέ τινες οἳ πρὸς φιλίαν ἄγουσι ;

Πάνυ μὲν οὖν.

59   Οὐκοῦν τούτων ὁ ἀγαθὸς μαστροπὸς τὰ συμφέροντα εἰς τὸ ἀρέσκειν διδάσκοι ἄν ;

Πάνυ μὲν οὖν.

Ἀμείνων δ' ἂν εἴη, ἔφη, ὁ ἑνὶ δυνάμενος ἀρεστοὺς ποιεῖν ἢ ὅστις καὶ πολλοῖς ;

Ἐνταῦθα μέντοι ἐσχίσθησαν, καὶ οἱ μὲν εἶπον Δῆλον ὅτι ὅστις πλείστοις, οἱ δὲ Πάνυ μὲν οὖν.

60   Ὁ δ' εἰπὼν ὅτι καὶ τοῦτο ὁμολογεῖται ἔφη· Εἰ δέ τις καὶ ὅλῃ τῇ πόλει ἀρέσκοντας δύναιτο ἀποδεικνύναι, οὐχ οὗτος παντελῶς ἂν ἤδη ἀγαθὸς μαστροπὸς εἴη ;

Σαφῶς γε νὴ Δία, πάντες εἶπον.

Οὐκοῦν εἴ τις τοιούτους δύναιτο ἐξεργάζεσθαι ὧν προστατοίη, δικαίως ἂν μέγα φρονοίη ἐπὶ τῇ τέχνῃ καὶ δικαίως ἂν πολὺν μισθὸν λαμβάνοι ;

61   Ἐπεὶ δὲ καὶ ταῦτα πάντες συνωμολόγουν, Τοιοῦτος μέντοι, ἔφη, μοι δοκεῖ Ἀντισθένης εἶναι οὗτος.

man's power to use the one pair of eyes to express both friendship and hostility?"

"Certainly."

"And again, it is possible to speak both modestly and boldly with the same voice?"

"Certainly."

"Moreover, are there not words that create ill feeling and others that conduce to friendliness?"

"Certainly."

"Now the good procurer would teach only the words that tend to make one attractive, would he not?"

"Certainly."

"Which one would be the better?" he continued, "the one who could make people attractive to a single person or the one who could make them attractive to many?"

This question brought a division; some said, "Clearly the one who could make them attractive to a great many"; the others merely repeated, "Certainly."

Remarking that they were all of one mind on this point as on the others, he went on: "If a person could render people attractive to the entire community, would he not satisfy the requirements of the ideal procurer?"

"Indubitably," they all said.

"And so, if one could produce men of this type out of his clients, he would be entitled to feel proud of his profession and to receive a high remuneration, would he not?"

All agreeing on this point, too, he added, "Antisthenes here seems to me to be a man of just that sort."

Καὶ ὁ Ἀντισθένης, Ἐμοί, ἔφη, παραδίδως, ὦ Σώκρατες, τὴν τέχνην;

Ναὶ μὰ Δί', ἔφη. ὁρῶ γάρ σε καὶ τὴν ἀκόλουθον ταύτης πάνυ ἐξειργασμένον.

Τίνα ταύτην;

Τὴν προαγωγείαν, ἔφη.

62 Καὶ ὃς μάλα ἀχθεσθεὶς ἐπήρετο· Καὶ τί μοι σύνοισθα, ὦ Σώκρατες, τοιοῦτον εἰργασμένῳ;

Οἶδα μέν, ἔφη, σε Καλλίαν τουτονὶ προαγωγεύσαντα τῷ σοφῷ Προδίκῳ, ὅτε ἑώρας τοῦτον μὲν φιλοσοφίας ἐρῶντα, ἐκεῖνον δὲ χρημάτων δεόμενον· οἶδα δέ σε Ἱππίᾳ τῷ Ἠλείῳ, παρ' οὗ οὗτος καὶ τὸ μνημονικὸν ἔμαθεν· ἀφ' οὗ δὴ καὶ ἐρωτικώτερος γεγένηται διὰ τὸ ὅ τι ἂν καλὸν ἴδῃ μη-

63 δέποτε ἐπιλανθάνεσθαι. ἔναγχος δὲ δήπου καὶ πρὸς ἐμὲ ἐπαινῶν τὸν Ἡρακλεώτην ξένον ἐπεί με ἐποίησας ἐπιθυμεῖν αὐτοῦ, συνέστησάς μοι αὐτόν. καὶ χάριν μέντοι σοι ἔχω· πάνυ γὰρ καλὸς κἀγαθὸς δοκεῖ μοι εἶναι. Αἰσχύλον δὲ τὸν Φλειάσιον πρὸς ἐμὲ ἐπαινῶν καὶ ἐμὲ πρὸς ἐκεῖνον οὐχ οὕτω διέθηκας ὥστε διὰ τοὺς σοὺς λόγους ἐρῶντες ἐκυ-

64 νοδρομοῦμεν ἀλλήλους ζητοῦντες; ταῦτα οὖν ὁρῶν δυνάμενόν σε ποιεῖν ἀγαθὸν νομίζω προαγωγὸν εἶναι. ὁ γὰρ οἷός τε ὢν γιγνώσκειν τοὺς ὠφελίμους αὑτοῖς καὶ τούτους δυνάμενος ποιεῖν ἐπιθυμεῖν ἀλλήλων, οὗτος ἄν μοι δοκεῖ καὶ πόλεις δύνασθαι φίλας ποιεῖν καὶ γάμους ἐπιτηδείους

---

[1] Zeuxippus, the painter. Cf. Plato, *Protag.* 318 B, C.

[2] Nothing further seems to be known of this man.

Antisthenes asked, "Are you resigning your profession to me, Socrates?"

"Assuredly," was the answer. "For I see that you have brought to a high state of perfection the complementary trade."

"What is that?"

"The profession of go-between," he said.

Antisthenes was much incensed and asked, "What knowledge can you possibly have of my being guilty of such a thing as that?"

"I know several instances," he replied. "I know that you acted the part between Callias here and the scholar Prodicus, when you saw that Callias was in love with philosophy and that Prodicus wanted money. I know also that you did the same for Hippias, the Elean, from whom Callias got his memory system; and as a result, Callias has become more amorous than ever, because he finds it impossible to forget any beauty he sees. And just recently, you remember, you introduced the stranger from Heraclea[1] to me, after arousing my keen interest in him by your commendations. For this I am indeed grateful to you; for I look upon him as endowed with a truly noble nature. And did you not laud Aeschylus the Phleiasian[2] to me and me to him until you brought us to such a pass that in mutual yearning, excited by your words, we went coursing like hounds to find each other? It is the witnessing of your talent at achieving such a result that makes me judge you an excellent go-between. For the man who can recognize those who are fitted to be mutually helpful and can make them desire one another's acquaintance, that man, in my opinion, could also create friendship between cities and arrange

597

XENOPHON

συνάγειν, καὶ πολλοῦ ἂν ἄξιος εἶναι καὶ πόλεσι καὶ¹ ἰδιώταις φίλος καὶ σύμμαχος κεκτῆσθαι. σὺ δὲ ὡς κακῶς ἀκούσας ὅτι ἀγαθόν σε ἔφην προαγωγὸν εἶναι, ὠργίσθης.

Ἀλλὰ μὰ Δί, ἔφη, οὐ νῦν. ἐὰν γὰρ ταῦτα δύνωμαι, σεσαγμένος δὴ παντάπασι πλούτου τὴν ψυχὴν ἔσομαι.

Καὶ αὕτη μὲν δὴ ἡ περίοδος τῶν λόγων ἀπετελέσθη.

V. Ὁ δὲ Καλλίας ἔφη· Σὺ δὲ δή, ὦ Κριτόβουλε, εἰς τὸν περὶ τοῦ κάλλους ἀγῶνα πρὸς Σωκράτην οὐκ ἀνθίστασαι;

Νὴ Δί, ἔφη ὁ Σωκράτης, ἴσως γὰρ εὐδοκιμοῦντα τὸν μαστροπὸν παρὰ τοῖς κριταῖς ὁρᾷ.

2 Ἀλλ' ὅμως, ἔφη ὁ Κριτόβουλος, οὐκ ἀναδύομαι· ἀλλὰ δίδασκε, εἴ τι ἔχεις σοφόν, ὡς καλλίων εἶ ἐμοῦ. μόνον, ἔφη, τὸν λαμπτῆρα ἐγγύς τις² προσενεγκάτω.

Εἰς ἀνάκρισιν τοίνυν σε, ἔφη, πρῶτον τῆς δίκης καλοῦμαι· ἀλλ' ἀποκρίνου.

Σὺ δέ γε ἐρώτα.

3 Πότερον οὖν ἐν ἀνθρώπῳ μόνον νομίζεις τὸ καλὸν εἶναι ἢ καὶ ἐν ἄλλῳ τινί;

Ἐγὼ μὲν ναὶ μὰ Δί, ἔφη, καὶ ἐν ἵππῳ καὶ βοῖ καὶ ἐν ἀψύχοις πολλοῖς. οἶδα γοῦν οὖσαν καὶ ἀσπίδα καλὴν καὶ ξίφος καὶ δόρυ.

4 Καὶ πῶς, ἔφη, οἷόν τε ταῦτα μηδὲν ὅμοια ὄντα ἀλλήλοις πάντα καλὰ εἶναι;

---

¹ καὶ ἰδιώταις φίλος καὶ σύμμαχος Finckh; καὶ φίλοις καὶ συμμάχοις MSS.; Sauppe brackets καὶ συμμάχοις.
² ἐγγύς τις Mehler; ἐγγὺς MSS.

suitable marriages, and would be a very valuable acquisition as friend or ally for both states and individuals. But you got indignant, as if you had received an affront, when I said that you were a good go-between."

"But, indeed, that is all over now," he replied; "for with this power mine I shall find my soul chock-full of riches."

And so this round of discourse was brought to a close.

V. Callias now said, "Critobulus, are you going to refuse to enter the lists in the beauty contest with Socrates?"

"Undoubtedly!" said Socrates; "for probably he notices that the procurer stands high in the favour of the judges."

"But yet in spite of that," retorted Critobulus, "I do not shun the contest. So make your plea, if you can produce any profound reason, and prove that you are more handsome than I. Only," he added, "let some one bring the light close to him."

"The first step, then, in my suit," said Socrates, "is to summon you to the preliminary hearing; be so kind as to answer my questions."

"And you proceed to put them."

"Do you hold, then, that beauty is to be found only in man, or is it also in other objects?"

CRIT. "In faith, my opinion is that beauty is to be found quite as well in a horse or an ox or in any number of inanimate things. I know, at any rate, that a shield may be beautiful, or a sword, or a spear."

SOC. "How can it be that all these things are beautiful when they are entirely dissimilar?"

Ἦν νὴ Δί, ἔφη, πρὸς τὰ ἔργα ὧν ἕνεκα ἕκαστα κτώμεθα εὖ εἰργασμένα ᾖ ἢ εὖ πεφυκότα πρὸς ἃ ἂν δεώμεθα, καὶ ταῦτ᾽, ἔφη ὁ Κριτόβουλος, καλά.

5 Οἶσθα οὖν, ἔφη, ὀφθαλμῶν τίνος ἕνεκα δεόμεθα; Δῆλον, ἔφη, ὅτι τοῦ ὁρᾶν.

Οὕτω μὲν τοίνυν ἤδη οἱ ἐμοὶ ὀφθαλμοὶ καλλίονες ἂν τῶν σῶν εἴησαν.

Πῶς δή;

Ὅτι οἱ μὲν σοὶ τὸ κατ᾽ εὐθὺ μόνον ὁρῶσιν, οἱ δὲ ἐμοὶ καὶ τὸ ἐκ πλαγίου διὰ τὸ ἐπιπόλαιοι εἶναι.

Λέγεις σύ, ἔφη, καρκίνον εὐοφθαλμότατον εἶναι τῶν ζῴων;

Πάντως δήπου, ἔφη· ἐπεὶ καὶ πρὸς ἰσχὺν τοὺς ὀφθαλμοὺς ἄριστα πεφυκότας ἔχει.

6 Εἶεν, ἔφη, τῶν δὲ ῥινῶν ποτέρα καλλίων, ἡ σὴ ἢ ἡ ἐμή;

Ἐγὼ μέν, ἔφη, οἶμαι τὴν ἐμήν, εἴπερ γε τοῦ ὀσφραίνεσθαι ἕνεκεν ἐποίησαν ἡμῖν ῥῖνας οἱ θεοί. οἱ μὲν γὰρ σοὶ μυκτῆρες εἰς γῆν ὁρῶσιν, οἱ δὲ ἐμοὶ ἀναπέπτανται, ὥστε τὰς πάντοθεν ὀσμὰς προσδέχεσθαι.

Τὸ δὲ δὴ σιμὸν τῆς ῥινὸς πῶς τοῦ ὀρθοῦ κάλλιον;

Ὅτι, ἔφη, οὐκ ἀντιφράττει, ἀλλ᾽ ἐᾷ εὐθὺς τὰς ὄψεις ὁρᾶν ἃ ἂν βούλωνται· ἡ δὲ ὑψηλὴ ῥὶς ὥσπερ ἐπηρεάζουσα διατετείχικε τὰ ὄμματα.

---

[1] Critobulus, of course, gets into trouble by his poor definition of beauty. In the Greek the ensuing discussion is made plausible by the fact that throughout both disputants use only one word, καλός, which means not only *beautiful* or *handsome* but also *glorious, noble, excellent, fine;* and though

"Why, they are beautiful and fine,"[1] answered Critobulus, "if they are well made for the respective functions for which we obtain them, or if they are naturally well constituted to serve our needs."

Soc. "Do you know the reason why we need eyes?"

Crit. "Obviously to see with."

"In that case, it would appear without further ado that my eyes are finer ones than yours."

"How so?"

"Because, while yours see only straight ahead, mine, by bulging out as they do, see also to the sides."

Crit. "Do you mean to say that a crab is better equipped visually than any other creature?"

Soc. "Absolutely; for its eyes are also better set to insure strength."

Crit. "Well, let that pass; but whose nose is finer, yours or mine?"

Soc. "Mine, I consider, granting that Providence made us noses to smell with. For your nostrils look down toward the ground, but mine are wide open and turned outward so that I can catch scents from all about."

"But how do you make a snub nose handsomer than a straight one?"

Soc. "For the reason that it does not put a barricade between the eyes but allows them unobstructed vision of whatever they desire to see; whereas a high nose, as if in despite, has walled the eyes off one from the other."

starting with the first meaning it soon shifts to the last. The translator is compelled to use different terms for this in the two parts of the argument.

XENOPHON

7 Τοῦ γε μὴν στόματος, ἔφη ὁ Κριτόβουλος,
ὑφίεμαι. εἰ γὰρ τοῦ ἀποδάκνειν ἕνεκα πεποίηται,
πολὺ ἂν σὺ μεῖζον ἢ ἐγὼ ἀποδάκοις. διὰ δὲ τὸ
παχέα ἔχειν τὰ χείλη οὐκ οἴει καὶ μαλακώτερόν
σου ἔχειν τὸ φίλημα;
Ἔοικα, ἔφη, ἐγὼ κατὰ τὸν σὸν λόγον καὶ τῶν
ὄνων αἴσχιον τὸ στόμα ἔχειν. ἐκεῖνο δὲ οὐδὲν
τεκμήριον λογίζῃ ὡς ἐγὼ σοῦ καλλίων εἰμί, ὅτι
καὶ Ναΐδες θεαὶ οὖσαι τοὺς Σειληνοὺς ἐμοὶ
ὁμοιοτέρους τίκτουσιν ἢ σοί;
8 Καὶ ὁ Κριτόβουλος, Οὐκέτι, ἔφη, ἔχω πρὸς σὲ
ἀντιλέγειν, ἀλλὰ διαφερόντων, ἔφη, τὰς ψήφους,
ἵνα ὡς τάχιστα εἰδῶ ὅ τι με χρὴ παθεῖν ἢ ἀποτεῖσαι. μόνον, ἔφη, κρυφῇ φερόντων· δέδοικα γὰρ
τὸν σὸν καὶ Ἀντισθένους πλοῦτον μή με κατα-
δυναστεύσῃ.
9 Ἡ μὲν δὴ παῖς καὶ ὁ παῖς κρύφα ἀνέφερον. ὁ
δὲ Σωκράτης ἐν τούτῳ διέπραττε τόν τε λύχνον
ἀντιπροσενεγκεῖν τῷ Κριτοβούλῳ, ὡς μὴ ἐξ-
απατηθείησαν οἱ κριταί, καὶ τῷ νικήσαντι μὴ
ταινίας ἀλλὰ φιλήματα ἀναδήματα παρὰ τῶν
10 κριτῶν γενέσθαι. ἐπεὶ δὲ ἐξέπεσον αἱ ψῆφοι καὶ
ἐγένοντο πᾶσαι σὺν Κριτοβούλῳ, Παπαῖ, ἔφη ὁ
Σωκράτης, οὐχ ὅμοιον ἔοικε τὸ σὸν ἀργύριον, ὦ
Κριτόβουλε, τῷ Καλλίου εἶναι. τὸ μὲν γὰρ τούτου δικαιοτέρους ποιεῖ, τὸ δὲ σὸν ὥσπερ τὸ πλεῖστον διαφθείρειν ἱκανόν ἐστι καὶ δικαστὰς καὶ
κριτάς.
VI. Ἐκ δὲ τούτου οἱ μὲν τὰ νικητήρια φιλήματα ἀπολαμβάνειν τὸν Κριτόβουλον ἐκέλευον,

"As for the mouth," said Critobulus, "I concede that point. For if it is created for the purpose of biting off food, you could bite off a far bigger mouthful than I could. And don't you think that your kiss is also the more tender because you have thick lips?"

Soc. "According to your argument, it would seem that I have a mouth more ugly even than an ass's. But do you not reckon it a proof of my superior beauty that the River Nymphs, goddesses as they are, bear as their offspring the Seileni, who resemble me more closely than they do you?"

"I cannot argue any longer with you," answered Critobulus; "let them distribute the ballots, so that I may know without suspense what fine or punishment I must undergo. Only," he continued, "let the balloting be secret, for I am afraid that the 'wealth' you and Antisthenes possess will overmaster me."

So the maiden and the lad turned in the ballots secretly. While this was going on, Socrates saw to it that the light should be brought in front of Critobulus, so that the judges might not be misled, and stipulated that the prize given by the judges to crown the victor should be kisses and not ribbons. When the ballots were turned out of the urn and proved to be a unanimous verdict in favour of Critobulus, "Faugh!" exclaimed Socrates; "your money, Critobulus, does not appear to resemble Callias's. For his makes people more honest, while yours is about the most potent to corrupt men, whether members of a jury or judges of a contest."

VI. At this some of the company urged Critobulus to take his kisses, the meed of victory; others advised him to get the consent of the young

οἱ δὲ τὸν κύριον πείθειν, οἱ δὲ καὶ ἄλλα ἔσκωπτον.
ὁ δὲ Ἑρμογένης κἀνταῦθα ἐσιώπα. καὶ ὁ Σωκρά
της ὀνομάσας αὐτόν, Ἔχοις ἄν, ἔφη, ὦ Ἑρμό
γενες, εἰπεῖν ἡμῖν τί ἐστὶ παροινία ;

Καὶ ὃς ἀπεκρίνατο· Εἰ μὲν ὅ τι ἐστὶν ἐρωτᾷς,
οὐκ οἶδα· τὸ μέντοι μοι δοκοῦν εἴποιμ᾽ ἄν.

Ἀλλ᾽ ὃ δοκεῖ, τοῦτ᾽, ἔφη.

2 Τὸ τοίνυν παρ᾽ οἶνον λυπεῖν τοὺς συνόντας,
τοῦτ᾽ ἐγὼ κρίνω παροινίαν.

Οἶσθ᾽ οὖν, ἔφη, ὅτι καὶ σὺ νῦν ἡμᾶς λυπεῖς
σιωπῶν ;

Ἦ καὶ ὅταν λέγητ᾽ ; ἔφη.

Οὔκ, ἀλλ᾽ ὅταν διαλίπωμεν.

Ἦ οὖν λέληθέ σε ὅτι μεταξὺ τοῦ ὑμᾶς λέγειν
οὐδ᾽ ἂν τρίχα, μὴ ὅτι λόγον ἄν τις παρείρειε ;

3 Καὶ ὁ Σωκράτης, Ὦ Καλλία, ἔχοις ἄν τι, ἔφη,
ἀνδρὶ ἐλεγχομένῳ βοηθῆσαι ;

Ἔγωγ᾽, ἔφη. ὅταν γὰρ ὁ αὐλὸς φθέγγηται,
παντάπασι σιωπῶμεν.

Καὶ ὁ Ἑρμογένης, Ἦ οὖν βούλεσθε, ἔφη, ὥσπερ
Νικόστρατος ὁ ὑποκριτὴς τετράμετρα πρὸς τὸν
αὐλὸν κατέλεγεν, οὕτω καὶ ὑπὸ τὸν αὐλὸν ὑμῖν
διαλέγωμαι ;

4 Καὶ ὁ Σωκράτης, Πρὸς τῶν θεῶν, ἔφη, Ἑρμό
γενες, οὕτω ποίει. οἶμαι γάρ, ὥσπερ ἡ ᾠδὴ ἡδίων
πρὸς τὸν αὐλόν, οὕτω καὶ τοὺς σοὺς λόγους ἡδύ
νεσθαι ἄν τι ὑπὸ τῶν φθόγγων, ἄλλως τε καὶ εἰ
μορφάζοις ὥσπερ ἡ αὐλητρὶς καὶ σὺ πρὸς τὰ
λεγόμενα.

604

people's legal guardian; and others indulged in other badinage. But even then Hermogenes kept silent. And Socrates, calling him by name, inquired, "Hermogenes, could you define 'convivial unpleasantness' for us?"

"If you ask me what it actually is," he answered, "I do not know; but I am willing to tell you what I think it is."

Soc. "Very well, tell us that."

HERM. "My definition of 'convivial unpleasantness' is the annoying of one's companions at their drink."

Soc. "Well, do you realize that at the present moment you conform to the definition by annoying us with your taciturnity?"

HERM. "What! while you are talking?"

"No, but in the intervals."

"Why, don't you see that a person could not insert even a hair in the interstices of your talk, much less a word?"

"Callias," said Socrates, appealing to him, "could you come to the rescue of a man hard put to it for an answer?"

"Yes, indeed," said he: "we are absolutely quiet every time the flute is played."

Hermogenes retorted, "Is it your wish that I should converse with you to the accompaniment of a flute, the way the actor Nicostratus used to recite tetrameter verses?"

"In Heaven's name, do so, Hermogenes," urged Socrates. "For I believe that precisely as a song is more agreeable when accompanied on the flute, so your discourse would be embellished somewhat by the music, especially if you were to gesticulate and pose, like the flute-girl, to point your words."

5 Καὶ ὁ Καλλίας ἔφη· Ὅταν οὖν ὁ Ἀντισθένης ὅδ᾽ ἐλέγχῃ τινὰ ἐν τῷ συμποσίῳ, τί ἔσται τὸ αὔλημα ;

Καὶ ὁ Ἀντισθένης εἶπε, Τῷ μὲν ἐλεγχομένῳ οἶμαι ἄν, ἔφη, πρέπειν συριγμόν.

6 Τοιούτων δὲ λόγων ὄντων ὡς ἑώρα ὁ Συρακό-σιος τῶν μὲν αὑτοῦ ἐπιδειγμάτων ἀμελοῦντας, ἀλλήλοις δὲ ἡδομένους, φθονῶν τῷ Σωκράτει εἶπεν· Ἆρα σύ, ὦ Σώκρατες, ὁ φροντιστὴς ἐπικα-λούμενος ;

Οὔκουν κάλλιον, ἔφη, ἢ εἰ ἀφρόντιστος [1] ἐκα-λούμην ;

Εἰ μή γε ἐδόκεις τῶν μετεώρων φροντιστὴς εἶναι.

7 Οἶσθα οὖν, ἔφη ὁ Σωκράτης, μετεωρότερόν τι τῶν θεῶν ;

Ἀλλ᾽ οὐ μὰ Δί᾽, ἔφη, οὐ τούτων σε λέγουσιν ἐπιμελεῖσθαι, ἀλλὰ τῶν ἀνωφελεστάτων.

Οὔκουν καὶ οὕτως ἄν, ἔφη, θεῶν ἐπιμελοίμην· ἄνωθεν μέν γε ὕοντες ὠφελοῦσιν, ἄνωθεν δὲ φῶς παρέχουσιν. εἰ δὲ ψυχρὰ λέγω, σὺ αἴτιος, ἔφη, πράγματά μοι παρέχων.

8 Ταῦτα μέν, ἔφη, ἔα· ἀλλ᾽ εἰπέ μοι πόσους

---

[1] ἀφρόντιστος Capps ; ἀφρόντιστος MSS.

---

[1] The Syracusan uses the word applied by the Greeks first to astronomical and then to philosophical (especially onto-logical) inquiry, a word of reproach for radical thinkers that was used against Socrates in Aristophanes' burlesque, the

"What is the tune to be," asked Callias, "when Antisthenes here gets some one at the banquet cornered in an argument?"

"For the discomfited disputant," said Antisthenes, "I think the appropriate music would be a hissing."

The Syracusan, seeing that with such conversation going on the banqueters were paying no attention to his show, but were enjoying one another's company, said spitefully to Socrates, "Socrates, are you the one nick-named the 'Thinker'?"

"Well, isn't that preferable," he rejoined, "to being called the 'Thoughtless'?"

"Yes, if it were not that you are supposed to be a thinker on celestial subjects."[1]

"Do you know," asked Socrates, "anything more celestial than the gods?"

Syr. "No; but that is not what people say you are concerned with, but rather with the most unbeneficial things."

Soc. "Even granting the expression, it would still be the gods that are my concern; for (1) they cause rain *under* the heavens and so are *beneficial*,[2] and (2) they produce light, also *under* the heavens, and are thus again *beneficial*. If the pun is strained," he added, "you have only yourself to blame for it, for annoying me."

Syr. "Well, let that pass. But tell me the

Clouds, and later played a more serious part in Socrates' trial.

[2] This translation is an attempt to reproduce Socrates' bad logic and worse pun whereby he takes the Syracusan's expression ἀν-ωφελεστάτων (" most useless," " most unbeneficial ") and not only splits it in two, but changes the negative prefix into the adverb ἄνωθεν (" from above ").

ψύλλης πόδας ἐμοῦ ἀπέχεις. ταῦτα γάρ σέ φασι γεωμετρεῖν.

Καὶ ὁ Ἀντισθένης εἶπε· Σὺ μέντοι δεινὸς εἶ, ὦ Φίλιππε, εἰκάζειν· οὐ δοκεῖ σοι ὁ ἀνὴρ οὗτος λοιδορεῖσθαι βουλομένῳ ἐοικέναι ;

Ναὶ μὰ τὸν Δί', ἔφη, καὶ ἄλλοις γε πολλοῖς.

9 Ἀλλ' ὅμως, ἔφη ὁ Σωκράτης, σὺ αὐτὸν μὴ εἴκαζε, ἵνα μὴ καὶ σὺ λοιδορουμένῳ ἐοίκῃς.

Ἀλλ' εἴπερ γε τοῖς πᾶσι καλοῖς καὶ τοῖς βελτίστοις εἰκάζω αὐτόν, ἐπαινοῦντι μᾶλλον ἢ λοιδορουμένῳ δικαίως ἂν εἰκάζοι μέ τις.

Καὶ νῦν σύγε λοιδορουμένῳ ἔοικας, εἰ πάντ' αὐτοῦ βελτίω φὴς εἶναι.

10 Ἀλλὰ βούλει πονηροτέροις εἰκάζω αὐτόν ;

Μηδὲ πονηροτέροις.

Ἀλλὰ μηδενί ;

Μηδενὶ μηδὲν τοῦτον εἴκαζε.

Ἀλλ' οὐ μέντοι γε σιωπῶν οἶδα ὅπως ἄξια τοῦ δείπνου ἐργάσομαι.

Καὶ ῥᾳδίως γ', ἂν ἃ μὴ δεῖ λέγειν, ἔφη, σιωπᾷς. Αὕτη μὲν δὴ ἡ παροινία οὕτω κατεσβέσθη.

VII. Ἐκ τούτου δὲ τῶν ἄλλων οἱ μὲν ἐκέλευον

---

[1] In a famous passage in the *Clouds* (144 ff., cf. also 830 f.), published two years before this banquet was supposed to have been held, Aristophanes had represented Socrates and Chaerephon as measuring a flea's jump in terms of its own feet.

[2] *i. e.* (if the text is sound), by saying that he resembles the virtuous, thus assuming that he is not actually one of them.

distance between us in flea's feet; for people say that your geometry includes such measurements as that." [1]

At this Antisthenes said to Philip: "You are clever at hitting off a person's likeness; wouldn't you say that our friend here resembles one with a penchant for abuse?"

"Yes, indeed," came the answer; "and I see a resemblance in him to many another kind of person, too."

"Nevertheless," interposed Socrates, "do not draw the comparison, lest you take on a similar likeness to one stooping to abuse."

"But suppose I am likening him to all the upright, the very élite; then I should deserve to be compared to a eulogist, rather than to a detractor."

"Ah, you resemble the latter right now, for you are asserting that every one is better than he." [2]

"Would you have me compare him to those who excel him in villainy?"

"No, not those, either."

"What, to no one?"

"No; don't compare him to any one in any particular."

"But if I hold my peace, I do not understand how I am going to render services suitable to such a fine dinner."

"That is easily effected," said Socrates, "if you will be reticent on matters that should not be talked about."

Thus was quenched this bit of convivial unpleasantness.

VII.   Then some among the rest of the banqueters kept urging Philip to go on with his com-

εἰκάζειν, οἱ δὲ ἐκώλυον. θορύβου δὲ ὄντος ὁ Σωκράτης αὖ πάλιν εἶπεν· Ἆρα ἐπειδὴ πάντες
ἐπιθυμοῦμεν λέγειν, νῦν ἂν μάλιστα καὶ ἅμα
ᾄσαιμεν; καὶ εὐθὺς τοῦτ᾿ εἰπὼν ἦρχεν ᾠδῆς.
2 ἐπεὶ δ᾿ ἦσαν, εἰσεφέρετο τῇ ὀρχηστρίδι τροχὸς
τῶν κεραμικῶν, ἐφ᾿ οὗ ἔμελλε θαυματουργή-
σειν.

Ἔνθα δὴ εἶπεν ὁ Σωκράτης· Ὦ Συρακόσιε,
κινδυνεύω ἐγώ, ὥσπερ σὺ λέγεις, τῷ ὄντι φροντιστὴς εἶναι· νῦν γοῦν [1] σκοπῶ ὅπως ἂν ὁ μὲν παῖς
ὅδε ὁ σὸς καὶ ἡ παῖς ἥδε ὡς ῥᾷστα διάγοιεν, ἡμεῖς
δ᾿ ἂν μάλιστ᾿ ἂν εὐφραινοίμεθα θεώμενοι αὐτούς·
3 ὅπερ εὖ οἶδα ὅτι καὶ σὺ βούλει. δοκεῖ οὖν μοι τὸ
μὲν εἰς μαχαίρας κυβιστᾶν κινδύνου ἐπίδειγμα
εἶναι, ὃ συμποσίῳ οὐδὲν προσήκει. καὶ μὴν τό
γε ἐπὶ τοῦ τροχοῦ ἅμα περιδινουμένου γράφειν
τε καὶ ἀναγιγνώσκειν θαῦμα μὲν ἴσως τί ἐστιν,
ἡδονὴν δὲ οὐδὲ ταῦτα δύναμαι γνῶναι τίν᾿ ἂν
παράσχοι. οὐδὲ μὴν τό γε διαστρέφοντας τὰ
σώματα καὶ τροχοὺς μιμουμένους ἥδιον ἢ ἡσυχίαν
4 ἔχοντας τοὺς καλοὺς καὶ ὡραίους θεωρεῖν. καὶ
γὰρ δὴ οὐδὲ πάνυ τι σπάνιον τό γε θαυμασίοις
ἐντυχεῖν, εἴ τις τούτου δεῖται, ἀλλ᾿ ἔξεστιν αὐτίκα
μάλα τὰ παρόντα θαυμάζειν, τί ποτε ὁ μὲν λύχνος
διὰ τὸ λαμπρὰν φλόγα ἔχειν φῶς παρέχει, τὸ δὲ
χαλκεῖον λαμπρὸν ὂν φῶς μὲν οὐ ποιεῖ, ἐν αὑτῷ
δὲ ἄλλα ἐμφαινόμενα παρέχεται· καὶ πῶς τὸ μὲν
ἔλαιον ὑγρὸν ὂν αὔξει τὴν φλόγα, τὸ δὲ ὕδωρ, ὅτι
5 ὑγρόν ἐστι, κατασβέννυσι τὸ πῦρ. ἀλλὰ γὰρ καὶ
ταῦτα μὲν οὐκ εἰς ταὐτὸν τῷ οἴνῳ ἐπισπεύδει· εἰ

___
[1] γοῦν L. Dindorf; οὖν MSS.

parisons, while others opposed. As the clamour rose to some height, Socrates once more interposed, saying: "Since we all want to talk, would this not be a fine time to join in singing?" And with the words he began a song. When they had finished, a potter's wheel was brought in for the dancing-girl on which she intended performing some feats of jugglery.

This prompted Socrates to observe to the Syracusan: "Sir, it is quite probable that, to use your words, I am indeed a 'thinker'; at any rate, I am now considering how it might be possible for this lad of yours and this maid to exert as little effort as may be, and at the same time give us the greatest possible amount of pleasure in watching them,—this being your purpose, also, I am sure. Now, turning somersaults in among knives seems to me to be a dangerous exhibition, which is utterly out of place at a banquet. Also, to write or read aloud on a whirling potter's wheel may perhaps be something of a feat; yet I cannot conceive what pleasure even this can afford. Nor is it any more diverting to watch the young and beautiful going through bodily contortions and imitating hoops than to contemplate them in repose. For it is of course no rare event to meet with marvels, if that is what one's mind is set on. He may marvel at what he finds immediately at hand,—for instance, why the lamp gives light owing to its having a bright flame, while a bronze mirror, likewise bright, does not produce light but instead reflects other things that appear in it; or how it comes about that olive oil, though wet, makes the flame higher, while water, because it is wet, puts the fire out. However, these questions also fail to promote the same object that wine does;

δὲ ὀρχοῖντο πρὸς τὸν αὐλὸν σχήματα ἐν οἷς
Χάριτές τε καὶ Ὧραι καὶ Νύμφαι γράφονται,
πολὺ ἂν οἶμαι αὐτούς τε ῥᾷον διάγειν καὶ τὸ
συμπόσιον πολὺ ἐπιχαριτώτερον εἶναι.

Ὁ οὖν Συρακόσιος, Ἀλλὰ ναὶ μὰ τὸν Δί, ἔφη,
ὦ Σώκρατες, καλῶς τε λέγεις καὶ ἐγὼ εἰσάξω
θεάματα ἐφ' οἷς ὑμεῖς εὐφρανεῖσθε.

VIII. Ὁ μὲν δὴ Συρακόσιος ἐξελθὼν συνεκρο-
τεῖτο· ὁ δὲ Σωκράτης πάλιν αὖ καινοῦ λόγου
κατῆρχεν. Ἆρ', ἔφη, ὦ ἄνδρες, εἰκὸς ἡμᾶς
παρόντος δαίμονος μεγάλου καὶ τῷ μὲν χρόνῳ
ἰσήλικος τοῖς ἀειγενέσι θεοῖς, τῇ δὲ μορφῇ νεωτά-
του, καὶ μεγέθει μὲν πάντα ἐπέχοντος, ψυχῇ δ'
ἀνθρώπου ἱδρυμένου,[1] Ἔρωτος, μὴ ἀμνημονῆσαι,
ἄλλως τε καὶ ἐπειδὴ πάντες ἐσμὲν τοῦ θεοῦ τού-
2 του θιασῶται; ἐγώ τε γὰρ οὐκ ἔχω χρόνον εἰπεῖν
ἐν ᾧ οὐκ ἐρῶν τινος διατελῶ, Χαρμίδην δὲ τόνδε
οἶδα πολλοὺς μὲν ἐραστὰς κτησάμενον, ἔστι δὲ
ὧν καὶ αὐτὸν ἐπιθυμήσαντα· Κριτόβουλός γε μὴν
ἔτι[2] καὶ νῦν ἐρώμενος ὢν ἤδη[3] ἄλλων ἐπιθυμεῖ.
3 ἀλλὰ μὴν καὶ ὁ Νικήρατος, ὡς ἐγὼ ἀκούω, ἐρῶν
τῆς γυναικὸς ἀντερᾶται. Ἑρμογένη γε μὴν τίς
ἡμῶν οὐκ οἶδεν ὡς, ὅ τι ποτ' ἐστὶν ἡ καλοκἀγαθία,
τῷ ταύτης ἔρωτι κατατήκεται; οὐχ ὁρᾶτε ὡς
σπουδαῖαι μὲν αὐτοῦ αἱ ὀφρύες, ἀτρεμὲς δὲ τὸ
ὄμμα, μέτριοι δὲ οἱ λόγοι, πραεῖα δὲ ἡ φωνή,
ἱλαρὸν δὲ τὸ ἦθος; τοῖς δὲ σεμνοτάτοις θεοῖς
φίλοις χρώμενος οὐδὲν ἡμᾶς τοὺς ἀνθρώπους

[1] ἱδρυμένου Blomfield ; ἰσουμένου MSS.
[2] μὴν ἔτι Bornemann ; ἔτι μὴν MSS. (one omitting the
words) ; μὴν Sauppe.
[3] ἤδη καὶ Sauppe (with one MS.).

but if the young people were to have a flute accompaniment and dance figures depicting the Graces, the Horae,[1] and the Nymphs, I believe that they would be far less wearied themselves and that the charms of the banquet would be greatly enhanced."

"Upon my word, Socrates," replied the Syracusan, "you are quite right; and I will bring in a spectacle that will delight you."

VIII. So the Syracusan withdrew amid applause. Socrates now opened up another new topic for discussion. "Gentlemen," said he, "it is to be expected of us, is it not, when in the presence of a mighty deity that is coëval with the eternal gods, yet youngest of them all in appearance, in magnitude encompassing the universe, but enthroned in the heart of man,—I mean Love,—that we should not be unmindful of him, particularly in view of the fact that we are all of his following? For I cannot name a time when I was not in love with some one, and I know that Charmides here has gained many lovers and has in some instances felt the passion himself; and Critobulus, though even yet the object of love, is already beginning to feel this passion for others. Nay, Niceratus too, so I am told, is in love with his wife and finds his love reciprocated. And as for Hermogenes, who of us does not know that he is pining away with love for nobility of character, whatever that may be? Do you not observe how serious his brows are, how calm his gaze, how modest his words, how gentle his voice, how genial his demeanour? That though he enjoys the friendship of the most august gods, yet he does not disdain us

---

[1] Or, the Seasons. Or it may be used here in the Homeric sense of the maidens who kept the cloud gate of Heaven.

XENOPHON

ὑπερορᾷ; σὺ δὲ μόνος, ὦ Ἀντίσθενες, οὐδενὸς
ἐρᾷς;

4 Ναὶ μὰ τοὺς θεούς, εἶπεν ἐκεῖνος, καὶ σφόδρα
γε σοῦ.

Καὶ ὁ Σωκράτης ἐπισκώψας ὡς δὴ θρυπτόμενος
εἶπε· Μὴ νῦν μοι ἐν τῷ παρόντι ὄχλον πάρεχε·
ὡς γὰρ ὁρᾷς, ἄλλα πράττω.

5 Καὶ ὁ Ἀντισθένης ἔλεξεν· Ὡς σαφῶς μέντοι
σύ, μαστροπὲ σαυτοῦ, ἀεὶ τοιαῦτα ποιεῖς· τοτὲ
μὲν τὸ δαιμόνιον προφασιζόμενος οὐ διαλέγῃ μοι,
τοτὲ δ' ἄλλου του ἐφιέμενος.

6 Καὶ ὁ Σωκράτης ἔφη· Πρὸς τῶν θεῶν, ὦ Ἀντίσθενες, μόνον μὴ συγκόψῃς με· τὴν δ' ἄλλην
χαλεπότητα ἐγώ σου καὶ φέρω καὶ οἴσω φιλικῶς.
ἀλλὰ γάρ, ἔφη, τὸν μὲν σὸν ἔρωτα κρύπτωμεν,
ἐπειδὴ καὶ ἔστιν οὐ ψυχῆς ἀλλ' εὐμορφίας τῆς
7 ἐμῆς. ὅτι γε μὴν σύ, ὦ Καλλία, ἐρᾷς Αὐτολύκου
πᾶσα μὲν ἡ πόλις οἶδε, πολλοὺς δ' οἶμαι καὶ τῶν
ξένων. τούτου δ' αἴτιον τὸ πατέρων τε ὀνομα-
στῶν ἀμφοτέρους ὑμᾶς εἶναι καὶ αὐτοὺς ἐπιφανεῖς.
8 ἀεὶ μὲν οὖν ἔγωγε ἠγάμην τὴν σὴν φύσιν, νῦν δὲ
καὶ πολὺ μᾶλλον, ἐπεὶ ὁρῶ σε ἐρῶντα οὐχ ἁβρό-
τητι χλιδαινομένου οὐδὲ μαλακίᾳ θρυπτομένου,
ἀλλὰ πᾶσιν ἐπιδεικνυμένου ῥώμην τε καὶ καρτερίαν καὶ ἀνδρείαν καὶ σωφροσύνην. τὸ δὲ τοιούτων ἐπιθυμεῖν τεκμήριόν ἐστι καὶ τῆς τοῦ ἐραστοῦ
9 φύσεως. εἰ μὲν οὖν μία ἐστὶν Ἀφροδίτη ἢ διτταί,
Οὐρανία τε καὶ Πάνδημος, οὐκ οἶδα· καὶ γὰρ
Ζεὺς ὁ αὐτὸς δοκῶν εἶναι πολλὰς ἐπωνυμίας ἔχει·

---

[1] See footnote on page 494 of the *Defence*.

mortals? Are you the only person, Antisthenes, in love with no one?"

"No, by Heaven!" replied he; "I am madly in love—with you."

And Socrates, banteringly, pretending to be coquettish, said: "Don't pester me just now; I am engaged in other business, as you see."

"How transparent you are, sir procurer of your own charms," Antisthenes rejoined, "in always doing something like this; at one time you refuse me audience on the pretext of your divine sign,[1] at another time because you have some other purpose in mind."

"In Heaven's name, Antisthenes," implored Socrates, "only refrain from beating me; any other manifestation of your bad temper I am wont to endure, and shall continue to do so, in a friendly spirit. But," he went on, "let us keep your love a secret, because it is founded not on my spirit but on my physical beauty. But as for you, Callias, all the city knows that you are in love with Autolycus, and so, I think, do a great many men from abroad. The reason for this is the fact that you are both sons of distinguished fathers and are yourselves in the public eye. Now, I have always felt an admiration for your character, but at the present time I feel a much keener one, for I see that you are in love with a person who is not marked by dainty elegance nor wanton effeminacy, but shows to the world physical strength and stamina, virile courage and sobriety. Setting one's heart on such traits gives an insight into the lover's character. Now, whether there is one Aphrodite or two, 'Heavenly' and 'Vulgar,' I do not know; for even Zeus, though considered one and the same, yet has

ὅτι γε μέντοι χωρὶς ἑκατέρᾳ βωμοί τέ εἰσι καὶ νεὼ
καὶ θυσίαι τῇ μὲν Πανδήμῳ ῥᾳδιουργότεραι, τῇ δὲ
10 Οὐρανίᾳ ἁγνότεραι, οἶδα. εἰκάσαις δ' ἂν καὶ
τοὺς ἔρωτας τὴν μὲν Πάνδημον τῶν σωμάτων
ἐπιπέμπειν, τὴν δ' Οὐρανίαν τῆς ψυχῆς τε καὶ
τῆς φιλίας καὶ τῶν καλῶν ἔργων. ὑφ' οὗ δὴ καὶ
σύ, ὦ Καλλία, κατέχεσθαί μοι δοκεῖς ἔρωτος.
11 τεκμαίρομαι δὲ τῇ τοῦ ἐρωμένου καλοκἀγαθίᾳ καὶ
ὅτι σε ὁρῶ τὸν πατέρα αὐτοῦ παραλαμβάνοντα
εἰς τὰς πρὸς τοῦτον συνουσίας. οὐδὲν γὰρ τούτων ἐστὶν ἀπόκρυφον πατρὸς τῷ καλῷ τε κἀγαθῷ
ἐραστῇ.
12   Καὶ ὁ Ἑρμογένης εἶπε, Νὴ τὴν Ἥραν, ἔφη, ὦ
Σώκρατες, ἄλλα τέ σου πολλὰ ἄγαμαι καὶ ὅτι
νῦν ἅμα χαριζόμενος Καλλίᾳ καὶ παιδεύεις αὐτὸν
οἷόνπερ χρὴ εἶναι.
      Νὴ Δί', ἔφη· ὅπως δὲ καὶ ἔτι μᾶλλον εὐφραίνη-
ται, βούλομαι αὐτῷ μαρτυρῆσαι ὡς καὶ πολὺ
κρείττων ἐστὶν ὁ τῆς ψυχῆς ἢ ὁ τοῦ σώματος
13 ἔρως. ὅτι μὲν γὰρ δὴ ἄνευ φιλίας συνουσία οὐδεμία ἀξιόλογος πάντες ἐπιστάμεθα. φιλεῖν γε μὴν
τῶν μὲν τὸ ἦθος ἀγαμένων ἀνάγκη ἡδεῖα καὶ ἐθε-
λουσία καλεῖται· τῶν δὲ τοῦ σώματος ἐπιθυ-
μούντων πολλοὶ μὲν τοὺς τρόπους μέμφονται
14 καὶ μισοῦσι τῶν ἐρωμένων· ἢν δὲ καὶ ἀμφότερα
στέρξωσι, τὸ μὲν τῆς ὥρας ἄνθος ταχὺ δήπου
παρακμάζει, ἀπολείποντος δὲ τούτου ἀνάγκη καὶ
τὴν φιλίαν συναπομαραίνεσθαι, ἡ δὲ ψυχὴ
ὅσονπερ ἂν χρόνον ἴῃ ἐπὶ τὸ φρονιμώτερον καὶ
15 ἀξιεραστοτέρα γίγνεται.   καὶ μὴν ἐν μὲν τῇ τῆς

many by-names. I do know, however, that in the case of Aphrodite there are separate altars and temples for the two, and also rituals, those of the 'Vulgar' Aphrodite excelling in looseness, those of the 'Heavenly' in chastity. One might conjecture, also, that different types of love come from the different sources, carnal love from the 'Vulgar' Aphrodite, and from the 'Heavenly' spiritual love, love of friendship and of noble conduct. That is the sort of love, Callias, that seems to have you in its grip. I infer this from the noble nature of the one you love and because I see that you include his father in your meetings with him. For the virtuous lover does not make any of these matters a secret from the father of his beloved."

"Marry," quoth Hermogenes, "you arouse my admiration in numerous ways, Socrates, but now more than ever, because in the very act of flattering Callias you are in fact educating him to conform to the ideal."

"True," he replied; "and to add to his pleasure, I wish to bear testimony to him that spiritual love is far superior to carnal. For we all know that there is no converse worth the mention that does not comprise affection. Now affection on the part of those who feel admiration for character is commonly termed a pleasant and willing constraint; whereas many of those who have a merely physical concupiscence reprehend and detest the ways of those they love. But suppose they are satisfied on both scores; yet the bloom of youth soon passes its prime, and as this disappears, affection also inevitably fades away as fast; but the soul becomes more and more lovable the longer it progresses toward wisdom. Besides, in

μορφῆς χρήσει ἔνεστί τις καὶ κόρος, ὥστε ἅπερ
καὶ πρὸς τὰ σιτία διὰ πλησμονήν, ταῦτα ἀνάγκη
καὶ πρὸς τὰ παιδικὰ πάσχειν· ἡ δὲ τῆς ψυχῆς
φιλία διὰ τὸ ἁγνὴ εἶναι καὶ ἀκορεστοτέρα ἐστίν,
οὐ μέντοι, ὥς γ' ἄν τις οἰηθείη, διὰ τοῦτο καὶ ἀνεπ-
αφροδιτοτέρα, ἀλλὰ σαφῶς καὶ ἀποτελεῖται ἡ
εὐχὴ ἐν ᾗ αἰτούμεθα τὴν θεὸν ἐπαφρόδιτα καὶ
16 ἔπη καὶ ἔργα διδόναι. ὡς μὲν γὰρ ἄγαταί τε καὶ
φιλεῖ τὸν ἐρώμενον θάλλουσα μορφῇ τε ἐλευθερίᾳ
καὶ ἤθει αἰδήμονί τε καὶ γενναίῳ ψυχῇ εὐθὺς ἐν
τοῖς ἥλιξιν ἡγεμονική τε ἅμα καὶ φιλόφρων οὖσα
οὐδὲν ἐπιδεῖται λόγου· ὅτι δὲ εἰκὸς καὶ ὑπὸ τῶν
παιδικῶν τὸν τοιοῦτον ἐραστὴν ἀντιφιλεῖσθαι, καὶ
17 τοῦτο διδάξω. πρῶτον μὲν γὰρ τίς μισεῖν δύναιτ'
ἂν ὑφ' οὗ εἰδείη καλός τε κἀγαθὸς νομιζόμενος,
ἔπειτα δὲ ὁρῴη αὐτὸν τὰ τοῦ παιδὸς καλὰ μᾶλλον
ἢ τὰ ἑαυτοῦ ἡδέα σπουδάζοντα, πρὸς δὲ τούτοις
πιστεύοι μήτ' ἂν παρά τι ποιήσῃ μήτ' ἂν καμὼν
ἀμορφότερος γένηται, μειωθῆναι ἂν τὴν φιλίαν;
18 οἷς γε μὴν κοινὸν τὸ φιλεῖσθαι, πῶς οὐκ ἀνάγκη
τούτους ἡδέως μὲν προσορᾶν ἀλλήλους, εὐνοϊκῶς
δὲ διαλέγεσθαι, πιστεύειν δὲ καὶ πιστεύεσθαι,
καὶ προνοεῖν μὲν ἀλλήλων, συνήδεσθαι δὲ ἐπὶ ταῖς
καλαῖς πράξεσι, συνάχθεσθαι δὲ ἤν τι σφάλμα
προσπίπτῃ, τότε δ' εὐφραινομένους διατελεῖν ὅταν
ὑγιαίνοντες συνῶσιν, ἢν δὲ κάμῃ ὁπότεροσοῦν,
πολὺ συνεχεστέραν τὴν συνουσίαν ἔχειν, καὶ

618

the enjoyment of physical beauty there is a point of surfeit, so that one cannot help feeling toward his favourite the same effect that he gets toward food by gratification of the appetite. But affection for the soul, being pure, is also less liable to satiety, though it does not follow, as one might suppose, that it is also less rich in the graces of Aphrodite; on the contrary, our prayer that the goddess will bestow her grace on our words and deeds is manifestly answered. Now, no further argument is necessary to show that a soul verdant with the beauty of freeborn men and with a disposition that is reverent and noble, a soul that from the very first displays its leadership among its own fellows and is kindly withal, feels an admiration and an affection for the object of its love; but I will go on to prove the reasonableness of the position that such a lover will have his affection returned. First, who could feel dislike for one by whom he knew himself to be regarded as the pattern of nobleness, and, in the next place, saw that he made his favourite's honour of more account than his own pleasure, and beside this felt assured that this affection would not be lessened under any circumstances, no matter whether he suffered some reverse or lost his comeliness through the ravages of illness? Moreover, must not those who enjoy a mutual affection unavoidably take pleasure in looking into each other's faces, converse in amity, and trust and be trusted, and not only take thought each for the other but also take a common joy in prosperity and feel a common distress if some ill fortune befall, and live in happiness when their society is attended by sound health, but be much more constantly together if one or the other become ill, and be even more solicitous, each for the other,

ἀπόντων ἔτι μᾶλλον ἢ παρόντων ἐπιμελεῖσθαι;
οὐ ταῦτα πάντα ἐπαφρόδιτα; διά γέ τοι τὰ
τοιαῦτα ἔργα ἅμα ἐρῶντες τῆς φιλίας καὶ χρώ-
19 μενοι αὐτῇ εἰς γῆρας διατελοῦσι. τὸν δὲ ἐκ τοῦ
σώματος κρεμάμενον διὰ τί ἀντιφιλήσειεν ἂν ὁ
παῖς; πότερον ὅτι ἑαυτῷ μὲν νέμει ὧν ἐπιθυμεῖ,
τῷ δὲ παιδὶ τὰ ἐπονειδιστότατα; ἢ διότι ἃ σπεύ-
δει πράττειν παρὰ τῶν παιδικῶν, εἴργει μάλιστα
20 τοὺς οἰκείους ἀπὸ τούτων; καὶ μὴν ὅτι γε οὐ
βιάζεται, ἀλλὰ πείθει, διὰ τοῦτο μᾶλλον μιση-
τέος. ὁ μὲν γὰρ βιαζόμενος ἑαυτὸν πονηρὸν ἀποδεικνύει, ὁ δὲ πείθων τὴν τοῦ ἀναπειθομένου
21 ψυχὴν διαφθείρει. ἀλλὰ μὴν καὶ ὁ χρημάτων
γε ἀπεμπολῶν τὴν ὥραν τί μᾶλλον στέρξει τὸν
πριάμενον ἢ ὁ ἐν ἀγορᾷ πωλῶν καὶ ἀποδιδόμενος;
οὐ μὴν ὅτι γε ὡραῖος ἀώρῳ, οὐδὲ ὅτι γε καλὸς
οὐκέτι καλῷ καὶ ἐρῶντι οὐκ ἐρῶν ὁμιλεῖ φιλήσει
αὐτόν. οὐδὲ γὰρ ὁ παῖς τῷ ἀνδρὶ ὥσπερ γυνὴ
κοινωνεῖ τῶν ἐν τοῖς ἀφροδισίοις εὐφροσυνῶν,
ἀλλὰ νήφων μεθύοντα ὑπὸ τῆς Ἀφροδίτης θεᾶται.
22 ἐξ ὧν οὐδὲν θαυμαστὸν εἰ καὶ τὸ ὑπερορᾶν ἐγγίγνεται αὐτῷ τοῦ ἐραστοῦ. καὶ σκοπῶν δ' ἄν τις
εὕροι ἐκ μὲν τῶν διὰ τοὺς τρόπους φιλουμένων
οὐδὲν χαλεπὸν γεγενημένον, ἐκ δὲ τῆς ἀναιδοῦς
23 ὁμιλίας πολλὰ ἤδη καὶ ἀνόσια πεπραγμένα. ὡς
δὲ καὶ ἀνελεύθερος ἡ συνουσία τῷ τὸ σῶμα μᾶλλον ἢ τῷ τὴν ψυχὴν ἀγαπῶντι, νῦν τοῦτο δηλώ-

when absent than when present? Are not all these things marked by Aphrodite's grace? It is by conducting themselves thus that men continue mutually to love friendship and enjoy it clear down to old age. But what is there to induce a favourite to make a return of affection to a lover who bases his feeling solely on the flesh? Would it be the consideration that the lover allots to himself the joys he desires but gives the favourite only what excites the deepest contempt? Or that he conceals, as best he can, from the favourite's relatives the ends that he is bent on attaining? As for his using entreaty rather than coercion, that is all the stronger reason for detestation. For any one who applies force merely discovers his rascality, but he who uses persuasion corrupts the soul of the one upon whom he prevails. Once more, how will he who traffics in his beauty feel greater affection toward the buyer than he who puts his produce up for sale and disposes of it in the open market? For assuredly he will not be moved to affection because he is a youthful companion to one who is not youthful, or because he is handsome when the other is no longer so, or because he is untouched by passion when the other is in its sway. For a youth does not share in the pleasure of the intercourse as a woman does, but looks on, sober, at another in love's intoxication. Consequently, it need not excite any surprise if contempt for the lover is engendered in him. If one looked into the matter, also, he would descry no ill effect when people are loved for their personality, but that many shocking results have come from companionship lost to shame. I will now go on to show also that the union is servile when one's regard is for the body

XENOPHON

σω. ὁ μὲν γὰρ παιδεύων λέγειν τε ἃ δεῖ καὶ
πράττειν δικαίως ἂν ὥσπερ Χείρων καὶ Φοῖνιξ
ὑπ᾽ Ἀχιλλέως τιμῷτο, ὁ δὲ τοῦ σώματος ὀρεγό-
μενος εἰκότως ἂν ὥσπερ πτωχὸς περιέποιτο. ἀεὶ
γάρ τοι προσαιτῶν καὶ προσδεόμενος ἢ φιλήματος

24 ἢ ἄλλου τινὸς ψηλαφήματος παρακολουθεῖ. εἰ
δὲ λαμυρώτερον λέγω, μὴ θαυμάζετε· ὅ τε γὰρ
οἶνος συνεπαίρει καὶ ὁ ἀεὶ σύνοικος ἐμοὶ ἔρως κεν-
τρίζει εἰς τὸν ἀντίπαλον ἔρωτα αὐτῷ παρρησιά-

25 ζεσθαι. καὶ γὰρ δὴ δοκεῖ μοι ὁ μὲν τῷ εἴδει τὸν
νοῦν προσέχων μεμισθωμένῳ χώρῳ ἐοικέναι. οὐ
γὰρ ὅπως πλείονος ἄξιος γένηται ἐπιμελεῖται,
ἀλλ᾽ ὅπως αὐτὸς ὅτι πλεῖστα ὡραῖα καρπώσεται.
ὁ δὲ τῆς φιλίας ἐφιέμενος μᾶλλον ἔοικε τῷ τὸν
οἰκεῖον ἀγρὸν κεκτημένῳ· πάντοθεν γοῦν φέρων
ὅ τι ἂν δύνηται πλείονος ἄξιον ποιεῖ τὸν ἐρώμενον.

26 καὶ μὴν καὶ τῶν παιδικῶν ὃς μὲν ἂν εἰδῇ ὅτι ὁ
τοῦ εἴδους ἐπαρκῶν ἄρξει τοῦ ἐραστοῦ, εἰκὸς
αὐτὸν τἆλλα ῥᾳδιουργεῖν· ὃς δ᾽ ἂν γιγνώσκῃ ὅτι
ἂν μὴ καλὸς κἀγαθὸς ᾖ, οὐ καθέξει τὴν φιλίαν,
τοῦτον προσήκει μᾶλλον ἀρετῆς ἐπιμελεῖσθαι.

27 μέγιστον δ᾽ ἀγαθὸν τῷ ὀρεγομένῳ ἐκ παιδικῶν
φίλον ἀγαθὸν ποιήσασθαι ὅτι ἀνάγκη καὶ αὐτὸν
ἀσκεῖν ἀρετήν. οὐ γὰρ οἷόν τε πονηρὰ αὐτὸν
ποιοῦντα ἀγαθὸν τὸν συνόντα ἀποδεῖξαι, οὐδέ γε
ἀναισχυντίαν καὶ ἀκρασίαν παρεχόμενον ἐγκρατῆ

28 καὶ αἰδούμενον τὸν ἐρώμενον ποιῆσαι. ἐπιθυμῶ
δέ σοι, ἔφη, ὦ Καλλία, καὶ μυθολογῆσαι ὡς οὐ
μόνον ἄνθρωποι ἀλλὰ καὶ θεοὶ καὶ ἥρωες τὴν τῆς

---

[1] Cheiron, the just Centaur, and Phoenix, an exile who was
received into the household of Peleus; both were tutors to
the young Achilles.

rather than when it is for the soul. For he who
inculcates right speech and conduct would merit the
honour given by Achilles to Cheiron and Phoenix;[1]
but the man who lusts only after the flesh would
with good reason be treated like a mendicant; for
he is always dogging the footsteps of his favourite,
begging and beseeching the favour of one more kiss
or some other caress. Do not be surprised at my
plain speaking; the wine helps to incite me, and
the kind of love that ever dwells with me spurs me
on to say what I think about its opposite. For, to
my way of thinking, the man whose attention is
attracted only by his beloved's appearance is like
one who has rented a farm; his aim is not to increase
its value but to gain from it as much of a harvest as
he can for himself. On the other hand, the man
whose goal is friendship is more like one possessing
a farm of his own; at any rate he utilizes all sources
to enhance his loved one's worth. Furthermore, the
favourite who realizes that he who lavishes physical
charms will be the lover's sovereign will in all likeli-
hood be loose in his general conduct; but the one
who feels that he cannot keep his lover faithful
without nobility of character will more probably give
heed to virtue. But the greatest blessing that
befalls the man who yearns to render his favourite
a good friend is the necessity of himself making
virtue his habitual practice. For one cannot produce
goodness in his companion while his own conduct
is evil, nor can he himself exhibit shamelessness and
incontinence and at the same time render his beloved
self-controlled and reverent. My heart is set on
showing you, Callias, on the basis of olden tales,
also, that not only humankind but also gods and

ψυχῆς φιλίαν περὶ πλείονος ἢ τὴν τοῦ σώματος
29 χρῆσιν ποιοῦνται. Ζεύς τε γὰρ ὅσων μὲν θνητῶν
οὐσῶν μορφῆς ἠράσθη, συγγενόμενος εἴα αὐτὰς
θνητὰς εἶναι· ὅσων δὲ ψυχαῖς ἀγασθείη, ἀθανά-
τους τούτους ἐποίει· ὧν Ἡρακλῆς μὲν καὶ Διόσ-
30 κοροί εἰσι, λέγονται δὲ καὶ ἄλλοι· καὶ ἐγὼ δέ
φημι καὶ Γανυμήδην οὐ σώματος ἀλλὰ ψυχῆς
ἔνεκα ὑπὸ Διὸς εἰς Ὄλυμπον ἀνενεχθῆναι. μαρτυρεῖ δὲ καὶ τοὔνομα αὐτοῦ· ἔστι μὲν γὰρ δήπου
καὶ Ὁμήρῳ,

> γάνυται δέ τ᾽ ἀκούων.

τοῦτο δὲ φράζει ὅτι ἥδεται δέ τ᾽ ἀκούων. ἔστι δὲ
καὶ ἄλλοθί που,

> πυκινὰ φρεσὶ μήδεα εἰδώς.

τοῦτο δ᾽ αὖ λέγει σοφὰ φρεσὶ βουλεύματα εἰδώς.
ἐξ οὖν συναμφοτέρων τούτων οὐχ ἡδυσώματος
ὀνομασθεὶς ὁ Γανυμήδης ἀλλ᾽ ἡδυγνώμων ἐν θεοῖς
31 τετίμηται. ἀλλὰ μήν, ὦ Νικήρατε, καὶ Ἀχιλλεὺς
Ὁμήρῳ πεποίηται οὐχ ὡς παιδικοῖς Πατρόκλῳ
ἀλλ᾽ ὡς ἑταίρῳ ἀποθανόντι ἐκπρεπέστατα τιμω-
ρῆσαι. καὶ Ὀρέστης δὲ καὶ Πυλάδης καὶ Θησεὺς
καὶ Πειρίθους καὶ ἄλλοι δὲ πολλοὶ τῶν ἡμιθέων
οἱ ἄριστοι ὑμνοῦνται οὐ διὰ τὸ συγκαθεύδειν ἀλλὰ

---

[1] Castor and Pollux.

[2] Nothing like the first expression, except the bare occurrence of γάνυται ("he joys"), is to be found anywhere in the
extant Homeric poems. The second phrase, also, is not in
these poems, although several different expressions much
resembling it are to be seen in the *Iliad*, vii. 278, xvii. 325,
xviii. 363, xxiv. 88, 282, 674 and the *Odyssey*, ii. 38, xi. 445,

demi-gods set higher value on the friendship of the spirit than on the enjoyment of the body. For in all cases where Zeus became enamoured of mortal women for their beauty, though he united with them he suffered them to remain mortal; but all those persons whom he delighted in for their souls' sake he made immortal. Among the latter are Heracles and the Sons of Zeus;[1] and tradition includes others also. And I aver that even in the case of Ganymede, it was not his person but his spiritual character that influenced Zeus to carry him up to Olympus. This is confirmed by his very name. Homer, you remember, has the words,

'He joys to hear';[2]

that is to say, 'he rejoices to hear;' and in another place,

'harbouring shrewd devices in his heart.'

This, again, means 'harbouring wise counsels in his heart.' So the name given Gany-mede, compounded of the two foregoing elements, signifies not *physically* but *mentally* attractive;[3] hence his honour among the gods. Or again, Niceratus, Homer pictures us Achilles looking upon Patroclus not as the object of his passion but as a comrade, and in this spirit signally avenging his death. So we have songs telling also how Orestes, Pylades, Theseus, Peirithous, and many other illustrious demi-gods wrought glorious deeds of valour side by side, not because

xix. 353, xx. 46. Either Xenophon's memory is faulty or he is quoting from some of the lost epics.

[3] Socrates takes the name Ganymede to be a compound of the two archaic words *ganytai* ("he joys," "exults") and *medea* ("devices," "thoughts").

διὰ τὸ ἄγασθαι ἀλλήλους τὰ μέγιστα καὶ κάλ-
32 λιστα κοινῇ διαπεπρᾶχθαι. τί δέ; τὰ νῦν καλὰ
ἔργα οὐ πάντ' ἂν εὕροι τις ἕνεκα ἐπαίνου ὑπὸ τῶν
καὶ πονεῖν καὶ κινδυνεύειν ἐθελόντων πραττόμενα
μᾶλλον ἢ ὑπὸ τῶν ἐθιζομένων ἡδονὴν ἀντ' εὐκλείας αἱρεῖσθαι; καίτοι Παυσανίας γε ὁ Ἀγάθω-
νος τοῦ ποιητοῦ ἐραστὴς ἀπολογούμενος ὑπὲρ τῶν
ἀκρασίᾳ ἐγκαλινδουμένων εἴρηκεν ὡς καὶ στράτευμα ἀλκιμώτατον ἂν γένοιτο ἐκ παιδικῶν τε
33 καὶ ἐραστῶν. τούτους γὰρ ἂν ἔφη οἴεσθαι
μάλιστα αἰδεῖσθαι ἀλλήλους ἀπολείπειν, θαυμαστὰ λέγων, εἴ γε οἱ ψόγου τε ἀφροντιστεῖν καὶ
ἀναισχυντεῖν πρὸς ἀλλήλους ἐθιζόμενοι οὗτοι
34 μάλιστα αἰσχυνοῦνται αἰσχρόν τι ποιεῖν. καὶ
μαρτύρια δὲ ἐπήγετο ὡς ταῦτα ἐγνωκότες εἶεν καὶ
Θηβαῖοι καὶ Ἠλεῖοι· συγκαθεύδοντας γοῦν αὐτοῖς
ὅμως παρατάττεσθαι ἔφη τὰ παιδικὰ εἰς τὸν
ἀγῶνα, οὐδὲν τοῦτο σημεῖον λέγων ὅμοιον. ἐκείνοις μὲν γὰρ ταῦτα νόμιμα, ἡμῖν δ' ἐπονείδιστα.
δοκοῦσι δ' ἔμοιγε οἱ μὲν παραταττόμενοι ἀπιστοῦ-
σιν ἐοικέναι μὴ χωρὶς γενόμενοι οἱ ἐρώμενοι οὐκ
35 ἀποτελῶσι τὰ τῶν ἀγαθῶν ἀνδρῶν ἔργα. Λακεδαιμόνιοι δὲ οἱ νομίζοντες, ἐὰν καὶ ὀρεχθῇ τις
σώματος, μηδενὸς ἂν ἔτι καλοῦ κἀγαθοῦ τούτου
τυχεῖν, οὕτως τελέως τοὺς ἐρωμένους ἀγαθοὺς
ἀπεργάζονται ὡς καὶ μετὰ ξένων κἂν μὴ ἐν τῇ

they shared a common bed but because of mutual admiration and respect. Moreover, take the splendid feats of the present day; would not a person discover that they are all done for glory's sake by persons willing to endure hardship and jeopardy, rather than by those who are drifting into the habit of preferring pleasure to a good name? Yet Pausanias, the lover of the poet Agathon, has said in his defence of those who wallow in lasciviousness that the most valiant army, even, would be one recruited of lovers and their favourites! For these, he said, would in his opinion be most likely to be prevented by shame from deserting one another,—a strange assertion, indeed, that persons acquiring an habitual indifference to censure and to abandoned conduct toward one another will be most likely to be deterred by shame from any infamous act. But he went further and adduced as evidence in support of his position both the Thebans and the Eleans, alleging that this was their policy; he stated, in fine, that though sharing common beds they nevertheless assigned to their favourites places alongside themselves in the battle-line. But this is a false analogy; for such practices, though normal among them, with us are banned by the severest reprobation. My own view is that those who assign these posts in battle suggest thereby that they are suspicious that the objects of their love, if left by themselves, will not perform the duties of brave men. In contrast to this, the Lacedaemonians, who hold that if a person so much as feels a carnal concupiscence he will never come to any good end, cause the objects of their love to be so consummately brave that even when arrayed with foreigners and even when not stationed in the same

αὐτῇ[1] ταχθῶσι τῷ ἐραστῇ, ὁμοίως αἰδοῦνται
τοὺς παρόντας ἀπολείπειν. θεὰν γὰρ οὐ τὴν
36 Ἀναίδειαν ἀλλὰ τὴν Αἰδῶ νομίζουσι. δοκοῦμεν
δ᾽ ἄν μοι πάντες ὁμόλογοι γενέσθαι περὶ ὧν λέγω,
εἰ ὧδε ἐπισκοποῖμεν, τῷ ποτέρως παιδὶ φιλη-
θέντι μᾶλλον ἄν τις πιστεύσειεν ἢ χρήματα ἢ
τέκνα ἢ χάριτας παρακατατίθεσθαι. ἐγὼ μὲν
γὰρ οἶμαι καὶ αὐτὸν τὸν τῷ εἴδει τοῦ ἐρωμένου
χρώμενον μᾶλλον ἂν ταῦτα πάντα τῷ τὴν ψυχὴν
37 ἐρασμίῳ πιστεῦσαι. σοί γε μήν, ὦ Καλλία,
δοκεῖ μοι ἄξιον εἶναι καὶ θεοῖς χάριν εἰδέναι ὅτι
σοι Αὐτολύκου ἔρωτα ἐνέβαλον. ὡς μὲν γὰρ
φιλότιμός ἐστιν εὔδηλον, ὃς τοῦ κηρυχθῆναι ἕνεκα
νικῶν παγκράτιον πολλοὺς μὲν πόνους, πολλὰ δ᾽
38 ἄλγη ἀνέχεται. εἰ δὲ οἴοιτο μὴ μόνον ἑαυτὸν καὶ
τὸν πατέρα κοσμήσειν, ἀλλ᾽ ἱκανὸς γενήσεσθαι
δι᾽ ἀνδραγαθίαν καὶ φίλους εὖ ποιεῖν καὶ τὴν
πατρίδα αὔξειν τρόπαια τῶν πολεμίων ἱστάμενος,
καὶ διὰ ταῦτα περίβλεπτός τε καὶ ὀνομαστὸς
ἔσεσθαι καὶ ἐν Ἕλλησι καὶ ἐν βαρβάροις, πῶς
οὐκ οἴει αὐτόν, ὅντιν᾽ ἡγοῖτο εἰς ταῦτα συνεργὸν
εἶναι κράτιστον, τοῦτον ταῖς μεγίσταις ἂν τιμαῖς
39 περιέπειν; εἰ οὖν βούλει τούτῳ ἀρέσκειν, σκεπτέον
μέν σοι ποῖα ἐπιστάμενος Θεμιστοκλῆς ἱκανὸς
ἐγένετο τὴν Ἑλλάδα ἐλευθεροῦν, σκεπτέον δὲ
ποῖά ποτε εἰδὼς Περικλῆς κράτιστος ἐδόκει τῇ
πατρίδι σύμβουλος εἶναι, ἀθρητέον δὲ καὶ πῶς
ποτε Σόλων φιλοσοφήσας νόμους κρατίστους τῇ

[1] αὐτῇ ; αὐτῇ πόλει MSS. ; Sauppe brackets πόλει.

line with their lovers they just as surely feel ashamed
to desert their comrades. For the goddess they
worship is not Impudence but Modesty. We could
all come to one mind, I think, on the point I am
trying to make, if we were to consider the question
in this way : of two lads, the objects of the different
types of love, which one would a person prefer to
trust with his money, or his children, or to lay under
the obligation of a favour ? My own belief is that
even the person whose love is founded on the loved
one's physical beauty would in all these cases rather
put his trust in him whose loveliness is of the spirit.
In your case, Callias, I deem it meet that you should
thank Heaven for inspiring you with love for
Autolycus. For his ardour for glory is manifest,
inasmuch as he undergoes many toils and many
bodily discomforts to ensure his being proclaimed
victor in the pancratium. Now if he were to believe
that he is going not merely to shed lustre on himself
and his father but also to acquire through his manly
virtue the ability to serve his friends and to exalt his
country by setting up trophies of victory over its
enemies, and for these reasons draw the admiring
glances of all and be famous among both Greeks and
barbarians, do you not suppose that he would esteem
and honour highly any one whom he looked upon
as the best partner in furthering these designs ? If,
then, you would be in his good graces, you must try
to find out what sort of knowledge it was that made
Themistocles able to give Greece liberty ; you must
try to find out what kind of knowledge it was that
gave Pericles the name of being his country's wisest
counsellor ; you must reflect, further, how it was that
Solon by deep meditation established in his city laws

πόλει κατέθηκεν, ἐρευνητέον δὲ καὶ ποῖα Λακεδαιμόνιοι ἀσκοῦντες κράτιστοι δοκοῦσιν ἡγεμόνες
εἶναι· πρόξενος δ' εἰ καὶ κατάγονται ἀεὶ παρὰ
40 σοὶ οἱ κράτιστοι αὐτῶν. ὡς μὲν οὖν σοι ἡ πόλις
ταχὺ ἂν ἐπιτρέψειεν αὐτήν, εἰ βούλει, εὖ ἴσθι.
τὰ μέγιστα γάρ σοι ὑπάρχει· εὐπατρίδης εἶ, τῶν¹
ἀπ' Ἐρεχθέως, ἱερεὺς θεῶν οἳ καὶ ἐπὶ τὸν βάρβα-
ρον σὺν Ἰάκχῳ ἐστράτευσαν, καὶ νῦν ἐν τῇ ἑορτῇ
ἱεροπρεπέστατος δοκεῖς εἶναι τῶν προγεγενημέ-
νων, καὶ σῶμα ἀξιοπρεπέστατον μὲν ἰδεῖν τῆς
41 πόλεως ἔχεις, ἱκανὸν δὲ μόχθους ὑποφέρειν. εἰ
δ' ὑμῖν δοκῶ σπουδαιολογῆσαι μᾶλλον ἢ παρὰ
πότον πρέπει, μηδὲ τοῦτο θαυμάζετε. ἀγαθῶν
γὰρ φύσει καὶ τῆς ἀρετῆς φιλοτίμως ἐφιεμένων
ἀεί ποτε τῇ πόλει συνεραστὴς ὢν διατελῶ.
42   Οἱ μὲν δὴ ἄλλοι περὶ τῶν ῥηθέντων διελέγοντο,

¹ τῶν ἀπ' Ἐρεχθέως, ἱερεὺς θεῶν ; ἱερεὺς θεῶν τῶν ἀπ'
Ἐρεχθέως MSS.   The MS. reading should mean : "You are
of aristocratic birth, a priest serving the gods who succeeded
Erechtheus (or, gods of Erechtheus' line), who under the
leadership of Iacchus" etc. This involves two difficulties : (1)
in the numerous Attic references to this brilliant period, we
find no hint of any part taken in the Persian Wars by any
descendants or "successors" of Erechtheus ; and (2) there
is no evidence that Callias was a priest to any such descendants or "successors." The suggested transposition of the
text avoids these difficulties and provides for two well-
authenticated facts : (1) the tradition mentioned by Herodotus and Plutarch that the Eleusinian deities encouraged the
Greeks just before the battle of Salamis by a portentous
vision ; and (2) Callias's priesthood in the Eleusinian worship.

¹ In the absence of regular consular representation, any
Greek city-state could secure commercial and political agents in
other cities only by getting influential citizens there to consent
to use their good offices, as occasion might arise, in its behalf
or in behalf of its citizens when abroad. Such a local native
representative of another state was called a *proxenus.*

of surpassing worth; you must search and find out
what kind of practices it is that gives the Lacedaemonians the reputation of being pre-eminent military
commanders; for you are their proxenus,[1] and their
foremost citizens are always being entertained at
your house. You may regard it as certain, therefore,
that our city would be quick to entrust itself to your
hands, if you so desire. For you possess the highest
qualifications for such a trust: you are of aristocratic
birth, of Erechtheus' line,[2] a priest serving the gods
who under the leadership of Iacchus took the field
against the barbarian;[3] and in our day you outshine
your predecessors in the splendour of your priestly
office in the festival;[4] and you possess a person more
goodly to the eye than any other in the city and one
at the same time able to withstand effort and hardship. If what I say appears to you gentlemen to be
too grave and earnest for a drinking party, I beg you
again not to be surprised. For during practically all
my life I have been at one with the commonwealth
in loving men who to a nature already good add
a zealous desire for virtue."

  The rest of the company now engaged in a dis-

  [2] Callias's family belonged to the priestly clan of the
Ceryces, who traced their lineage back to Ceryx, son of
Hermes and Aglaurus. The latter, however, was not a
descendant of Erechtheus, but one of his nurses.
  [3] Herodotus (VIII, 65) and Plutarch (*Life of Themistocles*,
XV) report the tradition that while the Greek fleet was at
anchor near Salamis just before the critical sea-fight, great
elation was caused at sight of a big cloud of dust (or, in the
later version, a brilliant light) off toward Eleusis, and a
wonderful sound as of the Eleusinian festival with its cries to
Iacchus, followed by a cloud that drifted directly toward the
fleet.
  [4] In addition to being one of the priestly Ceryces, Callias
was an hereditary torch-bearer in the Eleusinian festival.

ὁ δ' Αὐτόλυκος κατεθεᾶτο τὸν Καλλίαν. καὶ ὁ
Καλλίας δὲ παρορῶν εἰς ἐκεῖνον εἶπεν· Οὐκοῦν σύ
με, ὦ Σώκρατες, μαστροπεύσεις πρὸς τὴν πόλιν,
ὅπως πράττω τὰ πολιτικὰ καὶ ἀεὶ ἀρεστὸς ὦ
αὐτῇ;

43   Ναὶ μὰ Δί', ἔφη, ἢν ὁρῶσί γέ σε μὴ τῷ δοκεῖν
ἀλλὰ τῷ ὄντι ἀρετῆς ἐπιμελούμενον. ἡ μὲν γὰρ
ψευδὴς δόξα ταχὺ ἐλέγχεται ὑπὸ τῆς πείρας· ἡ δ'
ἀληθὴς ἀνδραγαθία, ἢν μὴ θεὸς βλάπτῃ, ἀεὶ ἐν
ταῖς πράξεσι λαμπροτέραν τὴν εὔκλειαν συμ-
παρέχεται·

  IX. Οὗτος μὲν δὴ ὁ λόγος ἐνταῦθα ἔληξεν.
Αὐτόλυκος δέ, ἤδη γὰρ ὥρα ἦν αὐτῷ, ἐξανίστατο
εἰς περίπατον· καὶ ὁ Λύκων ὁ πατὴρ αὐτῷ συν-
εξιὼν ἐπιστραφεὶς εἶπε· Νὴ τὴν Ἥραν, ὦ Σώκρατες, καλός γε κἀγαθὸς δοκεῖς μοι ἄνθρωπος εἶναι.

2   Ἐκ δὲ τούτου πρῶτον μὲν θρόνος τις ἔνδον
κατετέθη, ἔπειτα δὲ ὁ Συρακόσιος εἰσελθὼν εἶπεν·
Ὦ ἄνδρες, Ἀριάδνη εἴσεισιν εἰς τὸν ἑαυτῆς τε καὶ
Διονύσου θάλαμον· μετὰ δὲ τοῦθ' ἥξει Διόνυσος
ὑποπεπωκὼς παρὰ θεοῖς καὶ εἴσεισι πρὸς αὐτήν,
ἔπειτα παιξοῦνται πρὸς ἀλλήλους.

3   Ἐκ τούτου πρῶτον μὲν ἡ Ἀριάδνη ὡς νύμφη
κεκοσμημένη παρῆλθε καὶ ἐκαθέζετο ἐπὶ τοῦ θρό-
νου. οὔπω δὲ φαινομένου τοῦ Διονύσου ηὐλεῖτο ὁ
βακχεῖος ῥυθμός. ἔνθα δὴ ἠγάσθησαν τὸν ὀρχηστοδιδάσκαλον. εὐθὺς μὲν γὰρ ἡ Ἀριάδνη ἀκού-

cussion of the views propounded by Socrates; but Autolycus kept his eyes fixed on Callias. And Callias, addressing Socrates, but looking beyond him and returning the gaze of Autolycus, said: "So you intend acting the procurer, do you, Socrates, to bring me to the attention of the commonwealth, so that I may enter politics, and the state may always look upon me with favour?"

"Assuredly," was the reply, "that is, if people see that you set your heart on virtue, not in pretence, but in reality. For false reputation is soon exposed when tried by experience, whereas true manly virtue,—barring the interposition of Providence,—confers ever more and more brilliant glory when put to the test of actual deeds."

IX. Their conversation ended here. Autolycus got up to go out for a walk (it being now his usual time); and his father Lycon, as he was departing to accompany him, turned back and said: "So help me Hera, Socrates, you seem to me to have a truly noble character."

After he had withdrawn, a chair of state, first of all, was set down in the room, and then the Syracusan came in with the announcement: "Gentlemen, Ariadne will now enter the chamber set apart for her and Dionysus; after that, Dionysus, a little flushed with wine drunk at a banquet of the gods, will come to join her; and then they will disport themselves together."

Then, to start proceedings, in came Ariadne, apparelled as a bride, and took her seat in the chair. Dionysus being still invisible, there was heard the Bacchic music played on a flute. Then it was that the assemblage was filled with admiration of the dancing master. For as soon as Ariadne heard the

σασα τοιοῦτόν τι ἐποίησεν ὡς πᾶς ἂν ἔγνω ὅτι
ἀσμένη ἤκουσε· καὶ ὑπήντησε μὲν οὐ οὐδὲ ἀνέστη,
4 δήλη δ' ἦν μόλις ἠρεμοῦσα. ἐπεί γε μὴν κατεῖδεν
αὐτὴν ὁ Διόνυσος, ἐπιχορεύσας ὥσπερ ἂν εἴ τις
φιλικώτατα ἐκαθέζετο ἐπὶ τῶν γονάτων καὶ
περιλαβὼν ἐφίλησεν αὐτήν. ἡ δ' αἰδουμένῃ μὲν
ἐῴκει, ὅμως δὲ φιλικῶς ἀντιπεριελάμβανεν. οἱ
δὲ συμπόται ὁρῶντες ἅμα μὲν ἐκρότουν, ἅμα δὲ
5 ἐβόων Αὖθις. ὡς δὲ ὁ Διόνυσος ἀνιστάμενος
συνανέστησε μεθ' ἑαυτοῦ τὴν Ἀριάδνην, ἐκ τούτου δὴ φιλούντων τε καὶ ἀσπαζομένων ἀλλήλους
σχήματα παρῆν θεάσασθαι. οἱ δ' ὁρῶντες ὄντως
καλὸν μὲν τὸν Διόνυσον, ὡραίαν δὲ τὴν Ἀριάδνην,
οὐ σκώπτοντας δὲ ἀλλ' ἀληθινῶς τοῖς στόμασι
6 φιλοῦντας, πάντες ἀνεπτερωμένοι ἐθεῶντο. καὶ
γὰρ ἤκουον τοῦ Διονύσου μὲν ἐπερωτῶντος αὐτὴν
εἰ φιλεῖ αὐτόν, τῆς δὲ οὕτως ἐπομνυούσης ὥστε
μὴ μόνον τὸν Διόνυσον ἀλλὰ καὶ τοὺς παρόντας
ἅπαντας συνομόσαι ἂν ἦ μὴν τὸν παῖδα καὶ τὴν
παῖδα ὑπ' ἀλλήλων φιλεῖσθαι. ἐῴκεσαν γὰρ οὐ
δεδιδαγμένοις τὰ σχήματα ἀλλ' ἐφειμένοις πράτ-
7 τειν ἃ πάλαι ἐπεθύμουν. τέλος δὲ οἱ συμπόται
ἰδόντες περιβεβληκότας τε ἀλλήλους καὶ ὡς εἰς
εὐνὴν ἀπιόντας, οἱ μὲν ἄγαμοι γαμεῖν ἐπώμνυσαν,
οἱ δὲ γεγαμηκότες ἀναβάντες ἐπὶ τοὺς ἵππους
ἀπήλαυνον πρὸς τὰς ἑαυτῶν γυναῖκας, ὅπως τού
των τύχοιεν. Σωκράτης δὲ καὶ τῶν ἄλλων οἱ
ὑπομείναντες πρὸς Λύκωνα καὶ τὸν υἱὸν σὺν
Καλλίᾳ περιπατήσοντες ἀπῆλθον.

Αὕτη τοῦ τότε συμποσίου κατάλυσις ἐγένετο.

strain, her action was such that every one might have perceived her joy at the sound; and although she did not go to meet Dionysus, nor even rise, yet it was clear that she kept her composure with difficulty. But when Dionysus caught sight of her, he came dancing toward her and in a most loving manner sat himself on her lap, and putting his arms about her gave her a kiss. Her demeanour was all modesty, and yet she returned his embrace with affection. As the banqueters beheld it, they kept clapping and crying "encore!" Then when Dionysus arose and gave his hand to Ariadne to rise also, there was presented the impersonation of lovers kissing and caressing each other. The onlookers viewed a Dionysus truly handsome, an Ariadne truly fair, not presenting a burlesque but offering genuine kisses with their lips; and they were all raised to a high pitch of enthusiasm as they looked on. For they overheard Dionysus asking her if she loved him, and heard her vowing that she did, so earnestly that not only Dionysus but all the bystanders as well would have taken their oaths in confirmation that the youth and the maid surely felt a mutual affection. For theirs was the appearance not of actors who had been taught their poses but of persons now permitted to satisfy their long-cherished desires. At last, the banqueters, seeing them in each other's embrace and obviously leaving for the bridal couch, those who were unwedded swore that they would take to themselves wives, and those who were already married mounted horse and rode off to their wives that they might enjoy them. As for Socrates and the others who had lingered behind, they went out with Callias to join Lycon and his son in their walk.

So broke up the banquet held that evening.

SOCRATES'
DEFENCE TO THE JURY

INTRODUCTION

In the year 399 B.C., Socrates, then about seventy years old, was brought to trial by Anytus, Meletus, and Lycon on an indictment charging him with subversion of religion and morals. The fullest account of Socrates at this crisis is to be found in Plato's *Euthyphro, Apology of Socrates, Crito,* and *Phaedo.* Apparently other admirers also of the great man had described the trial and the last days of his life, but Xenophon, who at that time was with the conglomerate army of Cyrus the Younger on its memorable trip into the heart of Persia, seems to have felt that these various accounts left out one essential point, which he proceeds to develop in the *Apology* or *Defence.*

The first sentence of this composition suggests an intimate connection with something preceding;[1] but this connection is now broken, and whether the *Defence,* as Mahaffy thought, is the original conclusion to Xenophon's *Memoirs of Socrates,* where, in the last chapter, we find practically the same material in smaller compass, or was meant to be part of some other writing, we have no means to determine. Almost equally indeterminate is the date. It is clear that when the *Defence* was written, both Socrates and Anytus (whose death occurred we

[1] Compare also the beginning of the *Oeconomicus.*

know not when) had been gone several years, and that several accounts of the trial had already appeared. But there is nothing to show how late the work was written, nor whether it preceded or followed the *Apology* of Plato.

Hermogenes, the authority on whom Xenophon relied, the indigent brother of the rich Callias, appears, both from Xenophon's *Defence* and *Symposium* and from Plato, to have been an intimate in the Socratic circle. Although he is not mentioned in the doubtless incomplete list given in Plato's *Apology* (33 D–34 A) of friends and disciples present at the trial, he is named (in Plato's *Phaedo* 59B) as one of those who were with Socrates at the time of his execution, and so may be presumed to have been cognizant of what happened in those tragic days.

Xenophon's design in writing the present account was not to give a full report of the trial or even of Socrates' address to the jury, but to show that because Socrates believed it time for him to die he had a common-sense basis for his sublime attitude before the court; but while Plato, the only eye-witness whose work is extant, represents Socrates as telling the jury that he can face death calmly because of his confidence in a life hereafter,—a doctrine greatly elaborated in the *Phaedo*,—Xenophon does not even mention this faith either in this partial report of the trial or in his *Memoirs of Socrates*, but says that in conversation with Hermogenes before the trial as well as with other friends after it Socrates founded his contentment on the prospect of avoiding the disabilities of old age. Dread of such ills had doubtless filled many a Greek's heart; at any rate the theme comes out a number of times in poetry, from the haunting elegy of Mimnermus on. And it seems quite likely that in conversation Socrates had mentioned this commonplace comfort as one reason for his willingness to die;[1] but whether Plato did not hear it, or thought it not worth recording beside more spiritual thoughts, at any rate he nowhere reports it,[2] and it is certain that in the publicity of the court-room Socrates dwelt rather on his hope of immortality and of communion with the great men of the past. The reader who wishes to get a true picture of this great man at the climax of his life should therefore not fail to supplement Xenophon's professedly incomplete account by the fuller one of Plato.

[1] Perhaps with the feeling that here at least was an argument that would appeal to his friends.

[2] The nearest approach to such a sentiment is found in the closing words of Socrates' defence as reported by Plato (*Apology*, 41D): " . . . but this is clear to me, that it were better for me now to die and once and for all be rid of troubles."

ΑΠΟΛΟΓΙΑ ΣΩΚΡΑΤΟΥΣ

ΠΡΟΣ ΤΟΥΣ ΔΙΚΑΣΤΑΣ[1]

1. Σωκράτους δὲ ἄξιόν μοι δοκεῖ εἶναι μεμνῆσθαι καὶ ὡς ἐπειδὴ ἐκλήθη εἰς τὴν δίκην ἐβουλεύ-
σατο περί τε τῆς ἀπολογίας καὶ τῆς τελευτῆς τοῦ
βίου. γεγράφασι μὲν οὖν περὶ τούτου καὶ ἄλλοι
καὶ πάντες ἔτυχον τῆς μεγαληγορίας αὐτοῦ· ᾧ
καὶ δῆλον ὅτι τῷ ὄντι οὕτως ἐρρήθη ὑπὸ Σωκράτους. ἀλλ' ὅτι ἤδη ἑαυτῷ ἡγεῖτο αἱρετώτερον
εἶναι τοῦ βίου θάνατον, τοῦτο οὐ διεσαφήνισαν·
ὥστε ἀφρονεστέρα αὐτοῦ φαίνεται εἶναι ἡ μεγαλη-
2 γορία. Ἑρμογένης μέντοι ὁ Ἱππονίκου ἑταῖρός
τε ἦν αὐτῷ καὶ ἐξήγγειλε περὶ αὐτοῦ τοιαῦτα
ὥστε πρέπουσαν φαίνεσθαι τὴν μεγαληγορίαν
αὐτοῦ τῇ διανοίᾳ. ἐκεῖνος γὰρ ἔφη ὁρῶν αὐτὸν
περὶ πάντων μᾶλλον διαλεγόμενον ἢ περὶ τῆς
3 δίκης εἰπεῖν, Οὐκ ἐχρῆν μέντοι σκοπεῖν, ὦ Σώκρατες, καὶ ὅ τι ἀπολογήσῃ; τὸν δὲ τὸ μὲν πρῶτον ἀποκρίνασθαι, Οὐ γὰρ δοκῶ σοι ἀπολογεῖσθαι
μελετῶν διαβεβιωκέναι; ἐπεὶ δ' αὐτὸς[2] ἐρέσθαι,
Πῶς; Ὅτι οὐδὲν ἄδικον διαγεγένημαι ποιῶν·
ἥνπερ νομίζω μελέτην εἶναι καλλίστην ἀπολο-
4 γίας. ἐπεὶ δὲ αὐτὸς[3] πάλιν λέγειν, Οὐχ ὁρᾷς τὰ
Ἀθηναίων δικαστήρια ὡς πολλάκις μὲν οὐδὲν

---

[1] Sauppe omits ΠΡΟΣ ΤΟΥΣ ΔΙΚΑΣΤΑΣ.
[2] αὐτὸς Schenkl ; αὐτὸν MSS.
[3] αὐτὸς Schenkl ; αὐτὸν MSS.

SOCRATES'
DEFENCE TO THE JURY

It seems to me fitting to hand down to memory,
furthermore, how Socrates, on being indicted, de-
liberated on his defence and on his end. It is
true that others have written about this, and that
all of them have reproduced the loftiness of his
words,—a fact which proves that his utterance really
was of the character intimated;—but they have not
shown clearly that he had now come to the conclusion
that for him death was more to be desired than life;
and hence his lofty utterance appears rather ill-
considered. Hermogenes, the son of Hipponicus,
however, was a companion of his and has given us
reports of such a nature as to show that the sub-
limity of his speech was appropriate to the resolve
he had made. For he stated that on seeing Socrates
discussing any and every subject rather than the
trial, he had said: "Socrates, ought you not to be
giving some thought to what defence you are going
to make?" That Socrates had at first replied,
"Why, do I not seem to you to have spent my
whole life in preparing to defend myself?" Then
when he asked, "How so?" he had said, "Because
all my life I have been guiltless of wrong-doing;
and that I consider the finest preparation for a
defence." Then when Hermogenes again asked,
"Do you not observe that the Athenian courts

ἀδικοῦντας λόγῳ παραχθέντες ἀπέκτειναν, πολλάκις δὲ ἀδικοῦντας ἢ ἐκ τοῦ λόγου οἰκτίσαντες ἢ
ἐπιχαρίτως εἰπόντας ἀπέλυσαν; Ἀλλὰ ναὶ μὰ
Δία, φάναι αὐτόν, καὶ δὶς ἤδη ἐπιχειρήσαντός μου
σκοπεῖν περὶ τῆς ἀπολογίας ἐναντιοῦταί μοι τὸ
5 δαιμόνιον. ὡς δὲ αὐτὸς[1] εἰπεῖν, Θαυμαστὰ λέγεις, τὸν δ' αὖ ἀποκρίνασθαι, Ἦ θαυμαστὸν νομίζεις εἰ καὶ τῷ θεῷ δοκεῖ ἐμὲ βέλτιον εἶναι ἤδη
τελευτᾶν; οὐκ οἶσθα ὅτι μέχρι μὲν τοῦδε οὐδενὶ
ἀνθρώπων ὑφείμην ἂν βέλτιον ἐμοῦ βεβιωκέναι;
ὅπερ γὰρ ἥδιστόν ἐστιν, ᾔδειν ὁσίως μοι καὶ δικαίως ἅπαντα τὸν βίον βεβιωμένον· ὥστε ἰσχυρῶς ἀγάμενος ἐμαυτὸν ταὐτὰ εὕρισκον καὶ τοὺς
ἐμοὶ συγγιγνομένους γιγνώσκοντας περὶ ἐμοῦ.
6 νῦν δὲ εἰ ἔτι προβήσεται ἡ ἡλικία, οἶδ' ὅτι
ἀνάγκη ἔσται τὰ τοῦ γήρως ἀποτελεῖσθαι καὶ
ὁρᾶν τε χεῖρον καὶ ἀκούειν ἧττον καὶ δυσμαθέστερον εἶναι καὶ ὧν ἔμαθον ἐπιλησμονέστερον.
ἢν δὲ αἰσθάνωμαι χείρων γιγνόμενος καὶ κατα-
μέμφωμαι ἐμαυτόν, πῶς ἄν, εἰπεῖν, ἐγὼ ἔτι ἂν
7 ἡδέως βιοτεύοιμι; ἴσως δέ τοι, φάναι αὐτόν, καὶ
ὁ θεὸς δι' εὐμένειαν προξενεῖ μοι οὐ μόνον τὸ
ἐν καιρῷ τῆς ἡλικίας καταλῦσαι τὸν βίον, ἀλλὰ
καὶ τὸ ᾗ ῥᾷστα. ἢν γὰρ νῦν κατακριθῇ μου,[2]
δῆλον ὅτι ἐξέσται μοι τῇ τελευτῇ χρῆσθαι ἣ
ῥᾷστη μὲν ὑπὸ τῶν τούτου ἐπιμεληθέντων κέκρι-
ται, ἀπραγμονεστάτη δὲ τοῖς φίλοις, πλεῖστον δὲ
πόθον ἐμποιοῦσα τοῦ τελευτῶντος. ὅταν γὰρ

---

[1] αὐτὸς Schenkl; αὐτὸν MSS.
[2] Sauppe reads (by a misprint ?) μοι.

have often been carried away by an eloquent speech and have condemned innocent men to death, and often on the other hand the guilty have been acquitted either because their plea aroused compassion or because their speech was witty?" "Yes, indeed!" he had answered; "and I have tried twice already to meditate on my defence, but my divine sign interposes." And when Hermogenes observed, "That is a surprising statement," he had replied, "Do you think it surprising that even God holds it better for me to die now? Do you not know that I would refuse to concede that any man has lived a better life than I have up to now? For I have realized that my whole life has been spent in righteousness toward God and man,—a fact that affords the greatest satisfaction; and so I have felt a deep self-respect and have discovered that my associates hold corresponding sentiments toward me. But now, if my years are prolonged, I know that the frailties of old age will inevitably be realized,—that my vision must be less perfect and my hearing less keen, that I shall be slower to learn and more forgetful of what I have learned. If I perceive my decay and take to complaining, how," he had continued, "could I any longer take pleasure in life? Perhaps," he added, "God in his kindness is taking my part and securing me the opportunity of ending my life not only in season but also in the way that is easiest. For if I am condemned now, it will clearly be my privilege to suffer a death that is adjudged by those who have superintended this matter to be not only the easiest but also the least irksome to one's friends and one that implants in them the deepest feeling of loss for the dead. For when a person leaves behind in

ἄσχημον μὲν μηδὲν μηδὲ δυσχερὲς ἐν ταῖς γνώμαις
τῶν παρόντων καταλίπηται, ὑγιὲς δὲ τὸ σῶμα ἔχων
καὶ τὴν ψυχὴν δυναμένην φιλοφρονεῖσθαι ἀπο-
μαραίνηται, πῶς οὐκ ἀνάγκη τοῦτον ποθεινὸν
8 εἶναι; ὀρθῶς δὲ οἱ θεοὶ τότε μου ἠναντιοῦντο,
φάναι αὐτόν, τῇ τοῦ λόγου ἐπισκέψει ὅτε ἐδόκει
ἡμῖν¹ ζητητέα εἶναι ἐκ παντὸς τρόπου τὰ ἀποφευ-
κτικά. εἰ γὰρ τοῦτο διεπραξάμην, δῆλον ὅτι
ἡτοιμασάμην ἂν ἀντὶ τοῦ ἤδη λῆξαι τοῦ βίου ἢ
νόσοις ἀλγυνόμενος τελευτῆσαι ἢ γήρᾳ, εἰς ὃ
πάντα τὰ χαλεπὰ συρρεῖ καὶ μάλα ἔρημα τῶν
9 εὐφροσυνῶν. μὰ Δί', εἰπεῖν αὐτόν, ὦ Ἑρμόγενες,
ἐγὼ ταῦτα οὐδὲ προθυμήσομαι, ἀλλ' ὅσων νομίζω
τετυχηκέναι καλῶν καὶ παρὰ θεῶν καὶ παρ'
ἀνθρώπων καὶ ἣν ἐγὼ δόξαν ἔχω περὶ ἐμαυτοῦ,
ταύτην ἀναφαίνων εἰ βαρυνῶ τοὺς δικαστάς,
αἱρήσομαι τελευτᾶν μᾶλλον ἢ ἀνελευθέρως τὸ ζῆν
ἔτι προσαιτῶν κερδᾶναι τὸν πολὺ χείρω βίον ἀντὶ
θανάτου.

10   Οὕτως δὲ γνόντα αὐτὸν ἔφη, ἐπειδὴ κατηγό-
ρησαν αὐτοῦ οἱ ἀντίδικοι ὡς οὓς μὲν ἡ πόλις νομίζει θεοὺς οὐ νομίζοι, ἕτερα δὲ καινὰ δαιμόνια
εἰσφέροι καὶ τοὺς νέους διαφθείροι, παρελθόντα
11 εἰπεῖν· Ἀλλ' ἐγώ, ὦ ἄνδρες, τοῦτο μὲν πρῶτον
θαυμάζω Μελήτου ὅτῳ ποτὲ γνοὺς λέγει ὡς ἐγὼ
οὓς ἡ πόλις νομίζει θεοὺς οὐ νομίζω· ἐπεὶ θύοντά
γέ με ἐν ταῖς κοιναῖς ἑορταῖς καὶ ἐπὶ τῶν δημοσίων
βωμῶν καὶ οἱ ἄλλοι οἱ παρατυγχάνοντες ἑώρων
12 καὶ αὐτὸς Μέλητος, εἰ ἐβούλετο. καινά γε μὴν
δαιμόνια πῶς ἂν ἐγὼ εἰσφέροιμι λέγων ὅτι θεοῦ

---

¹ Sauppe adopts Weiske's emendation ὑμῖν.

the hearts of his companions no remembrance to cause a blush or a pang, but dissolution comes while he still possesses a sound body and a spirit capable of showing kindliness, how could such a one fail to be sorely missed? It was with good reason," Socrates had continued, "that the gods opposed [1] my studying up my speech at the time when we held that by fair means or foul we must find some plea that would effect my acquittal. For if I had achieved this end, it is clear that instead of now passing out of life, I should merely have provided for dying in the throes of illness or vexed by old age, the sink into which all distresses flow, unrelieved by any joy. As Heaven is my witness, Hermogenes," he had gone on, "I shall never court that fate; but if I am going to offend the jury by declaring all the blessings that I feel gods and men have bestowed on me, as well as my personal opinion of myself, I shall prefer death to begging meanly for longer life and thus gaining a life far less worthy in exchange for death."

Hermogenes stated that with this resolve Socrates came before the jury after his adversaries had charged him with not believing in the gods worshipped by the state and with the introduction of new deities in their stead and with corruption of the young, and replied: "One thing that I marvel at in Meletus, gentlemen, is what may be the basis of his assertion that I do not believe in the gods worshipped by the state; for all who have happened to be near at the time, as well as Meletus himself,—if he so desired,— have seen me sacrificing at the communal festivals and on the public altars. As for introducing 'new divinities,' how could I be guilty of that merely in

---

[1] See note on p. 494.

μοι φωνὴ φαίνεται σημαίνουσα ὅ τι χρὴ ποιεῖν;
καὶ γὰρ οἱ φθόγγοις οἰωνῶν καὶ οἱ φήμαις ἀνθρώπων χρώμενοι φωναῖς δήπου τεκμαίρονται. βρον-
τὰς δὲ ἀμφιλέξει τις ἢ μὴ φωνεῖν ἢ μὴ μέγιστον
οἰωνιστήριον εἶναι; ἢ δὲ Πυθοῖ ἐν τῷ τρίποδι
ἱέρεια οὐ καὶ αὐτὴ φωνῇ τὰ παρὰ τοῦ θεοῦ διαγ-
13 γέλλει; ἀλλὰ μέντοι καὶ τὸ προειδέναι γε τὸν
θεὸν τὸ μέλλον καὶ τὸ προσημαίνειν ᾧ βούλεται,
καὶ τοῦτο, ὥσπερ ἐγώ φημι, οὕτω πάντες καὶ
λέγουσι καὶ νομίζουσιν. ἀλλ' οἱ μὲν οἰωνούς τε
καὶ φήμας καὶ συμβόλους τε καὶ μάντεις ὀνομάζουσι τοὺς προσημαίνοντας εἶναι, ἐγὼ δὲ τοῦτο
δαιμόνιον καλῶ, καὶ οἶμαι οὕτως ὀνομάζων καὶ
ἀληθέστερα καὶ ὁσιώτερα λέγειν τῶν τοῖς ὄρνισιν
ἀνατιθέντων τὴν τῶν θεῶν δύναμιν. ὥς γε μὴι
οὐ ψεύδομαι κατὰ τοῦ θεοῦ καὶ τοῦτ' ἔχω τεκμή-
ριον· καὶ γὰρ τῶν φίλων πολλοῖς δὴ ἐξαγγείλας
τὰ τοῦ θεοῦ συμβουλεύματα οὐδεπώποτε ψευσάμενος ἐφάνην.

14 Ἐπεὶ δὲ ταῦτ' ἀκούοντες οἱ δικασταὶ ἐθορύβουν,
οἱ μὲν ἀπιστοῦντες τοῖς λεγομένοις, οἱ δὲ καὶ φθονοῦντες εἰ καὶ παρὰ θεῶν μειζόνων ἢ αὐτοὶ τυγχά-
νοι, πάλιν εἰπεῖν τὸν Σωκράτην· Ἄγε δὴ ἀκούσατε
καὶ ἄλλα, ἵνα ἔτι μᾶλλον οἱ βουλόμενοι ὑμῶν

---

[1] Or "divine sign." Here, as earlier, the mere adjective
is used; but in Plato's *Theages* (128 D ff.) and *Apology* (31 D)
this admonitory something is described as a voice sent by
heavenly dispensation, and is called variously "the sign"
(*Apology* 41 D), "the usual sign" (*Apology* 40 C), "the divine
sign" (*Rep.* 496 C), "the usual divine sign" (*Euthyd.* 272 E,
Phaedrus 242 B, *Theages* 129 B), "the sign from God" (*Apology*
40 B), "something God-sent and divine" (*Apology* 31 D). Plato

648

asserting that a voice of God is made manifest to me indicating my duty? Surely those who take their omens from the cries of birds and the utterances of men form their judgments on 'voices.' Will any one dispute either that thunder utters its 'voice,' or that it is an omen of the greatest moment? Does not the very priestess who sits on the tripod at Delphi divulge the god's will through a 'voice'? But more than that, in regard to God's foreknowledge of the future and his forewarning thereof to whomsoever he will, these are the same terms, I assert, that all men use, and this is their belief. The only difference between them and me is that whereas they call the sources of their forewarning 'birds,' 'utterances,' 'chance meetings,' 'prophets,' I call mine a 'divine' thing;[1] and I think that in using such a term I am speaking with more truth and deeper religious feeling than do those who ascribe the gods' power to birds. Now that I do not lie against God I have the following proof: I have revealed to many of my friends the counsels which God has given me, and in no instance has the event shown that I was mistaken."

Hermogenes further reported that when the jurors raised a clamour at hearing these words, some of them disbelieving his statements, others showing jealousy at his receiving greater favours even from the gods than they, Socrates resumed: "Hark ye; let me tell you something more, so that those of you who feel so inclined may have still greater

reports Socrates' description of this as a voice not directing his actions but serving only as a deterrent when he or his friends were contemplating doing something inadvisable.

ἀπιστῶσι τῷ ἐμὲ τετιμῆσθαι ὑπὸ δαιμόνων. Χαι-
ρεφῶντος γάρ ποτε ἐπερωτῶντος ἐν Δελφοῖς περὶ
ἐμοῦ πολλῶν παρόντων ἀνεῖλεν ὁ Ἀπόλλων μηδένα εἶναι ἀνθρώπων ἐμοῦ μήτε ἐλευθεριώτερον
μήτε δικαιότερον μήτε σωφρονέστερον.

15 Ὡς δ᾽ αὖ ταῦτ᾽ ἀκούσαντες οἱ δικασταὶ ἔτι μᾶλλον εἰκότως ἐθορύβουν, αὖθις εἰπεῖν τὸν Σωκρά-
την· Ἀλλὰ μείζω μέν, ὦ ἄνδρες, εἶπεν ὁ θεὸς ἐν
χρησμοῖς περὶ Λυκούργου τοῦ Λακεδαιμονίοις
νομοθετήσαντος ἢ περὶ ἐμοῦ. λέγεται γὰρ εἰς
τὸν νεὼ εἰσιόντα προσειπεῖν αὐτόν, Φροντίζω
πότερα θεόν σε εἴπω ἢ ἄνθρωπον. ἐμὲ δὲ θεῷ
μὲν οὐκ εἴκασεν, ἀνθρώπων δὲ πολλῷ προέκρινεν
ὑπερφέρειν. ὅμως δὲ ὑμεῖς μηδὲ ταῦτ᾽ εἰκῇ
πιστεύσητε τῷ θεῷ, ἀλλὰ καθ᾽ ἓν ἕκαστον
16 ἐπισκοπεῖτε ὧν εἶπεν ὁ θεός. τίνα μὲν γὰρ ἐπίστασθε ἧττον ἐμοῦ δουλεύοντα ταῖς τοῦ σώματος
ἐπιθυμίαις; τίνα δὲ ἀνθρώπων ἐλευθεριώτερον,
ὃς παρ᾽ οὐδενὸς οὔτε δῶρα οὔτε μισθὸν δέχομαι; δικαιότερον δὲ τίνα ἂν εἰκότως νομίσαιτε τοῦ οὕτω¹
πρὸς τὰ παρόντα συνηρμοσμένου ὡς τῶν ἀλλοτρίων
μηδενὸς προσδεῖσθαι; σοφὸν δὲ πῶς οὐκ ἄν τις
εἰκότως ἄνδρα φήσειεν εἶναι ὃς ἐξ ὅτουπερ ξυνιέ-
ναι τὰ λεγόμενα ἠρξάμην οὐπώποτε διέλιπον καὶ
17 ζητῶν καὶ μανθάνων ὅ τι ἐδυνάμην ἀγαθόν; ὡς
δὲ οὐ μάτην ἐπόνουν οὐ δοκεῖ ὑμῖν καὶ τάδε τεκμήρια εἶναι, τὸ πολλοὺς μὲν πολίτας τῶν ἀρετῆς
ἐφιεμένων, πολλοὺς δὲ ξένων ἐκ πάντων προαιρεῖσθαι ἐμοὶ ξυνεῖναι; ἐκείνου δὲ τί φήσομεν αἴτιον

¹ οὕτω added by Cobet.

---

¹ A very enthusiastic follower of Socrates.

disbelief in my being honoured of Heaven. Once on a time when Chaerephon[1] made inquiry at the Delphic oracle concerning me, in the presence of many people Apollo answered that no man was more free than I, or more just, or more prudent."

When the jurors, naturally enough, made a still greater tumult on hearing this statement, he said that Socrates again went on: "And yet, gentlemen, the god uttered in oracles greater things of Lycurgus, the Lacedaemonian law-giver, than he did of me. For there is a legend that, as Lycurgus entered the temple, the god thus addressed him: 'I am pondering whether to call you god or man.' Now Apollo did not compare me to a god; he did, however, judge that I far excelled the rest of mankind. However, do not believe the god even in this without due grounds, but examine the god's utterance in detail. First, who is there in your knowledge that is less slave to his bodily appetites than I am? Who in the world more free,—for I accept neither gifts nor pay from any one? Whom would you with reason regard as more just than the one so reconciled to his present possessions as to want nothing beside that belongs to another? And would not a person with good reason call me a wise man, who from the time when I began to understand spoken words have never left off seeking after and learning every good thing that I could? And that my labour has not been in vain do you not think is attested by this fact, that many of my fellow-citizens who strive for virtue and many from abroad choose to associate with me above all other men? And what shall we say is accountable for

εἶναι, τοῦ πάντας εἰδέναι ὅτι ἐγὼ ἥκιστ' ἂν
ἔχοιμι χρήματα ἀντιδιδόναι, ὅμως πολλοὺς ἐπιθυμεῖν ἐμοί τι δωρεῖσθαι ; τὸ δ' ἐμὲ μὲν μηδ' ὑφ'
ἑνὸς ἀπαιτεῖσθαι εὐεργεσίας, ἐμοὶ δὲ πολλοὺς
18 ὁμολογεῖν χάριτας ὀφείλειν ; τὸ δ' ἐν τῇ πολιορκίᾳ
τοὺς μὲν ἄλλους οἰκτίρειν ἑαυτούς, ἐμὲ δὲ μηδὲν
ἀπορώτερον διάγειν ἢ ὅτε τὰ μάλιστα ἡ πόλις
ηὐδαιμόνει[1] ; τὸ δὲ τοὺς ἄλλους μὲν τὰς εὐπα-
θείας ἐκ τῆς ἀγορᾶς πολυτελεῖς πορίζεσθαι, ἐμὲ
δὲ ἐκ τῆς ψυχῆς ἄνευ δαπάνης ἡδίους ἐκείνων
μηχανᾶσθαι ; εἴ γε μὴν ὅσα εἴρηκα περὶ ἐμαυτοῦ
μηδεὶς δύναιτ' ἂν ἐξελέγξαι με ὡς ψεύδομαι, πῶς
οὐκ ἂν ἤδη δικαίως καὶ ὑπὸ θεῶν καὶ ὑπ' ἀνθρώ-
19 πων ἐπαινοίμην ; ἀλλ' ὅμως σύ με φῄς, ὦ Μέλητε,
τοιαῦτα ἐπιτηδεύοντα τοὺς νέους διαφθείρειν ;
καίτοι ἐπιστάμεθα μὲν δήπου τίνες εἰσὶ νέων δια-
φθοραί· σὺ δὲ εἰπὲ εἴ τινα οἶσθα ὑπ' ἐμοῦ γεγενημένον ἢ ἐξ εὐσεβοῦς ἀνόσιον ἢ ἐκ σώφρονος
ὑβριστὴν ἢ ἐξ εὐδιαίτου πολυδάπανον ἢ ἐκ
μετριοπότου οἰνόφλυγα ἢ ἐκ φιλοπόνου μαλακὸν
20 ἢ ἄλλης πονηρᾶς ἡδονῆς ἡττημένον. Ἀλλὰ ναὶ
μὰ Δί', ἔφη ὁ Μέλητος, ἐκείνους οἶδα οὓς σὺ
πέπεικας σοὶ πείθεσθαι μᾶλλον ἢ τοῖς γειναμέ-
νοις. Ὁμολογῶ, φάναι τὸν Σωκράτην, περί γε
παιδείας· τοῦτο γὰρ ἴσασιν ἐμοὶ μεμεληκός. περὶ
δὲ ὑγιείας τοῖς ἰατροῖς μᾶλλον οἱ ἄνθρωποι πείθονται ἢ τοῖς γονεῦσι· καὶ ἐν ταῖς ἐκκλησίαις γε

---

[1] εὐδαιμόνει one MS. ; εὐδαιμονεῖ Sauppe with the other MSS.

---

[1] The blockade of Athens by the Spartans in the last year of the Peloponnesian War.

this fact, that although everybody knows that it is quite impossible for me to repay with money, many people are eager to make me some gift? Or for this, that no demands are made on me by a single person for the repayment of benefits, while many confess that they owe me a debt of gratitude? Or for this, that during the siege,[1] while others were commiserating their lot, I got along without feeling the pinch of poverty any worse than when the city's prosperity was at its height? Or for this, that while other men get their delicacies in the markets and pay a high price for them, I devise more pleasurable ones from the resources of my soul, with no expenditure of money? And now, if no one can convict me of misstatement in all that I have said of myself, do I not unquestionably merit praise from both gods and men? But in spite of all, Meletus, do you maintain that I corrupt the young by such practices? And yet surely we know what kinds of corruption affect the young; so you tell us whether you know of any one who under my influence has fallen from piety into impiety, or from sober into wanton conduct, or from moderation in living into extravagance, or from temperate drinking into sottishness, or from strenuousness into effeminacy, or has been overcome of any other base pleasure." "But, by Heaven!" said Meletus: "there is one set of men I know,—those whom you have persuaded to obey you rather than their parents." "I admit it," he reports Socrates as replying, "at least so far as education is concerned; for people know that I have taken an interest in that. But in a question of health, men take the advice of physicians rather than that of their parents; and

πάντες δήπου οἱ Ἀθηναῖοι τοῖς φρονιμώτατα
λέγουσι πείθονται μᾶλλον ἢ τοῖς προσήκουσιν.
οὐ γὰρ δὴ καὶ στρατηγοὺς αἱρεῖσθε καὶ πρὸ πατέρων καὶ πρὸ ἀδελφῶν καὶ ναὶ μὰ Δία γε ὑμεῖς
πρὸ ὑμῶν αὐτῶν, οὓς ἂν ἡγῆσθε περὶ τῶν πολεμικῶν φρονιμωτάτους εἶναι ; Οὕτω γάρ, φάναι τὸν
Μέλητον, ὦ Σώκρατες, καὶ συμφέρει καὶ νομίζε-
21 ται. Οὔκουν, εἰπεῖν τὸν Σωκράτην, θαυμαστὸν
καὶ τοῦτό σοι δοκεῖ εἶναι, τὸ ἐν μὲν ταῖς ἄλλαις
πράξεσι μὴ μόνον ἰσομοιρίας τυγχάνειν τοὺς κρατίστους ἀλλὰ καὶ προτετιμῆσθαι, ἐμὲ δέ, ὅτι περὶ
τοῦ μεγίστου ἀγαθοῦ ἀνθρώποις, περὶ παιδείας,
βέλτιστος εἶναι ὑπό τινων προκρίνομαι, τούτου
ἕνεκα θανάτου ὑπὸ σοῦ διώκεσθαι ;
22 Ἐρρήθη μὲν δῆλον ὅτι τούτων πλείονα ὑπό τε
αὐτοῦ καὶ τῶν συναγορευόντων φίλων αὐτῷ. ἀλλ᾽
ἐγὼ οὐ τὰ πάντα εἰπεῖν τὰ ἐκ τῆς δίκης ἐσπού-
δασα, ἀλλ᾽ ἤρκεσέ μοι δηλῶσαι ὅτι Σωκράτης τὸ
μὲν μήτε περὶ θεοὺς ἀσεβῆσαι μήτε περὶ ἀνθρώπους ἄδικος φανῆναι περὶ παντὸς ἐποιεῖτο· τὸ δὲ
μὴ ἀποθανεῖν οὐκ ᾤετο λιπαρητέον εἶναι, ἀλλὰ
23 καὶ καιρὸν ἤδη ἐνόμιζεν ἑαυτῷ τελευτᾶν. ὅτι δὲ
οὕτως ἐγίγνωσκε καταδηλότερον ἐγίγνετο ἐπειδὴ
ἡ δίκη κατεψηφίσθη. πρῶτον μὲν γὰρ κελευό-
μενος ὑποτιμᾶσθαι οὔτε αὐτὸς ὑπετιμήσατο οὔτε
τοὺς φίλους εἴασεν, ἀλλὰ καὶ ἔλεγεν ὅτι τὸ ὑποτιμᾶσθαι ὁμολογοῦντος εἴη ἀδικεῖν. ἔπειτα τῶν
ἑταίρων ἐκκλέψαι βουλομένων αὐτὸν οὐκ ἐφεί-
654

moreover, in the meetings of the legislative assembly all the people of Athens, without question, follow the advice of those whose words are wisest rather than that of their own relatives.   Do you not also elect for your generals, in preference to fathers and brothers,—yes, by Heaven! in preference to your very selves,—those whom you regard as having the greatest wisdom in military affairs?"   "Yes," Meletus had said ;   "for that is both expedient and conventional."   "Well, then," Socrates had rejoined, "does it not seem to you an amazing thing that while in other activities those who excel receive honours not merely on a parity with their fellows but even more marked ones, yet I, because I am adjudged by some people supreme in what is man's greatest blessing, — education, — am being prosecuted by you on a capital charge?"

More than this of course was said both by Socrates himself and by the friends who joined in his defence. But I have not made it a point to report the whole trial ; rather I am satisfied to make it clear that while Socrates' whole concern was to keep free from any act of impiety toward the gods or any appearance of wrong-doing toward man, he did not think it meet to beseech the jury to let him escape death ; instead, he believed that the time had now come for him to die.   This conviction of his became more evident than ever after the adverse issue of the trial.   For, first of all, when he was bidden to name his penalty, he refused personally and forbade his friends to name one, but said that naming the penalty in itself implied an acknowledgment of guilt.   Then, when his companions wished to remove him clandestinely from prison, he would not accom-

πετο, ἀλλὰ καὶ ἐπισκῶψαι ἐδόκει, ἐρόμενος εἴ
**που εἰδείέν τι χωρίον ἔξω τῆς Ἀττικῆς ἔνθα οὐ
προσβατὸν θανάτῳ.**

24 Ὡς δὲ τέλος εἶχεν ἡ δίκη, εἰπεῖν αὐτόν· Ἀλλ᾽,
ὦ ἄνδρες, τοὺς μὲν διδάσκοντας τοὺς μάρτυρας ὡς
χρὴ ἐπιορκοῦντας καταψευδομαρτυρεῖν ἐμοῦ καὶ
τοὺς πειθομένους τούτοις ἀνάγκη ἐστὶ πολλὴν
ἑαυτοῖς συνειδέναι ἀσέβειαν καὶ ἀδικίαν· ἐμοὶ δὲ
τί προσήκει νῦν μεῖον φρονεῖν ἢ πρὶν κατακριθῆ-
ναι, μηδὲν ἐλεγχθέντι ὡς πεποίηκά τι ὧν ἐγρά-
ψαντό με; οὔτε γὰρ ἔγωγε ἀντὶ Διὸς καὶ Ἥρας
καὶ τῶν σὺν τούτοις θεῶν οὔτε θύων τισὶ καινοῖς
δαίμοσιν οὔτε ὀμνὺς οὔτε ὀνομάζων ἄλλους θεοὺς
ἀναπέφηνα. τούς γε μὴν νέους πῶς ἂν διαφθεί-
25 ροιμι καρτερίαν καὶ εὐτέλειαν προσεθίζων; ἐφ᾽
οἷς γε μὴν ἔργοις κεῖται θάνατος ἡ ζημία, ἱεροσυ-
λία, τοιχωρυχία, ἀνδραποδίσει, πόλεως προδοσία,
οὐδ᾽ αὐτοὶ οἱ ἀντίδικοι τούτων πρᾶξαί τι κατ᾽
ἐμοῦ φασιν. ὥστε θαυμαστὸν ἔμοιγε δοκεῖ εἶναι
ὅπως ποτὲ ἐφάνη ὑμῖν τοῦ θανάτου ἔργον ἄξιον
26 ἐμοὶ εἰργασμένον. ἀλλ᾽ οὐδὲ μέντοι ὅτι ἀδίκως
ἀποθνῄσκω, διὰ τοῦτο μεῖον φρονητέον· οὐ γὰρ
ἐμοὶ ἀλλὰ τοῖς καταγνοῦσι τοῦτο αἰσχρόν ἐστι.
παραμυθεῖται δέ τί με καὶ Παλαμήδης ὁ παρα-
πλησίως ἐμοὶ τελευτήσας· ἔτι γὰρ καὶ νῦν πολὺ
καλλίους ὕμνους παρέχεται Ὀδυσσέως τοῦ ἀδίκως
ἀποκτείναντος αὐτόν· οἶδ᾽ ὅτι καὶ ἐμοὶ μαρτυρή-

---

[1] One of the Greek warriors at Troy ; put to death on a
charge of treason trumped up by Odysseus, or by Odysseus,
Diomedes, and Agamemnon.

pany them, but seemed actually to banter them, asking them whether they knew of any spot outside of Attica that was inaccessible to death.

When the trial was over, Socrates (according to Hermogenes) remarked: "Well, gentlemen, those who instructed the witnesses that they must bear false witness against me, perjuring themselves to do so, and those who were won over to do this must feel in their hearts a guilty consciousness of great impiety and iniquity; but as for me, why should my spirit be any less exalted now than before my condemnation, since I have not been proved guilty of having done any of the acts mentioned in the indictment? For it has not been shown that I have sacrificed to new deities in the stead of Zeus and Hera and the gods of their company, or that I have invoked in oaths or mentioned other gods. And how could I be corrupting the young by habituating them to fortitude and frugality? Now of all the acts for which the laws have prescribed the death-penalty — temple robbery, burglary, enslavement, treason to the state—not even my adversaries themselves charge me with having committed any of these. And so it seems astonishing to me how you could ever have been convinced that I had committed an act meriting death. But further, my spirit need not be less exalted because I am to be executed unjustly; for the ignominy of that attaches not to me but to those who condemned me. And I get comfort from the case of Palamedes,[1] also, who died in circumstances similar to mine; for even yet he affords us far more noble themes for song than does Odysseus, the man who unjustly put him to death. And I know that time to come as well as

σεται ὑπό τε τοῦ ἐπιόντος καὶ ὑπὸ τοῦ παρελη-
λυθότος χρόνου ὅτι ἠδίκησα μὲν οὐδένα πώποτε
οὐδὲ πονηρότερον ἐποίησα, ηὐεργέτουν δὲ τοὺς
ἐμοὶ διαλεγομένους προῖκα διδάσκων ὅ τι ἐδυνάμην
ἀγαθόν.

27 Εἰπὼν δὲ ταῦτα μάλα ὁμολογουμένως δὴ τοῖς
εἰρημένοις ἀπῄει καὶ ὄμμασι καὶ σχήματι καὶ
βαδίσματι φαιδρός. ὡς δὲ ᾔσθετο ἄρα τοὺς παρ-
επομένους δακρύοντας, Τί τοῦτο; εἰπεῖν αὐτόν,
ἢ ἄρτι δακρύετε; οὐ γὰρ πάλαι ἴστε ὅτι ἐξ ὅτουπερ ἐγενόμην κατεψηφισμένος ἦν μου ὑπὸ τῆς
φύσεως ὁ θάνατος; ἀλλὰ μέντοι εἰ μὲν ἀγαθῶν
ἐπιρρεόντων προαπόλλυμαι, δῆλον ὅτι ἐμοὶ καὶ
τοῖς ἐμοῖς εὔνοις λυπητέον· εἰ δὲ χαλεπῶν προσ-
δοκωμένων καταλύω τὸν βίον, ἐγὼ μὲν οἶμαι ὡς
εὐπραγοῦντος ἐμοῦ πᾶσιν ὑμῖν εὐθυμητέον εἶναι.

28 Παρὼν δέ τις Ἀπολλόδωρος, ἐπιθυμητὴς μὲν
ὢν ἰσχυρῶς αὐτοῦ, ἄλλως δ' εὐήθης, εἶπεν ἄρα·
Ἀλλὰ τοῦτο ἔγωγε, ὦ Σώκρατες, χαλεπώτατα
φέρω ὅτι ὁρῶ σε ἀδίκως ἀποθνήσκοντα. τὸν δὲ
λέγεται καταψήσαντα αὐτοῦ τὴν κεφαλὴν εἰπεῖν·
Σὺ δέ, ὦ φίλτατε Ἀπολλόδωρε, μᾶλλον ἂν ἐβού-
λου με ὁρᾶν δικαίως ἢ ἀδίκως ἀποθνήσκοντα;
καὶ ἅμα ἐπιγελάσαι.

29 Λέγεται δὲ καὶ Ἄνυτον παριόντα ἰδὼν εἰπεῖν·
Ἀλλ' ὁ μὲν ἀνὴρ ὅδε κυδρός, ὡς μέγα τι[1] καὶ καλὸν
διαπεπραγμένος εἰ ἀπέκτονέ με ὅτι αὐτὸν τῶν
μεγίστων ὑπὸ τῆς πόλεως ὁρῶν ἀξιούμενον οὐκ

[1] Sauppe reads τε (a misprint?).

time past will attest that I, too, far from ever doing any man a wrong or rendering him more wicked, have rather profited those who conversed with me by teaching them, without reward, every good thing that lay in my power."

With these words he departed, blithe in glance, in mien, in gait, as comported well indeed with the words he had just uttered. When he noticed that those who accompanied him were in tears, " What is this ? " Hermogenes reports him as asking. " Are you just now beginning to weep ? Have you not known all along that from the moment of my birth nature had condemned me to death ? Verily, if I am being destroyed before my time while blessings are still pouring in upon me, clearly that should bring grief to me and to my well-wishers; but if I am ending my life when only troubles are in view, my own opinion is that you ought all to feel cheered, in the assurance that my state is happy."

A man named Apollodorus, who was there with him, a very ardent disciple of Socrates, but otherwise simple, exclaimed, " But, Socrates, what I find it hardest to bear is that I see you being put to death unjustly ! " The other, stroking Apollodorus' head, is said to have replied, " My beloved Apollodorus, was it your preference to see me put to death justly ? " and smiled as he asked the question.

It is said also that he remarked as he saw Anytus[1] passing by : " There goes a man who is filled with pride at the thought that he has accomplished some great and noble end in putting me to death, because, seeing him honoured by the state with the highest

[1] One of the three plaintiffs in Socrates' trial.

ἔφην χρῆναι τὸν υἱὸν περὶ βύρσας παιδεύειν. ὡς
μοχθηρὸς οὗτος, ἔφη, ὃς οὐκ ἔοικεν εἰδέναι ὅτι
ὁπότερος ἡμῶν καὶ συμφορώτερα καὶ καλλίω εἰς
τὸν ἀεὶ χρόνον διαπέπρακται, οὗτός ἐστι καὶ ὁ
30 νικῶν. ἀλλὰ μέντοι, φάναι αὐτόν, ἀνέθηκε μὲν
καὶ Ὅμηρος ἔστιν οἷς τῶν ἐν καταλύσει τοῦ βίου
προγιγνώσκειν τὰ μέλλοντα, βούλομαι δὲ καὶ ἐγὼ
χρησμῳδῆσαί τι. συνεγενόμην γάρ ποτε βραχέα
τῷ Ἀνύτου υἱῷ, καὶ ἔδοξέ μοι οὐκ ἄρρωστος τὴν
ψυχὴν εἶναι· ὥστε φημὶ αὐτὸν ἐπὶ τῇ δουλο-
πρεπεῖ διατριβῇ ἣν ὁ πατὴρ αὐτῷ παρεσκεύακεν οὐ
διαμενεῖν· διὰ δὲ τὸ μηδένα ἔχειν σπουδαῖον ἐπι-
μελητὴν προσπεσεῖσθαί τινι αἰσχρᾷ ἐπιθυμίᾳ καὶ
31 προβήσεσθαι μέντοι πόρρω μοχθηρίας. ταῦτα
δ᾽ εἰπὼν οὐκ ἐψεύσατο, ἀλλ᾽ ὁ νεανίσκος ἡσθεὶς
οἴνῳ οὔτε νυκτὸς οὔτε ἡμέρας ἐπαύετο πίνων, καὶ
τέλος οὔτε τῇ ἑαυτοῦ πόλει οὔτε τοῖς φίλοις οὔτε
αὐτῷ ἄξιος οὐδενὸς ἐγένετο. Ἄνυτος μὲν δὴ διὰ
τὴν τοῦ υἱοῦ πονηρὰν παιδείαν καὶ διὰ τὴν αὑτοῦ
ἀγνωμοσύνην ἔτι καὶ τετελευτηκὼς τυγχάνει κακο-
32 δοξίας. Σωκράτης δὲ διὰ τὸ μεγαλύνειν ἑαυτὸν
ἐν τῷ δικαστηρίῳ φθόνον ἐπαγόμενος μᾶλλον
καταψηφίσασθαι ἑαυτοῦ ἐποίησε τοὺς δικαστάς.
ἐμοὶ μὲν οὖν δοκεῖ θεοφιλοῦς μοίρας τετυχηκέναι·
τοῦ μὲν γὰρ βίου τὸ χαλεπώτατον ἀπέλιπε, τῶν
33 δὲ θανάτων τοῦ ῥᾴστου ἔτυχεν. ἐπεδείξατο δὲ
τῆς ψυχῆς τὴν ῥώμην· ἐπεὶ γὰρ ἔγνω τοῦ ἔτι ζῆν
τὸ τεθνάναι αὐτῷ κρεῖττον εἶναι, ὥσπερ οὐδὲ
πρὸς τἆλλα τἀγαθὰ προσάντης ἦν, οὐδὲ πρὸς τὸν

offices, I said that he ought not to confine his son's
education to hides.[1] What a vicious fellow," he
continued, "not to know, apparently, that whichever one of us has wrought the more beneficial and
noble deeds for all time, *he* is the real victor. But,"
he is reported to have added, "Homer has attributed
to some of his heroes at the moment of dissolution
the power to foresee the future; and so I too wish
to utter a prophecy. At one time I had a brief
association with the son of Anytus, and I thought
him not lacking in firmness of spirit; and so I
predict that he will not continue in the servile
occupation that his father has provided for him;
but through want of a worthy adviser he will fall
into some disgraceful propensity and will surely go
far in the career of vice." In saying this he was
not mistaken; the young man, delighting in wine,
never left off drinking night or day, and at last
turned out worth nothing to his city, his friends,
or himself. So Anytus, even though dead, still
enjoys an evil repute for his son's mischievous education and for his own hard-heartedness. And as for
Socrates, by exalting himself before the court, he
brought ill-will upon himself and made his conviction
by the jury all the more certain. Now to me he seems
to have met a fate that the gods love; for he escaped
the hardest part of life and met the easiest sort of
death. And he displayed the stalwart nature of his
heart; for having once decided that to die was better
for him than to live longer, he did not weaken in
the presence of death (just as he had never set his
face against any other thing, either, that was for

---

[1] The tanning trade had been in the family from at least
the time of the boy's grandfather.

XENOPHON

θάνατον ἐμαλακίσατο, ἀλλ᾽ ἱλαρῶς καὶ προσ-
εδέχετο αὐτὸν καὶ ἐπετελέσατο.

24 Ἐγὼ μὲν δὴ κατανοῶν τοῦ ἀνδρὸς τήν τε σοφίαν
καὶ τὴν γενναιότητα οὔτε μὴ μεμνῆσθαι δύναμαι
αὐτοῦ οὔτε μεμνημένος μὴ οὐκ ἐπαινεῖν. εἰ δέ τις
τῶν ἀρετῆς ἐφιεμένων ὠφελιμωτέρῳ τινὶ Σωκράτους συνεγένετο, ἐκεῖνον ἐγὼ τὸν ἄνδρα ἀξιομα-
καριστότατον νομίζω.

his good), but was cheerful not only in the expectation of death but in meeting it.

And so, in contemplating the man's wisdom and nobility of character, I find it beyond my power to forget him or, in remembering him, to refrain from praising him. And if among those who make virtue their aim any one has ever been brought into contact with a person more helpful than Socrates, I count that man worthy to be called most blessed.

INDEX TO THE MEMORABILIA

(References are to Book, Chapter, and Section)

665

INDEX TO THE MEMORABILIA

667

INDEX TO THE MEMORABILIA

INDEX TO THE OECONOMICUS

(References are to Chapter and Section)

669

INDEX TO THE OECONOMICUS

INDEX TO SYMPOSIUM
AND APOLOGY

671

INDEX TO SYMPOSIUM AND APOLOGY

INDEX TO SYMPOSIUM AND APOLOGY

THE LOEB CLASSICAL LIBRARY

VOLUMES ALREADY PUBLISHED

Latin Authors

AMMIANUS MARCELLINUS. Translated by J. C. Rolfe. 3 Vols.

APULEIUS: THE GOLDEN ASS (METAMORPHOSES). W. Adlington (1566). Revised by S. Gaselee.

ST. AUGUSTINE: CITY OF GOD. 7 Vols. Vol. I. G. E. McCracken. Vol. II. and VII. W. M. Green. Vol. III. D. Wiesen. Vol. IV. P. Levine. Vol. V. E. M. Sanford and W. M. Green. Vol. VI. W. C. Greene.

ST. AUGUSTINE, CONFESSIONS OF. W. Watts (1631). 2 Vols.

ST. AUGUSTINE, SELECT LETTERS. J. H. Baxter.

AUSONIUS. H. G. Evelyn White. 2 Vols.

BEDE. J. E. King. 2 Vols.

BOETHIUS: TRACTS and DE CONSOLATIONE PHILOSOPHIAE. Rev. H. F. Stewart and E. K. Rand. Revised by S. J. Tester.

CAESER: ALEXANDRIAN, AFRICAN and SPANISH WARS. A. G. Way.

CAESER: CIVIL WARS. A. G. Peskett.

CAESER: GALLIC WAR. H. J. Edwards.

CATO: DE RE RUSTICA; VARRO: DE RE RUSTICA. H. B. Ash and W. D. Hooper.

CATULLUS. F. W. Cornish; TIBULLUS. J. B. Postgate; PERVIGILIUM VENERIS. J. W. Mackail.

CELSUS: DE MEDICINA. W. G. Spencer. 3 Vols.

CICERO: BRUTUS, and ORATOR. G. L. Hendrickson and H. M. Hubbell.

[CICERO]: AD HERENNIUM. H. Caplan.

CICERO: DE ORATORE, etc. 2 Vols. Vol. I. DE ORATORE, BOOKS I. and II. E. W. Sutton and H. Rackham. Vol. II. DE ORATORE, Book III. De Fato; Paradoxa Stoicorum; De Partitione Oratoria. H. Rackham.

CICERO: DE FINIBUS. H. Rackham.

CICERO: DE INVENTIONE, etc. H. M. Hubbell.

CICERO: DE NATURA DEORUM and ACADEMICA. H. Rackham.

CICERO: DE OFFICIIS. Walter Miller.

CICERO: DE REPUBLICA and DE LEGIBUS: SOMNIUM SCIPIONIS. Clinton W. Keyes.

2

OVID: HEROIDES and AMORES. Grant Showerman. Revised by G. P. Goold
OVID: METAMORPHOSES. F. J. Miller. 2 Vols. Vol. 1 revised by G. P. Goold.
OVID: TRISTIA and EX PONTO. A. L. Wheeler.
PERSIUS. Cf. JUVENAL.
PETRONIUS. M. Heseltine; SENECA; APOCOLOCYNTOSIS. W. H. D. Rouse.
PHAEDRUS AND BABRIUS (Greek). B. E. Perry.
PLAUTUS. Paul Nixon. 5 Vols.
PLINY: LETTERS, PANEGYRICUS. Betty Radice. 2 Vols.
PLINY: NATURAL HISTORY. Vols. I.–V. and IX. H. Rackham. VI.–VIII. W. H. S. Jones. X. D. E. Eichholz. 10 Vols.
PROPERTIUS. H. E. Butler.
PRUDENTIUS. H. J. Thomson. 2 Vols.
QUINTILIAN. H. E. Butler. 4 Vols.
REMAINS OF OLD LATIN. E. H. Warmington. 4 Vols. Vol. I. (ENNIUS AND CAECILIUS.) Vol. II. (LIVIUS, NAEVIUS, PACUVIUS, ACCIUS.) Vol. III. (LUCILIUS and LAWS OF XII TABLES.) Vol. IV. (ARCHAIC INSCRIPTIONS.)
SALLUST. J. C. Rolfe.
SCRIPTORES HISTORIAE AUGUSTAE. D. Magie. 3 Vols.
SENECA, THE ELDER: CONTROVERSIAE, SUASORIAE. M. Winterbottom. 2 Vols.
SENECA: APOCOLOCYNTOSIS. Cf. PETRONIUS.
SENECA: EPISTULAE MORALES. R. M. Gummere. 3 Vols.
SENECA: MORAL ESSAYS. J. W. Basore. 3 Vols.
SENECA: TRAGEDIES. F. J. Miller. 2 Vols.
SENECA: NATURALES QUAESTIONES. T. H. Corcoran. 2 Vols.
SIDONIUS: POEMS and LETTERS. W. B. Anderson. 2 Vols.
SILIUS ITALICUS. J. D. Duff. 2 Vols.
STATIUS. J. H. Mozley. 2 Vols.
SUETONIUS. J. C. Rolfe. 2 Vols.
TACITUS: DIALOGUS. Sir Wm. Peterson. AGRICOLA and GERMANIA. Maurice Hutton. Revised by M. Winterbottom, R. M. Ogilvie, E. H. Warmington.
TACITUS: HISTORIES AND ANNALS. C. H. Moore and J. Jackson. 4 Vols.
TERENCE. John Sargeaunt. 2 Vols.
TERTULLIAN: APOLOGIA and DE SPECTACULIS. T. R. Glover. MINUCIUS FELIX. G. H. Rendall.
VALERIUS FLACCUS. J. H. Mozley.
VARRO: DE LINGUA LATINA. R. G. Kent. 2 Vols.
VELLEIUS PATERCULUS and RES GESTAE DIVI AUGUSTI. F. W. Shipley.
VIRGIL. H. R. Fairclough. 2 Vols.
VITRUVIUS: DE ARCHITECTURA. F. Granger. 2 Vols.

Greek Authors

ACHILLES TATIUS. S. Gaselee.

AELIAN: ON THE NATURE OF ANIMALS. A. F. Scholfield. 3 Vols.

AENEAS TACTICUS, ASCLEPIODOTUS and ONASANDER. The Illinois Greek Club.

AESCHINES. C. D. Adams.

AESCHYLUS. H. Weir Smyth. 2 Vols.

ALCIPHRON, AELIAN, PHILOSTRATUS: LETTERS. A. R. Benner and F. H. Fobes.

ANDOCIDES, ANTIPHON, Cf. MINOR ATTIC ORATORS.

APOLLODORUS. Sir James G. Frazer. 2 Vols.

APOLLONIUS RHODIUS. R. C. Seaton.

THE APOSTOLIC FATHERS. Kirsopp Lake. 2 Vols.

APPIAN: ROMAN HISTORY. Horace White. 4 Vols.

ARATUS. Cf. CALLIMACHUS.

ARISTIDES: ORATIONS. C. A. Behr. Vol. I.

ARISTOPHANES. Benjamin Bickley Rogers. 3 Vols. Verse trans.

ARISTOTLE: ART OF RHETORIC. J. H. Freese.

ARISTOTLE: ATHENIAN CONSTITUTION, EUDEMIAN ETHICS, VICES AND VIRTUES. H. Rackham.

ARISTOTLE: GENERATION OF ANIMALS. A. L. Peck.

ARISTOTLE: HISTORIA ANIMALIUM. A. L. Peck. Vols I.--II.

ARISTOTLE: METAPHYSICS. H. Tredennick. 2 Vols.

ARISTOTLE: METEOROLOGICA. H. D. P. Lee.

ARISTOTLE: MINOR WORKS. W. S. Hett. On Colours, On Things Heard, On Physiognomies, On Plants, On Marvellous Things Heard, Mechanical Problems, On Indivisible Lines, On Situations and Names of Winds, On Melissus, Xenophanes, and Gorgias.

ARISTOTLE: NICOMACHEAN ETHICS. H. Rackham.

ARISTOTLE: OECONOMICA and MAGNA MORALIA. G. C. Armstrong; (with METAPHYSICS, Vol. II.).

ARISTOTLE: ON THE HEAVENS. W. K. C. Guthrie.

ARISTOTLE: ON THE SOUL. PARVA NATURALIA. ON BREATH. W. S. Hett.

ARISTOTLE: CATEGORIES, ON INTERPRETATION, PRIOR ANALYTICS. H. P. Cooke and H. Tredennick.

ARISTOTLE: POSTERIOR ANALYTICS, TOPICS. H. Tredennick and E. S. Forster.

ARISTOTLE: ON SOPHISTICAL REFUTATIONS.
On Coming to be and Passing Away, On the Cosmos. E. S. Forster and D. J. Furley.

ARISTOTLE: PARTS OF ANIMALS. A. L. Peck; MOTION AND PROGRESSION OF ANIMALS. E. S. Forster.

ARISTOTLE: PHYSICS. Rev. P. Wicksteed and F. M. Cornford. 2 Vols.
ARISTOTLE: POETICS and LONGINUS. W. Hamilton Fyfe; DEMETRIUS ON STYLE. W. Rhys Roberts.
ARISTOTLE: POLITICS. H. Rackham.
ARISTOTLE: PROBLEMS. W. S. Hett. 2 Vols.
ARISTOTLE: RHETORICA AD ALEXANDRUM (with PROBLEMS. Vol. II). H. Rackham.
ARRIAN: HISTORY OF ALEXANDER and INDICA. 2 Vols. Vol. I. P. Brunt. Vol. II. Rev. E. Iliffe Robson.
ATHENAEUS: DEIPNOSOPHISTAE. C. B. Gulick. 7 Vols.
BABRIUS AND PHAEDRUS (Latin). B. E. Perry.
ST. BASIL: LETTERS. R. J. Deferrair. 4 Vols.
CALLIMACHUS: FRAGMENTS. C. A. Trypanis. MUSAEUS: HERO AND LEANDER. T. Gelzer and C. Whitman.
CALLIMACHUS, Hymns and Epigrams, and LYCOPHRON. A. W. Mair; ARATUS. G. R. Mair.
CLEMENT OF ALEXANDRIA. Rev. G. W. Butterworth.
COLLUTHUS. Cf. OPPIAN.
DAPHNIS AND CHLOE. Thornley's Translation revised by J. M. Edmonds: and PARTHENIUS. S. Gaselee.
DEMOSTHENES I.: OLYNTHIACS, PHILIPPICS and MINOR ORATIONS. I.–XVII. AND XX. J. H. Vince.
DEMOSTHENES II.: DE CORONA and DE FALSA LEGATIONE. C. A. Vince and J. H. Vince.
DEMOSTHENES III.: MEIDIAS, ANDROTION, ARISTOCRATES, TIMOCRATES and ARISTOGEITON, I. and II. J. H. Vince.
DEMOSTHENES IV.–VI.: PRIVATE ORATIONS and IN NEAERAM. A. T. Murray.
DEMOSTHENES VII: FUNERAL SPEECH, EROTIC ESSAY, EXORDIA and LETTERS. N. W. and N. J. DeWitt.
DIO CASSIUS: ROMAN HISTORY. E. Cary. 9 Vols.
DIO CHRYSOSTOM. J. W. Cohoon and H. Lamar Crosby. 5 Vols.
DIODORUS SICULUS. 12 Vols. Vols. I.–VI. C. H. Oldfather. Vol. VII. C. L. Sherman. Vol. VIII. C. B. Welles. Vols. IX. and X. R. M. Geer. Vol. XI. F. Walton. Vol. XII. F. Walton. General Index. R. M. Geer.
DIOGENES LAERTIUS. R. D. Hicks. 2 Vols. New Introduction by H. S. Long.
DIONYSIUS OF HALICARNASSUS: ROMAN ANTIQUITIES. Spelman's translation revised by E. Cary. 7 Vols.
DIONYSIUS OF HALICARNASSUS: CRITICAL ESSAYS. S. Usher. 2 Vols.
EPICTETUS. W. A. Oldfather. 2 Vols.
EURIPIDES. A. S. Way. 4 Vols. Verse trans.
EUSEBIUS: ECCLESIASTICAL HISTORY. Kirsopp Lake and J. E. L. Oulton. 2 Vols.

GALEN: ON THE NATURAL FACULTIES. A. J. Brock.

THE GREEK ANTHOLOGY. W. R. Paton. 5 Vols.

GREEK ELEGY AND IAMBUS with the ANACREONTEA. J. M. Edmonds. 2 Vols.

THE GREEK BUCOLIC POETS (THEOCRITUS, BION, MOSCHUS). J. M. Edmonds.

GREEK MATHEMATICAL WORKS. Ivor Thomas. 2 Vols.

HERODES. Cf. THEOPHRASTUS: CHARACTERS.

HERODIAN. C. R. Whittaker. 2 Vols.

HERODOTUS. A. D. Godley. 4 Vols.

HESIOD AND THE HOMERIC HYMNS. H. G. Evelyn White.

HIPPOCRATES and the FRAGMENTS OF HERACLEITUS. W. H. S. Jones and E. T. Withington. 4 Vols.

HOMER: ILIAD. A. T. Murray. 2 Vols.

HOMER: ODYSSEY. A. T. Murray. 2 Vols.

ISAEUS. E. W. Forster.

ISOCRATES. George Norlin and LaRue Van Hook. 3 Vols.

[ST. JOHN DAMASCENE]: BARLAAM AND IOASAPH. Rev. G. R. Woodward, Harold Mattingly and D. M. Lang.

JOSEPHUS. 9 Vols. Vols. I.–IV. H. Thackeray. Vol. V. H. Thackeray and R. Marcus. Vols. VI.–VII. R. Marcus. Vol. VIII. R. Marcus and Allen Wikgren. Vol. IX. L. H. Feldman.

JULIAN. Wilmer Cave Wright. 3 Vols.

LIBANIUS. A. F. Norman. Vols. I.–II.

LUCIAN. 8 Vols. Vols. I.–V. A. M. Harmon. Vol. VI. K. Kilburn. Vols. VII.–VIII. M. D. Macleod.

LYCOPHRON. Cf. CALLIMACHUS.

LYRA GRAECA. J. M. Edmonds. 3 Vols.

LYSIAS. W. R. M. Lamb.

MANETHO. W. G. Waddell: PTOLEMY: TETRABIBLOS. F. E. Robbins.

MARCUS AURELIUS. C. R. Haines.

MENANDER. I New edition by W. G. Arnott.

MINOR ATTIC ORATORS (ANTIPHON, ANDOCIDES, LYCURGUS, DEMADES, DINARCHUS, HYPERIDES). K. J. Maidment and J. O. Burtt. 2 Vols.

MUSAEUS: HEOR AND LEANDER. Cf. CALLIMACHUS.

NONNOS: DIONYSIACA. W. H. D. Rouse. 3 Vols.

OPPIAN, COLLUTHUS, TRYPHIODORUS. A. W. Mair.

PAPYRI. NON-LITERARY SELECTIONS. A. S. Hunt and C. C. Edgar. 2 Vols. LITERARY SELECTIONS (Poetry). D. L. Page.

PARTHENIUS. Cf. DAPHNIS and CHLOE.

PAUSANIAS: DESCRIPTION OF GREECE. W. H. S. Jones. 4 Vols. and Companion Vol. arranged by R. E. Wycherley.

PHILO. 10 Vols. Vols. I.–V. F. H. Colson and Rev. G. H. Whitaker. Vols. VI.–IX. F. H. Colson. Vol. X. F. H. Colson and the Rev. J. W. Earp.

PHILO: two supplementary Vols. (*Translation only.*) Ralph Marcus.

PHILOSTRATUS: THE LIFE OF APOLLONIUS OF TYANA. F. C. Conybeare. 2 Vols.

PHILOSTRATUS: IMAGINES; CALLISTRATUS: DESCRIPTIONS. A. Fairbanks.

PHILOSTRATUS and EUNAPIUS: LIVES OF THE SOPHISTS. Wilmer Cave Wright.

PINDAR. Sir J. E. Sandys.

PLATO: CHARMIDES, ALCIBIADES, HIPPARCHUS, THE LOVERS, THEAGES, MINOS and EPINOMIS. W. R. M. Lamb.

PLATO: CRATYLUS, PARMENIDES, GREATER HIPPIAS, LESSER HIPPIAS. H. N. Fowler.

PLATO: EUTHYPHRO, APOLOGY, CRITO, PHAEDO, PHAEDRUS, H. N. Fowler.

PLATO: LACHES, PROTAGORAS, MENO, EUTHYDEMUS. W. R. M. Lamb.

PLATO: LAWS. Rev. R. G. Bury. 2 Vols.

PLATO: LYSIS, SYMPOSIUM, GORGIAS. W. R. M. Lamb.

PLATO: Republic. Paul Shorey. 2 Vols.

PLATO: STATESMAN, PHILEBUS. H. N. Fowler; Ion. W. R. M. Lamb.

PLATO: THEAETETUS and SOPHIST. H. N. Fowler.

PLATO: TIMAEUS, CRITIAS, CLITOPHO, MENEXENUS, EPISTULAE. Rev. R. G. Bury.

PLOTINUS: A. H. Armstrong. Vols. I.–III.

PLUTARCH: MORALIA. 17 Vols. Vols. I.–V. F. C. Babbitt. Vol. VI. W. C. Helmbold. Vols. VII. and XIV. P. H. De Lacy and B. Einarson. Vol. VIII. P. A. Clement and H. B. Hoffleit. Vol. IX. E. L. Minar, Jr., F. H. Sandbach, W. C. Helmbold. Vol. X. H. N. Fowler. Vol. XI. L. Pearson and F. H. Sandbach. Vol. XII. H. Cherniss and W. C. Helmbold. Vol. XIII 1–2. H. Cherniss. Vol. XV. F. H. Sandbach.

PLUTARCH: THE PARALLEL LIVES. B. Perrin. 11 Vols.

POLYBIUS. W. R. Paton. 6 Vols.

PROCOPIUS: HISTORY OF THE WARS. H. B. Dewing. 7 Vols.

PTOLEMY: TETRABIBLOS. Cf. MANETHO.

QUINTUS SMYRNAEUS. A. S. Way. Verse trans.

SEXTUS EMPIRICUS. Rev. R. G. Bury. 4 Vols.

SOPHOCLES. F. Storr. 2 Vols. Verse trans.

STRABO: GEOGRAPHY. Horace L. Jones. 8 Vols.

THEOPHRASTUS: CHARACTERS. J. M. Edmonds. HERODES, etc. A. D. Knox.

7

THEOPHRASTUS: ENQUIRY INTO PLANTS. Sir Arthur Hort, Bart. 2 Vols.

THEOPHRASTUS: DE CAUSIS PLANTARUM. G. K. K. Link and B. Einarson. 3 Vols. Vol. I.

THUCYDIDES. C. F. Smith. 4 Vols.

TRYPHIODORUS. Cf. OPPIAN.

XENOPHON: CYROPAEDIA. Walter Miller. 2 Vols.

XENOPHON: HELLENCIA. C. L. Brownson. 2 Vols.

XENOPHON: ANABASIS. C. L. Brownson.

XENOPHON: MEMORABILIA AND OECONOMICUS. E. C. Marchant. SYMPOSIUM AND APOLOGY. O. J. Todd.

XENOPHON: SCRIPTA MINORA. E. C. Marchant. CONSTITUTION OF THE ATHENIANS (Athenians.) G. W. Bowersock